LARGE-SAMPLE INFERENCE
$(n \geq 30)$

Parameter (Population Value)	Statistic (Sample Value)	Hypothesis (Example)	Standard Error	Test Statistic	Confidence Interval
μ (Mean)	$\bar{X}$	$H_0: \mu = 50$ $H_A: \mu \neq 50$	$\sigma_{\bar{x}} = \dfrac{\sigma}{\sqrt{n}}$ or $S_{\bar{x}} \approx \dfrac{S}{\sqrt{n}}$	$Z = \dfrac{\bar{X} - \mu}{\frac{\sigma}{\sqrt{n}}}$ or $Z = \dfrac{\bar{X} - \mu}{\frac{S}{\sqrt{n}}}$	$\bar{X} \pm Z\dfrac{\sigma}{\sqrt{n}}$ or $\bar{X} \pm Z\dfrac{S}{\sqrt{n}}$
$\mu_1 - \mu_2$ (Two means)	$\bar{X}_1 - \bar{X}_2$	$H_0: \mu_1 - \mu_2 = 0$ $H_A: \mu_1 - \mu_2 \neq 0$	$\sigma_{\bar{x}_1 - \bar{x}_2} = \sqrt{\dfrac{\sigma_1^2}{n_1} + \dfrac{\sigma_2^2}{n_2}}$ or $S_{\bar{x}_1 - \bar{x}_2} \approx \sqrt{\dfrac{S_1^2}{n_1} + \dfrac{S_2^2}{n_2}}$	$Z = \dfrac{(\bar{X}_1 - \bar{X}_2) - (\mu_1 - \mu_2)}{\sqrt{\dfrac{\sigma_1^2}{n_1} + \dfrac{\sigma_2^2}{n_2}}}$ or $Z = \dfrac{(\bar{X}_1 - \bar{X}_2) - (\mu_1 - \mu_2)}{\sqrt{\dfrac{S_1^2}{n_1} + \dfrac{S_2^2}{n_2}}}$	$(\bar{X}_1 - \bar{X}_2) \pm Z\sqrt{\dfrac{\sigma_1^2}{n_1} + \dfrac{\sigma_2^2}{n_2}}$ or $(\bar{X}_1 - \bar{X}_2) \pm Z\sqrt{\dfrac{S_1^2}{n_1} + \dfrac{S_2^2}{n_2}}$
p (Proportion)	$\hat{p}$	$H_0: p \leq 0.10$ $H_A: p > 0.10$	$\sigma_{\hat{p}} = \sqrt{\dfrac{pq}{n}}$ or $S_{\hat{p}} \approx \sqrt{\dfrac{\hat{p}\hat{q}}{n}}$	$Z = \dfrac{\hat{p} - p}{\sqrt{\dfrac{pq}{n}}}$	$\hat{p} \pm Z\sqrt{\dfrac{\hat{p}\hat{q}}{n}}$
$p_1 - p_2$ (Two proportions)	$\hat{p}_1 - \hat{p}_2$	$H_0: p_1 - p_2 = 0$ $H_A: p_1 - p_2 \neq 0$	$\sigma_{\hat{p}_1 - \hat{p}_2} = \sqrt{\dfrac{p_1 q_1}{n_1} + \dfrac{p_2 q_2}{n_2}}$ or $S_{\hat{p}_1 - \hat{p}_2} = \sqrt{\dfrac{\hat{p}_1 \hat{q}_1}{n_1} + \dfrac{\hat{p}_2 \hat{q}_2}{n_2}}$	$Z = \dfrac{(\hat{p}_1 - \hat{p}_2) - (p_1 - p_2)}{\sqrt{\bar{p}(1-\bar{p})\left(\dfrac{1}{n_1} + \dfrac{1}{n_2}\right)}}$	$\hat{p}_1 - \hat{p}_2 \pm Z\sqrt{\dfrac{\hat{p}_1 \hat{q}_1}{n_1} + \dfrac{\hat{p}_2 \hat{q}_2}{n_2}}$

Second Edition

ESSENTIALS OF BUSINESS STATISTICS:
A Decision-Making Approach

Second Edition

ESSENTIALS OF BUSINESS STATISTICS: A Decision-Making Approach

David F. Groebner
Patrick W. Shannon
Boise State University

Macmillan College Publishing Company
New York

Maxwell Macmillan Canada
Toronto

Editor: Robert Pirtle
Project Management: J. Carey Publishing Service
Production Manager: Aliza Greenblatt
Text Designer: Proof/Positive/Farrowlyne Associates, Inc.
Cover Designer: Hothouse Designs

This book was set in Sabon by York Graphic Services,
and printed and bound by R. R. Donnelley & Sons.
The cover was printed by Lehigh Press.

Macmillan College Publishing Company
866 Third Avenue, New York, New York 10022

Macmillan College Publishing Company is part of
the Maxwell Communication Group of Companies.

Maxwell Macmillan Canada, Inc.
1200 Eglinton Avenue East
Suite 200
Don Mills, Ontario M3C 3N1

Library of Congress Cataloging-in-Publication Data

Groebner, David F.
    Essentials of business statistics / David F. Groebner, Patrick W.
    Shannon. —2nd ed.
        p.   cm.
    Includes index.
    ISBN 0-02-347862-4
      1. Commercial statistics.   2. Statistical decision—Case studies.
    I. Shannon, Patrick W.   II. Title.
    HF1017.G733   1994
    519.5—dc20
                                                                    93-39925
                                                                    CIP

Printing: 1 2 3 4 5 6 7   Year: 4 5 6 7 8 9 0

Preface

Business statistics is a course that introduces students to concepts and techniques used extensively in public- and private-sector decision making. The statistical techniques covered in an introductory course are used in functional areas, including accounting, finance, marketing, production, and personnel management.

We believe the beginning statistics course should be rich with applications involving decision-making situations. These applications will enable students to understand why statistics is useful to decision makers, and to appreciate the role that statistics plays in their academic education. The text used in the course should, therefore, contain a wide variety of realistic decision-making applications and should help convince the students how important statistics is to their academic curriculum.

Essentials of Business Statistics is designed for a one-term statistics course and contains those topics considered most essential. However, while this text has reduced topic coverage to be consistent with one-term course time limitations, it has retained many features of our two semester text, *Business Statistics: A Decision-Making Approach, Fourth Edition* (Macmillan, 1993). For example, this text uses actual databases and contains many case studies based on real business situations. Problems related to the databases are provided in most chapters and students are encouraged to use available computer software to help solve the problems. An enhanced computer orientation is present throughout the text. Numerous figures show computer output from software programs such as MINITAB and GB-STAT. We have an expanded discussion of descriptive statistics in chapters 2 and 3 to emphasize the various methods of graphically presenting data and to explain the meaning of important concepts associated with describing data.

Every chapter contains a large set of problems to emphasize business applications. The problems have been ordered by the section of the chapter they address. This makes it easy for instructors to develop homework assignments and for students to review text material when they have trouble arriving at the correct approach to a problem.

An important feature of this text is the short cases at the end of most chapters. These cases present realistic business applications for students and reinforce the importance of statistics in decision making. *Essentials of Business Statistics* has accompanying it one of the widest range of supplementary materials on the market. First a carefully developed study guide written by Susan Fry is available with a comprehensive set of notes for each chapter in the test and worked out solutions to each of the odd-numbered problems in the text. Also included in the study guide are sample test questions pertaining to each chapter. We believe that this study guide is ideally suited to the student who wishes to obtain the maximum amount of knowledge from the statistics course.

For the instructor, we offer an instructor's manual containing worked out solutions to all the problems and cases in the text. In addition a set of transparency masters is available, designed to be used as the basis for the course lectures from each chapter in the text. Several databases are available in ASCII format on IBM PC diskette form. Instructors will be provided complete documentation for these data sets for dissemination to their students.

Essentials of Business Statistics benefitted from the comments and constructive criticisms of the following reviewers: Professor Lee Ash, Yakima Community College; Professor Timothy Hoskins, Gulf Coast Community College; Dr. Charles Zeis, University of South Colorado. We are grateful for their input.

Finally, a text and all the supplementary materials that accompany it do not get completed without the professional assistance of the editorial staff. We are deeply grateful to Robert Pirtle, Executive Editor at Macmillan Publishing Company, for his direction and support. Also, we wish to thank Jennifer Carey, Project Manager, for her thoughtful copyediting and attention to detail that is so vital to determining how the end product looks.

In writing the first edition of *Essentials of Business Statistics* we learned a great deal about ourselves and our attitude toward education. Working on the second edition of *Essentials of Business Statistics* has extended our learning process a great deal and we are grateful for the opportunity. We know that we are better teachers for having written this text; we hope that after students have had the chance to read this text they will consider themselves better off for the experience too. With hope they will understand the importance of statistics as a decision-making tool.

D.F.G.
P.W.S.

Contents

9 INTRODUCTION TO HYPOTHESIS TESTING 315

10 ADDITIONAL HYPOTHESIS-TESTING TECHNIQUES 357

11 STATISTICAL ESTIMATION AND HYPOTHESIS TESTING—SMALL SAMPLES 389

12 TESTS OF VARIANCES AND AN INTRODUCTION TO ANOVA 431

13 INTRODUCTION TO REGRESSION AND CORRELATION ANALYSIS   481

14 CONTINGENCY TABLES AND GOODNESS-OF-FIT TESTS   557

Data Collection for Decision Making

WHY DECISION MAKERS NEED TO KNOW

The production vice-president for Chrysler Motors has just completed a meeting with his United States plant managers. The emphasis of the meeting was on production quality control and plant productivity. A number of sessions were held to discuss steps being taken by the company to build the highest-quality cars possible. These sessions focused on the use of statistical quality control techniques. Everyone at the meeting knew that foreign auto makers such as Toyota are committed to statistical quality control and in the 1970s and early 1980s developed a reputation for high-quality products. They applied basic statistical techniques to help solve many forms of quality control problems. American car manufacturers such as Chrysler Motors are now making great strides toward applying these same basic statistical tools. Therefore, decision makers in this industry must understand statistics.

However, statistical quality control extends far beyond the automobile industry. Virtually every production and service industry in this country has turned its attention to quality. Decision makers in industries such as wood products, electronics, steel, garments, and food processing must have a basic understanding of statistics to effectively deal with the quality control issues facing their organizations.

Other business issues also present a need for understanding statistics. Decisions such as those involving new product introductions, market identification, desired inventory levels, production volume, and financial investment strategy can be improved by using statistics.

There is no functional business area that operates today without using statistics. This means that a business student who graduates without a good understanding of statistics will be at a disadvantage when hired into a decision-making position and also when trying to advance within the organization.

As the competitive nature of business increases, it is becoming apparent that to make good decisions, the decision maker must carefully analyze all alternatives in light of all available information. The primary role of statistics is to provide decision makers with methods for obtaining and converting data into useful information. **Data** are values, facts, observations, or measurements.

This text introduces many statistical techniques that are used by decision makers in the functional areas of business. Regardless of whether you plan a career in marketing, finance, accounting, economics, management, real estate, or the public sector, you will benefit from knowing how to apply the basic statistical tools introduced in this text.

Statistics, like most academic disciplines, has its own terminology. As a student and future decision maker, you must learn the language of statistics. Throughout this and the subsequent chapters, we will present terms that have special statistical meaning. Each chapter contains a glossary that summarizes the important terms introduced in the chapter.

CHAPTER OBJECTIVES

The objectives of this chapter are to introduce business statistics and emphasize its role in the decision-making process. This chapter will focus on the process of data collection. We will point out some potential problems associated with collecting data. Our discussion will include an introduction to the more commonly used sampling techniques.

This chapter also introduces a case study that describes the data collection process and presents you with a small database. Both the case study and database will be referred to throughout the text.

STUDENT OBJECTIVES

After studying the material in this chapter, you should be able to do the following:

1. Understand the role of statistics in the decision-making process.
2. Discuss the four levels of data measurement.
3. Identify some of the more commonly used methods of data collection.
4. Know the strengths and weaknesses of the different data collection methods.
5. Understand the differences between a population and a sample.

1-1 WHAT DOES STATISTICS INVOLVE?

All too often individuals think of statistics as only numerical measures of some item of interest. For example, the unemployment rate is a statistic published monthly by the U.S. Department of Labor. The Dow Jones Industrial Average is a statistic that interests many stock market investors. Another statistic important to everyone is the inflation rate. Although the numbers these examples yield are a type of statistics, the philosophy of statistics introduced in this text is something quite different.

Statistics can be described by three terms: (1) *data description*, (2) *probability*, and (3) *inference*.

1. Data description, or descriptive statistics, is an important area of statistics. Descriptive statistics consists of techniques and measures that help decision makers describe data. Graphs, charts, tables, and summary numerical measures are tools that decision makers use to help turn data into meaningful information. For example, Figure 1-1 illustrates two approaches for meaningfully presenting education-related data. One shows the distribution of scores in a freshman psychology course; the other compares university and college of business enrollment over several years. Chapters 2 and 3 introduce some basic methods and procedures of descriptive statistics.

2. Probability is a bridge that carries us from merely describing a particular set of data to developing an understanding of what the source of the data is like. Probability is important to statistics because it helps measure a decision maker's level of uncertainty about whether some outcome will occur. For example, suppose an investment manager for a bank in California is considering investing $10 million of her bank's money in a government bond. The manager recognizes that this investment may earn an acceptable rate of return or, because of increasing inflation, may result in an actual loss to the bank. Although the investment manager is uncertain which will occur, she has analyzed the available information and believes there is a 75% chance of the investment being profitable and a 25% chance of a loss. These percentages, or probabilities, reflect her attitude about the chances of the two outcomes occurring and thus measure her uncertainty about which outcome will result. The fact that she has assigned a 0.75 probability to the profit outcome indicates that she thinks a profit is three times as likely as a loss.

3. Inference, or inferential statistics, is an area of statistics in which conclusions about a large body of data are reached by examining only part of those data. For example, an accountant in charge of auditing a client's financial records may select a subset, or *sample,* of accounts from the ledger of all accounts. Then, based on the accuracy rate of the sampled accounts, the accountant can make inferences about the accuracy rate of all accounts.

   In another instance, quality control testing relies heavily on statistical inference to accept or reject production output. Suppose a semiconductor production process is designed to produce less than 1% defective items. To determine whether the production process is in control, the quality control manager may select a sample of items from the production process. If he finds too many defectives in the sample, he will infer that the defective rate of all items is too high. He will probably then decide that the production process needs to be adjusted.

FIGURE **1-1**

Descriptive
Statistics Graph
Examples

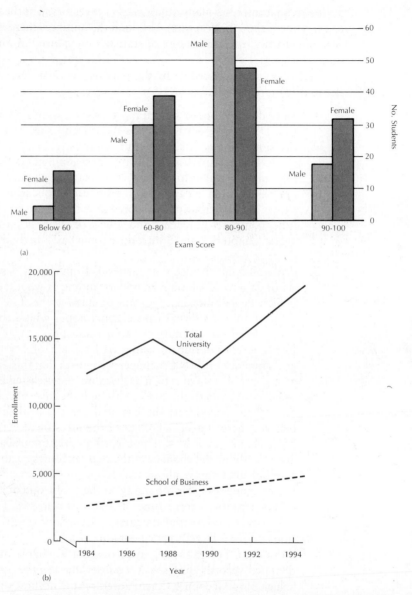

(a)

(b)

Statistics, as defined in this text, is a collection of techniques to describe data and provide a means for making inferences about a total group based on observations from part of the total. Statistics will then allow us to make a statement about the chance that our inferences are true. The primary purpose of statistics is to provide information for the decision-making process. If you keep this in mind, you should understand why statistics is called a partner in decision making.

Probably the greatest misconception about statistics is that it is "just another math course." Certainly, if statistics is approached from a theoretical viewpoint, as is the case in many mathematical statistics courses, the required mathematics can be considerable. However, the concepts introduced in this text can be discussed with a minimum amount of math. In fact, one objective in this text is to present the statistical material at a precalculus level. The text emphasizes how statistics is applied in decision-making settings and stresses the intuitive logic of the techniques. This is not to say, however, that some basic math skills are not required, because some statistical tools have a mathematical format. In particular, summation notation is a frequently used tool. A brief review of summation notation is presented in the appendix to this chapter. We suggest you review this material.

1-2 DATA LEVELS

The statistical techniques introduced in this text deal with different forms of data. The data, in turn, come from observations that can be measured. However, the level of measurement may vary greatly from application to application. In some cases the observed value can be expressed in purely numerical terms, such as dollars, pounds, inches, percentages, and so forth. In other cases the observation may be quantifiable only to the extent that it has more of some characteristic than does a second observation; such observations can be ranked only in a greater-than, equal-to, or less-than form. For example, we may be firmly convinced that the quality of one product is greater than that of another product but be unable to state that the quality is, say, twice as great. In still other cases we may only be able to count the number of observations having a particular characteristic. For instance, we may count the number of males and females in a statistics class.

To use statistical tools, we must, in one manner or another, be able to attach some quantifiable measure to the observations we are making. Thus the measurement technique used to gather data becomes important in determining how the data can be analyzed. We shall discuss and give examples of four levels of measurements: **nominal, ordinal, interval,** and **ratio.**

NOMINAL

Nominal measurement is the weakest data measurement technique. In nominal measurements, numbers or other symbols are used to describe an item or characteristic. For example, when developing a computerized payroll system, designers will generally assign a number to each employee. Most of the data processing is then performed by employee number, not name. Employee numbers make up a nominal measurement scale; they are used to represent the employees but contain no additional information. Most colleges and universities require each student to have a unique student number—another example of nominal measurement.

ORDINAL

Ordinal, or *rank,* measurement is one notch above nominal data in the measurement hierarchy. At this level, the data elements can be rank-ordered on the basis of some relationship between them; the assigned values indicate this order. For example, a typical market-research technique is to offer potential customers the chance to use two unidentified brands of a product. The customers are then asked to indicate which brand they prefer. The brand eventually offered to the general public depends on how often it was the preferred test brand. The fact that an ordering of items took place makes this an ordinal measure.

A corporate management hierarchy offers another example of ordinal measurement. The president, vice-president, division manager, plant manager, and so on form an ordinal scale; the president is "greater than" the vice-president, who is "greater than" the division manager, who is "greater than" the plant manager, and on down the line.

Ordinal measurement allows decision makers to equate two or more observations or to rank-order the observations. In contrast, nominal data can be compared only for equality. You cannot order nominal measurements. Thus a primary difference between ordinal data and nominal data is that ordinal data contain both an equality ($=$) and a greater-than ($>$) relationship, whereas nominal data contain only an equality ($=$) relationship.

INTERVAL

If you have data with ordinal properties ($>$, $=$) and can also measure on some scale the distance between two data items, you have an **interval** measurement. Interval measurements are preferred over ordinal measurements because, with them, decision makers can precisely determine the difference between two observations.

Frozen-food packagers have daily contact with a common interval measurement—temperature. Both the Fahrenheit and Celsius temperature scales have equal distances between points on the scales, which is an interval scale property, along with the ordinal properties of ">" and "=." For example, 32°F > 30°F and 8°C > 4°C. The difference between 32°F and 30°F is the same as the difference between 80°F and 78°F, two degrees in each case.

Our ordinal example about the corporate hierarchy—president > vice-president > division manager > plant manager—could not be interval unless we could measure the difference between the various titles using some scale.

RATIO

Data that have all the characteristics of interval data but also have a unique or true zero point (where zero means "none") are called **ratio data.** Ratio measurement is the highest level of measurement.

Packagers of frozen foods encounter ratio measures when they pack their products by weight. Weight, whether measured in pounds or grams, is a ratio measurement because it has a unique zero point. Many other types of data encountered in business environments involve ratio measurements—for example, distance, money, and time.

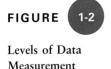

FIGURE 1-2

Levels of Data
Measurement

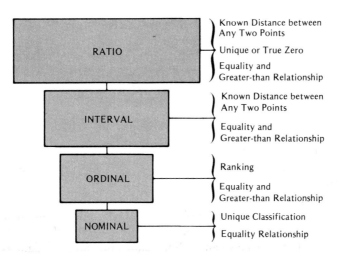

The difference between interval and ratio measurements can be confusing because it involves the definition of a true zero. If you have five dollars and your brother has ten dollars, he has twice as much money as you. If you convert your dollars to pounds, lire, yen, or marks, your brother will still have twice as much as you. If you have zero dollars, then you have none. Therefore, money has a true zero. Likewise, if you travel 100 miles today and 200 miles tomorrow, the ratio of distance traveled will be 2/1, even if you convert the distance to kilometers. Distance has a true zero. Conversely, if today's temperature is 35°F and tomorrow's is 70°F, is tomorrow twice as warm as today? The answer is no. One way to see this is to convert the Fahrenheit temperature to Celsius and the ratio will no longer be 2/1. Temperature, measured with either the Fahrenheit or Celsius scale, does not have a true zero. A temperature of 0°F does not mean no temperature.

Figure 1-2 illustrates the four levels of data measurement and summarizes the properties of each. The level of data measurement largely influences the type of statistical technique that can be used to analyze the data. As statistical techniques are introduced in this text, the data levels appropriate for analysis will be indicated.

1-3 METHODS OF OBTAINING DATA

Statistical tools are used to transform data into useful information. However, data must be available before the decision maker can use the statistical tools. Data are available from many sources, both within the organization and outside it.

Many data are originally generated in the day-to-day operations of the firm or from sources outside the firm such as government agencies. This type of data is extremely useful for resolving normal operational problems in an organization. However, many important decisions made in any organization involve actions that will occur in the future or that have future consequences. And, specifically, much of the information needed by decision makers can be found only in the actions or thoughts of individuals. The problems of gathering information on human actions are important for almost all managers and decision makers. This kind of information can be gathered in many ways. The following paragraphs will outline some basic techniques.

OBSERVATION

Conceptually, the simplest way to gather data on human behavior is to watch people. If you are trying to decide whether a new method of displaying your product at the supermarket will be more pleasing to customers, change a few displays and watch their reactions. If you would like some information on whether your new movie will be a success, have a preview screening and listen to the comments of patrons as they exit.

Time and motion study is actually a detailed method for watching people and determining their responses to environmental conditions. Much of what has been learned by psychologists has come from watching individuals' reactions when confronted with a new situation or a series of stimuli.

The conceptually simple method of watching human reactions or behavior patterns is not, however, without problems. The major constraints are time and money—a person or an organization never has enough of either. When time and money are considered, personal observation is a very expensive method of gathering data. For this method to be effective, trained observers must be used, and this increases the cost. Personal observation is also time-consuming, and to be certain that enough observations are taken, a long observation period is generally necessary. Also, since personal perception is subjective, you have no guarantee that two observers will see a situation in the same way, much less report it in the same way.

Personal observation is, however, a frequently used initial process improvement tool. For instance, in its Ranger pickup assembly operations Ford selects a number of trucks each day to be analyzed on numerous quality characteristics. Characteristics such as finish are analyzed using personal observation. Data may be gathered using checksheets where marks are made indicating the number of defects found on the right door, the left front fender, the hood, and so forth. Alternatively, an outline of the truck could be used to determine the exact location of each finish defect.

PERSONAL INTERVIEWS

Primarily to reduce cost and time wasted, personal interviews are used much more frequently than observation as a means of data collection. Individuals are asked a series of questions with the hope that they will supply useful information to the decision makers. Almost everyone has at one time or another been asked to fill out a questionnaire giving information on such items as product preference, activities, work habits, transportation choices, and so on. If these questions were asked by an interviewer, it was a personal interview.

The questions asked in personal interviews fall into two categories: *closed-ended* questions and *open-ended* questions. If the question is phrased in such a way that only certain answers are possible, it is a closed-ended question. Examples of this would be

1. Are you considering buying a new car this year?
   Yes_____ No_____
2. How would you rate the food at the student union?
   a. Excellent b. Good c. Average d. Poor e. Flushable

If the question is phrased so that the respondents are required to formulate their own answers, it is open-ended. For instance:

1. What qualities do you look for in a car?
2. Why did you decide to major in business administration?

In general, open-ended questions will gather more accurate information than closed-ended questions, but statistically analyzing open-ended answers is often difficult. When open-ended questions are analyzed, the answers are usually grouped into subjective categories. There is always room for disagreement, both about the categories and about which responses belong in which category. Data collected from closed-ended questions are much easier to analyze statistically than data from open-ended questions.

Although the time and money spent on personal interviews are generally less than for personal observations, both may still be high. This method of data gathering has additional problems:

1. Interviewers may unconsciously predetermine the answer to a question by indicating the socially acceptable answer. Consequently, the interviewer can influence the response given. This problem is compounded as the number of interviewers used increases. Each interviewer may indicate different acceptable answers.
2. Many people are uncomfortable answering certain questions in person. For instance, most individuals are reluctant to give information about their incomes. However, these people may give the information on an anonymous questionnaire.
3. An increasingly common problem with using personal interviews is that many door-to-door salespeople use questionnaires as a ploy to gain entry to a house. Individuals who have answered questions involving their children's education only to find themselves listening to a sales pitch for encyclopedias may have little sympathy for the person asking legitimate questions for the local school board.

TELEPHONE INTERVIEWS

A common method of gathering data is the telephone interview. The main advantage of a telephone interview is that it provides a rapid method of gathering data.

It has the added benefit of relatively low cost, especially when compared with personal observations and personal interviews.

In spite of the advantages of low cost and short time, the telephone interview has several disadvantages. First, people are not as likely to answer questions over the telephone as they are in person. Second, people are able to lie easily over the telephone, and unfortunately often do. During a personal interview, the interviewer can do some screening to determine whether the answers given appear to be correct. This screening can be done for questions involving relative socioeconomic status, age, sex, and so forth. This screening is generally not possible over the telephone. The telephone interview generally limits the sample to people listed in the phone book. This eliminates that segment of the population who do not have phones or who are not listed in the directory.

Thus, when telephone questionnaires are used, the time and cost advantages must be weighed against the disadvantages of potentially poorer information. Since the hardest phase of telephone interviewing is holding a person's attention, only short-answer questions should be asked.

MAIL QUESTIONNAIRES

Certainly the cheapest method of gathering data is a mail questionnaire. Many questionnaires can be printed and sent for the cost of one personal interview. The mail questionnaire also eliminates the possibility of interviewer bias. However, mail questionnaires have definite disadvantages. Probably the largest of these is a characteristically poor response. Most response rates to mail questionnaires run less than 10%. Also, the individuals who do answer are often those who have a particular interest in the subject, and consequently may not accurately represent the overall population. In addition, individuals will often interpret the same question differently, and so similar answers may not mean the same thing.

A poor questionnaire response can be followed up with letters, phone calls, or even personal visits. However, these procedures add greatly to the cost of data gathering.

Questionnaire writers should always remember that whenever they gather data from people, the problems of confidentiality are great. If the questions are asked incorrectly or concern sensitive information, many people will refuse to answer or will give wrong answers.

1-4 POPULATIONS AND SAMPLES

Two of the most important terms in statistics are *population* and *sample*. A **population** is a collection of all the items or observations of interest to the decision makers. Decision makers can specify the population in any manner they choose. A **sample** is a subset of the population. The following examples should clarify what is meant by a population and a sample.

One of the problems a certified public accounting firm faces when auditing a business is determining the number of accounts to examine. Until recently, good accounting practice dictated that the auditors verify the balance of every account and trace through each financial transaction. Though this is still done in some audits, the size and complexity of most businesses have forced accountants to select only some accounts and some transactions to audit.

The accountant's first problem is to determine just what she wishes to examine. Suppose one part of the financial audit involves verifying the accounts-receivable balances. By definition a population includes all the items of interest to the data gatherer. The accountant defines the population of interest as all receivable accounts on record. Next she selects from this population a representative group of accounts and determines their level of accuracy or inaccuracy. The representative group of accounts is the sample. The accountant uses the sample results to make inferences about the population. How these inferences are drawn will be discussed at great length in later chapters.

The short example just discussed, where the population was defined as all account-receivable balances, implies all members of the population exist at one point in time. All accounts receivable have balances. However, sometimes a population is defined as the output of a stable process. For instance, Hewlett-Packard makes disk drives at one of its production facilities. In monitoring the quality of its drives, the company would select a sample from the continuing production process. The results from this sample would be used to draw conclusions about how the production process is operating.

The process of selecting a subset of data from the population of interest is called *sampling*. George Odiorne, a widely published author on the subject of management, makes a very intuitive analogy about sampling. He says, in effect, that managers will take little buckets and row their boats over an ocean of data, dipping the buckets here and there. By examining what they find in the buckets, they will be able to draw firm conclusions not only about what is in the buckets, but also about the entire ocean.[1]

This managerial process of rowing over an ocean of data and occasionally dipping in a bucket should not be viewed as unscientific. Rather, decision makers have available both a procedure to tell them where to row their boats and dip their buckets (*sampling techniques*) and a method of scientifically drawing conclusions based on what they find in the sample buckets (*statistical inference*).

We have defined a population as all items of interest to the decision maker. If we have access to the entire population, we could collect measurements from each item. A set of measurements from the whole population is called a **census**. There are trade-offs between taking a census and a sample. Usually the trade-off is whether the cost of taking a census is worth the extra information gathered by the census. In organizations where many census-type data are stored on computer files, the additional time and effort of gathering all information are not substantial. In other cases, technology in testing equipment has advanced to the point where many companies can run a 100% acceptance sample. Thus, a census should not automatically be eliminated as an information-gathering technique.

[1] George S. Odiorne, *Management Decisions by Objectives*, 196.

Generally a census should be considered if two factors exist. First, the needed information has already been gathered as a by-product of another operation or the available technology allows information to be gathered rapidly from the population. Second, the gathering process will not change or destroy the item being observed. If these factors do not exist, a sample will most likely offer the best means of obtaining the needed information. Even if a decision maker can take a census, there are often reasons to sample. These reasons fall into the following four categories:

1. *Time constraints.* Obviously, asking a question of 100 people will take much less time than asking the same question of 10,000 people. Thus a major advantage of sampling is that it is much faster than taking a census. An additional advantage, and one that is often overlooked, is that sample data can be processed much faster than census information. Although actual processing of data is now almost always done by computer, coding and putting the data into machine-readable form is time-consuming. For instance, it takes the U.S. Census Bureau several years to make final 10-year census data available. Most managerial decisions have a time limit. The manager must make a good decision, but often this involves making a decision now instead of next year. A manager does not want to still be gathering data when the decisions must be made.

2. *Cost constraints.* The cost of taking a census may be tremendous. Consider, for example, the cost to General Motors of determining exactly what the U.S. population thinks of its latest automobiles. Gathering that data would be an astronomical undertaking. Even the federal government, with its large financial resources, attempts a nationwide census only once every 10 years, and, indeed, much of its information is based on a sample.

   This is not to say, however, that the cheapest approach is the best. In all cases the decision makers must balance the cost of obtaining information against the value of the information. Often decision makers can obtain more relevant and meaningful information from a sample than from a census. This generally occurs because more care can be taken with a sample since the data are gathered from fewer sources. Basically, if a certain amount of time is allotted to gather information, we can either gather a little information from many observations, or a lot of information from a few observations. Often the value of the additional information from a few sources outweighs the advantage of having a census.

3. *Improved accuracy.* The results of a sample may be more accurate than the results of a census. A person obtaining data from fewer sources tends to be more complete and thorough in both gathering and tabulating the data. There are likely to be fewer human errors. However, if these measurement errors can be eliminated, a census will be more accurate than a sample.

4. *Impossibility of a census.* Sometimes taking a complete census to gather information is economically impossible. In addition, obtaining informa-

tion often requires a change in, or destruction of, the item from which information is being gathered. For instance, light-bulb manufacturers have to determine the average lifetime of their bulbs. The way to determine how long a bulb will last is to plug it in and wait until it burns out. Once the bulb fails, they have determined how long it would have lasted, but obviously are unable to sell the bulb. Many other information-gathering methods are destructive and therefore cannot be used on a census basis.

A slightly different problem occurs when gathering information involves legal restrictions or personal freedoms. An example is testing new drugs. Ill people are generally unwilling to take a new drug until its effectiveness has been determined; certainly individuals cannot be forced to test a drug. However, you cannot determine a drug's effectiveness until it has been used. In fact, the Food and Drug Administration will not allow a drug to be sold until it has been extensively tested. Thus, using a census to test a new drug's effectiveness is difficult, if not impossible.

In practice, most important managerial decisions are made on the basis of sample data, and the whole issue of correctly selecting a sample from a population is one of the most complicated, and most important, in statistics. In a later chapter we will introduce some common sampling techniques and briefly consider potential problems found when applying these techniques. However, throughout this text we will assume any sample data given were gathered using correct sampling procedures. We will leave an in-depth consideration of the important subject of sampling to a later course.

At the end of this chapter, a case study involving a research effort conducted by a state transportation department is presented. This case study is designed to illustrate the steps taken to collect data and also to provide a *database* that will be referred to throughout the remainder of the text.

1-5 QUALITY IMPROVEMENT AND STATISTICS

Anyone who has studied business for any period of time, or has been following the economic events in the world, must be aware of the rapid ascent of Japan as a major economic power. In most surveys of consumer attitudes, Japanese products are given the highest marks for quality of any produced in the world. Lee Iacocca, the president of Chrysler Corporation, has complained that a car produced on a joint assembly line with Mitsubishi and given the Japanese name plate is viewed as being of higher quality than the next car given a Chrysler label. Yet, anyone aware of the history of world industry knows that during the 1950s and early 1960s Japanese products were seen as having inferior quality. Then, "Made in the U.S." was viewed as a mark of quality in world manufacturing. The story of what happened to cause the change in perception is long, and not the subject of this book, but it does have something to do with statistics.

The modern procedures of quality improvement, used so well by Japanese companies and less well by companies from other countries in the world, are a continuation of work done in the Bell Telephone system in the United States. The initial work in quality improvement, much of it statistically based, was performed at the Bell Laboratories by a group led by Walter Shewhart. Under Shewhart's leadership, many of the tools used in companies today were developed by the 1940s. While these tools were used extensively in the Bell system, their use was slow to spread to other companies in the United States.

During the 1940s, W. Edwards Deming, the person most associated with quality improvement throughout the world, gave a series of lectures on process control techniques to American companies engaged in manufacturing products for the World War II effort. Many of the correct process control procedures were installed in companies during this time, but immediately forgotten in the years after the war. In 1950 Deming gave the same series of lectures to a group of Japanese companies, which implemented his techniques. While the procedures he initially suggested have been expanded, both by him and by other pioneers of modern quality improvement techniques, the summer of 1950 is cited as the start of Japanese industrial ascendancy, and Deming is considered the "Father of Japanese Quality and Productivity." Today the Deming Award is the highest industrial prize in Japan.

Deming was rediscovered in the United States during the 1980s and continued to teach his procedures of quality improvement. He has constantly insisted that modern quality improvement procedures be based on a good understanding of basic statistical procedures. Further, he states strongly that process control cannot be implemented by people without an understanding of statistics. While this may not be a popular opinion, few are willing to debate him.

It remains somewhat of a mystery as to why U.S. companies were so slow to implement the statistical quality improvement procedures Deming recommended. Possible explanations range from complacency to ignorance. What is true, however, is that the statistical procedures being instituted today are based on the statistical concepts every business student has covered over the past 40 years.

Since quality, or process control, has become such an important issue, and may be required for the survival of many industries, we have included a separate section on quality improvement procedures in many of the chapters in the text. We will describe how the statistical concepts introduced in those chapters apply in a quality improvement setting. We will also introduce the terms used in process control situations to describe the statistical concepts covered in that chapter. Unfortunately, some of the implementation problems may be caused by semantical differences. We cannot think of an industry that has not been affected by a move to quality improvement and process control.

1-6 CONCLUSIONS

Decision makers, by definition, make decisions. They are willing to use any technique that will help them make better decisions. The primary objective of the statistical tools presented in this and the remaining chapters is to provide decision makers with a means of transferring data into meaningful information that can be used to make better decisions.

Before a decision can be made, data must often be gathered. Unfortunately, all methods used to gather data have inherent problems. This chapter has presented some methods used to gather data and some problems that can occur when data are gathered. These problems do not imply that decision makers should throw up their hands and just guess at the best decision. Rather, they should view statistical techniques as tools to be used in making decisions. We will continually emphasize, and you should never forget, that statistical techniques do not make decisions—people make decisions.

The tools presented in this text give decision makers added information to use in arriving at decisions, but the degree to which the information is useful depends on the degree to which the problems associated with data gathering have been avoided.

CHAPTER **GLOSSARY**

census A measurement of each item in the population.

data A set of values, facts, or observations.

interval data Data with the "=" and ">" comparative relationships and known scale distances between any two items or numbers.

nominal data The weakest form of data. Numbers or other symbols are used to describe an item or characteristic. The "=" relationship is the highest level of comparison.

ordinal data Data elements that can be placed in a rank ordering based on some specific relationship between them. The relationships for comparison are "=" and ">".

population A collection of measurements, items, or individuals that make up the total of all possible measurements within the scope of the study.

ratio data Data with all the characteristics of interval data, but with a unique zero point. These data are considered to be the highest data level.

sample A subset of a population. The members of a sample may be selected using either probability or nonprobability sampling.

QUESTIONS AND PROBLEMS

1. Look up the course description of your college statistics course. Relate this description to the description of statistics presented in this chapter.

2. List some examples of television and radio commentators referring to or giving descriptive statistics. When are they discussing statistical inference?

3. In connection with other classes, discuss instances when you have been exposed to descriptive statistics and when you have seen statistical inference used.

4. The Ford Motor Company has been advertising a series of comparisons between its cars and competitors' cars. What level of data measurement would each of the following be?
   a. The sound level inside the car
   b. Drivers' ratings of the handling characteristics of the car

       c. The mileage ratings for the cars

       d. The indication of whether a stereo radio is standard equipment on a car

5. This chapter presented four levels of data measurement. List these four levels and provide examples of each.

6. A company financial manager recently made a presentation showing that during the previous sixteen quarters (three months per quarter) the company showed a profit twelve times and a loss four times. What possible levels of data is the manager working with? Show what you mean with an example.

7. Discuss the advantages and disadvantages of telephone surveys. As you answer this question think in terms of a survey of small businesses in your hometown regarding employee turnover.

8. Suppose you work at a local fast-food restaurant. The manager has asked you to begin compiling a database that may be helpful later in marketing decisions. Identify five internal sources of data and three external sources of data that might prove useful for the database.

9. Suppose the U.S. Post Office is interested in obtaining feedback about how satisfied the public is with its Express Mail service. Which method of data collection would you recommend and why? Outline the procedure by which they could collect the data and discuss any potential problems.

10. Develop a short questionnaire that will be administered as a mail survey. The questionnaire will be used to collect data regarding undergraduate opinion on a proposal to institute a fee for computer usage to be paid by all undergraduate students at your college or university. Be sure to include both closed-ended and open-ended questions in your questionnaire.

11. Referring to Problem 10, modify your questionnaire so that it can be administered as a telephone survey. Also comment on how you would go about selecting the telephone numbers of those to be surveyed.

12. Comment on how it might be possible for data collected through personal interviews or observation to be inaccurate or biased. If you know of any examples of when this may have happened, discuss them.

13. Go to the library and locate three articles written by W. Edwards Deming. Write a brief review of these articles. Contrast his opinions with those of other business writers you have studied to this point.

14. Locate a company in your area that is implementing quality management. Determine the extent to which Deming has influenced its thinking.

15. (*This is best given as a group project.*) Compare and contrast the ideas of Deming with those of other pioneers of modern quality control procedures, such as Feigenbaum, Juran, Ishikawa, and Crosby.

CASE

State Department of Transportation Insurance Division Case Study and Database

This case study describes the efforts undertaken by the director of the Insurance Division for the State Department of Transportation to assess the magnitude of the uninsured motorist problem in the state. The objective of the case study is to introduce you to a data collection application and show how one organization developed a database. The actual database will be supplied to your instructor upon request. The database that appears at the end of the case study is a subset of the data found by the state department. A copy of the raw data subset has been included so that you can apply different statistical techniques introduced in subsequent chapters using a computer and appropriate statistical software.

The impetus for the case came from the Legislative Transportation Committee, which heard much testimony during the recent legislative session about the problems that occur when an uninsured motorist is involved in a traffic accident where damages to individuals and property occur. The state's law enforcement officers also testified that a large number of vehicles are not covered by liability insurance.

Because of both political pressure and a sense of duty to do what is right, the legislative committee spent many hours wrestling with what to do about drivers who do not carry the *mandatory* liability insurance. Because the actual magnitude of the problem was unknown, the committee finally arrived at a compromise plan, which required the State Transportation Department's Insurance Division to perform random audits of vehicles to determine whether the vehicle was covered by liability insurance. The audits are to be performed on approximately 5% of the state's 1 million registered vehicles each year. If a vehicle is found not to have liability insurance, the vehicle license and the owner's driver's license will be revoked for 3 months and a $250 fine will be imposed.

However, before actually implementing the audit process, which is projected to cost $1.5 million per year, Herb Kriner, director of the Insurance Division of the State Transportation Department, was told to conduct a study of the uninsured motorist problem in the state and to report back to the legislative committee in 6 months.

The Study

A random sample of twelve counties in the state was selected in a manner that gave the counties with higher numbers of registered vehicles proportionally higher chances of being selected. Then two locations were selected in each county and the state police set up roadblocks on a randomly selected day. Vehicles with in-state license plates were stopped at random until approximately 100 vehicles had been stopped at each location. The target total was about 2,400 vehicles statewide.

The issue of primary interest was whether the vehicle was insured. This was determined by observing whether the vehicle was carrying the required certificate of insurance. If so, the officer took down the insurance company name and address and the policy number. If the certificate was not in the car, but the owner stated that insurance was carried, the owner was given a postcard to return within 5 days supplying the required information. A vehicle was determined to be uninsured if no postcard was returned or if, subsequently, the insurance company reported that the policy was not valid on the day of the survey.

In addition to the issue of insurance coverage, Herb Kriner wanted to collect other information about the vehicle and the owner. This was done using a personal interview during which the police officer asked a series of questions and observed certain things such as seat belt usage and driver's and vehicle license expiration status. Also, the owner's driving records were obtained through the Transportation Department's computer division and added to the information gathered by the state police.

The Data

In all, a file consisting of 2,434 valid observations (vehicles) with all associated data was developed. Seventeen different variables were measured for each vehicle. Table 1-1 contains a listing of the data for 100 vehicles. These data should be available from your instructor on computer diskette. The diskette also contains the data set (called LIABINS) for the entire group of 2,434 observations.

The first few variables on the data set relate to the owner's driving record:

X_1 = Number of DUI (Driving Under the Influence) occurrences during the past 3 years

X_2 = Number of DUI points on the driving record in the past 3 years; different categories of DUI offenses result in different numbers of points being assigned

X_3 = Number of occurrences of failure to maintain liability insurance within the past 3 years

X_4 = Number of points on the driving record for failure to maintain insurance within the past 3 years

X_5 = Total convictions for driving-related citations within the past 3 years

X_6 = Total cancellations and suspensions of driver's license within the past 3 years

The following variables deal with the vehicle and the owner of the vehicle:

X_7 = Vehicle year

X_8 = Sex of the owner/driver; coded 1 if male, 2 if female

X_9 = Age of the owner/driver

X_{10} = Driver's seat belt status, coded

    0 = Not observed

    1 = Yes, was wearing seat belt

    2 = No, was not wearing seat belt

    3 = Not required because of age of vehicle

X_{11} = Knowledge of the state's mandatory liability insurance law, coded

    0 = No response

    1 = Yes, aware of law

    2 = No, not aware of law

    3 = Uncertain about the law

T A B L E **1-1** State Transportation Department Insurance Division Database

X_1	X_2	X_3	X_4	X_5	X_6	X_7	X_8	X_9	X_{10}	X_{11}	X_{12}	X_{13}	X_{14}	X_{15}	X_{16}	X_{17}	Case No.
0	0	0	0	0	0	60	1	29	3	1	1	4	2	12	1	1	1
0	0	0	0	0	0	69	2	24	2	1	2	17	1	10	2	1	2
0	0	0	0	0	0	77	1	50	2	1	2	0	1	12	1	1	3
0	0	0	0	0	0	82	1	64	2	2	2	37	1	12	1	1	4
0	0	0	0	0	0	77	2	18	2	1	1	9	0	11	1	1	5
0	0	0	0	0	0	87	2	18	2	1	2	10	0	11	1	1	6
0	0	0	0	0	0	81	1	52	1	1	2	52	3	17	1	1	7
0	0	0	0	0	0	79	2	38	2	1	1	7	1	2	1	1	8
0	0	0	0	2	0	87	1	31	1	1	1	30	2	12	1	1	9
0	0	0	0	0	0	82	1	58	2	1	1	57	2	9	1	1	10
0	0	0	0	1	0	74	1	69	2	1	2	4	2	10	1	1	11
0	0	0	0	0	0	78	2	45	2	1	1	12	0	13	2	1	12
0	0	0	0	0	0	86	1	35	1	1	1	10	3	14	2	1	13
0	0	0	0	0	0	80	2	42	2	1	1	13	3	12	1	1	14
0	0	0	0	0	0	85	2	22	1	1	1	21	1	12	1	1	15
0	0	0	0	1	0	87	2	20	1	1	2	17	1	12	1	1	16
0	0	0	0	0	0	79	1	36	1	1	1	35	3	12	1	1	17
0	0	0	0	0	0	0	1	23	2	0	1	11	2	12	2	1	18
0	0	0	0	0	0	82	1	55	1	1	1	45	1	13	2	1	19
0	0	0	0	0	0	68	2	61	2	1	2	7	3	16	2	1	20
0	0	0	0	1	0	87	1	68	1	1	2	9	2	12	1	1	21
0	0	0	0	0	0	86	2	65	1	1	2	2	1	18	1	1	22
0	0	0	0	0	0	80	1	61	0	1	1	59	1	16	2	1	23
0	0	0	0	0	0	86	1	37	2	1	1	25	2	14	1	1	24
0	0	0	0	1	0	76	1	38	2	1	2	37	1	14	2	1	25
0	0	0	0	0	0	79	2	49	2	1	1	48	2	13	1	1	26
0	0	0	0	5	0	79	1	21	2	1	1	20	1	12	1	1	27
0	0	0	0	0	0	77	2	39	1	1	2	1	3	12	2	1	28
0	0	0	0	2	0	74	1	38	2	1	1	21	2	1	1	1	29
0	0	0	0	0	0	78	1	18	2	1	2	17	1	10	2	1	30
0	0	0	0	1	0	0	1	27	1	1	1	2	1	10	2	0	31
0	0	0	0	0	0	84	2	58	2	1	1	57	2	12	1	1	32
0	0	0	0	0	0	78	1	26	2	1	2	10	2	10	1	1	33
0	0	0	0	0	0	82	1	37	1	1	2	9	2	12	2	1	34
0	0	0	0	1	0	79	2	31	2	1	2	9	1	15	2	1	35
0	0	0	0	1	0	85	1	56	2	1	1	55	2	10	1	1	36
0	0	0	0	1	0	72	1	18	3	1	1	16	1	12	1	1	37
0	0	0	0	0	0	78	2	61	2	1	2	60	1	12	2	1	38
0	0	0	0	0	0	78	1	42	2	1	1	17	3	14	2	1	39
0	0	0	0	0	0	84	2	41	1	1	1	26	4	12	2	1	40
0	0	0	0	2	0	79	1	19	2	1	1	14	1	12	1	1	41
0	0	0	0	0	0	79	1	55	2	3	2	30	2	6	2	1	42
0	0	0	0	0	0	83	2	67	2	1	1	66	2	12	1	1	43
0	0	0	0	0	0	78	2	50	1	1	2	49	4	18	1	1	44
0	0	0	0	0	0	79	1	48	2	1	2	47	2	8	2	1	45
0	0	0	0	0	0	68	1	49	2	1	1	46	7	12	1	1	46
0	0	0	0	0	0	75	1	38	2	1	1	11	3	12	2	1	47
0	0	0	0	0	0	77	1	27	2	1	1	26	1	12	2	1	48
0	0	0	0	1	0	84	2	22	1	1	1	21	1	13	1	1	49
0	0	0	0	1	0	86	2	23	2	1	1	20	2	13	1	1	50

T A B L E **1-1** State Transportation Department Insurance Division Database (*Continued*)

X_1	X_2	X_3	X_4	X_5	X_6	X_7	X_8	X_9	X_{10}	X_{11}	X_{12}	X_{13}	X_{14}	X_{15}	X_{16}	X_{17}	Case No.
0	0	0	0	3	1	81	1	20	2	1	1	18	1	12	2	0	51
0	0	0	0	0	0	81	2	42	1	1	1	11	4	17	1	1	52
0	0	0	0	0	0	0	1	24	2	1	1	6	0	1	1	1	53
0	0	0	0	0	0	73	2	70	2	1	2	69	1	14	1	1	54
0	0	0	0	0	0	83	2	42	2	1	2	36	3	12	1	1	55
0	0	0	0	1	0	74	1	29	2	1	1	28	1	16	1	1	56
0	0	0	0	0	0	84	1	50	2	1	1	39	2	9	1	1	57
0	0	0	0	0	0	86	2	45	2	0	1	40	1	12	2	1	58
0	0	0	0	1	0	87	2	62	1	1	2	60	3	11	1	1	59
0	0	0	0	0	0	0	1	18	2	1	1	16	3	12	1	1	60
0	0	0	0	0	0	80	2	38	2	1	1	27	2	13	1	1	61
0	0	0	0	0	0	59	1	66	2	1	2	65	5	13	1	1	62
0	0	0	0	0	0	73	2	43	1	1	2	9	4	16	1	1	63
0	0	0	0	0	0	77	2	19	2	2	1	3	1	10	2	1	64
0	0	0	0	0	0	75	1	65	2	1	2	64	6	12	1	1	65
0	0	0	0	0	0	81	1	62	2	1	1	40	2	8	1	1	66
0	0	0	0	0	0	79	1	72	1	1	1	68	4	8	1	1	67
0	0	0	0	0	0	76	1	28	2	1	1	27	2	16	2	1	68
0	0	0	0	0	0	86	2	44	2	1	1	43	1	12	1	1	69
0	0	0	0	0	0	86	1	80	2	1	2	75	1	18	2	1	70
0	0	0	0	0	0	75	2	48	2	1	1	47	1	12	1	0	71
0	0	0	0	1	0	72	1	27	2	1	2	26	2	12	1	1	72
0	0	0	0	0	0	86	2	41	2	1	2	25	3	9	1	1	73
0	0	0	0	0	0	0	1	29	2	1	1	27	2	12	1	1	74
0	0	0	0	1	0	78	1	44	2	1	1	43	3	12	1	1	75
0	0	0	0	0	0	77	1	38	2	1	1	37	2	15	1	1	76
0	0	0	0	0	0	70	1	19	2	1	2	18	0	12	1	1	77
4	0	0	0	5	4	88	1	31	2	1	1	30	2	16	2	1	78
0	0	0	0	1	0	87	2	36	1	1	2	3	0	12	1	1	79
0	0	0	0	0	0	82	1	33	2	1	1	32	2	10	1	1	80
0	0	0	0	0	0	79	1	83	2	1	2	65	4	8	1	1	81
0	0	0	0	0	0	86	1	45	2	1	1	44	2	15	2	1	82
0	0	0	0	0	0	80	2	79	1	1	2	1	1	13	2	0	83
0	0	0	0	0	0	87	2	39	2	2	1	13	3	14	1	0	84
0	0	0	0	0	0	0	1	61	2	1	1	39	3	12	1	1	85
0	0	0	0	0	0	71	2	23	2	1	2	12	0	12	2	0	86
0	0	0	0	0	0	73	1	41	1	1	1	35	5	13	1	1	87
0	0	0	0	0	0	86	1	30	1	1	1	14	2	12	1	0	88
0	0	0	0	0	0	77	1	24	2	1	1	21	2	12	1	1	89
1	0	0	0	2	1	76	1	39	1	1	1	3	3	16	1	1	90
0	0	1	0	1	3	78	1	22	1	1	1	19	1	12	2	1	91
1	0	0	0	1	0	85	1	65	1	1	1	64	1	12	1	1	92
1	0	0	0	4	2	71	1	22	1	1	2	21	2	12	2	1	93
2	0	1	0	1	3	0	1	70	3	3	2	45	3	6	2	1	94
1	0	0	0	0	2	66	1	26	2	1	1	25	2	14	1	1	95
2	0	0	0	1	1	74	1	27	2	1	1	3	3	10	1	1	96
1	0	0	0	1	1	80	1	32	2	1	1	6	2	12	1	1	97
2	0	0	0	3	1	78	1	24	2	1	1	15	1	11	1	1	98
2	0	0	0	5	5	60	1	32	2	1	1	15	1	12	2	1	99
1	0	1	0	3	4	65	1	21	2	1	1	5	1	11	1	1	100

X_{12} = Employment status coded

   0 = No response
   1 = Yes, is employed
   2 = No, unemployed
   3 = Other (retired)

X_{13} = Number of years lived in this state
X_{14} = Number of vehicles registered in this state
X_{15} = Number of years of formal education
X_{16} = Insurance certificate status coded

   0 = Not observed
   1 = Yes, certificate in vehicle
   2 = No, certificate not in vehicle
   3 = Other

X_{17} = Liability insurance status coded

   0 = Uninsured
   1 = Insured

The data collected by this survey are designed to help Herb Kriner and his staff respond to the legislative committee and to provide background information that should be helpful if the decision is to continue with the random audit enforcement process currently proposed.

ADDITIONAL DATABASES

In addition to the database called LIABINS described on the previous pages, several other databases accompany this text. Your instructor has these data files on diskette and can make them available to you.

Discussions of each of these databases along with a description of their variables follow. You will need to refer to these pages as you work the database problems in subsequent chapters of the text.

One important point to note is that in each of the following databases, if there are variables that have missing values for one or more cases, the missing value is designated by a code of −99. You must remember this when using a statistical software package.

CITIES

In September 1990, Art Lee, general manager for the Peripherals Equipment Division for a major electronics company, was given the assignment of selecting the location for the division's new research and development laboratory. Art asked his administrative assistant, Phyllis Rigg, to compile some pertinent information on 50 U.S. cities. She compiled data on eight variables for each of the 50 cities and formed a database called CITIES. The descriptions of the variables for the database are as follows:

Variable 1: 1990 population based on U.S. census estimates

Variable 2: Estimated population growth between 1990 and 1995 as a percentage of 1990 population

Variable 3: 1989 unemployment rate as a percentage

Variable 4: Average SAT or ACT score for city dwellers (*Note:* ACT scores are indicated by values less than 30. Thus, any value for variable 4 higher than 30 is an SAT score.)

Variable 5: Average SAT or ACT score for suburb dwellers (*Note:* ACT scores are indicated by values less than 30. Thus, any value for variable 5 higher than 30 is an SAT score.)

Variable 6: Average 1987 annual earnings for manufacturing workers

Variable 7: Average 1987 annual earnings for white-collar employees

Variable 8: Labor Market Stress Index (*Note:* This is an index that indicates availability of workers. High values mean a tight labor supply. The U.S. average in 1990 was 100.)

FAST100

D. L. Green & Associates is a regional investment management company that specializes in working with clients who wish to invest in smaller companies with high growth potential. To aid the investment firm in locating appropriate investments for its clients, Sandra Williams, an assistant client manager, put together a database on 100 fast-growing companies. The data were compiled in late summer of 1991. The database consists of data on eight variables for each of the 100 companies. Note that in some cases data are not available. A code of −99 has been used to signify missing data. The data are described as follows:

Variable 1: Annual 3–5-year growth rate in sales as a percentage

Variable 2: Total sales in millions of dollars for last four quarters

Variable 3: Earnings per share annual growth rate as a percentage

Variable 4: Profits for last four quarters

Variable 5: Stock price as of 9/6/91

Variable 6: Stock price 1 year earlier

Variable 7: Price earnings (P/E) ratio over last four quarters

Variable 8: Where stock is traded [1 = OTC (over the counter), 2 = NYSE (New York Stock Exchange), 3 = ASE (American Stock Exchange)]

PACRIM

The Pacific Rim countries, including Japan, South Korea, Australia, Malaysia, New Zealand, and Taiwan, are a growing factor in the world economic situation. The database named PACRIM contains data on ten variables for 150 Pacific Rim companies. The data are defined as follows:

Variable 1: Country code (1 = Japan, 2 = South Korea, 3 = Australia, 4 = Taiwan, 5 = New Zealand, 6 = Malaysia)

Variable 2: 1989 annual sales in millions of U.S. dollars

Variable 3: 1989 after-tax profits in millions of U.S. dollars

Variable 4: Profit ranking among Pacific Rim companies

Variable 5: Year-end assets in millions of U.S. dollars

Variable 6: Asset ranking among Pacific Rim companies

Variable 7: Year-end stockholder's equity in millions of U.S. dollars

Variable 8: Stockholder's equity ranking among Pacific Rim companies

Variable 9: Number of employees

Variable 10: Ranking among Pacific Rim companies by number of employees

TRUCKS

In every state, a governmental unit is charged with the responsibility of weighing trucks that drive on the state's highway system. Truck weighing serves two primary purposes: (1) to assure that the trucks operate at weights that are within the legal limit for the permit carried by the truck, and (2) to collect data on truck weights that can be factored into the studies done by engineers in designing roads and surface materials.

Typically, trucks are weighed at port-of-entry (POE) locations throughout the state. At each POE there is a platform scale on which the truck sits while being weighed. The scale can be used to measure the weight on each axle of the truck and also the gross weight of the truck. Officials at the POE also measure the length of the truck. The weights and measurements taken at the POE are assumed to be accurate.

An alternative weighing and measuring system is being studied in some states that would allow the trucks to be weighed and measured as they drive down the highway. This system, referred to as weigh-in-motion (WIM), was first developed for use in Germany. Several years ago, the state of Idaho undertook a study to determine whether a German manufactured WIM scale could be effectively used in Idaho. The actual study involved 2,000 trucks, which were weighed and measured by both the WIM scale and the POE scale. Twenty-two different measurements were observed for each truck. For the purposes of this text, the database has been reduced to 200 trucks (every 10th truck) and nine variables. The database description is as follows:

Variable 1:   Month (1 = January, 2 = February, etc.)

Variable 2:   WIM front axle weight

Variable 3:   WIM gross weight

Variable 4:   WIM total length of truck

Variable 5:   POE front axle weight

Variable 6:   POE gross weight

Variable 7:   POE total length of truck

Variable 8:   Speed of truck crossing WIM scale

Variable 9:   Temperature at time truck crossed WIM scale

DATABASE PROBLEMS

Most of the chapters in this text contain questions or problems that pertain to the State Department of Transportation database and case study. It is expected that you will be using a computer and appropriate software to work these problems. The following questions for this chapter relate to the case study but do not actually require you to do any computations with the data.

1.   For each of the seventeen variables in the database, indicate the level of data measurement for each variable.

2.   The data collection method consisted of a combination of observation and personal interview. Indicate which of the seventeen variables were obtained through observation. What potential problems might result from collecting data through observation?

3.   It would probably have been less expensive to collect the data via a telephone survey. What variables would have been difficult to collect over the telephone? Discuss.

4.   If a mail questionnaire or telephone survey had been used, what would some of the problems have been and what would some of the advantages have been? Discuss.

5.   Write a short statement outlining the objectives for which the data were collected. Assuming there was more than one objective, list the objectives in order of priority.

ADDITIONAL DATABASE PROBLEMS

The questions and problems in this section refer to the various databases that accompany this text and which are described in Chapter 1. Your instructor has been provided a diskette with these databases. It is expected that you will be using computer software to access these data and to perform the required calculations.

DATABASE: **CITIES** (*Refer to the database description in Chapter 1.*)

1. Access the CITIES database on your computer. If your software permits, provide a label for each variable and then print out the data. Determine how many variables and how many cases there are in the data set. Make sure that these data match the description in Chapter 1. (If possible, save the data and labels on your own data diskette or in your own hard disk file for later use.)
2. For each variable in the data set, determine the level of data measurement.
3. Based on the description of the database in Chapter 1, discuss how you think the data might have been collected.
4. Put yourself in the position of those responsible for collecting and analyzing these data. Identify at least two questions that you would like to answer from these data.

DATABASE: **FAST100** (*Refer to the database description in Chapter 1.*)

1. Access the FAST100 database on your computer. If your software permits, provide a label for each variable and then print out the data. Determine how many variables and how many cases there are in the data set. Make sure that these data match the description in Chapter 1. (If possible, save the data and labels on your own data diskette or in your own hard disk file for later use.)
2. For each variable in the data set, determine the level of data measurement.
3. Based on the description of the database in Chapter 1, discuss how you think the data might have been collected.
4. Put yourself in the position of those responsible for collecting and analyzing these data. Identify at least two questions that you would like to answer from these data.

DATABASE: **PACRIM** (*Refer to the database description in Chapter 1.*)

1. Access the PACRIM database on your computer. If your software permits, provide a label for each variable and then print out the data. Determine how many variables and how many cases there are in the data set. Make sure that these data match the description in Chapter 1. (If possible, save the data and labels on your own data diskette or in your own hard disk file for later use.)
2. For each variable in the data set, determine the level of data measurement.
3. Based on the description of the database in Chapter 1, discuss how you think the data might have been collected.
4. Put yourself in the position of those responsible for collecting and analyzing these data. Identify at least two questions that you would like to answer from these data.

DATABASE: **TRUCKS** (*Refer to the database description in Chapter 1.*)

1. Access the TRUCKS database on your computer. If your software permits, provide a label for each variable and then print out the data. Determine how many variables and how many cases there are in the data set. Make sure that these data match the description in Chapter 1. (If possible, save the data and labels on your own data diskette or in your own hard disk file for later use.)
2. For each variable in the data set, determine the level of data measurement.
3. Based on the description of the database in Chapter 1, discuss how you think the data might have been collected.
4. Put yourself in the position of those responsible for collecting and analyzing these data. Identify at least two questions that you would like to answer from these data.

REFERENCES

Kish, Leslie. *Survey Sampling*. Melbourne, Fla.: Krieger Publishing, 1983.

Loether, H. J., and McTavish, D. *Descriptive and Inferential Statistics*. 3d ed. Boston: Allyn and Bacon, 1988.

Neter, John; Wasserman, William; and Whitmore, G. A. *Applied Statistics*. 3d ed. Boston: Allyn and Bacon, 1988.

Odiorne, George S. *Management Decisions by Objectives*. Englewood Cliffs, N.J.: Prentice-Hall, 1969.

Siegel, S. *Nonparametric Statistics for the Behavioral Sciences*. New York: McGraw-Hill, 1956.

Yamane, Taro. *Elementary Sampling Theory*. Englewood Cliffs, N.J.: Prentice-Hall, 1967.

APPENDIX: SUMMATION NOTATION

Statistics relies heavily on **summation notation** to simplify equations involving sums of numbers. Consider the following sequence of numbers in Examples 1–3:

$$1, 2, 3, 4, 5, 6, 7, \ldots$$

Example 1

The notation summing the first five numbers is

$$\sum_{X=1}^{5} X = 1 + 2 + 3 + 4 + 5$$

$$= 15$$

Note that we read this as "the sum of the X values where X goes from 1 through 5 is equal to 15." The capital form of the Greek letter sigma (Σ) stands for the summation of these numbers.

Example 2

$$\sum_{X=1}^{4} X^2 = 1 + 4 + 9 + 16$$

$$= 30$$

This is read "the sum of the squared X values where X ranges from 1 through 4."

Example 3

$$\sum_{X=1}^{3} (X - 3) = (1 - 3) + (2 - 3) + (3 - 3)$$

$$= -3$$

Subscripts and Summation Notation

Suppose we have

i	X_i
1	5
2	7
3	3
4	1
5	12
6	5

where $i = 1, 2, 3, 4, 5, 6$
$X_i = i$th value of X (i.e., $X_1 = 5$, $X_2 = 7$, etc.)

Example 4

$$\sum_{i=1}^{3} X_i = X_1 + X_2 + X_3$$

$$= 5 + 7 + 3$$

$$= 15$$

Example 5

$$\sum_{i=1}^{5} X_i^2 = X_1^2 + X_2^2 + X_3^2 + X_4^2 + X_5^2$$

$$= 5^2 + 7^2 + 3^2 + 1^2 + 12^2$$

$$= 25 + 49 + 9 + 1 + 144$$

$$= 228$$

Example 6

$$\sum_{i=1}^{3} X_i - 4 = X_1 + X_2 + X_3 - 4$$

$$= 5 + 7 + 3 - 4$$

$$= 11$$

Rule

If c is a constant (an element that does not contain a subscript), the summation of the constant is

$$\sum_{i=1}^{n} c = nc$$

Example 7

$$\sum_{i=1}^{5} 3 = 3 + 3 + 3 + 3 + 3$$

$$= 5 \cdot 3 = 15$$

Rule

If c is a constant, then

$$\sum_{i=1}^{n} cX_i = c\sum_{i=1}^{n} X_i$$

Example 8

$$\sum_{i=1}^{5} cX_i = cX_1 + cX_2 + cX_3 + cX_4 + cX_5$$

$$= c(X_1 + X_2 + X_3 + X_4 + X_5)$$

$$= c\sum_{i=1}^{5} X_i$$

Example 9

Suppose

i	X_i
1	11
2	14
3	3
4	9
5	15

Then

$$\sum_{i=1}^{3} 5X_i = 5\sum_{i=1}^{3} X_i = 5(X_1 + X_2 + X_3)$$
$$= 5(11 + 14 + 3)$$
$$= 140$$

Rule

The summation of two or more different elements can be found by summing each element and adding the summed quantities. That is,

$$\sum_{i=1}^{n}(X_i + Y_i) = \sum_{i=1}^{n} X_i + \sum_{i=1}^{n} Y_i$$

Example 10

Given

i	X_i	Y_i
1	3	14
2	8	6
3	5	9
4	2	7

Then

$$\sum_{i=1}^{4}(X_i + Y_i) = (3 + 8 + 5 + 2) + (14 + 6 + 9 + 7)$$
$$= \quad 18 \quad + \quad 36$$
$$= 54$$

Organizing and Presenting Data

WHY DECISION MAKERS NEED TO KNOW

The element most common to the decision maker's environment is uncertainty. This is true, at least in part, because other people make up much of the managerial environment. Whenever you interact with other individuals, you can never be certain of their actions. Other parts of the managerial environment also are characterized by uncertainty. Unpredictable events such as machine breakdowns and weather changes affect output or productivity, making them anything but consistent.

The problem most decision makers must resolve is how to deal with the uncertainty that is inherent in almost all aspects of their jobs. In making decisions with uncertain results, decision makers should use all available data to analyze the possible alternatives. In many cases the data available are in *raw* form. Unfortunately, raw data are often not useful and cannot be considered to be information. Take the personnel manager who is concerned that employee absenteeism is becoming excessive. The available data consist of absentee rates for each of the last 500 days. Without being organized, these raw data provide little, if any, information about the pattern or growth of absenteeism in the company.

Decision makers need a means of converting the raw data into useful information. A first step in transforming data into information is to organize and present the data in a meaningful way. Therefore, decision makers must be aware of the basic techniques for effectively organizing and presenting data.

The ability to effectively organize and present data can mean a great deal to you in your advancement through the organization. Recently, a vice-president for the General Motors Company spoke at his former university business school's awards banquet. During a question-and-answer period that followed his speech, he was asked what single factor he considered most important in his rise to vice-president of one of the world's largest companies. He responded that a short time after he joined General Motors he took part in a departmental presentation before a group of upper-management personnel. He noted that he was able to *effectively organize and present* the complex data and that the upper-management people were outwardly impressed with his presentation. Further, he said that he is convinced that this presentation and several others like it were remembered by upper management when they needed a person for a special project a couple of years later. One thing led to another and he advanced to become vice-president.

The vice-president stressed the importance of knowing how to organize and present data and pointed out that no matter how high in an organization you reach, these skills are still an important part of the job.

CHAPTER OBJECTIVES

The objective of this chapter is to introduce some methods for handling the uncertainty that managers continually face. Practical managers often are not interested in attempting to eliminate the uncertainty or variation they face because they recognize that variation will always exist. Rather, managers often are mainly interested in determining whether the uncertainty they face is what would normally be expected or if somehow the extent of the uncertainty or variation has changed. Production managers are interested in whether their production processes are continuing in a normal fashion or whether they have been altered. A change may indicate the need for corrective action. Personnel managers are interested in knowing if overall employee skill levels have changed over time. A change may indicate that the managers need to institute a training procedure or that a new training program is paying off.

This chapter will introduce some tools decision makers need for examining the uncertainty they face. The first tools managers need are those necessary to "picture" the situation around them. To this end, several frequently used methods of presenting data will be discussed.

STUDENT OBJECTIVES

After studying the material in this chapter, you should be able to do the following:

1. Determine how to separate large volumes of data into more workable forms.
2. Describe several different methods to graph and present data in order to transform raw data into usable information.

2-1

METHODS OF REPRESENTING DATA

The process of gathering information is often complicated not because of a lack of potential information, but because the body of raw data is too large to analyze. Consider the problems facing merchandising managers interested in sales data from a series of stores, or even from one store. They are interested in which product lines are selling best, what the inventory levels are, which store areas have the highest sales levels, and numerous related questions. Imagine the managers being given a box of sales-slip copies each day and being asked to answer the questions just presented. The data cannot be effectively used in that form and therefore must be converted to a more useful form. This section introduces several useful techniques of data presentation.

FREQUENCY DISTRIBUTION

Perhaps the easiest method of organizing data is to construct a **frequency distribution.** To do this, we first establish **classes,** where a class is simply a category of interest. In a study of weather, the classes might be "clear days" and "cloudy days." In another example the categories of loan balances might be "$0 and under $500," "$500 and under $1,000," and "$1,000 and under $2,000."

The second step in developing a frequency distribution is to count the number of observations that fall into each class. Table 2-1 presents the raw data and a frequency distribution of salaries for 134 employees in a hypothetical company. We see that forty persons have salaries in the class "$20,000 and under $22,500" and that only six individuals earn $27,500 or more. Note how confusing the salary data are in their raw form.

Although developing a frequency distribution is fairly straightforward, two factors must be considered: how many classes should be used and the limits for each class. These are considered in the following paragraphs.

Decision makers want to organize data in the first place so that they can picture what the data look like. However, they immediately face a dilemma. The data must be grouped into separate classes. If the number of classes is too small, much detail available in the data is lost and the amount of potential information is reduced. On the other hand, having too many classes often makes the representation as confusing as the raw data.

No firm rule exists for determining the appropriate number of classes for a particular application, but one rule that is sometimes employed is that the number of classes, k, be the smallest integer such that $2^k \geq n$, where n is the number of raw data values. Using this rule, we get

Number of Observations	Number of Classes
9 to 16	4
17 to 32	5
33 to 64	6
65 to 128	7
129 to 256	8

TABLE 2-1

Employee Salaries

Raw Data

$12,525	$13,346	$13,850	$19,400	$13,300	$13,100	$17,204	$16,250
15,950	16,450	19,200	20,700	17,100	16,000	19,300	19,200
21,000	22,000	21,000	25,400	22,000	21,250	22,000	21,275
21,400	23,350	24,200	14,425	23,250	23,000	23,750	26,000
29,500	14,852	14,750	19,650	20,700	14,000	12,950	17,000
16,000	15,700	17,100	21,000	17,005	16,300	17,620	19,000
18,300	22,210	21,000	24,750	19,800	22,210	21,400	21,000
20,900	22,200	22,950	13,950	20,283	24,100	23,475	23,800
27,000	30,000	14,900	17,480	26,500	21,750	17,704	18,000
15,105	29,000	16,300	20,800	19,305	17,700	17,950	18,750
19,000	18,900	22,175	23,000	19,600	20,003	22,400	22,000
22,400	21,175	20,983	12,800	22,100	21,240	24,200	24,900
24,000	26,900	21,005	15,500	25,250	27,800	18,120	19,120
14,300	15,250	15,403	21,290	18,900	17,950	18,200	18,300
16,475	18,800	18,605	22,800	19,250	20,100	21,900	21,000
20,500	21,000	22,150	29,000	22,450	22,175	23,700	24,750
23,000	24,000	27,200	16,250	25,300	29,200		

Frequency Distribution

Class Interval	Frequency
$12,500 and under $15,000	14
15,000 and under 17,500	20
17,500 and under 20,000	27
20,000 and under 22,500	40
22,500 and under 25,000	19
25,000 and under 27,500	8
27,500 and over	6

Remember that this is just a rule of thumb; specific applications may require that the number of classes be more or less than implied by this rule.

Determining class size and class limits is essentially arbitrary. Two individuals will often come up with different ways of arranging data into classes. Nevertheless, certain rules and guidelines are available. The only firm rule in grouping data is that the classes be both mutually exclusive and all-inclusive. **Mutually exclusive classes** means that the classes must be arranged so that every piece of data can be placed in only one class. In particular, this means selecting class limits so that an item cannot fall into two classes. **All-inclusive classes** are classes that together contain all the data.

Every class in a frequency distribution has *expressed* class limits. Expressed class limits are those shown in the frequency distribution. For example, a frequency distribution of employee ages might have the following expressed class limits:

$$\text{Expressed lower limits} \quad \left\{ \begin{array}{l} 21\text{–}30 \\ 31\text{–}40 \\ 41\text{–}50 \\ 51\text{–}60 \\ 61\text{–}70 \end{array} \right\} \quad \text{Expressed upper limits}$$

The **class width** is determined by counting the number of units between (and including) the lower and upper expressed class limits. For instance, the class width of the first class of the employee age frequency distribution is 10 years because 21, 22, 23, . . . , 30 gives 10 years.

To find the center of a class, called the **midpoint,** we apply the half-the-sum rule:

$$\text{Midpoint} = \frac{\text{Lower limit} + \text{Upper limit}}{2}$$

For the employee age frequency distribution the midpoints are

Expressed Class Limits	Sum	Midpoint = Sum/2
21 to 30	51	25.5
31 to 40	71	35.5
41 to 50	91	45.5
51 to 60	111	55.5
61 to 70	131	65.5

Thus, for the first class, the value 25.5 is midway between the expressed class limits and is therefore the midpoint of this class.

As mentioned, the classes of a frequency distribution need to be developed such that they are mutually exclusive and all-inclusive. In addition, it is desirable to select class limits so that the actual observations are evenly distributed throughout the class interval. This means that if an age class has limits of "21–30," the ages within this class should be evenly spread between 21 and 30 inclusive. If most of the people are younger than 25, the limits "21–30" are not very representative of the data in this class.

An easy way to determine an approximate class width is to take the smallest and largest values in the raw data, subtract the two, and divide by the desired number of classes:

$$\text{Class width} = \frac{\text{Largest value} - \text{Smallest value}}{\text{Number of classes}}$$

This will give a starting figure for class widths. You should also apply some common sense in developing the frequency distribution. For example, if the division gives class sizes of 4.817 years, round this up to 5 years. Also, start your class limits at some easy-to-use value. If you have data on automobile weights, do not initiate 100-pound intervals at 1,805.6 pounds; start with 1,800 pounds.

If possible, have class intervals of equal size. Frequency distributions with equal class intervals are not only easier to understand, but will make later statistical analysis much simpler. However, constant intervals are not possible in many managerial applications because the data are **skewed.** Data are *skewed* when most observations are located relatively close together, but a few points are located in one direction far from the majority. Data that are not skewed are *symmetrical.* These concepts are discussed more fully in Chapter 3.

Many data of interest to managers are skewed. Incomes in the United States form a skewed frequency distribution. The vast majority of incomes are less than $50,000, but a few individuals make much more than that. Class intervals wide enough to contain all observations using even twenty classes would be hundreds of thousands of dollars wide. Thus almost everyone would fall in the first interval, totally obscuring information in the data. However, if the intervals were $2,000, $5,000, or even $10,000 wide, many more than twenty intervals would be needed to contain all data points. The way out of this dilemma is to use open-ended intervals, or intervals of unequal sizes. *Open-ended intervals* occur when the first class contains no lower limit or the last data class contains no upper limit. Table 2-1 contains an open-ended interval, "$27,500 and over."

Data may be skewed in either direction; thus open-ended intervals or unequal intervals are common. Once again, they are necessary when the majority of data are contained within a limited range of values and relatively few observations exist with extreme values.

Constructing a Frequency Distribution

The manager of a local department store is interested in what her store's sales values look like. Table 2-2 presents the raw data from a sample of sixty-four sales. What do the data in this form indicate to you?

TABLE 2-2

Raw Sales Data
for Department
Store Example
($n = 64$)

$ 6.49	$ 8.90	$22.95	$16.30
7.19	11.97	74.95	13.39
18.63	4.44	24.99	11.99
1.29	13.88	69.99	4.44
34.98	8.12	8.99	61.98
12.95	64.88	35.95	6.99
21.25	24.99	1.26	11.99
68.99	9.97	3.97	9.97
9.98	3.99	4.35	7.49
0.97	14.99	5.99	12.49
2.19	7.75	11.99	21.50
41.69	67.29	5.25	1.69
4.65	4.50	9.85	49.99
3.19	34.95	6.50	13.89
10.45	7.49	29.97	19.97
23.85	5.69	3.57	2.77

The manager decides to construct a frequency distribution of the sample data. She elects to apply the $2^k \geq n$ rule. Since $n = 64$, she will start with six classes. To determine the class width, she divides the difference between the highest ($74.95) and the lowest ($0.97) values in the sample by the number of classes, as follows:

$$\text{Class width} = \frac{\$74.95 - \$0.97}{6}$$

$$= \$12.33$$

She rounds up to $12.50. She then picks a starting point of $0.00 and forms the following expressed classes:

$ 0.00 and under $12.50

12.50 and under   25.00

25.00 and under   37.50

37.50 and under   50.00

50.00 and under   62.50

62.50 and under   75.00

Note that the class limits are mutually exclusive and that no overlap exists between classes. Also, the classes are all-inclusive since the smallest and largest elements are included. You should also note that the decision maker could have rounded the class width to a value such as $13.00 or even $15.00. Remember that the reason for grouping raw data into a frequency distribution is to make things easier to understand, so always develop class limits that are easy to work with.

With the class limits determined as shown, the manager now counts the number of values that fall into each class. The resulting frequency distribution is shown in Table 2-3. The midpoint of each class has also been recorded for future use. For example, the midpoint for the second class is found using the half-the-sum rule, as follows:

$$\text{Midpoint} = \frac{12.50 + 25.0}{2}$$

$$= \frac{37.50}{2}$$

$$= \$18.75$$

Referring to Table 2-3, the frequency column shows the number of sales values falling in each class. The **relative frequency** is the ratio of observations in a class to the total observations in all classes. Thus 21.875% of the sample sales values were in the class $12.50 and under $25.00. The relative frequency values are very useful for comparing two or more frequency distributions that have been developed from data sets with different amounts of raw data. For example, this department store manager can say that slightly over 59% of the individual sales were under $12.50. This percentage could be compared meaningfully with the percentage of sales under $12.50 for another store regardless of the amount of raw data available from the second store. A comparison of actual frequencies would not be meaningful if the sample sizes differed.

Table 2-3 contains two other columns: the **cumulative frequency** and the **relative cumulative frequency**. The *cumulative frequency* is the sum of the frequency of a particular class and all preceding classes. For example, we see in Table 2-3 that fifty-six of the sales values in the sample were under $37.50. The *relative cumulative frequency* in a class is the cumulative frequency divided by the total observations in all classes. For example, 87.5% of the sales values in this sample were under $37.50. Note also the sum of the relative frequencies equals 1.

TABLE 2-3

Frequency Distribution for Department Store Sales

Sales Class	Midpoint	Frequency	Relative Frequency	Cumulative Frequency	Relative Cumulative Frequency
$ 0 and under $12.50	6.25	38	0.59375	38	0.59375
12.50 and under 25.00	18.75	14	0.21875	52	0.81250
25.00 and under 37.50	31.25	4	0.06250	56	0.87500
37.50 and under 50.00	43.75	2	0.03125	58	0.90625
50.00 and under 62.50	56.25	1	0.01563	59	0.92188
62.50 and under 75.00	68.75	5	0.07812	64	1.00000
Total		64	1.00000		

SKILL DEVELOPMENT PROBLEMS FOR **SECTION 2-1**

The following set of problems is meant to test your understanding of the material in this section.

1. Describe briefly each of the following:
   a. Class limits
   b. Relative frequency distribution
   c. Cumulative frequency distribution

2. Describe the difference between a frequency distribution and a relative frequency distribution.

3. Assume you are trying to construct a frequency distribution for the weights of people in this class. Describe the steps you would take.

4. Think of examples of skewed distributions. How would you select class limits for these distributions?

5. Go to the library, and from the *Statistical Abstract of the United States,* construct a frequency distribution for unemployment rate by state. Justify your choice of class limits and number of classes.

6. Suppose that the loan officer at Money First National Bank wants to obtain information about the loans she has made over the past 5 years. She has decided to develop a distribution showing the loan frequency by size of loan. A quick look at the data indicates that the smallest loan she made was for $1,000 and the largest loan was $25,000. She has decided to have ten classes in her distribution. Define the ten classes in terms of lower and upper limits. Determine the midpoints for each class developed.

7. The following data are a sample of sixty accounts receivable balances selected from accounts at the Wallingford Department Store.
   a. Decide how many classes would be appropriate for these data and justify your choice.

$ 39.93	$ 72.04	$ 69.04	$ 87.00	$ 55.55	$33.33
107.56	146.93	107.33	80.00	7.50	29.59
98.05	27.50	141.88	68.00	15.00	11.05
24.88	105.19	70.00	96.07	150.00	9.47
25.00	11.41	37.73	44.09	80.05	99.99
19.95	53.72	125.00	75.55	97.94	47.09
72.50	16.18	33.97	56.25	12.11	19.58
20.00	126.12	16.47	110.00	8.00	49.00
30.72	14.50	11.01	76.47	19.33	62.50
90.05	19.33	49.99	52.52	27.05	66.05

   b. Using the number of classes you selected, develop a frequency distribution for the accounts receivable.
   c. Write a one-paragraph statement describing the accounts receivable balances as reflected by the sample. (Remember that in business, report writing is an important way of conveying information.)

8. Comment on using the following classes in connection with the data given in Problem 7.
   a. $ 9.47–$19.46
      19.47– 29.46
         etc.
   b. $ 5–$15
      15– 25
      25– 30
         etc.
   c. $ 5 to under $35
      35 to under 45
      45 to under 55
         etc.
   d. $16 to under $30
      31 to under 45
      46 to under 60
         etc.

2-2 GRAPHICALLY PRESENTING DATA

The usefulness of a body of data depends on whether the individuals working with it are able to readily understand the information it contains. Data must be arranged in the most understandable manner possible. In addition, the information should be arranged in an eye-catching way. Unfortunately, frequency distributions are often neither totally meaningful nor eye-catching. Because of this, *graphical representations* are often used to display statistical information. There are almost as many ways to present data as there are persons doing the presenting. The following sections discuss some of the most common forms of graphical data representation.

PIE CHARTS

An effective manner of presenting statistical data is with a **pie chart.** This method is useful in showing proportional relationships, such as market share, budgets, and demographic rankings. A pie chart is often used by newspapers and magazines when national, state, or local government budgets are being determined. Perhaps the major advantage of a pie diagram is that it is extremely easy to understand. The entire circle, or "pie," represents the total amount available, and the pieces are proportional to the amount of the total they represent. Figure 2-1 illustrates how a property-tax dollar was distributed in a midwestern city in 1992.

Pie charts can also be developed quite easily from a frequency distribution by using relative frequencies. Consider again the department store sales frequency distribution shown in Table 2-2. Figure 2-2 shows the pie chart illustrating the percentage breakdown of sales in each of the six classes. In this example, the pie chart provides an effective picture of the relative frequency distribution.

FIGURE **2-1**

Pie Chart for
Property-tax
Example

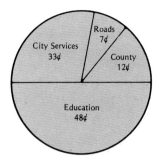

FIGURE **2-2**

Pie Chart for
Department Store
Sales

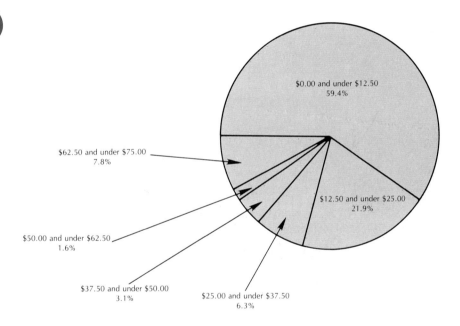

For easy understanding, limit the number of slices to five or six. This sometimes requires combining several small classes into an "other" category. Experienced presenters often put the most important slice in the upper right of the pie.

HISTOGRAMS

A **histogram** is a graphical picture of a frequency (or relative frequency) distribution. The number of observations in each class is represented by a rectangle whose base is equal to the class width and whose height is proportional to the frequency (or relative frequency) of cases belonging to that class. The vertical axis represents the class frequency and begins at the zero point. The horizontal axis represents the measure of interest, and the scale can begin with any conveniently low value.

The purpose of a histogram is to provide a visual picture of a frequency distribution. Relative differences in the areas of the rectangles correspond to relative differences in the number of observations between different classes.

When constructing a histogram, the measure for the item being considered is plotted on the horizontal axis, and the appropriate frequency measure on the vertical axis. Figure 2-3 shows a histogram representing the frequency distribution of sales data shown in Table 2-3.

FIGURE 2-3

Histogram
Showing the
Distribution of
Daily Store Sales

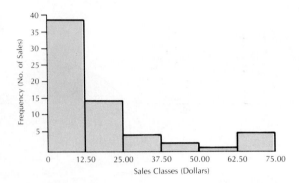

Histograms with Unequal Class Widths

Sometimes data can be most clearly and meaningfully presented by using *unequal-size class widths*. When this is the case, a slight modification must be made in the procedure for developing a histogram. For example, Table 2-4 shows a frequency distribution for department store sales with unequal-size class intervals. Note that the interval "15.00–29.99" is twice the width of the interval "7.50–14.99," and that the interval "45.00–74.99" is four times as wide. In developing a histogram for the relative frequency distribution, we must account for the extra width by reducing the height of the histogram proportionately. That

TABLE 2-4

Frequency
Distribution with
Unequal-size
Class Intervals
for Department
Store Data

Sales Class	Frequency	Relative Frequency
$ 0.00– 7.49	24	0.375
7.50–14.99	19	0.297
15.00–29.99*	10	0.156
30.00–37.49	3	0.047
37.50–44.99	1	0.016
45.00–74.99*	7	0.109
Total	64	1.000

*Intervals having widths greater than $7.50.

is, for an interval having a width twice the normal size, the height of the associated frequency rectangle must be cut in half. Figure 2-4 illustrates this concept for the department store sales data.

FIGURE **2-4**

Relative
Frequency
Histogram with
Unequal Class
Intervals for
Department Store
Sales Data

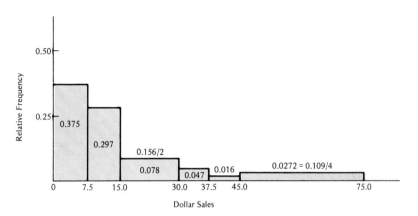

Special care should be taken when using histograms to represent frequency distributions with unequal intervals. Even though the area of each rectangle represents the relative frequency, many people will automatically look at the height of each rectangle instead. Therefore, the possibility of misrepresenting the data always exists.

Cumulative Histogram

Table 2-3 displays the cumulative frequency distribution for the department store sales data. Decision makers frequently find it useful to graph this cumulative frequency distribution to illustrate a particular point about the data. A **cumulative frequency histogram** is used to graph the cumulative frequency distribution values. Figure 2-5 shows a cumulative histogram developed from the information in Table 2-3. Note that the vertical axis represents the cumulative frequency and the height of each rectangle is the cumulative frequency of the class shown on the horizontal axis and all preceding classes. Figure 2-5 shows that most of the data (52 of 64 data points) are contained in the first two classes.

BAR CHARTS

Bar charts are variations of histograms and are often used to illustrate data or to emphasize classes or categories of interest. For example, Figure 2-6 shows a bar-chart representation of data collected in a recent survey of college students. In this example, each bar is the same length, representing 100% of those taking the course. From this we can visualize the relative rates of students passing and failing specific courses.

FIGURE 2-5

Cumulative
Frequency
Histogram for
Department Store
Sales

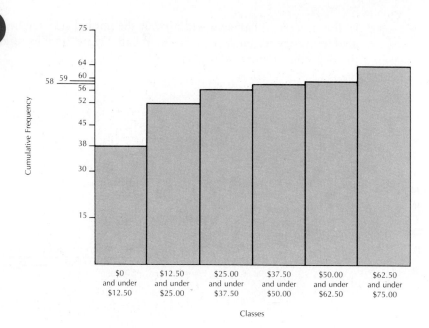

FIGURE 2-6

Bar Chart of Pass/
Fail Percentages
by Course

A horizontal bar chart, such as in Figure 2-6, is particularly effective in comparing values at the same point in time. For ease of viewing, the bars are often arranged in descending order. Note that the labels and appropriate numbers are contained in the bars themselves.

Vertical bar charts, such as Figure 2-7, showing the growth in number of homes heated by electricity in a western state, are effective for presenting the same data at different points in time. It is easy to see that electricity use has been rising rapidly in this western state since 1983. To avoid the possibility of misrepresenting the associated data, each bar in these graphs should be of equal width.

TIME SERIES PLOTS

A **time series plot** is a graph of data that have been measured over time. For example, consider the Beltview Printing Company, which does virtually all forms

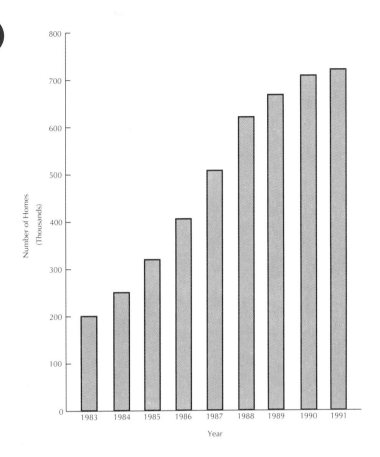

FIGURE 2-7

Number of
Homes with
Electric Heating

of printing for businesses in the Miami, Florida, area. Table 2-5 shows data for sales and advertising expenses for the company over the 10-year period beginning in 1983. These data constitute **time series data.** A major advantage of time series plots is the capability to use a large number of data points. Because of this, they

TABLE 2-5

Time Series Data
for Beltview
Printing
Company
Example

Year	Sales	Advertising
1983	$117,000	$11,000
1984	205,000	54,000
1985	190,000	39,000
1986	300,000	65,000
1987	325,000	90,000
1988	400,000	75,000
1989	375,000	80,000
1990	340,000	70,000
1991	300,000	60,000
1992	340,000	75,000

are often used to represent values companies measure continually, such as monthly inventory levels, daily customer demand, or weekly cash balances.

Figure 2-8 illustrates a time series plot where both sales and advertising are plotted against time. Time series plots like these are very useful for identifying how variables have changed over time. Here the plots show that both advertising and sales have increased over the 10-year period. Also, except for 1988 and 1989, relative changes in advertising and sales have been in the same direction.

FIGURE **2-8**

Time Series Plot for Beltview Printing Company Example

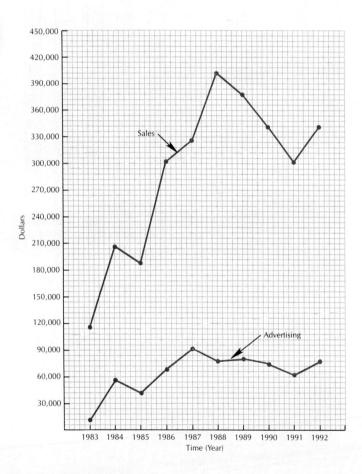

SCATTER PLOTS

A **scatter plot** is a two-dimensional graph of the ordered pairs of two variables. One variable is placed on the horizontal axis and the second variable is located on the vertical axis. For example, the J–Max Real Estate Agency has randomly selected a sample of eight homes from those that have sold during the past year in Madison, Wisconsin. For each of these eight homes, data have been recorded for the sales price, the number of square feet in the home, and the distance of the home from the airport. These data are presented in Table 2-6.

TABLE 2-6

Scatter Plot Data for J–Max Real Estate Company Example

Home	Sales Price	Square Feet	Miles to Airport
1	$ 95,000	1,750	0.50
2	117,000	2,150	1.00
3	95,000	1,500	3.00
4	145,000	2,200	2.50
5	80,000	1,900	0.25
6	70,000	1,800	0.20
7	110,000	2,000	1.50
8	77,000	1,900	0.30

Figures 2-9 and 2-10 show the scatter plots for sales price versus square feet and for sales price versus distance to the airport, respectively. Scatter plots like these are useful for helping identify what, if any, relationship exists between two variables. For instance, Figure 2-9 shows that, in general, larger homes tend to sell for more money. Figure 2-10 shows that, in general, the closer the home is to the airport, the lower the sales price.

FIGURE 2-9

Scatter Plot of Sales Price vs. Square Feet for J–Max Real Estate Company Example

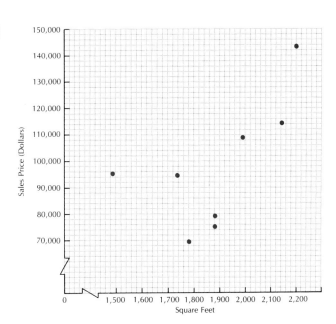

FIGURE **2-10**

Scatter Plot of
Sales Price vs.
Distance for
J–Max Real
Estate Company
Example

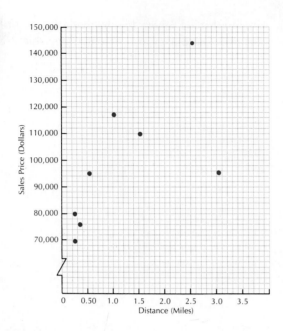

SKILL DEVELOPMENT PROBLEMS FOR **SECTION 2-2**

The following set of problems is meant to test your understanding of the
material in this section.

9. You work for the State Industrial Development Council. You are presently
working on a financial services brochure to send to out-of-state companies.
You are given the following data on banks in your state and are to present
them in an eye-catching manner with a two-paragraph summary of what the
data would mean to a company considering moving. Further, your boss has
just said you need to include relative frequencies in your presentation.

Deposit Size (× $1 million)	Number of Banks	Total Deposits (× $1 million)
Less than 5	2	7.2
5 to less than 10	7	52.1
10 to less than 25	6	111.5
25 to less than 50	3	95.4
50 to less than 100	2	166.6
100 to less than 500	2	529.8
Over 500	2	1,663.0

10. Your company is about to introduce a complete line of steel-belted radial
tires. Because you are late entering the market, you are supposed to develop a
new, hard-hitting advertising approach. You decide to put test tires on 100

taxis along the Alaskan pipeline. The following is a listing of how far the 100 taxis ran before one of the four tires did not meet minimum federal standards (rounded to the nearest thousand miles):

38	24	12	36	41	40	45	41	40	47
26	15	48	44	29	43	28	29	37	10
37	45	29	31	23	49	41	47	41	42
61	40	40	45	37	55	47	42	28	38
38	48	18	16	39	50	14	52	33	32
51	10	49	21	44	31	43	34	49	48
28	39	28	36	56	54	39	31	35	36
32	20	54	25	39	44	25	42	50	41
9	34	32	34	42	40	43	32	30	45
20	29	14	19	38	46	46	39	40	47

Although you do not want to be dishonest in presenting the results of your test, at the same time your job depends on showing the results in as favorable a light as possible. Organize and present the data using the methods discussed in this chapter and decide which method would be most favorable for selling the tires.

Your boss apparently delights in putting people on the spot. Make sure you can defend your choice, including how you determined the interval size and interval limits.

11. Ed Christianson has been asked by the director of marketing to make a presentation at next week's annual meeting of the Brown Manufacturing Company. The presentation concerns the company's advertising budget for the past year and the projected budget for the next year. In preparing for the meeting, Ed has obtained the following data:

Medium	This Year's Expenses	Next Year's Budget
Newspaper	$35,000	$40,000
Television	60,000	80,000
Trade publications	25,000	20,000
Miscellaneous	10,000	10,000

Use these data to develop a bar chart that effectively shows both this year's expenses for advertising and next year's proposed budget.

12. Referring to Problem 11, present the data in a pie chart. Do this presentation first using two separate pie charts, and then present both sets of data in one pie chart. Finally, develop a pie chart that shows how the increased advertising expenditure will be allocated the next year.

13. The American Accounting Association recently contracted with a consulting company to study issues pertaining to continuing education on the part of certified public accountants. As part of that study, the consulting firm selected

a random sample of twenty accountants in New York state and collected data on a variety of variables, including the number of years since each accountant entered public accounting, the number of continuing education courses taken the past year, and the annual salary of the accountant. These data are shown in the following table.

Years Since Entering Public Accounting X_1	Number of Courses Taken Last Year X_2	Annual Salary X_3
11	2	$ 45,000
4	3	29,000
17	0	71,000
6	4	38,000
15	1	40,000
12	0	31,000
2	6	32,500
21	0	104,000
4	6	36,000
10	3	39,500
7	2	29,500
11	1	54,000
13	0	44,000
15	0	47,000
4	3	29,500
9	1	37,000
23	0	41,000
10	1	36,000
14	0	56,000
3	5	23,500

a. Develop scatter plots of all three combinations of two variables. Discuss what (if anything) you can discern from the scatter plots.
b. Develop frequency distributions for each variable and then develop a histogram from each frequency distribution. Write a short report describing the data.
c. Develop a bar chart that shows (on the same chart) X_1 and X_2 by income (X_3). Discuss the advantage of presenting all these data together.

14. Discuss how bar charts and frequency histograms are similar and how they are different.

15. The Morrison Center for the Performing Arts has been operational since 1981. The annual ticket sales for the center for the years 1981 through 1991 are shown in the table.

Year	Sales
1981	$204,000
1982	275,000
1983	280,000
1984	299,000
1985	345,000
1986	368,000
1987	401,000
1988	344,000
1989	359,000
1990	405,000
1991	507,000

Prepare a time series plot for the sales data and write a short report describing what your graph illustrates.

2-3 COMPUTER GRAPHICS AND STATISTICAL SOFTWARE

Technological advances during the past several years have brought many changes to the way organizations operate. One area in which technological change has been widely implemented is in the employment of statistical techniques. Not too many years ago most statistical analysis was performed by hand or with a calculator; now, virtually every decision maker has access to a mainframe and/or a microcomputer that has statistics software.

Because computer output has become such a universal method of presenting the results of statistical analysis, we have integrated two statistical packages throughout the text. We have chosen these packages both for their ease of use and because they represent the types of statistical packages currently available. The first package, MINITAB, was originally designed for use on a central computer system and accessed by individual terminals.[1] MINITAB is a command-driven program, and so if you want to perform a statistical procedure you will have to enter the correct sequence of commands into the "command line" on the screen. This statistical package is widely used in colleges and universities, and you may well have access to this program. When showing MINITAB output in the text, we will also show the sequence of commands necessary to produce this output. MINITAB is also available for personal computers.

The second statistical package we will include is GB-STAT.[2] This is a more recently developed statistical program and was designed to be used on individual

[1] MINITAB was originally developed at Pennsylvania State University as a teaching aid for the introductory statistics course.

[2] GB-STAT is a product of Dynamic Microsystems, Inc., 13003 Buccaneer Road, Silver Spring, MD 20904.

personal computers. GB-STAT is menu-driven, which means the statistical procedures are chosen from a set of options presented on the screen in response to other
screen selections. Initially we will show some of the menu screens when discussing
GB-STAT output, but most often we will show only the output from this package.

These software programs allow the user to perform statistical analyses
quickly and accurately and to work with large or small data sets to do more
extensive analysis than would be feasible by manual methods. This is especially
true in the field of graphical analysis. Earlier in this chapter we described methods
for manually developing bar charts, histograms, pie charts, and other graphical
techniques for displaying data. All of these techniques and many others can be
performed using a computer and the right statistical software.

To illustrate, we will use data gathered for KIVZ-Channel 5, in Middleton.
KIVZ has started to slip in the Arbitron ratings. Alex McKinnon, the recently
hired station manager, has decided to survey viewers in the market area to develop an information base before trying to formulate a strategy to increase viewer
numbers. Table 2-7 provides the definition of each variable in the database.

Figures 2-11, 2-12, and 2-13 illustrate three different types of graphs created
using a graphics package and the KIVZ-Channel 5 data. In particular, note the
level of sophistication that can be included in the bar charts shown in Figures
2-11 and 2-12. Remember that the role of graphical data presentation is to help

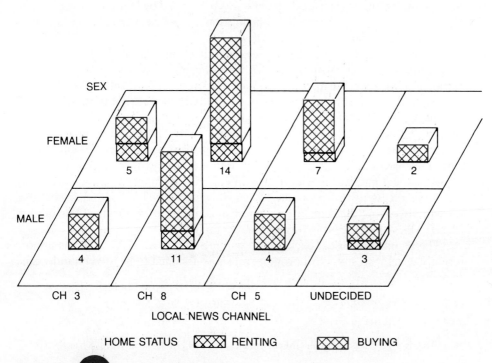

FIGURE **2-11** Three-dimensional Bar Chart for KIVZ-Channel 5 Home Ownership Analysis

Variable	Question & Response Code
X_1	On which of the following channels do you most frequently watch national network news at 5:30 P.M.? (1) Channel 5 (2) Channel 3 (3) Channel 8 (4) Undecided
X_2	On which of the following channels do you most frequently watch local news at 6:00 P.M.? (1) Channel 3 (2) Channel 8 (3) Channel 5 (4) Undecided
X_3	Considering the local news station you most frequently watch, how would you rate the station's coverage of local news? (1) Poor (2) Fair (3) Good (4) Very good (5) Excellent
X_4	Considering the local news station you most frequently watch, how would you rate the station's sports coverage? (1) Poor (2) Fair (3) Good (4) Very good (5) Excellent
X_5	Considering the local news station that you most frequently watch, how would you rate the station's weather report? (1) Poor (2) Fair (3) Good (4) Very good (5) Excellent
X_6	Considering the local news station that you most frequently watch, how would you rate the station's anchor newscaster? (1) Poor (2) Fair (3) Good (4) Very good (5) Excellent
X_7	Considering the local news station that you most frequently watch, how would you rate the station's sportscaster? (1) Poor (2) Fair (3) Good (4) Very good (5) Excellent
X_8	Considering the local news station that you most frequently watch, how would you rate the overall news performance? (1) Poor (2) Fair (3) Good (4) Very good (5) Excellent
X_9	I believe the network news station I prefer to watch at 5:30 P.M. is an important influence regarding which local news I usually watch. (1) True (2) False (3) Undecided
X_{10}	The head of this household is: (1) Male (2) Female
X_{11}	The head of this household is: (1) Single (2) Divorced (3) Married (4) Other
X_{12}	How many people living in this household are employed full time?____
X_{13}	Are you buying or renting (leasing) the home you now live in? (1) Renting/leasing (2) Buying
X_{14}	How many years have you lived at this residence?____
X_{15}	How many years have you lived in this state?____
X_{16}	Indicate the highest level of formal education of the head of this household: (1) Grade school (2) Some college (3) Vocational training (4) High school (5) College graduate (6) Graduate work
X_{17}	How old is the head of this household?____
X_{18}	Please indicate the total household annual income.____
X_{19}	Approximately how many hours per week is the television turned on in your household?____

TABLE 2-7

Identification of Variables for KIVZ-Channel 5

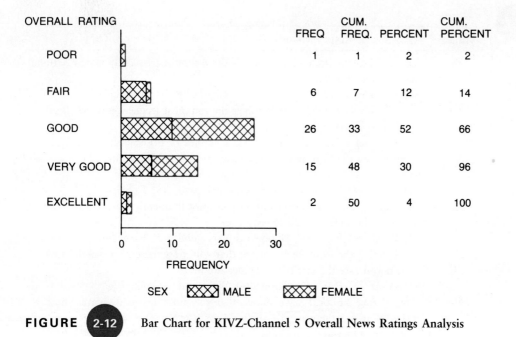

OVERALL RATING

	FREQ	CUM. FREQ.	PERCENT	CUM. PERCENT
POOR	1	1	2	2
FAIR	6	7	12	14
GOOD	26	33	52	66
VERY GOOD	15	48	30	96
EXCELLENT	2	50	4	100

FREQUENCY

SEX ⊠ MALE ⊠ FEMALE

FIGURE **2-12** Bar Chart for KIVZ-Channel 5 Overall News Ratings Analysis

the decision maker obtain information from a data set. Computer graphics is an important tool in this process.

The graphs shown in Figures 2-11, 2-12, and 2-13 are only a few examples of the graphics you can create with graphics software and a plotter. In Section 2-5

FIGURE **2-13**

Pie Chart for KIVZ-Channel 5 Education Level Distribution

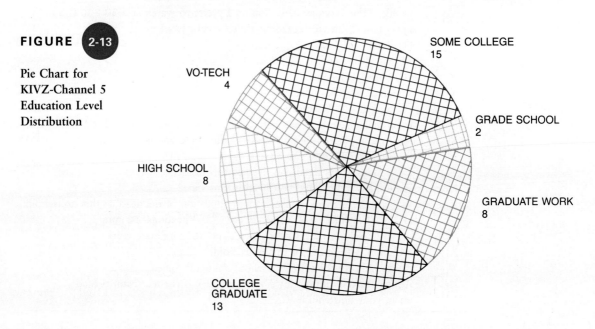

SOME COLLEGE
15

VO-TECH
4

GRADE SCHOOL
2

HIGH SCHOOL
8

GRADUATE WORK
8

COLLEGE GRADUATE
13

we show some alternative computer applications that can be performed without the aid of special graphics capabilities.

2-4 QUALITY IMPROVEMENT AND DESCRIPTIVE STATISTICS

Some of the most widely used quality improvement tools are based on the statistical concepts introduced in this chapter. The following examples will demonstrate these tools.

PROCESS CAPABILITY STUDIES

A fundamental concept of quality management is that the process providing the good or service must be able to meet the expectations of the organization's customer. You should not promise error-free products unless the process is capable of producing error-free products. You should not promise next-day delivery if your system is not capable of providing next-day deliveries.

Consider the case of a local fire department that has been charged by the city council to respond to all fires in less than 3 minutes from the time the call is received. Data are gathered for the last 100 calls indicating the time from when the call is received until the first unit arrives at the fire. The data are used to construct a **tally sheet.** This is shown in Figure 2-14.

FIGURE (2-14)

Tally of Fire Response Times

Time Range	Tally	Frequency	
Under 1 minute	₩Ⅲ Ⅰ	6	
1–1.49 minutes	₩Ⅲ ₩Ⅲ	10	
1.5–1.99 minutes	₩Ⅲ ₩Ⅲ ₩Ⅲ	15	69
2–2.49 minutes	₩Ⅲ ₩Ⅲ ₩Ⅲ ₩Ⅲ	20	
2.5–2.99 minutes	₩Ⅲ ₩Ⅲ ₩Ⅲ Ⅲ	18	
3–3.49 minutes	₩Ⅲ ₩Ⅲ Ⅰ	11	
3.5–3.99 minutes	₩Ⅲ Ⅲ	8	31
Over 4 minutes	₩Ⅲ ₩Ⅲ Ⅱ	12	
	Total	100	

Notice that this is simply a frequency distribution as described in Section 2-1. The corresponding bar chart is shown in Figure 2-15. This chart shows that the fire department is clearly not able to meet the 3-minute standard in all cases. For these sample data, the standard is not met for 31% of the calls. From a quality improvement perspective, the alternatives are either to make some change in the system to allow the response distribution to be lowered, or admit that the present system cannot always meet the standard.

FIGURE **2-15**

Bar Chart of Fire
Response Times

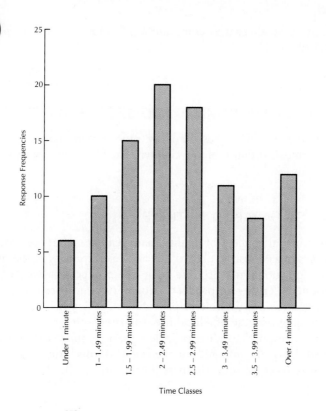

PARETO ANALYSIS

Pareto analysis is a technique introduced by Joseph Juran, one of the early pioneers in quality improvement procedures. It is named after Vilfredo Pareto, an Italian economist, who discovered that 85% of the world's wealth was owned by 15% of the population. This pattern of nonuniform distribution can be seen in many other areas, as the following example demonstrates.

A large home appliance repair company has launched a campaign to improve its customer service. To concentrate its efforts in the most important areas, the company has looked at the past 1,000 customer complaint cards. The negative comments were identified as falling into the categories shown in Table 2-8.

The frequency values to the right of each category identify the number of times each complaint was mentioned. Notice that the total is more than 1,000, since some people had more than one complaint. The distribution of complaints is shown in Figure 2-16. Notice that the complaints are not uniformly distributed. "Not arriving when scheduled" is the single most numerous complaint. In addition, the vast majority of complaints are associated with three of the ten categories. Figure 2-16 is called a Pareto chart, one of the most useful quality improvement tools. Note that the complaint categories are arranged in order of decreasing frequency. Pareto charts are always presented in this way to draw attention to the

TABLE 2-8

Customer
Complaint
Categories and
Frequencies

Categories	Frequency
Repairs taking longer than 1 day	289
Not having the correct parts	326
Not arriving when scheduled	445
Talking down to the customer	74
Can't describe how the product works	42
Need to call in help to finish repair	55
Repairs not being completed correctly	120
Being put on hold when calling for service	141
Not cleaning up the work area when complete	63
Not explaining how to prevent future errors	27
Total	1,582

FIGURE 2-16

Pareto Chart of
Customer
Complaint
Categories

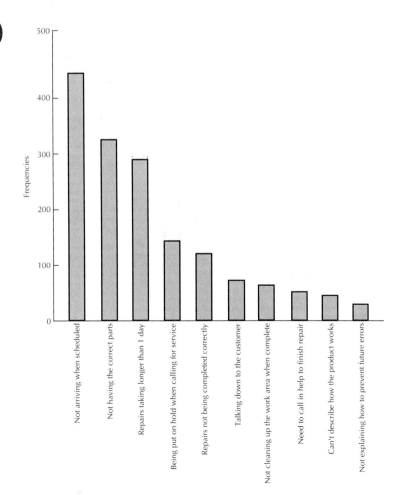

"few" most important factors. Based on the Pareto analysis, the company would begin to attack the problems with the greatest number of responses.

RUN CHART

Run charts are a special case of time series plots, which were introduced in Section 2-2. In a run chart, a quality-related measurement is plotted on the vertical axis and time on the horizontal axis. The purpose is to determine whether the quality characteristic is changing over time.

Consider again the example of the repair company which constructed the Pareto diagram of categories of customer complaints. To attack the primary complaint, the company decided to institute a major campaign to ensure that service technicians arrived at the scheduled time. Data on the number of complaints in this area were then gathered. But instead of waiting for customers to call in with complaints, the company called each customer after the service was complete to gather the information required to track customer satisfaction.

Table 2-9 shows the data, on a weekly basis, for the following 20 weeks of service calls. Notice that the quality measurement is the percentage who complained about on-time arrival, since a different number of calls were made each week.

TABLE 2-9

Dissatisfaction with On-time Arrivals

Week	% Dissatisfied	Week	% Dissatisfied
1	12	11	8
2	10	12	6
3	13	13	9
4	9	14	7
5	11	15	6
6	10	16	8
7	8	17	6
8	7	18	7
9	9	19	5
10	10	20	7

These data are plotted in Figure 2-17. The plot indicates that variation exists in the data, but the trend seems to be favorable. Apparently, the actions taken to improve on-time arrival rates have been working. If no improvement was seen, additional changes to the system would be needed.

In general, run charts are effective at showing how a process is performing over time. Sometimes, if the characteristic being measured is related to a product specification, such as length, the run chart will show the nominal (target) level and the upper and lower *specification limits*. The decision maker can then observe

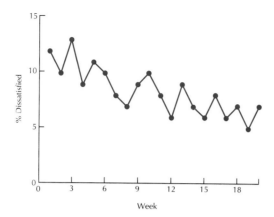

FIGURE 2-17

Run Chart of
Customer
Dissatisfaction
Rates by Week

how capable the process is of meeting specifications over time and whether trends
are occurring in the product measure.

2-5 COMPUTER APPLICATIONS

The purpose of this section is to show examples of computer output from two
software programs MINITAB and GB-STAT. We will use the KIVZ-Channel 5
data as the basis for these examples and demonstrate the type of output you can
expect if you run these programs or a similar statistical software package. If you
do not have access to a computer and statistical software, these examples provide
an overview of what the computer can offer. (Other chapters in the text also have
sections like this one showing computer applications based on the KIVZ-Channel
5 data.) Note that these data are arranged in matrix format, with columns representing variables and rows representing cases.

The TV station's staff conducted a survey of people in the station's viewing
area. For descriptive purposes, the manager would like to see a frequency distribution and histogram for education level of the viewers. Table 2-10 shows the
output obtained from the MINITAB software. This program formats the histo-

TABLE 2-10

MINITAB
Computer
Output:
Histogram and
Frequency
Distribution for
KIVZ-Channel 5
Survey Variable
X_{16} (Education)

```
EDUCAT

MIDDLE OF      NUMBER OF
INTERVAL       OBSERVATIONS
  1.00            2      **
  2.00           15      ***************
  3.00            4      ****
  4.00            8      ********
  5.00           13      *************
  6.00            8      ********
```

FIGURE **2-18**

MINITAB
Commands for
Frequency
Distribution and
Histogram of
Table 2-10

```
MTB> READ 'KIVZ5' INTO C1-C19
MTB> NAME C16 'EDUCAT'
MTB> OUTUNIT = 'PRINTER'
MTB> HISTOGRAM C16, 1, 1
```

gram a little differently than did the manual examples presented earlier in this chapter. Figure 2-18 shows the MINITAB commands that generated the output shown.

Next, suppose the station manager would like to see whether there is any relationship between income, X_{18}, and years of residence in the state, X_{15}. Using GB-STAT, the F4 key accesses the Graphics Utilities Options. The menu screen for this is shown in Figure 2-19. By selecting the option DEVELOP NEW GRAPH, and then selecting the plot option for the years in state and income variables, you can generate the scatter plot shown in Figure 2-20.

FIGURE **2-19**

Graphics Utilities
Options Screen of
GB-STAT
Software

GB-STAT Ver 2.0   GRAPHICS UTILITIES OPTIONS   CURRENT DATE
                  > 1. DEVELOP NEW GRAPH
                    2. LOAD/DRAW GRAPH FILE
                    3. LOAD/DRAW DIF FILE
                    4. PRINT CURRENT GRAPH
                    5. PLOT CURRENT GRAPH
                    6. SAVE GRAPH TO DISK
                    7. SAVE GRAPH DATA AS DIF FILE
                    8. VIEW CURRENT GRAPH
                    9. MODIFY CURRENT GRAPH

FIGURE **2-20**

GB-STAT
Computer
Output: Scatter
Plot for KIVZ-
Channel 5 Survey
Variable X_{18}
(Income) vs.
Variable X_{15}
(Years in State)

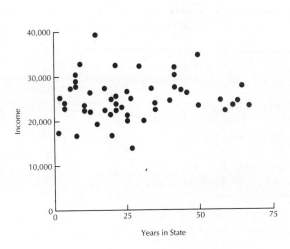

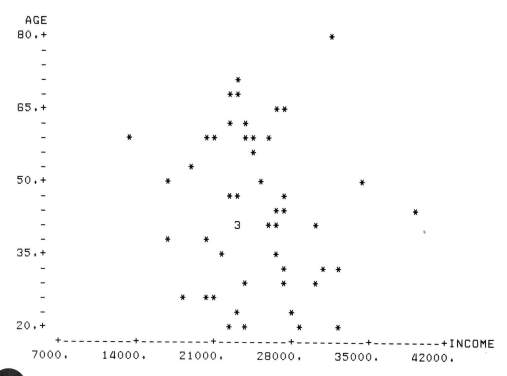

FIGURE **2-21** MINITAB Computer Output: Scatter Plot for KIVZ-Channel 5 Survey Variable X_{17} (Age) vs. Variable X_{18} (Income)

FIGURE **2-22**

MINITAB Commands for Scatter Plot

```
MTB> READ 'KIVZ5' INTO C1-C19
MTB> NAME C17 'AGE'
MTB> NAME C18 'INCOME'
MTB> OUTUNIT = 'PRINTER'
MTB> PLOT C17 VS C18
```

Both computer packages can produce other types of graphical output. For instance, Figure 2-21 shows a scatter plot for variables X_{17} (age) and X_{18} (income), which was developed using MINITAB (see Figure 2-22 for MINITAB program statements). Using the Main Menu screen (see Figure 2-23) from GB-STAT and then selecting the DISTRIBUTIONS option gives the Distribution & Plot Options menu screen shown in Figure 2-24. Selecting the HISTOGRAM command from this screen and then identifying the variable X_{14}, the years at residence, gives the distribution shown in Figure 2-25.

These are but a few examples of the descriptive outputs possible from these two software packages. Other software packages will have different options and

FIGURE 2-23

Main Menu
Screen of GB-
STAT Software

FIGURE 2-23

Main Menu
Screen of GB-
STAT Software

```
GB-STAT Ver 2.0     MAIN MENU          CURRENT DATE
                    1. ENTER DATA
                    2. LOAD SUBSET
                    3. OUTPUT
                    4. SAVE/EDIT
                    5. EDIT DATA
                  > 6. DISTRIBUTIONS
                    7. REDIMENSION
                    8. CONFIGURE
                    9. QUIT GB-STAT
```

FIGURE 2-24

Distribution &
Plot Options
Screen of GB-
STAT Software

```
GB-STAT Ver 2.0     DISTRIBUTION & PLOT OPTIONS          CURRENT DATE
                    1. FREQUENCY DISTRIBUTION
                    2. CUMULATIVE FREQ. DISTRIBUTION
                  > 3. HISTOGRAM
                    4. HISTOGRAM VS. NORMAL DISTR.
                    5. SURVIVAL ANALYSIS
                    6. NORMAL PROBABILITY PLOT
                    7. FREQUENCY POLYGON
                    8. CONTROL CHART
                    9. CASEWISE SEQUENCE PLOT
```

likely will format the output differently. However, these examples demonstrate the potential that computers hold in helping describe data.

2-6 CONCLUSIONS

This chapter has introduced some of the most commonly used statistical techniques for organizing data and presenting them in a meaningful way to aid in the decision-making process. Organizing raw data into a frequency distribution is a major step in transforming data into information. We have outlined the steps for developing frequency distributions and for producing histograms.

The chapter also has introduced other graphical techniques for displaying data to make them more usable to a decision maker. The choices for effective graphical data displays are numerous. Bar charts, pie charts, scatter plots, and time series plots are among the more commonly used techniques.

Recent developments in statistical software packages have made graphical representation of data much easier. In this chapter we have demonstrated some possible graphical output from two commonly used software packages: MINITAB and GB-STAT. Output from these packages will be presented following many of the chapters in this book.

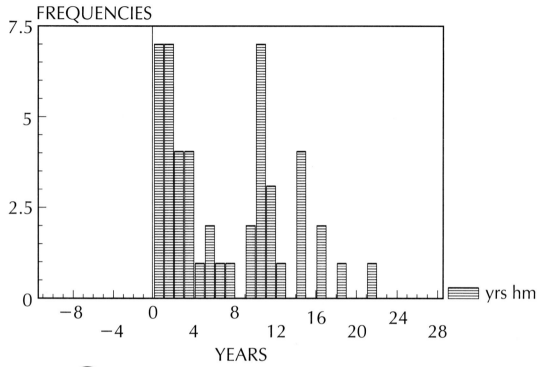

FIGURE (2-25) GB-STAT Computer Output: Bar Chart for KIVZ-Channel 5 Survey Variable X_{14}, Years at Residence

CHAPTER **GLOSSARY**

all-inclusive classes The frequency distribution classes that include all raw data.

bar chart A graph used to display data or to emphasize the categories into which data have been divided.

case Data recorded for each variable of interest.

class midpoint The center point between the upper and lower limits of a class in a frequency distribution.

class width The number of units between the lower class limit and upper class limit of a frequency class.

cumulative frequency distribution A distribution that represents the frequency of observations equal to or less than a particular class limit or value.

frequency distribution A way in which data are arranged, showing the number of cases in each category or class.

frequency histogram A graphical representation of a frequency or relative frequency distribution. The frequency of cases in each class is represented by a rectangle with a base equal to the class width and a height proportional to the frequency of cases belonging to the class.

mutually exclusive classes Frequency classes that have boundaries that do not overlap.

pie chart A graph drawn in the form of a circle, with slices sized proportionally to percentages of the whole that each category represents.

relative frequency The percentage of observations falling within a particular class.

scatter plot A two-dimensional plot of the ordered pairs of two variables.

skewed distribution A distribution that has more than half of the observations falling above or below the midpoint of the center class.

time series data Data measured over time.

time series plot A graph of time series data. Usually the horizontal axis is the time variable and the vertical axis is the variable being measured.

variable The label used to identify a factor being counted or measured.

CONCEPTUAL QUESTIONS AND ASSIGNMENTS

16. Locate two examples each of pie charts, histograms, and bar charts in current business periodicals and write a short report that summarizes what the charts are showing. Make sure you read the articles associated with the charts. Then comment on how effective you think these charts and graphs were in displaying the data.

17. The claims manager at Handover Insurance Company has been collecting data on the size of each claim paid by the company this month. A total of 500 claims were paid, with the smallest one being $44.00 and the largest one being $29,000.
    a. If a grouped data frequency distribution is to be constructed, how many class intervals would you suggest?
    b. Based on your answer to part **a** and assuming equal-width classes, what should the class width be for each class?
    c. Based on your responses to parts **a** and **b**, construct the intervals and determine the class midpoints.

18. A large supermarket in Dallas, Texas, has been having trouble with bad checks. A management intern was given the task of studying the bad checks to determine whether there was a way to anticipate which checks might be bad in advance. She began by examining 300 bad checks taken in the previous month and recording the check number and the amount of each check. The check numbers ranged from 0022 to 3456 and the amount of the bad checks ranged from $4.23 to $109.05. To begin, the intern planned to develop frequency distributions for each of these two factors.
    a. How many classes would you recommend that she use in developing a grouped data frequency distribution?
    b. If she wants equal class widths, what should the class width be for each variable being studied?
    c. In doing the analysis, do you think it would be helpful to look also at checks that were good? Explain why or why not.

ADDITIONAL PROBLEMS

19. The following data represent the commuting distances for employees of the Pay-and-Carry Department store. The personnel manager for Pay-and-Carry would like you to develop a frequency distribution for these data and write a short report describing the data.

Commuting Distance (Miles)

3.5	2.0	4.0	2.5	0.3	1.0	12.0	17.5	3.0	3.5	6.5	7.0	9.0
3.0	2.4	2.7	4.0	9.0	16.0	3.5	0.5	2.5	1.0	0.7	1.5	1.4
12.0	9.2	8.3	4.0	2.0	1.0	3.0	7.5	3.2	2.0	1.0	3.5	3.6
1.9	2.0	3.0	1.5	0.4	2.0	3.0	6.4	11.0	2.5			

20. Wendy Harrington is a staff accountant at a regional accounting firm in Miami, Florida. One of her clients has had a problem with balancing the cash register at the end of the day. Because several clerks work out of the same cash register, it is not possible to determine whether only one person is at fault. Wendy has made a study of the ending shortage or overage for the past 30 days when the cash register did not balance and has recorded the following data.

Amount Over or (Under)

$12.00	(2.55)	13.05	(55.20)	10.00	(18.00)
(11.00)	6.35	(19.02)	(33.00)	11.00	14.00
(10.00)	9.50	23.00	(16.00)	8.30	2.00
(24.00)	2.38	20.01	(43.50)	17.20	(41.04)
11.00	(19.33)	23.01	(0.34)	1.01	(23.04)

   a. Develop a frequency distribution for these data.

   b. Write a short report describing the data. Reference the frequency distribution, relative frequency distribution, cumulative frequencies, and any other pertinent factors in your report.

21. The Green Glow Lawn Company spreads liquid fertilizer on lawns. It charges by square footage of the lawn and so has records of the lawn sizes for each of its customers. The frequency distribution for lawn sizes is given.

Class	Frequency
Lawn Size (sq. ft.)	f_i
0 and under 400	8
400 and under 800	12
800 and under 1,200	20
1,200 and under 1,600	50
1,600 and under 2,000	125
2,000 and under 2,400	103
2,400 and under 2,800	24

   a. Develop a histogram from the frequency distribution.

    b. Determine the relative frequency distribution for the lawn sizes and make a pie chart that represents the data. Be sure to label the pie chart correctly.

22. The Minnesota State Fishing Bureau has contracted with a university biologist to study the length of fish caught in Minnesota lakes. The biologist has collected data on a sample of 1,000 fish caught and developed the following relative frequency distribution.

Class	Relative Frequency
Length (inches)	Rf_i
8 and under 10	0.22
10 and under 12	0.15
12 and under 14	0.25
14 and under 16	0.24
16 and under 18	0.06
18 and under 20	0.05
20 and under 22	0.03

    a. Construct a frequency distribution from this relative frequency distribution and then produce a histogram based on the frequency distribution.

    b. Construct a pie chart from the relative frequency distribution. Discuss which of the two graphs, the pie chart or histogram, you think is more effective in presenting the fish length data.

    c. Construct a cumulative ogive graph for the fish length data and write a short paragraph to accompany the graph.

23. Michael Gordon is the regional sales manager for American Toys, Inc. Recently, he collected data on weekly sales (in dollars) for the fifteen stores in his region. He also collected data on the number of sales clerk work hours during the week for each of the stores. The data are as follows:

Store	Sales	Hours	Store	Sales	Hours
1	$23,300	120	9	$27,886	140
2	25,600	135	10	54,156	300
3	19,200	96	11	34,080	254
4	10,211	102	12	25,900	180
5	19,330	240	13	36,400	270
6	35,789	190	14	25,760	175
7	12,540	108	15	31,500	256
8	43,150	234			

    a. Develop a scatter plot of these data.

    b. Based on the scatter plot, what, if any, conclusions might the sales manager reach with respect to the relationship between sales and number of clerk hours worked? Do any stores stand out as being different? Discuss.

24. Midlands Metal Works has recently begun supplying parts to a Japanese automaker. As part of its efforts to improve the quality of its products, the company has started keeping track of categories of defects. It has identified five general categories: incomplete (inc), surface scars (ss), cracks (cks), misshapen (mis), and others (oth). The company has categorized the last 100 defective parts as follows:

inc	cks	ss	oth	inc	ss	inc	ss	inc	inc
cks	inc	ss	cks	oth	ss	inc	inc	ss	ss
inc	cks	inc	inc	oth	mis	inc	ss	inc	cks
ss	cks	inc	oth	inc	ss	cks	inc	inc	inc
ss	cks	mis	oth	inc	ss	inc	cks	inc	inc
ss	inc	cks	inc	inc	oth	ss	cks	inc	ss
inc	inc	ss	ss	cks	inc	cks	ss	cks	inc
inc	mis	inc	ss	cks	inc	inc	cks	oth	inc
inc	ss	cks	mis	inc	inc	cks	inc	ss	ss
inc	inc	ss	oth	cks	ss	ss	inc	inc	oth

  a. Construct a tally sheet and frequency distribution using these data.
  b. Use the values in part **a** to construct a Pareto chart of the types of defective parts.

25. A computer software company has been looking at the amount of time customers spend on hold after their call is answered by the central switchboard. The company would like to have only 2% of the callers have to wait more than 2 minutes. The company's calling service has provided the following data showing how long each of last month's callers spent on hold.

Class	Number
Less than 15 seconds	456
15 to less than 30 seconds	718
30 to less than 45 seconds	891
45 to less than 60 seconds	823
60 to less than 75 seconds	610
75 to less than 90 seconds	449
90 to less than 105 seconds	385
105 to less than 120 seconds	221
120 to less than 150 seconds	158
150 to less than 180 seconds	124
180 to less than 240 seconds	87
More than 240 seconds	153

  What do these data say about the company's ability to meet its objective?

26. A local branch of the Government Employee's Credit Union has been keeping track of the types of errors its tellers have been making. You are responsible for providing training to reduce these errors. The following data show the categories of errors and the frequency of each for the last month.

Errors posting debits/credits	182
Errors posting other entries	158
Entries not posted	77
Cash letter errors	31
Claims	24
Adjustment tickets	16
Multiple postings	9
Incorrect totals	7

Use these data to justify in which areas to start your training effort.

27. The marketing director of a company manufacturing small disk drives for notebook computers has directed her sales force to accept orders based on a projected production rate of 3,000 disk drives per day. The production manager objected strongly when hearing this and presented the following frequency distribution to support his claim that this goal was impossible given the present production process.

Production Rate	Frequency
2,000–2,499	3
2,500–2,749	7
2,750–2,999	10
3,000–3,249	15
3,250–3,499	22
3,500–3,999	11
More than 4,000	2

Which manager do the data support? Justify your answer.

DATABASE PROBLEMS

The following questions and problems pertain directly to the State Department of Transportation case study and database introduced in Chapter 1. The questions and problems were written assuming that you will have access to a computer and appropriate statistical software. The database contains 100 observations and seventeen variables.

1. Prepare an ungrouped frequency distribution for the driving record variables, X_1–X_6. Construct a frequency histogram for each variable and then write a short report to Herb Kriner informing him of the results.

2. Variable X_9 is the age of the owner/driver. Develop a grouped data frequency distribution with six classes of equal width. Then construct a frequency histogram from this distribution.

3. Develop a cross-tabulation table with X_{17}, liability insurance status, as the row variable and variable X_{11}, knowledge of the law, as the column variable. Write a report to Herb Kriner describing the results of this cross-tabulation.

Also indicate the advantage of using cross-tabulation versus looking at the two variables individually.

4.   Herb Kriner is interested in knowing the percentage of owners/drivers who are not employed who also do not carry liability insurance. Determine this percentage for the entire sample. Then do the same for males and females separately.

ADDITIONAL DATABASE PROBLEMS

The questions and problems in this section reference the various databases that accompany this text and which are described in Chapter 1. Your instructor has been provided a diskette with these databases. It is expected that you will be using computer software to access these data and to perform the required calculations and graphs.

DATABASE: **CITIES** (*Refer to the database description in Chapter 1.*)

1.   Develop a grouped data frequency distribution for 1990 city population, X_1. Use the $2^k \geq n$ rule to determine the appropriate number of classes. Prepare a histogram from the frequency distribution. Write a one-paragraph statement that describes the frequency distribution.

2.   Develop a grouped data relative frequency distribution and histogram for X_6 and X_7. Determine an appropriate number of classes and class limits. Write a short report comparing the two distributions. Comment on why a relative frequency distribution would be appropriate. Then create a new variable that is the difference between manufacturing and white-collar earnings. Develop a frequency distribution and histogram for this new variable and write a short report describing this distribution.

3.   Develop a grouped data frequency distribution for X_8. Use the $2^k \geq n$ rule to determine the appropriate number of classes. Prepare a histogram from the frequency distribution. Write a one-paragraph statement that describes the frequency distribution.

4.   Prepare a scatter plot with X_3 on the Y-axis and X_1 on the X-axis. Write a short statement that describes the output of the scatter plot.

DATABASE: **FAST100** (*Refer to the database description in Chapter 1.*)

1.   Develop a grouped data frequency distribution for X_1 and X_2. Use the $2^k \geq n$ rule to determine the appropriate number of classes. Prepare a histogram from each frequency distribution. Write a one-paragraph statement describing the frequency distributions.

2.   Develop a grouped data relative frequency distribution and histogram for X_5 and X_6. Determine an appropriate number of classes and class limits. Write a

short report that compares the two distributions. Comment on why a relative frequency distribution would be appropriate. Then create a new variable that is the difference between X_5 and X_6. Develop a frequency distribution and histogram for this new variable and write a short report describing this distribution.

3. Prepare a scatter plot showing X_4 on the Y-axis and X_2 on the X-axis. Prepare a short statement describing the output of the scatter plot.

4. Prepare a pie chart for X_8 and write a statement that describes what the pie chart shows.

DATABASE: **PACRIM** (*Refer to the database description in Chapter 1.*)

1. Develop a grouped data frequency distribution for X_1 and X_2. Use the $2^k \geq n$ rule to determine the appropriate number of classes. Prepare a histogram from each frequency distribution. Write a one-paragraph statement that describes the frequency distributions.

2. Prepare a scatter plot showing X_4 on the Y-axis and X_9 on the X-axis. Prepare a short statement to describe the output of the scatter plot.

3. Prepare a grouped data frequency distribution and histogram for X_2 broken down by country where the company is located. Write a report that discusses the histogram.

DATABASE: **TRUCKS** (*Refer to the database description in Chapter 1.*)

1. Develop a frequency distribution and histogram to show the number of trucks weighed by month. Discuss this output and comment on whether the distribution is skewed.

2. Develop a grouped data frequency distribution for X_2, X_3, and X_4. Use the $2^k \geq n$ rule to determine the appropriate number of classes. Prepare a histogram from each frequency distribution. Write a report that describes the frequency distributions. Keep in mind that all these measurements come from the WIM scale.

3. Develop a grouped data frequency distribution for X_5, X_6, and X_7. Use the $2^k \geq n$ rule to determine the appropriate number of classes. Prepare a histogram from each frequency distribution. Write a report that describes the frequency distributions. Keep in mind that all these measurements come from the POE scale.

4. Create a new variable that represents $X_6 - X_3$. Then prepare a scatter plot showing the new variable on the Y-axis and X_8, speed, on the X-axis. Prepare a short statement to describe the output of the scatter plot. Does it appear that big differences between POE and WIM gross weights occurred when the trucks hit the WIM scale at higher speeds?

C A S E

Willburn & Associates

Willburn & Associates is a regional CPA firm located in upstate New York. The managing partner, Chad Willburn, is considered to be one of the more progressive accountants in the area in his use of statistical analysis and quantitative methods. When he hires new staff accountants, one of the criteria is that they have a basic understanding of statistics and an interest in applying statistics to their accounting work.

Elenor Douglas joined Willburn & Associates nearly 2 months ago after finishing her accounting degree at a nearby state university. She plans to sit for her CPA examination in the spring. Currently, Elenor is assigned to an audit project for a governmental client of the firm and has been assisting in all phases of the audit.

In the course of the audit, Elenor has collected data on inventory levels for parts and materials kept by the agency for carrying out its normal business operations. She has taken a sample of thirty inventory items and recorded data on the following variables:

X_1 = Number of items actually on hand

X_2 = Number of items stated to be on hand on the ledger

X_3 = Per-unit price of each item

X_4 = Number of days since last recorded withdrawal from inventory

These data are shown in Table 2A-1. Elenor plans to prepare a short presentation describing these data. Knowing Chad Willburn's interest in statistical methods, Elenor wants to make effective use of statistical methods of data presentation. She knows that the conclusions reached in her report need to be supported by the tables and graphs she uses. Of particular interest is whether the client is meeting its objective of keeping its inventory error to less than 5% of the total value of the inventory, in terms of both numbers and dollar value. If her report is of sufficient quality, it will be included as part of the final audit report, and conclusions about the agency's inventory control can be partially based on this study.

T A B L E 2A-1

Inventory Data for Willburn & Associates

Item No.	X_1	X_2	X_3	X_4
1	204	198	$ 3.42	8
2	18	18	89.50	34
3	44	49	49.80	2
4	7	5	2,004.40	74
5	14	14	5.49	11
6	33	38	14.70	6

TABLE 2A-1

Inventory Data
for Willburn &
Associates
(*Continued*)

Item No.	X_1	X_2	X_3	X_4
7	9	9	1,234.50	49
8	46	49	203.99	3
9	187	175	4.33	5
10	11	11	58.00	14
11	4	6	749.00	34
12	35	35	12.49	9
13	15	15	2.45	17
14	77	89	14.25	1
15	21	21	79.50	12
16	345	372	1.25	1
17	6	6	39.78	13
18	19	16	34.00	6
19	77	80	102.50	24
20	4	5	756.40	7
21	457	478	3.04	5
22	23	13	23.50	45
23	19	19	111.34	7
24	50	56	45.79	1
25	2	1	5.50	34
26	23	23	206.00	5
27	45	46	19.90	1
28	234	244	450.00	12
29	7	7	678.99	19
30	23	23	78.98	35

REFERENCES

Brightman, Harvey, and Schneider, Howard. *Statistics for Business Problem Solving.* Cincinnati: South-Western, 1992.

Hamburg, Morris. *Statistical Analysis for Decision Making,* 5th ed. Orlando, Fla.: Harcourt Brace Jovanovich, 1990.

Huntsberger, David V.; Billingsley, Patrick; Croft, D. James; and Watson, Collin J. *Statistical Inference for Management and Economics,* 3d ed. Boston: Allyn and Bacon, 1986.

Mendenhall, William; Reinmuth, James E.; and Beaver, Robert. *Statistics for Management and Economics,* 6th ed. Boston: PWS-Kent, 1989.

Measures of Location

and Spread

WHY DECISION MAKERS NEED TO KNOW

The methods for graphically presenting data discussed in Chapter 2 provide a starting point for analyzing data. However, these methods do not reveal all the information contained in a set of data. Managers who want to know as much as possible about their companies' sales divisions most likely will not be satisfied with frequency distributions showing the distribution of daily sales. Even frequency histograms or other graphical techniques probably will not provide all the required information. The managers will likely want to make comparisons between sales divisions to discern whether major differences exist. Although frequency distributions and histograms provide some basis for making this type of comparison, they may be misleading. In fact, histograms from two quite different sets of data may appear very similar owing to the number and width of the class intervals selected.

To overcome some limitations in the methods discussed in Chapter 2, decision makers need to become acquainted with some additional tools of descriptive statistics. Specifically, managers need to know some statistical measures that can be determined from any set of data. There are two broad categories within which these measures fall: *measures of location* and *measures of spread*.

CHAPTER OBJECTIVES

Statistics is often used to decide whether a true difference exists between two sets of data. Many statistical techniques used to test for differences between data groups attempt to determine whether the data from the two groups have the same distribution. That is, do the groups have the same central location and the same spread?

This chapter will discuss some techniques for measuring the central location of a data distribution. Although there are many ways of measuring data location, the three most common will be explored here: the arithmetic mean, the median, and the mode.

Techniques for measuring the spread, or dispersion, in a set of data will also be discussed. The measures that will receive the greatest emphasis are the range, variance, and standard deviation.

STUDENT OBJECTIVES

After studying the material in this chapter, you should be able to do the following:

1. Calculate the mean and median for both grouped and ungrouped data.
2. Determine the variance and standard deviation for grouped and ungrouped data.
3. Understand the relationship between process variation and quality improvement efforts.

3-1 MEASURES OF LOCATION

As implied by the name, the *central location* is the middle, or center, of a set of data. This section considers several common measures of central location. The important statistical properties will be discussed and some business applications for each of the measures will be introduced. The measures of location that will be covered are the mode, the median, and the arithmetic mean.

THE MODE

The **mode** is the observation that occurs most frequently in a data set. Suppose two business majors have just been hired for the summer to run the T-Shirt Shop in an eastern resort hotel. This is the first summer the shop will be open; although the owner has designated the total inventory investment allowed, the two co-managers will have to determine the inventory mix. T-shirts for adults come in five sizes: small (S), medium (M), large (L), extra large (XL), and extra extra large (XXL). To help in deciding the inventory levels for each size, the managers have selected a sample of fifty potential customers and have recorded their shirt sizes, as shown in Table 3-1.

T A B L E 3-1					
Adult T-shirt Sizes	L	L	L	S	S
	XL	L	XL	XL	M
	XL	M	M	XL	M
	M	M	XXL	L	M
	M	M	XL	M	L
	M	S	S	M	L
	M	XXL	M	M	XL
	S	M	M	XL	XL
	XXL	M	L	XL	XL
	XL	L	XL	XXL	S

Initially, the two managers might use this sample to estimate the T-shirt size that will be demanded most often. Recalling that the mode is the value occurring most often, the mode here is medium since this size was observed eighteen times in the sample, more than any other size. Note also the data here are ordinal. The mode can be found for data measured at any of the four levels considered in Chapter 1. This will not be true for the median and mean.

A set of data may have two or more values that tie for the most frequently occurring. When this happens the distribution is *multimodal* instead of unimodal (only one mode). Also, a data set may have no mode, if no one value occurs more frequently than another.

The following example illustrates how the mode can aid in the decision-making process. Fox Corporation executives saw that the existing corporate jets, such as Lear and Gulfstream, were expensive ($1 million or more each). Some of this cost was due to the fact that these jets were usually built to carry eight or more passengers. A study of passenger loads for a large number of trips for different corporate jets revealed that, although sometimes the jets were full, in a vast majority of trips there were empty seats. In fact, for the data studied, the number of passengers observed most often was three, including the pilot. Thus the value 3, the mode for the observed data, figured strongly in Fox Corporation's plans to build a "small," lower-priced, four-passenger jet.

THE MEDIAN

The **median** is the middle observation in data that have been arranged in ascending or descending numerical sequence. A numerical sequence of data is called an *array*. For example, Midstates Bank Corp. has been conducting a campaign to get small-account customers to use automated banking machines, which can process most transactions at less cost than tellers can. The following data represent the number of times each of nine customers used the banking machines last month. (Note that the data have been arranged in numerical order.)

2   4   4   5   7   8   10   10   12

When the array has an *odd* number of observations, the median is $(N + 1)/2$ observations from either end. Thus the median number of banking machines used by these nine customers is the fifth $[(9 + 1)/2]$ observation from either end. Therefore the median is 7.

If the array contains an *even* number of observations, the median is any point between the two middle values. Generally, the median is taken to be the average of the middle two values. For example, a company that supplies heating oil to residential customers has collected the following data on the quantity of oil (in gallons) purchased by eight households in December:

42   51   53   53   59   61   75   100

Since there are eight observations, the median is the average of the fourth and fifth observations.

$$\text{Median} = \frac{53 + 59}{2}$$
$$= 56 \text{ gallons}$$

The median is most useful as a measure of central tendency, or central location, in situations where the data contain some extreme observations. For instance, incomes in a market area are often characterized by a few very high incomes, but with the majority under \$40,000. Although the few high-income earners are worth noting, a person contemplating opening a drive-in restaurant would like to have a measure of central income that represents the majority of people in the area. The median might be the measure of choice, since it is relatively unaffected by extreme values.

To illustrate that the median is not sensitive to extreme cases, suppose the highest banking machine use rate for the nine customers discussed earlier was 75 rather than 12; the median would still be 7. Note also that data must be at least ordinal for the median to be determined.

THE MEAN

By far the most common statistical measure of location is the mean. The **mean** is often called the *arithmetic average* in nonstatistical applications and is found by summing all the observations and dividing the sum by the number of observations.

The notation used to represent the mean differs depending on whether the data represent an entire population or a sample from a population. If the data comprise an entire population, the mean is found from equation 3-1:

$$\mu_x = \frac{\sum\limits_{i=1}^{N} X_i}{N}$$

3-1

where

μ_x = Population mean (μ is pronounced m$\bar{\text{u}}$)
N = Population size
Σ = Summation symbol
X_i = Individual observations

Recall from your math class or from the algebra review in Chapter 1 that $\sum\limits_{i=1}^{N}$ requires us to sum all the elements with an i subscript from $i = 1$ to $i = N$ inclusive.

If the data are from a sample, the sample mean is found from equation 3-2:

$$\overline{X} = \frac{\sum\limits_{i=1}^{n} X_i}{n}$$

3-2

where

$\overline{X}$ = Sample mean (pronounced X bar)
n = Sample size
X_i = Individual observations

Now suppose the population of interest is the total sales of the T-Shirt Shop in the resort hotel for the first 10 days it is open. These sales values are listed in Table 3-2. The mean sales for these 10 days is

$$
\begin{aligned}
\mu_x &= \frac{\sum\limits_{i=1}^{N} X_i}{N} \\
&= \frac{\$216 + 255 + 330 + 254 + 348 + 317 + 292 + 267 + 310 + 295}{10} \\
&= \frac{\$2{,}884}{10} \\
&= \$288.40
\end{aligned}
$$

TABLE 3-2

Daily Sales of
Resort Hotel
T-Shirt Shop

$216	$317
255	292
330	267
254	310
348	295

We use equation 3-1 since we are dealing with the entire population of sales values.

Suppose we select a sample of 5 days' sales from this population, say, $216, $330, $348, $292, and $310. The sample mean is found using equation 3-2:

$$\overline{X} = \frac{\sum_{i=1}^{n} X_i}{n}$$

$$= \frac{\$216 + 330 + 348 + 292 + 310}{5}$$

$$= \frac{\$1,496}{5}$$

$$= \$299.20$$

Note that the sample mean in this example does not equal the population mean. This difference is called *sampling error*. Sampling error occurs whenever the sample does not perfectly represent the population. Sampling error generally occurs any time sampling is performed. We will look at the subject of sampling error in detail beginning in Chapter 7. Note also that the data must be either interval or ratio for the mean to be meaningful.

As we discussed previously, the median is not affected by extreme values. However, since the mean is determined by using all observations, it is affected by extreme values. Returning to the banking machine use rate for nine customers,

$$2, \quad 4, \quad 4, \quad 5, \quad 7, \quad 8, \quad 10, \quad 10, \quad 12$$

the mean is $\overline{X} = 62/9 = 6.889$, and the median is 7. We saw that increasing the largest observation to 75 would not affect the median but it would change the mean to

$$\overline{X} = \frac{125}{9} = 13.889$$

THE MEAN, MEDIAN, AND MODE FOR SKEWED DATA

The mean, median, and mode usually are not the same for a given set of data. Yet each of the three measures is an attempt to describe the central position of the data being considered. The only time the mean, median, and mode will all have

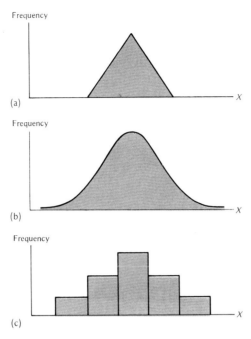

(a)

(b)

(c)

the same value is when the data distribution is both unimodal *and* symmetrical. Several unimodal and symmetrical distributions are shown in Figure 3-1.

The three measures of location do not have the same value if the data distribution is skewed. As mentioned in Chapter 2, data can be skewed to the left or right depending on the direction of the tail in the distribution. Skewed distributions affect the three measures of location differently. In the distribution shown in Figure 3-2, the mode, the most frequent observation, is at the highest point of the

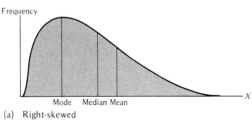

(a) Right-skewed

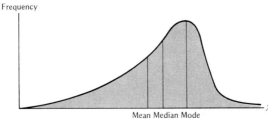

(b) Left-skewed

distribution. The median, the center observation, lies to the skewed side of the mode. The mean—the measure most affected by extreme values in the distribution's tail—lies beyond the median. Of the three common measures of location, the mean is most affected by a skewed distribution. For this reason, the mean, although the most commonly used statistical measure, is not always the best measure of location.

SKILL DEVELOPMENT PROBLEMS FOR SECTION 3-1

The following set of problems is meant to test your understanding of the material in this section.

1. Determine the mean, median, and mode for the following set of data:

16	23	17	24	9	11	13	15
18	21	16	23	17	16	10	14

2. Gail Pooley, the marketing director for South East Insurance, has been worried about the increasing age of their policyholder base. She wants to determine whether the new advertising campaign has had the desired effect of attracting more younger customers. She has taken a sample of ten new policies and has found the following ages:

32	22	24	27	27
33	28	23	24	21

Determine the mean, median, and mode of these data. Is there any indication from this group of data that the new policyholders may tend to be younger?

3-2 MEASURES OF SPREAD

As shown in the previous section, the mean, median, and mode describe the central location of a distribution. However, the location is only one data characteristic of interest to decision makers. Measures of *spread* are also important.

For example, the Fabcare Company is considering a new machine for filling 16-ounce bottles of its Brite-Wool cold-water wool fabric cleaner. The machine is guaranteed to put an average of 16 ounces of cleaner in each bottle. If the machine always put in 16 ounces, the Fabcare Company would have no worries. However, as in any production process, there will be variation. Here, variation occurs in the amount of cleaner going into each bottle. Even though the average may be 16 ounces, sometimes the fill may be slightly more than 16 ounces and at other times less than 16 ounces. Because of the legal ramifications of putting too little cleaner in bottles, and of the lost profit if too much cleaner is used, the Fabcare Company is concerned with the variation in the filling process.

You should also be aware that the mean by itself tells only part of the story in a set of data. For example, consider an oversimplified case where the fabric cleaner company selected two bottles of cleaner and measured the volume in each bottle, with the following results:

Bottle 1:   16.01 ounces

Bottle 2:   15.99 ounces

The average amount in a bottle is

$$\overline{X} = \frac{16.01 + 15.99}{2}$$
$$= 16.00 \text{ ounces}$$

Thus, these data show that the desired average of 16 ounces was reached for these two bottles. Suppose a couple of weeks later the manufacturer selected two more bottles of fabric cleaner and measured these bottles, with the following results:

Bottle 1:   18 ounces

Bottle 2:   14 ounces

The average amount per bottle is still 16 ounces. Thus if the manufacturer looked only at the averages, it would conclude that the filling mechanism was performing the same as 2 weeks ago. On the contrary, taking into account the spread in the data, there is a big difference in the filling process at present. It is important to look at both measures of location and measures of variation in analyzing a set of data.

Statistical measures of variation are also called measures of spread, or measures of dispersion. In this section we shall discuss the measures of dispersion most commonly used in statistical analysis. These measures are the *range, variance,* and *standard deviation.*

THE RANGE

The simplest measure of spread in a set of data is the range. The **range** is the difference between the largest and smallest observations in the data. For example, Table 3-3 lists the number of IBM System/2 personal computers sold by the PC

TABLE 3-3

Sales for 20 Days of IBM System/2

8	6	7	2	6
1	2	7	4	4
1	3	5	1	12
5	4	3	4	2

Shop during its first 20 days in business. The range for these data is found by equation 3-3:

$$\text{Range} = \text{Maximum} - \text{Minimum} \qquad \textbf{3-3}$$

Therefore,

$$\text{Range} = 12 - 1$$
$$= 11 \text{ personal computers}$$

Although the range is the easiest measure of dispersion to calculate, it also conveys the least information. Since the range is determined only by the two extreme values, it provides no indication about the spread of the other values. The range is therefore very sensitive to extreme values in the data. For example, if the PC Shop had on the one day sold twenty personal computers instead of twelve, the range would have been nineteen rather than eleven, even though no other values had changed.

The range is also sensitive to the number of observations in the data set. In general, if more observations are included, there is a greater chance of having extreme values in the data set.

THE VARIANCE AND STANDARD DEVIATION

As just illustrated, the range is an easy measure of spread to compute but is of limited value because it is computed from only the most extreme values in the data. This section introduces the two most frequently used measures of spread: the **variance** and the **standard deviation**. Unlike the range, the variance and the standard deviation consider all the data in their computation.

The variance and standard deviation provide numerical measures of how the data tend to vary around the mean. If the data are tightly clustered around the mean, both the variance and standard deviation will be relatively small. However, if the data are widely scattered around the mean, the variance and standard deviation will be relatively large.

Consider again the computer sales data shown in Table 3-3. The population mean for these data is computed as follows:

$$\mu_x = \frac{\sum_{i=1}^{N} X_i}{N}$$
$$= \frac{87}{20}$$
$$= 4.35$$

Thus, on the average, 4.35 computers were sold daily by the PC Shop during the 20 days of operation. You will note that the data in Table 3-3 tend to vary. Some values are larger than 4.35; others are smaller. The variance and standard deviation can be used to provide measures of this variation. We will concentrate first on computing the variance, using the information tabulated in Table 3-4.

TABLE 3-4

Variance Calculations for System/2 Sales Example

a X_i	b $(X_i - \mu_x)$	c $(X_i - \mu_x)^2$
8	$(8 - 4.35) = 3.65$	13.32
1	$(1 - 4.35) = -3.35$	11.22
1	$(1 - 4.35) = -3.35$	11.22
5	$(5 - 4.35) = 0.65$	0.42
6	$(6 - 4.35) = 1.65$	2.72
2	$(2 - 4.35) = -2.35$	5.52
3	$(3 - 4.35) = -1.35$	1.82
4	$(4 - 4.35) = -0.35$	0.12
7	$(7 - 4.35) = 2.65$	7.02
7	$(7 - 4.35) = 2.65$	7.02
5	$(5 - 4.35) = 0.65$	0.42
3	$(3 - 4.35) = -1.35$	1.82
2	$(2 - 4.35) = -2.35$	5.52
4	$(4 - 4.35) = -0.35$	0.12
1	$(1 - 4.35) = -3.35$	11.22
4	$(4 - 4.35) = -0.35$	0.12
6	$(6 - 4.35) = 1.65$	2.72
4	$(4 - 4.35) = -0.35$	0.12
12	$(12 - 4.35) = 7.65$	58.52
2	$(2 - 4.35) = -2.35$	5.52
	$\Sigma = 0.00$	$\Sigma = 146.50$

The first step in computing the variance is to find the algebraic difference between each X_i value and the mean, as shown in column **b** of Table 3-4. Note that the sum of these differences is zero. This will always be the case for any set of raw data. To overcome the problem of the negative differences cancelling the positive differences, we can square each of the differences as shown in column **c** of Table 3-4. The sum of the squared differences is 146.50.

The final step in computing the variance of the population is to divide the sum of squared differences by the population size, $N = 20$, in equation 3-4:

$$\sigma_x^2 = \frac{\sum\limits_{i=1}^{N}(X_i - \mu_x)^2}{N}$$

3-4

Then

$$\sigma_x^2 = \frac{146.50}{20}$$

$$= 7.33$$

The notation for the population variance is σ_x^2 (pronounced sigma sub x squared). Because we have squared all the differences between the individual data and the population mean, the variance is measured in units squared. Thus, the variance for the sales data is 7.33 computers squared. Although this terminology presents no statistical problems, we do have a problem interpreting the term "computers squared"!

If we take the square root of the variance, we return to the original units of measure, computers. The square root of the variance is called the **standard deviation.** We compute the standard deviation as in equation 3-5:

$$\sigma_x = \sqrt{\frac{\sum\limits_{i=1}^{N}(X_i - \mu)^2}{N}}$$

3-5

Then

$$\sigma_x = \sqrt{\frac{146.50}{20}}$$

$$= \sqrt{7.33}$$

$$= 2.71$$

The notation for the population standard deviation is σ_x (pronounced sigma sub x). Thus, the standard deviation for the population of the System/2 computers sold by the PC Shop dealer during the 20 days of operation is 2.71 computers.

Because the standard deviation is measured in the same units as the raw data, we generally use it as the measure of spread rather than variance. However, we will deal specifically with the variance in later chapters of this text.

THE MEANING OF THE STANDARD DEVIATION

Because the standard deviation plays such an important role in statistical analysis, it is important that you understand what it means. The standard deviation may be thought of as a measure of distance from the mean. For instance, in Figure 3-3 we see that a point on the line $1\sigma_x$ above the mean corresponds to $(4.35 + 2.71) = 7.06$ and a point on the line $2\sigma_x$ above the mean corresponds to $(4.35 + 5.42) = 9.77$. Likewise, a point on the line $2\sigma_x$ below the mean corresponds to $(4.35 - 5.42) = -1.07$.

FIGURE **3-3**

Standard Deviation—A Measure of Distance—for the System/2 Sales Example

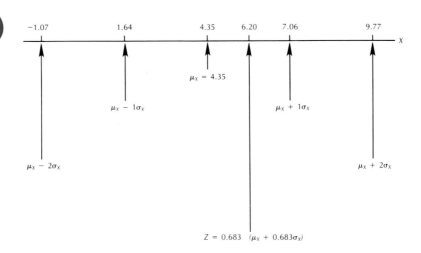

We can also pick any point on the line and determine how many standard deviations above or below the mean that point falls. For example, suppose we pick the value 6.2. To determine how many standard deviations 6.2 is from 4.35, we perform the following:

$$Z = \frac{X - \mu_x}{\sigma_x}$$

$$= \frac{6.2 - 4.35}{2.71}$$

$$= 0.683$$

Thus, the value 6.2 falls 0.683 standard deviation above the mean value of 4.35. The Z is sometimes referred to as a Z score. A Z score is the number of standard deviations a point is above or below the mean of a set of data. We will use Z scores a great deal in our study of statistics because it is a unitless number and will allow us to make comparisons between different data sets.

Keeping in mind that the standard deviation is a measure of distance from the mean, we can use the information contained in the mean and the standard deviation to provide us with greater insight about the data from which they have been computed. The *empirical rule* can be used to demonstrate this.

Empirical Rule

The empirical rule holds that if the distribution of the data is bell shaped, like that shown in Figure 3-4, then the interval

$(\mu_x \pm 1\sigma_x)$ contains approximately 68% of the values.

$(\mu_x \pm 2\sigma_x)$ contains approximately 95% of the values.

$(\mu_x \pm 3\sigma_x)$ contains virtually all the values.

Suppose we were to apply the empirical rule to the computer sales data in Table 3-3, which have a mean of 4.35 and standard deviation of 2.71. Applying the empirical rule, (4.35 ± 2.71) should contain approximately 68% of the twenty values.

We find that in the interval 1.64 to 7.06 there are actually fifteen values, or 75% of the population. If we look at (4.35 ± 5.42) according to the empirical rule, we should find approximately 95% of the twenty values. Indeed we find exactly nineteen of the twenty, or 95%, of the values between -1.07 and 9.77. The more the distribution resembles the bell-shaped curve in Figure 3-4, the more accurate the empirical rule is.

FIGURE 3-4

**Empirical Rule—
Bell-shaped
Distribution**

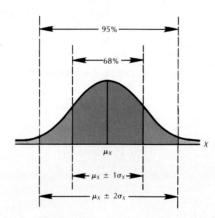

Suppose the time it takes to install a door on a new automobile is known to have a mean of 12 minutes and a standard deviation of 2 minutes. If the distribution of actual times is bell shaped, like that shown in Figure 3-5, then the production manager could expect about 68% of all doors to be mounted in 10 to 14 minutes (12 ± 2). Further, he could expect about 95% of all doors to take between 8 and 16 minutes to mount. Finally, he could expect virtually all doors to

FIGURE **3-5**

Distribution of
Door Installation
Times

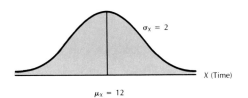

be mounted in between 6 and 18 minutes (12 ± 6). If he begins to observe too many doors that require over 18 minutes to mount, he might suspect that a problem exists.

THE STANDARD DEVIATION FOR SAMPLE DATA

The variance and standard deviation were introduced through an example that dealt with a population of data. However, as indicated several times already, decision makers will often be dealing with a sample from the population rather than the entire population. Therefore, in describing the sample data and making inferences about the population from which the sample was selected, these decision makers will have to compute the variance and standard deviation for the sample.

The method for computing the sample variance is almost exactly the same as for computing the population variance. Consider an example involving Julie Hanson, owner of Hanson Auto, Home, and Life, an insurance agency in Wichita, Kansas. Julie has selected a sample from long-term auto insurers (with the Hanson Agency for more than 3 years) and has determined the number of claims filed against these policies for the past 3-year period. These data for a sample of ten policies are shown in Table 3-5.

TABLE **3-5**

Auto Policy
Claims from
Sample Data for
Hanson Agency

3	5
0	2
6	0
2	3
2	2

To analyze these sample data, we first compute the sample mean from equation 3-6:

$$\overline{X} = \frac{\Sigma X}{n}$$

3-6

Then

$$\overline{X} = \frac{25}{10}$$

$$= 2.5 \text{ claims}$$

In computing the sample variance we determine the differences between the individual X values and the sample mean and then square each of these differences:

X	$X - \overline{X}$	$(X - \overline{X})^2$
3	$3 - 2.5 = 0.5$	0.25
0	$0 - 2.5 = -2.5$	6.25
6	$6 - 2.5 = 3.5$	12.25
2	$2 - 2.5 = -0.5$	0.25
2	$2 - 2.5 = -0.5$	0.25
5	$5 - 2.5 = 2.5$	6.25
2	$2 - 2.5 = -0.5$	0.25
0	$0 - 2.5 = -2.5$	6.25
3	$3 - 2.5 = 0.5$	0.25
2	$2 - 2.5 = -0.5$	0.25
	$\Sigma = 0.0$	$\Sigma = 32.50$

To compute the variance we divide the sum of the squared differences by $n - 1$. Note the divisor is $n - 1$ for the sample variance, S_x^2. The reason that $n - 1$, rather than n, is used in computing S_x^2 is that, for small samples, computing S_x^2 with n as the divisor will slightly underestimate σ_x^2, the population variance. When $n - 1$ is used as the divisor, S_x^2 is a better estimate for the population variance. Remember, the goal of statistics is to use information in a sample to estimate what is true for a population. Because division by $n - 1$ rather than n does a "better" job of estimating the population variance, division by $n - 1$ is used when calculating sample variances. We will discuss this more fully in Chapter 7. For now, just remember to divide by N when computing a population variance and by $n - 1$ when computing a sample variance.

Thus the formula for the sample variance is given by equation 3-7:

$$S_x^2 = \frac{\Sigma(X - \overline{X})^2}{n - 1} \qquad \textbf{3-7}$$

Then for this example,

$$S_x^2 = \frac{32.50}{9}$$

$$= 3.611$$

Like the population variance, the sample variance is measured in units squared. To convert to original units, we again take the square root. The *sample standard deviation* is the square root of the sample variance. This is shown in equation 3-8:

$$S_x = \sqrt{\frac{\Sigma(X - \overline{X})^2}{n - 1}} \qquad \textbf{3-8}$$

Then

$$S_x = \sqrt{\frac{32.50}{9}}$$
$$= \sqrt{3.611}$$
$$= 1.9 \text{ claims}$$

The sample standard deviation has the same meaning as the population standard deviation. It can be thought of as a measure of distance from the mean. The empirical rule can be applied in the same manner as for population data.

Note that in the equations for the sample variance and sample standard deviation we have dropped the subscript notation. We will follow this format for the remainder of the text whenever the summation involves all the data either in the sample or in a population. You should find this relaxed notation easier to work with.

SKILL DEVELOPMENT PROBLEMS FOR **SECTION 3-2**

The following set of problems is meant to test your understanding of the material in this section.

3. Determine the range, variance, and standard deviation for the following data set, assuming it represents the population:

16	23	17	24	9	11	13	15
18	21	16	23	17	16	10	14

Compare the values you just found with those found if you assume that the data came from a sample of the population.

4. Use the following set of sales data to test the empirical rule. Assume that the data represent a population.

$17.87	19.95	22.95	18.74	9.95
11.22	21.98	14.52	16.65	14.98

5. The Morgan Manufacturers Representative Company provides sales services for several small computer software developers. The company has been

worried about its increasing sales force expense accounts. A sample of fifteen daily expense logs shows the following total values:

$ 84.29	94.55	67.98	112.15	75.29
102.58	92.67	128.90	135.85	86.34
89.95	63.44	128.80	94.55	115.60

Calculate the mean, variance, and standard deviation of these data. Use the empirical rule in a short report analyzing these sales values.

3-3 MEASURES OF LOCATION AND SPREAD FOR GROUPED DATA (OPTIONAL)

The previous sections introduced the most commonly used measures of location and spread. The formulas presented are used when you are dealing with raw data either from a population or from a sample. For most applications in business, you probably will be working with raw data and those formulas will most likely be used. Even when you have large amounts of data, calculators with memory units or computers will more than likely be available for you to use in performing the calculations.

However, as illustrated in Chapter 2, one of the first steps that many decision makers take in transforming data into useful information is to form a frequency distribution. There may be instances in which you are given the frequency distribution but not the raw data from which it was constructed. Thus it is important to be able to compute measures of location and spread from the grouped data frequency distribution. This section introduces the methods for doing this and presents some examples.

You should note that computations made from grouped data frequency distributions are only *approximations* of the values that would be computed from the original raw data. The reason for this is that we lose detail by grouping the data into classes. We no longer know what the individual values are and must assume that the data in each class are spread evenly through each class, and therefore the midpoint is used to represent each value within a given class. This concept will become clear as we look at the computations of the measures of location and spread.

FINDING THE MEDIAN FOR GROUPED DATA

If the data have been grouped into a frequency distribution, calculating the median requires interpolation. For example, Table 3-6 gives the distribution of the last 5,000 awards given by the Fort Wayne, Indiana, small claims court. The *median class* contains the middle value in the array. Thus, if the frequency distribution has N items, the median class contains the N/2 item (in this case, the 2,500th item). Starting from either the top or bottom, item 2,500 is in the class "$100 and under $150."

TABLE **3-6**

Distribution of
Awards in Small
Claims Court

Class	Frequency f_i	Cumulative Frequency
$ 0 and under $ 50	600	600
50 and under 100	1,000	1,600
100 and under 150	1,200	2,800
150 and under 200	800	3,600
200 and under 250	600	4,200
250 and under 300	400	4,600
300 and under 350	200	4,800
350 and under 400	200	5,000
Total	5,000	

Although we know the class that contains the median, does it lie near $100, or is it closer to $150? This question is answered by interpolating the required distance from the lower limit of the median class, as shown in the median formula 3-9:

$$\text{Median} \approx L_{median} + \left(\frac{\frac{N}{2} - \Sigma f_{prec}}{f_{median}} \right)(W) \quad \text{3-9}$$

where

L_{median} = Lower limit of the median class
N = Total number of observations
Σf_{prec} = Sum of observations in classes preceding the median class
W = Width of the median class
f_{median} = Number of observations in the median class

Therefore,

$$\text{Median} \approx \$100 + \left(\frac{\frac{5,000}{2} - 1,600}{1,200} \right)(\$50)$$

$$\approx \$100 + \left(\frac{900}{1,200} \right)(\$50)$$

$$\approx \$137.50$$

We should discuss the rationale behind this procedure. Notice in Table 3-6 that there are 1,600 observations in the classes with awards less than $100. Because we want to find award 2,500 we need to go 900 awards into the next interval, "$100 and less than $150." Because 1,200 awards are contained in this interval, and the awards are assumed evenly spread through the interval, we need to move 900/1,200 of the way through this class. Because the class width is $50, we will go 900/1,200 of this $50 width, or $37.50 through the $50 interval. Because the interval starts at $100, the median award is

$$\$100 + \$37.50 = \$137.50$$

Remember, the median is not sensitive to extreme values in a data set and thus is particularly useful as a measure of location for skewed distributions.

FINDING THE MEAN FOR GROUPED DATA

If the data have been grouped into classes and a frequency distribution has been formed, we apply equation 3-10[1] to find the mean:

$$\mu_x \approx \frac{\sum\limits_{i=1}^{c} f_i M_i}{N} \qquad \textbf{3-10}$$

where

μ_x = Population mean
c = Number of classes
f_i = Frequency in the ith class
M_i = Midpoint of the ith class
N = Population size

[1] Equation 3-10 can also be used to define a weighted mean, or weighted average, where

f_i = Weight assigned to category or class i
N = Sum of all the weights

Using the grouped distribution of small claims awards given in Table 3-6, we can find the mean award as follows:

Class	Midpoint M_i	Frequency f_i	f_iM_i
$ 0 and under $ 50	$ 25	600	$ 15,000
50 and under 100	75	1,000	75,000
100 and under 150	125	1,200	150,000
150 and under 200	175	800	140,000
200 and under 250	225	600	135,000
250 and under 300	275	400	110,000
300 and under 350	325	200	65,000
350 and under 400	375	200	75,000

$$N = \sum_{i=1}^{c} f_i = 5,000 \qquad \sum_{i=1}^{c} f_iM_i = \$765,000$$

For this example,

$$\mu_x \approx \frac{\sum_{i=1}^{8} f_iM_i}{N}$$

$$\approx \frac{\$765,000}{5,000}$$

$$\approx \$153$$

Equation 3-10 also assumes the data are spread equally through the interval. Therefore, the midpoint can be assumed to be a good representative of each value.

Recall that the median for these data was $137.50. For any set of data, the mean and median need not be the same. Also, when the data are in grouped form, the calculations for the median and mean provide only approximations. When the data are grouped, we assume either that all observations fall at the class midpoint or that the observations are spread evenly throughout each class interval and can be represented by the midpoint. The closer these assumptions are to being true, the better the approximations will be.

THE VARIANCE AND THE STANDARD DEVIATION FOR GROUPED DATA

As illustrated, data are often best presented by grouping into classes. The variance and standard deviation can be calculated for grouped data in much the same manner as the mean is calculated for grouped data. The formulas for calculating the variance and standard deviation for grouped data are given in equations 3-11 to 3-14:

For populations

$$\sigma_x^2 \approx \frac{\Sigma f(M - \mu_x)^2}{N}$$

(3-11)

$$\sigma_x \approx \sqrt{\frac{\Sigma f(M - \mu_x)^2}{N}}$$

(3-12)

where

f = Number of values in each class
M = Midpoint of each class
μ_x = Mean of the population $\approx \Sigma fM/N$
N = Population size = Σf

For samples

$$S_x^2 \approx \frac{\Sigma f(M - \overline{X})^2}{n - 1}$$

(3-13)

$$S_x \approx \sqrt{\frac{\Sigma f(M - \overline{X})^2}{n - 1}}$$

(3-14)

where

$\overline{X}$ = Sample mean $\approx \dfrac{\Sigma fM}{n}$

n = Sample size = Σf

Table 3-7 illustrates the frequency distribution from a sample of 100 days of production at a lumber mill. The standard deviation for this sample is found as follows. First,

$$\overline{X} \approx \frac{\Sigma fM}{n}$$

$$\approx \frac{5,850}{100}$$

$$\approx 58.50$$

Then,

M	f	$(M - \overline{X})$	$(M - \overline{X})^2$	$f(M - \overline{X})^2$
20	5	$(20 - 58.50) = -38.50$	1,482.25	7,411.25
30	8	$(30 - 58.50) = -28.50$	812.25	6,498.00
40	15	$(40 - 58.50) = -18.50$	342.25	5,133.75
50	20	$(50 - 58.50) = -\ 8.50$	72.25	1,445.00
60	15	$(60 - 58.50) = \ \ \ 1.50$	2.25	33.75
70	10	$(70 - 58.50) = \ \ 11.50$	132.25	1,322.50
80	17	$(80 - 58.50) = \ \ 21.50$	462.25	7,858.25
90	5	$(90 - 58.50) = \ \ 31.50$	992.25	4,961.25
100	5	$(100 - 58.50) = \ \ 41.50$	1,722.25	8,611.25
	$n = 100$			$\Sigma = 43,275.00$

which makes the standard deviation

$$S_x \approx \sqrt{\frac{43,275}{100 - 1}}$$

$$\approx 20.91$$

TABLE 3-7

Lumber Production Sample (Board Feet × 1,000)

Class	M	f	fM
15 and under 25	20	5	100
25 and under 35	30	8	240
35 and under 45	40	15	600
45 and under 55	50	20	1,000
55 and under 65	60	15	900
65 and under 75	70	10	700
75 and under 85	80	17	1,360
85 and under 95	90	5	450
95 and under 105	100	5	500
		$n = 100$	$\Sigma = 5,850$

Now, based on these calculations, the production manager has estimates for both the central location and dispersion in the daily lumber production. Without the information contained in the mean and standard deviation, the production manager would be hard pressed to reasonably assess and monitor the mill's daily lumber production. For example, the large standard deviation in this example indicates high variability in production output. High variability in production is generally undesirable and is an indication that better production control is needed.

SKILL DEVELOPMENT PROBLEMS FOR **SECTION 3-3**

The following set of problems is meant to test your understanding of the material in this section.

6. Find the mean and median for the following set of grouped data:

Class	Frequency
0 to under 5	15
5 to under 10	22
10 to under 15	47
15 to under 20	34
20 to under 25	19
25 to under 30	9

7. Find the variance and standard deviation for the following set of grouped data. Assume the data came from a sample.

Class	Frequency
10 to under 20	29
20 to under 30	69
30 to under 40	81
40 to under 50	57
50 to under 60	44
60 to under 70	21

8. Several recent articles in *Fortune* and *The Wall Street Journal* about the potential health insurance problems being caused by the aging American work force have caused Harry Anderson, benefits director for AdvanceTech Manufacturing, to look at the age of its work force. He found the following values:

Class	Frequency
20 through 24	26
25 through 29	45
30 through 34	52
35 through 39	61
40 through 44	49
45 through 49	37
50 through 54	32
55 through 59	24
60 through 64	17
65 through 69	11

Find the mean, median, variance, and standard deviation of these data. Using these values, write a short report analyzing the age distribution of the work force. (Assume this represents the entire work force.)

3-4 MEASURES OF RELATIVE VARIATION

While the distribution of a set of data can be described by a measure of location and a measure of variation, in some cases combining these two measures makes comparisons easier. To this end, two measures are frequently used. The *coefficient of variation* compares the size of the distribution's standard deviation to its mean by forming a ratio of the two values. The *box and whisker plot* is a graphical technique based on the quartiles of the data set.

THE COEFFICIENT OF VARIATION

The standard deviation measures the variation in a set of data. For distributions having the same mean, the distribution with the largest standard deviation has the greatest relative spread. This is illustrated in Figure 3-6, where the distribution in (b) has greater dispersion than that in (a). For decision makers, the standard deviation indicates how spread out, or uncertain, a distribution is. Given two distributions with the same mean, decision makers should feel more certain about the decisions made from the distribution with the smaller standard deviation. However, when considering distributions with different means, decision makers cannot compare the uncertainty in distributions by comparing standard deviations only.

For instance, Agra-Tech has recently introduced feed supplements for both cattle and hogs that will increase the rate at which these animals gain weight. Three years of feedlot tests indicate that cattle fed the supplement will weigh an average of 125 pounds more than those not fed the supplement. The standard

FIGURE **3-6**

Distribution
Spread

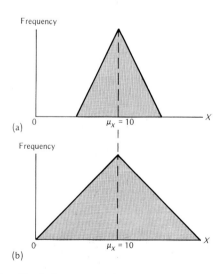

(a)

(b)

Note: The distribution in part (a) and the distribution in part (b) both have the same mean, but that in (b) has a larger standard deviation than that in (a) and is thus more spread out around the mean.

deviation of the additional weight gain is 10 pounds. Similar tests with hogs indicate those fed the hog supplement will gain an average of 40 pounds more than hogs not fed the supplement. The standard deviation associated with the average additional weight gain for hogs is also 10 pounds. Even though the standard deviation is 10 pounds for both distributions, the fact that the average increase in weight gain for cattle is 125 pounds and the average increase for hogs is 40 pounds indicates that there is a different degree of uncertainty associated with these two distributions.

The **coefficient of variation** is often used to indicate the relative uncertainty of distributions with different means. It does so by attempting to adjust the scales so that they are comparable. This is done by dividing the standard deviation by the mean, thus producing a unitless ratio.

The coefficients of variation for populations and samples are given in equations 3-15 and 3-16:

For populations

$$CV = \frac{\sigma_x}{\mu_x}(100)\%$$ **3-15**

For samples

$$CV = \frac{S_x}{\overline{X}}(100)\%$$ **3-16**

where

$$CV = \text{coefficient of variation}$$

When the coefficients of variation for different distributions are compared, the distribution with the largest CV value has the greatest relative spread. For the Agra-Tech example, the two coefficients of variation are

$$CV(\text{cattle}) = \frac{10}{125}(100)\% = 8\%$$

$$CV(\text{hogs}) = \frac{10}{40}(100)\% = 25\%$$

Clearly, the distribution associated with the additional weight gain for hogs has a greater relative spread.

The coefficient of variation is an excellent example of both the advantages and disadvantages of many statistical aids to decision making. When the mean and standard deviation of a distribution are combined to form the coefficient of variation, the effect of different mean values tends to be eliminated. However, many decisions must be based on both central location *and* spread of distributions. By combining the measure of location and measure of spread into one value, decision makers lose some information. The point is that any statistical tool should be used as an aid to good managerial judgment, not in place of managerial judgment.

THE BOX AND WHISKER PLOT

The box and whisker plot is a graphical method for indicating the shape of the distribution of a set of data. This technique is based on the quartiles of a data set. Quartiles are found by first arranging the data in rank order and then determining the values that divide the data into four equal-sized groups. The lower quartile is the value below which 25% of the data points fall. The middle quartile is the median, the value below which 50% of the data points fall (also called the 50th percentile). The upper quartile is the 75th percentile (75% of the observations lie below this point). Many computer packages now have box and whisker options. Figure 3-7 shows the MINITAB plot for the salary data presented in Table 2-1.

FIGURE **3-7**   MINITAB Box and Whisker Plot for Data in Table 2-1

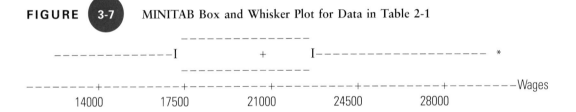

The meaning of a box and whisker plot is partially evident from Figure 3-7, but how the plot is constructed needs some explanation, as follows:

1. The box in the middle of the figure contains the middle 50% of the observations, or the values between the 25th and 75th percentiles. The I's at the end of the box, indicating the 25th and 75th percentiles, are called **hinges.** The distance between the hinges is called the **interquartile range.**
2. The median of the distribution is represented by the + inside the box. (Note: Some software allows you to indicate the mean, instead of the median.)
3. The lines extending from either side of the box are **whiskers.** Their length is determined by the relationship between values in the data set and two fences located on each side of the box. The inner fence is determined by starting at the appropriate hinge and moving up (or down) a distance of 1.5 times the interquartile range. For this data set:

$$\text{Interquartile range} = 22{,}400 - 17{,}500 = 4{,}900$$
$$\text{Lower inner fence} = 17{,}500 - 1.5(4{,}900) = 10{,}150$$

The lower whisker will extend to the smallest value in the data set inside the inner fence.

4. The upper inner fence is given by:

$$\text{Upper inner fence} = 22{,}400 + 1.5(4{,}900) = 29{,}750$$

The upper whisker extends to the largest data point still inside this fence. Observations falling outside the inner fences should receive special attention since they represent rare events. Note in Figure 3-7 that no values fall below the lower inner fence, but one value (represented by the *) falls above the upper inner fence.

5. A second fence, the outer fence, is found by starting at the appropriate hinge and moving up (or down) a distance of 3 times the interquartile range. Values falling outside the outer fence are represented by a 0 on the plot. These values are considered **outliers** and probably do not represent the population of interest. At the least, we should closely consider how these outlying data points were determined. Note that this data set contains no outliers.

SKILL DEVELOPMENT PROBLEMS FOR **SECTION 3-4**

The following set of problems is meant to test your understanding of the material in this section.

9. Determine the coefficient of variation for the following set of population data. Also construct a box and whisker plot.

33	42	39	17	27	32	40	37
30	35	37	19	34	37	41	35

10. Sportway Manufacturing has been experimenting with new materials to use for golf ball covers. Two recently developed compounds have been shown to be equally resistant to cutting, and the Development Lab is now looking at the distance the balls will travel during a simulated drive. However, both distance and consistency are important for a golf ball. A sample of ten balls with each type of cover was selected and the following distances were measured (in yards) using a mechanical driver that struck each ball with the same force.

Type A		Type B	
298	291	290	310
296	299	300	305
289	285	297	315
291	292	301	286
287	290	302	321

Write a report analyzing the performance of the two types of balls.

3-5 VARIATION AND QUALITY IMPROVEMENT

All physical processes exhibit variation. The amount of time you need to walk to your next class, or to your car after class, will not be the same each day. The amount of time needed by your barber or hair dresser the next time you get your hair cut will not be the same as that needed the last time you had your hair cut. The diameters of pistons made at the Ford engine plant will not all be the same. Hopefully, after studying the material in this chapter you will feel comfortable with the idea of variation in a physical process. This natural variation is central to many efforts to improve quality.

VARIATION IN A SERVICE PROCESS

In the quality control section of Chapter 2, we briefly considered an appliance repair company that was interested in improving its customer relations. The single largest cause of complaints against the company was that repair technicians did not arrive as scheduled. While this has been cited as the single most common complaint against the company, let's look at the problem from the company's perspective. Suppose we were scheduling only washing machine repairs. While the average repair may take 1 hour to complete, some repairs will take less than 1 hour and some more. Also, the time spent traveling between houses will vary.

If the time spent to service a washing machine were exactly 1 hour and the time spent traveling between any two service calls took exactly 20 minutes, the scheduling issue would be easy to resolve. However, since variation exists in both times, the possibility of late (or even early) arrivals exists. Any actions that would reduce the variability in either repair time or travel time would make scheduling easier, and therefore increase customer satisfaction. Consequently, the effort to improve quality in many organizations is equivalent to locating sources of variation in the physical process and finding ways to reduce these sources. The following example will expand on this point.

VARIATION IN A MANUFACTURING PROCESS

The key to improving the quality of manufactured products often lies in being able to reduce the variation in the output of the manufacturing process. For instance, the engine in today's automobile is a complex machine dependent on the correct fit of numerous parts. Certainly, one of the most critical fits is that of the pistons in the cylinders.

A simplified version of the piston–cylinder arrangement is shown in Figure 3-8. Assume that the design diameter of the cylinder is 3.00 inches. Since cylinders are bored by a mechanical process, not all will have exactly the same dimension. For this example, assume the diameters are distributed around a mean of 3.00 inches with a standard deviation of 0.001 inch. Using the empirical rule, this means that almost all the diameters will fall between 2.997 and 3.003 inches.

FIGURE **3-8**

Cylinder–Piston
Arrangement

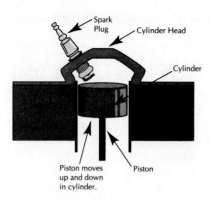

Since a tight fit between the cylinder wall and the piston is crucial for correct engine performance and good gas mileage, the question is, What dimension should be specified for the pistons? If the pistons were made with an outside diameter of 3.00 inches, but also had a standard deviation of 0.001 inch, half the pistons would not fit the average cylinder. However, if the average piston dimension were less than 3.00 inches, as will have to be the case, those at the lower end of the distribution will not fit tightly enough in cylinders with diameters at the upper end of their distribution. Also, some pistons would still be too large for the smaller cylinders.

The problem of establishing the correct fit in engines is so critical that a typical American manufacturer stocks thirteen different sizes of pistons. The engines are hand fitted by a technician using a trial-and-error procedure. Even then, not all pistons have a correct fit. By spending years finding the sources of variation in the physical process and acting to reduce this variation, some Japanese manufacturers are able to assemble engines with only one piston size.

VARIATION AND PROCESS CAPABILITY

Both service and manufacturing organizations rely on process and product specifications to plan present and future operations. In a typical service operation, for example, the number of tellers scheduled at banks is based on a forecast of customer arrival rates and the rate at which customers can be serviced. Banks may set a standard service rate for their tellers. With regard to the piston example, design engineers will set specifications on the dimensions of both the piston and cylinder. Unfortunately, in both service and manufacturing organizations, specifications are sometimes set without a consideration of process capability. There should be a relationship between what an organization claims a process can do and the actual capability of the process.

In Chapter 2, we addressed the issue of process capability by looking at a frequency distribution computed from sample measurements from the process. If too many of the measurements fell outside the specification limits, we concluded that the process was not capable of achieving the desired results. However, process capability can also be approached directly by understanding the standard deviation of the output measure. For example, consider the engine manufacturer example we have been discussing. Suppose that engineering specifications call for the cylinder diameter to be between 2.9985 inches and 3.0015 inches. Further, suppose that the company studies outputs from the process long enough to realize that the standard deviation in cylinder diameter is 0.001 inch.

A measure called the process capability ratio (PCR) can be computed to help assess the capability of the process. The PCR is computed as follows:

$$PCR = \frac{USL - LSL}{6\sigma}$$

where

$$USL = \text{Upper specification limit}$$
$$LSL = \text{Lower specification limit}$$
$$\sigma = \text{Output standard deviation}$$

For this example, the PCR is

$$PCR = \frac{3.0015 - 2.9985}{6(0.001)}$$
$$= 0.5000$$

A value of PCR = 1.0 implies that the specification limits are exactly equal to the natural process limits of ±3 standard deviations. A value of PCR > 1.0 implies that the specification limits are wider than the natural process limits, which is good. However, a value of PCR < 1.0 indicates that the process variation exceeds the specification limits, which is bad. It means that the process is not capable of meeting the specifications. Thus, the engine manufacturer has a process that is not capable of meeting product specifications consistently. (*Note:* Some quality improvement references use the notation Cp to indicate the process capability ratio.)

3-6 COMPUTER APPLICATIONS

This chapter has introduced several descriptive measures that can be computed from data. These measures, such as the mean, median, variance, and standard deviation, provide insight regarding the central location and spread in a data set.

The formulas for computing these measures are straightforward but the task can be burdensome if the data set has a large number of cases. Computer software is ideally suited to making computations quickly and accurately for very large databases.

MINITAB and GB-STAT have routines for computing a variety of descriptive statistics. In this section, we illustrate three examples of the type of output avail-

```
AGE        N =   50    MEAN =      44.060   ST.DEV. =      15.5
INCOME     N =   50    MEAN =      24846.   ST.DEV. =      4800.
HOURSTV    N =   50    MEAN =      12.080   ST.DEV. =      4.36
```

FIGURE 3-9 MINITAB Computer Output for the DESCRIBE Command for KIVZ-Channel 5 Data

FIGURE 3-10

MINITAB
Commands—
Descriptive
Statistics

```
MTB> READ 'KIVZ5' INTO C1-C19
MTB> NAME C17 'AGE'
MTB> NAME C18 'INCOME'
MTB> NAME C19 'HOURSTV'
MTB> OUTFILE = 'PRINTER'
MTB> DESCRIBE C17-C19
```

able from these programs. Figure 3-9 shows the results of using the DESCRIBE command in MINITAB for the KIVZ-Channel 5 television data (see Chapter 2, Table 2-7). The output shows the sample size, mean, and standard deviation for three variables: age, income, and hours of TV watched per week. Figure 3-10 shows the MINITAB program statements.

GB-STAT can also be used to determine many descriptive measures. Selecting the F3 key for STATISTICS and then the descriptive statistics option from the menu yields these values. Figure 3-11 shows the output of the mean and standard

FIGURE 3-11

GB-STAT Output
for Descriptive
Statistics Option

VAR NAME	SIZE	MEAN	SAMPLE STD DEV	SAMPLE VARIANCE	COEF. OF VARIATION
NATNEW	50	2.36	1.06445	1.13306	.45104
LOCNEW	50	2.24	.87037	.75755	.38856
NEWRAT	50	3.26	1.00631	1.01265	.30868
SPTRAT	50	3.36	1.20814	1.45959	.35956
WTRRAT	50	3.14	1.27791	1.63306	.40698
ANCRAT	50	3.38	1.06694	1.13837	.31566
SPCRAT	50	3.4	1.17803	1.38775	.34648
OVRALL	50	3.22	.78999	.62408	.24534
NATINF	50	1.78	.54548	.29755	.30645
SEX	50	1.56	.50143	.25143	.32143
MSTAT	50	2.88	.5206	.27102	.18076
NUMEMP	50	1.38	.60238	.36286	.4365
HSTAT	50	1.84	.37033	.13714	.20127
YRRES	50	8.68	8.00877	64.14041	.92267
YRSTAT	50	26.78	18.43498	339.8485	.68839
EDUCAT	50	3.78	1.59451	2.54245	.42183
AGE	50	44.06	15.50959	240.5474	.35201
INCOME	50	24846	4800.477	2.304458E+07	.19321
HRSTV	50	12.08	4.35581	18.97305	.36058

FIGURE 3-12

GB-STAT
Output, Mean
and Standard
Deviation of
Overall Anchor
Rating by Male
and Female
Respondents

BREAKDOWN OF 'ANCRAT'

SEX	N	MEAN	STD DEV
2 (FEMALE)	28	3.428571	1.168366
1 (MALE)	22	3.318182	.9454837
TOTAL	50	3.38	1.066943

deviation command from the descriptive statistics menu for all variables in the data set. Figure 3-12 shows the overall anchor rating means and standard deviations broken down by men and women respondents.

The role of these numerical statistics is to provide the decision maker with information about a set of data. The computer is a useful tool for calculation and almost any statistical software you might use will have the capability of computing the measures shown in this section.

3-7 CONCLUSIONS

Measures of central location and measures of variation, or spread, are statistical tools for transforming data into meaningful information. When used together, measures of location and dispersion allow managerial decision makers to compare distributions and determine whether they are statistically the same or whether a difference exists between them. Although we have discussed several measures of both location and spread for a distribution, the most widely used measures are the mean and standard deviation.

Throughout the chapter new statistical concepts have been discussed in general managerial terms. The chapter glossary presents a list of more formal statistical definitions for these concepts. To test your understanding, reconcile the managerial discussion with these definitions.

The important equations introduced in this chapter are presented in a special section following the glossary.

CHAPTER GLOSSARY

box and whisker plot A graphical method of representing a distribution based on the quartiles and extreme values in a data set.

coefficient of variation A measure that can be used to compare relative dispersion between two or more data sets. It is formed by dividing the standard deviation by the mean of a data set.

hinges In a box and whisker plot, lines indicating the 25th and 75th percentiles.

interquartile range The range containing the middle 50% of the values in a data set. The distance from the 25th to 75th percentiles.

mean   The mean of a set of n measurements is equal to the sum of the measurements divided by n. The mean is the most commonly used measure of location.

median   A measure of location. The middle item in a set of measurements that have been arranged according to magnitude.

mode   A measure of location. The value in a series of measurements that appears more frequently than any other. The mode may not be unique.

outliers   The extreme values in a data set, considered not to represent the population of interest. In a box and whisker plot, values beyond the outer fence.

range   The difference between the largest and the smallest values in a set of data.

standard deviation   The positive square root of the variance.

variance   A measure of data dispersion. The average of the squared differences between the individual measurements and the mean.

whiskers   Lines extending on each side of the box in a box and whisker plot.

CHAPTER FORMULAS

Median
Grouped

$$\text{Median} = L_{\text{median}} + \left(\frac{\frac{N}{2} - \Sigma f_{\text{prec}}}{f_{\text{median}}} \right)(W)$$

Mean
Population
Ungrouped

$$\mu_x = \frac{\Sigma X}{N}$$

Grouped

$$\mu_x \approx \frac{\Sigma f M}{N}$$

Sample
Ungrouped

$$\overline{X} = \frac{\Sigma X}{n}$$

Grouped

$$\overline{X} \approx \frac{\Sigma f M}{n}$$

Variance

Population

Ungrouped

$$\sigma_x^2 = \frac{\Sigma(X - \mu_x)^2}{N}$$

Grouped

$$\sigma_x^2 \approx \frac{\Sigma f(M - \mu_x)^2}{N}$$

Sample

Ungrouped

$$S_x^2 = \frac{\Sigma(X - \overline{X})^2}{n - 1}$$

Grouped

$$S_x^2 \approx \frac{\Sigma f(M - \overline{X})^2}{n - 1}$$

Standard deviation

Population

Ungrouped

$$\sigma_x = \sqrt{\frac{\Sigma(X - \mu_x)^2}{N}}$$

Grouped

$$\sigma_x \approx \sqrt{\frac{\Sigma f(M - \mu_x)^2}{N}}$$

Sample

Ungrouped

$$S_x = \sqrt{\frac{\Sigma(X - \overline{X})^2}{n - 1}}$$

Grouped

$$S_x \approx \sqrt{\frac{\Sigma f(M - \overline{X})^2}{n - 1}}$$

Coefficient of variation

Population

$$CV = \frac{\sigma_x}{\mu_x}(100)\%$$

Sample

$$CV = \frac{S_x}{\overline{X}}(100)\%$$

SOLVED PROBLEMS

1. A retail store manager has selected a sample of sales slips during the past month and now needs your assistance in answering some questions about the sample. The sixty-four sales values have been numerically ordered as follows:

$ 0.97	$ 1.23	$ 1.29	$ 1.69	$ 2.19	$ 2.77	$ 3.19	$ 3.57
3.97	3.99	4.35	4.44	4.44	4.50	4.65	5.25
5.69	5.99	6.49	6.50	6.99	7.19	7.44	7.49
7.75	8.12	8.90	8.99	9.85	9.97	9.97	9.98
10.48	11.97	11.99	11.99	11.99	12.49	12.95	13.39
13.88	13.89	14.99	16.30	18.63	19.97	21.25	21.50
22.95	23.85	24.99	24.99	29.97	34.95	34.98	35.95
41.69	49.99	61.98	64.88	67.29	68.99	69.99	74.96

a. What is the mean sales level for the sixty-four sales values?
b. What is the median sales level for these data?
c. What is the mode?
d. Note that the median and mode are fairly close but that the mean is much larger. Why is this?
e. What is the standard deviation from the sample of sales values?

Solution

a. The formula for finding the mean is

$$\overline{X} = \frac{\Sigma X}{n}$$

If we sum the sixty-four values, we get

$$\Sigma X = \$1,149.86$$

Dividing by $n = 64$,

$$\overline{X} = \frac{\$1,149.86}{64}$$

$$= \$17.97$$

Thus the mean sale for the sample is $17.97.

b. The median is the center item when the data have been rank-ordered. When the number of observations is an even number, the median is the average of the two middle observations. Thus, the median for these data is midway between the thirty-second and thirty-third sales values:

$$\text{Median} = \frac{\$9.98 + \$10.48}{2}$$

$$= \$10.23$$

c. The mode is the value in the data that appears most often. In this data set, the value $11.99 occurred three times, which is more often than any other value. Thus the mode is $11.99.

d. Whenever the mean, median, and mode differ in value, the data distribution is skewed. The farther the mean is from the median and the mode, the greater the skewness. The mean is sensitive to extreme observations, and in this example, although the majority of the observations are less than $15.00, the few high sales values over $60.00 have pulled the mean up to $17.97.

e. The sample standard deviation is found using the following formula:

$$S_x = \sqrt{\frac{\Sigma (X - \overline{X})^2}{n - 1}}$$

Recalling that $\overline{X} = 17.97$, we can find the standard deviation as follows:

X	$(X - \overline{X})$	$(X - \overline{X})^2$
0.97	$(0.97 - 17.97) = -17.00$	289.00
1.23	$(1.23 - 17.97) = -16.74$	280.23
1.29	$(1.29 - 17.97) = -16.68$	278.22
1.69	$(1.69 - 17.97) = -16.28$	265.04
.	. .	.
.	. .	.
.	. .	.
74.96	$(74.96 - 17.97) = 56.99$	3,247.86
		$\Sigma = 23,385.71$

$$S_x = \sqrt{\frac{23,385.71}{64 - 1}}$$
$$= \sqrt{371.20}$$
$$= \$19.27$$

Thus the sample standard deviation is $19.27.

CONCEPTUAL QUESTIONS AND ASSIGNMENTS

11. Discuss the circumstances under which you would prefer the median as a measure of location instead of the mean.

12. Considering the relative positions of the mean, median, and mode:
    a. Draw a symmetrical distribution and label the three measures of location.
    b. Draw a left-skewed distribution and label the three measures of location.
    c. Draw a right-skewed distribution and label the three measures of location.

13. The marketing manager for Sweetright Cola has just received the results of two separate marketing studies performed in the Ohio Valley market region. One study was based on a random sample of 300 people and the study

indicated that the mean income is $2,450.00 per month. The second study was based on a random sample of 400 people and indicated that the mean income in the region is $2,375.00 per month. The manager is confused. Should he have expected the two samples to yield exactly the same mean? Why or why not? Also, is it reasonable to believe that a sample mean should exactly equal the mean of the population? Discuss.

14. Discuss the advantages and disadvantages of using the range as a measure of spread in a set of data.

15. Explain why the mean calculated for a set of ungrouped data might differ from the mean if the same data were grouped into a frequency distribution. Would this also be the case for the standard deviation? Why?

ADDITIONAL PROBLEMS

16. Ivan Horton is a building contractor whose company builds many homes every year. In planning for each job, Ivan needs some idea about the direct labor hours required to build a home. He has collected sample information on the labor hours for ten jobs during the past year.

    245   402   291   351   353   242   118   595   152   175

    a. Calculate the mean for this sample and explain what it means.
    b. Calculate the median for this sample.
    c. Calculate the variance and standard deviation.
    d. If Ivan had to select the mean or the median as the measure of location for direct labor hours, what factors about each should he consider before making the decision?

17. The Hillside Bowling Alley manager has selected a random sample of his league customers. He asked them to record the number of lines they bowl during the month of December, including both league and open bowling. The sample of twenty people produced the following data:

    4   13   22   12   9   16   17   16   12   12   20
    11   16   15   12   12   14   32   12   18   15

    a. Compute the mean for these sample data.
    b. Compute the median for these sample data.
    c. Compute the mode for these sample data.
    d. Calculate the variance and standard deviation for these sample data.
    e. Note that one person in the sample bowled thirty-two lines. What effect, if any, does this large value have on each of the three measures of location? Discuss.
    f. For these sample data, which measure of location provides the best measure of the center?

18. The Indiana Transportation Department recently set up a speed check station on one of the interstate highways and collected speed data on forty vehicles selected at random during a 4-hour period. The data collected (in miles per hour) are presented.

1409 ↗   ↘   1408

68	72	62	75	81	64	81	66
65	68	70	70	69	73	72	75
71	70	80	74	62	59	81	69
66	88	66	65	65	77	70	65
64	77	68	70	72	66	73	68

  a. Compute the average speed for the sample.
  b. Compute the median speed for the sample data.
  c. Compute the mode for these sample data.
  d. Compute the variance and standard deviation of these sample data.
  e. The speed limit on the highway where the data were collected is 65 mph. Write a short report describing the sample data and include both graphical analyses and measures of location and spread. The report should address the issue of whether the vehicles traveling on this highway tend to obey the speed limit.

19. The Norton Oil Company has twenty oil wells operating in the Gulf of Mexico. The output of these twenty oil wells has been recorded in terms of barrels per day pumped, as follows:

| 800 | 100 | 230 | 700 | 1,900 | 300 | 400 | 700 | 250 | 500 |
| 340 | 670 | 340 | 250 | 450 | 700 | 500 | 200 | 75 | 1,200 |

  a. Compute the mean daily production for these twenty wells. Assume the data represent the population of interest.
  b. What is the median oil production per day for this population of oil wells?
  c. Write a short report describing the daily oil production for the Norton Oil Company wells in the Gulf of Mexico.

20. Refer to the Norton Oil Company data in Problem 21. Select a sample of six oil wells from this population.
  a. Discuss the method you used to determine your sample and list the sample data.
  b. Compute the median for the sample.
  c. Compute the mean for the sample.
  d. Write a short report comparing the sample measures of location with the population measures.

21. In the past few years many companies using trees as raw material have become interested in growing trees. One company has collected the following information on tree growth per year for samples from three species of trees:

Growth Class (feet)	Pine Frequency	Redwood Frequency	Cedar Frequency
0 and under 1	10	15	5
1 and under 2	5	10	10
2 and under 3	9	2	4
3 and under 4	4	2	4
4 and under 5	2	1	7
Total	30 trees	30 trees	30 trees

Write a report to management analyzing this information. Be sure to discuss the location and spread in the growth for each type of tree.

22. Suppose you are considering purchasing an apartment house. There would be many things to consider in the analysis of whether to buy. One of these would be the maintenance costs you might incur. The following frequency distribution reflects the historical weekly costs (rounded to the nearest dollar) based on the current owner's records for the past 30 weeks:

Expense Class	Frequency
$ 0–$100	12
101– 200	5
201– 300	6
301– 400	4
401– 500	3
Total	30 weeks

a. Calculate the mean weekly expense.
b. Calculate the variance and standard deviation.
c. Suppose you have made a deal with the current owner to keep the maintenance records yourself for 1 week. You find that $600 was spent. Assuming this was a typical week, what would you conclude about the current owner's records? Why?

23. The manager of the Clark Fork Station Restaurant recently selected a random sample of fifty customers and kept track of how long the customers were required to wait from the time they arrived at the restaurant until they were actually served dinner. This study resulted from several complaints the manager had received from customers saying that their wait time was unduly long and that it appeared that the objective was to keep people waiting in the lounge for as long as possible to increase the lounge business. The following data were recorded, with time measured in minutes.

34	24	43	56	74	20	19	33	55	43
45	23	43	56	67	45	26	57	78	41
30	19	36	32	65	24	54	34	27	34
36	24	54	39	43	23	56	36	34	45
67	54	32	18	40	35	67	53	23	47

a. Compute the mean waiting time for this sample of customers.
b. Compute the median waiting time for this sample of customers.
c. Compute the variance and standard deviation of waiting time for this sample of customers. Develop a frequency distribution using seven classes with class width of 10. Make the lower limit of the first class 15.
d. For each class, determine the class midpoint.
e. Develop a frequency histogram for the frequency distribution.
f. Compute the mean waiting time from the grouped data and compare this value with the mean computed from the raw data in part a.

g. Compute the median waiting time from the grouped data and compare this value with the median computed from the raw data in part **b.**

h. Compute the variance and standard deviation of the waiting times from the grouped data and compare these values with the variance and standard deviation computed from the raw data in part **c.**

i. Discuss whether it is preferable to compute measures of location and spread from grouped data versus raw data if a decision maker has the option.

j. If you have the appropriate software, construct a box and whisker plot of this data.

24. The C. A. Whitman Investment Company recently offered two mutual funds to its customers. A mutual fund is a group of stocks and bonds that is managed by an investment company. Individuals purchase shares of the mutual fund and the investment company uses the money to buy stocks. Many investors feel comfortable with a mutual fund because their money is not tied up in one or two stocks but is spread over many stocks, thereby, they hope, reducing the risk.

Each of the two mutual funds offered by C. A. Whitman currently has sixty stocks. During the past 6 months the average stock in fund A has increased $3.30 in price, with a standard deviation of $1.25. The stocks in fund B have shown an average increase of $8.00, with a standard deviation of $3.50.

Based on this information, which of the two funds has stocks that have shown the greater relative variability? Compute the appropriate measures and explain why we cannot simply compare standard deviations in this case.

25. The Smithfield Agricultural Company operates in the Midwest. The company owns and leases a total of 34,000 acres of prime farmland. Most of the crops are grain. Because of its size, the company can afford to do a great amount of testing to determine what seed types produce greatest yields. Recently, the company tested three types of corn seed on test plots. The following values were observed after the first test year:

	Seed Type A	Seed Type B	Seed Type C
Mean bushels/acre	88	56	100
Standard deviation	16	15	25

a. Based on the results of this testing, which seed seems to produce the greatest average yield per acre? Comment on the type of testing controls that should have been used to make this study valid.

b. Suppose the company is interested in consistency. Which seed type shows the least relative variability?

c. Using the empirical rule, describe the production distribution for each of the three seed types.

26. The B. L. Williams Company makes tennis balls. The company has two manufacturing plants. The plant in Portland, Maine, is a unionized plant with average daily production of 34,000 tennis balls. The output varies, with a

standard deviation of 4,500 tennis balls per day. The San Antonio, Texas, plant is nonunion and quite a bit smaller than the Portland plant. The San Antonio plant averages 12,000 tennis balls per day, with a standard deviation of 3,000.

Recently, the production manager was giving a speech to the Association of Sporting Goods Manufacturers. In that speech he stated that the B. L. Williams Company has been having real problems with its union plant maintaining consistency in production output and that the problem was not so great at the nonunion plant.

Based on the production data, was the manager justified in drawing the conclusions he made in the speech? Discuss and support your discussion with any appropriate calculations.

DATABASE PROBLEMS

The following questions and problems pertain directly to the State Department of Transportation case study and database introduced in Chapter 1. The questions and problems were written assuming that you will have access to a computer and appropriate statistical software. The database contains 100 observations and seventeen variables.

1. Herb Kriner is interested in determining the demographic characteristics of his sample. In particular, he would like to know the mean, median, and standard deviation for each interval or ratio level variable in the data set. Prepare one summary table that contains these statistics and write a short report describing the results.

2. Referring to Problem 1, Herb Kriner would like the same type of summary prepared for two groups: those determined to have insurance and those determined not to have insurance. Make one table showing the statistics for the two groups and write a report comparing the two groups.

3. Determine whether the variation in age of insured drivers exceeds that of uninsured drivers. Remember, the standard deviations should not be compared directly if the means are different!

4. One of his staff members asked Herb why he did not request means, medians, and standard deviations for all variables (see Problems 1 and 2)—for instance, X_8 and X_{12}. Herb has asked you to write a letter of response indicating whether it is all right to compute this type of descriptive measure on nominal and ordinal data and to indicate what interpretation should be made if such calculations are performed.

ADDITIONAL DATABASE PROBLEMS

The questions and problems in this section reference the various databases that accompany this text and which are described in Chapter 1. Your instructor has been provided a diskette with these databases. It is expected that you will be using computer software to access these data and to perform the required calculations and graphs.

DATABASE: **CITIES** (*Refer to the database description in Chapter 1.*)

1. Find the mean, median, range, variance, and standard deviation for X_1 assuming that the data reflect a population. Write a short report that incorporates these values and provides information to the reader about the data for this variable.
2. For those cities that reported ACT scores, find the mean and standard deviation assuming the data reflect a population.
3. Compute a new variable that is the difference between X_6 and X_7. Compute the mean, median, range, variance, and standard deviation for this new variable. Write a short report that utilizes these measures in describing this new variable.
4. Find the coefficient of variation for X_6 and X_7 and then write a paragraph that discusses the relative variation in earnings for manufacturing and white-collar workers.

DATABASE: **FAST100** (*Refer to the database description in Chapter 1.*)

1. Treating these data as a sample, compute the mean, median, range, variance, and standard deviation for X_1 and X_2. Write a short report that discusses these measures.
2. Convert X_5 and X_6 to Z values and develop a frequency distribution and histogram for each new variable. How many data points for each variable have Z values greater than 3.00 or less than -3.00? Using the empirical rule, what percentage of the data for each variable should have Z values between -2.00 and $+2.00$? How do these data compare with what would be expected under the empirical rule? What would be the case if Tchebysheff's theorem were employed? Discuss.
3. What numerical descriptive measures does your computer software provide that are not specifically discussed in this text? If there are some, go to your user's manual or another source to determine what these measures mean and how they might be used to describe data.

DATABASE: **PACRIM** (*Refer to the database description in Chapter 1.*)

1. For those companies located in Japan, find the mean, median, range, variance, and standard deviation for X_2 and X_3. Do the same for companies located in South Korea and Australia. Then write a report that compares these data for the companies from the three Pacific Rim countries.

2. Break down X_5 by country (X_1) and compute the coefficient of variation for each country on this variable. Write a short report that discusses the results and compares relative variability.

3. Find the mean, median, range, variance, and standard deviation for X_9 for all data combined, treating the data as a sample. Then compute the same measures on a country-by-country basis. Finally, compare the individual countries to the Pacific Rim as a whole based on these statistics. Prepare a report that discusses your results.

DATABASE: **TRUCKS** (*Refer to the database description in Chapter 1.*)

1. Find the mean, median, range, variance, and standard deviation for X_2–X_4. Write a short report that uses these statistics in describing the WIM measurements.

2. Find the mean, median, range, variance, and standard deviation for X_5–X_7. Write a short report that uses these statistics in describing the POE measurements.

3. Convert X_8 to Z values and find the mean and standard deviation for the new variable. Do the same thing for X_9. Write a short report that compares these statistics for the two variables. Do you see anything of importance about the mean and standard deviation? Discuss.

4. Compute a new variable by taking the difference between X_6 and X_3. Compute descriptive statistics for this new variable including the mean, median, and standard deviation. Write a report that discusses these statistics in light of the objective of the study. What conclusions might you reach based on the statistics?

5. Compute the coefficient of variation for X_3 and X_6 and write a report that discusses the relative variation between these two variables.

CASE

The Association of Independent Homeowners

The Association of Independent Homeowners has been spurred into action by the success of tax-limitation efforts in many states. However, although members are not particularly happy with the property-tax levels in their state, they are more concerned with the possibility of assessment errors. They do not think the county assessors are doing anything illegal, but they have all heard stories of how some properties are assessed at a much lower rate than other properties, when in fact they are of equal value.

The property-tax level in each county depends on the assessed valuation of all property in the county. One person's or business's property tax will depend on the levy set by the county and on the property value. Because the value of property changes from year to year, the association is particularly concerned that the assessed value accurately reflect the changing market value, as specified by state law.

Ruth Powers, an active member of the association, has heard of a recent study performed by the State Tax Commission. The commission gathers information on the sale price of recently marketed property and compares the true market price with the assessed value. Using the gathered data, the commission computes a mean assessment-to-market-value ratio for each county in the state. Since property is divided into four categories for assessment purposes ("residential," "rural investment," "business and industrial," and "other rural"), the commission also computes an adjusted mean value based on the number of parcels in each of these categories in each county. The State Tax Commission determined these values, plus the standard deviations of the individual ratios, for each county in the state. Ruth gathers the values for the seven counties nearest hers and for her own. They are as follows:

County	Ratio Mean Value	Ratio Weighted Mean	Ratio Standard Deviation
Box	18.38%	18.36%	1.96%
Elm	12.93	13.39	3.48
Canyon	15.93	15.90	6.91
Valley	11.92	13.45	7.97
Rice	15.42	16.90	6.24
Washington	20.44	19.69	11.74
Grant	13.82	17.07	2.25
Sandstone*	13.72	14.50	6.50

*Ruth's county.

Ruth wants to discuss the implications of these figures at the next meeting of the association's directors.

REFERENCES

Daniel, Wayne W., and Terrell, James C. *Business Statistics for Management and Economics.* 6th ed. Boston: Houghton Mifflin, 1989.

Hamburg, Morris. *Statistical Analysis for Decision Making.* 5th ed. Orlando, Fla.: Harcourt Brace Jovanovich, 1990.

McClave, James T., and Benson, P. George. *Statistics for Business and Economics.* 5th ed. San Francisco: Dellen-Macmillan, 1991.

Mendenhall, William; Reinmuth, James E.; and Beaver, Robert. *Statistics for Management and Economics.* 6th ed. Boston: PWS-Kent, 1989.

Introduction to

Probability Concepts

WHY DECISION MAKERS NEED TO KNOW

Decision making means selecting among two or more alternatives. To make good decisions, managers must establish general criteria for deciding among these alternatives. Certainly the criteria must somehow be related to the objective of the decision-making situation. This objective may involve a profit level, a sales level, or even creating an orderly situation from near chaos.

Once the objective has been established, managers often assess the chances that each alternative will reach this objective. The managers may make this assessment while saying something like, "The chances are good that if we build a parking garage, we will make a higher return on our investment than if we build an office building. On the other hand, the chances are fair that building a shopping mall will produce a higher return than a parking garage."

When managers refer to the chances of something occurring, they are using *probability* in the decision-making process. The decision makers are establishing in their minds the probability that some result will occur if a particular action is taken. If the business world were a place of certainty, decision makers would have little need to understand probability; but, as emphasized in the previous chapters, much in the world is not certain. In practice, probability assists managers in dealing with uncertainty.

Chapter 1 pointed out that managers must often operate with sample information collected from the population of interest. They are uncertain about the population, but know a great deal about the sample. Probability theory allows managers to make inferences about the population based on knowledge of the sample and to have confidence in these inferences. As you shall see in later chapters, because statistical inference is based on probability, decision makers must have a solid grasp of basic probability theory.

CHAPTER OBJECTIVES

This chapter will present the fundamentals of probability needed to understand statistical inference. It will also cover some rules and concepts associated with probability theory. Such topics as sample space, the addition rule, the multiplication rule, independent events, and conditional probability will be included in this discussion.

STUDENT OBJECTIVES

All too often decision makers, when dealing with probability, rely on intuition rather than on well-established probability principles. This intuitive approach often proves faulty. After studying the material in this chapter, you should be able to do the following:

1. Discuss the reasoning behind assessing probability.
2. Discuss and use the common rules of probability.
3. Discuss and use three methods of counting large numbers of possible outcomes.

In studying the material in this chapter, concentrate initially on how probability helps decision makers rather than on the formulas necessary to use probability. The formulas are useless unless they are applied in the correct situation, and concentrating on applications often will remove the mystery sometimes associated with probability.

4-1 WHAT IS PROBABILITY?

Before we can apply probability to the decision-making process, we must first discuss just what is meant by *probability*. The mathematical study of probability originated over 300 years ago. A Frenchman named Gombauld, who today would probably be a dealer in Las Vegas, began asking questions about games of chance. He was mostly interested in the probability of observing various outcomes (probably 7s and 11s) when a pair of dice was repeatedly rolled. The French mathematician Blaise Pascal (you may remember studying Pascal's triangle in a mathematics class) was able to answer Gombauld's questions. Of course, Pascal began asking more and more complicated questions of himself and his colleagues, thus beginning the formal study of probability.

Several explanations of what probability is have come out of this mathematical study. Although probabilities will help managers in a decision-making process, managers often have trouble determining how to assign probabilities.

As discussed in Chapter 1, data come in many forms and are gathered in many ways. In a business environment, when a sample is selected or a decision is made, there are generally many possible outcomes. A **sample space** is the collection of all possible outcomes that can result from the selection or decision. In probability language, the process that produces the outcomes is an *experiment*. In business situations, the experiment can range from an investment decision to a personnel decision to a choice of warehouse location. The individual outcomes from an experiment are called **elementary events**. Thus the sample space for an experiment consists of all the elementary events that the experiment can produce. A collection of elementary events is called an *event*. An example will help clarify these terms.

Suppose the vice-president for project development for Spectrum Electronics is interested in analyzing the performance of her many project development teams. She is particularly interested in whether the projects are finished by the projected completion date. The vice-president can define the elementary events for one project for one team to be

e_1 = Project done early

e_2 = Project done on time

e_3 = Project done late

The sample space for the experiment, which would be a single project, is

$$SS = (e_1, e_2, e_3)$$

where SS is the notation for sample space.

If the experiment is expanded to include two projects, the sample space is

$$SS = (e_1, e_2, e_3, e_4, e_5, e_6, e_7, e_8, e_9)$$

where the events are defined as follows:

Elementary Event	Project 1	Project 2
e_1	early	early
e_2	early	on time
e_3	on time	early
e_4	early	late
e_5	late	early
e_6	late	on time
e_7	on time	late
e_8	late	late
e_9	on time	on time

Here, each elementary event consists of the combined outcomes of project 1 and project 2.

The manager might be interested in the event "At least one project is completed late." This event (E) is

$$E = (e_4, e_5, e_6, e_7, e_8)$$

In another example, the Wright National Bank classifies all outstanding installment loans into one of four categories. The experiment in this case is the loan classification. The elementary events for each loan are

e_1 = Very solid

e_2 = Solid

e_3 = Doubtful

e_4 = Uncollectable

Then the sample space for a loan is

$$SS = (e_1, e_2, e_3, e_4)$$

The manager in charge of installment loans might be interested in the event "The loan is doubtful or uncollectable." If too many loans are in one or the other of these categories, the bank examiners will issue an unfavorable report. This event is

$$E = (e_3, e_4)$$

Keeping in mind the definitions for *experiment, sample space, elementary events,* and *events,* we introduce two additional concepts. The first is the concept of *mutually exclusive events.* Two events are mutually exclusive if the occurrence of one event precludes the occurrence of the other. For instance, consider again the Spectrum Electronics example. The possible elementary events for different projects done by two teams are as follows:

Elementary Event	Project 1	Project 2
e_1	early	early
e_2	early	on time
e_3	on time	early
e_4	early	late
e_5	late	early
e_6	late	on time
e_7	on time	late
e_8	late	late
e_9	on time	on time

Suppose we define one event as consisting of the elementary events in which at least one of the two projects is late:

$$E_1 = (e_4, e_5, e_6, e_7, e_8)$$

Further, suppose we define two more events as follows:

$$E_2 = \text{Neither project is late}$$
$$= (e_1, e_2, e_3, e_9)$$
$$E_3 = \text{Both projects are done at the same time}$$
$$= (e_1, e_8, e_9)$$

Events E_1 and E_2 are mutually exclusive: If E_1 occurs, E_2 cannot occur, and conversely. That is, if at least one project is late, then it is not also possible for neither project to be late. This can be verified by observing that no elementary events in E_1 appear in E_2. This provides another way of defining mutually exclusive events: Two events are mutually exclusive if they have no common elementary events.

The second additional probability concept is that of *independent* versus *dependent* events. Two events are independent if the occurrence of one event in no way influences the probability of the occurrence of the other event. For instance, again consider the Spectrum Electronics example. The experiment is to check the completion times of two projects that had been assigned to different teams. Each pair of projects would be one trial of the experiment.

Suppose that two projects are checked and the elementary event is

Elementary Event	Project 1	Project 2
e_8	late	late

If a new pair of projects were observed and the elementary event

Elementary Event	Project 1	Project 2
e_1	early	early

occurred, the two trials would be *independent* if the probability of the occurrence of e_1 for the second pair is in no way influenced by elementary event e_8 occurring for the first pair of projects. This might be the case if the problems that caused the first pair of projects to be late had no impact on the second pair of projects. On the other hand, if the fact that the first pair of projects was late caused the people on the second pair of projects to work overtime, the trials would be considered *dependent*.

Another example of dependence and independence might be an assembly-line operation. Each item produced could be an experimental trial. On each trial the outcome is either a *good* or a *defective* item. Thus, the sample space is

$$SS = (\text{good, defective})$$

As long as the machine is properly adjusted, it may produce some good outcomes and some defective outcomes with no apparent pattern, or dependency, between trials. That is, the production of one good item has no influence on the probability of the outcome of subsequent trials. However, if the machine goes out of adjustment, problems begin to occur. A defective item may cause still further adjustment problems and increase the chances that subsequent items will be defective. In this case the trials are dependent because the probability of the outcome of one trial is in some way influenced by the outcome of a previous trial.

4-2 COUNTING PRINCIPLES

In many business applications of probability you will have to count the number of elementary events in the sample space in order to determine a desired probability. Many times, actually listing the sample space would prove difficult and time-consuming. Instead, counting methods exist which do not require that we actually list the sample space to determine the number of elementary events. This section introduces four specific counting techniques you will need to know and discusses the conditions under which each should be used.

THE BASIC COUNTING PRINCIPLE

Suppose the Top Flight Air Freight Company has its package-sorting hub in Denver, Colorado. A package sent from anywhere in the United States and destined for anywhere else in the United States is first sent to Denver, where it is sorted and sent to its destination via airline and truck. Recently, a package mailed from Miami to Chicago was lost in shipment. The company has a sophisticated tracking system that logs in all packages every step of the way. In this particular instance, the package was tracked to Denver, but never reached its final destination in Chicago. Top Flight has six flights nightly to Chicago and fourteen delivery trucks on the ground in Chicago. If the manager of lost parcels wishes to check each possible route, how many routes will he have to check?

This type of question could, of course, be answered by listing all the routes. However, we can also take advantage of the basic counting principle to determine the number of routes without listing them.

Basic Counting Principle

If an event, A, can occur in n_1 ways, and if following the occurrence of event A, a second event, B, can occur in n_2 ways, regardless of which way event A occurs, then the number of ways A and B can occur in that order is $n_1 \cdot n_2$.

Thus, in our example, the package could have traveled using $n_1 = 6$ possible airlines and $n_2 = 14$ possible trucks. Thus, the total number of routes the package could have taken is

$$6 \cdot 14 = 84 \text{ ways}$$

The basic counting principle can easily be extended to a general counting principle for cases involving more than two events.

General Counting Principle

If k events can occur where event A_1 can occur in n_1 ways, followed by event A_2, which can occur in n_2 ways (regardless of how A_1 occurs), . . . , followed by event A_k, which can occur in n_k ways (regardless of how the previous events occur), then the events A_1 through A_k can together occur in $n_1 \cdot n_2 \cdot n_3 \cdots \cdot n_k$ ways.

Suppose a state issues car license plates that have six numerical digits. The State Licensing Bureau wishes to know how many possible license plates can be made if no two have the same six-digit number. To find this number, we can employ the general counting principle.

$$\text{Number of ways} = n_1 \cdot n_2 \cdot n_3 \cdots \cdot n_6$$

Since each of the digits can take on a value of zero through nine, there are ten possible values for each digit. Therefore, the total number of license plates is

$$\text{Total number} = 10 \cdot 10 \cdot 10 \cdot 10 \cdot 10 \cdot 10$$
$$= 1{,}000{,}000$$

The state can make 1 million plates without duplicating a number, but most states need more than 1 million license plates. Suppose the State Licensing Bureau decides to have the first three positions on the plate be letters and the next three positions be numbers. Then the first three positions can be any one of twenty-six letters and the last three can be any numerical value. Using the general counting principle, we can find the number of possible license plates as follows:

$$\text{Total number} = 26 \cdot 26 \cdot 26 \cdot 10 \cdot 10 \cdot 10$$
$$= 17{,}576{,}000$$

Thus, the state could make 17,576,000 plates without a duplication.

PERMUTATIONS AND COMBINATIONS

The general counting principle forms the basis of two other useful counting techniques: **permutations** and **combinations**. An arrangement of a set of n objects in a given order is called a permutation of the n objects. An arrangement of $r \leq n$ objects in a given order is called a permutation of n objects taken r at a time. For example, suppose a movie complex has four possible theaters and four movies. How many different ways can the four movies be shown in the four theaters? We will represent the movie complex as follows:

The first theater can show any of the four possible movies. After the first movie is placed in its theater, the second theater can show any of the three remaining movies. In a like manner, the next theater can show either of the remaining two movies. Finally, there is only one choice for the last theater. This can be depicted as

4	3	2	1

Thus, using the general counting principle, there are $4 \cdot 3 \cdot 2 \cdot 1 = 24$ possible arrangements of the four movies. Therefore, the number of permutations of four things taken four at a time is twenty-four.

A general equation for permutations can be given using factorial notation. Factorial notation refers to the practice of denoting the product of the positive integers from n down to 1 as $n!$ (read n factorial). We also define $0! = 1$. Thus, the formula for the number of permutations of n items taken n at a time is

$$_nP_n = n!$$

For our example,

$$_4P_4 = 4! = 4 \cdot 3 \cdot 2 \cdot 1 = 24$$

Now suppose the theater complex had six movies to choose from for its four theaters. How many possible arrangements are possible? To answer this question, we recognize that there are six choices for the first theater, five choices for the second, four choices for the third theater, and three choices for the last. We represent this by

6	5	4	3

Using the general counting principle, we get $6 \cdot 5 \cdot 4 \cdot 3 = 360$ possible arrangements. Thus, there are 360 permutations of six items taken four at a time. In general notation, the number of permutations of n items taken r at a time is

$$_nP_r = n \cdot (n-1) \cdot (n-2) \cdot \cdots \cdot (n-r+1)$$

Then,

$$_nP_r = \frac{n!}{(n-r)!}$$

Thus, for our example,

$$_6P_4 = \frac{6!}{2!} = \frac{6 \cdot 5 \cdot 4 \cdot 3 \cdot 2 \cdot 1}{2 \cdot 1} = 6 \cdot 5 \cdot 4 \cdot 3 = 360$$

As another example we determine the number of permutations of seven objects taken five at a time as follows:

$$_7P_5 = \frac{7!}{(7-5)!} = \frac{7 \cdot 6 \cdot 5 \cdot 4 \cdot 3 \cdot 2 \cdot 1}{2 \cdot 1} = 7 \cdot 6 \cdot 5 \cdot 4 \cdot 3 = 2,520$$

Frequently, we want to determine the number of permutations of objects of which some are alike. When this is the case, we need a method for finding the **permutations of like items.** One example of this is sailing ships that use flags to pass messages to shore and to other ships. A ship might have flags of four colors—say red, yellow, green, and white—with three flags of each color. Suppose a message is sent by arranging the twelve flags in a particular order. For example, the order, "red, red, red, white, white, white, yellow, yellow, yellow, green, green, green," may indicate the ship is carrying an injured person. Since we cannot distinguish between flags of the same color, but rather only the difference between colors, we can use permutations of like items to determine how many different messages can be sent with the twelve flags by finding the number of permutations of like items as follows:

$$\frac{n!}{x_1! \cdot x_2! \cdot x_3! \cdot \cdots \cdot x_k!}$$

where

$$x_1, x_2, x_3, \ldots, x_k = \text{Number of items belonging to a}$$
$$\text{particular category}$$

$$k = \text{Number of categories}$$

$$n = \text{Total number of items}$$

In our flag example,

$$\text{Number of messages} = \frac{12!}{3!3!3!3!}$$
$$= 369,600$$

We have seen in the previous discussion that permutations take into account the order of objects in a group, as in the example of movies and theaters in which they are shown. However, there are many applications in which the particular ordering of the objects is not a consideration. When this is the case, instead of finding the permutations of n items taken r at a time, we need to determine the number of *combinations* of n items taken r at a time. A combination of n objects taken r at a time is any subset of r items from the original n.

Consider a marketing research study in which participants are asked to select the three cars they think are of highest quality from a list of four luxury-class automobiles. How many possible groupings of three automobiles could a given participant select? To answer this, suppose we label the cars W, X, Y, and Z. Then we can list the combinations as

Combinations	*Permutations*
W, X, Y	WXY, WYX, XWY, XYW, YXW, YWX
W, X, Z	WXZ, WZX, XWZ, XZW, ZXW, ZWX
W, Y, Z	WYZ, WZY, ZWY, ZYW, YWZ, YZW
X, Y, Z	XYZ, XZY, ZXY, ZYX, YXZ, YZX

We see that, for each of the four possible combinations, there are $_3P_3 = 3! = 6$ permutations. Using notation for combinations similar to that for permutations, we obtain

$$3!\,_4C_3 = \,_4P_3$$

Then to find the number of combinations without listing them, we use

$$_4C_3 = \frac{_4P_3}{3!}$$

$$_4C_3 = \frac{\dfrac{4!}{1!}}{3!} = \frac{4!}{3!}$$

$$= \frac{24}{6}$$

$$= 4$$

In general notation we have the following formula for combinations:

$$_nC_r = \frac{_nP_r}{r!} = \frac{\dfrac{n!}{(n-r)!}}{r!}$$

or

$$_nC_r = \frac{n!}{r!(n-r)!}$$

Suppose the list of automobiles has seven names rather than four. Now how many combinations of three can a research participant select? Using the formula for combinations, we get

$$
\begin{aligned}
{}_7C_3 &= \frac{7!}{3!(7-3)!} \\
&= \frac{7!}{3!4!} \\
&= \frac{7 \cdot 6 \cdot 5 \cdot 4 \cdot 3 \cdot 2 \cdot 1}{(3 \cdot 2 \cdot 1)(4 \cdot 3 \cdot 2 \cdot 1)} \\
&= \frac{7 \cdot 6 \cdot 5}{6} \\
&= 35 \text{ combinations}
\end{aligned}
$$

CALCULATING PROBABILITIES

The probability that event A will occur for equally likely outcomes is:

$$
P(A) = \frac{\text{Number of ways } A \text{ can occur}}{\text{Number of ways any event can occur}}
$$

Finding $P(A)$ is straightforward when values in the numerator and denominator are known. However, in many business situations these will not be easily determined. For example, a local company has been in trouble recently over hiring male applicants rather than female applicants. The last three employees hired were all male even though the six applicants for the three positions included three females. The company personnel director claims that in each case the remaining applicants were given an equal chance of selection because the name of the person hired was drawn from a hat. One female applicant claims that if the selections were made in this fashion, the process must have been "rigged." She says that the probability of fairly selecting three consecutive males is so low that it would be extremely doubtful that it would have happened without "some assistance from the company." How do we find this probability?

To answer this, we first let A be the event of hiring three males and no females. (We must stipulate that we started with three qualified males and three qualified females.) Then

$$
P(A) = \frac{\text{Number of ways to hire three males}}{\text{Number of ways to hire three people from six}}
$$

Our problem is to determine values for the numerator and denominator. However, the "number of ways" for each may not be immediately apparent. We

TABLE 4-1

Sample Space

Elementary Event	Outcomes		
1	M_1	M_2	M_3
2	M_1	M_2	F_1
3	M_1	M_2	F_2
4	M_1	M_2	F_3
5	M_1	M_3	F_1
6	M_1	M_3	F_2
7	M_1	M_3	F_3
8	M_2	M_3	F_1
9	M_2	M_3	F_2
10	M_2	M_3	F_3
11	M_1	F_1	F_2
12	M_1	F_1	F_3
13	M_1	F_2	F_3
14	M_2	F_1	F_2
15	M_2	F_1	F_3
16	M_2	F_2	F_3
17	M_3	F_1	F_2
18	M_3	F_1	F_3
19	M_3	F_2	F_3
20	F_1	F_2	F_3

where

M_1 = Male number 1

M_2 = Male number 2

M_3 = Male number 3

F_1 = Female number 1

F_2 = Female number 2

F_3 = Female number 3

might approach this problem in several ways. The most elementary way is to list the sample space as shown in Table 4-1. Notice that the order of hiring is not important. We are interested only in the three jobs as a group. We find by listing the entire sample space that there are only twenty possible ways of hiring three people from the six applicants. Of these, only one satisfies the requirement of event A: All three hires are male, that is, (M_1, M_2, M_3). Thus

$$P(A) = \frac{1}{20}$$
$$= 0.05$$

The probability of hiring three males and no females is 0.05, assuming the selection process was random as implied by drawing names from the hat. It would now be up to the decision makers to decide whether they think the company was "fair" in the selection process. The answer to this will depend on whether the probability of 0.05 is viewed as being a very small probability.

Listing the entire sample space is fine for a limited situation. However, suppose that instead of six applicants for the three positions, there were twelve applicants, five male and seven female. Now what is the probability that all three positions would go to males if the selection process is fair? Although listing the sample space is possible, doing so would be time-consuming and there would be a good chance of accidentally omitting one or more of the elementary events. To avoid listing the sample space, you can use the combinations method, as follows:

$$P(A) = \frac{\text{Number of ways three males can be hired}}{\text{Number of ways any three people can be hired}}$$

Using combinations, we get

$$P(A) = \frac{{}_5C_3}{{}_{12}C_3} = \frac{\dfrac{5!}{3!2!}}{\dfrac{12!}{3!9!}}$$

$$= \frac{10}{220}$$

$$= 0.045$$

Thus, if all applicants received an equal chance, the probability is 0.045 that all three jobs would go to male applicants.

SKILL DEVELOPMENT PROBLEMS FOR SECTION 4-2

The following set of problems is meant to test your understanding of the material in this section.

1. Find the number of different ordered groups of five that can be made from ten items.

2. Find the number of different groupings of four, with order not being important, that can be made from nine items.

3. Find the number of distinct permutations of fifteen letters that can be made from a set of four As, five Bs, and six Cs.

4. The year has been good to the Finch and Nagle Investment Banking Firm. At present, the firm has more potential new issues to place than it can accept. Although general manpower is not a problem, only five members of the firm have the necessary experience to handle the twelve possible new issues being considered. How many possible groupings of five new issues can the firm handle? Once the five are selected, how many possible ways can they be arranged among the five experienced firm members?

5.   The Carlisle Medical Clinic has five doctors on staff. The doctors have agreed to keep the office open on Saturdays but with only three doctors. The office manager has decided to make up Saturday schedules in such a way that no set of three doctors will be in the office together more than once. How many weeks can be covered by this schedule?

6.   The White Aviation Company runs a charter air service with eight planes. However, because of pilot availability, only four planes can be in the air at one time. The dispatcher has decided to set up a plane usage schedule that will include the planes to be used on a particular day in order of usage. How many different schedules are possible without repeating a schedule?

4-3   PROBABILITY RULES

The probability attached to an event represents the likelihood the event will occur on a specified trial of an experiment. This probability also measures the perceived uncertainty about whether the event will occur. If we are not uncertain at all, we will assign the event a probability of 0.0 or 1.0: $P(E_1) = 0.0$ indicates that the event E_1 will not occur, and $P(E_1) = 1.0$ means that E_1 will definitely occur. These values represent the outside limits on a probability value. If, in fact, we are uncertain about the result of an experiment, we measure this uncertainty by assigning a probability between 0.0 and 1.0. Probability rule 1 shows the range for probability values.

Probability Rule 1

For any event E_i,

$$0.0 \leq P(E_i) \leq 1.0 \quad \text{for all } i$$

All possible elementary events associated with an experiment form the sample space. Probability rule 2 indicates that the probabilities of all elementary events must add up to 1.0.

Probability Rule 2

$$\sum_{i=1}^{K} P(e_i) = 1.0$$

where

K = Number of elementary events in the sample space

e_i = ith elementary event

For example, suppose we assign probabilities to each possible outcome of a roll of one die. Since the possible outcomes are equally likely, let the sample space be

$$SS = (1, 2, 3, 4, 5, 6)$$

Then the probability the die will turn up "1" is

$$P(1) = \frac{\text{Number of ways "1" can occur}}{\text{Number of ways any value can occur}}$$

Since there is only one way to roll a "1" and six possible outcomes, the probability is

$$P(1) = \frac{1}{6}$$

The same is true for each elementary event in the sample space.

e_i	$P(e_i)$
1	$\frac{1}{6}$
2	$\frac{1}{6}$
3	$\frac{1}{6}$
4	$\frac{1}{6}$
5	$\frac{1}{6}$
6	$\frac{1}{6}$
	$\Sigma = \overline{1.0}$

Note that the probabilities of the individual elementary events sum to 1.0.

Closely connected with probability rules 1 and 2 is the *complement* of an event. The complement of an event E is the collection of all possible outcomes that are not contained in event E. The complement of event E is represented by $\overline{E}$. Thus a corollary to probability rules 1 and 2 is

$$P(\overline{E}_i) = 1 - P(E_i)$$

That is, the probability of the complement of event E is 1.0 minus the probability of event E.

ADDITION RULES

When making a decision involving probabilities, you will often need to combine elementary event probabilities to find the probability associated with the event of interest. Combining probabilities requires *addition*. There are three rules that govern the addition of probabilities.

Ted's Big Boy Restaurant is thinking about opening an establishment in Appleton, Wisconsin, and has recently performed a resident survey as part of its decision-making process. Probabilities are often used in analyzing the results of questionnaires and surveys. One question of particular interest is how often the respondent dines out. Table 4-2 shows the results of the survey for this question.

TABLE ● **4-2**

Appleton Resident Responses

How Often Dines Out	Frequency	Relative Frequency
10 or more times a week	400	0.08
3 to 9 times a week	1,900	0.38
1 or 2 times a week	1,500	0.30
Less than once a week	1,200	0.24
Total	5,000	1.00

We can define the sample space for the experiment for each respondent as

$$SS = (e_1, e_2, e_3, e_4)$$

where

$e_1 = $ Dines out 10 or more times a week

$e_2 = $ Dines out 3 to 9 times a week

$e_3 = $ Dines out 1 or 2 times a week

$e_4 = $ Dines out less than once a week

Using the relative frequencies in Table 4-2, we assign the following probabilities to events in the sample space:

$$P(e_1) = 0.08$$
$$P(e_2) = 0.38$$
$$P(e_3) = 0.30$$
$$P(e_4) = \underline{0.24}$$
$$\Sigma = 1.00$$

Suppose we define an event from these elementary events as follows:

$$E_1 = \text{Respondent dines out 1 to 9 times a week}$$

The elementary events that make up E_1 are

$$E_1 = (e_2, e_3)$$

We can find the probability $P(E_1)$ by using probability rule 3.

Probability Rule 3

Addition rule for elementary events
The probability of an event E_i is equal to the sum of the probabilities of the elementary events forming E_i. That is, if

$$E_i = (e_1, e_2, e_3)$$

then

$$P(E_i) = P(e_1) + P(e_2) + P(e_3)$$

The probability a respondent dines out one or two times a week or three to nine times a week is

$$P(E_1) = P(e_2) + P(e_3) = 0.38 + 0.30$$
$$= 0.68$$

Suppose the restaurant survey also contained questions about the respondent's age. Ted's Big Boy considers age an important factor in the location decision since its restaurants do better in areas with an older population base. Table 4-3 shows the breakdown of the sample by age group and by the number of times

TABLE 4-3

Frequency of
Dining Out by
Age Group

How Often Dines Out	Age Group			
	E_5: Less than 30	E_6: 30 to 50	E_7: Over 50	
E_1: 10 or more times a week	e_1 200	e_2 100	e_3 100	400
E_2: 3 to 9 times a week	e_4 600	e_5 900	e_6 400	1,900
E_3: 1 or 2 times a week	e_7 400	e_8 600	e_9 500	1,500
E_4: Less than once a week	e_{10} 700	e_{11} 500	e_{12} 0	1,200
	1,900	2,100	1,000	5,000

the respondent dines out per week. This table illustrates two important concepts in data analysis, namely, *joint frequencies* and *marginal frequencies*. Joint frequencies are represented by the values inside the table and represent information concerning age group and dining out jointly. Marginal frequencies are the row and column totals. These values, found in the margins, represent information concerning just age group or just dining out.

For example, 2,100 people in the survey are in the 30–50-year age group. This column total is a marginal frequency and is represented by E_6. Also, 600 respondents are less than 30 years old and dine out from three to nine times a week. Thus, 600 is a joint frequency represented by e_4. In this table the joint frequencies are elementary events and can be represented in terms of the two marginal frequencies making up the joint frequency. Here

$$e_4 = (E_2 \text{ and } E_5)$$

The key word here is *and,* which indicates a joint frequency. (You may have covered this same concept as an *intersection* in a math class.)

Table 4-4 shows the relative frequencies for the data in Table 4-3.

Now let E_1 be the event that the respondent dines out ten or more times a week:

$$E_1 = (e_1, e_2, e_3)$$

Further, let event E_5 indicate the person is less than 30:

$$E_5 = (e_1, e_4, e_7, e_{10})$$

TABLE 4-4

Relative Frequency of Dining Out by Age Group

How Often Dines Out	Age Group			
	E_5: Less than 30	E_6: 30 to 50	E_7: Over 50	
E_1: 10 or more times a week	e_1 200/5,000 = 0.04	e_2 100/5,000 = 0.02	e_3 100/5,000 = 0.02	400/5,000 = 0.08
E_2: 3 to 9 times a week	e_4 600/5,000 = 0.12	e_5 900/5,000 = 0.18	e_6 400/5,000 = 0.08	1,900/5,000 = 0.38
E_3: 1 or 2 times a week	e_7 400/5,000 = 0.08	e_8 600/5,000 = 0.12	e_9 500/5,000 = 0.10	1,500/5,000 = 0.30
E_4: Less than once a week	e_{10} 700/5,000 = 0.14	e_{11} 500/5,000 = 0.10	e_{12} 0/5,000 = 0.00	1,200/5,000 = 0.24
	1,900/5,000 = 0.38	2,100/5,000 = 0.42	1,000/5,000 = 0.20	5,000/5,000 = 1.00

Using rule 3, we find the probabilities for E_1 and E_5 as follows (we are using relative frequencies to assign probabilities):

$$P(E_1) = P(e_1) + P(e_2) + P(e_3)$$
$$= 0.08$$
$$P(E_5) = P(e_1) + P(e_4) + P(e_7) + P(e_{10})$$
$$= 0.38$$

Suppose we now wish to find the probability of a respondent dining out less than once a week *or* being in the 30 to 50 age group. That is,

$$P(E_4 \text{ or } E_6) = ?$$

To find this probability, we must use probability rule 4.

Probability Rule 4

Addition rule for any two events E_1, E_2

$$P(E_1 \text{ or } E_2) = P(E_1) + P(E_2) - P(E_1 \text{ and } E_2)$$

The key word in knowing when to use rule 4 is *or*. The word *or* indicates addition. (You may have covered this concept as a *union* in a math class.)

Table 4-5 shows the relative frequencies, with the events of interest shaded.

TABLE **4-5**

Joint Occurrence of Being in the 30 to 50 Age Group and Dining Out Less Than Once a Week

How Often Dines Out	E_5: Less than 30	Age Group E_6: 30 to 50	E_7: Over 50	
E_1: 10 or more times a week	e_1 200/5,000 = 0.04	e_2 100/5,000 = 0.02	e_3 100/5,000 = 0.02	400/5,000 = 0.08
E_2: 3 to 9 times a week	e_4 600/5,000 = 0.12	e_5 900/5,000 = 0.18	e_6 400/5,000 = 0.08	1,900/5,000 = 0.38
E_3: 1 or 2 times a week	e_7 400/5,000 = 0.08	e_8 600/5,000 = 0.12	e_9 500/5,000 = 0.10	1,500/5,000 = 0.30
E_4: Less than once a week	e_{10} 700/5,000 = 0.14	e_{11} 500/5,000 = 0.10	e_{12} 0/5,000 = 0.00	1,200/5,000 = 0.24
	1,900/5,000 = 0.38	2,100/5,000 = 0.42	1,000/5,000 = 0.20	5,000/5,000 = 1.00

TABLE 4-6

Joint Occurrence of Being in the Over-50 Age Group and Dining Out Less Than Once a Week

How Often Dines Out	Age Group			
	E_5: Less than 30	E_6: 30 to 50	E_7: Over 50	
E_1: 10 or more times a week	e_1 200/5,000 = 0.04	e_2 100/5,000 = 0.02	e_3 100/5,000 = 0.02	400/5,000 = 0.08
E_2: 3 to 9 times a week	e_4 600/5,000 = 0.12	e_5 900/5,000 = 0.18	e_6 400/5,000 = 0.08	1,900/5,000 = 0.38
E_3: 1 or 2 times a week	e_7 400/5,000 = 0.08	e_8 600/5,000 = 0.12	e_9 500/5,000 = 0.10	1,500/5,000 = 0.30
E_4: Less than once a week	e_{10} 700/5,000 = 0.14	e_{11} 500/5,000 = 0.10	e_{12} 0/5,000 = 0.00	1,200/5,000 = 0.24
	1,900/5,000 = 0.38	2,100/5,000 = 0.42	1,000/5,000 = 0.20	5,000/5,000 = 1.00

The overlap corresponds to the *joint occurrence* of dining out less than once a week and being in the 30 to 50 age group. The relative frequency of this overlap is $P(E_4 \text{ and } E_6)$ and must be subtracted to avoid double counting when calculating $P(E_4 \text{ or } E_6)$. Thus

$$P(E_4 \text{ or } E_6) = 0.24 + 0.42 - 0.10$$
$$= 0.56$$

Therefore, the probability that a respondent will either be in the 30 to 50 age group or eat out less than once a week is 0.56.

What is the probability a respondent will dine out less than once a week or be in the over-50 age group? We can again use rule 4:

$$P(E_4 \text{ or } E_7) = P(E_4) + P(E_7) - P(E_4 \text{ and } E_7)$$

Table 4-6 shows the relative frequencies for these events. We have

$$P(E_4 \text{ or } E_7) = 0.24 + 0.20 - 0.00 = 0.44$$

As can be seen, no one both dines out less than once a week and is in the over-50 age group.[1] When the joint probability of two events is 0, the events are mutually

---

[1] This example illustrates a potential weakness in using relative frequencies to represent probabilities. In this case, no person both dined out less than once a week and was over 50. Thus, using relative frequencies, we conclude that the probability of the joint event is 0. A larger sample may well have included one or more persons in this joint category, in which case the true probability is not 0. However, for the purposes of this example, we will assume these events are mutually exclusive.

exclusive. This is consistent with our earlier definition of mutually exclusive events. When events are mutually exclusive, probability rule 5, a special form of rule 4, applies.

Probability Rule 5

Addition rule for mutually exclusive events E_1, E_2

$$P(E_1 \text{ or } E_2) = P(E_1) + P(E_2)$$

This section has presented three rules for adding probabilities. You should become familiar with these rules and understand how they are used. To test your understanding, use the information in Table 4-6 and let

$$E_8 = (E_1, E_2)$$
$$E_9 = (E_5, E_6)$$

Find

$$P(E_8 \text{ or } E_9)$$

Your answer should be 0.90. Do you know why?

CONDITIONAL PROBABILITY

In dealing with probabilities, you will often need to determine the chances of two or more events occurring either at the same time or in succession. For example, a quality control manager for a manufacturing company may be interested in the probability of selecting two successive defectives from an assembly line. If the probability is low, this manager would be surprised at such a result and might readjust the production process.

In other instances, the decision maker may know that an event has occurred and may want to know the chances of a second event occurring. For instance, suppose an oil company geologist believes oil will be found at a certain drilling site. The oil company exploration vice-president might well be interested in the probability of finding oil, given the favorable report.

These situations require tools different from those presented in the section on addition rules. Specifically, you need to become acquainted with rules for *conditional probability* and *multiplication* of probabilities.

West-Air, Inc., a regional airline, has performed a study of its customers' traveling habits. Among the information collected are the data shown in Table 4-7. Lee Hansel, the operations manager, is aware the average traveler has changed over the years. Given the recent increase in discount fares, Lee is particularly interested in maintaining good relations with business travelers. However, since a business traveler is no longer necessarily dressed in a suit, or even always a man, Lee has trouble telling a business traveler from a nonbusiness traveler. Yet he wants to know the present composition of people traveling on his company's airline.

TABLE 4-7

West-Air, Inc.,
Data

		Sex		
Trips per Year	E_4: Female	E_5: Male	
E_1: 1 or 2	e_1 $f = 450$	e_2 $f = 500$	$\Sigma = 950$
E_2: 3–10	e_3 $f = 300$	e_4 $f = 800$	$\Sigma = 1{,}100$
E_3: Over 10	e_5 $f = 100$	e_6 $f = 350$	$\Sigma = 450$
	$\Sigma = 850$	$\Sigma = 1{,}650$	$\Sigma = 2{,}500$

Suppose Lee knows a traveler is female and wants to know the chances this woman will travel between three and ten times a year. We let

$$E_2 = (e_3, e_4) = \text{Event: Person travels 3–10 times per year}$$
$$E_4 = (e_1, e_3, e_5) = \text{Event: Traveler is female}$$

Then Lee needs to know the probability of E_2 given E_4 has occurred. Table 4-8 shows the frequencies and relative frequencies of interest. One way to find the desired probability is as follows:

1. We know E_4 has occurred. There are 850 females in the survey.
2. Of the 850 females, 300 travel between three and ten times per year.
3. Then

$$P(E_2|E_4) = \frac{300}{850}$$
$$= 0.3529$$

The notation $P(E_2|E_4)$ is read "probability of E_2 given E_4."

TABLE 4-8

West-Air, Inc.,
Relative
Frequencies

		Sex		
Trips per Year	E_4: Female	E_5: Male	
E_1: 1 or 2	e_1 $RF = 450/2{,}500 = 0.18$	e_2 $RF = 500/2{,}500 = 0.20$	$950/2{,}500 = 0.38$
E_2: 3–10	e_3 $RF = 300/2{,}500 = 0.12$	e_4 $RF = 800/2{,}500 = 0.32$	$1{,}100/2{,}500 = 0.44$
E_3: Over 10	e_5 $RF = 100/2{,}500 = 0.04$	e_6 $RF = 350/2{,}500 = 0.14$	$450/2{,}500 = 0.18$
	$850/2{,}500 = 0.34$	$1{,}650/2{,}500 = 0.66$	$2{,}500/2{,}500 = 1.00$

Although this approach produces the desired probability, probability rule 6 offers a general rule for conditional probability.

Probability Rule 6

Conditional probability for any two events E_1, E_2

$$P(E_1|E_2) = \frac{P(E_1 \text{ and } E_2)}{P(E_2)}$$

where

$$P(E_2) \neq 0$$

Rule 6 uses a *joint probability*, $P(E_1$ and $E_2)$, and a *marginal probability*, $P(E_2)$, to calculate the conditional probability, $P(E_1|E_2)$. Note that to find a conditional probability, we find the ratio of how frequently E_1 occurs to the total number of observations, given that we restrict our observations to only those cases where E_2 has occurred.

Applying rule 6 in our previous problem,

$$P(E_2|E_4) = \frac{0.12}{0.34}$$
$$= 0.3529$$

where

$$P(E_2 \text{ and } E_4) = 0.12$$
$$P(E_4) = 0.34$$

An earlier section stated that two events are independent if the occurrence of one event has no bearing on the probability that the second event occurs. Therefore, when two events are independent, the rule for conditional probability takes a special form, as indicated in probability rule 7.

Probability Rule 7

Conditional probability for independent events, E_1, E_2

$$P(E_1|E_2) = P(E_1)$$

and

$$P(E_2|E_1) = P(E_2)$$

As rule 7 shows, the conditional probability of one event occurring, given a second independent event that has already occurred, is simply the probability of the first event occurring.

Table 4-9 shows some more data from the West-Air passenger survey which we can use to demonstrate rule 7.

T A B L E 4-9 **Payment Method by Sex of Traveler**

Payment Method	Sex		
	E_3: Female	E_4: Male	
E_1: Cash	e_1 $f = 272$, $RF = 272/2{,}500 = 0.1088$	e_2 $f = 528$, $RF = 528/2{,}500 = 0.2112$	$\dfrac{800}{2{,}500} = 0.3200$
E_2: Credit card	e_3 $f = 578$, $RF = 578/2{,}500 = 0.2312$	e_4 $f = 1{,}122$, $RF = 1{,}122/2{,}500 = 0.4488$	$\dfrac{1{,}700}{2{,}500} = 0.6800$
	$850/2{,}500 = 0.3400$	$1{,}650/2{,}500 = 0.6600$	$\dfrac{2{,}500}{2{,}500} = 1.0000$

Suppose Lee Hansel wants to know the probability a passenger will pay cash for the airline ticket given the passenger is a male. To find this probability, let

$$E_1 = (e_1, e_2) = \text{Event: Pay with cash}$$
$$E_4 = (e_2, e_4) = \text{Event: Passenger is male}$$

Then, using rule 6, $P(E_1|E_4)$ is as follows:

$$P(E_1|E_4) = \frac{P(E_1 \text{ and } E_4)}{P(E_4)} = \frac{0.2112}{0.6600}$$
$$= 0.32$$

But, from Table 4-9, $P(E_1) = 0.32$. Thus,

$$P(E_1|E_4) = P(E_1)$$

Therefore these two events are independent.

You should become comfortable with the rules for conditional probability since they are used heavily in statistical decision making.

MULTIPLICATION RULES

We needed the joint probability of two events in the preceding discussion. We were able to find $P(E_1 \text{ and } E_4)$ simply by examining the frequencies in Table 4-9. However, often we need to find $P(E_1 \text{ and } E_2)$ when we do not know the joint relative frequencies. To illustrate how to find a joint probability, consider an example involving classical probability.

Suppose a game of chance involves selecting two cards from a standard deck of fifty-two cards. If both cards are aces, the participant receives a specified payoff. What is the probability of selecting two aces? To answer this question, we must recognize that two events are required to form the desired outcome. Therefore, let

$$A_1 = \text{Event: Ace on the first draw}$$

$$A_2 = \text{Event: Ace on the second draw}$$

The question really being asked is: What are the chances of observing both A_1 and A_2? The key word here is *and*, as contrasted with the addition rule, where the key word is *or*. The *and* signifies that we are interested in the joint probability of two events, as noted by

$$P(A_1 \text{ and } A_2)$$

To find this probability, we employ rule 8, the multiplication rule.

Probability Rule 8

Multiplication rule for two events E_1, E_2

$$P(E_1 \text{ and } E_2) = P(E_1)P(E_2|E_1)$$

and

$$P(E_2 \text{ and } E_1) = P(E_2)P(E_1|E_2)$$

Note that rule 8 is an algebraic rearrangement of rule 6.

We use the classical approach to probability assessment to find the value of $P(A_1 \text{ and } A_2)$ as follows:

$$P(A_1) = \frac{\text{Number of aces}}{\text{Number of possible cards}}$$

$$= \frac{4}{52}$$

Then, since we are not replacing the first card, we find $P(A_2|A_1)$ by

$$P(A_2|A_1) = \frac{\text{Number of remaining aces}}{\text{Number of remaining cards}}$$

$$= \frac{3}{51}$$

Thus, by rule 8,

$$P(A_1 \text{ and } A_2) = P(A_1)P(A_2|A_1) = \left(\frac{4}{52}\right)\left(\frac{3}{51}\right)$$

$$= 0.0045$$

Therefore, there are slightly more than four chances in 1,000 of selecting two successive aces from a fifty-two-card deck *without* replacement.

Note that rule 8 requires that conditional probability be used since the result on the second draw depends on the card selected on the first draw. The chance of obtaining an ace on the second draw was lowered from 4/52 to 3/51 given that the first card was an ace. However, if the two events of interest are *independent*, the conditional aspect is not important, and the multiplication rule takes the form shown in probability rule 9.

Probability Rule 9

Multiplication rule for independent events E_1, E_2

$$P(E_1 \text{ and } E_2) = P(E_1)P(E_2)$$

Thus, the joint probability of two independent events is simply the product of the marginal probabilities of the two events.

The probability rules presented in this section are vital to managers who will use statistical decision-making techniques. Remember the key words *or* and *and*. Know with what rules they are associated, and you should have little trouble with basic probability theory.

SKILL DEVELOPMENT PROBLEMS FOR SECTION 4-3

The following set of problems is meant to test your understanding of the material in this section.

7. Find the following probabilities associated with rolling two dice:
   a. Rolling an 11
   b. Rolling a 7
   c. Rolling a 5
   d. Rolling two 7s in a row
   e. Rolling first a 7 and then a 5
   f. Rolling first a 5 and then a 7

8. From a population of five As, ten Bs, and fifteen Cs:
   a. What is the probability of randomly selecting a B?
   b. What is the probability of randomly selecting a B and then a C if sampling is done with replacement? Is there a change if sampling is done without replacement?

c. What is the probability of selecting either an A or a B?

d. What is the probability of selecting three straight Cs if sampling is done without replacement?

9. Using the following joint frequency distribution table:

	A	B	C	Sum
D	20	32	18	70
E	12	28	40	80
F	8	20	22	50
	40	80	80	200

a. What is $P(C)$?

b. What is $P(E)$?

c. What is $P(A$ and $F)$?

d. What is $P(D$ or $F)$?

e. What is $P(E$ or $B)$?

f. What is $P(D$ and $E)$?

10. Your neighbor has just returned from a trip to Atlantic City and claims to have a foolproof method to make money on the roulette wheel. She knows the odds are slightly with the house on any single roll. However, she claims that all you need to do is to watch the wheel and anytime three successive rolls have the same color bet the next roll on the opposite color. Comment on her technique.

11. In the late 1960s the U.S. government instituted a lottery system for determining how young men between the ages of eighteen and twenty-six would be drafted into military service. Three hundred sixty-five balls, each with a different day of the year, were placed in a large drum and mixed. Balls were selected from the drum randomly.

a. What is the probability that the first two balls selected were for birthdays in March?

b. What is the probability that the first ball selected was a December birthday or a birthday on the first of any month?

c. If the first ball selected was a March birthday, what is the probability that the second ball selected was a June birthday?

d. What is the probability that the first three balls selected were for birthdays in the same month?

12. The Ace Construction Company has submitted a bid on a state government project in Delaware. The price of the bid was predetermined in the bid specifications. The contract is to be awarded on the basis of a blind drawing from those who have bid. Five other companies have also submitted bids.

a. What is the probability of the Ace Construction Company winning the bid?

b. Suppose that there are two contracts to be awarded by a blind draw. What is the probability of Ace winning both contracts?

c. Referring to part **b,** what is the probability of Ace not winning either contract?

d. Referring to part **b,** what is the probability of Ace winning exactly one contract?

e. Referring to part **b,** what is the probability of Ace winning at least one contract?

4-4 CONCLUSIONS

Probability provides decision makers a quantitative measure of the chance a particular outcome will occur. It allows decision makers to quantify uncertainty. The objectives of this chapter have been to discuss the various types of probability and to provide the basic rules that govern probability operations.

We have discussed many probability concepts from a managerial perspective. The chapter glossary lists a set of strict definitions for important probability concepts introduced in this chapter. To test your understanding of these concepts, reconcile the managerial definitions with the more formal definitions. The list of chapter formulas follows the glossary.

CHAPTER GLOSSARY

combinations The method of counting possible selections from a set of elementary events when order is not important:

$$_nC_r = \frac{n!}{r!(n-r)!}$$

elementary events The single outcomes resulting from an experiment.

permutations The method of counting possible arrangements from a set of elementary events when order is important:

$$_nP_r = \frac{n!}{(n-r)!}$$

permutations of like items The method of counting possible selections from a set of elementary events when order is important but the simple events within particular categories are indistinguishable:

$$\text{Permutations of like items} = \frac{n!}{x_1!x_2!x_3!\cdots x_k!}$$

sample space The set of all possible elementary events, or outcomes, that can result from a single trial or experiment.

CHAPTER FORMULAS

Probability rule 1

$$0.0 \leq P(E_i) \leq 1.0 \quad \text{for all } i$$

for any event E_i (including elementary events)

Probability rule 2

$$\sum_{i=1}^{K} P(e_i) = 1.0$$

Probability rule 3   Addition rule for elementary events
The probability an event E_i is equal to the sum of the probabilities of the elementary events forming E_i. That is, if

$$E_i = (e_1, e_2, e_3)$$

then

$$P(E_i) = P(e_1) + P(e_2) + P(e_3)$$

Probability rule 4   Addition rule for any two events E_1, E_2

$$P(E_1 \text{ or } E_2) = P(E_1) + P(E_2) - P(E_1 \text{ and } E_2)$$

Probability rule 5   Addition rule for mutually exclusive events E_1, E_2

$$P(E_1 \text{ or } E_2) = P(E_1) + P(E_2)$$

Probability rule 6   Conditional probability for any two events E_1, E_2
$[P(E_2) \neq 0]$

$$P(E_1|E_2) = \frac{P(E_1 \text{ and } E_2)}{P(E_2)}$$

Probability rule 7   Conditional probability for independent events E_1, E_2

$$P(E_1|E_2) = P(E_1)$$

and

$$P(E_2|E_1) = P(E_2)$$

Probability rule 8   Multiplication rule for two events E_1, E_2

$$P(E_1 \text{ and } E_2) = P(E_1)P(E_2|E_1)$$

and

$$P(E_2 \text{ and } E_1) = P(E_2)P(E_1|E_2)$$

Probability rule 9   Multiplication rule for independent events E_1, E_2

$$P(E_1 \text{ and } E_2) = P(E_1)P(E_2)$$

SOLVED PROBLEMS

1.   There are four defective power supplies in a package of ten. If two power supplies are randomly selected one after another, what is the probability of
    a.   One defective and one good power supply being selected?
    b.   Two defectives being selected?
    c.   At least one defective being selected?
    d.   Three good power supplies being selected?

Solution:

a. We will solve this problem two ways. First we list the sample space as follows:

$$G, G$$
$$G, D$$
$$D, G$$
$$D, D$$

where

G = Good power supply

D = Defective power supply

Then we attach probabilities to each sample event:

$$P(G_1) = P(\text{good on first draw})$$
$$= \frac{6}{10}$$
$$P(D_1) = P(\text{defective on first draw})$$
$$= \frac{4}{10}$$

Notice that the probabilities on the second draw depend on what took place on the first draw. Thus,

$$P(G_2|G_1) = \frac{5}{9}$$

$$P(G_2|D_1) = \frac{6}{9}$$

$$P(D_2|G_1) = \frac{4}{9}$$

$$P(D_2|D_1) = \frac{3}{9}$$

Then we find the probability of one defective power supply and one good power supply in a sample of two by using both the addition rule and the conditional probability rule:

$$P(G_1 \text{ and } D_2) + P(D_1 \text{ and } G_2) = P(G_1)P(D_2|G_1) + P(D_1)P(G_2|D_1)$$

$$= \left(\frac{6}{10}\right)\left(\frac{4}{9}\right) + \left(\frac{4}{10}\right)\left(\frac{6}{9}\right)$$

$$= \frac{24}{90} + \frac{24}{90} = \frac{48}{90}$$

$$= \frac{8}{15}$$

A second method uses the combinations counting method. We are looking for the sample event of selecting two power supplies by picking one of the four defectives and one of the six good supplies. This is represented in the following picture.

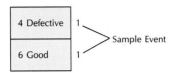

$$P(1 \text{ defective and } 1 \text{ good}) = \frac{\text{Number of ways to get 1 defective and 1 good}}{\text{Number of ways to draw 2 power supplies}}$$

$$= \frac{{}_4C_1 \text{ and } {}_6C_1}{{}_{10}C_2} = \frac{\left(\dfrac{4!}{1!3!}\right)\left(\dfrac{6!}{1!5!}\right)}{\dfrac{10!}{2!8!}}$$

$$= \frac{(4)(6)}{45} = \frac{24}{45}$$

$$= \frac{8}{15}$$

b. We want the following situation:

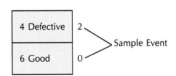

Again using combinations, we obtain

$$P(2 \text{ defective}) = \frac{\text{Number of ways to draw 2 defective and 0 good}}{\text{Number of ways to draw 2 power supplies}}$$

$$= \frac{({}_4C_2)({}_6C_0)}{{}_{10}C_2} = \frac{\left(\dfrac{4!}{2!2!}\right)\left(\dfrac{6!}{0!6!}\right)}{45}$$

$$= \frac{6}{45}$$

$$= \frac{2}{15}$$

Remember that $0! = 1$.

c. We are looking for the following sample event:

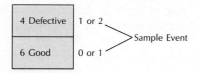

We know that

$$P(0 \text{ defective}) + P(1 \text{ defective}) + P(2 \text{ defective}) = 1$$

or

$$P(0 \text{ defective}) + P(1 \text{ or more defective}) = 1$$

So

$$P(1 \text{ or more defective}) = 1 - P(0 \text{ defective})$$

To find $P(1 \text{ or more defective})$, we find $P(0 \text{ defective})$. Using combinations,

$$P(0 \text{ defective}) = \frac{(_4C_0)(_6C_2)}{_{10}C_2} = \frac{(1)(15)}{45}$$

$$= \frac{1}{3}$$

Therefore,

$$P(1 \text{ or more defective}) = 1 - \frac{1}{3}$$

$$= \frac{2}{3}$$

d. $P(3 \text{ good}) = 0$, since only two power supplies are selected.

2. A small town has two ambulances. Records indicate that the first ambulance is in service 60% of the time and the second one is in service 40% of the time. What is the probability that when an ambulance is needed, one will not be available?

Solution

The sample space is as follows:

$$A, A = \text{Both available}$$
$$A, B = \text{One available}$$
$$B, A = \text{One available}$$
$$B, B = \text{Both busy}$$

If we assume that the availabilities of the ambulances are *independent* events (no large accidents), the probability of both ambulances being busy is

$$P(\text{B and B}) = (0.60)(0.40)$$
$$= 0.24$$

3. For the information given in Problem 2, what is the probability that at least one ambulance will be available?

Solution

Since

$$P(0 \text{ available}) + P(1 \text{ or more available}) = 1$$

then

$$P(1 \text{ or more available}) = 1 - P(0 \text{ available}) = 1 - 0.24$$
$$= 0.76$$

CONCEPTUAL QUESTIONS AND ASSIGNMENTS

13. Define and list five business examples of each of the following:
    a. Mutually exclusive events
    b. Independent events
14. The Goldberg Construction Company recently bid on three contracts, each of which the company could be either awarded or not awarded.
    a. Define the elementary events for a given bid.
    b. List the sample space for a bid on one contract.
    c. List the sample space for all three contracts.
15. The Harrison Corporation manufactures electronic components for the U.S. government. One particular component can be made without defect, with a minor defect, or with a major defect.
    a. If the company makes only one of these components, list the sample space.
    b. If the company makes three of the components, list the sample space.
    c. Grouping the minor defect and major defect elementary events together, list the sample space if the company makes six components.

ADDITIONAL PROBLEMS

16. The Sullivan Stables Company owns and races expensive racehorses. One of its horses placed second in the Kentucky Derby 2 years ago. Suppose Sullivan Stables recently purchased a new racehorse from a European breeder. Sullivan plans to race the horse four times this year.
    a. If the company is interested only in winning versus losing a particular race, list the sample space for the four races. Let W indicate win and L indicate lose.

b. Suppose the stable is interested in the chances of the horse placing first, second, third, or lower in each race. List the sample space for the first two races.

17. Assume that the outcomes of a lottery are equally likely.
    a. What is the probability that an individual will win if he or she holds one ticket out of the 500 sold?
    b. What is the probability of winning if he or she holds three tickets out of the 500 sold?

18. A bicycle manufacturer offers five color options, three handlebar options, and four seat options on its deluxe bicycle. How many different configurations could the company possibly make?

19. A computer program designed to prepare time and billing reports for an accounting firm has six subroutines. The first subroutine has three alternative paths that the program can take depending on the type of application. The second has four paths, the third has only one path, the fourth has eleven paths, the fifth has four paths, and the final subroutine has only two paths.
    a. If the program designer were considering testing the first three subroutines, how many different tests would she have to conduct to make sure that all paths had been taken at least once? (For example, one test might be subroutine 1—path 1, subroutine 2—path 1, and subroutine 3—path 1.)
    b. If the programmer wished to test the entire program and each possible path through it, how many different tests would be required?

20. A photography studio recently ran a Christmas special for children's photographs. It offered three poses with a nature backdrop, four poses with a fireside backdrop, and four poses with a schoolroom backdrop. If the parents must purchase one picture of each backdrop, how many possible choices will each customer have per child?

21. The United Way campaign has fifteen applicants for funding this year. If the committee will fund only seven of these, how many possible lists of successful applicants are there?

22. The Devor Corporation recently planned to test market a new product in an Arizona community. Management decided that it could put its product in five of the ten possible stores. The manager said that he would like to see a list of the possible store combinations before he picked the five stores to be used. How long will this list be?

23. A production manager has eleven people in his crew. A special project that will require five people for about a week has been assigned to this crew. Since any of the eleven people could successfully serve on the special crew, the manager wishes to select the crew randomly. How many different five-person crews can be selected from the eleven people?

24. The KYLT radio station program manager has started a call-in request program from noon to 1 P.M. Time permits ten requested songs, news, sports, and some special features to be broadcast. Listeners place their calls before 11:00 A.M. to have them played during the hour slot.

a. Suppose that the first day, fifteen people called to request different songs. If the order the songs are played is not considered important, in how many ways can ten songs be played from among the fifteen requested?

b. If the order of the songs played is important, how many different sequences of ten records can be played from among the fifteen requested?

25. The Phillips Publishing Company publishes technical manuscripts for the Defense Department. The contract specifies the allowable error rate, and so the company has a policy of having three reviewers check each manuscript.

   a. If the company has eight available reviewers, how many different groupings of three reviewers are possible to assign to a particular manuscript?

   b. Suppose the payment to a reviewer depends on the order in which he or she reviewed the manuscript (the first reviewer receives the highest payment and so forth). How many different arrangements can be made with three reviewers from among the eight?

26. Suppose $P(A) = 0.50$, $P(B) = 0.40$, and $P(A \text{ and } B) = 0.20$.

   a. Are A and B mutually exclusive? Why or why not?

   b. Are A and B independent events? Why or why not?

27. If the probability of a particular stock increasing in value is assessed at 0.60 and the probability of a second stock increasing is 0.70, are the two stocks independent if the probability of both stocks increasing is 0.15? Discuss.

28. A board of directors consists of ten members, six of whom are loyal to the current company president and four of whom want to fire the president. The chairman of the board, who is a loyal supporter of the president, decides to randomly select four other board members to serve with him on a committee to decide the president's fate.

   a. What is the probability that all five members will vote to keep the president if no one changes sides?

   b. What is the probability that a majority of the five members will vote to keep the president if no one changes sides? A majority vote will decide the issue.

   c. What is the probability that the vote will be four to one in favor of firing the current president if no one on the board changes sides?

29. The Town-Pump service station has performed an analysis of its customers and found that 80% pay on credit and the rest pay cash. If five customers are sampled, what is the probability that three or fewer of them will pay on credit?

30. In the sales business, repeat calls to finalize a sale are common. Suppose a particular salesperson has a 0.70 probability of selling on the first call and that the probability of selling drops by 0.10 on each successive call. If the salesperson is willing to make up to four calls on any client, what is the probability of a sale?

31. Of a batch of twenty television picture tubes, five are known to be defective. What is the probability that a sample of five without replacement will result in each of the following?

    a. Exactly one defective

    b. No defectives

    c. Two or fewer defectives

32. Recreational developers are considering opening a skiing area near a western U.S. town. They are trying to decide whether to open an area catering to family skiers or to some other group. To help make their decision, they gather the following information. If

$$A_1 = \text{Family will ski}$$
$$A_2 = \text{Family will not ski}$$
$$B_1 = \text{Family has children but none in the 8–16 age group}$$
$$B_2 = \text{Family has children in the 8–16 age group}$$
$$B_3 = \text{Family has no children}$$

then, for this location,

$$P(A_1) = 0.40$$
$$P(B_2) = 0.35$$
$$P(B_3) = 0.25$$
$$P(A_1|B_2) = 0.70$$
$$P(A_1|B_1) = 0.30$$

    a. Use the probabilities given to construct a joint probability distribution table.

    b. What is the probability a family will ski *and* have children who are not in the 8–16 age group? How do you write this probability?

    c. What is the probability a family with children in the 8–16 age group will not ski?

    d. Are the categories "skiing" and "family composition" independent?

33. A company is considering changing its starting hour from 8:00 A.M. to 7:30 A.M. A census of the company's 1,200 office and production workers shows 370 of its 750 production workers favor the change and a total of 715 workers favor the change. To further assess worker opinion, the region manager decides to talk with random workers.

    a. What is the probability a randomly selected worker will be in favor of the change?

    b. What is the probability a randomly selected worker will be against the change *and* be an office worker?

    c. Is the relationship between job type and opinion independent? Explain.

34. An investment advisor has a portfolio of eighty stocks: fifty blue-chip and thirty growth stocks. Of the fifty blue-chip stocks, thirty have increased in price during the past month, while twenty of the thirty growth stocks have increased in price.

    a. If a stock is selected at random from the portfolio, what is the probability it will be a blue-chip stock that has not increased in price?

    b. What is the probability of selecting a stock that has increased in price?

c. If the stock selected has not increased in price, what is the probability that it is a growth stock?

35. Bill Jones and Herman Smith are long-time business associates. They know that regular exercise improves their productivity and have made a practice of playing either tennis or golf every Saturday for the past 10 years. Jones enjoys tennis, but Smith prefers golf. Each Saturday they flip a coin to decide which sport to play. Jones beats Smith at tennis 80% of the time, whereas he beats Smith at golf only 30% of the time.
    a. Suppose Jones walks into the Monday morning staff meeting and announces he beat Smith on Saturday. What sport do you think they played and why?
    b. Assume open tennis courts are hard to find on Saturday, so instead of flipping a coin, Smith and Jones always first look for a tennis court. If they find one open, they play tennis; if not, they play golf. Further, suppose the chance of finding an open court is 30%. Given this, what sport do you think they played on Saturday, given that Jones won?

36. A marketing research team is considering using a mailing list for an advertising campaign. They know that 40% of the people on the list have only a MasterCard and that 10% have only an American Express card. Another 20% hold both MasterCard and American Express. Finally, 30% of those on the list have neither card.

    Suppose a person on the list is known to have a MasterCard. What is the probability that person also has an American Express card?

C A S E

Southwest Regional Medical Center

Mary Crozier was beginning to think she had begun an impossible task. Six months ago she was appointed to the new position of Vice-President of Patient Services at the Southwest Regional Medical Center. One of her first tasks was to try to change the perception of the staff about where patients fit in the hospital setting. Mary's position, supported by the Board of Directors, was that the hospital should move toward a system of customer-oriented services. The traditional position of the staff, in Mary's opinion, was that the role of the hospital is to offer the best medical treatment possible and the role of the patient is to "be quiet and take it."

Mary has made some limited inroads in changing this thinking and is now trying to gather data to show that her approach will actually lead to lower costs and improved medical care. The current issue she is considering is re-admissions—patients who were treated, discharged, and then readmitted for the same condition or something related to their first treatment. Mary contends the readmission rate could be lowered, particularly for medication-related reasons, if better instructions were given upon discharge. Mary created a medication instruction sheet which she asked all physicians to discuss with their patients upon discharge. Unfortunately, she has no way of forcing physicians to use the sheet, or determining how many actually do use it.

However, Mary was able to add a question about medication instruction to the health care questionnaire given to every patient upon discharge. While not all discharged patients fill out the questionnaire, Mary is able to use the questionnaire number to identify patients by name. This is necessary to differentiate the responses of patients who were, and were not, readmitted. Mary is looking at the following summary data gathered since the medication instruction sheet was implemented:

Patients discharged	2,250
Questionnaires returned	1,340
Total patients readmitted	280
Patients readmitted who returned questionnaire	155
Patients readmitted who returned questionnaire and said medication instructions were good	14

Mary is frustrated because she does not see anything in these data that will help her convince people that the medication instruction sheet was effective.

REFERENCES

Blyth, C. R. "Subjective vs. Objective Methods in Statistics." *American Statistician* 26 (June 1972): 20–22.

Brightman, Harvey, and Schneider, Howard. *Statistics for Business Problem Solving.* Cincinnati: South-Western, 1992.

Hogg, R. V., and Elliot, A. T. *Probability and Statistical Inference.* 3d ed. New York: Macmillan, 1988.

Raiffa, H. *Decision Analysis: Introductory Lectures on Choices Under Uncertainty.* Reading, Mass.: Addison-Wesley, 1968.

Discrete Probability

Distributions

WHY DECISION MAKERS NEED TO KNOW

Thus far we have seen that a frequency distribution transforms ungrouped data into more meaningful form. Therefore, frequency distributions help decision makers deal with the uncertainty in their decision environments. We also learned in Chapter 4 that probability is a fundamental part of statistics. Because all managers operate in an uncertain environment, they must be able to make the connection between descriptive statistics and probability. This connection is made by moving from frequency distributions to *probability distributions.*

Constructing and analyzing a frequency distribution for every decision-making situation would be time-consuming. Just deciding on the correct data-gathering procedures, the appropriate class intervals, and the right methods of presenting the data is not a trivial problem. Fortunately, many physical events that appear to be unrelated have the same underlying characteristics and can be described by the same probability distribution. If decision makers are dealing with an application described by a predetermined *theoretical* probability distribution, they can use a great deal of developmental statistical work already known and save considerable personal effort in analyzing their situation. Therefore decision makers need to become comfortable with probability distributions if they are to apply them effectively in the decision-making process.

CHAPTER OBJECTIVES

This chapter introduces general discrete probability distributions and then considers three commonly used discrete probability distributions: the uniform distribution, the binomial distribution, and the Poisson distribution. These distributions describe situations with discrete values for the variables of interest. Many business applications can use one of these distributions.

The chapter also discusses how discrete probability distributions are developed and indicates what type of events these distributions describe. In addition, several descriptive measures that help define discrete probability distributions will be covered.

STUDENT OBJECTIVES

After studying the material in this chapter, you should be able to do the following:

1. Identify the types of processes that are represented by discrete probability distributions in general and by the uniform, binomial, and Poisson distributions in particular.
2. Find the probabilities associated with particular outcomes in discrete distributions.
3. Determine the mean and standard deviation for general discrete probability distributions and for the binomial and Poisson probability distributions.
4. Be able to discuss how the best use of sample information can still lead to the wrong managerial decision.

5-1 DISCRETE RANDOM VARIABLES

As discussed in Chapter 4, when a random experiment or trial is performed, some outcome, or event, must occur. When the trial or experiment has a quantitative characteristic, we can associate a number with each outcome. For example, suppose the quality control manager at the American Plywood plant examines three pieces of plywood. Letting "G" stand for a good piece of plywood and "D" stand for a defective piece, the sample space is

G,	G,	G
G,	G,	D
G,	D,	G
D,	G,	G
G,	D,	D
D,	G,	D
D,	D,	G
D,	D,	D

We can let X be the number of *good* pieces of plywood in the sample of three pieces. Then X can only be 0, 1, 2, or 3, depending on how many defectives are found. Although the quality control manager knows these are the possible values of X before she samples, she would be uncertain about which would occur in any given trial; further, the value of X may vary from trial to trial. Under these conditions we say that X is a *random variable*. A **random variable** is a variable whose numerical value is determined by the outcome of a random experiment or trial.

In another example, if an accountant randomly examines fifteen accounts, the number of inaccurate account balances can be represented by the variable X. Then X is a random variable with the following possible values:

$$0 \quad 1 \quad 2 \quad \cdots \quad 15$$

Two classes of random variables exist, namely, *discrete* random variables and *continuous* random variables. A **discrete random variable** is a random variable that can assume values only from a distinct predetermined set. The two previous examples illustrate discrete random variables. The pieces of good plywood could assume only the values 0, 1, 2, or 3, and the number of incorrect account balances had to be one of the values 0, 1, 2, . . . , 15.

On the other hand, **continuous random variables** are random variables that may assume any value on a continuum. For example, weight is often thought to be continuous. The weight of a truck load of corn being delivered to a Green Giant processing plant may be any value between two points, say 8,000 pounds and 12,000 pounds.

This chapter discusses discrete random variables and introduces the concept of discrete probability distributions. Chapter 6 covers continuous random variables.

5-2 DISCRETE PROBABILITY DISTRIBUTIONS

A discrete probability distribution is actually an extension of the relative frequency distribution first introduced in Chapter 2. For example, the Magnetic Scan Corporation has introduced a magnetic resonance scanning system for use as a medical diagnostic tool. This system is a major commitment for Magnetic Scan. Not only is the system very expensive, but some much larger companies, like General Electric, have introduced competing equipment. To keep inventory investment to the lowest possible level, the company will carry no finished units in stock but will build only to order. However, production-line limitations mean a maximum of four units can be built in any week. Cory Rickbeil, the production vice-president for Magnetic Scan, has recorded how many units were built in each of the 30 weeks the system has been on the market (see Table 5-1). Note that X is a discrete random variable whose value equals the number of scanning systems built. The possible values of X are 0, 1, 2, 3, and 4.

The relative frequencies for each value of X have been computed in Table 5-1. For instance, over this 30-week period the company has built none of its systems during twelve, or 40%, of the weeks. During 8, or 27%, of the weeks one system was built. Recall from Chapter 4 that one way to assess probability is to use the relative frequency of occurrence; that is, the probability of an outcome (or value of the random variable) occurring can be assessed by the relative frequency of that outcome.

TABLE 5-1

Scanning Systems Built per Week

Systems Built (X)	Frequency	Relative Frequency
0	12	12/30 = 0.40
1	8	8/30 = 0.27
2	4	4/30 = 0.13
3	4	4/30 = 0.13
4	2	2/30 = 0.07
	$\Sigma = 30$	$\Sigma = 1.00$

The probability distribution for a discrete random variable shows each value of the random variable and its associated probability. The Magnetic Scan probability distribution is

X	P(X)
0	0.40
1	0.27
2	0.13
3	0.13
4	0.07
	$\Sigma = 1.00$

Since X represents all possible production values, the probability distribution must add up to 1.0. Figure 5-1 shows this probability distribution in graphical form.

Consider another example involving the McMillin Manufacturing Company, which makes an efficient wood-burning stove for use in homes. It manufactures all parts of the stove except for the chimney pipe, which it purchases from a supplier in Pennsylvania. The purchasing agent for McMillin has just received notification that this supplier is no longer going to make the type of chimney pipe that McMillin needs. The notification listed another company in Maryland that could supply the chimney pipe.

FIGURE **5-1**

Probability
Distribution for
Magnetic Scan
Corporation
Example

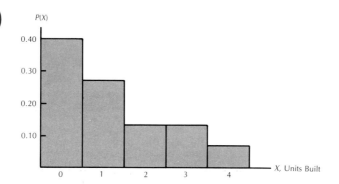

A call to the Maryland company confirmed that it could be used as the source of chimney pipe. The price was comparable to that of the Pennsylvania company, but it could not guarantee a fixed time between order and delivery. This time, referred to as *lead time,* would be anywhere between 1 and 4 weeks. Having nothing else to go on, the McMillan purchasing agent developed the following discrete probability distribution for lead time.

X	P(X)
1 week	0.25
2 weeks	0.25
3 weeks	0.25
4 weeks	0.25
	$\Sigma = \overline{1.00}$

In this example, the probability distribution for lead time was subjectively assessed by the purchasing agent. Note that the probabilities assigned to each of the discrete outcomes of the random variable, X, are the same. Since the purchasing agent had nothing other than the supplier's statement that lead time would be between 1 and 4 weeks, he chose to assign equal probabilities to each of the four outcomes. A discrete probability distribution that has equal probabilities for all possible outcomes of the random variable is called a **uniform probability distribution.**

The uniform probability distribution is sometimes called the distribution of little knowledge. In this example, the purchasing agent is unable to reflect any information in his probability assessments other than that the lead time will be either 1, 2, 3, or 4 weeks. Many instances arise in business when it is appropriate to assess a uniform probability distribution. These occur when the decision maker believes the outcomes of the random variable are equally likely.

5-3

THE BINOMIAL DISTRIBUTION

Managers could face innumerable discrete probability distributions such as those illustrated in the previous sections. Fortunately, there are several theoretical discrete distributions that have extensive application in business decision making. A probability distribution is called *theoretical* when it is well defined and the probabilities associated with values of the random variable can be computed from a well-established equation. This section introduces the first of two such distributions presented in this chapter, the **binomial probability distribution.**

Theoretical distributions are useful because, over time, they have been well analyzed and often provide a good approximation to the situation being studied. However, you should be aware that they rarely provide perfect descriptions. In those cases where a theoretical distribution can be used, this analysis can be accomplished with far fewer data than if a distribution had to be constructed.

The simplest probability distribution we will consider is one that describes processes with only *two* possible outcomes. The physical events described by this type of process are widespread. For instance, a quality control system in a manufacturing plant labels each tested item as either "defective" or "acceptable." A firm bidding for a contract either will get the contract or will not. A marketing research firm may receive responses to a questionnaire in the form of "Yes, I will buy" or "No, I will not buy." The personnel manager in an organization is faced with a two-stage process each time he offers a job: The applicant will either accept the offer or not accept it.

Suppose the management of a firm that makes radio transistors considers its production process operating correctly if 10% of the transistors produced are defective and 90% are acceptable. In a random sample of ten transistors, how often would we expect to find no defectives? Exactly one defective? Two defectives? The quality control manager may have a real reason for asking this type of question. She depends on the sample to provide the information necessary to decide whether to let the production process continue as is or to take corrective action.

A process in which each trial or observation can assume only one of two states is called a **binomial** or **Bernoulli process.** In a true Bernoulli process the following conditions are necessary:

1. The process has only two possible outcomes: successes and failures.
2. There are n identical trials or experiments.
3. The trials or experiments are independent of each other. In a production process, this means that if one item is found defective, this fact does not influence the chances of another being found defective.
4. The process must be consistent in generating successes and failures. That is, the probability, p, associated with a success remains consistent from trial to trial.
5. If p represents the probability of a success, then $(1 - p) = q$ is the probability of a failure.

Condition 3 states that the trials or experiments must be independent in order for a random variable to be considered a binomial random variable. This can be assured in a finite population if the sampling is performed **with replacement.** For instance, if the quality control manager for the transistor manufacturer selects her sample one transistor at a time, records whether that item is defective or not, and then replaces it into the population before selecting a second item, and so forth, the trials can be considered independent. This also assures that the probability of selecting a defective item will remain constant from trial to trial.

However, sampling with replacement is the exception rather than the rule in business applications. Most often the sampling is performed **without replacement.** For instance, if in testing the transistor the quality control manager is forced to destroy the transistor, the item obviously should not be replaced into the population. In many other cases, sampling without replacement is used because it is undesirable to potentially sample the same item more than once.

Thus, strictly speaking, when sampling is performed without replacement, the conditions for the binomial distribution cannot be satisfied. However, the conditions are approximately satisfied if the sample selected is quite small relative to the size of the population from which the sample is selected. A commonly used rule of thumb is that the binomial distribution can be applied if $n/N < 1/20$. Thus, if the sample is less than 5% of the size of the population, the conditions for the binomial will be approximately satisfied. Consider the following example. E. M. International produces and installs upgrade conversion units for automatic teller machines for banks. The upgrade conversion unit allows customers a wider variety of services, such as receiving checking and savings balances from remote locations and the ability to split deposits between different accounts. E. M. International prices the units to include 1-day installation service by two technicians. A defective conversion unit arriving at a site will require more than 1 day to install. Unfortunately, defective units can be a result of either the production process or shipping.

E. M. International has completed an extensive study of its production and distribution systems. The information shows that if the company is operating at standard quality, 10% (0.10) of the conversion units will be defective (require more than 1 day to install) by the time they reach the customer's bank location. Assuming the production, inventory, and distribution process are such that the Bernoulli process applies, the following conditions are true:

1. There are only two possible outcomes when a unit is produced: The conversion unit is good or it is defective (will take more than 1 day to install).
2. Each conversion unit is made by the same process.
3. The outcome of a conversion unit (defective or good) is independent of whether the preceding unit was good or defective.
4. The probability of a defective conversion unit, $p = 0.10$, remains constant from unit to unit.
5. The probability of a good unit, $q = (1 - p) = 0.90$, remains constant from unit to unit.

Suppose the quality assurance group at E. M. International has developed a plan for dismantling four conversion units each week to help determine whether the company is maintaining its quality standard. The sampling will be performed without replacement. Since the sample ($n = 4$) is small relative to the size of the population, the conditions of independence and constant probability will be approximately satisfied.

When the conditions satisfy the binomial requirements, the probability of X successes in n trials can be computed directly using equation 5-1.

$$P(X_1) = \frac{n!}{X_1!X_2!}p^{X_1}q^{X_2}$$

5-1

where

n = Sample size

X_1 = Number of successes (where a success is what we are looking for)[1]

X_2 = Number of failures ($n - X_1$)

p = Probability of a success

$q = 1 - p$ = Probability of a failure

[1] Students are often confused about the definition of success and failure. A success occurs when we observe the outcome of interest. If we are looking for defective machines, finding one is a success.

You should recognize the quantity $n!/(X_1!X_2!)$ as the expression for the number of *permutations of like items* discussed in Chapter 4. This expression determines the number of ways that X_1 successes can occur in a sample of size n. The expression $p^{X_1}q^{X_2}$ represents the probability of one way that X_1 successes can occur. Table 5-2 shows the resulting probability distribution for the E. M. International example.

USING THE BINOMIAL DISTRIBUTION TABLE

Using equation 5-1 to develop the binomial distribution is not difficult, but it can be time-consuming. To make binomial probabilities easier to find, you can use the binomial probability table in Appendix A. This table is constructed to give individual probabilities for different sample sizes and p values. Within the table for each specified sample size you will find columns of probabilities. Each column is headed by a probability value, p, which is the probability associated with a success. The column headings correspond to p values ranging from 0.01 to 0.50. At the bottom of each column are p values corresponding to probabilities of suc-

TABLE 5-2

Binomial
Probability
Distribution
for E. M.
International
Example
$(n = 4, p = .10)$

No. Defectives	Binomial Formula	Probability
x_1	$\dfrac{n!}{X_1!X_2!}p^{X_1}q^{X_2}$	$p(X_1)$
0	$\dfrac{4!}{0!4!}(0.10)^0(0.90)^4 =$	0.6561
1	$\dfrac{4!}{1!3!}(0.10)^1(0.90)^3 =$	0.2916
2	$\dfrac{4!}{2!2!}(0.10)^2(0.90)^2 =$	0.0486
3	$\dfrac{4!}{3!1!}(0.10)^3(0.90)^1 =$	0.0036
4	$\dfrac{4!}{4!0!}(0.10)^4(0.90)^0 =$	0.0001
		$\Sigma = 1.0000$

cesses ranging from 0.50 to 0.99. Down both sides of the table are integer values that correspond to the number of successes. The X_1 values on the *left* side are used with p values between 0.01 and 0.50. The X_1 values on the *right* side are used for p values greater than 0.50. Note that the values on the extreme right also correspond to the number of failures, X_2, for p values between 0.01 and 0.50.

Instead of using equation 5-1, you can find the appropriate binomial probability by turning to the part of the table with the correct sample size. Then look down the column headed by the appropriate p value until you locate the probability corresponding to the desired X_1 value. For example, if $n = 5$ and $p = 0.5$, the probability of exactly three successes is 0.3125. This is the same value we find using the binomial formula

$$P(X_1 = 3) = \frac{5!}{3!2!}(0.5^3)(0.5^2)$$
$$= 0.3125$$

Using the binomial table, we can find the probabilities of selecting zero, one, two, and three defectives in a sample of ten from a production process producing 10% defectives. We go to the table for $n = 10$, $p = 0.10$ and find

$$P(X_1 = 0) = 0.3487$$
$$P(X_1 = 1) = 0.3874$$
$$P(X_1 = 2) = 0.1937$$
$$P(X_1 = 3) = 0.0574$$

As another example, assume you are working for an automobile manufacturer. Based on engineering reports, 2% of the cars your company produces will receive a "below standard" rating from the Environmental Protection Agency (EPA) on the pollution control devices. Thus, even a correctly operating production process will have variation, and not all cars will be produced exactly as designed. If twenty cars are selected at random from the inventory in Detroit, what is the probability of each of the following?

1. Finding no below-standard cars
2. Finding two or three below-standard cars
3. Finding more than three below-standard cars

The answers to these questions can be found directly from the binomial table in Appendix A, if we assume a binomial distribution applies.

Using the binomial table with $n = 20$ and $p = 0.02$, we find

$$P(X_1 = 0) = 0.6676$$

and

$$P(X_1 = 2 \text{ or } 3) = P(X_1 = 2) + P(X_1 = 3) = 0.0528 + 0.0065$$
$$= 0.0593$$

There are two ways to find the probability of *more than* three below-standard cars in a sample of twenty. The first way is to add the probabilities of

$$P(X_1 = 4) + P(X_1 = 5) + P(X_1 = 6) + \cdots + P(X_1 = 20) = 0.0006$$

Alternatively, we could find the probability of selecting three or fewer below-standard cars and subtract this probability from 1. That is,

$$P(X_1 = 3 \text{ or fewer}) = P(X_1 = 3) + P(X_1 = 2) + P(X_1 = 1) + P(X_1 = 0)$$
$$= 0.0065 + 0.0528 + 0.2725 + 0.6676$$
$$= 0.9994$$

and

$$P(X_1 = \text{more than } 3) = 1 - 0.9994$$
$$= 0.0006$$

Suppose the EPA has been given a mandate by Congress to determine whether automobiles manufactured in the United States meet pollution standards. The EPA wishes to allow no more than 2% of the cars produced by any manufacturer to receive a substandard rating. A southern U.S. state with strict pollution control standards has decided to base its enforcement policy on the EPA 2% standard. Since the state enforcement agency cannot test every car sold in the state, it randomly samples twenty cars of each make and model. If it finds more than one car in the sample with a substandard pollution rating, the manufacturer receives a stiff fine and is ordered to recall all cars of that make and model sold in the state. The state's rule says that if more than one substandard car is found, the conclusion is that the automobile company is exceeding the 2% limit.

Of course the automobile manufacturers are concerned about the chances of being unjustly accused. That is, a company may in fact be producing 2% or fewer cars with substandard pollution control devices, but the state could find more than one such car in its sample of twenty. The binomial probability table can be used to find the probability of this happening. The company wants

$$P(X_1 > 1) = 1 - P(X_1 \le 1)$$

Going to the binomial table with $n = 20$ and $p = 0.02$ we find that

$$P(X_1 > 1) = 1 - [P(0) + P(1)]$$
$$= 1 - (0.6676 + 0.2725) = 1 - 0.9401$$
$$= 0.0599$$

This means that, under the proposed sampling plan, there is just under a 6% chance the auto makers will be unjustly accused of making too many substandard cars (by pollution standards).

Because of the high potential costs of being unjustly accused, the manufacturers would be likely to challenge the sample plan. They would probably argue that more cars should be sampled and that the cutoff point for recalling should be altered to reduce the probability of being unjustly accused.

In order not to look at the situation entirely from the manufacturer's perspective, let us consider the situation where 10% of a manufacturer's cars do exceed the pollution standards. What is the probability that a sample of twenty cars will have only one or fewer exceed the standards and thus allow the manufacturer to pass the test? This time we want

$$P(X_1 \leq 1)$$

Going to the binomial table with $n = 20$ and $p = 0.10$, we find

$$P(X_1 \leq 1) = P(0) + P(1)$$
$$= 0.1216 + 0.2702$$
$$= 0.3918$$

This relatively large chance of incorrectly passing the test may lead EPA officials to argue for stricter standards.

SKILL DEVELOPMENT PROBLEMS FOR **SECTION 5-3**

The following set of problems is meant to test your understanding of the material in this section.

1. Use the binomial distribution table to construct the distribution for a situation where $n = 15$ and $p = 0.35$.

2. Use the binomial distribution table to construct the distribution for a situation where $n = 20$ and $q = 0.40$.

3. For a sample of $n = 10$, assuming that the binomial probability distribution applies, find the following:
   a. The probability of $X_1 = 3$ successes if the probability of a success is 20%.
   b. The probability of $X_1 = 3$ successes if the probability of a success is 80%.
   c. The probability of $X_1 = 4$ successes if the probability of a success is 33%.
   d. The probability of $X_1 = 4$ successes if the probability of a success is 15%.

4. Assuming that the binomial distribution applies, given a sample size of $n = 25$, find the following:
   a. The probability of $X_1 = 5$ successes if the probability of a success is 75%.

    b. The probability of $X_1 = 4$ failures if the probability of a success is 20%.

    c. The probability of $X_1 = 11$ successes if the probability of a failure is 33%.

    d. The probability of $X_1 = 5$ successes if the probability of a success is 40%.

5. The Lexington School Board has agreed to help the A. P. Stevens School Furniture Company test a new type of elementary school chair. Using the present school furniture, school administrators have found that 15% of the chairs must be replaced each year. A. P. Stevens claims its chair will average a 10% replacement rate.

    a. In a sample of 100 chairs, determine the distribution that describes the number of present chairs that would be replaced each year.

    b. What is the distribution that describes the A. P. Stevens chairs if its claim of a 10% replacement rate is correct?

    c. Assume 100 Stevens chairs are tested for 1 year and twelve need to be replaced. Comment on Stevens' claim that this proves its chair is superior to the present brand.

5-4   MEAN AND STANDARD DEVIATION OF THE BINOMIAL DISTRIBUTION

The mean of a discrete probability distribution is referred to as its *expected value*. This is the long-run average number of occurrences we can expect to find over time. The expected value of a discrete random variable, X, is found using equation 5-2:

$$E(X) = \Sigma X P(X)$$

    5-2

where

    $E(X)$ = Expected value of X

        X = Value of the random variable

    $P(X)$ = Probability of each value of X

Suppose we wish to find the expected number (value) of defective upgrade conversion units in a sample of $n = 4$ with a 0.10 probability of a single unit being defective. This probability distribution for E. M. International was given in Table 5-2. We find the expected value as follows:

No. Defectives X	P(X)	XP(X)
0	0.6561	0.0000
1	0.2916	0.2916
2	0.0486	0.0972
3	0.0036	0.0108
4	0.0001	0.0004
		$\Sigma = 0.4000$

Thus,

$$\mu_x = E(X) = \Sigma XP(X)$$
$$= 0.4000$$

Therefore, if the probability of a single upgrade unit being defective is 0.10, the average number of defectives found in repeated samples of four is 0.4000. Of course, for any single sample we could not find 0.4000 defective since defectives must occur in discrete values, in this case 0, 1, 2, 3, or 4. However, if we are working with a binomial distribution, the mean can be found using equation 5-3.

$$\mu_x = np$$

5-3

where

n = Sample size

p = Probability of a success

Using the E. M. International example with a sample of four selected from a population with 10% defective upgrade units, the distribution mean is

$$\mu_x = np = (4)(0.10)$$
$$= 0.40$$

Notice that this is the same value we found earlier using the expected value equation.

STANDARD DEVIATION OF THE BINOMIAL DISTRIBUTION

To calculate the standard deviation for a discrete probability distribution, we use equation 5-4.

$$\sigma_x = \sqrt{\Sigma(X - \mu_x)^2 P(X)}$$

5-4

where

X = Value of the random variable

σ_x = Standard deviation of X

μ_x = Mean = $E(X)$

$P(X)$ = Probability of X

Continuing with the E. M. International example for a sample of $n = 4$ and $p = 0.10$, we find the standard deviation for the distribution of defective upgrade conversion units as follows:

$$\mu_x = E(X) = \Sigma X P(X) = np = (4)(0.10)$$
$$= 0.4000$$

X	$P(X)$	$X - \mu_x$	$(X - \mu_x)^2$	$(X - \mu_x)^2 P(X)$
0	0.6561	−0.4000	0.16	0.1050
1	0.2916	0.6000	0.36	0.1050
2	0.0486	1.6000	2.56	0.1244
3	0.0036	2.6000	6.76	0.0243
4	0.0001	3.6000	12.96	0.0013
				$\Sigma = 0.3600$

$$\sigma_x^2 = 0.3600$$
$$\sigma_x = \sqrt{0.3600}$$
$$= 0.60$$

Thus the mean and standard deviation for this distribution are 0.4000 and 0.60, respectively.

If a discrete probability distribution meets the binomial distribution conditions, the standard deviation is defined in equation 5-5.

$$\sigma_x = \sqrt{npq}$$

5-5

where

n = Sample size

p = Probability of a success

$q = (1 - p)$ = Probability of a failure

For the E. M. International example with $n = 4$ and $p = 0.10$, the standard deviation is

$$\sigma_x = \sqrt{npq} = \sqrt{(4)(0.10)(0.90)}$$
$$= \sqrt{0.3600}$$
$$= 0.60$$

SKILL DEVELOPMENT PROBLEMS FOR SECTION 5-4

The following set of problems is meant to test your understanding of the material in this section.

6. Assuming the binomial distribution applies, find the mean and standard deviation of the distribution determined by $n = 75$ and $p = 0.3$.

7. Assuming the binomial distribution applies, find the mean, variance, and standard deviation of the distribution determined by $n = 90$ and $q = 0.75$.

8. Assuming the binomial distribution applies, find the mean, variance, standard deviation, and coefficient of variation of the distribution determined by $n = 250$ and $p = 0.7$.

9. The A. B. C. Institute offers classes in state-of-the-art technical repair services. It has recently started teaching classes in fiber-optic repair. Because many long-distance companies have been converting to fiber-optic systems, the institute has been advertising that 90% of its graduates should expect job offers within their communities. The first class of five has just graduated.
   a. Assuming the claim of 90% community job offers is valid, and the class of five can be considered to be a representative sample of all possible future graduates, develop the probability distribution describing the possible number of home community job offers.
   b. Find the mean and standard deviation of the distribution found in part a.
   c. If the first graduating class had four people receiving home community job offers, what would you conclude about the 90% claim?

5-5 SOME COMMENTS ABOUT THE BINOMIAL DISTRIBUTION

The binomial distribution has many applications, such as the elementary quality control example discussed in Section 5-3. In later chapters on decision making under uncertainty, we will use this distribution for applications in the other functional areas of business.

At this point, several comments about the binomial distribution are worth making. If p, the probability of a success, is 0.5, the binomial distribution is *symmetrical* regardless of the sample size. This is illustrated in Figure 5-2, which shows frequency histograms for samples of $n = 5$, $n = 10$, and $n = 15$. Notice that all three distributions are centered at the expected value, μ_x.

FIGURE **5-2**

The Binomial
Distribution with
Varying Sample
Sizes ($p = 0.5$)

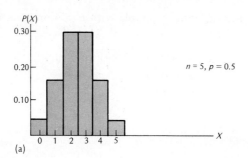

(a)

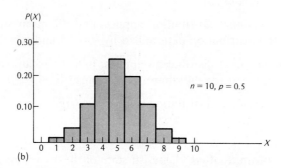

(b)

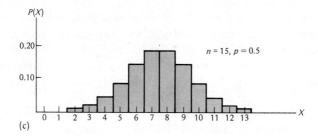

(c)

When the value of p differs from 0.5 in either direction, the binomial distribution is *skewed*. This was the case for the E. M. International examples with $n = 4$ and $p = 0.10$. The skewness will be most pronounced when n is small and p approaches 0 or 1.0. However, the binomial distribution approaches symmetry as n increases. The frequency histograms shown in Figure 5-3 bear this out. This fact will be used in Chapter 6, where we will show that the *normal distribution* (a symmetrical continuous distribution) can be used to approximate probabilities from a binomial distribution.

5-6 THE POISSON PROBABILITY DISTRIBUTION

To use the binomial distribution, we must be able to count the number of successes and the number of failures. Whereas in many applications you may be able

FIGURE **5-3**

The Binomial
Distribution with
Varying Sample
Sizes ($p = 0.05$)

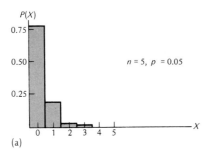

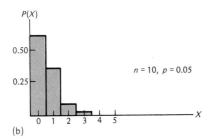

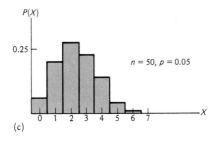

to count the number of successes, you often cannot count the number of failures. For example, suppose a company builds freeways in Vermont. The company could count the number of chuckholes that develop per mile (here a chuckhole is a success since it is what we are looking for), but how could it count the number of non-chuckholes? Or what about the emergency medical service in Los Angeles? It could easily count the number of emergencies its units respond to in 1 hour, but how could it determine how many calls it did not receive? Obviously, in these cases the number of possible outcomes (successes + failures) is difficult, if not impossible, to determine. If the total number of possible outcomes cannot be determined, the binomial distribution cannot be applied as a decision-making aid.

Fortunately, the **Poisson probability distribution** can be applied in these situations without knowing the total possible outcomes. To apply the Poisson distribution, we need only know the *average* number of successes for a given segment. For instance, we could use the Poisson distribution for our freeway construction company if we were able to determine the average number of chuckholes per mile. Likewise, the emergency medical service in Los Angeles could apply the Poisson distribution if it could find the average number of responses per hour. Of course, before the Poisson distribution can be applied, certain conditions must be satisfied.

CHARACTERISTICS OF THE POISSON DISTRIBUTION

A physical situation must possess certain characteristics before it can be described by the Poisson distribution, namely,

1. The physical events must be considered *rare* events. Considering all the chuckholes that could form, only a few actually do form. Considering all the medical emergencies that might result, only a few do occur.[2]
2. The physical events must be *random* and *independent* of each other. That is, an event occurring must not be predictable, nor can it influence the chances of another event occurring.

The Poisson distribution is described by a single parameter, λ (lambda), which is the average occurrence per segment. The value of λ depends on the situation being described. For instance, λ could be the average number of machine breakdowns per month or the average number of customers arriving at a checkout stand in a 10-minute period. It could also be the average number of emergency responses for the emergency medical service or the average number of chuckholes in a section of freeway.

Once λ has been determined, we can calculate the average occurrence rate for any multiple segment, t. This is λt. Note that λ and t must be in compatible units. If we have $\lambda = 20$ arrivals per hour, we cannot multiply this by a time period measured in minutes. That is, if we have

$$\lambda = \frac{20}{h} \quad \text{and} \quad t = 30 \text{ min}$$

we must set

$$t = \frac{1}{2}h$$

Then,

$$\lambda t = 10$$

The average number of occurrences is not necessarily the number we will see if we observe the process one time. We might expect an average of twenty people

---

[2] Another explanation of *rare* is that we are able to define a sufficiently small interval, perhaps of distance or time, such that at most, one occurrence of the event is possible. In addition, any increase in the width of this interval will lead to a proportional increase in the probability of an occurrence.

to arrive at a checkout stand in any given hour, but we do not expect to find exactly that number arriving every hour. The actual arrivals will form a distribution with an expected value, or mean, equal to λt. So, for the Poisson distribution,

$$\mu_x = \lambda t$$

The Poisson distribution is a discrete distribution. This means that if we are dealing with airplane arrivals at the San Francisco International Airport, in any given hour only 0, 1, 2, and so on, airplanes can arrive; 1.5 airplanes cannot land.

THE POISSON DISTRIBUTION FORMULA

Once λt has been specified, the probability for any discrete value in the Poisson distribution can be found using equation 5-6:

$$P(X_1) = \frac{(\lambda t)^{X_1} e^{-\lambda t}}{X_1!} \qquad \textbf{5-6}$$

where

X_1 = Number of successes in segment t

λt = Expected number of successes in segment t

e = Base of the natural number system (2.71828)

Consider the case where the predetermined average number of airplane arrivals at the San Francisco International Airport is sixty per hour. Thus $\lambda = 60$/hour. We can find the probability of exactly seven planes arriving in a 10-minute period as follows:

$$t = \text{One 10-min period} = \frac{1}{6}\,\text{h}$$

$$\lambda = \frac{60}{\text{h}}$$

$$\lambda t = (60)\left(\frac{1}{6}\right)$$

$$= 10$$

Then,

$$P(X_1 = 7) = \frac{(10)^7 e^{-10}}{7!}$$

$$= 0.0901$$

USING THE POISSON PROBABILITY TABLES

As was the case with the binomial distribution, a table of probabilities exists for the Poisson distribution. (This table appears in Appendix B at the end of the book.) The Poisson table is easy to use, as demonstrated through the following example.

The Acme Taxi Service has studied the demand for taxis at the local airport and found that, on the average, six taxis are demanded per hour. Thus, $\lambda = 6$/hour. If the company is considering locating six taxis at the airport during each hour, what is the probability that demand will exceed six and people will have to wait for taxi service?

To answer this question, we recognize that the segment of interest, t, equals one hour, so $\lambda t = 6$. We are interested in

$$P(X > 6) = 1 - P(X \leq 6)$$

To use the Poisson probability tables, we turn to Appendix B and locate the column with $\lambda t = 6$. Then we locate the values of X down the left-hand side of the table. We wish first to determine the sum of the probabilities for $X = 0$ to $X = 6$. This sum is found by adding the probabilities under the column for $\lambda t = 6$ from $X = 0$ through $X = 6$. These values are

X	$P(X)$
0	0.0025
1	0.0149
2	0.0446
3	0.0892
4	0.1339
5	0.1606
6	0.1606
	$\Sigma = 0.6063$

Thus,

$$P(X \leq 6) = 0.6063$$

Then the desired probability is

$$P(X > 6) = 1 - P(X \leq 6)$$
$$= 1 - 0.6063$$
$$= 0.3937$$

Thus, there is a 0.3937 probability that demand for taxis at the airport will exceed supply if the company puts only six taxis at the airport.

Suppose the Acme Taxi Service did a similar study at the town's largest hotel and found that demand averaged four taxis per hour. If the company planned to locate two taxis during each half-hour time segment, what is the probability that demand would exceed the supply within a half-hour time segment?

We first recognize that $\lambda = 4$ and the segment of interest is 0.5 hour. Thus $t = 0.5$ and $\lambda t = 2$. Then the probability of interest is

$$P(X > 2) = 1 - P(X \le 2)$$

We go to the Poisson probability table in Appendix B and look at the column headed $\lambda t = 2$. We sum the probabilities from $X = 0$ to $X = 2$ as follows:

X	P(X)
0	0.1353
1	0.2707
2	0.2707
	$\Sigma = 0.6767$

Then the probability of interest is

$$P(X > 2) = 1 - P(X \le 2)$$
$$= 1 - 0.6767$$
$$= 0.3233$$

As you can see, the Poisson tables allow you to determine probabilities much more quickly than does the Poisson formula.

APPLYING THE POISSON PROBABILITY DISTRIBUTION

Consider the problem facing a Boise Cascade Corporation lumber mill manager. Logs arrive by truck and are scaled (measured to determine the number of board feet) before they are dumped into the log pond. Figure 5-4 illustrates the basic flow. The mill manager must determine how many scale stations to have open during various times of the day. If he has too many stations open, the scalers will have excessive idle time and the cost of scaling will be unnecessarily high. On the other hand, if too few scale stations are open, some log trucks will have to wait.

The manager has studied the truck arrival patterns and has determined that during the first open hour (7:00–8:00 A.M.), the trucks randomly arrive at six per hour. He knows that if eight or fewer arrive during an hour, two scale stations can keep up with the work. If more than eight trucks arrive, three scale stations are required. He recognizes that the distribution of log truck arrivals during this hour can be represented by a Poisson distribution with $\lambda = 6.0$ per hour. The mill manager can use the Poisson distribution table to determine the probability that three scale stations will be needed.

The Boise Cascade mill manager would select $\lambda t = 6.0$ and find the probability that more than eight trucks will arrive during the 7:00–8:00 A.M. time slot. He could add the probabilities for $X_1 = 9, 10, 11, \ldots$ as follows:

$$P(9 \text{ or more trucks}) = P(9) + P(10) + P(11) + \cdots + P(17)$$
$$= 0.0688 + 0.0413 + 0.0225 + \cdots + 0.0001$$
$$= 0.1526$$

FIGURE 5-4

Truck Flow for
Boise Cascade
Mill Example

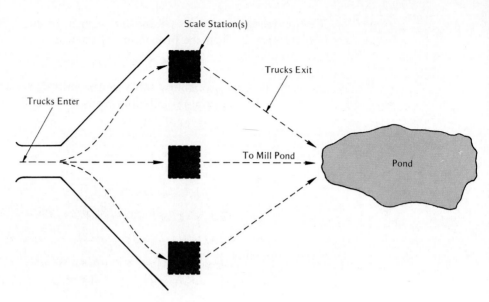

Notice that the probability of more than seventeen trucks arriving is so small that it has been rounded to zero.

The probability of needing three scale stations is 0.1526, and the probability that only two stations will be needed is $(1 - 0.1526)$ or 0.8474. The manager must now make the decision. He must balance the cost of an additional scale station against the potential dissatisfaction of both log truck drivers and the companies they represent.

Suppose this Boise Cascade manager studies the log truck arrivals in the hour between 11:00 A.M. and 12:00 noon and finds the average number of trucks arriving is 3.5. Assuming truck arrivals can be represented by the Poisson distribution, what is the probability of eight or fewer trucks arriving? We can determine this probability using the column under $\lambda t = 3.5$ in the Poisson probability table. We sum the individual probabilities from $X_1 = 0$ to $X_1 = 8$:

$$
\begin{aligned}
P(8 \text{ or fewer trucks}) &= P(0) + P(1) + P(2) + \cdots + P(8) \\
&= 0.0302 + 0.1057 + 0.1850 + \cdots + 0.0169 \\
&= 0.9902
\end{aligned}
$$

This indicates there is a 99% chance of needing only two scale stations from 11:00 A.M. to 12:00 noon.

SKILL DEVELOPMENT PROBLEMS FOR **SECTION 5-6**

The following set of problems tests your understanding of the material in this section.

10. Determine the Poisson probability distribution associated with $\lambda = 6$ and $t = 2$. Find $P(X \leq 3)$.

11. Determine the Poisson probability distribution associated with $\lambda = 20$ and $t = 1/2$. Find $P(X \geq 14)$.

12. If $\lambda = 8$ and $t = 1$, and the Poisson probability distribution applies, find
    a. $P(X > 4)$
    b. $P(X \leq 9)$
    c. $P(6 \leq X \leq 12)$

13. If $\lambda = 16$ and $t = 1/2$, and the Poisson probability distribution applies, find
    a. $P(X < 10)$
    b. $P(X \leq 7)$
    c. $P(3 \leq X \leq 7)$

14. East-West Translations publishes textbooks of ancient Oriental teachings for English-speaking universities. The company is presently testing a computer-based translation service. Since Oriental symbols are difficult to translate, East-West assumes the computer program will make some errors, but then so do human translators. The computer service claims its error rate will average three per 400 words of translation. East-West randomly selects a 1,200-word passage. If the computer company's claim is accurate:
    a. What is the probability no errors will be found?
    b. What is the probability more than fourteen errors will be found?
    c. What is the probability fewer than nine errors will be found?
    d. If fifteen errors are found in the 1,200-word passage, what would you conclude about the computer company's claim? Why?

$5\text{-}7$ MEAN, VARIANCE, AND STANDARD DEVIATION OF THE POISSON DISTRIBUTION

The mean of the Poisson distribution is

$$\mu_x = \lambda t$$

Thus, for the Boise Cascade lumber mill example, the mean number of arrivals was 6.0 trucks between 7:00 A.M. and 8:00 A.M. Since the Poisson distribution is a discrete distribution, we can calculate the mean, or expected value, using

$$\mu_x = E(X) = \Sigma X P(X)$$

and the variance using

$$\sigma_x^2 = \Sigma (X - \mu_x)^2 P(X)$$

The appropriate calculations are shown in Table 5-3.

Note that both the mean and the variance equal 6.0. This is no accident. The variance for the Poisson distribution always equals the mean, as given by equation 5-7:

TABLE 5-3

Poisson
Distribution for
Log Truck
Arrivals
$(\lambda t = 6.0)$

X	$P(X)$	$XP(X)$	$X - \mu_x$	$(X - \mu_x)^2$	$(X - \mu_x)^2 P(X)$
0	0.0025	0.0000	− 6	36	0.0900
1	0.0149	0.0149	− 5	25	0.3725
2	0.0446	0.0892	− 4	16	0.7136
3	0.0892	0.2676	− 3	9	0.8028
4	0.1339	0.5356	− 2	4	0.5356
5	0.1606	0.8030	− 1	1	0.1606
6	0.1606	0.9636	0	0	0.0000
7	0.1377	0.9639	1	1	0.1377
8	0.1033	0.8264	2	4	0.4132
9	0.0688	0.6192	3	9	0.6192
10	0.0413	0.4130	4	16	0.6608
11	0.0225	0.2475	5	25	0.5625
12	0.0113	0.1356	6	36	0.4068
13	0.0052	0.0676	7	49	0.2548
14	0.0022	0.0308	8	64	0.1408
15	0.0009	0.0135	9	81	0.0729
16	0.0003	0.0048	10	100	0.0300
17	0.0001	0.0017	11	121	0.0121
		$\Sigma = 5.9979 \approx 6.0^*$			$\Sigma = 5.9859 \approx 6.0^*$

$$\mu_x = \Sigma XP(X) = 6.0 = \lambda t$$
$$\sigma_x^2 = \Sigma(X - \mu_x)^2 P(X) = 6.0 = \lambda t$$

*Difference due to rounding.

$$\sigma_x^2 = \lambda t \qquad \text{5-7}$$

The standard deviation of the Poisson distribution is the square root of the mean:

$$\sigma_x = \sqrt{\lambda t} \qquad \text{5-8}$$

Thus, for those processes that can be assumed to follow a Poisson distribution, variance can be controlled directly by controlling the mean. If, as noted in Chapter 3, the variance can be considered a measure of uncertainty, then for those applications where a Poisson distribution applies, the uncertainty can be reduced by reducing the mean. Often this can be achieved by effective scheduling.

SKILL DEVELOPMENT PROBLEMS FOR **SECTION 5-7**

The following set of problems is meant to test your understanding of the material in this section.

15. If $\lambda = 5$ and $t = 2$, determine the mean and standard deviation of the corresponding Poisson distribution.

16. If $\lambda = 18$ and $t = 1/3$, find the expected value, variance, and standard deviation of the corresponding Poisson distribution.

17. The O'Rilley Office Worker Company has agreed to supply 100 part-time office employees to Mid-East Insurance each day. The O'Rilley Company knows that on the average 7% of the workers it schedules for any day will not come to work for one of many reasons. Mid-East Insurance is O'Rilley's biggest customer and so O'Rilley wants to have fewer than the scheduled 100 people show up less than one day in twenty workdays per month. Assuming the Poisson distribution can be used to describe the number of workers not coming to work on any day, how many workers should O'Rilley schedule?

5-8 QUALITY IMPROVEMENT USING THE BINOMIAL DISTRIBUTION

The binomial distribution serves as the base for an important part of process control efforts of many companies that use a technique known as **acceptance sampling.** Acceptance sampling can be used by a firm to help assure that incoming parts and materials meet predetermined quality standards. For example, consider the example involving the Harrison Construction Company, a worldwide organization with many operations including freeway and rail system construction. Recently, the firm entered into a $1.3 billion contract to rebuild part of the subway system in a major U.S. city. Included among the many parts and materials needed for this project is a certain spring-loaded clamp. The company will use thousands of these clamps during the course of the 3-year project.

The Harrison purchasing staff has entered into a contract with a company to supply these clamps. Included in the contract are points covering price, delivery dates, clamp specifications, etc. If the clamp is to work properly, a spring must be properly attached to the clamp. If it is not, the clamp will not work and must be discarded. The contract calls for no more than 5% of all clamps to have defectively attached springs. This defective rate is called the **acceptable quality level.** The Harrison Company plans to have the clamps delivered in lots of 5,000 clamps. One option for Harrison materials managers would be to assume that all the shipments contain clamps that meet the 0.05 defect level and not question the shipment. However, experience has shown that suppliers sometimes have quality problems and do not meet the contract specifications.

Therefore, Harrison materials managers have decided to set up an acceptance sampling plan whereby they will inspect a certain number of items from each incoming lot and, depending on the number of defective clamps in the sample, will either accept or reject the entire lot. Suppose for the sake of this discussion, the managers have decided to sample $n = 5$ clamps. If they find no defects, they will accept the lot. If they find two or more defects, they will reject the lot. If they find one defect, they are in the "gray area" and will sample $n = 5$ more. If the second sample contains one or more defects, they will reject the lot. The objectives of this sampling plan are as follows:

1. If the lot actually contains 5% or fewer defective clamps, the company wants to accept the shipment. Thus, an acceptance sampling plan should accept "good" shipments a high percentage of the time.
2. If a lot contains an unacceptably high percentage of defects, the company wants to reject the shipment. Thus, an acceptance sampling plan should reject "bad" shipments a high percentage of the time.

Based on the contract, a "good" shipment is one that contains no more than $p = 0.05$ defects. Suppose we consider for a minute the case of a "good" shipment. How can we determine the chances that our sampling plan will accept this shipment? The answer is fairly straightforward if we assume that the underlying distribution is binomial. On the first sample, the possible outcomes and associated probabilities from the binomial distribution are the following:

First Sample

No. of Defects X	Decision	Probability ($n = 5$, $p = 0.05$) P(X)
0	Accept	0.7738
1	Resample	0.2036
2	Reject	0.0214
3	Reject	0.0011
4	Reject	0.0000
5	Reject	0.0000

Thus, there is a 0.7738 chance that the sampling plan will accept the shipment on the first sample. However, there is a 0.2036 chance that one defect will be discovered in the first sample of $n = 5$ and resampling will be required. If this is a good shipment, the second sample has the same probability distribution as the first sample.

Second Sample

No. of Defects X	Decision	Probability ($n = 5$, $p = 0.05$) P(X)
0	Accept	0.7738
1	Reject	0.2036
2	Reject	0.0214
3	Reject	0.0011
4	Reject	0.0000
5	Reject	0.0000

There is a 0.7738 chance that the second sample also will accept the good shipment. Therefore, the overall probability of the good shipment being accepted is

$$P(\text{accept}|\text{good}) = 0.7738 + (0.2036)(0.7738)$$
$$= 0.9313$$

Thus, the chances are quite high at 0.9313 that the sampling plan will accept a good shipment. However, the flip side of this is that there is a $1 - 0.9313 = 0.0687$ probability that a good shipment will be rejected. This is called the **producer's risk** in quality control terminology.

Suppose the Harrison Company is satisfied with the sampling plan based on this analysis. However, there is another side to the picture. That is, how good is the sampling plan at rejecting "bad" shipments? To answer this question, we need to decide what a bad shipment is. A natural inclination would be to say that if a good shipment is one with at most 5% defects, then a bad shipment is one with defects greater than 5%, such as 5.1% defects. Therefore, if a good shipment has $5,000 \cdot 0.05 = 250$ defects, a bad shipment would be one with $5,000 \cdot 0.051 = 255$ defects. Unfortunately, short of checking all 5,000 clamps, there really is no way of distinguishing between a 5,000-unit lot with 250 defects and a 5,000-unit lot with 255 defects. A sample of size five from the shipment would certainly have no chance of making this distinction.

Consequently, the decision makers must establish a defect rate that defines a "bad" shipment at a higher level. This higher level defect rate is called the **lot tolerance percent defective (LTPD)**. Suppose for the purposes of this example, the materials managers set the rate at 0.10, twice the defective rate of a good shipment. Now, suppose, a shipment arrives containing 10% defects and is thus a bad shipment. The question is: What are the chances that the sampling plan will reject this bad shipment? To answer this question, we turn to the binomial table once again. This time we use $n = 5$ and $p = 0.10$ as follows:

First Sample

No. of Defects X	Decision	Probability $(n = 5, p = 0.10)$ $P(X)$
0	Accept	0.5905
1	Resample	0.3280
2	Reject	0.0729
3	Reject	0.0081
4	Reject	0.0004
5	Reject	0.0000

Therefore, the probability that the first sample will reject this "bad" shipment is

$$P(\text{reject}|\text{bad}) = 0.0729 + 0.0081 + 0.0004$$
$$= 0.0814$$

However, there is a 0.3280 probability that the first sample will uncover one defect and a second sample will be required. The probability distribution for this sample is the same as for the first sample.

Second Sample

No. of Defects X	Decision	Probability ($n = 5$, $p = 0.10$) P(X)
0	Accept	0.5905
1	Reject	0.3280
2	Reject	0.0729
3	Reject	0.0081
4	Reject	0.0004
5	Reject	0.0000

Now, the overall probability of rejecting a bad shipment is

$$P(\text{reject}|\text{bad}) = 0.0814 + (0.3280)(0.3280 + 0.0729 + 0.0081 + 0.0004)$$
$$= 0.21568$$

Thus, there is just over a 21% probability that if the shipment contains 10% defects (a bad shipment), this sampling plan will reject it. As you can see, this probability is quite low compared to what the materials managers would no doubt want to see and the sampling plan may not meet the needs of the Harrison Company. The alternative would be for the Harrison Company to increase its sample size and adjust its decision rule for accepting and rejecting a shipment. You are encouraged to try alternative sampling plans to see whether an improvement can be made.

Comments About Acceptance Sampling While acceptance sampling is still heavily used by many companies, the emphasis in quality control is to reduce the need for acceptance sampling by working with suppliers to improve their quality. If a customer can rely on the supplier to meet the contract requirements, there is no need for acceptance sampling. There would be no need to reject shipments.

5-9 CONCLUSIONS

This chapter has introduced discrete random variables and showed how a probability distribution is developed for a discrete random variable. Additionally, it has showed how to compute the mean and standard deviation for any discrete distribution.

As indicated in this chapter, there is virtually no end to the possible discrete probability distributions decision makers might use. However, the binomial and Poisson distributions represent two of the most commonly used theoretical distributions. In spite of some seemingly strong restrictions on the situations these distributions represent, they can be used in a surprising number of managerial applications.

This chapter has discussed some concepts connected with discrete distributions from a managerial perspective. The chapter glossary defines these concepts in more formal terms. Test your understanding of the material in this chapter by comparing the chapter's managerial discussion with the more formal definitions.

The important statistical equations presented in the chapter are summarized following the glossary.

CHAPTER **GLOSSARY**

Bernoulli process A sequence of random experiments such that the outcome of each trial has one of two complementary outcomes (success or failure), each trial is independent of the preceding trials, and the probability of a success remains constant from trial to trial.

binomial distribution A probability distribution that gives the probability of X_1 successes in n trials of a Bernoulli process.

discrete random variable A variable that can assume only integer or specific fractional values.

expected value A measure of location for a probability distribution. The expected value of an experiment is the weighted average of the values the outcomes of the experiments may assume. The weighting factors are the probabilities associated with each outcome.

Poisson probability distribution A probability distribution that gives the probability of X_1 occurrences from a Poisson process when the average number of occurrences is λt.

Poisson process A process describing the random occurrences of independent rare events.

random variable A function or rule that assigns numerical values to the possible outcomes of a trial or experiment.

sample space A set representing the universe of all possible outcomes from a statistical experiment.

sampling with replacement The process of replacing an item into the population before selecting the next item in the sample.

sampling without replacement The most common type of sampling, where items are not replaced into the population until after the entire sample has been selected.

uniform probability distribution A probability distribution that has equal probabilities for all values of the random variable.

CHAPTER FORMULAS

Binomial formula

$$P(X_1) = \frac{n!}{X_1!X_2!} p^{X_1} q^{X_2}$$

Expected value of a discrete probability distribution

$$E[X] = \Sigma X P(X)$$

Standard deviation of a discrete probability distribution

$$\sigma_x = \sqrt{\Sigma (X - \mu_x)^2 P(X)}$$

Mean of a binomial distribution

$$\mu_x = np$$

Standard deviation of a binomial distribution

$$\sigma_x = \sqrt{npq}$$

Poisson formula

$$P(X_1) = \frac{(\lambda t)^{X_1} e^{-\lambda t}}{X_1!}$$

Mean of a Poisson distribution

$$\mu_x = \lambda t$$

Variance of a Poisson distribution

$$\sigma_x^2 = \lambda t$$

SOLVED PROBLEMS

1. The Ace Electronics Corporation produces electronic calculators and markets them on a national basis. These calculators are sent to the division warehouses in lots of 1,000. You, as the warehouse manager, will not accept a lot of calculators if you think more than 5% are defective. You sample twenty calculators ($n = 20$) and test to see how many are defective and how many are good. Using the binomial distribution, find the following if $n = 20$ and $p = 0.05$:
    a. The probability of finding exactly one defective.
    b. The probability of finding more than one defective.
    c. The probability of finding from one to three defectives.
    d. The variance and standard deviation.
    e. Suppose you have just found three defectives in the sample. Would your recommendation be to keep the lot of 1,000 calculators or return them?
    f. How many defectives would you expect to find in a sample of $n = 20$ if there is actually 0.05 defective in a lot?

Solution:

a. Using the binomial equation,

$$P(1 \text{ defective}) = \frac{20!}{1!19!}(0.05^1)(0.95^{19})$$

$$= 0.3774$$

From the binomial table in Appendix A, with $n = 20$ and $p = 0.05$,

$$P(1) = 0.3774$$

b. $P(2 \text{ or more defective}) = P(2) + P(3) + P(4) + \cdots + P(20)$

or, by using the complement,

$$P(2 \text{ or more defective}) = 1 - [P(1) + P(0)]$$

From the binomial table,

$$P(2 \text{ or more defective}) = 1 - (0.3774 + 0.3585)$$
$$= 0.2641$$

c. $P(1 \le X_1 \le 3) = P(1) + P(2) + P(3)$

From the binomial table,

$$P(1 \le X_1 \le 3) = 0.3774 + 0.1887 + 0.0596$$
$$= 0.6257$$

d. $$\sigma_x^2 = npq = (20)(0.05)(0.95)$$
$$= 0.95$$
$$\sigma_x = \sqrt{0.95}$$
$$= 0.9747$$

e. The recommendation should depend on the probability of observing three or more defective calculators if, in fact, only 5% are defective. If this probability is very small, we would conclude that the lot must actually contain more than 5% defectives and should be returned. If the probability is not small, the recommendation should be to keep the calculators. Thus, with $n = 20$ and $p = 0.05$,

$$P(3 \text{ or more defective}) = 1 - P(2 \text{ or fewer defective})$$
$$= 1 - [P(2) + P(1) + P(0)]$$
$$= 1 - (0.1887 + 0.3774 + 0.3585)$$
$$= 1 - 0.9246$$
$$= 0.0754$$

Thus 0.0754 is the probability of finding three or more defectives in a sample of $n = 20$ when the population is supposed to contain, at most, 5% defective calculators. You make the final decision. (This type of question and the complete method for analysis will be discussed in Chapters 9 and 10, which cover statistical inference and hypothesis testing.)

f. The number of expected defectives is

$$E[X] = \Sigma X P(X)$$

For a binomial distribution,

$$\mu_x = E[X] = np$$

Therefore,

$$\mu_x = (20)(0.05)$$
$$= 1.0$$

2. In a study for a local hospital you have found that the average number of arrivals at the emergency room between 6 P.M. and 9 P.M. on Friday night is five patients. Using a Poisson distribution, answer the following:

    a. What is the probability distribution describing emergency room arrivals?
    b. Is this distribution skewed? If so, in what direction? Are all Poisson distributions skewed?
    c. What is the probability that only one or two patients will arrive during the 3-hour period on any Friday night?
    d. What is the probability exactly five patients will arrive?
    e. What is the probability more than eight patients will arrive?
    f. What are the mean and standard deviation of this probability distribution?
    g. Would you expect the same distribution to apply between 6 A.M. and 9 A.M. on Friday morning? Why or why not?

Solution:

a. The probability distribution relates the discrete arrivals to the probability of each arrival occurring. The following distribution is taken from the table of Poisson probabilities in Appendix B.

X_1	$P(X_1)$	X_1	$P(X_1)$
0	0.0067	8	0.0653
1	0.0337	9	0.0363
2	0.0842	10	0.0181
3	0.1404	11	0.0082
4	0.1755	12	0.0034
5	0.1755	13	0.0013
6	0.1462	14	0.0005
7	0.1044	15	0.0002

b. Yes, the distribution is skewed to the right. Looking at the probability columns in Appendix B, we see that all Poisson distributions are skewed. However, as λt becomes very large, the Poisson distribution approaches a symmetrical distribution.

c. From the Poisson table,

$$P(1) + P(2) = 0.0337 + 0.0842$$
$$= 0.1179$$

d. Again, from the Poisson distribution table,

$$P(5) = 0.1755$$

e.
$$
\begin{aligned}
P(\text{more than 8 arrive}) &= P(9) + P(10) + P(11) + P(12) \\
&\quad + P(13) + P(14) + P(15) \\
&= 0.0363 + 0.0181 + 0.0082 + 0.0034 \\
&\quad + 0.0013 + 0.0005 + 0.0002 \\
&= 0.068
\end{aligned}
$$

f. The mean is given as five per 3 hours. The standard deviation, by definition, is the square root of the mean; that is,

$$
\sigma_x = \sqrt{\mu_x} = \sqrt{5}
$$
$$
= 2.236
$$

g. Since the underlying conditions that give rise to the Friday night distribution would not remain constant, we would expect a different distribution to apply during the morning hours.

3. Assume you are responsible for operating a large fleet of taxis. The average number of taxis under repair during any day is four. The Poisson distribution applies.

   a. What is the probability that during any day fewer than three taxis will be under repair?
   b. What is the probability that eight or more taxis will be under repair?
   c. How many spare taxis must you have if you want the probability of not being able to assign a driver a spare taxi to be a maximum of 5%? Assume it takes an entire day to repair a taxi.

Solution:

a. Again, from the Poisson table, in the column under $\lambda t = 4.00$,

$$
\begin{aligned}
P(\text{fewer than 3}) &= P(0) + P(1) + P(2) = 0.0183 + 0.0733 + 0.1465 \\
&= 0.2381
\end{aligned}
$$

b.
$$
\begin{aligned}
P(\text{8 or more}) &= P(8) + P(9) + P(10) + P(11) + P(12) + P(13) + P(14) \\
&= 0.0298 + 0.0132 + 0.0053 + 0.0019 + 0.0006 \\
&\quad + 0.0002 + 0.0001 \\
&= 0.0511
\end{aligned}
$$

c. To answer this part, start at the bottom of the $\lambda t = 4.00$ probability column and work toward the top in the following manner. If you have thirteen spare taxis, you will be short only when fourteen or more break down. The probability of this happening is 0.0001. If you have twelve spare taxis, you will be short if thirteen or more taxis break down. The probability of this happening is

$$
\begin{aligned}
P(13) + P(14) &= 0.0001 + 0.0002 \\
&= 0.0003
\end{aligned}
$$

If you have seven spare taxis, the probability of being short is the probability of eight or more taxis being under repair. This is

$$P(8 \text{ or more}) = 0.0511 \quad (\text{See part } \textbf{b}.)$$

Since having seven taxis gives a probability of being short *more* than 5%, you will have eight spare taxis with a probability of being caught short equal to

$$P(9 \text{ or more}) = 0.0213$$

CONCEPTUAL QUESTIONS AND ASSIGNMENTS

18. Discuss the characteristics that must be present for the binomial probability distribution to apply. Relate these to a particular business application and show how the application meets the binomial requirements.

19. Discuss why, in the strictest sense, if the sampling is performed without replacement, the binomial distribution does not apply. Also, indicate under what conditions it is considered acceptable to use the binomial distribution even when the sampling is without replacement. Identify a business application that supports your answer.

20. How is the shape of a binomial distribution changed for a given sample size as p approaches 0.50 from either side? Discuss.

21. How is the shape of the binomial distribution changed for a given value of p as the sample size is increased? Discuss.

22. Discuss the basic differences and similarities between the binomial distribution and the Poisson distribution.

23. Through an example, discuss why, if the mean of the Poisson distribution can be reduced, the spread of the distribution can also be reduced.

ADDITIONAL PROBLEMS

24. The Question Research Company performs research work in which opinion surveys are administered. In a recent survey regarding the acceptability of a particular product, the respondents were asked to indicate (*yes* or *no*) whether they would consider using the product regularly after having tried it. The product's manufacturer thought that the chance of an individual saying *yes* was 0.70.

   a. Assuming that the 0.70 is correct, develop a probability distribution for the number of *yes* responses in a sample of five, assuming that the binomial distribution applies. Use the binomial formula.

   b. Use equation 5-2 to compute the expected value of this probability distribution. Interpret this value.

   c. Suppose the Question Research Company did survey five people and found no one who said *yes*. What is the probability of this happening, assuming the manufacturer's 0.70 probability value is correct? What might be concluded about the manufacturer's probability value? Why?

25. Suppose a study performed at St. Jude's Hospital shows that 30% of all patients arriving at the emergency room are subsequently admitted to the

hospital for at least one night. Assuming that in a sample of seven who arrived at the emergency room the number of people needing to be admitted to the hospital meets the requirements for the binomial distribution:
  a. Determine the probabilities for each of the possible values of the random variable. Use the binomial formula.
  b. What is the probability that five or more in the sample of seven will require admittance to the hospital?
  c. What is the expected number of patients in the sample that will require admittance to the hospital?

26. The Bayhill city council claims that 40% of the parking spaces downtown are used by employees of the downtown businesses. A sample of five parking spaces was selected from the 4,000 parking spaces.
  a. Assuming that the number of spaces filled by employees can be described by the binomial distribution, develop the binomial probability distribution for the sample of size five using the binomial formula.
  b. Suppose the sample results showed four or more of the spaces were actually filled by employees. What would you conclude about the council's claim? Discuss.
  c. What is the expected number of employees' cars in a sample of five parking spaces?

27. Suppose you were given a 10-question multiple-choice examination where each question had four optional answers.
  a. What is the probability of getting a perfect score if you were forced to guess at each question?
  b. Suppose it takes at least seven correct answers out of ten to pass the test. What is the probability of passing if you are forced to guess at each question? What does this indicate about studying for such an exam?
  c. Suppose through some late-night studying you are able to correctly eliminate two answers on each question. Now answer parts **a** and **b**.

28. The Sertan Corporation makes replacement parts for videocassette recorders (VCRs) sold under a variety of name brands. The company has a contract with one of the leading VCR manufacturers to supply a certain part. The contract calls for 95% of all parts to be "good." Before shipping a lot of 5,000 parts, Sertan selected a random sample of fifty parts and found that four were defective.
  a. What is the probability that a sample will contain four or more defectives if the population of all parts meets the contract specifications? What conditions must be satisfied to employ the binomial distribution?
  b. Based on the probability computed in part **a**, would you conclude that the shipment is likely to meet the specifications in the contract? Discuss.

29. The Sertan Corporation discussed in the last problem has a contract to supply 5,000 parts to a company producing videocassette recorders. The contract specifies that 95% of the parts must be "good." Suppose the company sets up the following sampling plan before shipping out the parts. If a sample of fifty contains three or fewer defectives, the shipment will be considered acceptable. If it contains six or more defectives, it will be considered unacceptable.

Between three and six defectives in the sample will result in a second sample of fifty items.

  a. If the shipment really does meet the 95% "good" requirement, what is the probability that the first sample of fifty parts will lead the company to conclude incorrectly that the shipment is unacceptable?

  b. Suppose the shipment contains only 90% good parts. What is the probability that the first sample will lead to the company thinking the shipment actually does meet the 95% requirements?

  c. Based on your answers to parts **a** and **b,** what do you think of the sampling plan and why?

  d. What is the probability that the sample results on the first sample will lead to the necessity of a second sample? (Assume 95% good.)

30. After a recent freeze in Florida, the Sweetbrand Citrus Company was concerned about the quality of its grapefruit. Estimates by the Department of Agriculture indicated that 25% of the grapefruit were damaged by the freeze. The problem is that there seems to be no pattern to indicate which grapefruit suffered freeze damage. For instance, given two grapefruit growing side by side on a tree, one could be perfect and the other damaged. Suppose the Sweetbrand Company selected a random sample of fifty grapefruit.

  a. What conditions must be satisfied in order that the number of damaged grapefruit has a probability distribution described by the binomial distribution?

  b. Assuming that the binomial distribution does apply, what is the probability of finding less than five damaged grapefruit, given that the 25% estimate is correct?

  c. Assuming that the binomial distribution applies, what is the probability of finding more than twenty damaged grapefruit if the 25% estimate is correct?

  d. Referring to your answer to part **c,** suppose that the company actually did observe more than twenty damaged grapefruit in a sample of fifty. What might be concluded about the Department of Agriculture's 25% estimate? Discuss.

31. The Dade County Emergency Services dispatcher is trained to determine from the call received whether an emergency exists or whether the problem can be handled on a nonemergency basis. Past evidence indicates that 50% of calls are true emergencies.

  a. If the binomial distribution applies, develop the probability distribution for a sample of ten, and graph the distribution in histogram form. Does the distribution appear to be symmetric? Discuss.

  b. Referring to part **a,** suppose that the probability of a call being a true emergency is actually 70%. Develop the probability distribution, and graph the distribution in histogram form. Compare the distribution in part **a** with this one in terms of symmetry. Discuss.

32. Recently four women and eight men applied for a job at the Baxter Company. The personnel manager claimed that the applicants were so equally qualified that he made the selection of the three people hired by a totally

random process. The selection resulted in three men and no women being selected. The women have filed discrimination charges against the company. Based on probability, what would you conclude about the suit? Discuss.

33. Assuming that the customer arrivals at the Fidelity Credit Union drive-through window are Poisson-distributed with a mean of five per hour, find

   a. The probability that in a given hour more than eight customers will arrive at the drive-through window.

   b. The probability that between three and six customers, inclusive, will arrive at the drive-through window in a given hour.

   c. The probability that fewer than three customers will arrive at the window in a given 30-minute period.

34. The Hilgren Map Company produces topographical maps covering all parts of Utah, Arizona, and New Mexico. Past studies have indicated that the number of errors per map is Poisson-distributed, with an average of 0.5 error per map.

   a. What is the probability that a map will contain no errors?

   b. What is the probability that a map will contain fewer than three errors?

   c. What is the probability that a series of three maps will contain no errors?

   d. What is the probability that a map will have five or more errors? What would you conclude if this did occur? Discuss.

35. The State of Maine has an inspector who checks all painting work performed by the state's painting crew. Past experience indicates that the average number of mistakes per 500 square feet of painting is 3.5 and the distribution of mistakes follows a Poisson distribution.

   a. What is the probability that if the inspector checks 1,000 square feet she will not find a mistake?

   b. What is the probability in an inspection of 500 square feet that over seven mistakes are observed? What could be concluded if this did occur?

   c. Suppose the 3.5 figure is considered to be a standard for good work. If the inspector wants at most a 10% probability of unjustly criticizing the painters, how many errors should she allow before she makes a criticism for 500 square feet of painting?

36. It has been determined that vehicles arriving at a drive-through pharmacy window arrive according to a Poisson distribution at the rate of twelve per hour.

   a. In a half-hour time period, what is the probability that three or fewer cars will arrive at the window?

   b. In a 15-minute period, what is the probability that three or fewer cars will arrive at the window?

   c. If the pharmacist can serve four cars per half-hour, what is the probability that during the first half-hour of business a customer will not be served and will still be waiting in line when the half-hour period ends?

   d. Compute the variance and standard deviation for the probability distribution in part a.

37. The Askot Publishing Company publishes paperback romantic novels. At the page-proof stage, it has been determined that spelling errors appear randomly

and are independent of each other at an average rate of 1.3 errors per page ($\lambda = 1.3$). Suppose a proofreader has been hired to read a new book.

a. Develop the appropriate discrete probability distribution describing the number of errors in two pages of a book to be published.

b. If the proofreader does a perfect job, what is the average number of errors he will find for each two pages read?

c. What is the variance of the number of errors per two pages? What is the standard deviation?

d. Suppose a proofreader has just finished four pages and has found no errors. What are some of the possible conclusions you might reach and why?

38. Continue with the acceptance sampling example of Section 5-12. Consider the two probabilities given in the example. Use the binomial distribution to determine the probability distributions associated with samples of $n = 10$ and $n = 20$. Based on your experiences, which decision would you make for each of the possible outcomes for the two sample sizes?

CASES

5A   Great Plains Oil Company

Margaret Clemonts, operations vice-president of Great Plains Oil, is putting together a proposal for the board of directors. Great Plains has several refineries in the mid-central United States. For years it has relied on crude oil from its fields in Texas and the Gulf area. However, these fields are very mature and have declining outputs. Margaret has recently been buying foreign crude delivered to eastern United States ports. In addition, she has been considering trying to buy some extra Alaska crude from the West Coast. Her main problem up until now has been the extra cost of transporting Alaska oil to Great Plains refineries.

Margaret has recently learned about an unused natural gas pipeline that would drastically reduce the cost of bringing oil from the West Coast to the Great Plains refineries. Great Plains can buy the pipeline for a reasonable price and, in fact, could use the excess distribution capability to add to its cash flow by selling excess crude. The main drawback to the proposal is that the pipeline was built for gas and, therefore, may not be strong enough for the additional forces generated by transmitting crude oil. The pipe material is strong enough; however, the welds may not be.

The vast majority of the pipe is buried approximately 10 feet underground. The pipeline is made of 50-foot sections and, since it is approximately 1,000 miles long, there are some 110,000 separate welds. If the welds were solidly made, they will be strong enough to handle the crude oil. If the welds were not carefully made, they will need to be redone.

An industrial X-ray company has recently developed a small, portable machine that will travel through a pipe and X-ray each weld. However, this machine is very expensive to rent and requires the pipe to be cut periodically to extend the machine's power cables. Margaret does not want to use the machine unless she is sure she will recommend buying the pipeline. Once the line is bought, any faulty welds will have to be located and redone.

As part of the negotiation procedure, the pipeline owners have agreed to let Great Plains dig up sections of the pipe and X-ray a sample of welds. Margaret's industrial engineers have estimated that if 1% or fewer of the welds need to be redone, the pipeline will be a good investment. If 2% or more need to be redone, the pipeline should not be bought. Unfortunately, taking the sample X-rays will not be easy, and Margaret estimates that each X-ray will cost $5,000.

Margaret recognizes the problems of sampling, but thinks a representative random sample can be taken. She would be willing to spend up to $175,000 to determine whether the pipeline should be bought, but would not want to spend this entire amount if it is obvious that the pipeline should not be bought. She is presently devising her sampling plan.

5B   Midwest Van Lines, Part 1

Two years ago Midwest Van Lines signed a contract with Gray Manufacturing to be the exclusive hauler of Gray's complete line of major home appliances. Gray's previous policy was to award quarterly contracts for particular portions of its business, generally to the low-cost bidder. This policy was changed after its president started reading about the exclusive contracts many Japanese manufacturers sign.

Of particular concern to Gray's director of transportation was the shipping damage that seemed to occur with all transporters. Damaged appliances are sold at a markdown, which means less profit for Gray Manufacturing. A joint team of Midwest and Gray employees worked on a method to change the packing procedure, loading techniques, and tie-down points. Trial loads indicated that the expected damage rate during transport would be about 6%, a major reduction in the long-term average.

Periodic audits, while showing some variability in damage, indicated that 6% seemed to be an accurate assessment of the overall damage rate. However, the director of transportation just received a fax message from a major distributor of Gray's appliances in Cleveland. The fax stated that the last shipment of fifty appliances included six that were damaged. The distributor thought this was an excessive number and suggested that the director look into the possibility of some change in procedures that could have caused this level of damage.

The director faces two issues: how to respond to the distributor's complaint and whether to perform an extensive audit of shipping procedures. She is not sure these are necessarily related.

5C   Midwest Van Lines, Part 2

Shortly after resolving the complaint from the Cleveland distributor (see Case 5B), the director of transportation for Gray manufacturing received a call from the New England sales manager. The sales manager was upset because he had just given a major price reduction to the largest appliance distributor in New London, Connecticut. The distributor showed evidence that twelve of the last 100 appliances received had shipping damage. The sales manager said that he would suggest contracting with a new carrier if this trend continued. He closed the conversation by commenting, "Things like this didn't happen in the past when we expected a 10% damage rate."

Two complaints, coming so closely together after months of no problems, cause the director of transportation obvious concern. However, she does not want to panic if there is no cause.

REFERENCES

Daniel, Wayne W., and Terrell, James C. *Business Statistics for Management and Economics,* 6th ed. Boston: Houghton Mifflin, 1989.

Duncan, Acheson J. *Quality Control and Industrial Statistics.* 5th ed. Homewood, Ill.: Irwin, 1986.

Hogg, R. V., and Craig, A. T. *Introduction to Mathematical Statistics.* 4th ed. New York: Macmillan, 1978.

Mendenhall, William, Reinmuth, James E., and Beaver, Robert. *Statistics for Management and Economics,* 6th ed. Boston: PWS-Kent.

Continuous

Probability

Distributions

WHY DECISION MAKERS NEED TO KNOW

Chapter 5 introduced discrete random variables and discussed discrete probability distributions as they apply to the decision process. It also discussed three theoretical discrete probability distributions: the uniform, binomial, and Poisson. For discrete distributions, the variable of interest can take on only specific values. For example, the number of defective tires produced by the day shift at General Tire Company can have only integer values (0, 1, 2, etc.).

In many business applications the variable of interest is not restricted to integer values. For example, checkout times through a supermarket checkout stand can take on any value between zero and some large number, and the load weight carried by a freight truck can take on values between zero and some large number. Variables that are measured in units of time, weight, volume, or distance are often assumed to be *continuous* variables. Technically, a continuous variable is one that can take on an infinite number of values (measured to as many decimal places as necessary). Because of measuring limitations, some argue that there is no such thing as a truly continuous variable. They consider all variables discrete even though they can take on decimal values. This text defines a *continuous random variable* as a variable that can assume a large number of values between any two points.

Because many business applications involve continuous or quasi-continuous variables, decision makers need to become acquainted with continuous probability distributions and learn how to use them in decision making.

197

CHAPTER OBJECTIVES

This chapter will discuss the characteristics of continuous probability distributions. It will emphasize the normal distribution and illustrate how to apply this distribution in a decision-making environment.

STUDENT OBJECTIVES

After studying the material in this chapter, you should be able to do the following:

1. Discuss the important properties of the normal probability distribution.
2. Recognize when the normal distribution might apply in a decision-making process.
3. Calculate probabilities using the normal distribution table.
4. Use the normal distribution to describe how physical processes fail.

6-1 CONTINUOUS RANDOM VARIABLES

A discrete random variable has been defined as a variable that can have only a specific finite set of values. In many cases these discrete values are limited to integers. As illustrated in Chapter 5, many decision situations can be analyzed using discrete random variables and their associated probability distributions.

In many instances decision makers will be faced with random variables that can take on a seemingly unlimited number of values. Such a random variable is a continuous random variable. Figure 6-1 illustrates a continuous random variable and contrasts it with a discrete random variable. Here, the actual waist measurement is a continuous variable because it can assume any value along the scale. However, when the scale is divided into intervals, a discrete value can be assigned

FIGURE 6-1

Classification of Random Variables

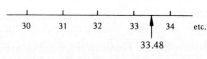

Men's Waist Measurements (Inches)

(a) Continuous Random Variable

Class No.

(b) Discrete Random Variable

to each waist size depending on where the size falls. In business decision making, many variables are defined as continuous, including:

Time measurements

Interest rates

Financial ratios

Income levels

Weight measurements

Distance measures

Volume measures

Chapter 5 discussed the problems facing the Boise Cascade Lumber mill manager when deciding how many log-scaling stations to open during a certain hour. The number of trucks arriving in that hour is a *discrete* random variable, but the time between arrivals (the interarrival time) is a *continuous* random variable. The time it takes to scale a truckload of logs is also a continuous random variable, and the amount of board feet of lumber on a truck still another.

In general, the value of a continuous random variable is found by *measuring*, whereas the value of a discrete random variable is determined by *counting*.

6-2 CONTINUOUS PROBABILITY DISTRIBUTIONS

In contrast to discrete case situations where the appropriate probability distribution can be represented by the areas of rectangles (histogram), the probability distribution of a continuous random variable is represented by a *probability density function*. Figure 6-2 illustrates a probability density function and shows its relationship to discrete probability distributions. Note that as the class width in the discrete examples becomes narrower, the top of the histogram approaches a smooth curve. This smooth curve represents the probability density function for a continuous variable.

Remember, discrete probability distributions have two characteristics. First, the rectangle representing each discrete value has an area corresponding to the probability of that value occurring. Second, the areas (probabilities) of all the rectangles must sum to 1.0. These two characteristics generally apply also to probability density functions. First of all, the total area (probability) under the density function curve must equal 1.0. In addition, the probability that the variable will have a value between any two points on the continuous scale equals the area under the curve between these two points. However, the probability that the variable will have any specific value cannot be determined because that probability would correspond to the area directly above a point. Because the area above a point is a line, and because a line has no width, it has no area and zero probability.

FIGURE **6-2**

FIGURE **6-2**

Comparison of a
Probability
Density Function
and Discrete
Probability
Distributions

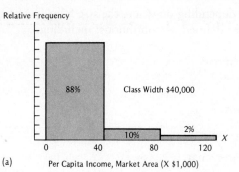

(a)

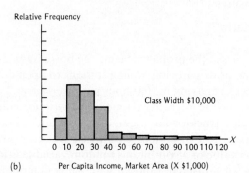

(b)

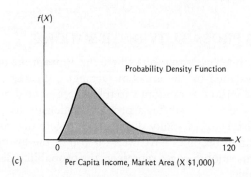

(c)

Since the probability of a single point on a continuous scale is zero, when dealing with continuous random variables we never consider the probability of a single value occurring. Rather, we consider the probability of a range of values occurring by finding the area under the density function for this range. For instance, we might ask, "What is the probability of a student in this class weighing 160 pounds?" If we mean exactly 160.0000 . . . , the probability is zero. If we mean any weight that would round to 160 pounds, i.e., 159.5 to 160.5 pounds, the question makes sense and we could find a probability.

6-3 CHARACTERISTICS OF THE NORMAL DISTRIBUTION

The most important continuous distribution in statistical decision making is the **normal distribution.** The normal distribution describes many physical situations where variation in a measured value occurs due to random, or unassignable, sources. Therefore, the distribution in populations such as the average weight gain of cattle in a feed lot, the power drain in a batch of integrated circuits, the rate of growth in a cloned planting of Douglas fir trees, and the average mileage among cars of the same type could all form a normal distribution. Most important, the normal distribution has a special place in statistical decision making, as we shall see in later chapters.

The normal distribution has the following properties:

1. It is *unimodal;* that is, the normal distribution peaks at a single value.
2. It is *symmetrical,* with the mean, median, and mode being equal. Symmetry assures us that 50% of the area under the curve lies left of the center and 50% lies right of the center.
3. It approaches the horizontal axis on either side of the mean toward plus and minus infinity ($\pm\infty$). In more formal terms, the normal distribution is *asymptotic* to the X-axis.

Figure 6-3 illustrates a typical normal distribution and highlights these three characteristics.

Although all normal distributions have the shape shown in Figure 6-3, their central locations and spreads can vary greatly depending on the situation being considered. The horizontal-axis scale is determined by the process being represented. It may be pounds, inches, dollars, or any other physical attribute with a continuous or quasi-continuous measurement. Figure 6-4 shows several normal distributions with different centers and different spreads. Note that the area under each normal "curve" equals 1.0.

FIGURE **6-3**

Characteristics
of a Normal
Distribution

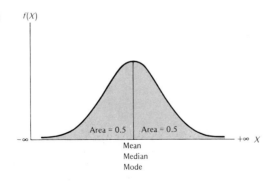

Characteristics:

1. Unimodal
2. Symmetric
3. Asymptotic to the X-axis in both directions

FIGURE **6-4**

Normal
Distributions
with Different
Locations and
Spreads

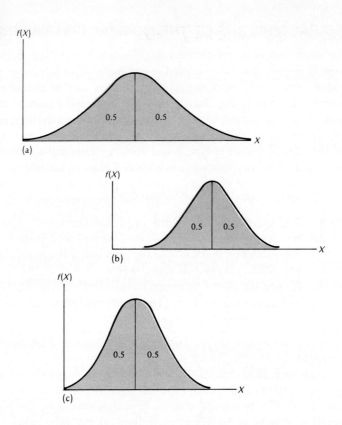

The normal distribution is defined by two parameters: μ_x, the population mean, and σ_x, the population standard deviation. Given these two values, the normal distribution is described by the probability density function of equation 6-1:

$$f(X) = \frac{1}{\sigma_x\sqrt{2\pi}}e^{-(X-\mu_x)^2/(2\sigma_x^2)}$$

6-1

where

X = Any value of the continuous random variable

σ_x = Population standard deviation

e = Base of the natural log ≈ 2.7183

μ_x = Population mean

Equation 6-1 will determine the height of the normal distribution curve for each possible value of the random variable X. If we were to substitute values for μ_x and

σ_x along with many values for X, the plot of $f(X)$ would be a curve similar to those shown in Figures 6-3 and 6-4.

Determining $f(X)$ requires only basic algebra. However, in business applications decision makers will rarely need to plot the normal distribution.

6-4 FINDING PROBABILITIES FROM A STANDARD NORMAL DISTRIBUTION

As indicated earlier, the probability of any particular value of a discrete random variable can be represented by an area in a relative frequency histogram. For example, Figure 6-5 shows a histogram for a binomial distribution with $n = 6$ and $p = 0.5$. The probabilities (areas) sum to 1.0, and the area above each value on the horizontal axis represents the probability of that value occurring. For example, the probability of exactly two successes in six trials ($n = 6$) is 0.2344. Likewise, the probability of observing values between any two points in a normal distribution is equal to the area under the normal curve between those two points. Figure 6-6 shows several examples.

Integral calculus is used to find the area under a normal distribution curve. However, we can avoid using calculus by transforming all normal distributions to fit the **standard normal distribution.** The principle behind the standard normal

FIGURE **6-5**

Binomial Distribution ($n = 6$, $p = 0.5$)

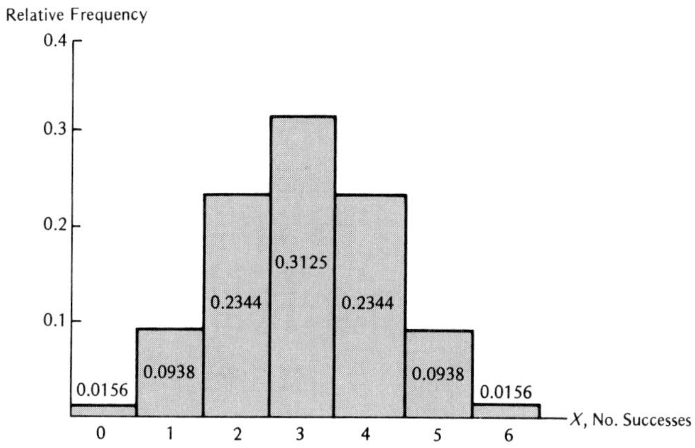

X	$P(X)$
0	0.0156
1	0.0938
2	0.2344
3	0.3125
4	0.2344
5	0.0938
6	0.0156
	$\Sigma = 1.0001^*$

*Difference due to rounding.

FIGURE 6-6

Areas and
Probabilities
for a Normal
Distribution

FIGURE 6-6

Areas and
Probabilities
for a Normal
Distribution

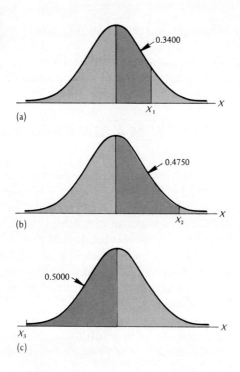

distribution is that all normal distributions can be converted to a common normal distribution with a common mean and standard deviation. This conversion is done by *rescaling* the normal distribution axis from its true units (time, weight, dollars, and so forth) to the standard measure referred to as a Z *value*. Thus, any value of the normally distributed continuous random variable can be represented by a unique Z value. The Z value is determined by equation 6-2:

$$Z = \frac{X - \mu_x}{\sigma_x} \qquad \text{6-2}$$

where

Z = Scaled value / standardscore

X = Any point on the horizontal axis / raw data

μ_x = Mean of the normal distribution / μ

σ_x = Standard deviation of the normal distribution / σ

FIGURE 6-7

Distribution of
Increases in Oil
Output Due to
Adding New
Enzyme

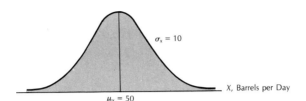

To use a simplified example to show how the standard normal distribution works, consider Westex Oil, which has home offices in Midland, Texas. Westex, an independent oil exploration and production company, was built by Tom Sanders after the oil embargo in the early 1970s. Tom had some initial success in finding small deposits of new oil, but most of the company's cash flow comes from wells it owns on established, and maturing, oil fields.

Even though most oil fields in the lower forty-eight states are maturing and facing declining production rates, substantial oil remains that is not recoverable by conventional means. Therefore, most oil producers experiment with ways to increase production from mature wells. One method is to inject water into a well to force out additional oil. Tom Sanders is considering adding a newly developed enzyme to the injected water but will do so only if the increased production is sufficient to cover the additional costs. Suppose the new enzyme will increase oil output by an average of fifty barrels a day, but because of differences in rock structures this output varies and has a standard deviation of ten barrels a day. Assuming the output increases can be represented by a normal distribution, Figure 6-7 shows the distribution of potential increases in oil output.

Suppose we select an increase level of $X = 50$ barrels per day. (Note that 50 is also μ_x, the mean increase.) We can find the Z value for this point using equation 6-2:

$$Z = \frac{X - \mu_x}{\sigma_x} = \frac{50 - 50}{10}$$
$$= 0$$

Thus, the Z value corresponding to the population mean, μ_x, is zero. This will be the case for all applications. Suppose we select sixty barrels per day as X. The Z value for this point is

$$Z = \frac{X - \mu_x}{\sigma_x} = \frac{60 - 50}{10} = \frac{10}{10}$$
$$= 1.00$$

Verify for yourself that $X = 40$ barrels per day corresponds to a Z value of -1.00. Note that a negative Z value indicates only that the specified value of X is less than the mean.

If we examine equation 6-2 and the previous examples carefully, we see that the Z value actually represents the number of standard deviations a point, X, is away from the population mean. In this Westex Oil example, σ_x, the standard deviation, is ten barrels per day. Therefore, an output increase of sixty barrels per day is exactly 1.00 standard deviation above $\mu_x = 50$ barrels per day. Likewise, an output increase of seventy barrels per day is 2.00 standard deviations above the mean.

Suppose Westex Oil can make an engineering change in injection techniques that will reduce the standard deviation to five barrels per day without changing the mean. Now an increase in output of sixty barrels per day is two standard deviations above the mean of fifty, and seventy barrels per day is 4.00 standard deviations above μ_x.

Thus, scaling an actual normal distribution to the standard normal distribution requires that we determine the Z values (number of standard deviations from μ_x) for any point on the horizontal axis. As shown, this is not a difficult process. Therefore, regardless of what situation we are dealing with, if the random variable is normally distributed, we can use the standard normal distribution, which is a special distribution with a mean of 0 and a standard deviation of 1. This offers some specific advantages when finding probabilities for ranges of values under the normal curve because a table of standard normal distribution probabilities has been developed. This table, which appears in Appendix C, lists a series of Z values and the corresponding probability that a random variable value will fall between that Z value and the mean of the distribution. Remember that the Z value is simply the number of standard deviations a point, X, is from the mean, μ_x. Therefore, if you want to know the probability that a value will lie within 1.00 standard deviation of the population mean, use the normal table as follows:

1. Go down the left-hand column of the table to $Z = 1.0$.
2. Go across the top row of the table to 0.00 for the second decimal place in $Z = 1.00$.
3. Find the value where the row and column found in steps 1 and 2 intersect.

Thus, the value 0.3413 is the probability that a value in a normal distribution will lie within 1.00 standard deviation *above* the population mean. Since the normal distribution is symmetrical, the probability that a value will lie within 1.00 standard deviation *below* the population mean is also 0.3413. Therefore the probability that a value will lie within 1.00 standard deviation of the population mean in *either* direction is $(0.3413 + 0.3413) = 0.6826$.

The same procedure is used to find the probability that a value will be within 2.00 standard deviations of the mean and within 3.00 standard deviations of the mean. Figure 6-8 illustrates these probabilities.

Let's return to the Westex Oil example. Recall that the mean increase in oil output was fifty barrels per day and the original standard deviation was ten barrels per day. However, Tom must try the enzyme on the wells he has and cannot afford to play the averages. He has estimated that the output level must be increased by at least forty-five barrels per day to pay for the additional cost of the enzyme injection. Therefore, if he tries the enzyme on one well, he is interested in the probability that production will be increased by forty-five or more barrels per

FIGURE 6-8

Standard Normal
Distribution
Probabilities

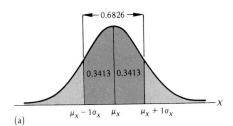

(a)

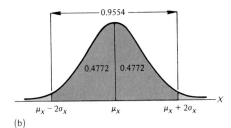

(b)

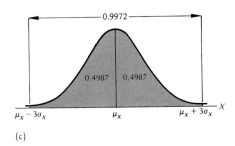

(c)

day. This probability corresponds to the area under the curve to the right of forty-five barrels per day:

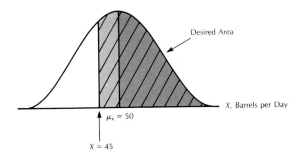

To use the standard normal table, we need to convert forty-five barrels per day to a Z value. This is equivalent to determining the number of standard deviations forty-five is from the mean:

$$Z = \frac{X - \mu_x}{\sigma_x} = \frac{45 - 50}{10}$$
$$= -0.50$$

The area corresponding to $Z = -0.50$ is 0.1915, shown under the normal curve:

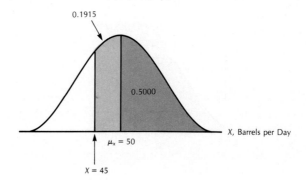

Since the normal curve is symmetrical and half the total area lies on each side of the mean, we can find $P(X \geq 45$ barrels per day) by adding 0.1915 to 0.5000:

$$0.1915 + 0.5000 = 0.6915$$

Thus, the probability that the well will increase production by enough to pay for the new enzyme is 0.6915.

As stressed many times in the preceding chapters, variation in a process cannot be completely avoided. Because of ever-present variation in the business world, decision makers face uncertainty. The best we can hope for is that this variation, and thus uncertainty, can be reduced. For example, we just calculated the probability as 0.6915 that introducing an enzyme in a mature oil well will be cost-effective. This means that slightly more than 30% of the time adding the enzyme will reduce profits. Tom Sanders, who must decide whether to try the new process, knows it is more likely to increase profits than to reduce them, yet is uncertain about what will happen with any single well. If he could find a way to reduce the standard deviation associated with output increases to five barrels per day, the uncertainty would be reduced because the probability of having a cost-effective well will be increased. We can calculate this probability as follows:

$$Z = \frac{X - \mu_x}{\sigma_x} = \frac{45 - 50}{5}$$
$$= -1.00$$

The following normal curve shows the area corresponding to the probability that adding the enzyme to a well will be cost-effective. Note that by developing a more consistent process, and thus reducing the standard deviation, we have increased the probability the enzyme injection will be cost-effective from 0.6915 to 0.8413.

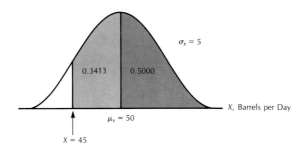

SKILL DEVELOPMENT PROBLEMS FOR SECTION 6-4

The following set of problems is meant to test your understanding of the material in this section.

1. Assuming that we have a normal distribution, find the following probabilities if the mean is 60 and the standard deviation is 10.
   a. $P(X > 60)$
   b. $P(X \geq 70)$
   c. $P(50 \leq X \leq 70)$
   d. $P(X \leq 40)$

2. For a normal distribution with a mean of 7.5 and a variance of 9, find the following probabilities:
   a. $P(X \geq 8.5)$
   b. $P(X \geq 6.5)$
   c. $P(X \geq 9.5)$
   d. $P(3 \leq X \leq 5.5)$

3. Find the following probabilities assuming a normal distribution with a mean of 7,450 and a standard deviation of 300:
   a. $P(X \leq 7,000)$
   b. $P(X \geq 8,000)$
   c. $P(X \geq 8,250)$
   d. $P(7,400 \leq X \leq 7,700)$

4. The average number of acres burned in August by forest and range fires in the western United States is 430,000, with a standard deviation of 75,000 acres. The distribution of the number of acres burned is normal.
   a. What is the probability in any year that more than 500,000 acres will be burned?
   b. What is the probability in any year that fewer then 400,000 acres will be burned?
   c. What is the probability that between 250,000 and 420,000 acres will be burned?
   d. In those years when more than 550,000 acres are burned, help is needed from eastern-region fire teams. What is the probability help will be needed in any year?

6-5 NORMAL APPROXIMATION TO THE BINOMIAL DISTRIBUTION

The binomial distribution discussed in Chapter 5 is not easy to work with when the sample size is larger than those found in the binomial table, or when the p values are not given in the table. In these cases, we would have to apply the binomial formula, which can be cumbersome. Fortunately, for large samples an *approximation* can be used.

As a rule of thumb, the normal distribution generally provides good approximations for binomial problems if the sample size is large enough to meet the following two conditions:

$$np \geq 5$$
$$nq \geq 5$$

where

n = Sample size

p = Probability of a success

$q = 1 - p$ = Probability of a failure

These conditions help ensure that the histogram formed by the binomial distribution is reasonably symmetrical and "looks like" a normal distribution. The best approximations occur when p approaches 0.5 and the sample size becomes large, because the binomial distribution approaches symmetry as p approaches 0.5. If $np \geq 5$ and $nq \geq 5$, the normal distribution can be used if we recall that for the binomial distribution, $\mu_x = np$ and $\sigma_x = \sqrt{npq}$. We can substitute these values into the Z formula and use the normal distribution table, as the following example illustrates.

A large retail store has discovered that 5% of its sales receipts contain some form of human error. Out of the next 1,000 sales made, the credit manager wants to know the probability that more than sixty errors will be made.

Since

$$np = (1,000)(0.05)$$
$$= 50 \geq 5$$

and

$$nq = (1,000)(0.95)$$
$$= 950 \geq 5$$

we will use the normal distribution to approximate the binomial. The first step is to determine the mean and standard deviation:

$$\mu_x = np = (1,000)(0.05)$$
$$= 50$$
$$\sigma_x = \sqrt{npq} = \sqrt{(1,000)(0.05)(0.95)}$$
$$= 6.89$$

Because the binomial distribution is a discrete distribution, we must make a slight modification when using the normal approximation. Specifically, we must treat sixty errors as the unit interval "59.5 to 60.5." Thus, the probability of *exactly* sixty errors will correspond to the area between 59.5 and 60.5 errors and the probability of *more* than sixty errors is found as follows:

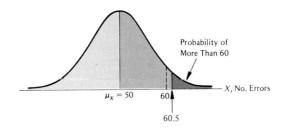

$$Z = \frac{X - \mu_x}{\sigma_x} = \frac{60.5 - 50.0}{6.89}$$
$$= 1.52$$

From the normal distribution table, the area between 60.5 and 50 ($Z = 1.52$) is 0.4357. Therefore the approximate probability of more than sixty incorrect sales slips is $(0.5000 - 0.4357) = 0.0643$.

Consider another example where the appropriate distribution is binomial but we can choose to approximate the probability using the normal approximation approach. In this example, we will compute both the exact probability, using the binomial distribution, and the approximate probability, using the normal distribution.

The American Chip Company manufactures computer memory chips for use in such products as digital watches and microwave oven controls. After checking and rechecking the product, records indicate that 6% of the chips actually delivered to customers are faulty. Recently the company was informed that a shipment of 100 chips contained four defectives. The quality control manager was asked to determine the probability of four or more defectives being shipped if, in fact, the 6% defective level was still valid.

To help her answer this question, we recognize that the appropriate probability distribution might likely be the binomial distribution since the random variable is discrete, with only two possible outcomes (*defective* or *nondefective*) per chip. Assuming that the binomial distribution does apply, we can find the exact probability of four or more defectives using either the binomial formula or, preferably, the binomial tables in the appendix. We do this as follows:

$$P(X_1 \geq 4) = 1 - P(X_1 < 4)$$

Using the binomial table with $n = 100$ and $p = 0.06$, we find

$$\begin{aligned} P(X_1 \geq 4) &= 1 - (0.0021 + 0.0131 + 0.0414 + 0.0864) \\ &= 1 - 0.1430 \\ &= 0.8570 \end{aligned}$$

Thus, the exact probability of four or more defectives being shipped by the American Chip Company is 0.8570. We say this is the exact probability because we assumed the underlying distribution is binomial and we did, in fact, use the binomial distribution to compute the probability.

Suppose, however, that we did not have available the binomial tables with $n = 100$ and $p = 0.06$, and we did not wish to use the binomial formula, which could be quite cumbersome for this problem. Instead, we can use the normal approximation to the binomial probability since

$$np = (100)(0.06) = 6 \qquad (6 \geq 5)$$

and

$$nq = (100)(0.94) = 94 \qquad (94 \geq 5)$$

In order to use the normal approximation, we need to know the mean and standard deviation. For the binomial distribution

$$\mu_x = np = 6$$

and

$$\sigma_x = \sqrt{npq} = 2.375$$

Then we draw a normal distribution as follows. The area of interest has been labeled. Take special notice that the 0.5 unit adjustment has been made, which is required anytime we use the normal distribution to approximate a discrete distribution such as the binomial.

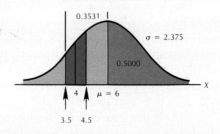

As we wish to find the probability of $X_1 \geq 4$, we will solve for the Z value using $X = 3.5$, which would include any value 4 or higher. This is shown as follows:

$$Z = \frac{3.5 - 6.0}{2.375}$$

$$= -1.0526 = -1.05$$

We next go to the normal distribution table for $Z = -1.05$ and find the area between 3.5 and the mean 6.0, which we find is 0.3531. As the diagram shows, the desired area can be found by adding 0.5000 to 0.3531, giving 0.8531. Thus, the normal approximation for the probability of four or more defective chips is 0.8531.

This approximation compares favorably with the exact probability of 0.8570 computed earlier from the binomial tables. Thus, the normal approximation can offer a good alternative under certain conditions to computing binomial probabilities using the binomial formula or the binomial tables.

SKILL DEVELOPMENT PROBLEMS FOR **SECTION 6-5**

The following set of problems is meant to test your understanding of the material in this section.

5. Using the normal approximation to the binomial distribution with $n = 250$ and $p = 0.1$:
    a. What is the probability a value from the distribution will have a value between 20 and 35?
    b. What is the probability a value from the distribution will have a value greater than 18?
    c. What is the probability a value from the distribution will have a value less than 22?
    d. What is the probability a value from the distribution will have a value less than 35?

6. Sun City Stages promotes 3-day weekend excursions to Las Vegas. A typical promotion will be staged for 150 people, who will be transported in three buses. Historical records indicate the no-show rate for people who call in to sign up for a tour will be 20%. If fewer than 115 people take part in a tour, Sun City will lose money. What is the probability the next tour will be profitable?

7. A quality control process at the Guidian Manufacturing plant calls for a random sample of 150 parts to be inspected. If the defective rate in the population is thought to be 0.076 and the underlying distribution is binomial, what is the probability of finding fewer than twenty-one defectives in the sample?

8. The X-Color Lab in Los Angeles attempts to produce pictures with a 98% success rate. To check on the quality control, a sample of 500 pictures has been selected. The distribution is assumed to be binomial.
    a. What is the expected number of defective pictures in the sample?

b. What is the standard deviation of the distribution?

c. What is the probability of finding between seven and thirteen defectives in the sample if the defective level is 2%?

6-6 QUALITY IMPROVEMENT AND CONTINUOUS DISTRIBUTIONS

Many modern quality improvement and process control ideas are based on the fact that the output of physical processes can be represented by a continuous distribution. In the context of the tools introduced in this chapter, the idea is to quantitatively measure the location and spread associated with output of the physical process. These measurements, when correctly applied, will allow decision makers not only to monitor the results of efforts to improve the quality of products or services, but also to determine when problems are occurring in the production process.

As discussed earlier in the chapter, the normal distribution describes more physical situations than any other distribution. So we will base the following discussion of using measures of location and spread on the normal distribution, although the concepts will apply no matter what underlying distribution describes the physical process we are considering.

HOW PHYSICAL PROCESSES FAIL

A key aspect of process control is maintaining a stable process. Only if the process is stable can changes be made to improve its operations. Unfortunately, much effort is required to maintain a stable process, and some mechanism is needed to determine when the process is not stable or is changing. While processes change in many ways, most of these can be categorized as being either a catastrophic failure or a gradual wearing out. Consider the following example.

Some people we know keep track of the mileage driven, and amount of gas bought, at each fill-up and then calculate the miles per gallon for their car. Not all fill-ups result in the same miles-per-gallon figure. Assume many of these values were calculated and plotted. A normal distribution would be the likely result. Assume that the normal distribution shown in Figure 6-9 represents the distribution of mileage values for one car. If a scatter plot of values taken from this distribution were made, we would see the graph shown in Figure 6-10, with the observations scattered around 32 miles per gallon. However, as cars age their

FIGURE 6-9

Normal
Distribution of
Mileage Values

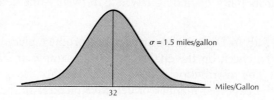

FIGURE **6-10**

Scatter Plot of
Average Mileage
Per Fill-Up

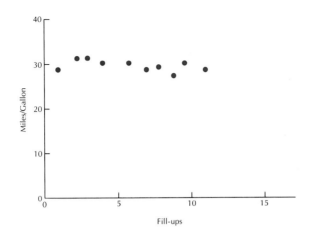

FIGURE **6-10**

Scatter Plot of
Average Mileage
Per Fill-Up

engines become less efficient and the mean of the normal distribution would
gradually decrease; then we would see the trend shown in Figure 6-11. A catastrophic failure, such as the fuel injector suddenly failing, would cause a sudden
shift in the distribution, as shown in Figure 6-12. Notice that the mean of the
distribution has dropped dramatically, but variation still exists around the lower

FIGURE **6-11**

Scatter Plot for
Trend as Engine
Ages

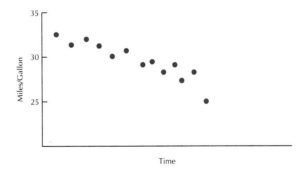

FIGURE **6-12**

Result of
Catastrophic
Failure

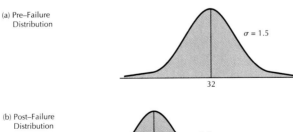

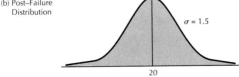

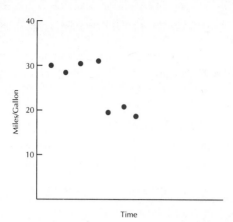

FIGURE 6-13

Scatter Plot
Showing
Catastrophic
Failure

mean. This sudden failure would be seen in the scatter plot of average mileage figures as shown in Figure 6-13.

Since physical processes fail either suddenly or gradually, a quality control system must have tools to detect both. These tools are based on continuous distributions and the measures of location and spread considered in this chapter. We will discuss them further in later chapters.

6-7 CONCLUSIONS

This chapter introduced continuous probability distributions, concentrating on the normal distribution. It showed the normal distribution, with its special properties, is used extensively in statistical decision making. It discussed in some detail the standard normal distribution and showed how it can be adapted to any normal distribution application. It also showed that the normal distribution can be used to approximate the binomial distribution under certain circumstances.

Subsequent chapters will introduce other continuous probability distributions. Among these will be the *t distribution,* the *chi-square distribution,* and the *F distribution.* These additional distributions play important roles in statistical decision making. The basic concept that the area under a continuous curve is equivalent to the probability is true for all continuous distributions.

The important statistical terms introduced in this chapter are summarized in the chapter glossary. The main statistical formulas presented in this chapter are listed following the glossary.

CHAPTER GLOSSARY

continuous probability distribution The probability distribution of a variable that can assume an infinitely large number of values. The probability of any single value is theoretically 0.

normal distribution A continuous distribution that is symmetrical (mean, median, and mode are all equal) and in theory has an infinite range.

standard normal distribution A normal distribution with a mean equal to 0 and a standard deviation equal to 1.0. All normal distributions can be standardized by forming a standard normal distribution of Z values.

CHAPTER FORMULAS

Normal distribution

$$f(X) = \frac{1}{\sigma_x \sqrt{2\pi}} e^{(X-\mu_x)^2/(2\sigma_x^2)}$$

Standard Z value

$$Z = \frac{X - \mu_x}{\sigma_x}$$

where

Z = Scaled value

X = Any point on the horizontal axis

μ_x = Mean of the normal distribution

σ_x = Standard deviation of the normal distribution

SOLVED PROBLEMS

1. The length of steel I-beams made by the Smokers City Steel Company is normally distributed, with $\mu_x = 25.1$ feet and $\sigma_x = 0.25$ foot.
   a. What is the probability that a steel beam will be less than 24.8 feet long?
   b. What is the probability that a steel beam will be more than 25.25 feet long?
   c. What is the probability that a steel beam will be between 24.9 and 25.7 feet long?
   d. What is the probability that a steel beam will be between 24.6 and 24.9 feet long?
   e. For a particular application, any beam less than 25 feet long must be scrapped. What is the probability that a beam will have to be scrapped?

Solution

To answer all these questions, we will use the following procedure:

1. Draw a picture to show what area we are interested in.
2. Find the desired Z value.

3. Use the normal distribution table to find the desired area under the normal distribution curve (the needed probability).

a.

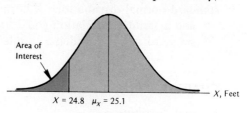

$$Z = \frac{X - \mu_x}{\sigma_x} = \frac{24.8 - 25.1}{0.25}$$

$$= \frac{-0.3}{0.25}$$

$$= -1.20$$

The negative sign means only that we are on the left half of the distribution.

From the normal distribution table, the area associated with a Z value of -1.20 is 0.3849. However, this is the area between 24.8 and 25.1 feet. We want the area less than 24.8 feet. We proceed as follows:

1. The total area under the curve (probability the beam will have some length) is 1.0.
2. The area under half the curve is 0.5.
3. The area we want is $0.5 - 0.3849 = 0.1151$.

b.

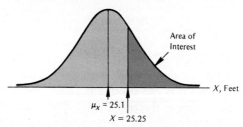

$$Z = \frac{X - \mu_x}{\sigma_x} = \frac{25.25 - 25.1}{0.25} = \frac{0.15}{0.25}$$

$$= 0.60$$

The area between 25.1 and 25.25 from the table is 0.2257. The area greater than 25.25 is $0.5 - 0.2257 = 0.2743$.

c.

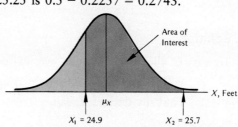

We do this problem in three steps:

1. Find the area between 25.1 and 25.7 feet.
2. Find the area between 24.9 and 25.1 feet.
3. Add the probabilities found in steps 1 and 2.

Therefore,

1. $Z = \dfrac{25.7 - 25.1}{0.25} = \dfrac{0.6}{0.25}$

   $= 2.40$

   From the table, area = 0.4918.

2. $Z = \dfrac{24.9 - 25.1}{0.25} = \dfrac{-0.2}{0.25}$

   $= -0.80$

   From the table, area = 0.2881.

3. Total area = 0.4918 + 0.2881 = 0.7799.

d.

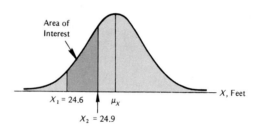

We also do this problem in three steps:

1. Find the area between 25.1 and 24.6.
2. Find the area between 25.1 and 24.9.
3. Subtract the area in step 2 from the area in step 1.

Therefore,

1. $Z = \dfrac{24.6 - 25.1}{0.25}$

   $= -2.0$

   From the table, area = 0.4772.

2. $Z = \dfrac{24.9 - 25.1}{0.25}$

   $= -0.80$

   From the table, area = 0.2881.

3. Desired area = 0.4772 − 0.2881 = 0.1891.

e.

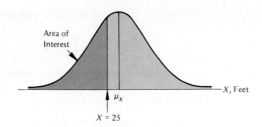

$$Z = \frac{25 - 25.1}{0.25} = \frac{-0.1}{0.25}$$

$$= -0.40$$

From the table, area = 0.1554. The probability we want is

$$0.5 - 0.1554 = 0.3446$$

Thus slightly more than 34% of the beams will have to be scrapped because they will not meet the required length.

2. The average absentee rate in large economics lecture sections has always been 15%. In a section of 200 students:
    a. What is the probability that on a given day 160 or more students will attend class?
    b. What is the probability that 180 or fewer students will attend?
    c. What is the probability that between 165 and 185 students will attend?

Solution

Since

$$np = (200)(0.15) = 30 \geq 5$$
$$n(1 - p) = (200)(0.85) = 170 \geq 5$$

we can use the normal approximation to the binomial. For all parts of this problem,

$$\mu_x = np = (200)(0.15)$$
$$= 30$$
$$\sigma_x = \sqrt{np(1 - p)} = \sqrt{(200)(0.15)(0.85)}$$
$$= 5.05$$

a. This part asks for the probability that forty or fewer students will be absent. We must use $X = 40.5$ because we are using a continuous distribution to approximate a discrete distribution. This is illustrated as follows:

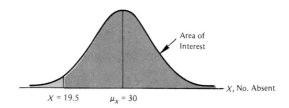

$$Z = \frac{40.5 - 30}{5.05} = 2.08$$

From the table, $Z = 2.08$ gives an area of 0.4812. We have

$$P(X \leq 40.5) = P(30 \text{ to } 40.5) + P(\text{less than } 30)$$

but since $P(\text{less than } 30) = 0.5$,

$$P(X \leq 40.5) = 0.4812 + 0.5$$
$$= 0.9812$$

b. We want the probability that twenty or more will be absent.

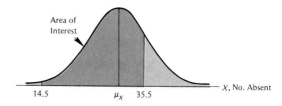

$$Z = \frac{19.5 - 30}{5.05}$$
$$= -2.08$$

From the table,

$$P(19.5 \text{ to } 30) = 0.4812$$

therefore,

$$P(X \geq 19.5) = P(19.5 \text{ to } 30) + P(\text{more than } 30) = 0.4812 + 0.5$$
$$= 0.9812$$

c. We want the probability that from fifteen to thirty-five students will be absent.

$$P(14.5 \text{ to } 35.5) = P(14.5 \text{ to } 30) + P(30 \text{ to } 35.5)$$

$$Z = \frac{14.5 - 30}{5.05} \qquad\qquad Z = \frac{35.5 - 30}{5.05}$$

$$= -3.07 \qquad\qquad\qquad = 1.09$$

$$\text{Area} = 0.4989 \qquad\qquad \text{Area} = 0.3621$$

So,

$$P(14.5 \text{ to } 35.5) = 0.4989 + 0.3621$$
$$= 0.8610$$

CONCEPTUAL QUESTIONS AND ASSIGNMENTS

9. Go to the library and locate two articles that use the normal distribution to describe the population of interest. Prepare a short report that discusses both the specific application being considered and how well the normal distribution represents the population being considered.

10. Discuss the requirements for using the normal distribution to approximate the binomial. Support your discussion by selecting a value of p and several sample sizes, n, and demonstrate that the approximation becomes better as the sample size increases.

11. Discuss the reasoning behind using the one-half unit correction factor when using the normal distribution to approximate the binomial. Formulate an example to support your discussion.

12. Discuss the difference between discrete and continuous probability distributions. Discuss two situations where a variable of interest may be considered either continuous or discrete.

ADDITIONAL PROBLEMS

13. The manager of consumer loans at Swiftview National Bank has determined that the average account balance is $700.00, with a median balance of $600.00. He has indicated that the distribution of account balances is a normal distribution. Comment on whether it is possible for a distribution to be normal if the mean and median are different.

14. The time spent by patients at a particular hospital has averaged 4.2 days, which is also the number of days in a median stay. In order for the distribution of patient length of stay to be normally distributed, what must the mode for length of stay be?

15. Suppose personal daily water usage in California is normally distributed, with a mean of 18 gallons and a standard deviation of 6 gallons.
    a. What percentage of the population uses more than 18 gallons?
    b. What percentage of the population uses between 10 and 20 gallons?
    c. What is the probability of finding a person who uses less than 10 gallons?

16.   Cattle are often fattened in a feedlot before being shipped to a slaughterhouse. Suppose the weight gain per steer at a feedlot averaged 1.5 pounds per day, with a standard deviation of 0.25 pound. Assume a normal distribution.
    a. What is the probability a steer will gain over 2 pounds on a given day?
    b. What is the probability a steer will gain between 1 and 2 pounds in any given day?
    c. What is the probability of selecting two steers that both gain less than 1.5 pounds on a given day, assuming the two are independent?
    d. Compute the probabilities found in parts **a, b,** and **c** assuming a standard deviation of 0.2 pound. Why are these probabilities different?

17.   The dollar amount of dairy products consumed per week by adults is thought to be normally distributed, with a mean of $4.50 and a standard deviation of $1.10.
    a. What is the probability that an individual adult from the population will consume over $4.90 in dairy products in a week?
    b. What is the probability that an individual selected at random from the population will consume less than $6.25 in dairy products in a week?
    c. What is the probability that a person will consume between $3.25 and $5.75 in dairy products in a week?

18.   Jamieson Airlines has a central office that takes reservations for all flights flown by the airline. The calls received during any week are normally distributed, with a mean of 12,000 and a standard deviation of 2,500.
    a. During what percentage of weeks does the airline receive more than 11,000 calls?
    b. During what percentage of weeks does it receive fewer than 12,300 calls?
    c. During what percentage of weeks does it receive between 10,800 and 13,400 calls?
    d. During what percentage of weeks does the airline receive more than 12,800 or fewer than 11,000 calls?

19.   The Ziegler Lumber Company sets the cut length on its 2 × 12 lumber a little longer than the specified length because its trim saw is fairly old. The mill foreman had discovered that the saw would cut any set length short by an average of 3 inches, with a standard deviation of 1.5 inches. Fortunately, the errors seem to be normally distributed.
    a. If the foreman is setting up the trim saw to cut 2 × 12 boards 10 feet long, what should the trim saw length setting be if he wants no more than a 5% chance of a board being shorter than 10 feet?
    b. Suppose the machine can be fixed so that the standard deviation in cut error can be controlled to a specified level. What would the standard deviation have to be in order that trim length could be set 1 inch shorter than the answer to part **a**?

20.   Problem 19 refers to the Ziegler Lumber Company, which discovered its old trim saw would cut any set length short by an average of 3 inches, with a standard deviation of 1.5 inches. The errors seen are normally distributed. Suppose an adjustment is made to the machine that reduces the average error

to 2 inches, but increases the standard deviation to 2 inches. What should the trim saw length setting be if the foreman wants no more than a 5% chance of a board being cut shorter than 10 feet?

21. The personnel manager for a large company is interested in the distribution of sick-leave hours for employees of her company. A recent study revealed the distribution to be approximately normal, with a mean of 58 hours per year and a standard deviation of 14 hours.

    An office manager in one division has reason to believe that during the past year, two of his employees have taken excessive sick leave relative to everyone else. The first employee used 74 hours of sick leave, and the second used 90 hours. What would you conclude about the office manager's claim and why?

22. Problem 21 considers a company's distribution of sick-leave hours for its employees. The personnel manager has found the distribution to be approximately normal, with a mean of 58 hours per year and standard deviation of 14 hours. Suppose the company grants 40 hours of paid sick leave per year. Given the sick-leave distribution, what would you conclude about the adequacy of the company's sick-leave policy? Why?

23. The preceding two problems deal with a company's distribution of sick-leave hours for its employees. The personnel manager has found the distribution to be approximately normal, with a mean of 58 hours per year and a standard deviation of 14 hours.

    Suppose the company is considering a change in its sick-leave policy for next year. The objective is to have the number of paid sick-leave hours at a level that will require 10% or fewer people to incur unpaid sick time. Assuming the historical sick-leave pattern holds true next year, how many sick-leave hours should be paid by the company?

24. This is the last of several problems dealing with a company's distribution of sick-leave hours for its employees, which the personnel manager has found to be approximately normal, with a mean of 58 hours per year and a standard deviation of 14 hours.

    Suppose a consultant has suggested the company hold its paid sick-leave hours to 40 hours per year and hire a physician who will serve employees at the plant in an attempt to reduce the average number of sick-leave hours used to a more acceptable level. What would the mean have to be if the probability of an individual needing more than 40 hours of sick leave is to be, at most, 10%? Assume the standard deviation remains 14 hours and the distribution is normal.

25. Suppose light bulbs are packed in boxes of 1,000 bulbs. Although the packers try their best, 10% of the bulbs get broken before they reach the retail stores.
    a. Using the normal approximation to the binomial distribution, find the probability that from 110 to 130 bulbs will be broken in a box.
    b. Using the normal approximation, find the probability that more than 130 bulbs will be broken.
    c. Suppose you have just found a box with 200 broken bulbs. Would you consider this unusual? Why or why not?

26. A market-research firm was hired to determine the percentage of people in a market area who would purchase *Playboy* magazine if a door-to-door sales campaign were undertaken. The firm stated that 40% would buy if contacted at home. Suppose the publisher has tried the sales campaign at 300 randomly selected homes.
    a. If the market research was accurate, what is the probability that fewer than 100 individuals will buy? Use the normal approximation to the binomial distribution.
    b. Suppose the publisher actually sells *Playboy* to seventy people out of the 300 contacted. What would you conclude about the market research and about the sales campaign, respectively?
    c. Assuming the market research was done properly and the 40% is representative, how many sales are expected if the publisher attempts to sell to 5,000 homes?

27. The firm of Anderson, Barnhart, and DuPuis is a C.P.A. firm in Lincoln, Nebraska. When its accountants perform audits, they often use sampling as a way of reducing the cost of audits. Recently they audited an automobile dealership, including the parts inventory. The inventory has 4,000 different part numbers. For each part number there is a stated inventory quantity on a computer listing.

    The accountants plan on sampling 100 part numbers and counting the actual inventory. They will then compare the actual inventory with the stated amount shown on the printout. They will record the number of "material" differences between actual and stated in the sample of 100 parts.
    a. If the true proportion of "material" errors is 10%, what is the probability that the sample will contain fewer than five parts with "material" errors? Use the normal approximation to the binomial.
    b. Use the binomial tables to solve part **a** and compare the two answers. Discuss why they are not exactly the same.

28. A market-research study indicates that 80% of all homes have a videocassette recorder for recording television programs.
    a. In a sample of 500 homes, what is the probability that from 375 to 425, inclusive, will have a videocassette recorder?
    b. In a sample of 1,000 homes, what is the probability that between 600 and 800 homes will have a recorder?

29. The Internal Revenue Service (IRS) has estimated that 60% of its audits find that there is either no change in the individual's tax or that the individual actually paid too much.
    a. If the IRS estimate is true, what is the probability that in a sample of 1,000 audits, from 500 to 600 individuals will not owe additional taxes?
    b. What is the probability in a random sample of 1,500 IRS audits that fewer than 800 will owe additional tax?

CASES

6A   East Mercy Medical Center

Dorothy Jacobs was recently hired as assistant administrator of the East Mercy Medical Center. She is a new graduate of a well-regarded master's degree program in hospital administration and is expected to incorporate some advanced thinking into the apparently lax practices at East Mercy.

Hospitals have recently been under increasing pressure from both government and local sources because of escalating costs. Although members of the board of directors of East Mercy feel that cost considerations are secondary to quality care, its members also are sensitive to the increasing public pressure.

East Mercy is located in a rapidly growing area and is experiencing capacity limitations. In particular, according to staff personnel, the obstetrics, adult medical/surgical, and pediatric wards are "bursting at the seams." East Mercy is considering an extensive expansion program, including expansion of the obstetric, adult medical/surgical, and pediatric wards. The board has allocated a total of $400,000 for new beds in these three wards. Dorothy is presently trying to determine how many beds current demand levels justify for each ward and how many beds to actually add, given the $400,000 cost constraint.

Dorothy and her staff have computed statistics based on the current year's patient census data in each of the three wards. These figures are as follows:

Ward	Average No. Beds Used per Day	Standard Deviation
Obstetrics	24	6.1
Surgery	13	4.3
Pediatrics	19	4.7

Histogram plots of bed usage show a remarkably close approximation to a normal distribution for each department.

The present capacity of each ward is

Obstetrics: 30

Surgery: 20

Pediatrics: 24

The hospital's architects have given the following estimates for the cost of adding one bed and all necessary supporting equipment to each of the wards:

Obstetrics: $20,000

Surgery: $26,000

Pediatrics: $15,500

It is possible for a ward to exceed its capacity, but according to state guidelines, this should not occur more than 5% of the time.

Dorothy is in the process of preparing a report to the administrator showing how many beds are to be added to each of the three wards.

6B High Country Ale

Ed Sharperson returned to his office dumbfounded by the reception he received on the carefully crafted marketing plan he created for High Country Ale, a potential new entry in the nonalcoholic beer market. Ed contended a well-planned entry into this market had a high probability of success for two reasons:

1. Recent data showed that the North American public is increasing its beer consumption.
2. The health and safety concerns about alcohol continue.

Ed's in-house testing has indicated that the product development group has done an outstanding job designing a process for removing the alcohol from beer and that the average person could not tell the difference between High Country Ale and any of the leading brands. His marketing campaign would be based on a take-off of the famous Schlitz Beer commercials of the early 1980s. The Schlitz commercials, which were run live, involved 100 Budweiser drinkers who were given two unidentified glasses of beer and asked to indicate which they liked better. Since the typical person cannot tell the difference between beers, about 50% said they preferred Schlitz.

Ed's plan was to run a series of live commercials, have 100 beer drinkers taste an unidentified glass of High Country Ale and each of the leading brands, find the same 50% preferring High Country Ale, and follow this with a campaign featuring the slogan,

Nonalcoholic—but tastes like real beer.

Christina Horowitz, the vice-president of marketing, complimented Ed on his "open-minded approach to marketing campaigns"—a phrase that always made him uneasy. She then asked a series of questions that Ed was unable to answer directly, such as,

"What procedures are you going to use to select the 100 people for the ad to ensure that the viewers do not think we have stacked the deck?"

"While the overall average may well be 50%, getting one group that had only 45%, or 40%, or even 35% prefer High Country Ale would be hard to explain. Could that happen?"

"What would be the implications of a series of tests, all of which show less than 50% prefer High Country? How about three or four tests where less than 40% prefer High Country? Could anything like this happen?"

"Also, viewers would probably not believe a group that showed 65% or 70% preferring High Country Ale. Could that happen?"

Ed assured her none of these issues would be a problem, but Christina said she needed more than his statement to approve the marketing campaign. Ed walked back to his office thinking about how some people always see problems where none exist. But he also vowed to be able to provide logical answers to her questions.

REFERENCES

Lapin, Lawrence. *Statistics for Modern Business Decisions.* 5th ed. New York: Harcourt Brace Jovanovich, 1990.

McClave, James T., and Benson, P. George. *Statistics for Business and Economics,* 5th ed. San Francisco: Dellen Publishing Co., 1991.

Neter, John; Wasserman, William; and Whitmore, G. A. *Applied Statistics.* 3d ed. Boston: Allyn and Bacon, 1988.

Sampling Techniques and the Sampling Distribution of $\overline{X}$

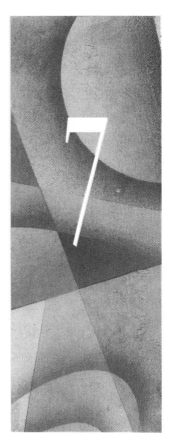

WHY DECISION MAKERS NEED TO KNOW

Many business decisions involve determining the average, or mean, of a set of data. For example, when deciding what brand of tires to purchase, the manager of a car-rental company wants to know which brand will give the longest average wear. In another example, light-bulb manufacturers are now required to indicate the average life of each type of bulb they make. These companies must somehow determine the mean life of the bulbs they manufacture.

Calculating the mean of a set of data presents no particular problem as long as the data are available. However, few business problems allow decision makers to measure the entire population of values. Either cost or time constraints limit the number of values they can use to calculate the mean. As stated in Chapter 1, these constraints are the main reason for sampling.

In practice, selecting a sample from a population in such a manner that valid statistical conclusions can be drawn about the population is a complicated task. Few managers need to be experts on sampling techniques, but all managers who rely on sample information should be aware of what is generally required for a sample to yield statistically sound results. This chapter introduces some commonly used sampling techniques.

After a sample is taken, and the mean of that sample calculated, the decision maker needs to recognize that the sample mean observed depends on which sample of the many possible samples is selected. Consequently, decision makers need to understand how the possible sample means are distributed. This chapter introduces the very important concept of *sampling distributions*.

CHAPTER OBJECTIVES

This chapter begins our discussion of how sample values are used to allow a decision maker to draw inferences about population values. But before any statistical relationships between sample values and population values can be drawn, a statistically valid sample must be taken. This chapter discusses some common sampling techniques.

This chapter also introduces the sampling distribution of $\overline{X}$. It will show that the value of $\overline{X}$ obtained depends on the particular sample selected. Thus, $\overline{X}$ comes from a distribution of possible sample means. The chapter also introduces one of the most important theorems in statistics—the central limit theorem—and will show how it is used in the decision-making process.

STUDENT OBJECTIVES

After studying the material in this chapter, you should be able to do the following:

1. Discuss the difference between statistical and nonstatistical sampling and describe four statistical sampling techniques: simple random sampling, stratified random sampling, systematic random sampling, and cluster random sampling.
2. Discuss the relationship between a population and the many samples that can be selected from it.
3. Explain why the central limit theorem is so important to statistical decision making.
4. Discuss the relationship between the sample size and the decisions that can be based on sample information.
5. Discuss how variation in the population affects decisions that can be based on sample information.

7-1 AN INTRODUCTION TO SAMPLING

Once a manager decides to gather information by sampling, there are many ways to select the sample. This section introduces several of the sampling techniques most often employed.

All sampling techniques fall into one of two categories: *statistical* or *nonstatistical*. *Statistical sampling* techniques include all those using *random* or *probability sampling*. With a random or probability sample, data items are selected by chance alone. Once the probabilities of selecting the items in the population are known, the individual selecting the sample does not change those probabilities. *Nonstatistical sampling*, or *nonprobability sampling*, is *nonrandom* in nature.

Both statistical and nonstatistical sampling techniques are commonly used by decision makers. However, nonstatistical sampling techniques have some widely recognized problems. For example, when a judgmental sample is selected, there is no objective means of evaluating the results. Because the results depend on personal judgment, their reliability cannot be measured using probability theory.

This does not imply that judgmental sampling is bad or should not be used. In fact, in many cases it represents the only feasible way to sample. For example, the J. R. Simplot Corporation, a manufacturer of frozen french fries, tests potatoes from each truck arriving at its manufacturing plant. The company uses the results of the sample to determine whether each truckload should be accepted. The quality control people use their judgment to select a few potatoes from the top of each truck rather than from throughout the load, as statistical sampling would require. It just is not feasible to take a statistical sample.

The remainder of this section discusses statistical and nonstatistical sampling techniques. While many techniques fall within each of these categories, only the most common will be covered.

STATISTICAL (PROBABILITY) SAMPLING TECHNIQUES

Simple Random Sampling

The most fundamental statistical sample is called a *simple random sample*. Simple random sampling is a method of selecting items from a population such that every possible sample of a specific size has an equal chance of being selected.

As an example, suppose a new insurance salesperson wishes to estimate the percentage of people in a local subdivision who already have life insurance policies. This would be important since the result would be an indication of the potential market in the subdivision. The population of interest consists of all families living in the subdivision.

For the purposes of our example, we will simplify the situation. Suppose there are five families in the subdivision: James, Sanchez, Lui, White, and Fitzpatrick. We will let N be the population size and n be the sample size. Then, from the five families ($N = 5$), we select three ($n = 3$) for the sample. Now we list the possible samples of size three that could be selected as follows:

James, Sanchez, Lui

James, Sanchez, White

James, Sanchez, Fitzpatrick

James, Lui, White

James, Lui, Fitzpatrick

James, White, Fitzpatrick

Sanchez, Lui, White

Sanchez, Lui, Fitzpatrick

Sanchez, White, Fitzpatrick

Lui, White, Fitzpatrick

In a correctly performed simple random sample, each of these samples would have an equal chance of being selected.

This example did not allow for a family to be selected more than once in a given sample. This condition is *sampling without replacement* and is the most common sampling condition. However, sometimes after an item has been selected for the sample it is replaced into the population and may be reselected. This is called *sampling with replacement*.

In some cases we will not be able to easily count the number of possible samples that could be selected due to the nature of the population. However, from a practical point of view, if every effort is made to select the individual items in a random fashion, the decision maker can be fairly sure that the sample will have the attributes of a simple random sample.

Simple random samples can be obtained in a variety of ways. We will present several examples to illustrate how simple random samples are selected in practice.

The Lottery   In those situations where a perception of fairness is important, simple random sampling is useful. For instance, shortly before the military draft ended, the U.S. Selective Service Commission adopted a *lottery* system to select draftees. The purpose was to eliminate any possible favoritism in determining who would be drafted. The lottery was held every year and the population consisted of all males who had turned 19 years old since the last lottery. Each male in this population was assigned a lottery number corresponding to his birthday. To assure a random selection of numbers, the following procedure was used:

1.   A rotating drum was filled with 365 balls, each corresponding to a specific day of the year.
2.   In front of a group of questioning members of Congress, news reporters, and television floodlights, the first ball (date) was selected from the drum. All individuals with this birthday were ranked number 1 in the draft priority system.
3.   After the first date was removed, the drum was closed, turned, and the next date selected. The procedure was repeated for all 365 dates. However, constructing a fair lottery is difficult since, as in this example, you must be sure that the balls in the drum are adequately mixed.

If you have given this procedure some thought, you should realize it would result in a random sample of days, but not necessarily of draft-age men. A random sample of draft-age men would occur if births were evenly distributed throughout the year.

The Random Number Table   Another way of selecting a random sample is to use a *random number table* like the one in Appendix H. Random number tables are constructed by recording values from a process that produces numbers which have the properties of randomness. Generally, random numbers are generated by computer routines.

Suppose the personnel department at a large retail store in Seattle is considering changing the pay period from once a month to every 2 weeks. Since the decision will affect all 400 Seattle employees, the personnel manager has decided to select a simple random sample of ten employees and ask their opinion about the change.

To select a random sample, each employee is assigned a number between 000 and 399. (For this application, no two employees will be assigned the same number.) The personnel manager decides on the following procedure for using the random number table:

1. Since each page of Appendix H has seventy rows and forty columns, pick two numbers, the first between one and seventy and the second between one and forty.
2. Use the first number to locate the *row* for the starting random number and the second number to locate the *column*.
3. Beginning with this starting point, select ten three-digit numbers by moving according to some predetermined pattern through the random number table. Assume we decide to move down the column. If the bottom of the table is reached before ten numbers are selected, go to the top of the next column and continue. If a number exceeds 399 or is repeated, skip it and go to the next number.

Assume the personnel manager picks 12 and 17 as the numbers used to locate the starting point. The starting point is the 2 found in row 12, column 17. The three-digit numbers and the actions associated with them are:

Number	Action
216	Select employee (1)
459	Skip number
134	Select employee (2)
834	Skip number
519	Skip number
378	Select employee (3)
031	Select employee (4)
966	Skip number
815	Skip number
096	Select employee (5)
192	Select employee (6)
026	Select employee (7)
831	Skip number
531	Skip number
441	Skip number
107	Select employee (8)
697	Skip number
530	Skip number
230	Select employee (9)
952	Skip number
344	Select employee (10)

The individuals whose numbers correspond to these three-digit numbers would be asked their opinions regarding the proposed change in pay periods.

Stratified Random Sampling

Suppose we have been asked to estimate the average cash holdings of Oregon financial institutions on July 1. We will base our estimate on a sample. However, not all of these financial institutions are the same size. A majority are classified as small, some are medium-sized, and only a few large-sized. However, the few large institutions have a substantial percentage of the total cash on hand in the state.

To ensure that the sample is representative of the cash holdings of institutions in the population, we could divide the institutions into three *classes:* small, medium, and large. We could then select a simple random sample of institutions from each group and estimate the average cash on hand from this combined sample.

What we have done is break the population (Oregon's financial institutions) into *subpopulations* called *strata.* Selecting simple random samples from predetermined subpopulations, or strata, is called *stratified random sampling.* Stratified random sampling is particularly useful when some subpopulations are relatively small and may be missed in a simple random sample. A stratified random sample guarantees we will obtain sample information from these subpopulations.

Populations can be stratified if they have a readily identifiable characteristic that can be used to separate the population members into subgroups. In our example, the identifiable characteristic is institution size. In other cases, the characteristic may be family size, location, or disposable personal income. In looking at company employees, we may stratify on the basis of sex, age, education, or race.

If done correctly, stratified sampling can be used to estimate a population's characteristics with *less error* than the same-size simple random sample. Since sample size is directly related to cost (in both time and money), this means a stratified sample can be more cost-effective than a simple random sample. Stratification is particularly useful when the population contains extreme points that can be grouped into separate strata. This will guarantee that some of the sample values include the extremes.

Let us look at another example where stratified random sampling could be used. A manufacturer of automotive replacement parts recently landed a contract with several national retailers to manufacture parts to be sold under the retailers' brand names. Because of these large contracts, the company was forced to move from a single-shift operation to a three-shift operation. The manufacturing company has begun to receive complaints about the quality of its parts. Before operations were expanded, quality complaints were rare. The company owner is concerned about the increasing complaints and discusses the situation with her production manager. The production manager thinks the increase in complaints could be due to any one of several things. First, because the plant is now used more extensively, the machines may go out of adjustment more quickly than in the past. Consequently, the solution may be to increase periodic maintenance.

Second, most of the quality control problems could be occurring in the two added shifts, in which case additional training is needed. Third, the complaints may be increasing because the national retailers offer well-advertised money-back guarantees, in which case the complaints will likely continue.

The production manager has some historical quality information and therefore decides to sample the present output. He has decided to perform a stratified sample by shift. With results from the stratified sample, the production manager feels he will be able to identify the cause of the complaints and to recommend the correct course of action. Note, however, that once the population has been stratified, simple random sampling is used to select items from each stratum.

Systematic Sampling

Recently, the National Association of Accountants (the NAA is an association of managerial accountants as opposed to public accountants) was considering establishing a code of ethics. To determine the opinion of the 20,000 members about this issue, a questionnaire was sent to a sample of 500 members.

Simple random sampling would involve assigning a unique number to each member and using a random number table to select the sample of 500. (A computer could also be used if the membership lists are stored on disk or tape files. The computer could be programmed to generate random numbers similar to those in the table in Appendix H.)

An alternative to selecting a simple random sample would be to send the questionnaire to every 40th member from the list of members. The procedure would involve using a random number table to select a number between 1 and 40 for the starting point. Using the random starting point, each 40th member would be selected. If the starting point were 25, the sample would be

$$
\left.\begin{array}{r}
25 \\
65 \\
105 \\
145 \\
. \\
. \\
. \\
19{,}985
\end{array}\right\} \quad n = 500
$$

Selecting a sample based on this type of predetermined system is called *systematic sampling*. Systematic sampling is frequently used in business applications. Systematic sampling should be used as an alternative to simple random sampling only when the population is randomly ordered. For example, NAA members were listed alphabetically. To use systematic sampling in this case, we must assume that individual opinion is randomly distributed through the alphabet.[1]

---

[1] There are more statistically precise indications of when systematic sampling can be used instead of simple random sampling. See Leslie Kish, *Survey Sampling*, 113–142.

Systematic sampling, when applicable, has specific advantages. First, a systematic sample is easy to select. A highly trained expert is not needed to select, say, every 100th name from a membership list or every third house in a subdivision. Also, depending on the characteristics of the population, a systematic sample can be more evenly distributed across the population and thus be more representative.

Cluster Sampling

Taking a random sample requires not only that we randomly determine who or what from the population will be in the sample, but also that those selected be contacted and measured. This is not a problem when the population is an incoming shipment of transistors. This is a problem when the population members selected for the sample are scattered across the country or the world.

Suppose the Morrison–Knudsen Company, one of the largest construction companies in the world, wants to develop a new corporate bidding strategy. Upper management wants input on possible new strategies from its middle-level managers. Figure 7-1 illustrates the hypothetical distribution of middle-level managers throughout the world. For example, there are twenty-five middle-level managers in Algeria, forty-seven in Illinois, and so forth. Upper management decided to have personal interviews with a sample of these employees.

FIGURE 7-1 Number of Middle-level Managers at Various Geographical Locations of Morrison–Knudsen

One sampling technique is to select a simple random sample of size n from the population of middle managers. Unfortunately, this technique would likely require that the interviewer(s) go to each state or country where Morrison–Knudsen has middle-level managers. This would prove an expensive and timeconsuming process. A systematic or stratified sampling procedure also would probably require visiting each location.

A sampling technique that overcomes the traveling (time and money) problem is *simple cluster sampling*. Cluster sampling is a method by which the population is divided into groups, or clusters, and a sample of clusters is taken to represent the population. Once the clusters are chosen, sampling of items from each cluster may be undertaken. In the Morrison–Knudsen example, the clusters are the geographical locations of the middle-level managers. As shown in Figure 7-1, this example has ten clusters. Notice that clusters are determined by the physical locations of the population. This is different from stratified sampling, where strata are determined by some measurable characteristic of the items in the population.

The first step in the simple cluster sampling is to randomly select various clusters (m) from the total possible clusters (M). Suppose Morrison–Knudsen randomly selects the following three clusters:

The interview team can either question all middle managers in these three locations or select a random sample at each location, depending on the desired sample size and the cost of sampling. Suppose they randomly sample from each primary cluster, and they select the following number of managers from the chosen clusters:

$$
\left.
\begin{array}{ll}
\text{Mexico} & 15 \\
\text{Alaska} & 8 \\
\text{Algeria} & 12
\end{array}
\right\} \text{Ultimate clusters}
$$

Cluster sampling can be used in a variety of ways. Table 7-1 illustrates the relationship between population, population members, and clusters for this example and several other possible clusters.

TABLE 7-1

Examples of Possible Clusters

Population	Variable of Interest	Individual Elements	Clusters
Middle managers	Ideas on bidding strategies	Persons	Area locations
People in Boston	Political preference	Persons	City block
San Francisco workers	Commuting distance	Persons	Office building
Houses in Atlanta	Price	Houses	Subdivisions
Automobiles produced in Detroit	Mileage	Automobiles	State of current location
Harvard University students	Parents' income	Persons	Class standing

NONPROBABILITY SAMPLING TECHNIQUES

The simple random, stratified random, systematic, and cluster sampling techniques discussed up to now are all examples of probability samples. When a probability sample is selected, there are a variety of statistical techniques available to analyze the sample data, as you will see in the remaining chapters of this text.

However, sometimes a probability sample is either not possible or not desirable. In these instances, *nonprobability sampling* is used. One example of nonprobability sampling is *judgment sampling*. In judgment sampling, the person taking the sample has direct or indirect control over which items are selected for the sample. Judgment sampling is appropriate when decision makers believe that some population members have more or better information than other members.

Judgment sampling is also used when the decision makers think that some population members are more representative of the population than others. For instance, if you had to pick only one city in the United States in which to test market a new product, you probably would not select that city randomly. You would be likely to pick the city for a reason, such as, "Los Angeles is good for new products and it tends to lead the country," or "Never introduce anything new in the Midwest." You would probably also use a judgment sample if you could select only two cities, or three, or four. However, if you could select twenty-five cities to test market your product, you might very well choose these cities randomly.

Of course a judgment sample is only as good as the people doing the sampling. If poor judgment is used, the information gathered may be nonrepresentative and misleading. For example, a decision maker can easily bias an opinion survey by sampling only individuals who share similar opinions.

Other nonprobability samples include *quota sampling* and *convenience sampling*. In quota sampling, the decision maker requires the sample to contain a certain number of items with a given characteristic. For example, suppose an opinion survey is to be taken in a factory employing 60% males and 40% females. If the sample size is 1,000, the sampling quota might be 600 randomly selected males and 400 randomly selected females. Many political polls are, in part, quota samples.

With convenience sampling the decision maker selects a sample from the population in a manner that is relatively easy and convenient. For example, the Flathead Cherry Association operates a cherry warehouse in Polson, Montana. During the picking season in early August, cherry growers bring truckloads of cherries to the warehouse in lugs weighing about 20 pounds each. As the trucks are unloaded, each lug moves along a conveyor and over a scale that weighs it. Next, an individual selects several cherries from the top of each lug and places them into a sack marked with the grower's name and the load number. When the truck is completely unloaded, the sample of cherries in the sack is graded by inspectors and the price per pound paid to the grower is determined for that load of cherries.

In this case the sampling process would not meet the definition of random sampling, but it is a convenient method of sampling. The cherry association and the growers should be aware, however, of the risks associated with their sampling techniques. For example, it is possible that cherries on top of each lug may not be representative of the remaining cherries in the lugs. Also, the quality of cherries may not be evenly distributed throughout all lugs in the load.

Market research firms also use convenience sampling as a means of obtaining data on consumer buying habits. For example, you may have encountered individuals located outside supermarkets or department stores who ask people a series of questions related to their purchases, the store, and general demographics. No effort is made to select a statistically valid sample. Rather, the researchers rely on the convenience of the sampling technique to allow them to interview a large number of people who they hope represent the targeted population.

Although nonprobability sampling is often used in decision-making situations, it has some serious potential problems. The greatest of these is that if you use a nonprobability sample you have no way of assessing the probability of reaching a correct conclusion from the sample information.

7-2 RELATIONSHIP BETWEEN SAMPLE DATA AND POPULATION VALUES

Decision makers are faced with a problem in addition to the problems associated with correctly gathering and arranging data in an understandable manner. This problem is that two samples from the same population are likely to have different sample values and therefore possibly lead to different decisions. The following examples will demonstrate what this means.

Suppose the investment officer at SeaSide State Bank handles the retirement fund for all state government employees. Although most of the retirement money is invested in government bonds, the officer has been increasing the amount invested in corporate stocks.

The retirement committee, composed of state government employees, is naturally concerned with the rate of return being earned by the invested dollars. The greater this return, the larger the retirement fund will be and the greater the benefits to the employees when they retire. The committee has asked the investment officer to determine the average return for money invested in stocks only.

For the purposes of this example, assume the money has been invested in five stocks, with an equal amount in each stock. The returns on each stock last year were

Stock	Return
A	7%
B	12%
C	-3%
D	21%
E	3%

With only five stocks, the investment officer could easily report the population mean, μ_x, to the employee committee. The population mean is given in equation 7-1:

$$\mu_x = \frac{\Sigma X}{N} \qquad \text{7-1}$$

where

X = Individual returns for the stocks

N = Population size

Thus,

$$\mu_x = \frac{7\% + 12\% + (-3\%) + 21\% + 3\%}{5}$$

$$= 8\%$$

To more fully describe the stock returns, the investment officer might also calculate the population standard deviation (equation 7-2):

$$\sigma_x = \sqrt{\frac{\Sigma(X - \mu_x)^2}{N}} \qquad \text{7-2}$$

Thus,

$$\sigma_x = \sqrt{\frac{(7 - 8)^2 + (12 - 8)^2 + (-3 - 8)^2 + (21 - 8)^2 + (3 - 8)^2}{5}}$$

$$= 8.15\%$$

However, for this example, the investment officer has decided to select a simple random sample of three stocks and base her report on this sample. Although she will select only one sample, there are several possible samples from which to choose. We can determine exactly how many possible samples of three stocks can be selected without replacement from a population size of five by recognizing this as a combinations problem (equation 7-3):

$$_NC_n = \frac{N!}{n!(N - n)!} \qquad \text{7-3}$$

Thus,

$$_5C_3 = \frac{5!}{3!(5-3)!}$$

$$= 10 \text{ possible samples}$$

Table 7-2 lists the ten possible samples and the sample mean, $\overline{X}$, of each. Since the $\overline{X}$ values range from 2.33% to 13.33%, the value of the sample mean reported to the employee committee will depend on the sample selected. The reported sample mean will also be different from the true population mean, although some samples have a mean closer to the true value than others.

TABLE **7-2**

Possible Samples
for SeaSide State
Bank Example

Sample Stocks	Returns	$\overline{X}$
A, B, C	7%, 12%, −3%	5.33
A, B, D	7%, 12%, 21%	13.33
A, B, E	7%, 12%, 3%	7.33
A, C, D	7%, −3%, 21%	8.33
A, C, E	7%, −3%, 3%	2.33
A, D, E	7%, 21%, 3%	10.33
B, C, D	12%, −3%, 21%	10.00
B, C, E	12%, −3%, 3%	4.00
B, D, E	12%, 21%, 3%	12.00
C, D, E	−3%, 21%, 3%	7.00

where

$$\overline{X} = \frac{\Sigma X}{n}$$

n = Sample size

SKILL DEVELOPMENT PROBLEMS FOR **SECTION 7-2**

The following set of problems is meant to test your understanding of the material in this section.

1.   Consider the following population of values:

   33   41   17   27   35   23   24   19

   a.   Determine the population mean and standard deviation.
   b.   If you were to select a sample of four from the population, how many possible samples could you select?
   c.   Use a random sampling procedure to select five samples of four and determine the mean and standard deviation of each sample.

2. Consider the following population of values:

   71 58 55 67 61 77 65 49 80 72

   a. Determine the population mean and standard deviation.
   b. If you were to select a sample of three from this population, how many possible samples could you select?
   c. Use a random sampling procedure to select five samples of three and determine the mean and standard deviation of each sample.

3. Tom Scott, Inc., distributes mining equipment made in several European Community countries. The company has midsize computers in each of its seven district sales offices. Last year the maintenance costs on the seven computers were as follows:

   $17,593 $14,295 $15,608 $10,255 $9,118 $19,895 $13,495

   a. What is the average maintenance cost?
   b. If the company auditors were to select three districts to do an extensive audit, how many different samples of three could they select?
   c. Randomly select three districts and determine the sample average maintenance cost.

7-3   SAMPLING ERROR

The investment officer at SeaSide State Bank is going to select only one of the ten possible samples. Notice in Table 7-2 that no sample mean equals the population mean of 8%. Thus, her report to the employee committee will contain *sampling error*.

   Sampling error is the difference between a population value and the corresponding sample value. The amount of sampling error is determined by which $\overline{X}$ value is found. In the SeaSide example, if $\overline{X} = 8.33\%$, the sampling error is fairly small. However, if $\overline{X} = 13.33\%$, the sampling error is quite large. Because the investment officer cannot know how large the sampling error will be before selecting the sample, she should know how the possible sample means are distributed. The distribution of possible sample means is called the **sampling distribution of $\overline{X}$.**

SAMPLING DISTRIBUTION OF $\overline{X}$

We can use the SeaSide State Bank example to illustrate two important concepts for statistical decision making. The first concerns the relationship between the population mean, μ_x, and the average of the possible sample means, $\mu_{\overline{x}}$. We often call $\mu_{\overline{x}}$ the *mean of the sample means*. We find $\mu_{\overline{x}}$ from equation 7-4:

$$\mu_{\overline{x}} = \frac{\sum\limits_{i=1}^{K} \overline{X}_i}{K}$$

where

$\overline{X}_i$ = ith sample mean

K = Number of possible samples

Then

$$\mu_{\overline{x}} = \frac{5.33\% + 13.33\% + 7.33\% + \cdots + 7.00\%}{10}$$

$$= 8\%$$

We see that $\mu_{\overline{x}}$, the average of all possible sample means, equals the true population mean, μ_x. This will always be true because $\overline{X}$ is an **unbiased estimator** of μ_x, the population mean. We will discuss the concept of unbiased estimates more fully in Chapter 8.

The second important concept concerns the relationship between the population standard deviation and the *standard deviation of the sample means*. The population returns ranged from -3% to 21%. However, Table 7-2 illustrates that the sample means range from 2.33% to 13.33%. The distribution of sample means is less variable than the population from which the samples were taken.

Recall that in our example, the population standard deviation, σ_x, is 8.15%. Since there are only ten possible samples, we can calculate the standard deviation of the sample means, $\sigma_{\overline{x}}$, as follows:

$$\sigma_{\overline{x}} = \sqrt{\frac{\sum\limits_{i=1}^{K} (\overline{X}_i - \mu_{\overline{x}})^2}{K}}$$

Therefore,

$$\sigma_{\overline{x}} = \sqrt{\frac{(5.33 - 8.0)^2 + (13.33 - 8.0)^2 + \cdots + (7.0 - 8.0)^2}{10}}$$

$$= \sqrt{11.07}$$

$$= 3.326$$

Note that $\sigma_{\overline{x}} = 3.326\%$ is less than $\sigma_x = 8.15\%$. In fact, $\sigma_{\overline{x}}$ will be less than the population standard deviation, σ_x, for any application.

The value $\sigma_{\overline{x}}$, also called the **standard error of the mean**, indicates the spread in the distribution of all possible sample means.

SKILL DEVELOPMENT PROBLEMS FOR **SECTION 7-3**

The following set of problems is meant to test your understanding of the material in this section.

4. Consider the following population of values:

    39   33   47   41   30   23   28   50

    a. Determine the population mean and standard deviation.
    b. If you were to select a sample of four from this population, how many possible samples could you select?
    c. Use a random sampling procedure to select five samples of four and determine the mean and standard deviation of each sample.
    d. For each of the five samples selected in part c, determine the sampling error.

5. Consider the following population of values:

    171   258   155   367   261   177   165   449   280   172

    a. Determine the population mean and standard deviation.
    b. If you were to select a sample of three from this population, how many possible samples could you select?
    c. Use a random sampling procedure to select five samples of three and determine the mean and standard deviation of each sample.
    d. For each of the five samples selected in part c, determine the sampling error.

6. Problem 3 in the preceding section considered Tom Scott, Inc., which distributes mining equipment made in several European Community countries. The company has midsize computers in each of its seven district sales offices. Last year the maintenance costs on the seven computers were

    $17,593 $14,295 $15,608 $10,255 $9,118 $19,895 $13,495

    The company auditors selected three districts to do an extensive audit.
    Randomly select four samples of three districts and determine the average maintenance cost for each sample. Give the sampling error associated with each sample and discuss how you think the auditors should deal with this error.

7-4 SAMPLING FROM NORMAL DISTRIBUTIONS

In more realistic situations with larger populations, the number of possible $\overline{X}$ values can become very large. For example, if a sample of five is selected from a population of 100, the number of possible samples is

$$_{100}C_5 = \frac{100!}{5!95!}$$

$$= 75,287,520$$

In applications where the number of possible samples is very large, we cannot possibly calculate all the possible sample means to find $\sigma_{\overline{x}}$ and $\mu_{\overline{x}}$. However, two important theorems allow decision makers to describe the distribution of sample means for any distribution. Theorem 7-1 is the first of these.

Theorem 7-1

If a population is normally distributed, with mean μ_x and standard deviation σ_x, the sampling distribution of $\overline{X}$ values is also normally distributed, with $\mu_{\overline{x}} = \mu_x$ and $\sigma_{\overline{x}} = \sigma_x/\sqrt{n}$.

Figure 7-2 shows a normal population distribution and two sampling distributions. As Theorem 7-1 states, the average of the sample means, $\mu_{\overline{x}}$, equals the population mean, μ_x. Figure 7-2 also shows that the spread of the sampling

FIGURE 7-2

Relationship between Normal Population and Sampling Distribution of $\overline{X}$

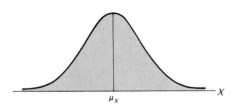

(a) Population Distribution

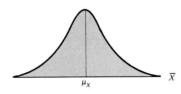

(b) Sampling Distribution, $n = 8$

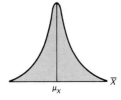

(c) Sampling Distribution, $n = 64$

distribution decreases as the sample size increases. From Theorem 7-1, the standard error of the mean is given by equation 7-5:

$$\sigma_{\bar{x}} = \frac{\sigma_x}{\sqrt{n}} \qquad \text{7-5}$$

where

σ_x = Population standard deviation

n = Sample size

Suppose scores for all students taking a standard college entrance examination are normally distributed, with $\mu_x = 80$ and $\sigma_x = 10$. If a random sample of 100 scores is selected, the sampling distribution of possible $\overline{X}$ values will be normally distributed, with

$$\mu_{\bar{x}} = \mu_x = 80$$

and

$$\sigma_{\bar{x}} = \frac{\sigma_x}{\sqrt{n}} = \frac{10}{\sqrt{100}} = 1.0$$

We see that the spread of the sampling distribution, $\sigma_{\bar{x}} = 1.0$, is considerably smaller than the spread of the population, $\sigma_x = 10$. Because the population standard deviation is divided by the square root of the sample size, as the sample size increases, the standard deviation of the sample means decreases. If the sample size were 400 instead of 100 scores, the mean of the sampling distribution would still be 80, but the standard deviation of the sampling distribution would be reduced to 0.50.

$$\sigma_{\bar{x}} = \frac{\sigma_x}{\sqrt{n}} = \frac{10}{\sqrt{400}} = 0.5$$

$\sigma_{\bar{x}}$ is a measure of average sampling error. Therefore, increasing the sample size will reduce the average sampling error.

SKILL DEVELOPMENT PROBLEMS FOR **SECTION 7-4**

The following set of problems is meant to test your understanding of the material in this section.

7. A population is normally distributed, with a mean of 58 and a standard deviation of 10.
   a. If a sample of nine is taken from the population (assume it is less than 5% of the population), what is the mean of all possible samples?

b. What is the measure of average sampling error?

c. How are the values changed if the sample size is changed to twenty?

8. A population is normally distributed, with a mean of 117 and a standard deviation of 30.

a. If a sample of twenty is taken from the population (assume less than 5% of the population), what is the mean of all possible samples?

b. What is the measure of average sampling error?

c. How are the values changed if the sample size is changed to forty?

d. What would the sample size have to be to reduce the standard error to half that found in part **b**?

9. The Adam's Food King chain employs over 3,000 people. The workers' ages are approximately normally distributed, with a mean of 31 and a standard deviation of 4.3 years. The company is thinking of introducing a health-care package, and its insurance company wants to sample twenty-five workers before quoting a price.

a. What is the probability the sample of twenty-five will have an average age less than 31?

b. What is the value of the standard error associated with this sample?

c. What can the insurance company do to reduce the standard error?

7-5 SAMPLING FROM NONNORMAL POPULATIONS

Theorem 7-1 applies only if the population from which the sample is selected is normally distributed. As discussed in Chapter 6, there are many instances where the population of interest can be assumed to be normally distributed. However, there are many other applications where the population of interest will not be normally distributed. If the population is nonnormal, Theorem 7-1 cannot be used. In this case, however, Theorem 7-2—the **central limit theorem**—does apply.

> Theorem 7-2
>
> **Central Limit Theorem**
>
> If random samples of n observations are taken from any population with mean μ_x and standard deviation σ_x, and if n is large enough, the distribution of possible $\overline{X}$ values will be approximately normal, with $\mu_{\overline{x}} = \mu_x$ and $\sigma_{\overline{x}} = \sigma_x/\sqrt{n}$, regardless of the population distribution. The approximation becomes increasingly more accurate as the sample size, n, increases.

An important question when using the central limit theorem is how large a "large" sample size is. Although there is no exact answer to this question, if the population is symmetric and unimodal about μ_x, sample sizes of four or five will produce approximately normal sampling distributions. In other cases where the

FIGURE 7-3

Central Limit
Theorem,
Population
Normally
Distributed

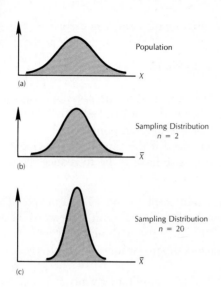

population is extremely skewed, sample sizes of more than twenty-five are required to produce a normal sampling distribution. Many have adopted the rule of
thumb that $n \geq 30$ will provide a distribution of sample means that is approximately normally distributed. We will also adopt this rule.

To more clearly see the relationship between increasing sample size and the
application of the central limit theorem, see Figures 7-3 through 7-6, which show
various population distributions and the resulting sampling distributions of $\overline{X}$ for
various sample sizes. These examples were originally developed using a computer
program that could quickly select large numbers of samples and plot the sampling

FIGURE 7-4

Central Limit
Theorem,
Uniform
Population
Distribution

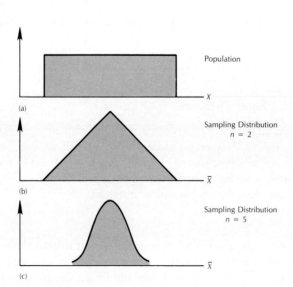

FIGURE 7-5

Central Limit
Theorem,
Exponential
Population
Distribution

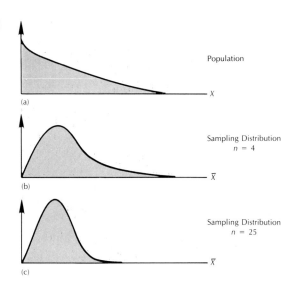

distributions. Note that in Figure 7-3 the population itself is normal, so the sampling distribution is also normal, even for sample sizes as small as two. Figure 7-4 shows, for a population that is uniformly distributed, that the sampling distribution is approximately normal for sample sizes as small as $n = 5$.

The populations in Figures 7-5 and 7-6 are less symmetrical and, as can be seen, larger samples are required before the sampling distribution approximates a normal distribution. Note also that Figures 7-3 through 7-6 show that the spread of the sampling distribution decreases as the size of the sample is increased, which is consistent with what the central limit theorem indicates should occur.

FIGURE 7-6

Central Limit
Theorem,
Triangular
Population
Distribution

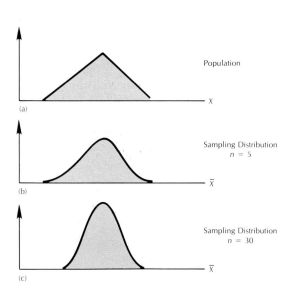

7-6 THE FINITE CORRECTION FACTOR

Both Theorems 7-1 and 7-2 assume either that sampling is done *with replacement* or that the population is large relative to the sample size. If sampling is done *without replacement* and the sample size is large relative to the population, a modification must be made in calculating $\sigma_{\bar{x}}$. If n is greater than 5% of the population size and sampling is performed without replacement, equation 7-6 applies:

$$\sigma_{\bar{x}} = \frac{\sigma_x}{\sqrt{n}} \sqrt{\frac{N - n}{N - 1}} \qquad \text{7-6}$$

where

$$\sigma_x = \text{Population standard deviation}$$
$$n = \text{Sample size}$$
$$N = \text{Population size}$$
$$\sqrt{\frac{N - n}{N - 1}} = \text{Finite correction factor}$$

In the SeaSide Bank example, the population mean, μ_x, was 8%, and the population standard deviation, σ_x, was 8.15%. Owing to the small number of possible samples (10), we were able to calculate $\sigma_{\bar{x}} = 3.326$. Because $n = 3$ is greater than 5% of $N = 5$ and sampling was without replacement, we can also use equation 7-6 to find $\sigma_{\bar{x}}$:

$$\sigma_{\bar{x}} = \frac{\sigma_x}{\sqrt{n}} \sqrt{\frac{N - n}{N - 1}} = \frac{8.15}{\sqrt{3}} \sqrt{\frac{5 - 3}{5 - 1}}$$
$$= 3.327$$

The term $\sqrt{(N - n)/(N - 1)}$ is called the **finite correction factor** and is used if we are sampling without replacement and the sample size is large relative to the population. Note that the finite correction factor is always less than 1.0 and that as the population gets large relative to the sample size, the factor approaches 1.0.

SKILL DEVELOPMENT PROBLEMS FOR **SECTIONS 7-5 AND 7-6**

The following set of problems is meant to test your understanding of the material in these sections.

10. A population of 100 has a mean of 17.5 and a standard deviation of 2.2. If a sample of thirty-five is taken from the population, what is the mean of the distribution of all possible samples of thirty-five? What is the standard deviation of the distribution of all possible sample means?

11. A population of 350 has a mean of 36.7 and a standard deviation of 6.3. If a sample of forty is taken from the population, what is the mean of the distribution of all possible samples of forty? What is the standard deviation of the distribution of all possible sample means?

12. SeaFair Fashions relies on its sales force of 217 to do an initial screen of all new fashions. The company is presently bringing out a new line of swimwear and has invited forty salespeople to its Orlando home office. An issue of constant concern to the SeaFair sales office is the volume of orders generated by each salesperson. Last year the overall company average was $417,330 with a standard deviation of $45,285.
   a. What is the probability the sample of forty will have a sales average less than that of the entire sales force?
   b. What shape do you think the distribution of all possible samples of forty will have? Discuss.
   c. What is the value of the standard deviation of the distribution of all possible samples of forty?
   d. How would the answers to parts **a, b,** and **c** change if the home office brought sixty salespeople to Orlando?

7-7 DECISION MAKING AND THE SAMPLING DISTRIBUTION OF $\overline{X}$

The concepts discussed in this chapter are extremely important to decision makers. The following example will demonstrate how the theorems are used in a decision environment. In this example, remember to distinguish among

1. The population distribution
2. The distribution of all possible sample means
3. The mean of a single sample

These are three different factors in the decision-making situation and should not be confused with one another.

Because of legislated mileage requirements, the major U.S. automobile makers are being forced to build smaller, lighter cars. In building cars with smaller exteriors, the auto makers want to maintain interior dimensions that are comfortable for the majority of U.S. car buyers. One important dimension for riding comfort is the distance between the floorboard and the bottom of the dashboard. If this distance is too small, the rider's knees will hit the dash. Unfortunately for the auto makers, the distance from the foot to the knee is not the same for all car buyers.

Suppose the average foot-to-knee length for the population is $\mu_x = 20$ inches and the population standard deviation is $\sigma_x = 3$ inches. One maker has decided to select a random sample of potential customers to test the riding comfort of its latest compact car. The product design manager wants the test group to represent the population as a whole. The average foot-to-knee length for the test sample of thirty-six people is 21.5 inches. The product design manager wishes to know whether this group is an unlikely selection from a population with $\mu_x = 20$ and $\sigma_x = 3$.

To help the product design manager, we employ the central limit theorem. Thus, the distribution of possible $\overline{X}$ values will be approximately normal, with $\mu_{\overline{x}} = \mu_x$ and $\sigma_{\overline{x}} = \sigma_x/\sqrt{n}$. This sampling distribution is shown as follows:

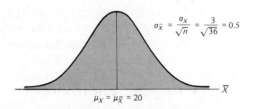

$$\sigma_{\overline{x}} = \frac{\sigma_x}{\sqrt{n}} = \frac{3}{\sqrt{36}} = 0.5$$

$$\mu_x = \mu_{\overline{x}} = 20$$

The sample mean selected is 21.5 inches. When the product design manager wonders if this sample mean is an unlikely selection, he is really wondering about the chances of finding an $\overline{X} \geq 21.5$ inches. This probability is represented by the darkest area in the following normal curve:

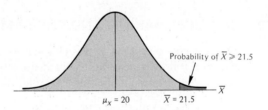

Probability of $\overline{X} \geq 21.5$

$\mu_x = 20$ $\overline{X} = 21.5$

Recall that to find areas under the normal curve, we first standardize the distribution so that we can work with Z values, where Z represents the number of standard deviations a value is from the mean. When working with a sampling distribution, we find the Z value from equation 7-7 or 7-8:

$$Z = \frac{\overline{X} - \mu_x}{\sigma_{\overline{x}}} \qquad \text{7-7}$$

or

$$Z = \frac{\overline{X} - \mu_x}{\dfrac{\sigma_x}{\sqrt{n}}} \qquad \text{7-8}$$

If sampling is done without replacement and n is greater than 5% of the population, equation 7-9 is used:

$$Z = \frac{\overline{X} - \mu_x}{\dfrac{\sigma_x}{\sqrt{n}}\sqrt{\dfrac{N - n}{N - 1}}}$$

7-9

In the auto maker example, the sample size, $n = 36$, is certainly small relative to the population size, so we will use equation 7-8:

$$Z = \frac{\overline{X} - \mu_x}{\dfrac{\sigma_x}{\sqrt{n}}} = \frac{21.5 - 20}{\dfrac{3}{\sqrt{36}}}$$

$$= 3.00$$

Thus, an $\overline{X}$ of 21.5 is 3.00 standard deviations above $\mu_x = 20$. From the standard normal distribution table in Appendix C, the area corresponding to $Z = 3.00$ is 0.4987:

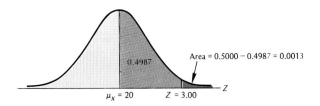

The probability of finding a sample mean equal to or greater than 21.5 inches is only 0.0013. Since this probability is so small, the product design manager would most likely not want to use these thirty-six people to test the new car's comfort because they have foot-to-knee lengths that apparently do not represent the population.

SKILL DEVELOPMENT PROBLEMS FOR SECTION 7-7

The following set of problems is meant to test your understanding of the material in this section.

13. A sample of forty is taken from a population with a mean of 87.6 and a standard deviation of 14.4.
    a. What is the probability the sample mean will be greater than 90?
    b. What is the probability the sample mean will be less than 86.5?

    c.   What is the probability the sample mean will be between 85 and 87.3?

    d.   What is the probability the sample mean will be either less than 86.2 or more than 88?

14.   A sample of thirty is taken from a population with a mean of 165 and a standard deviation of 25.

    a.   What is the probability the sample mean will be greater than 170?

    b.   What is the probability the sample mean will be less than 160?

    c.   What is the probability the sample mean will be between 150 and 160?

    d.   What is the probability the sample mean will be either less than 170 or more than 180?

15.   The UPSAT Company markets a computerized study guide that the company claims will greatly improve high school seniors' average SAT scores. In its advertising, the company says that students who have once taken the test will increase their overall score by an average of 40 points. The company is presently being sued in state court by an irritated student whose score did not go up at all. The company claims that its advertising refers to overall averages and so one individual score may go up by more or less than the advertised amount and that the standard deviation of the increases is 15 points.

    a.   Accepting the company's claim, what is the probability a student could show no increase in overall score?

    b.   The student's lawyer forces the company to allow her to see a random sample of thirty test scores. The sample average increase is 32. What is the probability of seeing a sample average this high or higher if the company's claim is correct?

    c.   Based on the available sample evidence, do you think the company's advertising claim is truthful?

7-8 CONCLUSIONS

When a manager selects a sample, it is only one of many samples that could have been selected. Consequently the sample mean, $\overline{X}$, is only one of the many possible sample means that could have been found. There is no reason to believe that the single $\overline{X}$ value will equal the population mean, μ_x. The difference between $\overline{X}$ and μ_x is called *sampling error*. Because sampling error exists, decision makers must be aware of how the sample means are distributed in order to discuss the potential sampling error.

This chapter introduced two important theorems. These theorems describe the distribution of sample means taken from any population. The more important of these theorems is the central limit theorem. Much of the material in Chapters 9, 10, and 11 is based on the central limit theorem.

The important aspect of the central limit theorem is that no matter how the population is distributed, if the sample size is large enough, the sampling distribution will be approximately normal.

    This chapter has presented the development of the sampling distributions for $\overline{X}$. Much of the discussion in the next few chapters is based on the concept of a normally distributed sampling distribution.

    The chapter also presented several new statistical terms, which are listed in the chapter glossary. Be sure you understand each one and how it applies to the material in this chapter. You will encounter these terms many times as you continue in this text.

    A summary of the statistical equations used in this chapter follows the glossary.

CHAPTER **GLOSSARY**

central limit theorem For random samples of n observations selected from any population with mean μ_x and standard deviation σ_x, if n is large, the distribution of possible $\overline{X}$ values will be approximately normal with $\mu_{\overline{x}} = \mu_x$ and $\sigma_{\overline{x}} = \sigma_x/\sqrt{n}$. The approximation improves as n becomes larger.

finite correction factor The factor used to adjust $\sigma_{\overline{x}}$ when sampling is done without replacement and the sample size is more than 5% of the population size.

sampling error The difference between a population value and the corresponding sample value. Sampling error occurs when the sample does not perfectly represent the population from which it was selected.

standard error of the mean A measure of the average sampling error. It is determined by dividing the population standard deviation by the square root of the sample size.

unbiased estimator An unbiased estimator of a population value is an estimator whose expected value equals the population value. For example, $E(\overline{X}) = \mu_x$. The average of all possible sample means will equal the population mean.

CHAPTER FORMULAS

Population mean

$$\mu_x = \frac{\Sigma X}{N}$$

Population standard deviation

$$\sigma_x = \sqrt{\frac{\Sigma(X - \mu_x)^2}{N}}$$

Combinations (number of possible samples of size n)

$$_NC_n = \frac{N!}{n!(N - n)!}$$

Sample mean

$$\overline{X} = \frac{\Sigma X}{n}$$

Standard error of the mean

$$\sigma_{\overline{x}} = \frac{\sigma_x}{\sqrt{n}}$$

and

$$\sigma_{\overline{x}} = \frac{\sigma_x}{\sqrt{n}} \sqrt{\frac{N-n}{N-1}}$$

Finite correction factor

$$\sqrt{\frac{N-n}{N-1}}$$

Z value for sample mean, $\overline{X}$

$$Z = \frac{\overline{X} - \mu_x}{\sigma_{\overline{x}}}$$

or

$$Z = \frac{\overline{X} - \mu_x}{\dfrac{\sigma_x}{\sqrt{n}}}$$

If sampling is done without replacement and $n > 5\%$ of the population,

$$Z = \frac{\overline{X} - \mu_x}{\dfrac{\sigma_x}{\sqrt{n}} \sqrt{\dfrac{N-n}{N-1}}}$$

SOLVED PROBLEMS

1. In a local agriculture reporting area, the average wheat yield is known to be 60 bushels per acre, with a standard deviation of 10 bushels.
   a. If a random sample of 64 acres is selected and the wheat yield recorded, what is the probability the sample mean will lie between 59 and 61 bushels?
   b. Suppose a sample size of 49 acres is selected. What is the probability the same mean will lie between 59 and 61 bushels?
   c. Why is the probability found in part **b** different from that found in part **a**?

Solution

a. The sampling distribution will be normally distributed with $\mu_{\bar{x}} = 60$ and $\sigma_{\bar{x}} = 10/\sqrt{64}$, as follows:

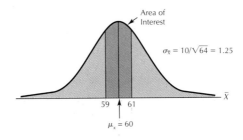

We standardize the sampling distribution by determining the Z values for $\overline{X} = 59$ and $\overline{X} = 61$:

$$Z = \frac{59 - 60}{\dfrac{10}{\sqrt{64}}} \quad \text{and} \quad Z = \frac{61 - 60}{\dfrac{10}{\sqrt{64}}}$$

$$= \frac{-1.0}{1.25} \qquad\qquad\qquad = \frac{1.0}{1.25}$$

$$= -0.80 \qquad\qquad\qquad = 0.80$$

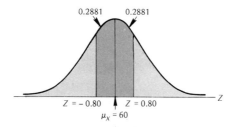

The probability can be determined by adding the areas corresponding to $Z = -0.80$ and $Z = 0.80$. From the normal distribution table in Appendix C, the area corresponding to a Z of -0.80 is 0.2881. The area corresponding to a Z of 0.80 is also 0.2881. Therefore, the probability that an $\overline{X}$ value will lie between 59 and 61 bushels for a sample of 64 acres is $(0.2881 + 0.2881) = 0.5762$.

b. The solution here is the same as for part **a** except that $\sigma_{\bar{x}}$ is increased because of the smaller sample size. Therefore,

$$\mu_{\bar{x}} = 60$$

$$\sigma_{\bar{x}} = \frac{10}{\sqrt{49}}$$

$$\approx 1.429$$

Thus,

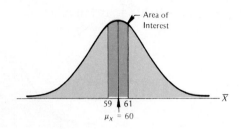

and

$$Z = \frac{59 - 60}{\dfrac{10}{\sqrt{49}}} \quad \text{and} \quad Z = \frac{61 - 60}{\dfrac{10}{\sqrt{49}}}$$

$$= \frac{-1.0}{1.429} \qquad\qquad = \frac{1.0}{1.429}$$

$$= -0.70 \qquad\qquad\qquad = 0.70$$

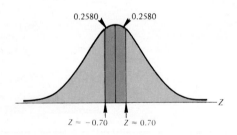

The probability, therefore, is $(0.2580 + 0.2580) = 0.5160$.

c. When the sample size is reduced (from 64 to 49), the probability of obtaining a sample mean between 59 and 61 is reduced. With a smaller sample size, the sampling distribution is more spread out, giving a greater opportunity for extreme $\overline{X}$ values.

2. A local insurance company has 240 employees, who have an average annual salary of $31,000. The standard deviation of annual salaries is $5,000.

a. In a random sample of 100 employees, what is the probability the average salary will exceed $31,500?

b. What is the probability the sample mean found in part **a** will be less than $32,000?

c. Why does the finite correction factor need to be used in determining $\sigma_{\overline{x}}$?

Solution

a.

$$\mu_{\overline{x}} = 31,000$$

$$\sigma_{\overline{x}} = \frac{\sigma_x}{\sqrt{n}} \sqrt{\frac{N-n}{N-1}}$$

$$= \frac{5,000}{\sqrt{100}} \sqrt{\frac{240-100}{239}}$$

$$= 382.68$$

$$Z = \frac{\overline{X} - \mu_x}{\dfrac{\sigma_x}{\sqrt{n}} \sqrt{\dfrac{N-n}{N-1}}}$$

$$= \frac{31,500 - 31,000}{382.68}$$

$$= 1.31$$

From Appendix C, the area corresponding to a Z of 1.31 is 0.4049.

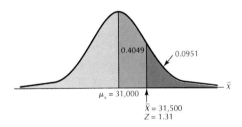

The probability of $\overline{X} \geq 31,500$ is 0.0951.

b. To find the probability the mean salary of 100 employees will be less than \$32,000, we must find the following area:

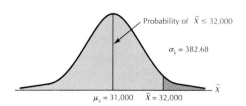

Then

$$Z = \frac{32,000 - 31,000}{382.68}$$

$$= 2.61$$

From the normal distribution table in Appendix C, the area corresponding to $Z = 2.61$ is 0.4955. The probability of an $\overline{X}$ value below 32,000 is, therefore, $(0.5000 + 0.4955) = 0.9955$.

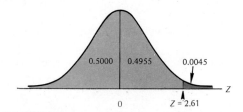

c. The finite correction factor must be used in determining $\sigma_{\overline{x}}$ because the sample size is quite large relative to the population size and the sampling is assumed to be without replacement.

CONCEPTUAL QUESTIONS AND ASSIGNMENTS

16. Define in your own words what a simple random sample is and provide a business example where such a sample could be used.

17. Define in your own words what a stratified random sample is and give a business example where such a sample could be used.

18. Suppose a retail store is considering expanding into a new market area. As part of the study, the store's managers wish to find out more about peoples' spending habits for the kind of goods the new store would sell. Assuming the market area is about the size of your hometown, how might the managers select a sample of individuals to talk to?

19. In Problem 18, the market area was reasonably small (the size of your hometown). How might your response change in terms of the type of sampling if the market area were about the size of your state?

20. Define in your own words what is meant by *cluster sampling* and indicate why it might offer an advantage over other types of statistical sampling.

21. Under what circumstances might a decision maker use nonprobability sampling techniques rather than probability sampling techniques?

22. Discuss the circumstances under which a systematic sample might be selected and provide an example of how such a sample might be obtained.

23. Discuss why the sampling distribution will be less variable than the population distribution. Give a short example to illustrate your answer.

24. Discuss why the standard error of a sampling distribution is considered a measure of average sampling error.

ADDITIONAL PROBLEMS

25. The maker of Creamy Good Ice Cream is concerned about the quality of ice cream being produced by its Illinois plant. Discuss a plan by which the Creamy Good managers might determine the percentage of defective cartons of ice cream. Would it be possible or feasible to take a census?

26. A random sample of skiers at the Aspen Ski Resort was selected by the makers of a particular brand of skiing equipment. Their method for selecting the sample required that individuals waiting in one of the lift lines be asked questions about various brands of skiing equipment. Comment on the method of sampling and indicate how you would design a sampling technique that might produce more statistically valid results.

27. If you were designing a stratified random sampling plan for a survey of city governments in your state to find out the amount of money they are spending on administrative salaries, what criteria might you use to form the strata? Provide several ideas and indicate the one that might give the best results.

28. Using the random number table in Appendix H, discuss how a simple random sample of service station operators in your city could be selected.

29. Student leaders often poll students to obtain opinions on topics of interest such as athletics, library hours, and so on. Using the last such poll on your campus, discuss the methods by which the sampling was performed, pointing out the strong and weak points of the process. If necessary, visit your student body officers and find out their approach to sampling student opinion.

30. The McMann Company has eight vehicles, which were purchased within the past 2 years. The service manager has recorded the current mileage on each vehicle as shown here. Consider these data to be a population.

    12,200   9,200   7,500   10,500   21,000   17,600   16,300   9,800

    a. Determine the mean number of miles for the population of eight vehicles.
    b. Suppose the service manager selected a random sample of six vehicles from the population. How many possible samples of size six could be selected?
    c. Referring to part **b**, use a random sampling procedure and select four samples of size six each. List the sample values and show the mean for each sample. Discuss why the sample means are likely to be different and why they do not necessarily equal the population mean.

31. The Doran Maintenance Company recently selected a random sample of businesses in the Dallas, Texas, area and asked the businesses to report their monthly budgets for office maintenance. The sample was randomly selected and contained 200 businesses. The mean budget for the sample was $750.00 per month. Does this indicate that the true average maintenance budget for all businesses in the Dallas area is $750.00 per month? Discuss.

32. The Doran Maintenance Company discussed in Problem 31 selected a random sample of 200 businesses and found that the average amount spent on office maintenance was $750. Suppose a second sample of 200 was taken by a rival maintenance company, which found an average of $680. Would you expect to see this difference between the two sample averages or does this indicate that one sample was incorrectly taken?

33. The Hardcone Baking Company recently performed a market study in which it asked people from the sample of 400 how much they spent on bakery products per week. The average of this sample was $3.45. Is it reasonable to

expect that another sample of size 400 would result in the same sample mean? Discuss.

34. Recently, a school system in the Midwest performed a study of its students' performance on mathematics examinations. If the population of all examination scores is thought to be normally distributed, with a mean of 68 points and a standard deviation of 12 points:

    a. What are the mean and standard deviation for the sampling distribution of the mean if the sample size is 100? Discuss why the sampling distribution has a smaller standard deviation than the population, but the same mean.

    b. Suppose we take a second sample of size 500. What is the difference between the two sampling distributions? Illustrate using graphs.

35. If the time it takes a mechanic to tune an engine is known to be normally distributed, with a mean of 45 minutes and a standard deviation of 14 minutes, what are the mean and standard error of a sampling distribution for a sample size of twenty tune-ups? Show a picture of the sampling distribution.

36. Suppose we are told that the sampling distribution developed from a sample of size 400 has a mean of 56.78 and a standard error of 9.6. If the population is known to be normally distributed, what are the population mean and population standard deviation? Discuss how these values relate to the values for the sampling distribution.

37. The Galusha C.P.A. Firm performs audits for the Allen Tool Company. As part of an audit, the accountant in charge of the audit selected a random sample of 300 accounts from the 2,000 accounts receivable on the Allen Company books. He was particularly interested in the average account balance.

    a. If the computer records indicate that the true average balance for all 2,000 accounts is $786.98, with a standard deviation of $356.75, describe the sampling distribution of the mean. Also draw an illustration of the sampling distribution.

    b. Describe the sampling distribution for the mean if the accountant changes the sample to 500 accounts. Also discuss why we need not be concerned with the shape of the population distribution.

38. The engineering staff for the Bentrim Manufacturing Company is considering sampling 100 parts produced by the company to determine the average diameter. If the population is 200 parts and the population standard deviation is known to be 0.15 inch, what is the standard error of the sampling distribution?

39. Dan Evko works for the *Morning Star* newspaper. He recently selected a random sample of forty issues of the daily newspaper during the past year. He was interested in determining the average number of column inches devoted to hard news. If the true standard deviation for the number of inches of hard news is 8 inches, what will the standard error of the sampling distribution be?

    Explain the effect the finite correction factor has on the mean of the sampling distribution.

40. The Chair Company repairs old furniture and restores it to "better than original" condition. Records indicate that the time it takes to refinish and otherwise restore a standard dining room set is normally distributed, with a mean of 30 hours and a standard deviation of 5 hours. Recently a customer complained that he was charged too much for work performed by The Chair Company. To settle the argument, the manager of the company offered the customer the following option. The company will select a random sample of past work performed on tables similar to the customer's. If the sample mean based on five work times turns out less than hers, The Chair Company will refund her money. If the mean of this sample turns out to be greater than or equal to her billed time, she will pay the company half again the amount of the bill.

    Taking into account the average and standard deviation of all work times on file, do you think the manager is wise to make such an offer if this customer's billed time was 32 hours? Discuss why or why not?

    What would be your response if the customer's billed time was 34 hours?

41. The Chair Company considered in the previous problem repairs and restores old furniture. Records indicate that the time needed to refinish and otherwise restore a standard dining room set is normally distributed, with a mean of 30 hours and a standard deviation of 5 hours. A customer was billed for 32 hours. What is the probability of a single customer being billed for these hours or more? What is the probability a sample of five customers will average 32 hours or more?

42. The Environmental Protection Agency (EPA) requires all U.S. automobile makers to test their cars for mileage in the city and on the highway. One company has indicated that a certain model will get 25 mpg in the city and 32 mpg on the highway. However, not all cars of a given model will get the same mileage; these mileage ratings are simply averages. Further, because there is variation among cars, the manufacturer has discovered that the standard deviation is 3 mpg for city driving and 2 mpg for highway driving.

    Given this information, suppose the San Francisco Police Department has purchased a random sample of sixty-four cars from this company. The police officers have driven these cars exclusively in the city and have recorded an average of 21 mpg. What would you conclude regarding the EPA mileage rating for this model car? Indicate the basis for your conclusion.

43. Problem 42 considered sixty-four cars bought by the San Francisco Police Department. The manufacturer advertised the cars would average 25 mpg in the city and 32 mpg on the highway. These values are, of course, averages and have standard deviations of 3 mpg for city driving and 2 mpg for highway driving. The police chief has asked his officers to drive the cars to Los Angeles and back to determine how the cars perform in highway driving. The sixty-four cars averaged 34 mpg. What can the chief conclude about the advertised highway mileage? Explain your answer.

44. The Mason Construction Company has built a total of fifty homes in the Seattle area in an average time of 35 days, with a standard deviation of 10 days. A prospective customer has interviewed forty of the fifty homeowners about the quality of construction, and so forth. One of the questions asked of

the homeowners was how long it took the builder to construct their homes. The forty responses averaged 46 days. What would you conclude about these responses? Explain.

45. The Sullivan Advertising Agency has determined that the average cost to develop a 30-second commercial is $20,000. The standard deviation is $3,000. Suppose a random sample of fifty commercials is selected and the average cost is $20,300. What are the chances of finding a sample mean this high or higher?

46. The Baily Hill Bicycle Shop sells ten-speed bicycles and offers a maintenance program to its customers. The manager has found the average repair bill during the maintenance program's first year to be $15.30, with a standard deviation of $7.00.
    a. What is the probability a random sample of forty customers will have a mean repair cost exceeding $16.00?
    b. What is the probability the mean repair cost for a sample of 100 customers will be between $15.10 and $15.80?

47. As part of a marketing study, the Food King Supermarket chain has randomly sampled 150 customers. The average dollar volume purchased by the customers in this sample was $33.14.

    Before sampling, the company assumed that the distribution of customer purchases had a mean of $30.00 and a standard deviation of $8.00. If these figures are correct, what is the probability of observing a sample mean of $33.14 or greater? What would this probability indicate to you?

48. The Bendbo Corporation has a total of 300 employees in its two manufacturing locations and the headquarters office. A study conducted 5 years ago showed that the average commuting distance to work for Bendbo employees was 6.2 miles, with a standard deviation of 3 miles.
    a. Recently, a follow-up study based on a random sample of 100 employees indicated an average travel distance of 5.9 miles. Assuming that the mean and standard deviation of the original study hold, what is the probability of obtaining a sample mean of 5.9 miles or less? Based on this probability, do you think the average travel distance may have decreased?
    b. A second random sample of size forty was selected. This sample produced a mean travel distance of 5.9 miles. If the mean for all employees is 6.2 miles and the standard deviation is 3 miles, what is the probability of observing a sample mean of 5.9 miles or less?
    c. Discuss why the probabilities differ even though the sample results were the same in each case.

49. An automatic saw at a local lumber mill cuts 2 × 4s to an average length of 120 inches. However, since the saw is a mechanical device, not all 2 × 4s are 120 inches. In fact, the distribution of lengths has a variance of 0.64. The saw operator took a sample of just thirty-six boards.
    a. If the saw is set correctly, what is the probability the average length of the sample boards is more than 120.6 inches?
    b. What is the probability the sample mean length is less than 119.3 inches?
    c. What should the saw operator conclude if she finds the sample to have an average length of 120.3 inches?

CASES

7A   Mountain West Gas and Electric Company

Jim Kelly called the meeting of the executive committee to order promptly at 9:00 A.M. in the plush McGiven Conference Room. In his capacity as operations vice-president for Mountain West Gas and Electric, Jim has day-to-day responsibility for the company and reports directly to the president, Willis Clayborn. Jim chairs the executive committee and can call it together for special meetings like the one being held today.

The purpose of the meeting was to discuss the latest ruling by the State Public Utilities Commission, the regulatory body responsible for overseeing all public utilities in the state. The PUC ruling requires that gas and electric companies in the state take into account peak day usage in setting their rates. As Jim explained to the executive committee, the ruling means that the amount of gas and electricity used on the peak day (the day with the greatest number of therms used) by the various classes of customers must be factored into the rates charged for the customer classes. The PUC logic, according to Jim, is that the company maintain adequate capacity to just meet the peak day demand. The classes of customers demanding a high share of this capacity should pay more of the capacity-related costs than those customers in classes who have a low demand on the peak day.

As Jim explained, this means that the company needs a way to monitor electricity and gas usage on a daily basis. Currently, customer meters are read once a month and the total power used for the month is known for each customer class. No information is currently available on a daily basis by customer class. However, Mountain West can measure the total gas and electricity supplied by the system each day, so the peak day during a year can be identified. Every year since records have been maintained, the peak day has occurred during January.

The company has four classes of customers: RES-1, RES-2, COM-1, and COM-2. The difference between RES-1 and RES-2 is that RES-1 customers have an electric water heater and RES-2 customers have gas water heaters. Both RES-1 and RES-2 are residential classes. There are approximately 42,000 RES-1 customers and 37,000 RES-2 customers. The COM-1 customer class consists of small- to medium-size commercial customers like retail stores and small manufacturing. The COM-1 customers number approximately 6,400. The last customer class, COM-2, consists of the large industrial users. While small in number (245), this class accounts for over 23% of the gas and electricity used throughout the year.

After a series of comments and questions from the other executive board members, Jim outlined the alternatives, as he saw them:

1.   Manually read the meters for every customer every day during the month of January.
2.   Manually read the meters for a sample of customers every day during January.

3. Install a microcomputer device for recording gas and electricity usage for a sample of customers.
4. Do nothing and justify the current rate structure to the Public Utilities Commission.

Options 1, 2, and 4 were easily understandable by the board members, but the microcomputer option was new to most members and Jim spent some extra time explaining what this involved. He pointed out that a California company has developed a "black box" that contains a small microprocessor capable of measuring natural gas and electricity usage in 15-minute intervals and can store up to a year's worth of data. The cost is $250.00 per unit plus installation and maintenance, estimated to be another $100.00 per unit.

The board members agreed that manually reading every customer's meter each day was impractical. They also agreed that doing nothing was not a desirable option in light of the PUC's interest in the issue. The group decided to investigate the sampling alternatives: either manually reading a sample of customer meters or using the new "black box" on a sample. Jim Kelly suggested that Elizabeth Kornfield, manager of data services, have her staff work up a report that would discuss the different sampling options available to Mountain West. The report should discuss the advantages and disadvantages of each sampling method considered.

When the meeting broke up at 11:15 A.M., Elizabeth headed back to her office. She knew whom she would ask to prepare the report on sampling and wanted to get it started right away!

7B   Carpita Bottling Company

Don Carpita owns and operates Carpita Bottling Company in Evertown, Maryland. The company bottles soda pop and beer, as well as distributes the products in the counties surrounding Evertown.

The company has four bottling machines, which can be adjusted to fill bottles at any mean fill level between 2 ounces and 72 ounces. The machines do exhibit some variation in actual fill from the mean setting. For instance, if the mean setting is 16 ounces, the actual fill may be slightly more or slightly less than that amount.

Three of the four filling machines are relatively new and their fill variation is not as great as that of the older machine. Don has observed that the standard deviation in fill for the three new machines is about 1% of the mean fill level when the mean fill is set at 16 ounces or less and 0.5% of the mean at settings exceeding 16 ounces. The older machine has a standard deviation of about 1.5% of the mean setting regardless of the mean fill setting. However, the older machine tends to underfill bottles more than overfill, so the older machine is set at a mean fill slightly in excess of the desired mean to compensate for the propensity to underfill. For example, when 16-ounce bottles are to be filled, the machine is set at a mean fill level of 16.05 ounces.

It is possible for the company to simultaneously fill bottles with two brands of soda pop using two machines and use the other two machines to bottle beer. Although each filling machine has its own warehouse and the products are loaded from the warehouse directly on a truck, products from two or more filling machines may be loaded on the same truck. However, an individual store almost always receives bottles on a particular day from just one machine.

Saturday morning Don received a call at home from the J. R. Summers Grocery store manager. She was very upset because the shipment of 16-ounce bottles of beer received yesterday contained several bottles that were not adequately filled. The manager wanted Don to replace the entire shipment at once.

Don gulped down his coffee and prepared to head for the store to check out the problem. He started thinking how he could determine which machine was responsible for the problem. If he could at least determine whether it was the old machine or one of the new ones, he could save his maintenance people a lot of time and effort checking all the machines.

His plan was to select a sample of 64 bottles of beer from the store and measure the contents. Don figured that he might be able to determine, on the basis of the average contents, whether it is more likely that the beer was bottled by a new machine or by the old one.

The results of the sampling showed an average of 15.993 ounces. Now Don needs some help in determining whether a sample mean of 15.993 ounces or less is more likely to come from the new machines or the older machine.

REFERENCES

Lapin, Lawrence. *Statistics for Modern Business Decisions*. 5th ed. New York: Harcourt Brace Jovanovich, 1990.

Mendenhall, William; Reinmuth, James E.; and Beaver, Robert. *Statistics for Management and Economics*. 6th ed. Boston: PWS-Kent, 1989.

Neter, John; Wasserman, William; and Whitmore, G. A. *Applied Statistics*. 3d ed. Boston: Allyn and Bacon, 1988.

Introduction to Statistical Estimation

WHY DECISION MAKERS NEED TO KNOW

Chapter 1 emphasized that decision makers cannot always measure an entire population but instead must often rely on information gained by sampling the population. Therefore, the decision made often depends on the sample information, which, as shown in Chapter 7, is subject to sampling error. Sampling error can cause problems for decision makers who are not familiar with statistical estimation. Suppose a market-research firm needs to know the average per capita income in a city before it can advise its client whether to open a new retail outlet in that city. This firm would likely select a statistical sample and compute the mean per capita income. However, as illustrated in Chapter 7, the sample mean will not likely be equal to the population mean. If the market-research firm does not recognize that sampling error can occur and assumes that the population mean is equal to the sample mean, it may be over- or understating the true population mean by a considerable amount. This may lead to a poor decision. However, the statistical estimation methods introduced in this chapter show the decision makers how to take into account the potential for sampling error.

Television networks rely on such rating services as Arbitron and Nielsen to provide them with information about the percentage of the viewing audience watching each network during a given time period. These organizations sample several hundred people from around the country and ask detailed questions about what television programs are viewed by the residents of the household. The ratings service can then combine the information from the sampled respondents and, through the application of statistical techniques such as those presented in this chapter, present an estimate of the viewing patterns for the population as a whole. From these estimates, the networks make decisions about which programs to retain and which to cancel.

As a decision maker, you will be called on to provide estimates of population values and make decisions based on the estimates. Therefore, it is very important that you understand the concepts of statistical estimation presented in this chapter.

CHAPTER OBJECTIVES

This chapter introduces the process of estimating population values based on samples from the population. Specifically, it introduces point estimates and interval estimates for such parameters as the population mean, the population proportion, the difference between two population means, and the difference between two population proportions. It will concentrate on estimation procedures for large sample sizes.

The chapter also introduces the concepts of precision and confidence level for an estimate and will show how to determine the sample size necessary to maintain a specified level of confidence and precision.

STUDENT OBJECTIVES

After studying the material in this chapter, you should be able to do the following:

1. Discuss the difference between a point estimate and an interval estimate.
2. Discuss the advantages of a confidence interval estimate and recognize applications of such an estimate.
3. Calculate a confidence interval estimate for each of the following:
   a. Population mean
   b. Population proportion
   c. Difference between two population means
   d. Difference between two population proportions
4. Determine the impact of sample size on the confidence interval.
5. Discuss the importance of precision in a confidence interval estimate.
6. Determine the required sample size for specific estimation problems involving population means and proportions.
7. Identify business decision applications that require statistical estimation.

8-1 POINT ESTIMATES AND INTERVAL ESTIMATES

You, no doubt, either have been a respondent or have seen the results of a political poll taken during an election year. These polls attempt to determine the percentage of voters who will favor a particular candidate or a particular issue. For example, suppose a poll indicates that 62% of people over 18 years old in your state favor setting the legal drinking age at 21 years. The pollsters have not contacted every person in the state, but rather have sampled only a relatively few people to arrive at the 62% figure. In statistical terminology, the 62% is the *point estimate* for the true population percentage who favor the 21-year drinking age. In general, a **point estimate** is a single number determined from a sample and is used to estimate the population value.

The Environmental Protection Agency (EPA) tests automobile models sold in the United States to determine their mileage ratings. Following the testing, each model is assigned an EPA mileage rating based on the test mileage. This rating is actually a point estimate for the true average of all cars of the given model.

Cost accountants make detailed studies of their company's production process to determine the costs of producing each product. These costs are often found by selecting a sample of items and following each item through the complete production process. The costs at each step in the process are determined, and the total cost is found when the process is completed. The accountants calculate the average cost for the items sampled and use this figure as the point estimate for the true average cost of all pieces produced. The point estimate becomes the basis for assigning a selling price to the finished product.

The federal government publishes many population estimates. Among these are estimates of the median family income and the proportion of unemployed persons. These values are calculated from samples and are point estimates of the population values.

Which point estimator the decision maker uses depends on the population characteristic the decision maker wishes to estimate. However, regardless of the population value being estimated, you can expect that the estimate will not equal the true population value. We always expect some sampling error. Recall that **sampling error** is the difference between the population value and the sample value. Chapter 7 discussed the distribution of potential sampling error. We cannot eliminate sampling error, but we can deal with it in our decision process. Thus, for example, when cost accountants use $\overline{X}$, the average cost of a sample of pieces, to establish the average production cost, the point estimate will most likely be wrong. But they will have no way of determining how wrong it is.

To overcome this problem with point estimates, the most common procedure is to calculate a **confidence interval** estimate.

The relationship between point estimates and confidence interval estimates might be better understood by considering the following analogy involving two well-known games—darts and horseshoes. To make the analogy, suppose we place a very thin peg firmly in the ground. This peg stands 18 inches above ground level and is the target that we wish to hit. Thus, the peg is analogous to the population parameter we wish to estimate.

We now take a sharply pointed dart, stand back at the throwing line, and throw the dart at the peg. In this game of darts we must hit the peg to win. However, because the peg is very thin and the dart has a very narrow point, we probably will not hit the peg, although we might come close. We might also miss by quite a margin. If we practice a long time, we should reach a level where most of our throws come very close, but we cannot count on hitting the peg. For the most part, we can expect to miss the target itself.

The dart is like the point estimate. The objective of point estimation is to "hit" the population value. However, as we have discussed before, we can expect sampling error; i.e., the point estimate will probably miss its target. We learned in Chapter 7 that if the sample size is increased, the potential for extreme sampling error is reduced. Just as practicing darts will result in more of our throws coming close to the target, point estimates from large samples have a better chance of being close to the population value.

Playing this type of dart game would be frustrating, since we would almost never hit our target. As a result, we might turn to another game, horseshoes. In horseshoes, the player throws a U-shaped horseshoe at the peg. But instead of having to hit the peg, the objective of horseshoes is to throw a ringer. It does not matter whether the peg is centered within the shoe. All that matters in this game is that the shoe encompass the peg. If we practice long enough, we could get to the point where we could throw a ringer 90%, or 95%, or even 99% of the time. If we use a wide horseshoe, we will not have to practice as long to achieve the level of accuracy we seek. A ringer thrown with a narrow horseshoe will be more impressive, but will require more practice.

Horseshoes is like confidence interval estimation. Our objective is to throw a ringer around the population value. We do not care where within our interval the population value falls, we just care that it be in the interval. We can attain a certain level of confidence (90%, 95%, 99%) that the interval estimate will be a good one. High confidence can be achieved with not so large samples, if we are willing to live with a wide interval. However, more meaningful estimates come from narrow intervals, and, like more horseshoe practice, this will require larger sample sizes.

CONFIDENCE INTERVAL ESTIMATION

The production manager of the Valley View Canning Company is responsible for monitoring the filling operations of cans. His company has recently installed a new machine that has been carefully tested and is known to fill cans of any size with a standard deviation of $\sigma_x = 0.2$ ounce. The manager's main problem is to adjust the average fill to the level specified on the can—for instance, 16 ounces, 24 ounces, and so forth.

Suppose he has just made a setting in an attempt to fill the peach cans to an average of 16 ounces. From the cans already filled he selects a random sample of 100 and carefully weighs each one. The sample mean, $\overline{X}$, provides a point estimate of the population mean, μ_x. Suppose this value is

$$\overline{X} = 16.8 \text{ ounces}$$

Because of the nature of any point estimate, the manager does not expect to find a sample mean that exactly equals 16 ounces. He also knows from the central limit theorem that the distribution of all possible sample means will be approximately normal around the true mean. This is illustrated in Figure 8-1.

FIGURE   8-1

Sampling
Distribution of $\overline{X}$
for the Valley
View Canning
Company
Example (Peach
Can Fill in
Ounces)

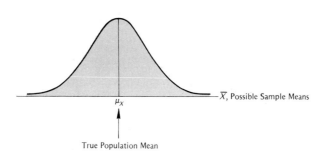

Thus, although the manager does not expect a sample mean of 16 ounces, he will likely allow the process to continue if the sample mean is close to 16 ounces. To determine just what "close" is, the manager needs to determine a confidence interval estimate of the population mean, μ_x.

8-2   CONFIDENCE INTERVAL ESTIMATE OF μ_x

LARGE SAMPLES, σ_x KNOWN

The Valley View Canning Company manager specifies that he wants a 95% confidence interval. This means that of all the intervals he might obtain, 95% will include the true mean. He figures that if the interval includes 16 ounces, the true mean might actually be 16 ounces and he will leave the machine setting as is. The general format for the confidence interval is

Point estimate ± (Interval coefficient)(Standard error)

The point estimate for our canning example is $\overline{X}$. The standard error is $\sigma_{\overline{x}}$, which is determined by equation 8-1:

$$\sigma_{\overline{x}} = \frac{\sigma_x}{\sqrt{n}}$$

  8-1

The remaining factor, the **interval coefficient,** is the number of standard errors on each side of the population mean necessary to include a percentage of the possible sample means equal to the confidence level. When the sample size is *large* and the population standard deviation is *known*, the interval coefficient is a Z value from the standard normal distribution table in Appendix C. For example, if the desired confidence level is 95%, the Z value (interval coefficient) is 1.96, as shown in Figure 8-2. Recall that the central limit theorem states that for sufficiently large samples, the sampling distribution will be normal.

FIGURE 8-2

Interval
Coefficient for a
95% Confidence
Interval

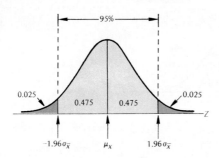

The format for a confidence interval for estimating μ_x, when the population standard deviation is known, is given in expression 8-2:

$$\overline{X} \pm Z\sigma_{\overline{x}} \qquad \boxed{8\text{-}2}$$

For this example, the confidence interval is given by formula 8-3:

$$\overline{X} \pm 1.96 \frac{\sigma_x}{\sqrt{n}} \qquad \boxed{8\text{-}3}$$

Any value of $\overline{X}$ between $\mu_x - 1.96\sigma_{\overline{x}}$ and $\mu_x + 1.96\sigma_{\overline{x}}$ will produce a confidence interval that contains μ_x. Using $Z = 1.96$ indicates that since 95% of the possible sample means come from this range, 95% of the potential confidence intervals will include the population mean. Figure 8-3 illustrates this important concept by showing a few of the possible intervals.

For the Valley View Canning Company example, the 95% confidence interval with a sample mean, $\overline{X}$, of 16.8 ounces a population standard deviation, σ_x of 0.2 and a sample size, n, of 100 is

$$\overline{X} \pm 1.96 \frac{\sigma_x}{\sqrt{n}}$$

$$16.8 \pm 1.96 \frac{0.2}{\sqrt{100}}$$

$$16.8 \pm 1.96(0.02)$$

$$16.8 \pm 0.0392$$

FIGURE 8-3

Possible
Confidence
Intervals

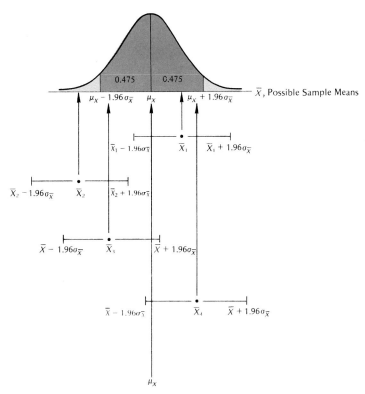

Note: Most intervals include μ_x, and some do not. Those intervals that do not contain the population mean are developed from sample means that fall in either tail of the sampling distribution.

Therefore, the 95% confidence interval estimate for the true average fill is

$$16.7608 \text{ ounces } \underline{\quad\quad} 16.8392 \text{ ounces}$$

This represents a 95% confidence interval because it is constructed by a procedure that will produce an interval containing μ_x 95% of the time. The manager is almost certain this interval *does* include the true mean. Since the desired average of 16 ounces is not contained within the limits, he will conclude (rightly or wrongly) that the true mean is not 16 ounces and will order further machine adjustment. The sampling and estimation process will be repeated.

Suppose after several adjustments the sample mean, $\overline{X}$, for a sample of size 100 cans is 16.02 ounces. The 95% confidence interval developed from this point estimate is

$$\overline{X} \pm 1.96\sigma_{\overline{x}}$$

$$16.02 \pm 1.96\frac{0.2}{\sqrt{100}}$$

$$15.9808 \text{ ounces } \underline{\quad\quad} 16.0592 \text{ ounces}$$

The production manager knows that 95% of all possible confidence intervals should include μ_x, the true population mean. Therefore, he is confident that the true mean is between 15.9808 ounces and 16.0592 ounces. Because the desired average fill, 16 ounces, falls in this interval, the manager should not make any further adjustments in the machine setting at this time.

Precision of the Estimate

The production manager for Valley View Canning is concerned about the width of his confidence interval. Though he is willing to believe, based on a sample of 100, that the true mean fill is 16 ounces because this value falls within the interval, he would also be willing to believe that the true mean fill is 16.02 ounces or 15.99 ounces because they also fall in the interval. The manager would like to decrease the width of the confidence interval estimate. The **precision** of a confidence interval estimate is inversely related to the width of the interval. As the width of the interval becomes narrower, the estimate becomes more precise.

One way to increase the precision of an estimate is to decrease the confidence level. For example, if the manager is willing to accept a 90% confidence level, the interval coefficient can be reduced from 1.96 to 1.645, as shown in Figure 8-4.

FIGURE **8-4**

Interval
Coefficient for a
90% Confidence
Interval

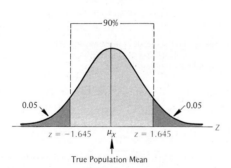

For a sample of 100 selected from the production run, the 90% confidence interval from a sample mean of 16.01 is

$$\overline{X} \pm Z\frac{\sigma_x}{\sqrt{n}}$$

$$16.01 \pm 1.645\frac{0.2}{\sqrt{100}}$$

$$16.01 \pm 0.0329$$

$$15.9771 \text{ ounces} \_\_\_\_ 16.0429 \text{ ounces}$$

This represents a slight *increase* in precision (narrowing the interval) compared with the 95% confidence level. A confidence level of 80% would increase the precision even further since the interval coefficient is reduced to 1.28:

$$\overline{X} \pm Z\frac{\sigma_x}{\sqrt{n}}$$

$$16.01 \pm 1.28\frac{0.2}{\sqrt{100}}$$

$$16.01 \pm 0.0256$$

$$15.9844 \text{ ounces} \underline{\qquad} 16.0356 \text{ ounces}$$

We have increased the precision by decreasing the confidence level, but what is the trade-off? Reducing the confidence from 95% to 80% means that now only 80% of all intervals are expected to include the true population mean. Thus the chances of obtaining an interval that includes the true mean have been decreased. The trade-off is between obtaining a narrow, more precise interval and decreasing the chances of obtaining an interval estimate that contains the true population mean. The extent to which a decision maker is willing to reduce the confidence level depends on the cost associated with an interval that does not contain μ_x. The higher this cost, the less willing the decision maker will be to reduce the confidence level.

If we have control over the confidence level, why do we not always use a very high confidence level such as 99%, so we can feel very confident about our estimation? The reason is that, other factors being held constant, higher confidence levels mean wider, less precise, intervals.

However, a second alternative for increasing the precision of an interval estimate is to increase the sample size. Since an increase in sample size will reduce the standard error, $\sigma_{\overline{x}}$, it will also reduce the confidence interval width. For example, suppose the production manager at Valley View Canning selects a random sample of 400 cans from the production run. Further, suppose the sample mean, $\overline{X}$, for this larger sample is also 16.01 ounces. The 95% confidence interval would be

$$\overline{X} \pm Z\frac{\sigma_x}{\sqrt{n}}$$

$$16.01 \pm 1.96\frac{0.2}{\sqrt{400}}$$

$$16.01 \pm 0.0196$$

$$15.9904 \text{ ounces} \underline{\qquad} 16.0296 \text{ ounces}$$

This interval is more precise (narrower) than the 95% interval based on a sample of 100 cans, which was calculated previously to be

$$15.9708 \text{ ounces} \underline{\qquad} 16.0492 \text{ ounces}$$

Thus, without losing any confidence in the estimate of the true average weight of a can, the manager has been able to reduce the width of the interval estimate from 2(0.0392) = 0.0784 ounce to 2(0.0196) = 0.0392 ounce by simply increasing the sample of cans from 100 to 400.

There are obvious trade-offs associated with selecting a larger sample size, generally in terms of time and money. Decision makers must decide on the benefit to be gained from increased precision and balance this gain against the increased costs.

Sample Size Determination (Simple Random Sample)

The Valley View Canning Company example illustrates some very important trade-offs associated with confidence interval estimation. We now know that the width of the confidence interval can be reduced by either decreasing the confidence level or increasing the sample size. While a narrow interval is desired, so is high confidence. Likewise, because of the costs associated with selecting sample items, we prefer to make our estimate with the smallest possible sample. Thus, a decision maker is faced with making difficult decisions about the confidence level, sample size, and interval width prior to actually taking the sample.

Possibly the most frequent question we hear from business decision makers who are faced with an estimation application is, "How large a sample do I need?" If their population standard deviation is known, we usually start by asking the decision maker two questions.

1. How much money do you have budgeted to do the sampling?
2. How much will it cost to select each item in the sample?

The answers to these questions dictate the upper limit on the sample size that can be selected. For instance, if the decision maker indicates that she has a $2,000.00 budget for selecting the sample and it will cost about $10.00 per unit to collect the sample, the upper limit is $n = \$2,000.00/\$10.00 = 200$.

Keeping in mind the estimation trade-offs discussed earlier, it is important that we discuss the issue more fully with the decision maker. For instance, is a sample of $n = 200$ sufficient to give the desired precision at a specified confidence level? Is $n = 200$ more than is needed to achieve the desired precision at the specified confidence level? Therefore, before we can give a firm answer about what sample size is needed, the decision maker must specify her confidence level and a desired precision. Then the required sample size can be computed.

Consider the following example. Ginger Davidson is the credit manager for a major public utility in the western United States. Her company has thousands of commercial customers in eleven western states. She is interested in estimating the average annual utility bill for all commercial customers and assumes that the standard deviation of annual utility bills is about $1,000.00, as reported in an earlier study. After considerable thought, she has decided that a 95% confidence interval is needed and that she wants the precision, or total width of the confidence interval, to be no more than $300. Given these requirements, what size sample is needed?

To answer this question, we must introduce a new concept, *tolerable error*. **Tolerable error** is one-half the width of the confidence interval. Recall that

$$\overline{X} \pm Z\frac{\sigma_x}{\sqrt{n}}$$

is the format of a confidence interval estimate of μ_x. Then tolerable error can be calculated from equation 8-4:

$$e = Z\frac{\sigma_x}{\sqrt{n}} \qquad \text{8-4}$$

where

e = Tolerable error

Z = Interval coefficient

σ_x = Population standard deviation

n = Sample size

Since tolerable error is half the width of a confidence interval, the credit manager, who wishes an interval width of $300, will accept a tolerable error of $150. Solving equation 8-4 for n, we get equation 8-5 for the sample size as follows:

$$n = \frac{Z^2\sigma_x^2}{e^2} \qquad \text{8-5}$$

Equation 8-5 applies to problems where the population is large or where the sampling is performed with replacement and simple random sampling is used.

For our example, we have

$$e = Z\frac{\sigma_x}{\sqrt{n}}$$

$$150 = 1.96\frac{1,000}{\sqrt{n}}$$

$$n = \frac{(1.96)^2(1,000)^2}{(150)^2} = 170.74$$

$$= 171 \text{ customers}$$

Thus, to obtain a 95% confidence interval with a tolerable error of $150 (precision = $300), the credit manager would need to sample 171 commercial customers.

Thus, Ginger Davidson, the decision maker who specified a $2,000 total sampling budget and a $10 per-unit sampling cost with an $n = 200$ maximum sample size, would be pleased to learn that a sample size of $n = 171$ is needed to satisfy her requirements.

While we have worked with decision makers who can firmly specify their desired precision and confidence level and stand by those values, more frequently we find decision makers expressing their sample size questions in "what if" form. What if I increased the precision? What if I lowered the confidence level? In these cases, we can compute the different required sample sizes using equation 8-5.

For example, what would be the impact on the sample size of increasing the required precision to $200? This means that the tolerable error is reduced to $100. The required sample size would be calculated as follows:

$$e = Z \frac{\sigma_x}{\sqrt{n}}$$

$$100 = 1.96 \frac{1,000}{\sqrt{n}}$$

$$n = \frac{(1.96)^2 (1,000)^2}{(100)^2} = 384.16$$

$$= 385 \text{ customers}$$

Recall that, originally, Ginger Davidson specified that the total interval width should not exceed $300 (tolerable error = $150) and a sample of 171 was required for a 95% confidence interval. That was within her budget limit of $n = 200$. However, if she wishes to have a more precise interval with a width of $200 (tolerable error = $100), she will be faced with the prospect of spending more money ($10.00 \cdot 385 = $3,850).

There is one other option open to her that will provide a narrower interval than originally planned at a lower sampling cost. She can lower her confidence level from 95%. For instance, suppose she asks, "What if the confidence level is 80% and I keep the total interval width at $200.00?" Now instead of $Z = 1.96$, we use $Z = 1.28$ for an 80% confidence interval. Then, the sample size is computed using equation 8-5 as follows:

$$n = \frac{(1.28)^2 (1,000)^2}{(100)^2}$$

$$= 163.84$$

$$= 164$$

Thus, by lowering the confidence level to 80%, she can get the precision she wants without having to exceed her original sample size limit of 200 customers. However, she is giving up some of the confidence that comes from a 95% confidence level.

LARGE SAMPLES, σ_x UNKNOWN

The previous section discussed confidence interval estimates for large samples with a known population standard deviation. In most business applications, if μ_x is not known, neither is σ_x. When σ_x is not known, it must also be estimated. The appropriate estimator is S_x, the *sample standard deviation,* calculated by equation 8-6:

$$S_x = \sqrt{\frac{\Sigma(X - \overline{X})^2}{n - 1}} \qquad \text{8-6}$$

where

S_x = Sample standard deviation

$\overline{X}$ = Sample mean

n = Sample size

If the sample size is *large,* the confidence interval estimate of the population mean, μ_x, is approximated by expression 8-7:

$$\overline{X} \pm Z\frac{S_x}{\sqrt{n}} \qquad \text{8-7}$$

Therefore, when the population standard deviation is not known and the sample size is large, we substitute the sample standard deviation and compute the confidence interval in the usual manner. Consider the estimation problem facing the flight scheduling manager for a major airline. He needs to know the average time it takes a ground crew to unload the baggage on international flights. To obtain the necessary data, he assigns an extra crew member to time the unloading process on a sample of $n = 100$ international flights at airports where his airline lands. Just as he does not know the population mean (average unloading time for all international flights), he also does not know the population standard deviation. Therefore, he must compute both the sample mean and the sample standard deviation, shown as follows:

$$\overline{X} = 852 \text{ seconds}$$
$$S_x = 210 \text{ seconds}$$

The manager wants a 98% confidence interval. Therefore,

$$\overline{X} \pm Z \frac{S_x}{\sqrt{n}}$$

$$852 \pm 2.33 \frac{210}{\sqrt{100}}$$

$$852 \pm 48.93$$

$$803.07 \text{ sec} \_\_\_\_ 900.93 \text{ sec}$$

One can state a proper interpretation of this estimate as: Based on the sample data, with 98% confidence, we think the mean unloading time for the population of all international flights is contained in the interval from 803.07 seconds to 900.93 seconds. Note that the tolerable error on this estimate is ±48.93 seconds. If the manager thinks this is too high and wishes to improve the precision, he is faced with the options of lowering the confidence level or increasing the sample size (or some of each).

A common error in interpreting a confidence interval estimate is to assign to the interval a probability that it contains the population mean. For instance, one might be tempted to say there is a 98% chance that the population mean unloading time falls within the range from 803.07 to 900.93 seconds. However, since the population mean is a fixed value, not a random variable, either it falls in this interval or it does not. Instead, the confidence level relates to the chances, prior to sampling, of obtaining an interval that contains the population mean.

A Quality Improvement Example

Consider another example where the population mean needs to be estimated from sample data. The Far West Window and Door Company converts dimension lumber into door and window frames. The dimension lumber is purchased from mills throughout the northwest. Unfortunately, not all pieces of wood are of suitable quality to be made into Far West's end products. These defective pieces must be scrapped. The Far West purchasing manager is planning to establish a quality partnership with a major supplier in the hopes of improving the quality of incoming lumber.

Before meeting with the supplier, the purchasing manager wants to have solid data about the product quality. One of the things he wants to estimate is the mean number of board feet of scrap per bundle from this supplier. To obtain this information, the purchasing manager assigned a management trainee the job of sampling $n = 80$ bundles and measuring the board feet of scrap in each bundle. When the measuring was finished, the sample mean and sample standard deviation were computed as follows:

$$\overline{X} = 245 \text{ bf}$$
$$S_x = 90 \text{ bf}$$

The manager can now use this sample information to estimate the mean scrap per bundle for all lumber coming from the supplier. The point estimate is the sample mean, $\overline{X} = 245$ board feet. While the purchasing manager might use this point estimate in his discussions, he is aware that the point estimate is subject to sampling error and may be higher or lower than the true population mean. Thus, he also wants to prepare a 95% confidence interval estimate as follows:

$$\overline{X} \pm Z\frac{S_x}{\sqrt{n}}$$

$$245 \pm 1.96\frac{90}{\sqrt{80}}$$

$$245 \pm 19.722$$

$$225.278 \text{ bf} \underline{} 264.722 \text{ bf}$$

The manager now believes, based on the sample data and with 95% confidence, that the mean board feet of scrap for all bundles coming from this supplier is between 225.278 and 264.722. This interval accounts for the potential sampling error.

SKILL DEVELOPMENT PROBLEMS FOR SECTION 8-2

The following set of problems is meant to test your understanding of the material in this section.

1. Given the following information:

$$\overline{X} = 580$$
$$\sigma_x = 75$$
$$n = 200$$

   a. Compute and interpret the 90% confidence interval estimate for the population mean.
   b. Compute and interpret the 95% confidence interval estimate for the population mean.

2. Given the following information:

$$\overline{X} = 7{,}200$$
$$\sigma_x = 800$$
$$n = 500$$

   a. Compute and interpret the 99% confidence interval estimate for the population mean.
   b. Compute and interpret the 95% confidence interval estimate for the population mean.

3. Given the following information:

$$Z = 1.96$$
$$\sigma_{\bar{x}} = 20$$

a. What is the required sample size necessary to estimate the population mean if the tolerable error is 3?

b. Determine the sample size necessary to estimate the population mean with a tolerable error of 2.

c. Discuss why there is a difference in the sample sizes determined in part **a** and part **b**.

4. Agri-Beef, Inc., is a large midwestern farming operation. The company has been a leader in employing statistical analysis techniques in its business. Recently, John Goldberg, operations manager, requested that a random sample of cattle be selected and that these cattle be fed a special diet. The cattle were weighed before the start of the new feeding program and at the end of the feeding program. He wished to estimate the average daily weight gain for cattle on the new feed program. Two hundred cattle were tested, with the following sample results:

$$\bar{X} = 1.2 \text{ lb per day gain}$$
$$S_x = 0.50 \text{ lb}$$

a. Develop the 95% confidence interval estimate for the true average daily weight gain.

b. Develop the 90% confidence interval estimate for the true average daily weight gain.

c. Discuss the difference between the two estimates found in parts **a** and **b** and indicate the advantages and disadvantages of each.

5. The Evergreen Company operates retail pharmacies in ten eastern states. Recently, the company's internal audit department selected a random sample of 300 prescriptions issued throughout the system. The objective of the sampling was to estimate the average dollar value of all prescriptions issued by the company. The following data were collected:

$$\bar{X} = \$14.23$$
$$S_x = 3.00$$

Determine the 90% confidence interval estimate for the true average sales value for prescriptions issued by the company. Interpret the interval estimate.

6. Marine World-Africa USA is a facility located near San Francisco, California, where people can see animals from the ocean and from Africa on display and performing in shows. Customers pay for a day ticket and can stay as long as they wish. The management is interested in determining the average length of time customers spend at the park per day. They plan to select a simple random sample of customers and ask them, as they leave the park, what time they arrived. The estimate is to be within plus or minus 5 minutes, with a

90% confidence level. A previous pilot sample indicated that the standard deviation is 28 minutes. Given this information, how many customers need to be sampled?

8-3 CONFIDENCE INTERVAL ESTIMATION OF A POPULATION PROPORTION

Chapter 5 introduced the binomial distribution. Recall that the binomial distribution applies when the following conditions are satisfied:

1. There are n identical trials, each of which results in one of two possible outcomes, success or failure.
2. The n trials are *independent* and the probability of a success remains constant from trial to trial.

Also, recall that the *average* of the binomial distribution is as given by equation 8-8:

$$\mu_x = np$$

where

> n = Sample size (number of trials)
>
> p = Probability of a success

8-8

and that the standard deviation of the binomial distribution is as given by equation 8-9:

$$\sigma_x = \sqrt{npq}$$

where

> $q = 1 - p$

8-9

The binomial distribution has many applications. However, rather than attempting to count the number of successes, decision makers will often want to determine the proportion or percentage of successes in the population. A Republican candidate for the U.S. Senate is concerned about the proportion of voters who will vote Republican. The quality control manager for a large toy manufacturer is concerned about the proportion of defective toys his company produces. The president of the United States and his economic advisors are concerned about the proportion of the labor force that is unemployed. These are but a few of the situations in which decision makers need to know the *population proportion*. The population proportion is determined by equation 8-10:

$$p = \frac{X}{N}$$

8-10

where

p = Population proportion

X = Total number of successes in the population

N = Population size

If decision makers have access to the entire population, the calculated p value is a **parameter**. However, rarely can decision makers measure the entire population. Consequently, a random sample must be selected and the population proportion estimated. The point estimate for the population proportion is given by equation 8-11:

$$\hat{p} = \frac{x}{n}$$

8-11

where

$\hat{p}$ = Sample proportion

x = Number of successes in the sample

n = Sample size

The sampling distribution of $\hat{p}$ values can be approximated by a normal distribution if the sample size is large and the population proportion, p, is not too close to 0 or 1.0. The expected value and standard deviation of the sampling distribution are given by equations 8-12 and 8-13:

$$E(\hat{p}) = \mu_{\hat{p}} = p$$

8-12

$$\sigma_{\hat{p}} = \sqrt{\frac{pq}{n}}$$

8-13

where

$\mu_{\hat{p}}$ = Expected proportion of successes

$\sigma_{\hat{p}}$ = Standard error of the sampling distribution of $\hat{p}$

$q = 1 - p$

n = Sample size

There is a problem with equations 8-12 and 8-13. The mean and standard deviation of the sampling distribution, $\mu_{\hat{p}}$ and $\sigma_{\hat{p}}$, are determined by knowing p, the population proportion. Yet, it is p that we want to estimate in the first place. We overcome this problem by substituting $\hat{p}$ and $\hat{q}$ ($\hat{q} = 1 - \hat{p}$) for p and q in equation 8-13, as shown in equation 8-14:

$$S_{\hat{p}} = \sqrt{\frac{\hat{p}\hat{q}}{n}}$$

8-14

The sample proportion, $\hat{p}$, is a point estimate for the population proportion. Consequently, it is subject to sampling error and we should develop a confidence interval estimate for p, the population proportion. Recall the usual format for a confidence interval:

Point estimate ± (Interval coefficient)(Standard error)

This general format applies to confidence interval estimates for any parameter including p, the population proportion. Expression 8-15 is used for computing confidence interval estimates for proportions.

$$\hat{p} \pm ZS_{\hat{p}}$$

8-15

where

$\hat{p}$ = Point estimate

Z = Interval coefficient

$S_{\hat{p}}$ = Estimated standard error of the sampling distribution

The Cedar River Construction Company operates in several U.S. western states. This company sells cedar shake roofs to people who currently have a different type of roof but want a more aesthetically pleasing look. Cedar River is considering opening an outlet in a Utah city, but before doing so, the manager wishes to estimate the proportion of homes in the city that already have cedar shake roofs. If this percentage is too high, the company will not operate in that city. The manager wants a 90% confidence interval and has selected a random sample of 200 homes, with the following results:

$$x = 72 \text{ homes with shake roofs}$$

$$\hat{p} = \frac{x}{n}$$

$$= \frac{72}{200}$$

$$= 0.36 \qquad \text{(Sample proportion of homes with cedar shakes)}$$

$$S_{\hat{p}} = \sqrt{\frac{(0.36)(0.64)}{200}}$$

$$= 0.0339$$

The 90% confidence interval estimate for the true proportion of homes currently with cedar shake roofs is

$$\hat{p} \pm 1.645 S_{\hat{p}}$$
$$0.36 \pm (1.645)(0.0339)$$
$$0.36 \pm 0.0558$$

$$0.3042 \underline{\qquad} 0.4158$$

Based on the sample data, the manager is confident that the true proportion is between 0.3042 and 0.4158. From this estimate, she will have to decide whether to open an outlet in this city.

A Quality Control Example

In the previous section we introduced an example involving the Far West Window and Door Company in which the purchasing manager was planning on working with one of his major suppliers to improve the quality of dimension lumber. In that example, he developed a confidence interval estimate for the mean board feet of scrap per bundle. In addition, the purchasing manager plans to present data to the supplier regarding the proportion of bundles that contain less than the specified 5,000 board feet.

To obtain the estimate, the manager has his trainee select a random sample of 140 incoming bundles and carefully measure the board feet in each bundle. The bundles with less than 5,000 board feet are tagged. The following data were observed:

$$x = 21 \text{ bundles with less than } 5,000 \text{ bf}$$

$$\hat{p} = \frac{x}{n} = \frac{21}{140} = 0.15$$

$$S_{\hat{p}} = \sqrt{\frac{\hat{p}\hat{q}}{n}} = \sqrt{\frac{(0.15)(0.85)}{140}} = 0.0302$$

Then the point estimate for "short" bundles is $\hat{p} = 0.15$. This point estimate is subject to sampling error and may be higher or lower than the true proportion of short bundles shipped by this supplier. Therefore, he also wants to develop a 95% confidence interval estimate for the population proportion as follows:

$$\hat{p} \pm ZS_{\hat{p}} = 0.15 \pm (1.96)(0.0302)$$
$$- 0.15 \perp 0.0592$$
$$0.0908 \underline{\qquad} 0.2092$$

Thus, based on the sample information and with 95% confidence, the proportion of bundles with less than 5,000 board feet is between 0.0908 and 0.2092.

Determining the Sample Size

The purchasing manager may not be satisfied with the relatively high tolerable error of ± 0.0592. If not, he is faced with the options of lowering his confidence level or increasing the sample size (or some of both). These are the same trade-offs that exist in the development of any confidence interval estimate.

Suppose the manager wishes to keep the confidence level at 95%, but wishes to reduce the tolerable error to ± 0.02. The sample must be increased, but to what level?

The appropriate sample size is found using equation 8-16:

$$e = Z \sqrt{\frac{pq}{n}} \qquad \text{8-16}$$

where

$$e = \text{Tolerable error} = \frac{\text{Precision}}{2}$$

Solving for n, we get equation 8-17:

$$n = \frac{Z^2 pq}{e^2} \qquad \text{8-17}$$

Equation 8-17 assumes that sampling is with replacement or that the sample size is less than 5% of the population and that the decision maker knows p. Of course, if p were already known, there would be no need to sample. There are two recommended ways of getting around this problem:

1. Use $p = 0.5$, since this will give the largest possible σ_p, and thus a conservatively large sample size.
2. Select a *pilot* sample smaller than the expected sample size and calculate p for this sample.

Since the Far West purchasing manager has already sampled 140 bundles and found 15% of these to have under 5,000 board feet, it makes sense to treat this sample as the pilot sample and to substitute $p = 0.15$ in equation 8-17 to solve for the required sample size. We do this as follows:

$$n = \frac{(1.96)^2 (0.15)(0.85)}{(0.02)^2}$$
$$= 1,224.51 \text{ or } 1,225 \text{ bundles}$$

Thus, the manager will need to sample 1,225 bundles to achieve the precision he seeks and maintain the 95% confidence level. Keep in mind that he already sampled 140 bundles, so he needs to sample an additional 1,085 bundles. If he thinks this is too many, he will be faced with increasing the tolerable error or decreasing the confidence level or both.

In this example, we used the pilot sample approach to assist in determining the required sample size. In cases where we cannot take a pilot sample, we could use $p = 0.50$ in equation 8-17. This will give a conservatively large sample size.

SKILL DEVELOPMENT PROBLEMS FOR **SECTION 8-3**

The following set of problems is meant to test your understanding of the material in this section.

7. Given the following information:

$$n = 200$$
$$x = 35$$

      a. Determine the 90% confidence interval for the population proportion.
      b. Determine the 95% confidence interval for the population proportion.

8. Given the following information:

$$n = 200$$
$$x = 155$$

      a. Determine the 80% confidence interval estimate for the population proportion.
      b. Determine the 95% confidence interval estimate for the population proportion.

9. Determine the sample size necessary to estimate the population proportion with a tolerable error of plus or minus 0.04 with 95% confidence. Assume $p = 0.50$ for the purpose of computing the required sample size.

10. What is the required sample size for estimating the population proportion within plus or minus 0.03 of the true value at 90% confidence? Assume that $p = 0.50$ for the purposes of determining the required sample size.

11. In determining the required sample size when estimating the population proportion, it is often recommended that the p value be set at 0.50. Discuss why this is and what the impact is on the computed sample size.

12. The Maine Department of Lands has recently selected a sample of 100 taxpayers. The taxpayers were asked whether the state should provide more state parks and camping facilities. A total of sixty answered "yes" to the question. A 95% confidence interval estimate was developed and provided to the director. However, the director was not satisfied with the precision of the estimate and asked that the width of the interval be cut in half. What size sample is necessary to achieve these results? How many new taxpayers need to be surveyed?

13. The Tree-Top Company sells franchise fast-food stores throughout the southeast. As part of the franchise service provided to the individual stores, Tree-Top managers provide a variety of marketing research services. Recently, they selected a random sample of 400 customers and asked them whether they would be interested in a new product called "finger-food." Of the 400 people surveyed, 45 indicated an interest in the new product. Based on these results, determine the 95% confidence interval estimate for the true population proportion of customers who would be interested. Interpret the estimate.

14. United Airlines is interested in the percentage of its fliers who think the service aboard their flights is either very good or excellent. They wish the estimate to be within plus or minus 0.02 of the true percentage and they wish to have 98% confidence. How large a sample size is necessary?

8-4 CONFIDENCE INTERVALS FOR ESTIMATING THE DIFFERENCE BETWEEN TWO POPULATION PARAMETERS—LARGE SAMPLES

Managers often have to estimate either the mean of a single population or the proportion of successes in a population. The tools we have discussed up to now are very useful for these estimates. However, managers will also often have to estimate either the difference between two population means or the difference between two population proportions. These situations involve two populations and require random samples to be selected *independently* from each.

DIFFERENCE BETWEEN TWO POPULATION MEANS

One of the procedures that have given the Japanese an advantage over North American manufacturers in many industries is machine set-up time. Set-up time is the total time required to make necessary changes on the machine after the last item of a given product type or model comes off the machine and before the first good item of a new product type or model is produced on the machine. Short set-up times increase manufacturing flexibility and reduce manufacturing lead times. One documented example of the difference between Japanese and U.S. manufacturers occurred in the corrugated container manufacturing industry. In one U.S. plant the typical set-up time on a box cutting machine was 30 minutes. At a plant in Japan, in a span of 5 hours, the same machine was set up 52 times!

To help improve set-up times in one U.S. firm, the director of productivity improvement implemented a training program known as SMED, which stands for single minute exchange of dyes. The training program, designed to help the operators make quicker set-ups, was introduced to machine operators in the Burley, Idaho, plant. The company also has a plant in Corvallis, Oregon. SMED training was not given at this plant. Six weeks following the training at Burley, the director is interested in determining the difference in average set-up times at the two manufacturing plants. Before the training, both plants had the same average set-up times.

The point estimator for the difference between population means, $(\mu_{x_1} - \mu_{x_2})$, is $(\overline{X}_1 - \overline{X}_2)$, the difference in sample means. As with a single sample mean, for large samples the sampling distribution of the difference, $(\overline{X}_1 - \overline{X}_2)$, will be approximately normally distributed, with the center of the sampling distribution determined by equation 8-18:

$$E(\overline{X}_1 - \overline{X}_2) = \mu_{x_1} - \mu_{x_2} \qquad \text{8-18}$$

The standard deviation of the difference between two sample means is determined by equation 8-19:

$$\sigma_{\bar{x}_1 - \bar{x}_2} = \sqrt{\frac{\sigma_{x_1}^2}{n_1} + \frac{\sigma_{x_2}^2}{n_2}}$$

8-19

Equation 8-19 assumes that the population variances are known. In some applications, this may be the case; however, far more frequently, these values will be unknown and must be estimated from the sample variances. If that is the case, then the estimated standard deviation of the sampling distribution is given by equation 8-20:

$$S_{\bar{x}_1 - \bar{x}_2} = \sqrt{\frac{S_1^2}{n_1} + \frac{S_2^2}{n_2}}$$

8-20

To arrive at an estimate for the true difference in average set-up times, the director has selected a random sample of 100 set-ups from each plant with the following results:

Burley Plant	Corvallis Plant
$\overline{X}_1 = 12.5$ min	$\overline{X}_2 = 17.9$ min
$S_1 = 3.2$ min	$S_2 = 5.2$ min
$n_1 = 100$	$n_2 = 100$

Note that when samples of equal size are selected from the two populations, the estimation is said to have a **balanced design.** However, the sample sizes do not have to be equal to estimate the difference between two population means.

The format for developing a confidence interval for estimating the difference between population means is the same as that for a single population mean. That is,

Point estimate ± (Interval coefficient) (Standard error)

Thus, the confidence interval for estimating the difference in average set-up times is given by expression 8-21 if the population variances are known, and by expression 8-22 if we must estimate the population variances.

$$(\overline{X}_1 - \overline{X}_2) \pm Z \sqrt{\frac{\sigma_{x_1}^2}{n_1} + \frac{\sigma_{x_2}^2}{n_2}}$$

8-21

$$(\overline{X}_1 - \overline{X}_2) \pm Z \sqrt{\frac{S_{x_1}^2}{n_1} + \frac{S_{x_2}^2}{n_2}} \qquad \text{8-22}$$

Since in this example, the population variances in set-up times are not known, we will use expression 8-22 to develop the confidence interval. If the director wants a 95% confidence interval estimate, we get:

$$(12.5 - 17.9) \pm (1.96) \sqrt{\frac{(3.2)^2}{100} + \frac{(5.2)^2}{100}}$$

$$-5.4 \pm 1.197$$

$$-6.597 \text{ min} \underline{\qquad} -4.203 \text{ min}$$

Thus, based on the sample data, the director can conclude with 95% confidence that the difference in average set-up times is between 4.203 and 6.597 minutes. The minus signs on the interval values indicate that the Burley plant set-up times are shorter than the Corvallis set-up times. Thus, if the director believes that set-up times were, on average, the same before the training, then the SMED training has apparently resulted in reduced average set-up times at Burley.

DIFFERENCE BETWEEN TWO POPULATION PROPORTIONS

The quality control manager for Morgan Electronics has been experimenting with two quality control systems. System 1 has been used on one assembly line, which has produced 15,000 computer power supplies. System 2 has been used on a second assembly line, which has produced 25,000 computer power supplies. The manager is interested in determining the difference in the proportion of defectives produced under each quality control system.

Although the quality control manager wants to know $(p_1 - p_2)$, he cannot test every power supply unit. Instead, he will select a sample of units produced under each system and calculate $(\hat{p}_1 - \hat{p}_2)$, the point estimate for the difference in population proportions. If the sample sizes are sufficiently large, the sampling distribution of $(\hat{p}_1 - \hat{p}_2)$ will be approximately normally distributed with a mean and standard error as shown in equations 8-23 and 8-24.

$$E(\hat{p}_1 - \hat{p}_2) = (p_1 - p_2) \qquad \text{8-23}$$

and

$$\sigma_{\hat{p}_1 - \hat{p}_2} = \sqrt{\frac{p_1 q_1}{n_1} + \frac{p_2 q_2}{n_2}} \qquad \text{8-24}$$

$$= \text{Standard error of the sampling distribution}$$

Equation 8-24, the standard error of the sampling distribution, contains p_1 and p_2, the population proportions. The quality control manager can substitute the estimates, $\hat{p}_1$ and $\hat{p}_2$, for these values (equation 8-25):

$$S_{\hat{p}_1 - \hat{p}_2} = \sqrt{\frac{\hat{p}_1 \hat{q}_1}{n_1} + \frac{\hat{p}_2 \hat{q}_2}{n_2}} \qquad \text{8-25}$$

Given equation 8-25, the quality control manager can develop a confidence interval estimate of $(p_1 - p_2)$ using expression 8-26:

$$(\hat{p}_1 - \hat{p}_2) \pm Z \sqrt{\frac{\hat{p}_1 \hat{q}_1}{n_1} + \frac{\hat{p}_2 \hat{q}_2}{n_2}} \qquad \text{8-26}$$

As you can see, the format of expression 8-26 is the same as for all other confidence intervals. That is,

Point estimate ± (Interval coefficient) (Standard error)

The quality control manager has selected a sample of 400 computer power supplies from each assembly line and tested them, with the following results:

Line 1	Line 2
$\hat{p}_1 = 0.08$	$\hat{p}_2 = 0.06$
$\hat{q}_1 = 0.92$	$\hat{q}_2 = 0.94$
$n_1 = 400$	$n_2 = 400$

The manager wants a 98% confidence interval estimate for the difference in the proportion of defectives produced under the two systems. He would find the estimate as follows:

$$(\hat{p}_1 - \hat{p}_2) \pm 2.33 \sqrt{\frac{\hat{p}_1 \hat{q}_1}{n_1} + \frac{\hat{p}_2 \hat{q}_2}{n_2}}$$

$$(0.08 - 0.06) \pm 2.33 \sqrt{\frac{(0.08)(0.92)}{400} + \frac{(0.06)(0.94)}{400}}$$

$$0.02 \pm 0.042$$

$$-0.022 \underline{\qquad} +0.062$$

The manager is very confident that this interval includes the true difference between the proportion of defectives produced under the two quality control systems. Since the interval contains 0, the manager will conclude that, even though there is a difference between the two sample proportions, this difference is not large enough to conclude that there is a significant difference between the two population proportions.

SKILL DEVELOPMENT PROBLEMS FOR **SECTION 8-4**

The following set of problems is meant to test your understanding of the material in this section.

15. Given the following information:

$$n_1 = 100 \qquad n_2 = 150$$
$$\overline{X}_1 = 50 \qquad \overline{X}_2 = 65$$
$$S_1 = 6 \qquad S_2 = 9$$

   a. Determine the 90% confidence interval estimate for the difference between population means. Interpret the estimate.
   b. Determine the 98% confidence interval estimate for the difference between population means. Interpret the estimate.

16. Given the following information:

$$n_1 = 300 \qquad n_2 = 400$$
$$\overline{X}_1 = 420 \qquad \overline{X}_2 = 300$$
$$S_1 = 24 \qquad S_2 = 20$$

   a. Determine the 95% confidence interval estimate for the difference between population means. Interpret the estimate.
   b. Determine the 90% confidence interval estimate for the difference between population means. Interpret the estimate.

17. Given the following information:

$$n_1 = 200 \qquad n_2 = 200$$
$$x_1/n_1 = 0.30 \qquad x_2/n_2 = 0.27$$

   a. Determine the 90% confidence interval estimate for the difference between population proportions. Interpret the estimate.
   b. Determine the 95% confidence interval estimate for the difference between population proportions. Interpret the estimate.

18. Given the following information:

$$n_1 = 100 \qquad n_2 = 200$$
$$x_1/n_1 = 0.60 \qquad x_2/n_2 = 0.67$$

   a. Determine the 95% confidence interval estimate for the difference between population proportions. Interpret the estimate.
   b. Determine the 80% confidence interval estimate for the difference between population proportions. Interpret the estimate.

19. The Phillips Oil Company is interested in estimating the difference in the population proportions of customers who purchase unleaded gasoline in eastern states versus western states. They have selected a random sample of 1,200 eastern-state customers and 900 western-state customers; 852 of the eastern-state customers and 643 of the western-state customers purchased unleaded gasoline. Using a 95% confidence level, determine the estimate for the difference in population proportions and interpret the estimate.

20. A marketing consulting firm was recently hired by a large retail hardware chain to study the buying habits of the chain's customers. As part of the study, the consultant selected a random sample of male customers and another random sample of female customers. The sampled customers were observed to determine how long they spent in the store per visit. The following data were recorded:

Male	Female
$n_1 = 250$	$n_2 = 350$
$\overline{X}_1 = 24$ min	$\overline{X}_2 = 53$ min
$S_{x_1} = 11$	$S_{x_2} = 32$

Based on these sample data, what is the 90% confidence interval estimate for the difference between true average shopping times for males and females? Interpret your estimate.

8-5 COMPUTER APPLICATIONS

This chapter has introduced large-sample estimation. We have demonstrated how confidence intervals can be developed based on sample data. If you are provided the summary statistics from a sample, such as the mean and standard deviation, the computations involved in developing a confidence interval are not too difficult. However, in many applications, a decision maker will have only the raw sample data. In these cases, a computer and appropriate statistical software can be very useful.

In this section, three computer applications for developing large-sample confidence intervals are shown. In the first two cases, we use the MINITAB software package and the KIVZ-Channel 5 survey data (see Table 2-10 in Chapter 2). First, we develop a 95% confidence interval estimate of the population's mean income, X_{18}. Table 8-1 shows the MINITAB output. Figure 8-5 shows the MINITAB

TABLE **8-1**

MINITAB Output for 95% Confidence Interval for Income

```
THE ASSUMED SIGMA = 95.0
 N     MEAN    STDEV    SE MEAN    95.0 PERCENT INCOME
50    24846.0   4800.5    678.9      (23513.5, 26178.5)
```

FIGURE **8-5**

MINITAB
Commands for
Confidence
Interval
Estimation

```
MTB> READ 'KIVZ5' into C1-C19
MTB> NAME C18 'INCOME'
MTB> OUTFILE = 'PRINTER'
MTB> ZINTERVAL 4800.5 C18
```

commands used to generate the output. You should review the printout and make sure that you can interpret the interval estimate.

In the second example, we want to estimate the difference in average income, X_{18}, between males and females, X_{10}. Table 8-2 shows the computer output generated when the MINITAB commands in Figure 8-6 were used. Be sure that you can interpret the 95% confidence interval estimate.

TABLE **8-2**

MINITAB
Output for
Two-Sample
Estimation of
Males vs. Females
Income (C10 =
2 = Female;
C10 = 1 = Male)

C10	N	MEAN	STDEV	SE MEAN
2	28	25661	5188	981
1	22	23809	4141	883

95 PCT CI FOR MU 2 − MU 1: (−803, 4507)

FIGURE **8-6**

MINITAB
Commands for
Confidence
Interval
Estimation of
Income by Sex

```
MTB> READ 'KIVZ5' into C1-C19
MTB> OUTFILE = 'PRINTER'
MTB> TWOT 95 C18 C10
```

For the third example, we use the microcomputer software package GB-STAT, which produces confidence interval estimates readily. Again using the KIVZ-Channel 5 data, the confidence interval estimate for average age of all viewers is shown in Table 8-3. Note that GB-STAT automatically provides both the 99% and 95% confidence intervals, along with a variety of other descriptive statistics pertaining to the age variable.

TABLE 8-3	DESCRIPTIVE ESTIMATES FOR... age			
GB-STAT Output for Confidence Intervals for KIVZ-Channel 5 Database	SAMPLE SIZE:	50	MINIMUM:	20
	NUMBER MISSING:	0	MAXIMUM:	81
	SUM:	2203	RANGE:	61
	SUM OF SQUARES:	108851	SEMI-INNER QT. RANGE:	13.75
	MEAN:	44.06	MEDIAN:	42.5
	LOWER 99% C.I.:	38.15979	5TH PERCENTILE:	21
	LOWER 95% C.I.:	39.64252	10TH PERCENTILE:	24
	UPPER 95% C.I.:	48.47748	25TH PERCENTILE:	30.5
	UPPER 99% C.I.:	49.96022	75TH PERCENTILE:	58
	ADJ. SUM SQUARES:	11786.82	90TH PERCENTILE:	65.5
	HARMONIC MEAN:	38.47844	95TH PERCENTILE:	67.5
	VARIANCE:	240.5474	STANDARD ERROR:	2.19339
	STANDARD DEVIATION:	15.50959	T-VALUE (MEAN=0):	20.08765
	COEF. OF VARIATION:	.35201	MEAN ABS. DEV:	12.9824
	SKEWNESS:	.25251	KURTOSIS:	−.80738

8-6 CONCLUSIONS

Many decision-making applications involve estimating a population value from a sample of the population. This chapter introduced the concepts of statistical estimation for large samples. We discussed two types of estimates: point estimates and interval estimates.

Point estimates are values such as $\overline{X}$, S_x^2, $\hat{p}$, $(\overline{X}_1 - \overline{X}_2)$, and $(\hat{p}_1 - \hat{p}_2)$, which are calculated from a sample. Confidence interval estimates are recommended when a decision maker wants to estimate a population value and have an idea of the estimate's error. The decision maker can control the estimate's level of confidence and precision, but constantly faces a trade-off between these two factors and the required sample size.

Even if a confidence interval that meets the decision maker's precision and confidence requirements is developed, there is no guarantee the calculated interval will actually include the population value of interest. The decision maker must recognize that there is always a chance of error anytime sampling and statistical estimation are involved. The best that can be said is that the decision maker has a measure of the chance that the interval includes the true population value. If the confidence level is increased, the decision maker can be even more confident. Formulas were presented for estimating population values when the population standard deviation is known and when it is unknown. Generally, the standard deviation will not be known, so the formulas that employ estimates of σ will be used most frequently.

The chapter glossary presents a summary of several new terms that were presented in this chapter. Several equations that can be used to develop interval estimates of various population parameters are listed immediately following the glossary.

CHAPTER **GLOSSARY**

confidence interval An interval developed from sample values such that if all possible intervals were calculated, a percentage equal to the confidence level would contain the population value of interest.

interval coefficient The table value (Z value in this chapter) associated with a particular level of confidence. For example:

Confidence	Interval Coefficient
90%	$Z = 1.645$
95%	$Z = 1.96$
98%	$Z = 2.33$
99%	$Z = 2.58$

parameter A descriptive measure of the population that has a fixed value. Examples are the population mean, μ_x, and the population standard deviation, σ_x.

point estimate A single number determined from a sample used to estimate a population parameter.

precision The width of the confidence interval.

tolerable error One-half the width of the confidence interval. Tolerable error is used in determining required sample size.

unbiased estimator An estimator whose expected value equals the population parameter. If μ_x is the population parameter, $\overline{X}$ is an unbiased estimate if $E(\overline{X}) = \mu_x$.

CHAPTER FORMULAS

Standard error of the mean

σ_x *known*

$$\sigma_{\overline{x}} = \frac{\sigma_x}{\sqrt{n}}$$

σ_x *unknown*

$$S_{\overline{x}} = \frac{S_x}{\sqrt{n}}$$

Sample mean

$$\overline{X} = \frac{\Sigma X}{n}$$

Sample variance

$$S_x^2 = \frac{\Sigma(X - \overline{X})^2}{n - 1}$$

Sample standard deviation

$$S_x = \sqrt{\frac{\Sigma(X - \overline{X})^2}{n - 1}}$$

Confidence interval for μ_x

$$\overline{X} \pm Z\sigma_{\overline{x}}$$

Standard error of the difference between two means
  Population variances known

$$\sigma_{\overline{x}_1 - \overline{x}_2} = \sqrt{\frac{\sigma_{x_1}^2}{n_1} + \frac{\sigma_{x_2}^2}{n_2}}$$

  Population variances unknown

$$S_{\overline{x}_1 - \overline{x}_2} = \sqrt{\frac{S_{x_1}^2}{n_1} + \frac{S_{x_2}^2}{n_2}}$$

Confidence interval for $\mu_{x_1} - \mu_{x_2}$

$$(\overline{X}_1 - \overline{X}_2) \pm Z\sqrt{\frac{\sigma_{x_1}^2}{n_1} + \frac{\sigma_{x_2}^2}{n_2}}$$

Sample proportion

$$\hat{p} = \frac{x}{n}$$

Standard error of proportions

$$\sigma_{\hat{p}} = \sqrt{\frac{pq}{n}}$$

and

$$S_{\hat{p}} = \sqrt{\frac{\hat{p}\hat{q}}{n}}$$

Confidence interval for p

$$\hat{p} \pm ZS_{\hat{p}}$$

Standard error of the difference between two proportions
  p_1 *and* p_2 *known*

$$\sigma_{\hat{p}_1 - \hat{p}_2} = \sqrt{\frac{p_1 q_1}{n_1} + \frac{p_2 q_2}{n_2}}$$

  p_1 *and* p_2 *unknown*

$$S_{\hat{p}_1 - \hat{p}_2} = \sqrt{\frac{\hat{p}_1 \hat{q}_1}{n_1} + \frac{\hat{p}_2 \hat{q}_2}{n_2}}$$

Confidence interval for $(p_1 - p_2)$

$$(\hat{p}_1 - \hat{p}_2) \pm ZS_{\hat{p}_1 - \hat{p}_2}$$

Sample size

One population mean

$$n = \frac{Z^2\sigma_x^2}{e^2}$$

One population proportion

$$n = \frac{Z^2pq}{e^2}$$

SOLVED PROBLEMS

1. The manager at a major U.S. airport wishes to estimate the proportion of flights that arrived late at the airport last year for a report she must submit to the Civil Aeronautics Board. She has indicated that a 95% confidence interval is required with a precision of 0.04.
   a. How large a sample should the airport manager select? (*Hint:* Use $\hat{p} = 0.5$ and explain why you can use this value.)
   b. Using the sample size determined in part **a,** suppose the sample proportion, $\hat{p}$, is 0.24. Develop the confidence interval and provide the appropriate interpretation for the airport manager.

Solution

a. To determine the appropriate sample size, we need the following information:

$$\text{Confidence level} = 95\%$$
$$\text{Interval coefficient} = 1.96$$
$$\text{Precision} = 0.04$$
$$\text{Tolerable error} = 0.02$$
$$\hat{p} = 0.5$$

(Note that using $\hat{p} = 0.5$ implies the greatest possible variance in the sampling distribution. Consequently, the sample size we find will always be large enough to meet the confidence level and precision requirements.) Then,

$$e = Z\sqrt{\frac{\hat{p}\hat{q}}{n}}$$

$$0.02 = 1.96\sqrt{\frac{(0.5)(0.5)}{n}}$$

$$n = \frac{(1.96)^2(0.5)(0.5)}{(0.02)^2}$$

$$= 2,401$$

b. The 95% confidence interval is

$$\hat{p} \pm 1.96\sqrt{\frac{(0.24)(0.76)}{2{,}401}}$$

$$0.24 \pm 0.017$$

$$0.223 \underline{\quad\quad} 0.257$$

Note that this interval is more precise than that required by the airport manager. The reason for this is that the calculated $\hat{p}$ is lower than the $\hat{p} = 0.5$ that was used to find the required sample size.

2. Suppose the airport manager in Problem 1 wishes to estimate the difference in the proportions of late flights for two airlines that use the airport. She has indicated that a 95% confidence interval is required, with precision equal to 0.03.

   a. What sample size is needed from each airline to provide an interval estimate with this confidence and precision? Let the sample sizes from the two airlines be equal. Also, use $\hat{p} = 0.24$ for both airlines since this value was calculated for a sample from all airlines using this airport.

   b. Using the sample size determined in part **a**, the airport manager found the following:

$$\hat{p}_1 = 0.22 \quad \text{and} \quad \hat{p}_2 = 0.27$$

   Develop the 95% confidence interval estimate for the difference between population proportions.

Solution

a. To determine the required sample size, we must perform the following calculation:

$$e = 1.96\sqrt{\frac{\hat{p}_1 \hat{q}_1}{n_1} + \frac{\hat{p}_2 \hat{q}_2}{n_2}}$$

Since $n_1 = n_2 = n$, we get

$$0.015 = 1.96\sqrt{\frac{(0.24)(0.76)}{n} + \frac{(0.24)(0.76)}{n}}$$

$$n = 6{,}228.5$$

$$= 6{,}229$$

Thus, the airport manager needs to study 6,229 flights from each airline. This is quite a large sample. Chances are the manager will have to decrease the confidence level, the desired precision, or both.

b. The 95% confidence interval is

$$(\hat{p}_1 - \hat{p}_2) \pm 1.96 \sqrt{\frac{\hat{p}_1 \hat{q}_1}{n_1} + \frac{\hat{p}_2 \hat{q}_2}{n_2}}$$

$$(0.22 - 0.27) \pm 1.96 \sqrt{\frac{(0.22)(0.78)}{6,229} + \frac{(0.27)(0.73)}{6,229}}$$

$$(0.22 - 0.27) \pm 0.015$$

$$-0.065 \underline{} -0.035$$

Thus, the manager is confident that the true difference is between -0.065 and -0.035 (airline 2 has a higher proportion of late flights).

CONCEPTUAL QUESTIONS AND ASSIGNMENTS

21.   Discuss in your own words the general advantage of an interval estimate over a point estimate.

22.   Discuss in your own words the difference between a point estimator and an interval estimator.

23.   Give at least one business-related example for which a point estimate would be used rather than an interval estimate.

24.   Give at least one business-related example for which an interval estimate would be preferred over a point estimate.

25.   This chapter stated that an increase in sample size will improve the precision of a confidence interval estimate. Discuss in your own words what the term *precision* means.

26.   Would you agree that an increase in sample size will increase the confidence level of an interval estimate? Why or why not?

27.   What is the effect on an estimate's precision of increasing the confidence level of the estimate? What is the reason for this change?

ADDITIONAL PROBLEMS

28.   For each of the following confidence levels, determine the appropriate interval coefficient:
   a.   90%
   b.   95%
   c.   99%
   d.   94%
   e.   50%
   f.   89%
   g.   80%

29.   The Texas Highway Department is studying traffic patterns on a busy highway near Dallas. As part of the study, the department needs to estimate the average number of vehicles that pass an off-ramp each day. A random sample of 65 days gives $\overline{X} = 14,205$ and $S_x = 1,000$. Develop the 90%

confidence interval estimate for μ_x, the average number of cars per day, and interpret your results.

30. Referring to Problem 29, suppose the Highway Department officials after careful analysis decide they really need 99% confidence.
   a. What is the 99% confidence interval estimate of μ_x, the average number of cars passing the off-ramp? Interpret your results.
   b. After calculating the confidence interval in part **a,** the Highway Department officials realize the precision is too low for their needs. They want the precision to be 330. Given this precision and 99% confidence, what size sample is required?

31. The optometrists at the Eye Care Center wanted to decide between two cleaning methods used by their staff when giving a patient a new contact lens. The main concern was lenses tearing while being cleaned. Staff members would obtain a lens from a sealed container, look at it under a microscope for defects, clean the lens either by hand or machine, and then give the lens to the patient to insert. The staff kept a record of patients finding their lens torn upon insertion after both types of cleaning methods were used 200 times each, with the following results:

	By hand	By machine
Percent torn	4.0	5.0

Using 90% confidence, can it be concluded that one cleaning method is safer in preventing tears than the other? Explain.

32. Each January an independent polling company conducts a survey of television viewers to provide an estimate of the average number of hours spent by Americans watching television per day. The January 1985 report showed that for a random sample of 1,800 people, the mean time spent watching television was 7.2 hours, with a standard deviation of 2.7 hours.
   a. What is the point estimate for the average number of hours Americans spend watching television per day?
   b. What is the 97% confidence interval estimate for the average number of hours Americans spend watching television per day?
   c. A representative for the polling company said that this survey sampled 450 more people than the previous year's survey. He said that the reason the point estimate jumped to 7.2 hours per day from 6.6 hours per day may have been because the larger sample might have included more extremes on the high side of the viewing time distribution. Therefore, the 7.2 value might be an "aberration." Comment on this statement and the soundness of the reasoning behind it.

33. The Army purchasing department is seeking suppliers of black oxfords because the previous supplier has stopped making this type of shoe. Since these shoes are issued to new recruits and these recruits do a lot of marching, the Army is particularly concerned with the durability of the soles. They have devised a shoe tester that rubs the shoe bottom against a slab of concrete. The testers monitor the time needed to rub a hole in the sole.

The Army asks for a sample of 100 from each of two shoe manufacturers, but part of one shipment is lost. The following results are found:

	Manufacturer A	Manufacturer B
Sample size	100	80
Average time	3.3 hours	2.8 hours
Standard deviation	0.86 hour	0.79 hour

What is the 97% confidence level estimate for the difference between the average wear times for the shoes of the two manufacturers?

34. Based on the interval found in problem 33, should the Army prefer one manufacturer over the other? Explain. How would a substantially lower price for shoe B affect your recommendation?

35. You have just completed a poll for a political candidate and have estimated the percentage of voters who will vote for her to be 0.51 ± 0.028. She is not happy with this estimate and would like a precision of 0.02. If each interview costs $1.75, how much will it cost to give her the interval width she wants? She will accept a 95% confidence level.

36. The Impact Service Corporation provides technical support for typewriters and word-processing equipment in the Seattle area. Recently, the company's manager for service was asked to recommend a word-processing system to an auto maker in Detroit. Although there were many systems she could have recommended, she narrowed the choice down to two brands: the Hawk/System 8000 and the Mercury–D750. Both systems are priced about the same, but the manager was uncertain about maintenance costs.

She decided to select a random sample of forty owners of each system and obtain their maintenance records for the first year of ownership. She recorded repair costs for each brand as follows:

Hawk/System 8000	Mercury–D750
$\overline{X}_1 = \$1,375.00$	$\overline{X}_2 = \$1,190.00$
$S_1 = \$203.00$	$S_2 = \$306.00$
$n_1 = 40$	$n_2 = 40$

a. Determine the point estimate for the difference in average repair costs for the two brands of word-processing systems.

b. Develop and interpret the 95% confidence interval for estimating the difference in population means for repair costs.

c. Based on your estimate in part **b**, what should the manager conclude with respect to word-processing-system average repair costs for the two systems? All other things being equal, which, if either, of these two systems should the manager recommend? Discuss.

37. Referring to Problem 36, the Impact Service Corporation knows the auto maker is also concerned with system down time. Suppose the service manager for Impact also recorded the down time during the first year for the systems

owned by each of the businesses sampled, and arrived at these summary statistics:

Hawk/System 8000	Mercury–D750
$\overline{X}_1 = 16.8$ hours	$\overline{X}_2 = 12.8$ hours
$S_1 = 2.1$ hours	$S_2 = 3.7$ hours
$n_1 = 40$	$n_2 = 40$

   a. Develop a 90% confidence interval estimate for the difference in average down time for the two machines. Interpret this estimate.

   b. Referring to the interval developed in part **a**, assuming all other things are equal, do the sample data provide evidence to support one system over the other based on average down time? Explain.

   c. Referring to your answers to parts **a** and **b** of this problem and also to parts **b** and **c** of Problem 36, what conclusions might be reached with respect to the word-processing systems? Discuss.

38. The manager of the Valley Sawmill needs to estimate the percentage of clear and standard redwood contained in a recent shipment of logs. (Standard boards have knots in them.) She samples a random selection of logs before they go to the drying kilns.

   a. If, out of a sample of 350 boards, she finds 92 clear, what is the 98% confidence interval estimate of the overall proportion of clear boards?

   b. Suppose, in an effort to increase the estimate's precision, the manager looks at an additional 350 boards and finds 245 of standard quality. What is her new estimate for the proportion of clear boards?

39. The Early Bird Egg Farm is trying to decide between two brands of egg containers. The major consideration is breakage prevention during shipment. Early Bird Egg Farm ships 500 eggs in each type of container, with the following results:

	Brand 1	Brand 2
Percent broken	2.0	2.6

Using 95% confidence, can one brand be concluded to be better than the other in preventing breakage? Explain.

40. The personnel director at a large southern electronics plant is not satisfied with the present training program. He observes that although the present program is extensive and expensive, too many people must be released because of inadequate work even after completing training. Unfortunately, he really does not know what percentage are released for inadequate work and what percentage are released for some other reason.

He has been considering implementing a new training program and would like to compare the results of the new program with those of the old. He decides to randomly separate the next group of new trainees into two groups, train each group entirely by one of the two methods, and monitor the results.

After several months, he has found the following:

	New Method	Old Method
Group size	215	216
Number released for poor work	65	73

a. Using a 96% confidence level, is there any reason to change training methods? Explain.

b. Suppose both methods are equivalent in cost, but trainees seem to like the new method better than the old. Is there any reason not to change training methods?

41. The federal government has mandated that to qualify for federal highway funds, states must ensure that at least 70% of the cars traveling on their highways are obeying the 55-mile-per-hour speed limit where required. A team of federal inspectors has gone to a western state and randomly checked the speed of 185 cars. They found 122 obeying this limit where required. Based on this evidence, and using a 96% confidence level, can the inspectors make a case for denying the state highway funds? Explain.

42. The district manager, upon reviewing the report submitted by the inspectors in Problem 41, objects strongly. He claims the sample size was much too small to draw any meaningful conclusions. Do you agree or disagree? If the district manager wants to limit the tolerable error of all future estimates to 0.02, how large a sample size is needed?

43. The makers of Data-Bank, a word-processing package for microcomputers, are interested in estimating the proportion of their packages that are being used in business settings rather than for personal uses. The sales manager believes the figure is close to 75%.

a. If the sales manager's figure is used, what random-sample size should the company select if it wishes to estimate the true proportion with 95% confidence with a precision of 0.08?

b. Suppose that the company does select a sample of the size computed in part a, and the p value equals 0.60. Comment on whether the sample size computed in part a was large enough to allow for a tolerable error of plus or minus 0.04 with 95% confidence.

44. Great Sky Chemical has developed a new, effective insect repellent. The leading spray on the market now advertises an effective time of 8 hours. From past experience, Great Sky knows that the time a spray is effective is a function of personal skin chemistry, and the variability remains the same no matter what the type of spray. This variability gives a variance of 2.5. Great Sky field tests its spray on sixty-five volunteers and finds it to be effective for an average of 8.75 hours.

Can Great Sky state, based on a 90% confidence interval estimate, that its spray is more effective than the leading brand?

45. The manager at the Bay Bridge Restaurant has started receiving complaints about the waiting time before being served in the dining room. The manager

takes a sample of 130 diners and finds that the mean time from entrance to serving is 18.56 minutes, with a standard deviation of 4.5 minutes.

   a. What is the confidence interval estimate of average serving time if the manager specifies a 94% confidence level?

   b. What should the manager say to the next irate customer who enters his office claiming to have waited in the dining room for 45 minutes without being served?

   c. Can you see any sampling problems that may affect the conclusions you can draw from the interval calculated in part **a**? Explain.

46. The United Automobile Association recently selected a random sample of 450 people who had purchased a new car 3 years ago. The U.A.A. is interested in estimating the average mileage for 3-year-old cars. If the sample showed a mean of 26,855 miles and a standard deviation of 4,350 miles:

   a. What is the point estimate for the population mean?

   b. Develop a 95% confidence interval estimate for the population mean and interpret this estimate.

   c. Develop a 90% confidence interval estimate and compare this estimate with the one developed in part **b**.

47. Referring to Problem 46, suppose the same sample results had been derived from a sample of 900 car owners.

   a. Develop a 95% confidence interval estimate for the population mean and interpret this value.

   b. Compare this interval estimate to the one developed in Problem 63b. Which interval would be preferred and why?

48. The manager whose department operates a fleet of company cars is trying to decide which brand of tires to use. Her choices are brand F and brand M, and the price per tire is the same for both brands. The manager takes a sample of sixty-four tires from brand F and fifty-five tires from brand M. She finds the following values:

	Brand F	Brand M
Average mileage	42,158	43,414
Sample standard deviation	3,465	2,980

   Based on this sample information, is there any reason to prefer one brand based on its average mileage? Explain. Use a confidence level of 95%.

49. Suppose the following confidence intervals estimating the mean age in a northern retail market area have been constructed from three different simple random samples. Assume the age distribution is normal.

Sample	Lower Limit	Upper Limit
1	38.0	50.0
2	40.0	51.9
3	42.0	50.0

   a. If the three samples had the same value for S_x^2 and all three intervals were constructed with a 95% confidence level, which sample was the largest?

Explain how you know this. Which sample was the smallest? How do you know this?

b. Suppose the size of sample 2 was thirty-six and had a sample variance of 255. Approximately what level of confidence should be associated with this interval?

c. Suppose each of the three samples contained sixty observations and all three intervals were constructed with an 85% confidence level. Which sample had the smallest standard deviation? Explain.

d. Compute the standard error for each sample, assuming the values in part c apply. Then determine what change in sample size would be necessary to cut the tolerable error by one-half.

e. Which sample had the smallest mean? How do you know?

50. A consumer organization has recently mounted a campaign to make the use of seat belts mandatory in a southern state. As part of the argument, the organization has sampled 1,000 accident records where no seat belts were used and found that in 130 cases, people were thrown from their vehicles. Based on this sample evidence, calculate and interpret a 95% confidence interval estimate for the true proportion of accidents in which people are thrown from their vehicles.

STATE DEPARTMENT OF TRANSPORTATION CASE STUDY PROBLEMS

The following questions and problems pertain directly to the State Department of Transportation case study and database introduced in Chapter 1. The questions and problems were written assuming that you will have access to a computer and appropriate statistical software. The database contains 100 observations and seventeen variables. *In the following problems, assume that the sampling was performed according to a simple random sampling procedure.*

1. Herb Kriner would like an estimate of the average age of the drivers in the state. He would like you to provide the estimate in the form of a 95% confidence level. Be sure to interpret your estimate.

2. The variable X_5 is the total convictions for driving-related citations in the past 3 years. Herb Kriner would like a 90% confidence interval estimate for the average number of convictions for drivers in the state. Be sure to interpret the interval.

3. For those drivers who were insured ($X_{17} = 1$), provide a 95% confidence interval estimate for the number of years of formal education. Interpret the interval estimate.

4. Referring to Problem 3, suppose the interval estimate is not precise enough to satisfy Herb Kriner. What must the sample size be to reduce the width by half without changing the confidence level? Show your calculations and prepare a short letter to Herb discussing your results.

5. Develop a 95% confidence interval estimate for the percentage of vehicles in the state that are insured. Interpret the interval.

6. Determine a 90% confidence interval estimate for the percentage of drivers in the state who use their seat belts. Interpret the interval.

7. Based on those drivers in the sample who were wearing a seat belt, what is the 90% confidence interval for the percentage of vehicles insured and driven by belted drivers? Interpret the interval estimate.

ADDITIONAL DATABASE PROBLEMS

The questions and problems in this section reference the various databases that accompany this text and which are described in Chapter 1. Your instructor has been provided a diskette with these databases. It is expected that you will be using computer software to access these data and to perform the required calculations and graphs.

DATABASE: **CITIES** (*Refer to the database description in Chapter 1.*)

1. The variable X_2 is the estimated population growth for the cities between 1990 and 1995. Assuming that these data reflect a random sample of all cities in the United States, determine the 95% confidence interval estimate for the true average growth rate. Interpret your estimate.
2. Provide a 90% confidence interval estimate for the average SAT score for cities in the United States. Assume that the sample is a random sample. Also, make sure you select only those cities that reported SAT scores. Interpret your estimate.
3. Assuming that the data are the result of a sample of cities in the United States, determine the 95% confidence interval for the average difference between earnings by manufacturing workers and white-collar workers. Interpret your estimate.
4. Provide an estimate for the percentage of U.S. cities that have a labor market stress index, X_8, which exceeds 105. Assume the data are a random sample and interpret your estimate. Does your computer software automatically produce the interval estimate or do you have to do some of the work manually?

DATABASE: **FAST100** (*Refer to the database description in Chapter 1.*)

1. Treating the data as a random sample, determine the 98% confidence interval estimate for the average earnings per share growth rate and interpret your estimate.
2. Provide a 90% confidence interval estimate for the average stock price as of 9/6/91. Assume that the data reflect a random sample of companies.
3. Determine a 90% confidence interval estimate for the difference in average profits over the past four quarters between companies traded on the New York Stock Exchange versus the American Stock Exchange. Assume that the data reflect a random sample. Interpret your estimate and comment on what, if anything, this implies about the two stock exchanges.

4. Provide a 95% confidence interval estimate for the difference in average earnings for companies traded over the counter versus those that are traded on one of the major stock exchanges. Assume the samples are random. Provide an interpretation of your result.

DATABASE: **PACRIM** (*Refer to the database description in Chapter 1.*)

1. Assuming that the data reflect a random sample, provide a 95% confidence interval estimate for the 1989 after-tax profits. Interpret your estimate.
2. Referring to Problem 1, suppose that you wished to cut the tolerable error in half. What must be done? Provide all options and discuss why they will accomplish the tolerable error reduction.
3. Provide a 90% confidence interval estimate for the difference in average year-end stockholder equity for companies located in Japan versus companies from the rest of the Pacific Rim area. Assume that the data reflect a random sample. Interpret your estimate.
4. Develop a 90% confidence interval estimate for the mean number of employees for companies located in Japan. Provide an interpretation of this estimate.

DATABASE: **TRUCKS** (*Refer to the database description in Chapter 1.*)

1. Provide a 95% confidence interval estimate for the average WIM gross weight. Assume that the data reflect a random sample. Interpret your estimate.
2. Assuming that the data reflect a random sample, determine a 90% confidence interval estimate for the average speed of vehicles that are weighed on the WIM scale. Interpret your estimate.
3. Determine the 80% confidence interval estimate for the difference between the average temperature during the first 6 months of the year versus the second 6 months. Interpret your estimate.
4. Compute a new variable that is the difference between POE gross weight and WIM gross weight. Then provide a 90% confidence interval estimate for the true average difference. Interpret your result and then comment on whether you believe that the two samples are independent samples. Discuss.
5. Provide a 90% confidence interval estimate for the percentage of trucks crossing the WIM scale at over 55 miles per hour. Interpret your estimate.

CASE

Amalgamated Trucking Company

The Amalgamated Trucking Company has just lost a labor arbitration suit in which it was accused of wrongly dismissing Al Farr, one of its drivers. The dismissal was ruled to be a violation of the union contract. In the current labor contract, both parties (union and management) agreed that all disputes that cannot be settled directly between the two parties be placed in binding arbitration. In the past few months there have been other cases arbitrated, and Amalgamated has always been the victor. However, in this case, the ruling states that Al Farr must be rehired and given back pay equivalent to the amount he would have earned in the 9 months since he was dismissed. The arbitrator stated, as is common in a case of this sort, that Al Farr must be "made whole."

Amalgamated Trucking pays its drivers an hourly wage with time-and-a-half for overtime and double-time for holidays. The hours worked each week depend on the routes assigned. The assignment of routes is done randomly. Thus, in some weeks certain drivers receive substantial overtime work and therefore more pay, while other drivers receive no overtime pay at all.

Dan Thomas, supervisor of Amalgamated Trucking personnel relations, has been assigned the task of determining the amount of back pay that should be awarded to Al Farr. The arbitrator will determine whether the amount proposed by Amalgamated Trucking is adequate, so Dan knows that he must be able to substantiate his figures.

The issue of back pay is complicated. The union has suggested a maximum-hours method in which Al Farr would receive pay equivalent to his pay rate multiplied by the maximum number of hours worked by any employee during the same 9-month period at Amalgamated Trucking. Dan is resisting this plan because of the precedent it would set. At the same time, he has admitted that he does not know the exact amount that Al Farr should receive.

Because he must have a figure by Wednesday, Dan has decided to use personnel records to attempt to arrive at a dollar amount for Al that will be fair. During the first 6 months that Al Farr was out of work, he would have been paid $7.75 per hour, and $8.10 per hour during the final 3 months. Personnel department records show hourly work records for all Amalgamated Trucking drivers. A sampling procedure Dan selected required him to pull a random sample of fifty employee records for each of the last three quarters (one quarter = 3 months). Table 8-4 shows the results of the sampling after several calculations have been made.

Dan faces a long evening trying to make sense out of this information so he can make an effective presentation to the arbitrator.

TABLE 8-4

	Quarter 1	Quarter 2	Quarter 3
Regular hours per week			
$\overline{X}$	39.4	39.7	39.6
S_x	1.6	2.1	1.3
Overtime hours per week			
$\overline{X}$	10.3	9.1	11.0
S_x	3.7	2.9	4.4
Holiday hours per quarter			
$\overline{X}$	12.7	6.2	8.8
S_x	3.1	4.7	2.6

REFERENCES

Berenson, Mark L., and Levine, David M. *Basic Business Statistics Concepts and Applications,* 5th edition. Englewood Cliffs, New Jersey: Prentice-Hall, 1992.

Daniel, Wayne W., and Terrell, James C. *Business Statistics for Management and Economics,* 6th edition. Boston: Houghton Mifflin, 1992.

Hayes, Glenn E., and Romig, Harry G. *Modern Quality Control.* Enrico, Calif.: Glencoe Publishing, 1982.

Iman, Ronald L., and Conover, W. J. *Modern Business Statistics,* 2d edition. New York: Wiley, 1989.

Levin, Richard I., and Rubin, David S. *Statistics for Management,* 5th edition. Englewood Cliffs, New Jersey: Prentice-Hall, 1991.

Pfaffenberger, Roger C., and Patterson, James H. *Statistical Methods for Business and Economics,* Revised edition. Homewood, Ill.: Irwin, 1981.

Winkler, Robert L., and Hays, William L. *Statistics: Probability, Inference, and Decision,* 2d ed. New York: Holt, Rinehart and Winston, 1975.

Wonnacott, Thomas H., and Wonnacott, Ronald J. *Introductory Statistics for Business and Economics,* 3d ed. New York: Wiley, 1984.

Introduction to

Hypothesis Testing

WHY DECISION MAKERS NEED TO KNOW

Chapter 8 introduced the basic techniques of large-sample statistical estimation. These techniques have many business applications. All applications, however, have a common bond: Sample information is used to help decision makers determine what the population is like. Although the marketing researcher, the accountant, and the operating manager all have their particular uses for statistical sampling, they all start out knowing very little about the population of interest. Through random sampling they are able to estimate population values such as the mean, variance, and proportion. This process of using sample information to statistically decide on the state of a population is called **statistical inference.**

The estimation process of going from sample to population is useful and is frequently applied. However, there is another class of problems where sampling and statistical techniques are employed. In this class, decision makers are faced with a claim, or **hypothesis,** about the population and must be able to substantiate or refute this claim, based on data from a sample of the population. For example, a producer of electronic components claims that no more than 3% of its components are defective. Before you buy 100,000 electronic components, you might want to test the manufacturer's claim. Since you could not feasibly test each component, you would select a sample and use the sample information to decide whether there really are fewer than 3% defectives in the shipment.

This chapter introduces statistical techniques used to test claims about several population values. All decision makers need to have a solid understanding of these techniques if they are to be able to use the information available in a sample effectively.

CHAPTER OBJECTIVES

This chapter will introduce statistical hypothesis testing for large-sample applications. Hypothesis testing requires that decision makers first formulate a position or make a claim regarding the decision environment they are dealing with. Then they select a sample and, based on its contents, either affirm that this position is correct or conclude that it is wrong. This chapter will demonstrate how these predetermined positions or claims are formulated and how data are used to substantiate or refute the positions. The two types of errors that can be made in hypothesis testing will be discussed. The material in this chapter will also show how to establish decision-making rules in light of the chances of making each type of error.

STUDENT OBJECTIVES

After studying the material in this chapter, you should be able to do the following:

1. Discuss three forms of statistical hypotheses and know how to use sample information to test each.
2. Correctly identify and formulate a decision rule to accompany each statistical hypothesis.
3. Identify the two forms of potential error in hypothesis testing and discuss these errors and their consequences.
4. Develop the operating characteristic curve and power curve associated with each decision rule.
5. Recognize business applications in which statistical hypothesis testing can be performed.

9-1 THE HYPOTHESIS-TESTING PROCESS

Denise Fitzgerald is manager of production for the Seltzer Bottling Company. Some soft-drink bottlers have recently been under pressure from consumer groups, which claim that bottlers have been increasing the price of soda and filling the bottles with less than the advertised amounts. Although Denise believes no manufacturer would purposely short-fill a bottle, she knows that filling machines sometimes fail to operate properly and fill the bottles less than full.

Since Denise is responsible for making sure the filling machines at her company operate correctly, she samples bottles every hour and, based on the sample results, decides whether to adjust the machines. She might identify two possible **states of nature** for 16-ounce bottles:

1. The bottles are filled with 16 or more ounces of soft drink on the average (machine is operating correctly).
2. The bottles are filled with less than 16 ounces on the average (machine is not operating correctly).

Denise must base her decision about the filling process on the results of her hourly sample. As indicated earlier, when a decision is based on sample results, sampling error must be expected. Therefore, sometimes when the process is operating correctly, the sample will indicate that the average soda bottle contains less than 16 ounces. At some other times, the process will actually need adjustments even though the sample results indicate it is operating correctly. To analyze such a situation and best select among the possible states of nature, decision makers need to formulate the problem in such a way that a hypothesis test can be conducted. The first step is to restate the states of nature in hypothesis-test notation.

In hypothesis testing, two hypotheses are formulated. The first is the *null hypothesis*—the hypothesis that the decision maker will either reject or "accept" based on the sample data. The null hypothesis traditionally contains an equality, such as "=", "≤", or "≥". The second hypothesis is the *alternative hypothesis*. The alternative includes all population values not covered by the null hypothesis. If the null hypothesis is rejected, then the decision maker will accept the alternative.

In addition to the null hypothesis containing the equality, the only other rule in the formulation of hypothesis testing is that both the null and alternative hypotheses must be stated in terms of the population value of interest. That is, if the test is about the population mean, the null and alternative hypotheses will be stated in terms of μ_x.

Decision makers sometimes have difficulty deciding how to formulate the null and alternative hypotheses. While several methods exist, we will look at the claim being made about the population value. If the claim contains the equality, then the claim becomes the null hypothesis. If the claim does not contain the equality, then the claim becomes the alternative. Consider the Seltzer Bottling Company example. The claim being made by consumer groups is that the bottlers are short-changing the customer with average fills of less than (<) 16 ounces. Since the claim does not contain the equality, the claim forms the alternative hypothesis. Thus, for the Seltzer Company we have the following:

$$\text{Null hypothesis—}H_0: \quad \mu_x \geq 16 \text{ ounces}$$
$$\text{Alternative hypothesis—}H_A: \quad \mu_x < 16 \text{ ounces} \quad \text{(Claim)}$$

where μ_x is the mean fill level for bottles.

Depending on the sample information, the null hypothesis will be either supported or refuted. Careful thought should be given to establishing the null and alternative hypotheses since the conclusion reached may depend on the hypotheses being tested. Many examples throughout this and subsequent chapters will illustrate how to develop proper statistical hypotheses.

If Denise decides the filling process is operating correctly, she will allow it to continue, but if she decides it is operating incorrectly, she will adjust the filling machines. The decision will be based on the results of her sample. She can make two possible errors when testing a hypothesis based on sample information:

1. She may decide that the process is filling bottles with an average of less than 16 ounces when, in fact, the average fill is 16 or more ounces. In this case she will *reject* a true null hypothesis. This error is a **Type I statistical error.**

2. She may decide the process is filling bottles with an average of 16 or more ounces when, in fact, it is not. Thus she might accept the null hypothesis when it is false. This error is a **Type II statistical error.**

Figure 9-1 shows the possible actions and possible states of nature associated with all hypothesis-testing problems. As you can see, there are three possible outcomes: no error, Type I error, and Type II error. Only one of these outcomes will occur for each test of a null hypothesis. From Figure 9-1, we can conclude that if the null hypothesis is true and an error is made, it must be a **Type I error.** On the other hand, if the null hypothesis is false and an error is made, it must be a **Type II error.**

Many statisticians argue that you cannot accept the null hypothesis, but instead you simply *do not reject it.* Thus, the only two hypothesis-testing decisions would be *reject H_0* or *do not reject H_0.* Our thinking is this argument is appropriate when hypothesis testing is employed in situations where some future action is not *required* based on the results of the hypothesis test. In most business applications a decision is required; the null hypothesis implies one course of action for the decision maker and the alternative hypothesis implies a different course of action. In the present situation Denise Fitzgerald must decide either to shut down the filling machine or to keep it running. She will shut down the machine if the sample evidence indicates H_0 should be rejected. She will keep the machine running if the sample evidence indicates H_0 should be accepted.

Since we are considering the decision-making implications of statistics, this text will adopt the policy of either rejecting H_0 or accepting H_0 and will deal with Type II errors in greater depth than do some basic statistics texts.

FIGURE 9-1

Hypothesis-
Testing Outcome
Possibilities

	State of Nature	
Action (Based on Sample)	H_0 True	H_0 False
Reject H_0	Type I Error	No Error
Accept H_0	No Error	Type II Error

ESTABLISHING THE DECISION RULE

The objective of a hypothesis test is to use sample information to decide whether to accept or reject the null hypothesis about a population value. How do decision makers determine whether the sample information supports or refutes the null hypothesis? The answer to this question is the key to understanding statistical hypothesis testing.

Returning to the Seltzer Bottling Company example, the null and alternative hypotheses are as follows:

Hypotheses:

$$\text{Null hypothesis—}H_0: \quad \mu_x \geq 16 \text{ ounces}$$
$$\text{Alternative hypothesis—}H_A: \quad \mu_x < 16 \text{ ounces}$$

Recall from the central limit theorem that for large samples, the distribution of possible sample means will be approximately normal with a center at the population mean, μ_x. The null hypothesis in the Seltzer Bottling Company example is $\mu_x \geq 16$ ounces; but even if the null hypothesis is true, we may get a sample mean less than 16 ounces due to sampling error. Assume that the population mean is exactly 16 ounces. Figure 9-2 shows the distribution of possible sample means for the company if μ_x equals 16 ounces.

Values of $\overline{X}$ greater than or equal to 16 ounces would tend to support the null hypothesis. By contrast, values of $\overline{X}$ below 16 ounces would tend to refute the null hypothesis. The smaller the value of $\overline{X}$, the greater the evidence that the null hypothesis should be rejected.

However, since we expect some sampling error, do we want to reject H_0 anytime $\overline{X}$ is found to be less than 16 ounces? Probably not, since the chances of $\overline{X}$ being less than 16 ounces when the population mean, μ_x, is 16 ounces is 50%. But what if the sample mean is only 15 ounces, or 14 ounces, or 13 ounces? Just how much sampling error do we expect to observe in our sample?

The job of the decision maker is to establish a cut-off point that can be used to separate sample results that should lead to rejecting H_0 from sample results that will lead to accepting H_0. This cut-off point is called a **critical value** and in this text is labeled A.

For example, the critical value, A, in the Seltzer example might be located as shown in Figure 9-3. The darkest area represents the rejection region. When $\overline{X}$ is

FIGURE 9-2

Sampling Distribution of $\overline{X}$ for the Seltzer Bottling Company Example

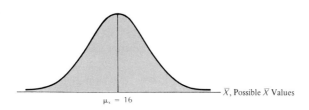

$\overline{X}$, Possible $\overline{X}$ Values

$\mu_x = 16$

FIGURE 9-3

Critical Value for
the Seltzer
Bottling
Company
Example

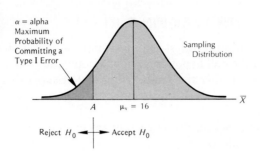

less than A, H_0 is rejected. When $\overline{X}$ is greater than or equal to A, H_0 will be accepted. Since it is possible to observe $\overline{X}$ less than A even if H_0 is true ($\mu_x \geq 16$), the area in the rejection region represents the maximum probability of a Type I statistical error. This probability is called **alpha (α)**. If A is moved farther to the left, the chances of committing a Type I error can be reduced. Figure 9-4 illustrates this point.

Ideally, we would like the chance of making both a Type I and a Type II error to be small. Unfortunately, if you make the chance of making a Type I error small, the chance of making a Type II error is increased. The decision maker must balance his or her choice for alpha against the probability of making a Type II error. This trade-off between the probabilities of making Type I and Type II errors is perhaps the most important part of hypothesis testing. We will discuss this more fully in Section 9-2.

To determine the appropriate value for A, decision makers must determine how large an alpha they want, keeping in mind the smaller the alpha, the larger the chance of making a Type II error.

Ultimately, decision makers must select the value of alpha in light of the costs involved in committing a Type I error versus a Type II error. For example, if Denise Fitzgerald rejects the null hypothesis when it is true, she will needlessly shut down production and incur the cost of machine adjustment. In addition, the adjustment might be incorrect, and future production could be affected. Calculating these costs and determining the probability of incurring them is a subjective management decision. Any two managers might well arrive at different alpha levels. The important thing is that each would specify his or her alpha level for the hypothesis test.

Suppose Denise decides that she is willing to incur a 0.10 chance of committing a Type I error. Assume that the population standard deviation of the production process is 0.5 ounce and the sample size is sixty-four bottles.

The critical value can be stated in either of two ways. First, we can establish the critical value as the number of standard deviations the critical value, A, is from μ_x. Figure 9-5 shows that if the rejection region on the lower end of the sampling distribution has an area of 0.10, the Z value from the standard normal table corresponding to the critical value is -1.28. Thus, if the sample mean lies more than 1.28 standard deviations below the population mean, 16 ounces, H_0 should be rejected. On the other hand, if the sample mean is between 0 and -1.28

FIGURE 9-4

Type I Error
Probabilities for
the Seltzer
Bottling
Company
Example

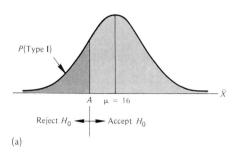

(a)

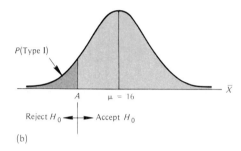

(b)

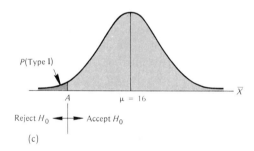

(c)

standard deviations from the mean, we will attribute that to sampling error and
will not reject the null hypothesis. Of course, in this example, if the sample mean
actually exceeds 16 ounces, the null hypothesis would be supported by the sample
data and should not be rejected.

The second way to state the critical value is in terms of the same units as the
sample mean. In the Seltzer example, A could be stated in terms of ounces such
that if $\overline{X}$ is less than A ounces, we should reject H_0, and if $\overline{X}$ is greater than or
equal to A ounces, we should accept H_0. Figure 9-6 shows how the value of A is
determined using this method. Thus, if $\overline{X}$ is less than 15.92 ounces, H_0 should be
rejected and the machine stopped for adjustment; otherwise, H_0 should be accepted and the machine left running. Likewise, any sample mean between 15.92
and 16 ounces will be attributed to sampling error and the null hypothesis would
not be rejected. Of course, a sample mean of 16 or greater would support the null
hypothesis.

FIGURE 9-5

FIGURE 9-5

Establishing the
Critical Value as
a Z Value

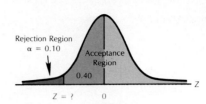

From the standard normal table,*

$$Z_{0.40} \approx -1.28$$

Then

$$A = Z_{critical} \approx -1.28$$

*The Z value from the standard normal table is used because the sampling distribution of $\overline{X}$ is approximately normal according to the central limit theorem for sample sizes $n \geq 30$. Remember also from Chapter 6 that if $Z_{critical}$ is to the left of the mean, it will be negative.

It makes no difference which approach you use in establishing the critical value. This text will mix the use of the methods throughout so that you become familiar with both.

Suppose the sample yields a sample mean of 15.75 ounces. We can test the null hypothesis two ways, depending on the procedure we used to establish the critical value. First using the Z-value method, we establish the following decision rule:

FIGURE 9-6

Determining the
Critical Value for
the Seltzer
Bottling
Company
Example

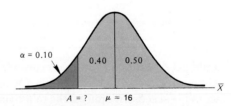

From the standard normal table,

$$Z_{0.40} \approx -1.28$$

Then

$$Z = \frac{A - \mu_x}{\frac{\sigma_x}{\sqrt{n}}}$$

Solving for A,

$$A = \mu_x + Z \frac{\sigma_x}{\sqrt{n}} = 16 + (-1.28)\left(\frac{0.5}{\sqrt{64}}\right)$$

$$= 15.92 \text{ oz.}$$

Hypotheses:

H_0: $\mu \geq 16$ ounces

H_A: $\mu < 16$ ounces

$\alpha = 0.10$

Decision Rule:

If $Z < Z_{\text{critical}}$, reject H_0.

If $Z \geq Z_{\text{critical}}$, accept H_0.

where

$Z_{\text{critical}} = -1.28$

Recall that the number of bottles tested is $n = 64$ and the population standard deviation is assumed known at 0.50 ounce. Then, Z is computed by what we call a test statistic, as follows:

$$Z = \frac{\overline{X} - \mu}{\dfrac{\sigma_x}{\sqrt{n}}}$$

$$= \frac{15.75 - 16}{\dfrac{0.50}{\sqrt{64}}}$$

$$= -4.00$$

Thus, the sample mean is 4 standard deviations below the hypothesized mean. Since $Z = -4.00$ is less than -1.28, we clearly reject H_0.

Now we use the second approach, which established a decision rule as follows:

Decision Rule:

If $\overline{X} < 15.92$ ounces, reject H_0.

If $\overline{X} \geq 15.92$ ounces, accept H_0.

Then, since 15.75 is less than 15.92, H_0 should be rejected.

Note that the two methods yield the same conclusion, as they always will if you perform the calculations correctly.

p-values

This example has illustrated two equivalent methods for testing a null hypothesis. These methods can be used in any hypothesis-testing application. However, still a third approach exists for testing a hypothesis. This is the *p*-**value approach.** Very simply, we compute a probability called a p-value. If the calculated p-value is smaller than the probability in the rejection region (α), the null hypothesis will be rejected. Otherwise, the hypothesis will not be rejected.

In the Seltzer Bottling Company example, recall that the sample mean fill of sixty-four bottles was 15.75 ounces. We previously found that 15.75 ounces is 4.00 standard deviations below the hypothesized mean of 16 ounces. We go to the standard normal table to find the probability of a Z value of -4.00. You will note that the table does not contain a Z value of 4.00, meaning that the probability of $Z \leq -4.00$ is essentially zero. Thus, to four decimal places, the p-value is 0.0000. Since this value is obviously less than our desired alpha of 0.10, the null hypothesis should be rejected.

Why do we need three methods to test the same hypothesis when they all give the same result? The answer is that we do not. However, you need to be aware of all three methods, since you will encounter each in business situations. The p-value approach is especially important since many statistical software packages output a p-value that you can use to test a hypothesis quite easily. This text will use both critical value approaches and the p-value approach interchangeably throughout the text.

SUMMARY OF HYPOTHESIS TESTING

The hypothesis-testing process discussed in this section can be summarized in six steps:

1. Determine the null hypothesis and the alternative hypothesis.
2. Determine the desired alpha level (α).
3. Choose a sample size.
4. Determine the critical value, A, or $Z_{critical}$.
5. Establish the decision rule.
6. Select the sample and perform the test.

These six steps can be followed to test any null hypothesis. Become well acquainted with the hypothesis-testing process, as it is a fundamental part of statistical decision making.

ONE-TAILED HYPOTHESIS TESTS

In the Seltzer Company example, the null hypothesis could be refuted only if the sample mean was too small (that is, too far to the left of $\mu_x = 16$ ounces). Consequently, the critical value, A, was placed in the left-hand (lower) tail of the normal curve. This example illustrates a **one-tailed hypothesis test.**

A one-tailed hypothesis test will assume one of two forms, depending on the way the null and alternative hypotheses are stated. Examples of these two forms are shown here.

1	2
H_0: $\mu_x \leq 50$	H_0: $\mu_x \geq 16$
H_A: $\mu_x > 50$	H_A: $\mu_x < 16$

If the first set of null and alternative hypotheses is used, we use a one-tailed hypothesis test with the critical value, A, in the right-hand (upper) tail of the normal curve, and we reject H_0 when $\overline{X}$ is greater than A. However, if the second set of null and alternative hypotheses is used (our Seltzer example), the critical value, A, is placed in the left-hand tail, and we reject H_0 when $\overline{X}$ is less than A.

The Marwick Chemical Company manufactures many different chemicals in an eastern U.S. state. The firm uses vast amounts of water in its processing and has a conditional-use permit from the Environmental Protection Agency. Marwick is allowed to return its waste water to the nearby river if it lowers the pollutant levels to allowable amounts. For a common toxic chemical, Marwick is required to reduce the amount in the waste water to 20 parts per million (ppm) or less.

Marwick's pollution-abatement equipment will easily reduce the toxic chemical levels below the upper limit of 20 ppm when working correctly but, like much pollution equipment, it needs checking and adjustment to maintain the standards. The waste water is continually monitored, and based on the periodic sample results, the pollution equipment is either adjusted—a costly process—or allowed to continue as is. The appropriate hypotheses and decision rule for this situation are stated as follows:

Hypotheses:

H_0: $\mu_x \leq 20$ ppm, process can continue.

H_A: $\mu_x > 20$ ppm, process requires adjustment.

Decision Rule:

Take a random sample of size n and calculate $\overline{X}$.

If $\overline{X} \leq A$, accept H_0.

If $\overline{X} > A$, reject H_0.

Marwick decides to limit alpha to a maximum of 3% and base the decision on a sample of forty trials. The decision rule is determined as shown in Figure 9-7. Note that the standard deviation, σ_x, is assumed to be 5 ppm. If the standard deviation is not known, we use S_x from the sample.

Suppose the Marwick Chemical Company has selected a sample of forty units of water that is scheduled to go into the river and has found an average of 23.4 ppm of the toxic chemical. What should it do based on this information? As with any hypothesis test, the sample results are compared to the decision rule and H_0 is either rejected or accepted. In this case, we formed two equivalent decision rules:

Option 1	Option 2
If $\overline{X} \leq 21.485$ ppm, accept H_0.	If $Z \leq 1.88$, accept H_0.
If $\overline{X} > 21.485$ ppm, reject H_0.	If $Z > 1.88$, reject H_0.

FIGURE 9-7

Decision Rule for
the Marwick
Chemical
Company
Example

Hypotheses:

$H_0: \mu_x \le 20$ p.p.m.
$H_A: \mu_x > 20$ p.p.m.

$\alpha = 0.03$

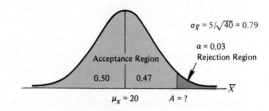

From the standard normal table,

$$Z_{0.47} \approx 1.88$$

Then

$$Z = \frac{\overline{X} - \mu_x}{\sigma_{\overline{x}}} = \frac{A - \mu_x}{\frac{\sigma_x}{\sqrt{n}}}$$

Solving for A,

$$A = \mu_x + Z\frac{\sigma_x}{\sqrt{n}} = 20 + 1.88(0.79)$$

$$= 21.485 \text{ ppm}$$

Decision Rule:

If $\overline{X} \le 21.485$ ppm, accept H_0.   If $Z \le 1.88$, accept H_0.
                                          or
If $\overline{X} > 21.485$ ppm, reject H_0.   If $Z > 1.88$, reject H_0.

Using option 1, our decision is to reject H_0, since the sample mean, 23.4, is greater than 21.485 ppm. Thus, the company would conclude that an adjustment is needed.

If the second decision rule is used, we will reject H_0 if the sample mean is more than 1.88 standard deviations greater than the hypothesized mean of 20 ppm. Based on the sample results, we compute the test statistic as follows:

$$Z = \frac{\overline{X} - \mu_x}{\frac{\sigma_x}{\sqrt{n}}}$$

$$= \frac{23.4 - 20}{\frac{5}{\sqrt{40}}}$$

$$\approx 4.30$$

Since 4.30 is greater than 1.88, we reject H_0. The sample mean is approximately 4.30 standard deviations above the hypothesized mean. This is beyond what we would attribute to sampling error at an alpha of 0.03.

Thus, again we see that regardless of which approach we take to test the hypothesis, the same conclusion is reached.

HYPOTHESIS TESTING—POPULATION STANDARD DEVIATION UNKNOWN, LARGE SAMPLE

In the previous example, we assumed that the population standard deviation was known. When we discussed statistical estimation, we stated that in most cases, the population standard deviation is not known. As in estimation, our solution to an unknown standard deviation is to estimate the population standard deviation, σ_x, by the sample standard deviation, S_x. For example, engineers at the American Lighting Company recently developed a new three-way light bulb that they say is more energy efficient than the company's existing three-way bulb. They also claim that the bulb will outlast the current bulb, which has an average lifetime of 700 hours.

The American Lighting Company has decided that before it begins full scale production on the new light bulbs, it should pick a test sample of 1,000 light bulbs (assumed to be a random sample) and determine whether the mean life of the new three-way bulb *exceeds* the old bulb's average of 700 hours. The sample results for the 1,000 bulbs were as follows:

$$\overline{X} = 704 \text{ h}$$
$$S_x = 150 \text{ h}$$

To test the claim about the bulbs, we formulate the null and alternative hypotheses as follows:

Hypotheses:

$H_0: \quad \mu_x \leq 700 \text{ h}$

$H_A: \quad \mu_x > 700 \text{ h} \qquad \text{(Claim)}$

$\alpha = 0.05$

Note that we have placed the claim in the alternative hypothesis. This puts the burden on the new product to "prove" it is superior to the old product.

Figure 9-8 shows the results of the hypothesis test. Note that S_x, the sample standard deviation, is used in place of σ_x in computing the test statistic. As Figure 9-8 shows, the null hypothesis is accepted, which means that the sample results (only 0.84 standard deviation from the hypothesized mean) are not sufficient to reject H_0. Thus, American Lighting may have a superior bulb energywise but, based on these sample data, it cannot say the same for average lifetime.

We can employ the *p*-value approach to test this hypothesis. To do so, after having computed $Z = 0.84$, we go to the standard normal table and find the probability of a value between $Z = 0.0$ and $Z = 0.84$ to be 0.2995. The *p*-value is

FIGURE 9-8

Hypothesis Test
for the American
Lighting
Company
Example

Hypotheses:

H_0: $\mu_x \leq 700$ h
H_A: $\mu_x > 700$ h

$\alpha = 0.05$

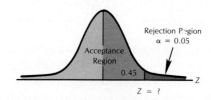

From the standard normal table

$$Z_{0.45} \approx 1.65 = Z_{\text{critical}}$$

Decision Rule:

If $Z > 1.65$, reject H_0.
If $Z \leq 1.65$, accept H_0.

Test Statistic:

$$Z = \frac{\overline{X} - \mu_x}{\dfrac{S_x}{\sqrt{n}}}$$

$$= \frac{704 - 700}{\dfrac{150}{\sqrt{1,000}}}$$

$$\approx 0.84$$

Since $0.84 \leq 1.65$, accept H_0.

computed as $0.5000 - 0.2995 = 0.2005$. Thus, since $p = 0.2005 > \alpha = 0.05$, we do not reject H_0. Recall that if the p-value is greater than or equal to alpha, do not reject H_0; if the p-value is less than alpha, reject H_0.

TWO-TAILED HYPOTHESIS TESTS

The hypothesis-testing examples presented thus far have been one-tailed. The entire rejection region (alpha) has been located in either the upper or the lower tail of the sampling distribution. However, there are instances in which a one-tailed hypothesis test is not appropriate. In these cases you will need to use a **two-tailed hypothesis test.** In a two-tailed test, the rejection region (alpha) is split into the two tails of the sampling distribution.

Consider the example involving the Dairy Fresh Ice Cream plant in Pittsburgh, Pennsylvania. The plant produces ice cream sold under the Dairy Fresh brand and a number of store brands in the East. The production process is highly automated. The filling machine for the 64-ounce cartons is good but not perfect.

There is some variation in the actual amount of ice cream that goes into the 64-ounce carton. The machine can go out of adjustment and put a mean amount either less than 64 ounces or more than 64 ounces in the cartons.

To monitor the filling process, the production manager selects a sample of 100 ice cream cartons at the end of each day. The sample information is used to test the following null and alternative hypotheses:

$$H_0: \quad \mu_x = 64 \text{ ounces} \qquad \text{(In adjustment)}$$
$$H_A: \quad \mu_x \neq 64 \text{ ounces} \qquad \text{(Out of adjustment)}$$

Due to potential sampling error, the sample mean may exceed 64 ounces or be less than 64 ounces. The production manager will not reject the null hypothesis as long as the difference appears to be due to sampling error. If the difference becomes too extreme, however, the null hypothesis will be rejected and the machine will be readjusted.

In establishing the decision rule, the production manager must decide which values of $\overline{X}$ will tend to refute the null hypothesis. In this example, values of $\overline{X}$ either too large or too small should lead to rejecting the null hypothesis. This situation is referred to as a **two-tailed hypothesis test,** meaning that the rejection region is divided into two tails. (Although not required, the general convention is to divide the rejection region equally between the two tails of the sampling distribution. The examples and problems in this text will follow this pattern.)

The correct decision rule to apply for a two-tailed hypothesis test about a population mean is

Decision Rule:

Select a sample size of n and determine $\overline{X}$.

If $A_L \leq \overline{X} \leq A_H$, accept H_0.

If $\overline{X} > A_H$, reject H_0.

If $\overline{X} < A_L$, reject H_0.

where

A_L = Critical value in the lower tail

A_H = Critical value in the upper tail

Suppose the production manager specifies an alpha level of 0.06 ($\alpha = 0.06$), meaning that she is willing to have a 6% chance of rejecting the null hypothesis when it is really true. At the end of a particular day, the sample of 100 cartons resulted in a sample mean of 64.12 ounces, with a sample standard deviation of 0.50 ounce. Figure 9-9 illustrates how the decision rule is developed. It shows that if $\overline{X} > 64.094$ ounces or if $\overline{X} < 63.906$ ounces, the null hypothesis should be rejected. For this particular day, the sample mean $\overline{X} = 64.12 > 64.094$, so the production manager should reject the null hypothesis and conclude that the machine is not filling the cartons with an average of 64 ounces of ice cream.

FIGURE 9-9

Decision Rule for
a Two-Tailed
Test for the Dairy
Fresh Example

Hypotheses:
$H_0: \mu_x = 64$ oz.
$H_A: \mu_x \neq 64$ oz.

$\alpha = 0.06$

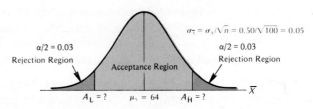

$\sigma_{\bar{x}} = \sigma_x/\sqrt{n} = 0.50/\sqrt{100} = 0.05$

$\alpha/2 = 0.03$
Rejection Region

$\alpha/2 = 0.03$
Rejection Region

Acceptance Region

$A_L = ?$ $\mu_x = 64$ $A_H = ?$ $\bar{X}$

From the standard normal table,

$$Z_{0.47} \approx \pm 1.88$$

Then, solving for A_L and A_H,

$$Z = \frac{A_L - \mu_x}{\sigma_{\bar{x}}} \qquad \text{and} \quad Z = \frac{A_H - \mu_x}{\sigma_{\bar{x}}}$$

$A_L = \mu_x + Z\sigma_{\bar{x}} = 64 + (-1.88)(0.05)$ $A_H = \mu_x + Z\sigma_{\bar{x}} = 64 + 1.88(0.05)$
  $= 63.906$ $= 64.094$

Decision Rule:
If $63.906 \leq \bar{X} \leq 64.094$, accept H_0.
If $\bar{X} < 63.906$, reject H_0.
If $\bar{X} > 64.094$, reject H_0.

Note: The $\alpha = 0.06$ is divided equally into the two rejection regions.

SKILL DEVELOPMENT PROBLEMS FOR **SECTION 9-1**

The following set of problems is meant to test your understanding of the material in this section.

1. Given the following null and alternative hypotheses:

$$H_0: \quad \mu \leq 200$$
$$H_A: \quad \mu > 200$$
$$\alpha = 0.05$$

and

$$\overline{X} = 204.50$$
$$\sigma_x = 45.00$$
$$n = 200$$

a. Establish the appropriate decision rule.
b. Indicate the appropriate decision based on the sample information and the decision rule.

2. Given the following null and alternative hypotheses:

$$H_0: \quad \mu \geq 4{,}000$$
$$H_A: \quad \mu < 4{,}000$$
$$\alpha = 0.05$$

and

$$\overline{X} = 3,980$$
$$S_x = 205$$
$$n = 100$$

a. Establish the appropriate decision rule.
b. Indicate the appropriate decision based on the sample information and the decision rule.

3. Given the following null and alternative hypotheses:

$$H_0: \quad \mu = 4,450$$
$$H_A: \quad \mu \neq 4,450$$
$$\alpha = 0.10$$

and

$$\overline{X} = 4,475.60$$
$$S_x = 340$$
$$n = 100$$

a. Establish the appropriate decision rule.
b. Indicate the appropriate decision based on the sample information and the decision rule.

4. A mail-order business prides itself in its ability to fill customers' orders in 6 calendar days or less on the average. Periodically, the operations manager selects a random sample of customer orders and determines the number of days actually taken to fill their orders. Based upon this sample information, he decides whether the desired standard is being met.
a. Establish the appropriate null and alternative hypotheses.
b. On one occasion where a sample of 100 customers was selected, the average number of days was 6.65, with a sample standard deviation of 1.5 days. If an alpha level of 0.08 is to be used, what is the appropriate decision rule to use and what should the operations manager conclude? Discuss.

5. The makers of Mini-Oats Cereal have an automated packaging machine that can be set at any targeted fill level between 12 and 32 ounces. It is expected that not every box of cereal will contain exactly the targeted weight, but the average of all boxes filled should. At the end of every shift (8 hours), 100 boxes are selected at random and the mean and standard deviation of the sample are computed. Based on these sample results, the production control manager determines whether the filling machine needs to be readjusted or whether it remains all right to operate. Use $\alpha = 0.05$.
a. Establish the appropriate null and alternative hypotheses to be tested.

b. At the end of a particular shift during which the machine was filling 24-ounce boxes of Mini-Oats, the sample mean of 100 boxes was 24.32 ounces, with a standard deviation of 0.70 ounce. Determine the appropriate decision rule and indicate what should be concluded about this machine based on these sample data.

c. Why do you suppose the production control manager would prefer to make this hypothesis test a two-tailed test? Discuss.

6. The makers of a new home furnace system claim that if the furnace is installed, homeowners will observe an average fuel bill of no more than $80.00 per month during January if their house has between 2,200 and 2,400 square feet of heated living space. A consumer agency plans to test this claim by taking a random sample of homes of this size where the new furnace has just been installed.

a. Establish the appropriate null and alternative hypotheses.

b. If the desired alpha level for the test is 0.05, what should be concluded about the company's claim if the following sample results are observed?

$$\overline{X} = \$81.40$$
$$S_x^2 = 625$$
$$n = 64$$

9-2 TYPE II ERRORS AND THE POWER OF THE HYPOTHESIS TEST

The previous examples have shown how decision rules for hypothesis tests of the population mean are determined and how the appropriate decision is based on the results of a sample from the population. In these examples, we have determined the critical values by first specifying alpha, the probability of committing a Type I error. As we indicated, if the cost of committing a Type I error is high, the decision maker should specify a small alpha. A small alpha results in a small rejection region. If the rejection region is small, the sample mean is less likely to fall there, and the chances of rejecting a true null hypothesis are small.

This logic provides a basis for establishing the critical value for the hypothesis test. However, it completely ignores the possibility of committing a Type II error. Recall that accepting a false null hypothesis is a Type II decision error. If the rejection region is made small by selecting a small alpha level, the acceptance region will be large since the area of the rejection region plus the area of the acceptance region must add to 1.0. This is illustrated in Figure 9-10.

To complete the logic, if the acceptance region is large, the probability of committing a Type II error [called **beta** (β)] will also tend to be large. This is a point many decision makers often forget in their efforts to control Type I errors. A decrease in alpha will increase beta. However, as will be shown, the increase in beta will not equal the decrease in alpha nor will the change be proportional.

Decision makers must examine carefully the costs of committing Type I and Type II errors and, in light of these costs, attempt to establish acceptable values for alpha and beta. Generally, the decision of what values of Type I and Type II

Acceptance and
Rejection Regions

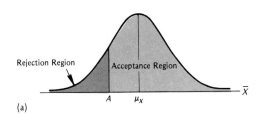

(a)

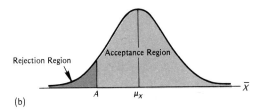

(b)

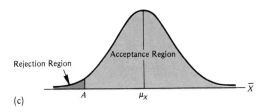

(c)

errors are acceptable depends on the relative cost associated with making each type of error. For instance, in the Marwick Chemical Company example considered previously, committing a Type I error would cause the pollution equipment to be adjusted needlessly, a costly process, and therefore alpha was limited to 3%. However, we did not consider the probability of making a Type II error, which would involve continuing a process producing too much pollution. Here, making a Type II error might have disastrous consequences. We will delay our discussion of how decision makers can simultaneously control the chances of making a Type I and a Type II error until the next section. We will now show how to calculate the probability of committing a Type II error.

CALCULATING BETA (PROBABILITY OF COMMITTING A TYPE II ERROR)

Once alpha has been specified for a hypothesis test involving a particular sample size, beta cannot also be specified. Rather, the beta value is fixed, and all the decision maker can do is calculate it. This does not imply that beta is a single value, because it is not. Since a Type II error occurs when a false null hypothesis is accepted (refer to Figure 9-1), there is a beta value for each possible population value for which the null hypothesis is false. For example, for the Marwick Chemical Company, the null and alternative hypotheses were

$$H_0: \quad \mu_x \leq 20 \text{ ppm}$$
$$H_A: \quad \mu_x > 20 \text{ ppm}$$

Therefore, the null hypothesis is false for all possible values of $\mu_x > 20$ ppm. Thus, for each of the infinite number of possibilities, a value of beta can be determined. Suppose we assume that μ_x is actually 21 ppm. If we use the alpha level of 0.03 and the decision rule determined in Figure 9-7, we can calculate beta using the following steps:

1. Draw a picture of the hypothesized sampling distribution showing the rejection region(s) and the acceptance region found by specifying an alpha level.
2. Immediately below the hypothesized sampling distribution, draw the "true" sampling distribution based on the assumed true population mean. Note that the shape of the true distribution will be the same as the shape of the hypothesized distribution. Only the central location will be different.
3. Extend the critical value(s) from the hypothesized distribution down to the true distribution and shade the rejection region on the true distribution.
4. The lightly shaded area in the true distribution is beta, the probability of committing a Type II error.

Figure 9-11 shows how beta is determined if the true value of μ_x is 21 ppm. Thus, by holding alpha to 0.03, the chance of committing a Type II error is approximately 0.7291. This means that if the true population mean is 21 ppm, there is nearly a 0.73 probability that the sampling plan the Marwick Chemical Company plans to use will not detect it and thus lead the decision makers to "accept" that the mean is 20 ppm. The decision makers might also be interested in the value of beta if the "true" mean is 22 ppm. Figure 9-12 shows the calculations. We see that beta is reduced to 0.2578 in this case. This points out a very important concept. That is, as the "true" mean moves farther from the hypothesized mean, beta will get smaller. This is logical, since it should be easier to tell the difference between populations with means of 22 versus 20 than it is between populations with means of 21 versus 20.

The darkly shaded area in the true distribution has also been calculated. This area is called the *power* of the hypothesis test. **Power** is the probability of rejecting a false hypothesis.[1] Naturally, decision makers want the power to be as large as

---

[1] Although this is a common definition of power, it is not universal. Some authors define power as the probability of rejecting the null hypothesis. For the purposes of an introductory text, this difference is not important.

FIGURE **9-11**

Beta Calculation for True $\mu_x =$ 21 ppm

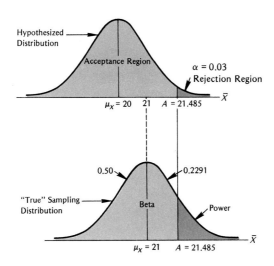

$$Z = \frac{\bar{X} - \mu_x}{\sigma_{\bar{x}}} \quad \text{(From the ''true'' distribution)}$$

$$= \frac{21.485 - 21}{0.79}$$

$$= 0.61$$

The area between $Z = 0.61$ and μ_x is 0.2291. Therefore

$$\text{Beta} = 0.5000 + 0.2291$$
$$= 0.7291$$
$$\text{Power} = 1 - \text{beta} = 1 - 0.7291$$
$$= 0.2709$$

possible, and this occurs if beta is made as small as possible, since power and beta are inversely related. Power is determined by equation 9-1:

Power = 1 − Beta   **9-1**

Like beta, power changes depending on what the "true" value for μ_x is assumed to be. In the calculation shown in Figure 9-9, for instance, power is 0.2709. This would likely be an unacceptably low value if it was important to be able to reject the null hypothesis when the true average pollution level is as high as 21.

Again, Figures 9-11 and 9-12 show that as the true μ_x value moves farther away from the hypothesized μ_x, beta becomes smaller. The greater the difference between the true mean and the hypothesized mean, the easier it is to tell the two apart, and the less likely we are to accept the null hypothesis when it is actually

FIGURE 9-12

Beta Calculation
for True $\mu_x =$
22 ppm

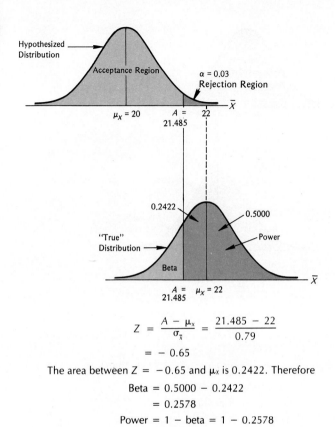

$$Z = \frac{A - \mu_x}{\sigma_{\bar{x}}} = \frac{21.485 - 22}{0.79}$$

$$= -0.65$$

The area between $Z = -0.65$ and μ_x is 0.2422. Therefore

$$\text{Beta} = 0.5000 - 0.2422$$

$$= 0.2578$$

$$\text{Power} = 1 - \text{beta} = 1 - 0.2578$$

$$= 0.7422$$

false. Of course the opposite is also true. As the true mean moves increasingly closer to the hypothesized mean, the harder it is for the hypothesis test to distinguish between the two.

IMPACT OF SAMPLE SIZE ON POWER AND BETA

Previous chapters have emphasized that the size of the sample influences the spread in the sampling distribution of $\bar{X}$. As the sample size increases, $\sigma_{\bar{x}}$ decreases. The smaller $\sigma_{\bar{x}}$ becomes, the lower the chance of extreme sampling error. This same concept applies in hypothesis testing and determining power and beta. As more information is available (larger sample size), with alpha held constant, the smaller beta (and the larger power) will be for any value of μ_x.

The previous example computed power and beta assuming a sample size of forty ($n = 40$). Suppose the sample size is increased to 100. Figure 9-13 shows how beta and power are determined for $\mu_x = 21$. Note that a shift in sample size from 40 to 100 has reduced beta and increased power. Notice also that the increase in sample size has changed the critical value, A, from 21.485 to 20.94. The reduced critical value occurs because $\sigma_{\bar{x}}$ has decreased.

FIGURE 9-13

Beta and Power Calculations for the Marwick Chemical Company Example

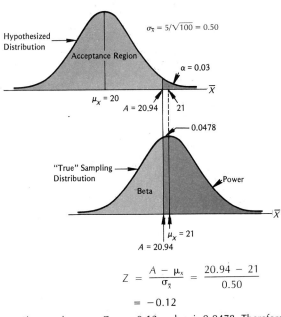

$$Z = \frac{A - \mu_x}{\sigma_{\bar{x}}} = \frac{20.94 - 21}{0.50}$$

$$= -0.12$$

The area between $Z = -0.12$ and μ_x is 0.0478. Therefore

$$\text{Beta} = 0.5000 - 0.0478$$

$$= 0.4522$$

$$\text{Power} = 1 - \text{beta} = 1 - 0.4522$$

$$= 0.5478$$

This example has illustrated that for a given level of alpha, the chances of making a Type II error can be reduced by increasing the sample size. Depending on the decision being made and the costs of making a Type II error, decision makers may want to control the chances of committing a Type II error.

SKILL DEVELOPMENT PROBLEMS FOR SECTION 9-2

The following set of problems is meant to test your understanding of the material in this section.

7. You are given the following null and alternative hypotheses:

$$H_0: \quad \mu_x \leq 1{,}200$$
$$H_A: \quad \mu_x > 1{,}200$$
$$\alpha = 0.05$$

a. If the true population mean is 1,204, what is the value of beta? Assume that the population standard deviation is known to be 20 and the sample size is 40.

b. Indicate clearly the decision rule that would be used to test the null hypothesis and determine what decision should be made if the sample mean was 1,201.3.

8. You are given the following null and alternative hypotheses:

$$H_0: \quad \mu_x \geq 4,350$$
$$H_A: \quad \mu_x < 4,350$$
$$\alpha = 0.05$$

a. If the true population mean is 4,345, what is the value of beta? Assume that the population standard deviation is known to be 200 and the sample size is 100.
b. Indicate clearly the decision rule that would be used to test the null hypothesis and determine what decision should be made if the sample mean was 4,337.50.

9. You are given the following null and alternative hypotheses:

$$H_0: \quad \mu_x = 12,000$$
$$H_A: \quad \mu_x \neq 12,000$$
$$\alpha = 0.05$$

a. If the true population mean is 12,004, what is the value of beta? Assume that the population standard deviation is known to be 500 and the sample size is 100. (*Hint:* Look at Solved Problem 3 at the end of this chapter to see the methodology for finding beta for a two-tailed hypothesis test.)
b. If the true population mean is 11,995, what is the value of beta? Assume that the population standard deviation is known to be 500 and the sample size is 100.
c. Find power for the conditions expressed in parts **a** and **b**.
d. Indicate clearly the decision rule that would be used to test the null hypothesis and determine what decision should be made if the sample mean was 11,987.40.

10. The Arrow Tire and Rubber Company plans to warranty its new Mountain Bike Tire for 12 months. However, before it does this, the company wants to be sure that the average tire will last at least 18 months under normal operations. It plans to test this statistically using a random sample of tires. Specify an alpha level and justify why you picked that value.
a. If the true average is actually 16.8 months, what is the probability that the hypothesis test will lead to accepting the null hypothesis incorrectly? Assume that the population standard deviation is known to be 2.4 months and the sample size is 60.
b. Determine the decision rule and test the hypothesis assuming that the sample mean turns out to be 17.4 months.

11. The union negotiations between labor and management at the Stone Container paper mill in Minnesota hit a snag when management asked labor to take a cut in health insurance coverage. As part of its justification, management claimed that the average dollars of insurance claims filed by union employees did not exceed $250 per employee. The union's chief negotiator requested that a sample of 100 employees' records be selected and that this claim be tested statistically. Specify an alpha level and justify why you picked that value.
    a. State the null and alternative hypotheses.
    b. Before the sample was selected, the negotiator was interested in the chances that her statistical test would incorrectly accept the null hypothesis if the true mean was $275. (Note that it was assumed the standard deviation in claims is $70.00, as determined in a similar study at another plant location.) Determine the value of beta.
    c. Referring to part **b,** suppose the negotiator was concerned about the value of beta if the true mean was really $260. Calculate beta under this condition.
    d. Based on your findings in parts **b** and **c,** would you recommend that the negotiator go ahead with the test as it is currently structured? Discuss.

9-3 CONCLUSIONS

This chapter has introduced the fundamentals of hypothesis testing. The focus has been on hypothesis tests for decisions with large sample sizes. The concepts presented in this chapter provide decision makers with tools for using sample information to decide whether a given null hypothesis should be rejected or accepted.

In this chapter we have concentrated on examples of large-sample hypothesis tests involving a single population mean. In following chapters you will see that the hypothesis-testing methodology is basically the same for all situations. The central issue is always to determine whether the sample information tends to support or refute the null hypothesis.

We have emphasized the importance of recognizing that when a hypothesis is tested, an error might occur. Type I and Type II statistical errors have been discussed. We have shown how to calculate the probability of committing each type of error for applications involving a single population mean.

You have probably noticed that the statistical estimation techniques discussed in Chapter 8 and hypothesis testing have much in common. Both estimation and hypothesis testing are used extensively by business decision makers. Estimation procedures are most useful when the decision makers have little or no idea of the value of a population parameter and are primarily interested in determining these values. On the other hand, hypothesis testing is used when a claim about a population value needs to be tested. Estimation and hypothesis testing are the central components of statistical inference and will be used throughout the remaining chapters of this text.

The chapter glossary contains important terms introduced in this chapter and the chapter formulas are summarized following the glossary.

CHAPTER **GLOSSARY**

alpha (α) The maximum probability of committing a Type I error.

beta (β) The probability of committing a Type II error.

critical value The value(s) in a hypothesis test that separate the rejection region from the acceptance region. The critical value can be in the same units as the population mean or it can be in standardized units.

hypothesis A supposition about a true state of nature.

one-tailed hypothesis test A hypothesis test in which the entire rejection region is located in one tail of the sampling distribution.

power The probability of rejecting a null hypothesis when it is false. Power is the complement of beta.

states of nature The uncertain events over which decision makers have no direct control.

statistical inference The process by which decision makers reach conclusions about a population based on sample information collected from the population.

two-tailed hypothesis test A hypothesis test in which the rejection region is split between the two tails of the sampling distribution.

Type I error Rejecting the null hypothesis when it is, in fact, true.

Type II error Accepting the null hypothesis when it is, in fact, false.

CHAPTER FORMULAS

Critical Value

$$A = \mu_x + Z\frac{\sigma_x}{\sqrt{n}}$$

Power

$$\text{Power} = 1 - \text{Beta}$$

SOLVED PROBLEMS

1. The personnel department of the East Coast Metal Fabrication Company needs help. A supervisor in the welding shop has repeatedly complained about one of her crew, a man named Robinson. The supervisor claims Robinson is a troublemaker, produces below-standard work, and is slow. East Coast Metal is bound by a strong union contract, and despite his poor work, Robinson is very active in union affairs. The personnel department believes

that if Robinson is fired, the union will challenge the case and claim that Robinson was fired because of his union activities.

Although the personnel department thinks Robinson cannot be challenged on vague issues such as below-standard work or being a troublemaker, there are some rather strong clauses in the contract dealing with output. If Robinson produces below-contract output, he can be released.

Robinson's crew is presently working on a prefabricated truck chassis unit. Robinson has been assigned a job where the time standard is 11 minutes per piece. No one is expected to finish every welding job in 11 minutes, but the average time is to be 11 minutes. The supervisor assures the personnel department that Robinson is not producing at this standard. The personnel department decides to take action or not take action against Robinson based on a sample of forty work times.

a. Formulate the null hypothesis for this decision.
b. Discuss the ramifications of making a Type I error in this decision.
c. If the standard deviation of times to perform this welding job is 2 minutes, what decision rule goes with your hypothesis if the personnel department is willing to commit a Type I error 5% of the time?
d. If the sample of forty welding operations showed an average completion time of 11.2 minutes, what decision would you make? Would your decision change if the sample average completion time were 12 minutes?
e. If Robinson actually is doing his work in an average of 12 minutes, what is the chance of his being fired using the decision rule found in part c?

Solution

a. **Hypotheses:**

$$H_0: \quad \mu_x \leq 11 \text{ min}$$

$$H_A: \quad \mu_x > 11 \text{ min}$$

b. If a Type I error is made, the company will conclude that Robinson is performing below standard and will fire him when, in fact, his true average time, μ_x, is less than or equal to 11 minutes. This type of error would be social in nature—that is, firing a good employee. Also, Robinson could sue the company and obtain damages for being unjustly fired. In addition, the union could challenge the firing, demand a new sample, and win.

c. **Decision Rule:**

Take a sample of size n and determine $\overline{X}$.

If $\overline{X} \leq A$, accept H_0.

If $\overline{X} > A$, reject H_0.

The appropriate figure for a 5% Type I error is

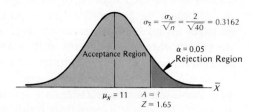

$$\sigma_{\bar{x}} = \frac{\sigma_X}{\sqrt{n}} = \frac{2}{\sqrt{40}} = 0.3162$$

Calculating A,

$$A = 11 + Z\sigma_{\bar{x}} = 11 + 1.65\frac{2}{\sqrt{40}}$$

$$= 11.522 \text{ min}$$

The rule becomes

Decision Rule:

If $\overline{X} \le 11.522$ min, accept H_0, keep Robinson.

If $\overline{X} > 11.522$ min, reject H_0, fire Robinson.

d.   If $\overline{X} = 11.2$ minutes, from the decision rule the hypothesis is thought to be true, and Robinson would be retained. If $\overline{X} = 12$ minutes, from the decision rule the null hypothesis is determined to be false, and Robinson would be fired.

e.

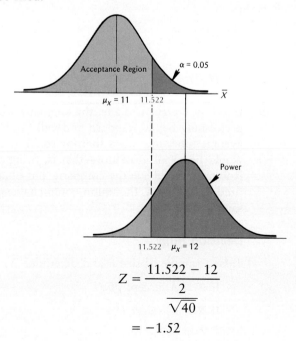

$$Z = \frac{11.522 - 12}{\dfrac{2}{\sqrt{40}}}$$

$$= -1.52$$

The area between $Z = -1.52$ and μ_x is 0.4357, so

$$P(\text{firing}) = 0.5000 + 0.4357$$
$$= 0.9357$$

This means there is greater than a 93% chance of firing Robinson when, in fact, he is actually producing the pieces in a time averaging 12 minutes. Note that beta = 1 − power is $1 - 0.9357 = 0.0643$. This means there is slightly over a 6% chance this decision rule will lead to keeping Robinson, if he is really producing at an average rate of 12 minutes per piece.

2. The Convoy Truck Company has been faced with steadily increasing fuel, labor, repair, and equipment costs. Although the company has raised rates as much as possible to reflect increased costs, many of the rates are subject to governmental regulation.

Four years ago Convoy completed an extensive study of the costs and revenues associated with its operations. The average profit per truckload shipment was found to be $158.12. Convoy does not want to go through such an extensive study again because of the costs involved and does not think it needs to because it has not altered operations. Rather than a complete study, the managers decide to select a random sample of invoices, determine the average profitability of this sample, and see if the per-run profitability has changed. The results of this sample are as follows:

Sample size = 800 invoices

Average sample profit = $149.76

Sample standard deviation = $189.90

a. Formulate the null hypothesis and decision rule for Convoy if the company wants to limit the chance of making a Type I error to 4%.

b. Based on your decision rule and the sample data, what conclusions should the Convoy Truck Company reach?

Solution

a. **Hypotheses:**

H_0: $\mu_x = \$158.12$

H_A: $\mu_x \neq \$158.12$

Note that this is a two-tailed hypothesis test.

Decision Rule:

Take a sample of 800 and determine $\overline{X}$.

If $A_L \leq \overline{X} \leq A_H$, accept H_0.

If $\overline{X} < A_L$, reject H_0.

If $\overline{X} > A_H$, reject H_0.

The appropriate figure is

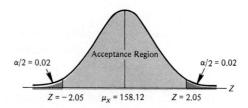

Note that we have split the rejection region into both tails.

$$A_L = \$158.12 + (-ZS_{\bar{x}}) \qquad \text{and} \qquad A_H = \$158.12 + ZS_{\bar{x}}$$

$$= \$158.12 - 2.05 \frac{\$189.90}{\sqrt{800}} \qquad\qquad = \$158.12 + 2.05 \frac{\$189.90}{\sqrt{800}}$$

$$= \$144.36 \qquad\qquad\qquad\qquad = \$171.88$$

The decision rule becomes

Decision Rule:

If $\$144.36 \leq \bar{X} \leq \$171.88$, accept H_0.

If $\bar{X} < \$144.36$, reject H_0.

If $\bar{X} > \$171.88$, reject H_0.

    b. Since $\bar{X} = \$149.76$, we should not reject H_0 and we conclude, based on the sample data, that the average profit has not changed.

3. The manager of a Chicago meat-packing plant has established a standard which says that from a 900-pound steer (live weight), the company should obtain an average of 550 pounds of meat (cut and wrapped). Past experience indicates that even though the average may change, the standard deviation remains fairly constant at 40 pounds. To determine whether current work deviates from the standard, the manager selects a sample of 100 ($n = 100$) 900-pound steers and compares the sample average with the standard.

    a. Establish the null and alternative hypotheses.

    b. If the manager wishes to have no more than a 0.05 chance of committing a Type I error, specify the appropriate decision rule for this hypothesis test.

    c. Given an alpha level of 0.05 and the decision rule found in part **b**, what is the probability of committing a Type II error if an average of 547 pounds is cut and wrapped from the 900-pound steers?

    d. Calculate the power of this hypothesis test if the true mean is 547 pounds. Discuss what power means in this example.

Solution

a. **Hypotheses:**

$$H_0: \quad \mu_x = 550 \text{ lb}$$

$$H_A: \quad \mu_x \neq 550 \text{ lb}$$

$$\alpha = 0.05$$

Note that because the manager is concerned with detecting departures from the mean in either direction, the hypothesis is two-tailed.

b. The appropriate decision rule is determined as follows:

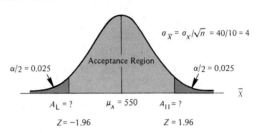

Solve for critical values.

$$\begin{aligned} A_L &= \mu_x + (-Z)\sigma_{\bar{x}} \\ &= 550 - 1.96(4) \\ &= 542.16 \end{aligned} \qquad \text{and} \qquad \begin{aligned} A_H &= \mu_x + Z\sigma_{\bar{x}} \\ &= 550 + 1.96(4) \\ &= 557.84 \end{aligned}$$

Decision Rule:

If $542.16 \leq \bar{X} \leq 557.84$, accept H_0.

If $\bar{X} < 542.16$, reject H_0.

If $\bar{X} > 557.84$, reject H_0.

c. To determine the probability of committing a Type II error if μ_x is actually 547 pounds, we use the following procedure:

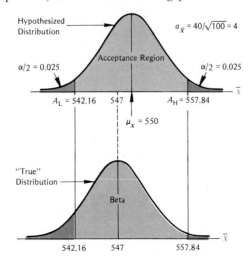

To find beta,

$$Z = \frac{A_L - \mu_x}{\sigma_{\overline{x}}} \quad \text{and} \quad Z = \frac{A_H - \mu_x}{\sigma_{\overline{x}}}$$

$$= \frac{542.16 - 547}{4} \qquad = \frac{557.84 - 547}{4}$$

$$= -1.21 \qquad\qquad = 2.71$$

The area between $Z = -1.21$ and μ_x is 0.3869. The area between $Z = 2.71$ and μ_x is 0.4966. Therefore, beta equals $0.3869 + 0.4966 = 0.8835$. Beta is the probability of accepting the null hypothesis when it is actually false.

d. Power is the probability of rejecting the null hypothesis. In this case, if μ_x is really 547 pounds, and not 550 as hypothesized, power $= 1 - \text{beta} = 1 - 0.8835 = 0.1165$. Thus, the chance of rejecting H_0 when μ_x is actually 547 pounds is only 0.1165. If this probability is too low, either alpha or the sample size can be increased.

CONCEPTUAL QUESTIONS AND ASSIGNMENTS

12. Discuss the two types of statistical errors that can occur when a hypothesis is tested. Illustrate what you mean by using a business example.
13. What is meant by the term *critical value* in a hypothesis-testing situation? Illustrate what you mean with a business example.
14. What is the probability of committing a Type I error called? How is this probability determined? Discuss.
15. Go to the library and, in a journal related to your declared major, locate two articles that use hypothesis testing. Discuss the problem being addressed, how the hypothesis was formulated, and any conclusions drawn based on the statistical test.
16. Consider a time when you had to make a personal decision. Discuss to what extent your decision followed the process: Formulate hypothesis—gather data—make decision.

ADDITIONAL PROBLEMS

17. The Ohio State Tax Commission attempts to set up payroll-tax withholding tables such that by the end of the year, an employee's income tax withholding is about $100 below his actual income tax owed to the state. The commission director claims that when all the Ohio tax returns are in, the average additional payment will be less than or equal to $100.

   A random sample of fifty accounts revealed on average additional payment of $114 with a sample standard deviation of $50. Testing at an alpha level of 0.10, do the sample data refute the director's claim?

18. The Television Advertising Institute claims that, on the average, adults spend 2.9 hours or more watching television on Thursday nights during the prime time hours of 8:00 to 11:00. Past studies have shown that the standard deviation is 0.6 hour. The National Education Association wishes to test this claim, but is uncertain how large the sample size should be to meet the following requirements: (1) no more than a 0.10 chance of rejecting the null hypothesis when it is true, and (2) no more than a 0.20 chance of accepting the null hypothesis when, in fact, the true mean is 2.20 hours. Determine the sample size sufficient to meet both of these restrictions.

    Also, develop the appropriate decision rule and test the hypothesis, assuming the sample information provides a sample mean of 2.35 hours. Which type of error may have been committed in this case? Discuss.

19. The TSR Testing Service prepares real estate license examinations for several states. Wisconsin officials are considering hiring this company to devise a test for their real estate brokers' license requirements. Wisconsin requires that the average test score be exactly 70 points. In order to evaluate the test prepared by TSR Testing, Wisconsin officials have selected a random sample of sixty potential brokers and have administered the exam. They found that the mean score was 68.55 points.
    a. State the appropriate null and alternative hypotheses.
    b. Assuming that the true standard deviation is 10 points and the hypothesis is to be tested at an alpha level of 0.08, what conclusions should be reached based on the sample data? Discuss.

20. The Cherry Hill Growers Association operates a fruit warehouse in California. Because of the volume of cherries that arrive at the warehouse during the picking season, the growers have agreed that instead of weighing each box of cherries, they would assume that the average box weighs 20 pounds. The total weight is then simply the number of boxes times 20 pounds.

    Past studies have shown that the standard deviation of weight from box to box is 0.5 pound. Suppose the manager of the warehouse has decided to select a random sample of seventy boxes of cherries from a particular grower's crop. He suspects that the grower may be underfilling the boxes and is concerned with detecting this, if it is the case. He is not concerned if the average box contains more than 20 pounds.
    a. State the appropriate null and alternative hypotheses.
    b. Establish the decision rule that the warehouse manager should use if he wishes to have at most a 10% chance of committing a Type I error.
    c. What is the probability of the warehouse manager making a Type II error if the true average weight is 19.55 pounds per box?
    d. What is the probability of the warehouse manager making a Type II error if the true average weight of a box is 19.85 pounds? Explain why the probability of a Type II error is larger in part **d** than in part **c**.

21. The owners of Fit and Trim, a fitness and diet club, would like to advertise that their clients lose at least 10 pounds on average during their first 3 months of membership at the club.

If the desired alpha level is 0.05, what should be concluded about this claim if the following results are observed? Be sure to first set up the appropriate decision rule.

$$\overline{X} = 9.1 \text{ lb}$$
$$S_x = 0.4 \text{ lb}$$
$$n = 150$$

22. The Oasis Chemical Company develops and manufactures pharmaceutical drugs for distribution and sale in the United States. The pharmaceutical business can be very lucrative when useful and safe drugs are introduced into the market. Whenever the Oasis research lab considers putting a drug into production, the company must actually establish the following sets of null and alternative hypotheses:

Set 1	Set 2
H_0: The drug is safe.	H_0: The drug is effective.
H_A: The drug is not safe.	H_A: The drug is not effective.

Taking each set of hypotheses separately, discuss the considerations that should be made in establishing alpha and beta.

23. The personnel manager for a large airline has claimed that, on the average, workers are asked to work no more than 3 hours overtime per week. Past studies show the standard deviation in overtime hours per worker to be 1.2 hours.

Suppose the union negotiators wish to test this claim by sampling payroll records for 250 employees. They believe that the personnel manager's claim is untrue, but want to base their conclusion on the sample results.

a. State the null and alternative hypotheses and discuss the meaning of Type I and Type II errors in this case.

b. Establish the appropriate decision rule if the union wishes to have no more than a 0.01 chance of a Type I error.

c. Determine the value of beta if the true mean overtime is 3.12 hours.

d. Compute the Type II error probability under the assumption that the true mean is 3.08 hours.

24. The managing partner of Patton and Associates, a CPA firm, has a basic knowledge of hypothesis testing. One of his clients, a retail store, would like Patton to perform an audit of the daily cash register tape against the actual dollar amount in the till.

The client recognizes that occasionally an error is going to occur. As long as the error is in the store's favor, the store manager is not concerned. However, when the store comes up short, the store manager is very concerned.

The Patton managing partner has indicated that he will perform the audit via sampling and hypothesis testing with the following hypotheses:

H_0: $\mu_x \geq \$0$ error; the store at least comes out even on the average

H_A: $\mu_x < \$0$ error; the store loses some money on the average

From past experience in this kind of audit, the CPA thinks that *A*, the critical value, should be set at $-\$2$. Therefore, if the average discrepancy between cash register tape and actual dollars is $2 or more at the store's expense, the null hypothesis will be rejected. If the null hypothesis is rejected, the clerk will be dismissed.

The CPA partner realizes that his client wants to be very sure any such employee is fired, but only if the firing is truly justified. Consequently, he is concerned with knowing beta for various values of the true, but unknown, population mean.

a. If the sample size is 47 days and the standard deviation is known to be $4.00, what is beta if the true mean is actually $-\$1.50$?

b. Calculate beta for a sample size of 64 days. The standard deviation remains $4, the critical value, *A*, is held at $-\$2$, and the true mean is $-\$1.50$.

c. Why has an increase in sample size caused an increase, rather than a decrease, in beta? Discuss how this undesirable event happened and how you could have prevented it from happening in this case. (Consult the following article if you need some help: Herbert H. Tsang, "The Effects of Changing Sample Size on the Alpha and Beta Errors: A Pedagogic Note," *Decision Sciences* 8 (October 1977): 757–759.)

25. The Bell Corporation is the parent corporation that franchises automobile lube and oil change centers around the United States. The standard set forth by the Bell Corporation is that the average time to lube and change oil in a car is 10 minutes or less.

Periodically, representatives from the Bell Company visit the franchises and perform a compliance test on this standard. They randomly select 150 cars (without the local operator's knowledge) and record how long it takes to service each car. Then, based on the sample mean, they will determine whether the franchise is operating within the standard. (The standard deviation is known to be 2.0 minutes.)

a. Establish the appropriate null and alternative hypotheses.

b. Determine the decision rule assuming that the company performs the compliance test using an alpha level of 0.05.

c. Determine the probability of committing a Type II error if the true average service time is 10.30 minutes.

d. Referring to part c, calculate power and explain what it means.

e. Develop an operating characteristic curve with values of beta obtained for the following values of the true mean:

$$\mu = 10.10 \text{ min}$$
$$\mu = 10.20 \text{ min}$$
$$\mu = 10.30 \text{ min}$$
$$\mu = 10.40 \text{ min}$$
$$\mu = 10.50 \text{ min}$$
$$\mu = 10.60 \text{ min}$$

Explain why a decision maker might be interested in developing an operating characteristic curve. Also, based on this O.C. curve, comment on the sampling procedure employed by the Bell Corporation in evaluating the performance of its franchises.

26. Suppose the manager in charge of compliance auditing for the Bell Corporation (see Problem 25) has decided that a larger sample size is necessary and thus has decided to select a random sample of 200 cars rather than 150. What general impact will this have on the probability of committing a Type II error for any level of the true mean? What impact will this have on the probability of committing a Type I error? Discuss.

27. A manufacturer of computer terminals claims that its product will last at least 50 weeks without needing repairs. The Quast Corporation is considering purchasing a great many of these computer terminals. A Quast data-processing manager has determined that given the price of the terminal and the total dollars involved, Quast should ask for some quality control records from the manufacturer.

   Suppose the manufacturer produces records of a random sample of 200 terminals. The average time before the first breakdown was 48 weeks. Assume the population standard deviation is known to be 24 weeks.
   a. Set up the appropriate null and alternative hypotheses.
   b. Determine the appropriate decision rule and indicate whether the sample information justifies rejecting the manufacturer's claim. Use an alpha level of 0.05.
   c. Discuss the ramifications of this decision and the potential costs of being wrong.

28. Referring to Problem 27, suppose the sample mean of 200 terminals had been 45 weeks rather than 48.
   a. What is the probability of finding a sample mean as small as or smaller than 45 if the true mean is 50 weeks?
   b. Now that you have determined the probability in part a, what does this mean to you with respect to whether the terminals can be expected to average at least 50 weeks before the first breakdown?
   c. "If the probability of a sample result, given the null hypothesis, is too small, the null hypothesis should be rejected." Comment on this statement with respect to your answers in parts a and b.
   d. What relationship does alpha have with a "too small" sample result, as discussed in part c?

29. The Larson & Sons Company sells dwarf fruit trees through the mail. It claims that the average pear tree will produce at least 2.5 bushels of pears the second year after it has been planted. If the standard deviation in production is known to be 0.70 bushel and the desired alpha level is 0.05, what should be concluded if the following data were recorded for a sample of forty trees showing the number of bushels produced the second year after planting?

1.6	3.3	4.0	2.6	2.6	2.8	3.2	2.9
3.4	2.4	3.0	3.9	2.7	3.3	2.6	1.9
2.8	3.0	2.8	1.6	3.0	2.5	1.9	3.0
3.0	4.5	1.0	2.3	1.8	2.9	0.4	3.6
2.0	2.5	2.2	2.6	2.4	1.8	3.5	2.0

30. The Inland Empire Food Store Company has stated in its advertising that the average shopper will save $5.00 or more per week by shopping at Inland stores. A consumer group has decided to test this assertion by sampling fifty shoppers who currently shop at other stores. It selects the customers and then notes each item purchased at their regular store. These same items are then priced at the Inland store and the total bill is compared. The following data reflect savings at Inland for the fifty shoppers. Note that those cases where the bill was higher at Inland are marked with a minus sign.

$14.00	$2.54	$11.33	$12.02	$ 4.55
12.00	8.45	− 0.75	1.83	12.04
− 5.04	2.80	2.09	− 3.10	8.02
12.10	3.31	2.20	4.65	1.03
2.93	9.75	1.73	− 1.54	9.80
3.56	3.29	1.34	− 4.08	9.70
10.02	1.33	4.56	− 1.52	3.25
− 0.85	−5.02	2.19	− 3.45	0.65
1.90	2.43	0.43	2.54	0.03
2.10	−0.56	7.89	− 0.65	1.34

   a. Set up the appropriate null and alternative hypotheses to test Inland's claim.
   b. Using an alpha level of 0.05, develop the decision rule and test the hypothesis. Discuss the results.

31. The Falcon Speedreading Course advertises that the average increase in reading speed for graduates of the course is at least 200 words per minute. Assuming that the standard deviation for the population is known to be forty words per minute, what should an independent reviewer conclude if a sample of 120 graduates showed an average improvement of 195 words per minute? Test at the alpha level of 0.10.

   Suppose the true population standard deviation is twenty words per minute rather than forty. Assuming that the sample results were the same and alpha was held to 0.10, what conclusion should be reached with respect to the speedreading course offered by Falcon? Discuss why the change in standard deviation would have this effect on the conclusion reached, considering that the sample information did not change.

32. The New York State (NYS) Insurance Company recorded the estimated number of labor hours the NY Capital Autobody Shop claimed to require for each repair job. The insurance company claims that the autobody shop took,

on average, 60 minutes or less time to actually repair the vehicle than estimated, but still charged NYS the full amount of estimated labor hours.

A random sample of 250 claims showed an average of 45 minutes less time with a sample standard deviation of 9 minutes. Testing at an alpha level of 0.05, do the sample data refute or support the insurance company's claim?

33. The maker of Super Saver paint advertises that its product will average at least 900 square feet per gallon coverage. A consumers' group that regularly tests these types of claims has budgeted enough money to sample 60 gallons of paint. It uses an alpha level of 0.10 to test claims like the one made by Super Saver. The consumers' group will base its analysis on findings of a previous study which showed the standard deviation in area covered to be 200 square feet.
    a. State the null and alternative hypotheses to be tested.
    b. Establish the appropriate decision rule for this hypothesis test.
    c. Determine the probability of accepting the null hypothesis when, in fact, the true average area covered is 875 square feet.
    d. Referring to part **c**, what is the probability of a Type II error if the sample size could be increased to 80 gallons? Discuss why the increase in sample size reduces the Type II error probability.

34. The manufacturer of a new car, CLM 3000, declares that the car runs like a camel—a long time on one tank of gas. The company claims that, on average, the CLM 3000 will get 52 mpg or more in the city.

A random sample of 500 car owners was asked to keep track of how many miles per gallon their newly purchased car was getting around town. The sample revealed an average of 49.5 mpg with a sample standard deviation of 1.25 mpg.
    a. Establish the appropriate null and alternative hypotheses.
    b. Assuming the alpha level equals 0.01, what conclusion can the car manufacturer make about its claim?

35. The Speedy Secretarial Service claims that its typists average at least 3.4 pages per hour. Before placing this information in its advertising brochures, Speedy wishes to determine whether this claim is true. A random sample of 450 records indicating typing productivity shows a mean of 3.2 pages per hour. Assuming the population standard deviation is known to be 0.5 page per hour and the desired alpha level is 0.05:
    a. Establish the appropriate null and alternative hypotheses.
    b. Develop the decision rule and test the null hypothesis. Indicate what the decision means to Speedy.
    c. Would the decision rule change if the same sample results had been obtained from a sample of thirty-six records? Discuss why or why not.
    d. Suppose the sample mean from a sample of size 350 is 3.34 pages per hour. What decision should Speedy make based on these sample data? Explain what this means to Speedy.

36. The Oat Crunch Cereal Company has a machine that automatically fills 16-ounce boxes of cereal. This machine may be set to any mean fill, but the

standard deviation of fill is known to be 0.5 ounce. The machine gets out of adjustment sometimes, even though the mean has been set at the desired fill level. The production manager has the responsibility of testing samples of filled cereal boxes to see whether the average fill has deviated from the desired level.

   a. Suppose the average fill level has been set at 16.2 ounces. If a sample of sixty boxes is tested and found to average 16.36 ounces, what should the production manager conclude about the machine's adjustment? Test at an alpha level of 0.05.

   b. Suppose the average fill setting is 16.2 ounces, but instead of a sample of sixty boxes, the sample size is 400 boxes. What conclusion should the production manager reach if the sample mean is the same as before, 16.36 ounces? Test at an alpha level of 0.05.

   c. Why are the conclusions different even though the sample mean was the same for both parts **a** and **b?** Discuss.

37.   The Cajun King restaurant recently ran a coupon advertisement in the local newspaper in which it offered a free soft drink with the purchase of a meal. Since the store did not define precisely what a meal was in the advertisement, the store manager was concerned with whether the average meal purchased using the coupon was less than or equal to $2.75.

   a. If the store manager wished to know whether the average meal purchase with a coupon was less than or equal to $2.75 without examining every cash receipt for the week, describe the procedure he might use to make a statistical inference about the average amount spent with the coupon.

   b. Formulate the appropriate null and alternative hypotheses and discuss in terms of the problem what a Type I error would be and what a Type II error would be.

   c. Suppose the manager wished to select a random sample of seventy-five cash register receipts. What would the critical value be if the population standard deviation were somehow known to be $0.50? Express the critical value in the same terms as the sample mean. Assume alpha equals 0.05.

   d. Referring to parts **b** and **c,** suppose the sample results showed a sample mean of $2.85. What conclusion should be reached, and why, if the test were performed with an alpha level of 0.05?

DATABASE PROBLEMS

The questions and problems in this section reference the various databases that accompany this text and which are described in Chapter 1. Your instructor has been provided a diskette with these databases. It is expected that you will be using computer software to access these data and to perform the required calculations and graphs.

DATABASE: **CITIES** (*Refer to the database description in Chapter 1.*)

1. It is claimed that the average white-collar 1987 earnings in U.S. cities was less than $25,000. Testing at an alpha level of 0.05, do these sample data support or refute this contention? Discuss your results.
2. The claim has been made that the average manufacturing salary in U.S. cities in 1987 exceeded $26,100. Based on the sample data, can this claim be supported or refuted at an alpha level of 0.05? Discuss your conclusion.
3. It was recently reported that SAT scores by students in cities average 908 points. Based on the sample data, can this claim be supported or refuted at an alpha level of 0.05? Discuss the results.

DATABASE: **FAST100** (*Refer to the database description in Chapter 1.*)

1. It has been claimed that for companies to be considered acceptable for investment by D. L. Green & Associates, they must have a growth rate of at least 100%. Based on the sample data, does the population of companies being evaluated by D. L. Green meet this requirement on average? Test at an $\alpha = 0.05$ level.
2. It has been hypothesized that growth companies traded over the counter have a price earnings ratio over the past 4 quarters (X_7) that will exceed 30. Based on these sample data, can this assertion be supported or refuted at the $\alpha = 0.05$ level?

DATABASE: **PACRIM** (*Refer to the database description in Chapter 1.*)

1. A recent report in a major business periodical has stated that profits for Japanese companies averaged in excess of $400 million dollars in 1989. Considering these data to be a statistical sample, can the periodical's claim be supported or refuted? Test using $\alpha = 0.10$.
2. Assuming your statistical software is capable of selecting random samples from an existing data set, first compute the average assets for all 150 companies. Then establish this as the hypothesized mean for the population of the 150 largest Pacific Rim companies. Now select a random sample of $n = 50$ companies. Use the sample information to test the null hypothesis using an $\alpha = 0.05$ level. If you rejected the null hypothesis, what type of error did you make? Discuss.

DATABASE: **TRUCKS** (*Refer to the database description in Chapter 1.*)

1. It is thought that the average speed of trucks crossing the WIM scale would exceed the posted speed limit of 55 miles per hour. Based on these sample data, what conclusion can be reached with respect to average speed? Test at an $\alpha = 0.10$ level.

2. A report published by the State of Idaho indicated that the average truck traveling through Idaho averages over 60 feet in length. Based on the sample data, can this claim be supported or refuted? Test at an $\alpha = 0.05$ level.

3. Compute a new variable which is the difference between X_6 and X_3. It is thought that, if the WIM scale is effective, the average difference would be 0. Based on these sample data, what can be concluded? Test at an $\alpha = 0.05$ level.

CASES

9A   Campbell Brewery, Inc., Part 1

Don Campbell and his younger brother Edward purchased Campbell Brewery from their father in 1983. The brewery makes and bottles beer under two labels and distributes it throughout the Southwest. Since purchasing the brewery, Don has been instrumental in modernizing operations.

One of the latest acquisitions is a filling machine that can be adjusted to fill at any average fill level desired. Since the bottles and cans filled by the brewery are exclusively the 12-ounce size, when they received the machine Don set the fill level to 12 ounces and left it that way. According to the manufacturer's specifications, the machine would fill bottles or cans around the average, with a standard deviation of 0.15 ounce.

Don just returned from a brewery convention where he attended a panel discussion related to problems with filling machines. One brewery representative discussed a problem her company had. It failed to learn that its machine's average fill went out of adjustment until several months later when its cost accounting department reported some problems with beer production in bulk not matching output in bottles and cans. It turns out that the machine's average fill had increased from 12 ounces to 12.07 ounces. With large volumes of production, this deviation meant substantial loss in profits.

Another brewery reported the same type of problem, but in the opposite direction. Its machine began filling bottles with slightly less than 12 ounces on the average. Although the consumers could not detect the shortage in a given bottle, the state and federal agencies responsible for checking the accuracy of packaged products discovered the problem in their testing and fined the brewery substantially for the underfill.

These problems were a surprise to Don Campbell. He had not considered the possibility that the machine might go out of adjustment and pose these types of problems. In fact, he became very concerned because both problems of losing profits and potentially being fined by the government were ones that he wished to avoid, if possible. Following the convention, Don and Ed decided to hire a consulting firm with expertise in these matters to assist them in setting up a procedure for monitoring the performance of the filling machine.

The consultant suggested that they set up a sampling plan whereby once a month they sample some number of bottles and measure their volumes precisely. If the average of the sample deviates too much from 12 ounces, they should shut the machine down and make the necessary adjustments. Otherwise, they should let the filling process continue. The consultant identified two types of problems that can occur from this sort of sampling plan:

1. They may incorrectly decide to adjust the machine when it is not really necessary to do so.
2. They may incorrectly decide to allow the filling process to continue when, in fact, the true average has deviated from 12 ounces.

After carefully considering what the consultant told them, Don indicated that he wanted no more than a 0.02 chance of the first problem occurring because of the costs involved. He also decided that if the true average fill had slipped to 11.99 ounces, he wanted no more than a 0.05 chance of not detecting this with his sampling plan. He wanted to avoid problems with the state and federal agencies. Finally, if the true average fill had actually risen to 12.007 ounces, he wanted to be able to detect this 98% of the time with his sampling plan. Thus, he wanted to avoid the lost profits that would result from such a problem.

Don needs to determine how large a sample size is necessary to meet his requirements.

9B   Campbell Brewery, Inc., Part 2

Don and Ed Campbell (see Case 9A) received assistance in setting up a sampling plan to help them detect whether their filling machine had gone out of adjustment. Upon hearing the results of the sample size calculations, both Don and Ed were shocked. It was simply not feasible to sample that many bottles and cans each month.

Don's letter to the consultant expressed his dissatisfaction with the sample size requirements. He requested a report back from the consultant advising him of his options regarding how the sample size could be reduced. The report was to contain specific options and the resulting sample sizes, as well as an overall review of the general trade-offs involved in this type of situation. You have been assigned the task by the consulting firm to prepare this report to the Campbell Brewery.

REFERENCES

Berenson, Mark L., and Levine, David M. *Basic Business Statistics Concepts and Applications,* 5th edition. Englewood Cliffs, New Jersey: Prentice-Hall, 1992.

Daniel, Wayne W., and Terrell, James C. *Business Statistics for Management and Economics,* 6th edition. Boston: Houghton Mifflin, 1992.

Iman, Ronald L., and Conover, W. J. *Modern Business Statistics,* 2nd edition. New York: Wiley, 1989.

Levin, Richard I., and Rubin, David S. *Statistics for Management,* 5th edition. Englewood Cliffs, New Jersey: Prentice-Hall, 1991.

Sincich, Terry. *Business Statistics by Example,* 4th edition. New York: Dellen, 1992.

Additional Hypothesis-Testing Techniques

WHY DECISION MAKERS NEED TO KNOW

Chapter 9 introduced the topic of hypothesis testing. Although it may initially appear to be only a statistical procedure, you should recognize the process as common in many decision-making situations. For instance:

On the basis of initial discussions with state party officials, a politician tentatively decides to run for office (hypothesizes she could win). She commissions a political poll to gauge her strength with voters (gathering sample information). Based on the results of the poll, she will make her final decision.

A bioengineering firm has developed a strain of corn that, in laboratory tests, appears to be more resistant to frost than current strains. The new strain appears to have commercial value (the hypothesis). The firm decides to perform a field trial (gather sample information) before making the final decision on whether to market the seeds.

A travel agency with many branches in Florida has been notified that the printing firm supplying its office forms is going out of business. Two competing firms are bidding for the agency's business. The travel agency's central office manager sees no reason to favor one firm over the other (the hypothesis), but asks to see samples of both firms' work (gather sample information) before making a decision between the two.

After listening to the weather report on the nightly news, you decide tomorrow may be rainy (the hypothesis) and so place your umbrella by the door. Before leaving in the morning you look up at the sky (gather sample information) and decide not to take the umbrella after all.

Clearly the hypothesis-testing procedure fits in well with the way many decisions are made. This chapter extends the hypothesis-testing discussion to include a wider range of applications involving parameters other than a single population mean.

CHAPTER OBJECTIVES

Chapter 9 introduced the steps taken when performing a statistical hypothesis test. These steps were discussed when considering only hypothesis tests about a population mean. This chapter will extend the hypothesis-testing discussion to include hypothesizing about a population proportion, about the difference between two population means, and about the difference between two population proportions. In each situation, this chapter will emphasize the use of the following steps in conducting a statistical hypothesis test:

1. Determine the null and alternative hypotheses.
2. Determine the desired alpha (α).
3. Choose a sample size.
4. Determine the critical value, A or Z_{critical}.
5. Establish the decision rule.
6. Select the sample and perform the test.

STUDENT OBJECTIVES

After studying the material in this chapter, you should be able to extend the hypothesis-testing procedure to do the following:

1. Perform hypothesis tests about a population proportion.
2. Perform hypothesis tests about the difference between two population means.
3. Perform hypothesis tests about the difference between two population proportions.

10-1 HYPOTHESIS TESTING ABOUT A POPULATION PROPORTION

The discussion in Chapter 9 involved hypothesis tests about a single population mean. Although there are many decision problems that involve a test of a population mean, there are many other cases where the value of interest is the **population proportion.** For example, the percentage of defective items produced on an assembly line might determine whether the assembly process should be restructured or left as it is, or the success of a life insurance salesperson might be measured by the percentage of renewals generated from his or her existing customers.

The internal auditors at First American Bank and Title Company routinely test the bank's system of internal controls. Recently, Jerry Millier, the audit manager, undertook an examination of the loan documentation on the bank's 22,500 outstanding automobile loans. Bank procedure requires that the file on each auto loan account contain certain specific documentation, such as a list of applicant assets, statement of monthly income, list of liabilities, and certificate of automobile insurance. If a particular account contains all the required documentation, that account is determined to be in compliance with bank procedures.

Jerry Millier has established a 1% noncompliance rate as the bank's standard. This means that if *more than* 1% of the 22,500 loans do not have appropriate documentation, the internal controls would be lacking and steps would need to be taken to improve the situation. It would be impractical to examine all 22,500 files to determine the noncompliance rate. Instead, Jerry instructed his staff to select a random sample of 600 files and determine how many contain deficient documentation. Then, based on the findings in the sample, Jerry will reach a conclusion about whether the bank exceeds the 1% noncompliance rate for the population of all 22,500 loan files.

The sample of 600 accounts uncovered nine files with inadequate loan documentation. The question facing Jerry is whether nine out of 600 is sufficient to conclude that the bank has a problem. To answer this question statistically, we need to recall our work in Chapters 7 and 8, in which we indicated that the sampling distribution for the population proportion is approximately normal for large sample sizes.

The basic claim about the population would be that the noncompliance rate is less than or equal to 1% (the internal controls are working). Since the claim contains the equality and since the population value of interest is a proportion, the null and alternative hypotheses are stated as follows:

$$H_0: \quad p \leq 0.01 \quad \text{(Claim)}$$
$$H_A: \quad p > 0.01$$

Note that Jerry wishes to test the null hypothesis using an alpha = 0.02 level. This means he is willing to reject a true null hypothesis 2% of the time. In this case, if a Type I statistical error is committed, the internal controls will be determined to be faulty when, in fact, they are working as designed.

Once the hypotheses and the alpha level have been specified, we can formulate the decision rule for testing the hypotheses. Figure 10-1 shows how this is done. As you can see in Figure 10-1, the critical value, A, is 2.06 standard deviations above $p = 0.01$. Thus, if the sample proportion exceeds 0.01824, the null hypothesis should be rejected.

Recall that for the $n = 600$ files sampled, nine were deficient in documentation. This means that $\hat{p} = 9/600 = 0.015$. Thus, since $0.015 < 0.01824$, the null hypothesis should not be rejected based on these sample data. Therefore, Jerry Millier will conclude that the system of internal controls is working effectively.

$$\sigma_{\hat{p}} = \sqrt{\dfrac{p(1-p)}{n}}$$

FIGURE 10-1

Decision Rule for First American Bank and Title Company Example

Hypotheses:

$H_0: p \le .01$
$H_A: p > .01$
$\alpha = 0.02$

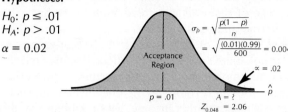

$$\sigma_{\hat{p}} = \sqrt{\dfrac{p(1-p)}{n}}$$

$$= \sqrt{\dfrac{(0.01)(0.99)}{600}} = 0.004$$

$A = p + Z\sigma_{\hat{p}}$
$A = 0.01 + (2.06)(0.004)$
$A = 0.01824$

Decision Rule:

If $\hat{p} > 0.01824$, reject H_0.
If $\hat{p} \le 0.01824$, do not reject H_0.

Since $\hat{p} = 0.015 < 0.01824$, do not reject H_0.

An important point to consider when testing hypotheses about a population proportion is that the standard deviation of the sampling distribution, $\sigma_{\hat{p}}$, is formed using the hypothesized proportion rather than the sample proportion. Equation 10-1 illustrates this:

$$\sigma_{\hat{p}} = \sqrt{\dfrac{p(1-p)}{n}} \qquad \text{10-1}$$

where

p = Hypothesized proportion

n = Sample size

SKILL DEVELOPMENT PROBLEMS FOR **SECTION 10-1**

The following set of problems is meant to test your understanding of the material in this section.

1. Given the following null and alternative hypotheses:

$$H_0: \quad p \le 0.24$$
$$H_A: \quad p > 0.24$$

test the null hypothesis based on a random sample of $n = 100$ where $\hat{p} = 0.27$. Assume an $\alpha = 0.05$ level. Be sure to show clearly the decision rule.

2. Given the following null and alternative hypotheses:

$$H_0: \quad p \geq 0.50$$
$$H_A: \quad p < 0.50$$

test the null hypothesis based on a random sample of $n = 200$ where $\hat{p} = 0.47$. Assume an $\alpha = 0.10$ level. Be sure to show clearly the decision rule.

3. Given the following null and alternative hypotheses:

$$H_0: \quad p = 0.20$$
$$H_A: \quad p \neq 0.20$$

test the null hypothesis based on a random sample of $n = 100$ where $\hat{p} = 0.23$. Assume an $\alpha = 0.05$ level. Be sure to show clearly the decision rule.

4. The College of Business at a state university has a computer literacy requirement for all graduates: Students must show proficiency with a computer spreadsheet software package and with a word-processing software package. To assess whether students are computer literate, a test is given at the end of each semester. The test is designed so that at least 70% of all students who have taken a special microcomputer course will pass the test. Suppose that, in a random sample of 100 students recently finishing the microcomputer course, 63 pass the proficiency test. Using an $\alpha = 0.05$ level, what conclusions should the administrators make regarding the difficulty of the test?

5. A shopping center developer claims in a presentation to a potential client that at least 40% of the adult female population in a community visit the mall one or more times a week. To test this claim, the developer selected a random sample of 100 households with an adult female present and asked if they visit the mall at least 1 day per week. Thirty-eight of the 100 respondents replied "yes" to the question. Based on the sample data and an $\alpha = 0.05$ level, what should be concluded about the developer's claim? Show the decision rule and your analysis clearly.

6. A large number of complaints have been received in the past 6 months regarding airlines losing fliers' baggage. The airlines claim the problem is nowhere near as great as the newspaper articles have indicated. In fact, one airline spokesman claimed that no more than 1% of all bags fail to arrive at the destination with the passenger. To test this claim, 200 bags were randomly selected at various airports in the United States when they were checked with this airline. Of these, six failed to reach the destination when the passenger (owner) arrived. Is this sufficient evidence to refute the airline spokesman's claim? Test at an $\alpha = 0.05$ level. Discuss.

10-2 HYPOTHESIS TESTING ABOUT THE DIFFERENCE BETWEEN TWO POPULATION MEANS

Many business decision problems require analyzing values from two or more populations. This section introduces methods to test hypotheses about the *difference between two population means*. These methods, however, are merely extensions of hypothesis tests for one population mean, introduced in Chapter 9.

The Peterson Toy Company designs and manufactures games for children and adults. The company has several popular games currently in production, but still finds itself with excess production capacity. Consequently, the company introduces new games as fast as they are designed and at the same time eliminates poor sellers from production. The marketing people push for games with recognizable themes and attempt to time their introduction for a holiday season, particularly Christmas.

The Peterson marketing people have performed extensive market research to determine what factors are most influential in a game's success or failure. A critical factor in children's games is the length of time needed to play the game. Games that are too complicated and too long are generally poor sellers, as are games that can be finished too quickly and are considered unchallenging.

After a new children's game has been designed, the company selects a sample of typical children to play it on a trial basis to determine the average time needed to finish. When the new game is similar to an existing game, the two are compared to determine whether they are equal with respect to average playing time.

For example, Peterson is currently developing an advertising plan for a game with the company identification "1." Some marketing department members fear that game 1 requires too much time to play. Recently, the research and design department has developed a game similar to game 1 in design but which it claims should take less time to play. However, the new game contains other features that are important in selling games. The new game is assigned the identification "2."

The marketing department at Peterson wishes to test the following hypotheses:

Hypotheses:

$$H_0: \quad \mu_1 \leq \mu_2 \quad \text{or} \quad \mu_1 - \mu_2 \leq 0$$
$$H_A: \quad \mu_1 > \mu_2 \quad \text{or} \quad \mu_1 - \mu_2 > 0$$

To simplify notation, we let μ_1 and μ_2 equal the population means, μ_{x_1} and μ_{x_2}, respectively. Also, we let σ_1^2 and σ_2^2 represent the population variances, $\sigma_{x_1}^2$ and $\sigma_{x_2}^2$, respectively. We shall follow this notation pattern throughout the remainder of the text whenever two or more populations are considered.

The null hypothesis states that the average playing time for game 1 is less than or equal to the average for game 2. If this is accepted, the company will continue with its marketing efforts for game 1. If the null hypothesis is rejected, the company will conclude that the average playing time for game 1 is *greater than the average* time for game 2. In this case, Peterson will abandon game 1 in favor of game 2.

The decision rule for the Peterson hypothesis is as follows:

Decision Rule:

Select two samples, of sizes n_1 and n_2, and calculate $\overline{X}_1$ and $\overline{X}_2$.

If $\overline{X}_1 - \overline{X}_2 \leq A$, accept H_0.

If $\overline{X}_1 - \overline{X}_2 > A$, reject H_0.

In Chapter 7 we introduced the central limit theorem for the sampling distribution of $\overline{X}$. The central limit theorem also applies for the sampling distribution of the difference between two sample means. Thus, if the sample sizes are sufficiently large, the sampling distribution of $(\overline{X}_1 - \overline{X}_2)$ will be approximately normally distributed, with a mean and standard error as shown in equations 10-2 and 10-3:

$$\mu_{\overline{X}_1 - \overline{X}_2} = \mu_1 - \mu_2 \qquad \textbf{10-2}$$

and

$$\sigma_{\overline{X}_1 - \overline{X}_2} = \sqrt{\frac{\sigma_1^2}{n_1} + \frac{\sigma_2^2}{n_2}} \qquad \textbf{10-3}$$

where

$\overline{X}_1$ and $\overline{X}_2$: Sample means for population 1 and population 2, respectively

$\mu_1 - \mu_2$ = Hypothesized difference between population means

σ_1^2 and σ_2^2: Variances of population 1 and population 2, respectively

n_1 and n_2: Sample sizes from population 1 and population 2, respectively

Thus, the critical value for the large-sample statistical test of the difference between two population means is found by solving equation 10-4 for A, as given by equation 10-5:

$$Z = \frac{A - (\mu_1 - \mu_2)}{\sqrt{\frac{\sigma_1^2}{n_1} + \frac{\sigma_2^2}{n_2}}} \qquad \textbf{10-4}$$

Then, solving for A,

$$A = (\mu_1 - \mu_2) + Z\sqrt{\frac{\sigma_1^2}{n_1} + \frac{\sigma_2^2}{n_2}} \qquad \textbf{10-5}$$

Hypotheses:

$H_0: \mu_1 - \mu_2 \leq 0$
$H_A: \mu_1 - \mu_2 > 0$

$\alpha = 0.07$
$n_1 = 100,\ n_2 = 100$
$\overline{X}_1 = 50,\ \overline{X}_2 = 46$
$\sigma_1 = 30,\ \sigma_2 = 30$
$\sigma_1^2 = 900,\ \sigma_2^2 = 900$

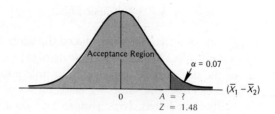

Acceptance Region

$\alpha = 0.07$

$(\overline{X}_1 - \overline{X}_2)$

0
$A = ?$
$Z = 1.48$

Decision Rule:

If $(\overline{X}_1 - \overline{X}_2) \leq A$, accept H_0.
If $(\overline{X}_1 - \overline{X}_2) > A$, reject H_0.

Solving for the critical level, A,

$$A = (\mu_1 - \mu_2) + Z\sqrt{\frac{\sigma_1^2}{n_1} + \frac{\sigma_2^2}{n_2}} = 0 + 1.48\sqrt{\frac{900}{100} + \frac{900}{100}}$$

$$= 6.279$$

Since $(\overline{X}_1 - \overline{X}_2) = 4 < 6.279$, accept H_0.

Suppose the standard deviations of the times needed to complete the games are 30 minutes for game 1 and 30 minutes for game 2. The company is willing to accept a 0.07 chance of a Type I error ($\alpha = 0.07$) and selects a sample of 100 people to play each game. Figure 10-2 shows the results of the sampling and the decision rule.

As shown in Figure 10-2, the critical value is 6.279. This means that if the difference between the two sample means exceeds 6.279 minutes, the null hypothesis that the two games take the same time to play, on average, should be rejected. Since the difference in sample means is 4, the company can attribute this to sampling error and the null hypothesis is not rejected. Thus, the company will continue to market game 1.

This hypothesis could also be tested using the p-value approach. Instead of solving for A, the critical value, we determine how many standard deviations $(\overline{X}_1 - \overline{X}_2) = 4$ is from the hypothesized value of 0. We use equation 10-4 and substitute $\overline{X}_1 - \overline{X}_2 = 4$ for A and solve for Z as follows:

$$Z = \frac{4 - 0}{\sqrt{\frac{900}{100} + \frac{900}{100}}}$$

$$= 0.943$$

Going to the standard normal table for $Z = 0.94$, we get a probability of 0.3264. The p-value is computed to be $0.5000 - 0.3264 = 0.1736$. Therefore, the null hypothesis would be rejected when alpha exceeds 0.1736. Otherwise, the null hypothesis will not be rejected. In the Peterson Toy Company example, the alpha level is 0.07. Thus, H_0 is not rejected.

WHEN THE POPULATION VARIANCES ARE UNKNOWN

As in decisions involving one population, often the variances for a two-population hypothesis test are not known. However, if the sample sizes are reasonably large (generally over 30), the sample variances can be substituted for the population variances. Then, the critical value in the decision rule is found by solving for A in equation 10-6:

$$Z = \frac{A - (\mu_1 - \mu_2)}{\sqrt{\dfrac{S_1^2}{n_1} + \dfrac{S_2^2}{n_2}}}$$

10-6

The decision rule is found exactly as in the previous examples. For example, in the Peterson Toy Company problem, instead of assuming that $\sigma_1^2 = 900$ and $\sigma_2^2 = 900$, suppose we found the sample variances $S_1^2 = 808$ and $S_2^2 = 933$. Figure 10-3 shows this situation. Thus, using the sample variances in place of the unknown population variances is the only change in the hypothesis-testing procedure. In this case, the decision to accept H_0 is unchanged from the previous example.

OTHER CONSIDERATIONS

The three basic forms for the null and alternative hypotheses for the two-sample test are as follows:

$$H_0: \quad \mu_1 \leq \mu_2 \quad \text{or} \quad \mu_1 - \mu_2 \leq 0$$
$$H_A: \quad \mu_1 > \mu_2 \quad \text{or} \quad \mu_1 - \mu_2 > 0$$

$$H_0: \quad \mu_1 = \mu_2 \quad \text{or} \quad \mu_1 - \mu_2 = 0$$
$$H_A: \quad \mu_1 \neq \mu_2 \quad \text{or} \quad \mu_1 - \mu_2 \neq 0$$

$$H_0: \quad \mu_1 \geq \mu_2 \quad \text{or} \quad \mu_1 - \mu_2 \geq 0$$
$$H_A: \quad \mu_1 < \mu_2 \quad \text{or} \quad \mu_1 - \mu_2 < 0$$

Also, the hypothesized difference between two population means need *not* be 0. For example, we might hypothesize that the average difference in attendance at

FIGURE 10-3

Two-sample
Decision Rule
with Variances
Unknown in the
Peterson Toy
Company
Example

Hypotheses:

H_0: $\mu_1 - \mu_2 \leq 0$
H_A: $\mu_1 - \mu_2 > 0$

$\alpha = 0.07$
$Z = 1.48$
$n_1 = 100, n_2 = 100$
$\bar{X}_1 = 50, \bar{X}_2 = 46$
$S_1^2 = 808, S_2^2 = 933$

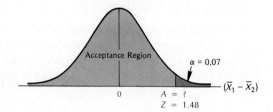

Decision Rule:

If $(\bar{X}_1 - \bar{X}_2) \leq A$, accept H_0.
If $(\bar{X}_1 - \bar{X}_2) > A$, reject H_0.

$$Z = \frac{A - (\mu_1 - \mu_2)}{\sqrt{\dfrac{S_1^2}{n_1} + \dfrac{S_2^2}{n_2}}}$$

$$A = (\mu_1 - \mu_2) + Z \sqrt{\frac{S_1^2}{n_1} + \frac{S_2^2}{n_2}} = 0 + 1.48 \sqrt{\frac{808}{100} + \frac{933}{100}}$$

$$= 6.175$$

Since $(\bar{X}_1 - \bar{X}_2) \leq 6.175$, accept H_0.

two movie theaters is at least 120 people per day. In this case, the null and alternative hypotheses would be

$$H_0: \quad \mu_1 - \mu_2 \geq 120$$
$$H_A: \quad \mu_1 - \mu_2 < 120$$

Another consideration is that the sample sizes selected from the two populations need *not* be equal. In the theater example, we might randomly sample 50 days ($n_1 = 50$) from theater 1 and 75 days ($n_2 = 75$) from theater 2. Generally, if the population variances are not equal, the larger sample size should be selected from the population with the larger variance.

SKILL DEVELOPMENT PROBLEMS FOR **SECTION 10-2**

The following set of problems is meant to test your understanding of the material in this section.

7.   Given the following null and alternative hypotheses:

$$H_0: \quad \mu_1 - \mu_2 = 0$$
$$H_A: \quad \mu_1 - \mu_2 \neq 0$$

and the following sample information:

Sample 1	Sample 2
$n = 100$	$n = 120$
$S = 20$	$S = 24$
$\overline{X} = 430$	$\overline{X} = 405$

a. Develop the appropriate decision rule, assuming an alpha level of 0.05 is to be used.
b. Test the null hypothesis and indicate whether the sample information leads you to reject or accept the null hypothesis.

8. Given the following null and alternative hypotheses:

$$H_0: \quad \mu_1 - \mu_2 \geq 0$$
$$H_A: \quad \mu_1 - \mu_2 < 0$$

and the following sample information:

Sample 1	Sample 2
$n = 64$	$n = 91$
$S = 30$	$S = 32$
$\overline{X} = 2,456$	$\overline{X} = 2,460$

a. Develop the appropriate decision rule, assuming an alpha level of 0.05 is to be used.
b. Test the null hypothesis and indicate whether the sample information leads you to reject or accept the null hypothesis.

9. Given the following null and alternative hypotheses:

$$H_0: \quad \mu_1 - \mu_2 \leq 0$$
$$H_A: \quad \mu_1 - \mu_2 > 0$$

and the following sample information:

Sample 1	Sample 2
$n = 200$	$n = 220$
$S = 5.5$	$S = 4.8$
$\overline{X} = 345$	$\overline{X} = 344.50$

a. Develop the appropriate decision rule, assuming an alpha level of 0.05 is to be used.
b. Test the null hypothesis and indicate whether the sample information leads you to reject or accept the null hypothesis.

10. The State College registrar is interested in determining whether there is a difference between male and female students in average number of credit hours taken during a term. She has selected a random sample of sixty males and sixty females and observed the following sample information:

	Male	*Female*
	$\overline{X} = 13.24$ credits	$\overline{X} = 14.65$ credits
	$S = 1.2$ credits	$S = 1.56$ credits

a. State the appropriate null and alternative hypotheses to be tested.
b. Develop the decision rule, based on an alpha = 0.05 level, and indicate whether the null hypothesis should be accepted or rejected.

11. The Nielson Product Testing Service in Detroit, Michigan, recently worked with a client who wished an independent determination of whether customers preferred its product to a particular competitor's product. The Nielson staff set up a rating scale and selected a random sample of 100 individuals to rate the client's product. A second random sample of 100 individuals was selected and asked to rate the competitor's product. The client believed that its product would be rated at least as high as the competitor's.

The following sample data were observed:

Client	*Competitor*
$\overline{X} = 88.5$	$\overline{X} = 90.05$
$S = 6.5$	$S = 5.0$

a. State the appropriate null and alternative hypotheses to be tested.
b. Based on the sample information and an alpha level = 0.10, what should be concluded about the average ratings? Be sure to state clearly the decision rule.

10-3 HYPOTHESIS TESTING ABOUT THE DIFFERENCE BETWEEN TWO POPULATION PROPORTIONS

Section 10-1 introduced the methodology for testing hypotheses involving population proportions. This section extends the analysis to testing hypotheses about the difference between two population proportions.

Pomona Fabrication, Inc., produces hand-held hair dryers that several major retailers sell as their house brands. Pomona was an early entrant into this market and has developed substantial manufacturing and technological skills. However, in recent years the firm has faced increased competition from both domestic and foreign manufacturers. Pomona has been forced to reduce its prices, and this, coupled with ever-increasing production costs, has caused a substantial reduction in the company's profit margin.

A critical component of a hand-held hair dryer is the motor-heater unit. This component accounts for the majority of the dryer's cost and also for a majority of the product's reliability problems. Product reliability is extremely important to Pomona since the company currently offers a standard 1-year warranty. Of course, Pomona is also interested in reducing production costs.

Pomona's research and development department has recently developed a new motor-heater unit that will offer a 15% cost savings. However, the company's vice-president of product development is unwilling to authorize the new component unless it is at least as reliable as the motor-heater currently being used.

The research and development department has decided to test samples of both units to see whether there is a difference in the proportions that will fail in 1 year. Two hundred fifty units of each type will be tested under conditions that simulate 1 year's use. Thus, the following hypotheses are formed:

Hypotheses:

$$H_0: \quad p_{new} \leq p_{old} \quad \text{or} \quad p_{new} - p_{old} \leq 0$$

$$H_A: \quad p_{new} > p_{old} \quad \text{or} \quad p_{new} - p_{old} > 0$$

where

p = Proportion of dryers that fail before 1 year

Decision Rule:

Select two samples, of sizes n_1 and n_2, and calculate $\hat{p}_1$ and $\hat{p}_2$, respectively, where $\hat{p}_1$ and $\hat{p}_2$ are estimates of the two population proportions, p_{new} and p_{old}, respectively.

If $Z \leq Z_{critical}$, accept H_0.

If $Z > Z_{critical}$, reject H_0.

If the null hypothesis is rejected, the company will continue to use the old motor-heater unit. Otherwise, the new motor-heater will be installed.

As with a hypothesis test of a single population proportion, the normal distribution can be used to test hypotheses about the difference between two population proportions, provided the sample sizes are sufficiently large. In this case, the critical value is found by solving equation 10-7 for Z:

$$Z = \frac{(\hat{p}_1 - \hat{p}_2) - (p_1 - p_2)}{\sqrt{\dfrac{p_1(1 - p_1)}{n_1} + \dfrac{p_2(1 - p_2)}{n_2}}} \qquad \textbf{10-7}$$

Note that the standard deviation of the sampling distribution for the difference between sample proportions is given by equation 10-8:

$$\sigma_{\hat{p}_1 - \hat{p}_2} = \sqrt{\dfrac{p_1(1 - p_1)}{n_1} + \dfrac{p_2(1 - p_2)}{n_2}} \qquad \textbf{10-8}$$

However, equation 10-8 requires that we know p_1 and p_2. Since these values are unknown and we have hypothesized zero difference between the two population proportions, we must calculate a **pooled estimator** $(\bar{p})$ by taking a weighted average of the observed sample proportions as in equation 10-9:

$$\bar{p} = \frac{n_1\hat{p}_1 + n_2\hat{p}_2}{n_1 + n_2}$$

10-9

The reason for taking a weighted average is to give more weight to the larger sample. Note that the numerator is the total number of successes in the two samples and the denominator is the total sample size.

The estimated standard deviation of the sampling distribution is given by equation 10-10:

$$S_{\hat{p}_1 - \hat{p}_2} = \sqrt{\bar{p}(1 - \bar{p})\left(\frac{1}{n_1} + \frac{1}{n_2}\right)}$$

10-10

Thus the Z formula is given by equation 10-11:

$$Z = \frac{(\hat{p}_1 - \hat{p}_2) - (p_1 - p_2)}{\sqrt{\bar{p}(1 - \bar{p})\left(\frac{1}{n_1} + \frac{1}{n_2}\right)}}$$

10-11

Assume that Pomona is willing to accept an alpha level of 0.05 and that seventy-five of the new motor-heaters and sixty-five of the originals failed the 1-year test. Figure 10-4 illustrates the decision rule development and the hypothesis test. As you can see in the figure, Pomona should *not* reject the null hypothesis. Rather, based on the sample information, the firm should conclude that the new motor-heater is at least as reliable as the old one. Since the new one is less costly, it should be used.

SKILL DEVELOPMENT PROBLEMS FOR **SECTION 10-3**

The following set of problems is meant to test your understanding of the material in this section.

FIGURE **10-4**

Hypothesis Test
of Two
Proportions for
the Pomona
Fabrication, Inc.
Example

Hypotheses:

H_0: $p_{new} - p_{old} \leq 0$
H_A: $p_{new} - p_{old} > 0$

$\alpha = 0.05$

$n_{new} = 250$, $n_{old} = 250$
$x_{new} = 75$, $x_{old} = 65$
$\hat{p}_{new} = 75/250 = 0.30$, $\hat{p}_{old} = 65/250 = 0.26$

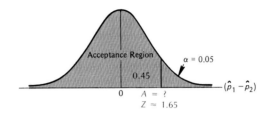

Decision Rule:

If $Z > 1.65$, reject H_0.
If $Z \leq 1.65$, accept H_0.

Test Statistic:

$$Z = \frac{(\hat{p}_1 - \hat{p}_2) - (p_1 - p_2)}{\sqrt{\bar{p}(1 - \bar{p})\left(\dfrac{1}{n_1} + \dfrac{1}{n_2}\right)}} = \frac{(0.30 - 0.26) - 0}{\sqrt{(0.28)(0.72)\left(\dfrac{1}{250} + \dfrac{1}{250}\right)}} = 0.996$$

where: $\bar{p} = \dfrac{250(0.30) + 250(0.26)}{250 + 250}$
$= 0.28$

Since $0.996 < 1.65$, accept H_0.

12. Given the following null and alternative hypotheses:

$$H_0: \quad p_1 - p_2 = 0$$
$$H_A: \quad p_1 - p_2 \neq 0$$

and the following sample information:

Sample 1	Sample 2
$n = 100$	$n = 100$
$x = 30$	$x = 34$

Based on $\alpha = 0.05$ and the sample information, what should be concluded with respect to the null and alternative hypotheses? Be sure to clearly show the decision rule.

13. Given the following null and alternative hypotheses:

$$H_0: \quad p_1 - p_2 \geq 0$$
$$H_A: \quad p_1 - p_2 < 0$$

and the following sample information:

Sample 1	Sample 2
$n = 100$	$n = 100$
$x = 70$	$x = 75$

Based on $\alpha = 0.05$ and the sample information, what should be concluded with respect to the null and alternative hypotheses? Be sure to clearly show the decision rule.

14. Given the following null and alternative hypotheses:

$$H_0: \quad p_1 - p_2 \leq 0$$
$$H_A: \quad p_1 - p_2 > 0$$

and the following sample information:

Sample 1	Sample 2
$n = 60$	$n = 80$
$x = 30$	$x = 24$

Based on $\alpha = 0.02$ and the sample information, what should be concluded with respect to the null and alternative hypotheses? Be sure to clearly show the decision rule.

15. The United Way Organization raises money for community charity activities. Recently in one community, the fund-raising committee was concerned whether there is a difference in the proportion of employees who give to United Way, depending on whether the employer is a private business or a government agency. It was decided to select a random sample of people who had been contacted about contributing last year. Seventy of those contacted worked for a private business and fifty worked for a government agency. Of the seventy private-sector employees, twenty-two had contributed some amount to United Way and nineteen of the government employees in the sample had contributed.

    Based on these sample data and $\alpha = 0.05$, what should be concluded? Be sure to show the decision rule.

16. Recently a nationwide television network commissioned a polling service to poll homeowners across the United States. Among the issues to be addressed in the survey was whether there is a difference in the proportions of homes that watch a national news broadcast depending on whether the household is headed by a man or a woman. The study surveyed 1,200 homes. In 745 of these, the head of household was listed as a man. In the others, the household head was a woman. The survey results showed that 62% of the households headed by men tuned in to a national network news program, whereas 49% of those homes headed by women did so. Based on these data, what could the network conclude overall? State the null and alternative hypotheses and test at an alpha level equal to 0.05.

10-4

HYPOTHESIS TESTING AND STATISTICAL PROCESS CONTROL

An important part of statistical process control has its foundation in the hypothesis-testing techniques introduced in both Chapter 9 and this chapter. To illustrate, consider an example involving a company called EasyGlide that makes the wheels used in rollerblade skates, the in-line roller skates that look like ice skates. The bearings in the wheels are self-contained and guaranteed for 1 year under "normal use." Company engineers and production managers agree that based on manufacturing controls, at most 4% of the wheels sold should require replacement within the 1-year warranty period.

Weekly output at the manufacturing facility is 30,000 wheels. Company engineers have devised a process whereby a year's use can be simulated in a relatively short amount of time. They can test a sample of the wheels that have been produced to verify the 4% "defect rate."

FORMULATE THE HYPOTHESES

Using the hypothesis-testing tools introduced so far, the first step in the test process might be to establish the appropriate null and alternative hypotheses. Since the standard is that the defect rate is 4% or less, the null and alternative hypotheses can be stated as follows:

$$H_0: \quad p \leq 0.04 \quad \text{(The standard)}$$
$$H_A: \quad p > 0.04$$

In quality control terminology, the 0.04 value is referred to as the **acceptable quality level** or **AQL.** In many instances, an AQL is negotiated between buyer and seller.

TYPE I AND TYPE II ERRORS

As you should understand by now, anytime sampling is involved, the possibility of sampling error exists. If extreme sampling error occurs, an incorrect decision may be made about the null hypothesis. For instance, the 30,000 wheels may actually meet the 4% standard, but the sample results could lead us to conclude otherwise. We refer to this as a Type I statistical error. In process control terminology, this type of error is called the **producer's risk.** Likewise, the 30,000 wheels may actually have a defect level higher than 4%, but the sample data do not detect that and we could "accept" the null hypothesis. This is called a Type II statistical error. The quality term for this error is the **consumer's risk.**

DETERMINING THE SAMPLING PLAN

If the managers at EasyGlide plan to use the simulation process to test the 30,000 wheels for durability, they must develop a sampling plan because not all wheels can be tested. The sampling plan consists of two elements:

1. The sample size
2. The decision rule

The number of units to be tested is determined by a combination of factors, including the cost of sampling and the time available to perform the sampling. However, crucial to determining the required sample size is an understanding of the trade-offs between the Type I error (producer's risk) and Type II error (consumer's risk). For a given sample size, a reduction in the probability of committing a Type I error, alpha, will result in an increase in the Type II error probability, beta.

Once the decision maker determines the sample size to be used, a decision rule must be established. The manager can then compare the sample result to the decision rule to decide whether the 4% defect level is being realized. Suppose the plan is to select a simple random sample of $n = 120$ wheels. Figure 10-5 shows how the decision rule would be determined assuming an alpha level of 0.05. Thus, if a sample of $n = 120$ is selected, the decision rule is as follows:

Decision Rule:

If $\hat{p} > 0.0694$, reject H_0.

If $\hat{p} \leq 0.0694$, do not reject H_0.

where $\hat{p}$ is the proportion of wheels in the sample that prove defective (i.e., will need to be replaced under warranty). We can convert the decision rule to number of wheels by multiplying $\hat{p}$ by 120, giving the following decision rule:

FIGURE 10-5

Decision Rule for the EasyGlide Example

Hypotheses:

$H_0: p \leq .04$
$H_A: p > .04$

$\alpha = 0.05$

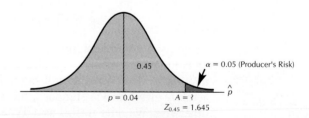

0.45

$\alpha = 0.05$ (Producer's Risk)

$p = 0.04$

$A = ?$

$Z_{0.45} = 1.645$

$\hat{p}$

$$\sigma_{\hat{p}} = \sqrt{\frac{p(1-p)}{n}} = \sqrt{\frac{0.04(0.96)}{120}}$$

$$= 0.0179$$

The critical value, A, is 1.645 standard deviations above $p = 0.04$. Therefore

$$A = 0.04 + 1.645(0.0179)$$
$$= 0.0694$$

Decision Rule:

If $\hat{p} > 0.0694$, reject H_0.
If $\hat{p} \leq 0.0694$, do not reject H_0.

Decision Rule:

If $X > 8$, reject H_0.

If $X \leq 8$, do not reject H_0.

where X is the number of defective wheels.

Thus far in this example, we have neglected the consumer's risk or Type II error. Does this sampling plan give adequate protection against a consumer's risk? A Type II error occurs if the null hypothesis is false, but the sample data lead us to accept it. Thus, if the EasyGlide null hypothesis is false, the rate of defects, p, would exceed 4%. In Chapter 9, we showed how to calculate beta. Recall that to find beta, we had to select a "what-if" value such that H_0 is false (i.e., $p > 0.04$). In quality control terminology, this value is referred to as the **lot tolerance percent defective** or **LTPD**. This is the highest possible defect rate that we can tolerate. For instance, suppose we set the LTPD at 0.10.

Then, if the decision rule for a sample of $n = 120$ is applied, the chance of making a Type II error, beta, can be calculated as shown in Figure 10-6. As this figure shows, the sampling plan provides for a 0.05 chance of a Type I error and a 0.1314 chance of a Type II error, if the true fraction defective (LTPD) is 10%. As a decision maker, you would have to determine whether this sampling plan is acceptable.

If we change the sample size, the decision rule will likely change. Likewise, if we choose to control the Type II error instead of the Type I error for a given sample size, the decision rule would change. If we elect to control both types of error, the required sample size will change as will the decision rule. The point is that hypothesis-testing tools, such as the one illustrated in this example, are useful in making decisions about whether quality standards are being satisfied. However, many operating personnel do not have the statistical education that you now

FIGURE 10-6

Consumer's Risk Computation for the EasyGlide Example

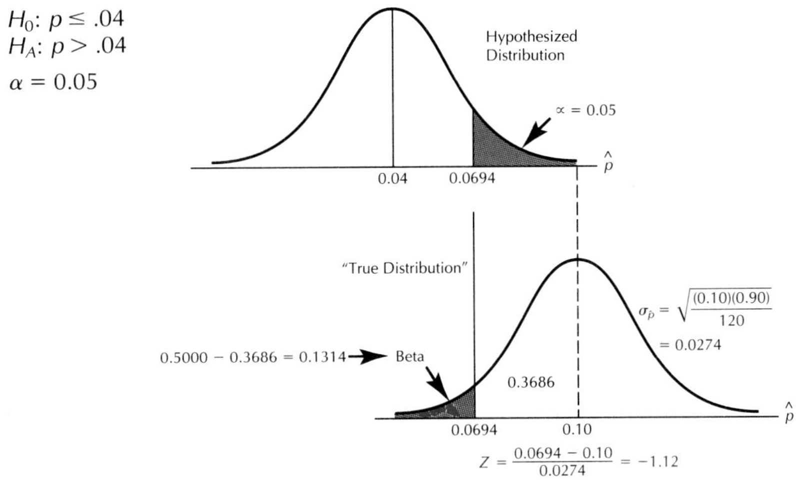

$H_0: p \leq .04$
$H_A: p > .04$

$\alpha = 0.05$

Hypothesized Distribution

$\alpha = 0.05$

$\hat{p}$

0.04   0.0694

"True Distribution"

$\sigma_{\hat{p}} = \sqrt{\dfrac{(0.10)(0.90)}{120}}$

$= 0.0274$

$0.5000 - 0.3686 = 0.1314 \rightarrow$ Beta

0.3686

0.0694   0.10

$\hat{p}$

$Z = \dfrac{0.0694 - 0.10}{0.0274} = -1.12$

have. They would have trouble understanding the hypothesis-testing process and the trade-offs we just described.

To help deal with this problem, tables have been developed that can lead us to appropriate sampling plans, including sample sizes and decision rules.

COMMENTS ON ACCEPTANCE SAMPLING

While acceptance sampling is a very common method of statistical process control, both W. Edwards Deming and Joseph Juran agree it cannot be considered the final method. First, it assumes some level of defect is acceptable, but the need is for continual improvement. Second, it has what Juran refers to as the fallacy of sampling, which means that if you sample enough times you will commit an error, either Type I or Type II, when the process has not changed.

Both quality experts agree that the process control chart methodology introduced in the next chapter presents a much more effective methodology for continually improving quality.

SKILL DEVELOPMENT PROBLEMS FOR **SECTION 10-4**

The following set of problems is meant to test your understanding of the material in this section.

17. What is the probability of accepting a lot whose incoming quality is 8% defective, using a sample size of 5 and a decision rule that says to accept only if no defects are found? What is the probability when using a decision rule that says accept if zero or one defect is found?

18. A production lot of 300,000 units is subjected to acceptance sampling. For an AQL of 1% and a sample size of 20, what is the appropriate decision rule if the manager wants at most a 10% chance of rejecting a "good" lot?

10-5 CONCLUSIONS

This chapter has expanded on the hypothesis-testing procedure introduced in Chapter 9. Again the focus has been on applications with large sample sizes.

You have seen examples of large-sample hypothesis tests involving the difference between two population means, a single population proportion, and the difference between two population proportions. If you paid close attention, you should have seen that the hypothesis-testing methodology is basically the same for all these situations. The central issue is always to determine whether the sample information supports or refutes the null hypothesis.

CHAPTER **GLOSSARY**

AQL (acceptable quality level) The level of defect that constitutes the standard. Also, the definition of a "good" batch or lot.

LTPD (lot tolerance percent defective) The maximum defect rate that could be tolerated. This is the defect rate used to determine consumer's risk.

population proportion The percentage of items in a population that possess a desired attribute.

p-value A value output by some computer software packages that indicates the probability of a sample result being as extreme as or more extreme than the one observed, given the hypothesized parameter is true.

CHAPTER FORMULAS

Critical value

One population proportion

$$A = p + Z\sqrt{\frac{p(1-p)}{n}}$$

Difference between means

$$A = (\mu_1 - \mu_2) + Z\sqrt{\frac{\sigma_1^2}{n_1} + \frac{\sigma_2^2}{n_2}}$$

Pooled estimator

$$\bar{p} = \frac{n_1\hat{p}_1 + n_2\hat{p}_2}{n_1 + n_2}$$

Z value

One population proportion

$$Z = \frac{\hat{p} - p}{\sqrt{\dfrac{p(1-p)}{n}}}$$

Two population proportions

$$Z = \frac{(\hat{p}_1 - \hat{p}_2) - (p_1 - p_2)}{\sqrt{\bar{p}(1-\bar{p})\left(\dfrac{1}{n_1} + \dfrac{1}{n_2}\right)}}$$

One population mean

$$Z = \frac{\overline{X} - \mu_x}{\dfrac{\sigma_x}{\sqrt{n}}}$$

Two population means

$$Z = \frac{(\overline{X}_1 - \overline{X}_2) - (\mu_1 - \mu_2)}{\sqrt{\dfrac{\sigma_1^2}{n_1} + \dfrac{\sigma_2^2}{n_2}}}$$

Two population means, variances unknown

$$Z = \frac{(\overline{X}_1 - \overline{X}_2) - (\mu_1 - \mu_2)}{\sqrt{\dfrac{S_1^2}{n_1} + \dfrac{S_2^2}{n_2}}}$$

Standard deviation of the proportion

$$\sigma_{\hat{p}} = \sqrt{\frac{p(1 - p)}{n}}$$

Standard deviation of difference between means

$$\sigma_{\overline{X}_1 - \overline{X}_2} = \sqrt{\frac{\sigma_1^2}{n_1} + \frac{\sigma_2^2}{n_2}}$$

SOLVED PROBLEMS

1. Property taxes are based on the assessed valuation of real estate. The higher the valuation, the greater the tax on that property. In one southern county, a controversy is taking place between some citizens and the county tax appraiser. The citizens claim that during a recent reappraisal, the residential property was increased in value by a greater average percentage than commercial property. If the citizens' claim is true, they will end up paying a greater relative share of property taxes than owners of commercial property.

   An outside consulting firm has been hired to study the situation. As part of their study, the consultants have selected a sample of 400 residential properties and 300 commercial properties and determined the average percent increase in assessed valuation for each class of property. The sample means along with the sample variances are

	Residential	*Commercial*
	$n_R = 400$	$n_C = 300$
	$\overline{X}_R = 108\%$	$\overline{X}_C = 102\%$
	$S_R^2 = 1,400$	$S_C^2 = 1,650$

Does this sample evidence support the citizens' claim? Test at the 0.10 alpha level.

Solution

Even though this problem deals with percentages, the problem is still one of hypothesis testing about two population means.

Hypotheses:

H_0: $\mu_R - \mu_C \le 0$

H_A: $\mu_R - \mu_C > 0$

The sampling distribution and the acceptance and rejection regions are as follows:

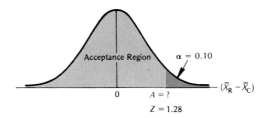

We can test the null hypothesis in two ways. First, we can solve for Z, using

$$Z = \frac{(\overline{X}_R - \overline{X}_C) - 0}{\sqrt{\dfrac{S_R^2}{n_R} + \dfrac{S_C^2}{n_C}}}$$

Note that we use the normal distribution even though the population variances are unknown, since the samples are large. Therefore,

$$Z = \frac{(108 - 102) - 0}{\sqrt{\dfrac{1,400}{400} + \dfrac{1,650}{300}}}$$

$$= 2.00$$

Since $Z = 2.00 > Z_{\text{critical}} = 1.28$, we reject the null hypothesis and conclude that the citizens' claim is true.

A second approach is to solve for A and then compare the difference between the two sample means to the decision rule.

$$A = 0 + 1.28 \sqrt{\frac{1,400}{400} + \frac{1,650}{300}}$$

$$= 3.84$$

Decision Rule:

If $(\overline{X}_R - \overline{X}_C) \le 3.84\%$, accept H_0.

If $(\overline{X}_R - \overline{X}_C) > 3.84\%$, reject H_0.

Since $(\overline{X}_R - \overline{X}_C) = 6\%$, we reject H_0. Rejecting the null hypothesis does not mean that the assessments are incorrect. They may actually reflect the change in market values or an adjustment from previous inequalities against commercial property.

2. The state legislature is deciding whether to remove the investment tax credit for capital investments. The Democrats in the legislature are generally in favor of removing the credit and the Republicans in favor of keeping the credit. Both parties have taken polls and claim the results support their position as shown:

Republican	Democratic
$n = 300$	$n = 350$
Keep credit: 165	Keep credit: 165

Both parties claim the other has taken a biased poll. Assuming the polls are both taken by simple random sampling techniques from the same population, could we expect to see the above results?

Solution

Since the question is whether both samples could have come from the same population, we formulate the following hypotheses:

Hypotheses:

H_0: $p_r = p_d$

H_A: $p_r \neq p_d$

Since we have specified an equal-to hypothesis, we have a two-tailed test. The sampling distribution and the acceptance and rejection regions for an alpha of 0.02 are as follows:

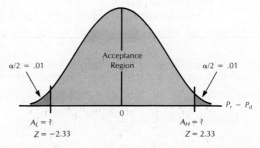

We can test the null hypothesis in two ways. First, we can solve for Z, using

$$Z = \frac{(\hat{p}_r - \hat{p}_d) - 0}{\sqrt{\bar{p}(1 - \bar{p})\left(\dfrac{1}{n_1} + \dfrac{1}{n_2}\right)}}$$

where

$$\bar{p} = \frac{165 + 165}{300 + 350} = 0.508$$

Since

$$\hat{p}_r = 165/300 = 0.55$$

and

$$\hat{p}_d = 165/350 = 0.47 \text{ (rounded)}$$

the Z value is

$$Z = \frac{(0.55 - 0.47) - 0}{\sqrt{0.508(0.492)\left(\dfrac{1}{350} + \dfrac{1}{350}\right)}}$$

$$= 2.12$$

Since this value of Z falls in the acceptance region (it is less than 2.33), we would accept the hypothesis that the two population means are equal. Note that if we had specified a different alpha value, say 10%, our conclusion would have been different.

A second approach is to solve for A_L and A_H and then compare the difference between the two sample means to the range defined by the decision rule. Again, assuming an alpha of 0.02,

$$A_L = 0 - Z\sqrt{\bar{p}(1 - \bar{p})\left(\frac{1}{n_1} + \frac{1}{n_2}\right)}$$

$$= 0 - 2.33\sqrt{0.508(0.492)\left(\frac{1}{300} + \frac{1}{350}\right)}$$

$$= -0.0916$$

Since the distribution is symmetrical,

$$A_H = 0.0916$$

Decision Rule:

If $-0.0916 \leq (\hat{p}_r - \hat{p}_d) \leq 0.0916$, accept H_0.

If $(\hat{p}_r - \hat{p}_d) < -0.0916$ or $(\hat{p}_r - \hat{p}_d) > 0.0916$, reject H_0.

Since $(\hat{p}_r - \hat{p}_d) = 0.08$, we accept the null hypothesis. Remember that accepting the null hypothesis does not "prove" the two populations are equal. It simply means that the observed difference could have occurred due to chance variation or sampling error.

ADDITIONAL PROBLEMS

19. A book publisher claims that undergraduates are more likely to buy used textbooks than are graduate students. The publisher's marketing department selected two random samples of 200 undergraduate students and 100 graduate students, respectively, at the Arizona State University. The students were asked whether they had purchased a used textbook this term. Sixty-two of the undergraduates said "yes," while forty-one of the graduates said "yes." Using an alpha level of 0.05, what should the publisher conclude?

    Based on the results of this survey, should the publisher extend its conclusions to all undergraduates and graduates at any university? Discuss.

20. The Maine Department of Transportation conducted a study of bridges in the state. To receive a federal grant, the department had to show that at least 40% of the bridges need repair, as claimed in its grant proposal. A random sample of fifty bridges revealed nineteen bridges in need of repair. Do these data support or refute the claim made in the grant proposal? Use an alpha level of 0.02.

21. A recent National Collegiate Athletic Association (NCAA) ruling requires that athletes progress toward a degree to remain eligible to play varsity sports. One athletic conference is considering defining *progress* as a situation under which, of the credits taken by the student, at least 75% of the credit hours are taken in courses leading toward the declared major at his or her institution.

    One of the college officials from this conference complained that this was too strict a requirement because, for the student body as a whole, less than 75% of the credit hours taken would be counted toward the declared major for the student taking those credits. To test this, a random sample of 420 individual 3-credit hour courses taken by students at the university was selected by going to the computerized transcript file. Each of the 3-credit-hour courses was evaluated to determine whether it would apply toward the degree program for the student involved. It was found that in 386 instances the course did apply toward degree requirements.

    a. State the appropriate null and alternative hypotheses to be tested.
    b. Based on the sample results, what should be concluded if the hypotheses are tested at an alpha level of 0.06?

22. The manager of a local engine repair service is considering mailing out a large number of coupons that offer substantial discounts on engine tune-ups. An industry trade publication indicates that no more than 20% of all such coupons will be used. He has decided to send out a test mailing of 250 coupons.

    a. State the null and alternative hypotheses to be tested based on the random sample.
    b. Suppose that of the 250 coupons mailed out, ninety-six are used within the specified period. At an alpha level of 0.10, what should the shop owner conclude?

c. Discuss in terms that the shop owner can understand what Type I and Type II errors are as they relate to this situation. Also discuss the relative costs associated with each type of error.

23. When planning the release of a new album, the record producers at ALM Artists base the number of initial copies to be produced at 60% of sales of the artist's last album. The winner of last year's Best New-Artist Award just finished recording a new album for ALM. Her agent believes that at least 50% of his client's fans who bought her last album will buy the new release, and, therefore, more than 2,400,000 (60% of 4,000,000) copies should be made.

The record company decided to select a random sample of 1,000 people and ask if they purchased the artist's last album. Two hundred forty-one people did say they had her album and 114 said they would buy her new release.

a. State the null and alternative hypotheses to be tested.
b. Establish the appropriate decision rule based on an alpha level of 0.03.
c. Based on the sample results, what should the record producer conclude about the number of albums to produce?

24. The manufacturer of one type of microcomputer has two options for the way in which the floppy disk drives are configured. One option is the horizontal configuration, in which the disk drives are laid flat and the disks are inserted horizontal to the table on which the microcomputer sits. The second is the vertical option, in which the diskettes are put into the disk drives in a position that is at a right angle with the table top.

Engineers at the company believe that there is no difference in maintenance problems with either configuration, but have never collected any data to support that contention. They have decided to select a random sample of 250 users of each option and determine their maintenance costs. The data are as follows:

Horizontal	Vertical
$n_H = 250$	$n_V = 250$
$\overline{X}_H = \$72.25$	$\overline{X}_V = \$40.30$
$S_H = \$20.50$	$S_V = \$18.80$

a. State the null and alternative hypotheses for this problem facing the microcomputer company.
b. Using an alpha level of 0.03, what conclusion should the engineers reach with respect to average maintenance costs for the two disk-drive configurations?

25. The makers of Hot Mix Chili in Houston, Texas, have a product that, by seasoning standards, is one of the hottest on the market. They have marketed this product under the assumption that there is no difference between men's and women's preference for spicy foods. The marketing manager decided that she would test this assumption by taking two samples of 280 men and 280 women, respectively, and letting them taste Hot Mix Chili and a milder

variety offered by a competitor. The people were asked to select which chili they liked better based on the criterion of seasoning.

The results showed that eighty-one men preferred Hot Mix Chili and seventy-four women preferred Hot Mix Chili. Using an alpha level of 0.10, what conclusions should the marketing manager reach based on these sample data?

26. Recently the city of Bellingham, Georgia undertook a campaign to consolidate the city and county governments. The premise was that proportionally more people in the city would favor the concept than in the outlying county area; this was because the county people might expect a tax increase from the consolidation even though the proponents of the plan promised a tax reduction in the long run.

    A polling agency was hired to conduct a study of this issue. It randomly selected 100 people in the city and seventy-five people in the county. It found sixty-two city dwellers favoring the idea and thirty-six county residents favoring the plan.
    a. State the appropriate null and alternative hypotheses to be tested.
    b. Based on the sample results, what should be concluded about the proportions favoring the consolidation when the city residents are compared with the county residents? Use an alpha level of 0.10. Discuss.

27. United States auto makers have been criticized in some circles for poor quality of U.S. cars compared with their foreign competitors. In fact, one trade publication has indicated that the percentage of U.S.-made cars having serious mechanical troubles within 2 years from purchase is greater than that for foreign cars after 5 years of ownership. If this allegation were to be substantiated, it would be a severe blow to the U.S. auto makers' efforts to contradict their poor quality image.

    To test this claim, a random sample of sixty U.S. car owners and another sample of seventy foreign car owners was selected. It was found that twelve owners of U.S. cars had severe mechanical problems within the first 2 years and thirteen foreign car owners had severe mechanical problems within the first 5 years of ownership.
    a. State the appropriate null and alternative hypotheses.
    b. Discuss what a Type I and a Type II error would be in this situation and attempt to provide an assessment of the relative costs of each.
    c. Based on an alpha level of 0.02, what conclusion should be reached? Discuss.

28. The makers of a new chemical fertilizer claim that hay yields will average at least 0.40 ton more per acre if this fertilizer is used than if the leading brand is used. The agricultural testing service at Oregon State University was retained to test this claim. Fifty-two 1-acre plots were selected at random and the new fertilizer was applied. A second sample of forty 1-acre plots was selected and the leading fertilizer was used. The following sample data were observed in tons per acre:

Old	New
$n_O = 40$	$n_N = 52$
Total $= 128$	Total $= 206$
$S_O^2 = 0.36$	$S_N^2 = 0.49$

    a. State the appropriate null and alternative hypotheses.

    b. If alpha is set at 0.05, what conclusion should be reached with respect to the claim made by the new fertilizer's company? Discuss.

29. A study of measles outbreaks was conducted by the Washington Department of Health and Welfare. In order to issue free immunizations to children 9 years old or younger, the department had to show that at least 50% of the children in that age category were not immunized. A random sample of 300 children aged 9 or younger revealed that 143 had not yet received their measles vaccination. Using an alpha level of 0.01, what should the department conclude?

30. The makers of Bounce Back glass backboards for basketball gymnasiums have claimed that their board is at least as durable, on the average, as the leading backboard made by Swoosh Company. Products Testing Services of Des Moines, Iowa, was hired to verify this claim. It selected a random sample of fifty backboards of each type and subjected the boards to a pressure test to determine the breaking point in terms of how much weight it would take to break the fiberglass backboard as it hung from a basketball rim. The following results were determined from the testing process:

Swoosh	Bounce Back
$n_S = 50$	$n_B = 50$
$\overline{X}_S = 685$ lb	$\overline{X}_B = 653$ lb
$S_S = 112$ lb	$S_B = 105$ lb

    a. Assuming that the more pounds it takes to break the backboard, the better it is, state the appropriate null and alternative hypotheses.

    b. At an alpha level of 0.01, what conclusion should be reached with respect to the claim made by the Bounce Back Company? Discuss.

    c. Suppose the hypothesis test was conducted at an alpha of 0.10 instead of 0.01. Would this change the conclusion reached based on the sample data? If so, discuss why; if not, discuss why not.

CASES

10A   Green Valley Assembly Company

The Green Valley Assembly Company assembles consumer electronics products for manufacturers that need temporary extra production capacity. As such, it has periodic product change. Since the products Green Valley assembles are marketed under the label of well-known manufacturers, high quality is a must.

Tom Bradley of the Green Valley personnel department has been very impressed by recent research concerning job-enrichment programs. In particular, he has been impressed with the increases in quality that seem to be associated with these programs. However, some studies have shown no significant increase in quality and imply that the money spent on such programs has not been worthwhile.

Tom has talked to Sandra Hansen, the production manager, about instituting a job-enrichment program in the assembly operation at Green Valley. Sandra was somewhat pessimistic about the potential, but agreed to introduce the program. The plan was to implement the program in one wing of the plant and continue with the current method in the other wing. The procedure was to be in effect for 6 months. Following that period, a test would be made to determine the effectiveness of the job-enrichment program.

After the 6-month trial period, a random sample of employees from each wing produced the following output measures:

	Old	Job-Enriched
	$n_1 = 50$	$n_2 = 50$
	$\overline{X}_1 = 11/h$	$\overline{X}_2 = 9.7/h$
	$S_1 = 1.2/h$	$S_2 = 0.9/h$

Both Sandra and Tom wonder whether the job-enrichment program has affected production output. They would like to use these sample results to determine whether the average output has changed and to determine whether the consistency of the employees was affected by the new program.

A second sample from each wing was selected. The measure was the quality of the products assembled. In the "old" wing, seventy-nine products were tested and 12% were found to be defectively assembled. In the "job-enriched" wing, 123 products were examined and 9% were judged defectively assembled.

With all these data, Sandra and Tom are beginning to get a little confused, but they realize that they must be able to use the information somehow in order to make a judgment about the effectiveness of the job-enrichment program.

10B Downtown Development: Bayview, North Dakota

Bayview, North Dakota, is a rapidly growing city with a large number of corporate headquarters. In addition, Bayview has a substantial amount of light industry and an increasing number of service businesses to support the population.

The city government has been involved in a controversy for the past 5 years over the issue of whether to build a regional shopping center in the downtown area or in the suburbs. The city council has gone on record as favoring the downtown site, but has received heavy opposition from a citizens' group called KNOW (Keep Nice Our World), which thinks that the best site is in the suburbs. KNOW's argument is that less energy will be needed to reach the shopping center if it is placed closer to the people. The city council, on the other hand, has passed a "Metro" plan calling for downtown development and mass transit of people to the downtown area, which it argues would save energy.

Endless meetings and hearings have been held on the issue, but a vote or poll of the people has not been taken. The city council and the KNOW representatives have agreed to hire a marketing consultant from Rock Springs, Wyoming, to select a random sample of citizens and ask which location is favored for the shopping center.

The city council claims that at least 50% of the population favor the downtown site and is quite confident that the sample will bear this out. However, the KNOW group claims that 50% or fewer prefer the downtown location and is equally confident in its claim.

The Rock Springs consultant selected a random sample of 384 persons and found 188 in favor of the downtown site and 196 opposed to the downtown site.

The day following the tabulation of the sample results, the *Bayview Gazette* ran a headline story relating the sample results and statements from the city council and KNOW, both of which stated that the results proved their claims. The story mentioned something about both parties testing their hypotheses at the 0.05 alpha level.

One citizen was heard that morning to say, "What does this mean? How can they both be right? This just doesn't make sense. It can't be."

REFERENCES

Berenson, Mark L., and Levine, David M. *Basic Business Statistics Concepts and Applications,* 5th edition. Englewood Cliffs, New Jersey: Prentice-Hall, 1992.

Daniel, Wayne W., and Terrell, James C. *Business Statistics for Management and Economics,* 6th edition. Boston: Houghton Mifflin, 1992.

Guldner, Francis J. *Statistical Quality Assurance.* Albany, New York: Delmar Publishers, 1987.

Iman, Ronald L., and Conover, W. J. *Modern Business Statistics,* 2nd edition. New York: Wiley, 1989.

Levin, Richard I., and Rubin, David S. *Statistics for Management,* 5th edition. Englewood Cliffs, New Jersey: Prentice-Hall, 1991.

Montgomery, Douglas C. *Introduction to Statistical Quality Control,* 2nd edition. New York: Wiley, 1991.

Sincich, Terry. *Business Statistics by Example,* 4th edition. New York: Dellen, 1992.

Statistical

Estimation and

Hypothesis Testing—

Small Samples

WHY DECISION MAKERS NEED TO KNOW

Chapter 8 introduced the fundamental concepts of statistical estimation. It emphasized the difference between point estimators and confidence interval estimators and showed how to calculate each. The discussion in Chapter 8 assumed that the decision makers were dealing with large samples of measurements from the populations of interest.

However, in many applications, obtaining measurements from large samples is not possible. Often the costs in time or money are prohibitive. In these instances, decision makers must rely on small samples from the populations of interest, so the estimation techniques presented in Chapter 8 are inappropriate. Yet decision makers still need to be able to estimate various population values. Thus, they need to understand the techniques for small-sample statistical estimation presented in this chapter.

Chapters 9 and 10 introduced the basics of hypothesis testing for large samples. When circumstances make it infeasible to work with large samples, decision makers need techniques for testing hypotheses based upon data from small samples. This chapter presents the fundamentals of hypothesis testing using small samples.

The small-sample estimation and hypothesis-testing techniques are very similar to those for large samples. If you understood the logic of estimation and hypothesis testing presented in Chapters 8, 9, and 10, you will have little trouble with the material in this chapter.

CHAPTER OBJECTIVES

This chapter introduces statistical estimation based on small samples. It will consider the Student t distribution and develop confidence intervals for estimates of the population mean, the difference between two population means for independent samples, and the difference between two population means for paired samples. This chapter will also show how hypothesis tests are carried out for each of the above population values when the decision maker is employing a small-size sample.

STUDENT OBJECTIVES

After studying the material presented in this chapter, you should be able to do the following:

1. Explain what the Student t distribution is.
2. Understand the fundamental differences between the t distribution and the normal distribution.
3. Be aware of the conditions under which the t distribution rather than the normal distribution should be used to determine the confidence interval estimate of a population value.
4. Know how to develop a small-sample confidence interval for estimating the population mean and how to test a small-sample hypothesis for this parameter.
5. Know how to develop a small-sample confidence interval and hypothesis test for estimating the difference between two population means for independent samples.
6. Know how to develop a small-sample confidence interval and hypothesis test for estimating the difference between two population means for paired samples.
7. Understand the trade-offs between sample size, confidence level, and precision.

11-1 SMALL-SAMPLE ESTIMATION

Chapter 8 introduced statistical estimation for several population values. The common bond for all the confidence intervals developed in that chapter was that the sample sizes were large and the interval coefficient was a Z value from the standardized normal distribution. Although differentiating between a large sample and a small sample is to some extent arbitrary, a widespread convention is to consider the sample large if the sample size is greater than or equal to 30 ($n \geq 30$).

The rationale for using a cutoff of $n = 30$ to define "large" sample size goes back to the central limit theorem, which was introduced in Chapter 7. The central limit theorem indicates that the sampling distributions for several statistics, including $\overline{X}$, $(\overline{X}_1 - \overline{X}_2)$, $\hat{p}$, and $(\hat{p}_1 - \hat{p}_2)$, will be approximately normally distributed if the sample size is sufficiently large. The term *sufficiently large* is a relative term. If the underlying population is symmetrical, a sufficiently large sample size might be $n = 3$ or $n = 4$. For other, more skewed populations, a sufficiently large sample size might be $n = 20$. Empirical studies indicate that regardless of the shape of the population, at $n = 30$, the sampling distribution will be approximately normal. Thus, to be conservative, we can use the $n \geq 30$ rule-of-thumb to define a large sample size.

Although many business applications involve large sample sizes, others do not. The cost in terms of dollars and time often prevents a large sample from being used to estimate a population value. In other instances, a large sample cannot be obtained because the population items are difficult to observe or few in number. In these cases, the large-sample procedures presented in Chapter 8 are simply not appropriate.

A major insurance company is conducting a study to determine whether a downward change in its automobile collision rates can be justified. As part of the study, the company needs to estimate the average damage in dollars to a new car that hits a barricade head-on at 15 miles per hour. Because of the high cost of this type of sampling, the insurance company has decided to crash only ten cars.

Since 10 is less than 30, the insurance company does not have a large sample. Thus, the company needs to use statistical techniques that are appropriate when dealing with small samples. Before these small-sample techniques are introduced, let's review four basic principles of interval estimation:

1. The format for any confidence interval is

   Point estimate $\pm$ (Interval coefficient)(Standard error of the estimate)

2. The higher the confidence, the lower the precision for a given sample size.
3. An increase in sample size will increase the precision of the estimate for a given confidence level. This occurs because an increase in sample size decreases the standard error of the estimate.
4. A confidence interval carries with it the following interpretation: If all possible samples of a given size are selected, and all possible confidence intervals for a given confidence level are calculated, the percentage of intervals containing the true population value will equal the confidence level.

These four principles were introduced in connection with large-sample estimation. They also apply to small-sample estimation. If you understand these four concepts, you should have little trouble understanding and applying the material presented in the remaining sections of this chapter.

11-2 THE STUDENT *t* DISTRIBUTION

The interval estimates in Chapter 8 were based on large samples. In developing the intervals, no concern was expressed about the shape of the population distribution because the central limit theorem tells us the sampling distribution will be approximately normal for large samples. Consequently, the interval coefficient we used for each interval was a Z value from the standard normal distribution. For example, the confidence interval estimate for μ_x is given by equation 11-1:

$$\overline{X} \pm Z\frac{\sigma_x}{\sqrt{n}} \qquad \textbf{11-1}$$

Even if σ_x is not known and must be estimated, the sampling distribution of $\overline{X}$ is still approximately normal if the sample size is large. The confidence interval estimate for μ_x with an unknown population standard deviation and a large sample size is given by equation 11-2:

$$\overline{X} \pm Z\frac{S_x}{\sqrt{n}} \qquad \textbf{11-2}$$

However, when σ_x is unknown and both μ_x and σ_x must be estimated from a small sample, the interval coefficient in equation 11-2 cannot be determined using the standard normal distribution.

If the population from which the small sample is selected is normally distributed, an exact solution to the problem of small-sample interval estimation is available. W. S. Gosset discovered the properties governing the sampling distribution of $\overline{X}$ for small samples. Gosset published his findings in 1908 under the pen name "Student" and called the sampling distribution the *t* **distribution.** He showed for small samples that the quantity of equation 11-3,

$$t = \frac{\overline{X} - \mu_x}{\dfrac{S_x}{\sqrt{n}}} \qquad \textbf{11-3}$$

follows a *t* distribution. "Student" (Gosset) set forth the following theorem:

If the population from which the sample is selected is *normally distributed* with *unknown standard deviation,* the sampling distribution of $(\overline{X} - \mu_x)/(S_x/\sqrt{n})$ will be described by a *t distribution* with $n - 1$ degrees of freedom.

The *t* distribution is similar to the Z distribution in that both distributions are symmetrical and range from $-\infty$ to $+\infty$. Both standardized distributions have a mean of 0. The basic difference occurs in the spread of the two distributions. The variance of the standard normal distribution is 1.0, whereas the variance of the t distribution is always greater than 1.0. The variance of the t distribution is determined by the following formula:

$$\frac{n-1}{n-1-2}$$

for $n \geq 4$. The exact variance of the t distribution depends on the sample size. If $n = 10$, the variance is 1.285. The variance for $n = 15$ is 1.167. The variance for $n = 25$ is 1.091.

Figure 11-1 illustrates the relationship between the t distribution and the Z distribution and shows how the variance of the t distribution changes as the sample size changes. When the sample size increases, the variance approaches 1.0. Thus, for large sample sizes, the t distribution approaches the standard normal distribution.

FIGURE 11-1

Comparison of
t and Z
Distributions

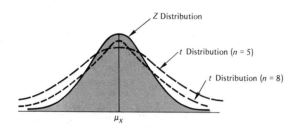

Chapter 7 showed that

$$Z = \frac{\overline{X} - \mu_x}{\frac{\sigma_x}{\sqrt{n}}}$$

and emphasized that Z represents the number of standard deviations $\overline{X}$ is from μ_x. Likewise,

$$t = \frac{\overline{X} - \mu_x}{\frac{S_x}{\sqrt{n}}}$$

where the t value is the number of standard deviations $\overline{X}$ is from μ_x.

As with the Z distribution, tables of t values have been developed. The standardized t-distribution table is contained in Appendix D. Across the top of the table are probabilities corresponding to areas in one tail and two tails and for various confidence levels. Down the left side is a column headed "d.f." (degrees of freedom).[1] You will learn how to determine the degrees of freedom for many

[1] The statistical concept of *degrees of freedom* is one of the most difficult for beginning students due to its many possible interpretations. The general expression for degrees of freedom is $n - k$, where n is the number of observations and k is the number of constants that must be calculated from the sample data to estimate the variance of the sampling distribution.

statistical procedures introduced in this text. For example, when we are developing a confidence interval for estimating μ_x, the number of degrees of freedom is $n - 1$.

The t value for a 90% confidence level with sample size $n = 10$ is 1.833. Note that we find this value by reading across the top to 0.90 and down the d.f. column to 9. The value found at the row and column intersection is the appropriate t value. As another example, the t value corresponding to a 95% confidence level and sample size $n = 19$ is 2.101. The t value for 95% confidence and sample size $n = 14$ is 2.160. Make sure you can locate these values in the t-distribution table in Appendix D. You will be required to use the t-distribution table extensively in this chapter.

SKILL DEVELOPMENT PROBLEMS FOR SECTION 11-2

The following set of problems is meant to test your understanding of the material in this section.

1. Referring to the t-distribution table in Appendix D, find the t value for each of the following:
   a. $n = 12$, confidence level = 0.99
   b. $n = 10$, confidence level = 0.90
   c. $n = 22$, confidence level = 0.95
   d. $n = 19$, confidence level = 0.90

2. Referring to the t-distribution table in Appendix D, find the t value for each of the following:
   a. $n = 12$, confidence level = 0.90
   b. $n = 23$, confidence level = 0.95
   c. $n = 29$, confidence level = 0.80
   d. $n = 14$, confidence level = 0.90

3. Given the following information:

$$\overline{X} = 1{,}300$$
$$\mu = 1{,}320$$
$$S_x = 80$$
$$n = 20$$

Find the t statistic and indicate what it measures.

4. Given the following information:

$$\overline{X} = 19.7$$
$$\mu = 18.0$$
$$S_x = 3.0$$
$$n = 25$$

Find the t statistic and indicate what it measures.

5. Discuss the difference between the standard normal distribution and the t distribution.

11-3 ESTIMATING THE POPULATION MEAN—SMALL SAMPLES

Let's return to the insurance company that needs to estimate the average damage to an automobile that crashes at 15 miles per hour.

The automobile industry in general has been attempting to build sturdier cars. Because of this, many insurance companies are examining their collision rates. The insurance company in our example needs to estimate each model's average damage for a 15-mile-per-hour crash to help the actuaries develop a premium rate for the model's owners.

Because of the costs involved, the company has selected a random sample of ten new cars and has crashed each one at 15 miles per hour. The resulting damage costs are shown in Table 11-1. Assuming the true distribution of damages is *normal,* the insurance actuaries can use these data to develop an interval estimate for the true average damage level by use of equation 11-4:

$$\overline{X} \pm t\frac{S_x}{\sqrt{n}} \qquad \text{11-4}$$

where

$\overline{X}$ = Point estimate

t = Interval coefficient from the t distribution

S_x = Estimate of σ_x

n = Sample size

Assuming a 95% confidence interval is specified, and using the values for $\overline{X}$ and S_x shown in Table 11-1, the interval is

$$\overline{X} \pm 2.262\frac{S_x}{\sqrt{n}}$$

$$\$3{,}121.5 \pm 2.262\frac{\$1{,}357.62}{\sqrt{10}}$$

$$\$3{,}121.5 \pm \$971.12$$

$$\$2{,}150.38 \underline{\qquad} \$4{,}092.62$$

Therefore, the actuaries are confident that the true average repair cost will be between \$2,150.38 and \$4,092.62.

TABLE **11-1**

Mean and
Standard
Deviation of
Automobile
Damage Costs at
15 Miles Per
Hour

$1,954.00	$6,109.00
2,702.00	3,311.00
3,605.00	3,702.00
1,627.00	2,151.00
4,105.00	1,949.00

$$\overline{X} = \frac{\Sigma X}{n}$$

$$= \$3,121.50$$

$$S_x^2 = \frac{\Sigma(X - \overline{X})^2}{n - 1}$$

$$= 1,843,142.7$$

$$S_x = \sqrt{1,843,142.7}$$

$$= 1,357.62$$

Of course, the true mean either will or will not fall in this interval. If this precision is too low (interval is too wide), the insurance company has two ways of increasing it. The company can increase the sample size *or* decrease the confidence level.

Suppose because of the costs involved, the number of cars tested cannot be increased. If the confidence level is reduced to 90%, the interval coefficient, t, is reduced to 1.833, giving the following confidence interval estimate for μ_x:

$$\overline{X} \pm 1.833 \frac{S_x}{\sqrt{n}}$$

$$\$3,121.50 \pm 1.833 \frac{\$1,357.62}{\sqrt{10}}$$

$$\$3,121.50 \pm \$786.94$$

$$\$2,334.56 \underline{\qquad} \$3,908.44$$

Thus, decreasing the confidence level from 95% to 90% has decreased the interval width from $1,942.24 to $1,573.88.

SKILL DEVELOPMENT PROBLEMS FOR **SECTION 11-3**

The following set of problems is meant to test your understanding of the material in this section.

6. Given the following sample information and assuming that the population is normally distributed:

$$n = 20$$
$$\overline{X} = 96.5$$
$$S_x = 7.4$$

a. Develop and interpret the 95% confidence interval estimate for the population mean.
b. Develop and interpret the 90% confidence interval estimate for the population mean.

7. Given the following sample information and assuming that the population is normally distributed:

$$n = 30$$
$$\overline{X} = 2,340.9$$
$$S_x = 220.50$$

a. Develop and interpret the 99% confidence interval estimate for the population mean.
b. Develop and interpret the 90% confidence interval estimate for the population mean.

8. Evergreen Hardware wishes to estimate the average number of board feet of lumber sold per day at its Eugene, Oregon, store. A random sample of 15 days of sales data has been collected, with the following results:

$$\overline{X} = 14,600$$
$$S_x = 3,005$$

a. If a small-sample interval estimate is to be made, what assumption is required? What distribution will be used to obtain the interval coefficient for an interval estimate?
b. Develop and interpret the 95% interval estimate for the average board feet of lumber sold per day at the Eugene store.

9. The Crane Creek Golf Club is interested in estimating the average number of times its members play golf during the month of September. In a pilot study, a random sample of twenty-five members was polled, with the following results:

$$\overline{X} = 3.45$$
$$S_x = 2.4$$

Determine the 90% confidence interval estimate for the true average number of rounds played by members in September. Interpret this estimate.

10. The U.S. National Park Service sells annual passes good for an unlimited number of visits to the country's national parks. Recently, a student intern for the Park Service surveyed ten randomly selected tourists holding passes and asked how many prior visits he or she had made to a national park. The following data were collected:

2   0   3   6   0   4   2   1   0   3

Based on these sample data, develop the 95% confidence interval estimate for the average number of prior visits to a national park made by the population members. Interpret.

11-4 ESTIMATING THE DIFFERENCE BETWEEN TWO POPULATION MEANS—SMALL SAMPLES

The C. J. Milne Corporation manufactures and distributes power hand tools in the Midwest. The plant managers at the two Milne locations have been responsible for their own quality control. They have always assumed that the quality of the tools coming from the two locations was the same. Recently, Milne has received more customer complaints than usual. A corporate vice-president thinks that one plant may have lost some control on quality. Since the finished goods from the two locations are mixed at a central warehouse before they are distributed to the retailers, she cannot tell which plant is producing the inferior product. Consequently, she has hired a testing company to examine twelve tools from each plant and assign a quality rating to each. The vice-president is interested in estimating the difference in the average ratings for tools produced at the two plants.

Chapter 8 discussed estimating the difference between two population means for large samples. We can estimate this difference for small samples using the t distribution, provided we make the following assumptions:

1. The two populations are normally distributed and independent.
2. The two populations have equal standard deviations.

If these two assumptions are satisfied, the small-sample confidence interval estimate of the difference between population means is shown by equation 11-5:

$$(\overline{X}_1 - \overline{X}_2) \pm tS_{\text{pooled}} \sqrt{\frac{1}{n_1} + \frac{1}{n_2}} \qquad \textbf{11-5}$$

where

$\overline{X}_1$ = Sample mean from population 1

$\overline{X}_2$ = Sample mean from population 2

t = Interval coefficient from the t distribution with d.f. = $(n_1 + n_2 - 2)$

$S_{\text{pooled}} = \sqrt{\dfrac{S_{x_1}^2(n_1 - 1) + S_{x_2}^2(n_2 - 1)}{n_1 + n_2 - 2}}$

n_1 and n_2: Sample sizes from populations 1 and 2, respectively

Note that the small-sample confidence interval for estimating the difference between two population means follows the usual format, that is,

Point estimate $\pm$ (Interval coefficient)(Standard error of the estimate)

As can be seen, the standard error of the estimate involves *pooling* the variances from each sample. The **pooled standard deviation, S_{pooled}**, is the square root of a weighted average of the sample variances, where the weights are $n_1 - 1$ and $n_2 - 1$. This pooled value is a better estimate of the common variance than either individual estimate.

The interval coefficient is a t value from the Student t distribution. An important point about this t value is that the appropriate degrees of freedom are $n_1 + n_2 - 2$. Note that this is equal to the denominator in the equation for the pooled standard deviation. This is also the sum of the individual degrees of freedom; that is, $n_1 + n_2 - 2 = (n_1 - 1) + (n_2 - 1)$.

Suppose the ratings for the twelve tools from each plant in the Milne Company example give the following results:

Plant 1	Plant 2
$n_1 = 12$	$n_2 = 12$
$\overline{X}_1 = 49$	$\overline{X}_2 = 46$
$S_{x_1}^2 = 147$	$S_{x_2}^2 = 154$

Notice that the two sample variances are nearly equal. This adds validity to the assumption of equal variances. We will introduce a technique for determining whether two population variances are equal in Chapter 12. In Section 11-6 of this chapter, we will comment on what can be done if we cannot assume that the variances are equal.

The 90% confidence interval for estimating the difference between the mean ratings for tools from plants 1 and 2 is

$$(\overline{X}_1 - \overline{X}_2) \pm 1.717 S_{pooled} \sqrt{\frac{1}{n_1} + \frac{1}{n_2}}$$

$$(49 - 46) \pm 1.717 S_{pooled} \sqrt{\frac{1}{12} + \frac{1}{12}}$$

where

$$S_{pooled} = \sqrt{\frac{(12 - 1)(147) + (12 - 1)(154)}{22}}$$

$$= 12.27$$

Note that the interval coefficient, t, is found in the t-distribution table with $n_1 + n_2 - 2 = 22$ degrees of freedom.

The confidence interval is

$$(49 - 46) \pm (1.717)(12.27)(0.4082)$$

$$3 \pm 8.60$$

$$-5.60 \text{ points} \underline{\quad\quad} 11.60 \text{ points}$$

The vice-president is confident, based on this interval estimate, that the true difference between the average quality ratings for the two plants is between 5.60 in favor of plant 2 and 11.60 in favor of plant 1. Since she believes that this interval contains the true mean difference, and since this interval includes 0, she would make no judgment about the quality control at either plant. However, she may dislike the low precision (wide interval) and suggest larger sample sizes or a decreased confidence level to increase the precision.

Note that the two sample sizes need not be equal when equation 11-5 is used to estimate the difference between two population means.

SKILL DEVELOPMENT PROBLEMS FOR SECTION 11-4

The following set of problems is meant to test your understanding of the material in this section.

11. Independent random samples from each of two populations have been selected, with the following results:

Sample 1	Sample 2
$n = 15$	$n = 10$
$\overline{X} = 43.5$	$\overline{X} = 52.4$
$S_x = 10$	$S_x = 9.6$

a. Determine the point estimate for the difference between the two population means.
b. Develop the 95% confidence interval estimate for the difference between the two population means. Be sure to provide an interpretation of the interval estimate.

12. Independent random samples from each of two populations have been selected, with the following results:

Sample 1	Sample 2
$n = 18$	$n = 12$
$\overline{X} = 1,234.6$	$\overline{X} = 1,198.45$
$S_x = 33.45$	$S_x = 35.70$

a. Determine the point estimate for the difference between the two population means.
b. Develop the 90% confidence interval estimate for the difference between the two population means. Be sure to provide an interpretation of the interval estimate.

13. The owner of a fast-food franchise outlet is considering two different promotions. In the first case, she will give out coupons that make the Big-Bite Burger half-price. The second alternative gives two Big-Bites for the price of one. She is interested in estimating the difference in average dollars spent on other products (such as fries, soft drinks, etc.) for the two alternatives. This estimate will help her decide which promotion to use.

The manager has selected a random sample of ten households and has mailed half-price coupons to each. A second sample of ten households was selected and two-for-one coupons were sent to each of these. By the week's end, eight half-price coupons and nine two-for-one coupons had been redeemed, with the following data for extra purchases:

Half-Price	Two-for-One
$n = 8$	$n = 9$
$\overline{X} = \$2.45$	$\overline{X} = \$2.10$
$S_x = 0.72$	$S_x = 0.86$

a. Develop a 95% confidence interval estimate for the difference in average dollar purchases between the two coupon offers. Interpret.
b. Based on the estimate in part **a,** can the manager conclude that a difference exists between the two promotions in terms of average extra dollar purchases? Discuss.

14. The Virginia Department of Highways recently conducted a study to estimate the difference in average damage to vehicles that crashed into an unprotected bridge abutment versus those that crashed into an experimental padded bridge abutment. Eight "identical" cars traveling 45 mph were crashed into the unprotected abutment; a second sample of seven "identical" cars were crashed into the experimental protected bridges. The following sample data were recorded based on figures supplied by the department's maintenance crew. The data are in thousands of dollars.

Unprotected		Experimental	
$4.34	$4.24	$3.65	$4.01
3.98	5.02	4.10	3.33
4.12	4.23	3.76	4.23
4.11	3.56	3.45	

a. Develop the 95% confidence interval estimate of the difference in average dollar damage to vehicles for crashes into the two types of bridges. Interpret your estimate.
b. Based on the estimate developed in part **a,** is there sufficient evidence to say that the experimental padding reduces average dollar damages? Discuss.

11-5 ESTIMATING THE DIFFERENCE BETWEEN TWO POPULATION MEANS—PAIRED SAMPLES

In the previous section, you learned how to develop and interpret small-sample confidence interval estimates for the difference between two population means. The assumption there is that the samples from the two populations are *independent.* There are many applications where this assumption will be appropriate. However, there are other estimation situations where the samples will not be independent. That is, a sample observation from one population might be affected by a sample value from the other population. For example, consider a market research study in which a family was asked to record its total monthly purchases at a regional shopping mall and its total monthly purchases at a downtown shopping center. The study wishes to estimate the difference in average monthly expenditures by families at the two shopping centers.

Clearly, there could be a relationship between how much a certain family spends at the mall and how much it spends downtown. For instance, a family might tend to shop at one location and not the other. Another family might be prone to do a lot of shopping regardless of location, while a third family would not shop much at either location. Thus, the sample data would not be independent because the data for the two samples are collected from the same families. The samples are called **paired samples,** and the confidence interval estimate for the true average paired difference is found using equation 11-6:

$$\bar{d} \pm t\frac{S_d}{\sqrt{n}}$$

11-6

where

$\bar{d}$ = Average of the paired differences

t = Interval coefficient

S_d = Standard deviation of the paired differences

n = Number of pairs

Table 11-2 shows the dollars spent for a sample of ten families at each location. Using equation 11-6, we can develop a 95% confidence interval in the following manner. (Note that the degrees of freedom associated with the interval coefficient, t, are $n - 1$. Here, degrees of freedom equal $10 - 1 = 9$.)

$$\bar{d} \pm 2.262\frac{S_d}{\sqrt{n}}$$

$$\$5 \pm (2.262)\frac{\$37.193}{\sqrt{10}}$$

$$\$5 \pm \$26.60$$

$$-\$21.60 \text{\_\_\_\_\_} \$31.60$$

Therefore, based on the sample data, the market researchers would conclude, with 95% confidence, that the difference in the average amount spent at the regional mall versus the downtown mall is between −$21.60 and +$31.60. The −$21.60 indicates that the difference may favor the downtown mall by as much

TABLE 11-2

Spending
Amounts for the
Market Research
Example

Family	Regional Mall	Downtown	d	$(d - \bar{d})^2$
1	$140	$100	+40	$(40 - 5)^2 =$ 1,225
2	120	150	−30	$(-30 - 5)^2 =$ 1,225
3	230	220	+10	$(10 - 5)^2 =$ 25
4	50	80	−30	$(-30 - 5)^2 =$ 1,225
5	70	110	−40	$(-40 - 5)^2 =$ 2,025
6	240	180	+60	$(60 - 5)^2 =$ 3,025
7	190	190	0	$(0 - 5)^2 =$ 25
8	120	140	−20	$(-20 - 5)^2 =$ 625
9	250	190	+60	$(60 - 5)^2 =$ 3,025
10	100	100	0	$(0 - 5)^2 =$ 25
			Total +50	12,450

$$\bar{d} = \frac{50}{10} = 5$$

$$S_d = \sqrt{\frac{\Sigma(d - d)^2}{n - 1}} = \sqrt{\frac{12,450}{10 - 1}} = 37.193$$

as $21.60, while the +$31.60 indicates that the difference in average spending might favor the regional mall by as much as $31.60. The fact that the confidence interval includes 0 means that, based on the sample data, there is no significant difference in average spending by families at the two malls.

Note that this estimate was obtained by pairing observations *before* the measurements were taken. The reason for this was to control for differences that might result because of family spending habits and income levels.

SKILL DEVELOPMENT PROBLEMS FOR **SECTION 11-5**

The following set of problems is meant to test your understanding of the material in this section.

15. Given two dependent samples with the following information:

Item	Sample 1	Sample 2
1	234	245
2	221	224
3	196	194
4	245	267
5	234	230
6	204	198

Develop a 90% confidence interval estimate for the paired difference between population means. Interpret.

16. Given two dependent samples with the following information:

Item	Sample 1	Sample 2
1	3.4	2.8
2	2.5	3.0
3	7.0	5.5
4	5.9	6.7
5	4.0	3.5
6	5.0	5.0
7	6.2	7.5
8	5.3	4.2

Develop a 99% confidence interval estimate for the paired difference between population means. Interpret.

17. Discuss the circumstances under which a paired sample estimate is desirable instead of taking two independent random samples.

18. A publisher of technical books on subjects such as computer documentation is considering going to a new publishing format. Before doing so, it is interested in getting some opinion about the old versus the new method. It has selected twenty people randomly from the population and has asked them to review a book in the old format and a book in the new format. Then they are to assign a point rating to each book between 1 and 1,000. The following results were obtained.

$$\bar{d} = -24.5$$
$$S_d = 40$$
$$n = 20$$

Considering this sampling to be paired sampling, construct the 95% confidence interval estimate for the true average paired difference in rating for the two publishing formats.

11-6 EFFECT OF VIOLATING THE ASSUMPTIONS FOR SMALL-SAMPLE ESTIMATION

When using the t distribution for statistical estimation with small samples, we assume that

1. The population(s) are normally distributed.
2. If two populations are involved, the populations have equal variances and the samples are independent.

Although applications may exist for which these assumptions are strictly satisfied, experience indicates that this rarely happens. Fortunately, however, the estimation methods presented in this chapter are fairly robust. That is, for small departures from the assumptions of normality and equal variances, the t distribution is still appropriate. However, if the populations differ extensively from normality (the populations are extremely skewed) or the variances are far from equal, the decision maker will need to employ different statistical procedures or select a large sample size and use the large-sample estimation techniques presented in Chapter 8.

In Chapter 12 we will consider techniques used to test whether two population variances are equal. Then, in Chapter 14, we will introduce goodness-of-fit tests that can be used to test a distribution for normality.

One other comment is in order here. You will note that this chapter has not presented examples for estimating a single population proportion or the difference between two population proportions when the sample sizes are small. The reason for this is that the underlying distribution for proportions is the binomial distribution. The binomial is discrete and is approximated by the normal distribution only for reasonably large sample sizes. To calculate a small-sample confidence interval for a population proportion, the binomial distribution would have to be used. We have chosen, therefore, to restrict our discussion of proportions to large-sample estimation procedures.

11-7 HYPOTHESIS TESTING WITH SMALL SAMPLES

Chapter 9 introduced the logic and techniques of hypothesis testing. The methods presented in Chapter 9 were based on the assumption that the sample size was sufficiently large to invoke the central limit theorem. However, as we have already discussed in this chapter, there will be many instances where business decisions must be based on small samples. In these cases, the standard normal distribution should not be used when developing confidence interval estimates. Instead, the t distribution is used.

The same situation exists in hypothesis-testing applications. Instead of using a Z value from the standard normal distribution for determining the critical value, when we have small sample sizes, a t value is used. However, the hypothesis-testing logic and methods are exactly the same as for large-sample situations. You are encouraged to refer to Solved Problem 3 at the end of this chapter. This solved problem demonstrates how the t distribution is employed in testing a null and alternative hypotheses. Additionally, there are several problems at the end of the chapter where the t distribution can be used in the hypothesis-testing process.

11-8 QUALITY IMPROVEMENT AND STATISTICAL ESTIMATION

Probably no tool in modern quality improvement is more important to increasing the quality of goods and services than the process control chart. While a complete discussion of how to construct and use all the different process control charts is not possible in this text, a list of quality control texts can be found in the references section at the end of the chapter for those who would like to read further. We will, however, discuss the construction and interpretation of the more common process control charts. As you will see, constructing this powerful quality improvement tool is simply an application of statistical estimation.

UNDERSTANDING THE CONCEPT OF STATISTICAL CONTROL

Statistical control is founded on the concept that variation is inherent in any process. Consider, for instance, walking to your next class or returning to your room or home after your last class. You have some idea about how long this should take, but not all trips take the same time—variation exists in the process. The question is: How much delay can occur in a trip home before someone starts worrying about you? How much of a delay is needed before it is considered "unusual"?

Most people who own cars have some idea about how far they should be able to drive before buying gas, but the distance between fill-ups varies. How much of a change in your expected driving distance would be needed before you would suspect a mechanical problem with your car?

Companies that produce integrated circuits do not expect a 100% yield rate. How much of a drop in yield is needed before an equipment problem is suspected?

The quality control answer to the questions posed in the above scenarios is based on the fact that variation in any physical process can be classified into two categories: *stable variation* and *unstable variation*. **Stable variation** represents the normal fluctuation in the output of any physical process and cannot be eliminated. No matter how hard you try, you will not be able to return to your room or walk to your next class in exactly the same amount of time. On the other hand, **unstable variation** occurs due to unusual events. Stopping at the library to work on your term paper will add considerable time to your return and be a source of unstable variation in the process of returning from class.

The key to improving quality is to determine the difference between stable and unstable variation. A process cannot be improved until the remaining variation is primarily due to stable causes. Statistical methods provide the only safe way to distinguish between stable and unstable variation. When the process contains only evidence of stable variation, the process is defined as being "under control."

The following examples will demonstrate how to provide evidence of statistical control. The primary statistical method is the **process control chart**.

Example 1

A customer service department has been monitoring the number of complaints about service representatives received each week. During the past 16 weeks the following complaint levels have been recorded.

Week	Complaints	Week	Complaints
1	7	9	6
2	10	10	4
3	9	11	3
4	6	12	1
5	5	13	10
6	4	14	7
7	8	15	8
8	5	16	7

Process control charts are constructed as three-standard-deviation (called 3-sigma) confidence interval estimates of a population value, using the correct statistical distribution. In this case the customer complaints can best be described using a Poisson distribution. With a Poisson distribution, the standard deviation is equal to the square root of the mean and the three-standard-deviation interval estimate is

$$\overline{C} \pm 3(\sqrt{\overline{C}})$$
$$6.25 \pm 3(2.5)$$

In the jargon of quality control, the upper value of the confidence interval is called the **upper control limit** (UCL) and the lower value is the **lower control limit** (LCL). For this example,

$$UCL = 13.75$$
$$LCL = -1.25 \rightarrow 0$$

Since we cannot have negative complaints, the lower control limit is rounded to 0.

The control limits are used to construct the process control chart (*c*-chart) shown in Figure 11-2. Process control charts are used both to determine whether the process is in control and to identify sources of unstable variation. In this example, since all the points are between the upper and lower control limits, the process is considered stable, or under control. Any point outside the control limits would indicate an unusual event, or source of unstable variation, and would be investigated to determine the cause.

FIGURE **11-2**

c-Chart of
Customer
Complaints

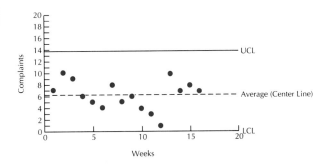

Weeks

Example 2

The key to constructing a process control chart is often to correctly identify the statistical distribution that best represents the situation being investigated. Consider the following example. You are the newly appointed Customer Satisfaction Manager for the manufacturer of a new laser printer. To develop a baseline from which to gauge any service improvements, you have your department call 1,000 randomly selected new customers in each of the next 10 weeks. They ask the customers if they received satisfactory service when installing the printer on their system. You find the following data:

Week	Number with Unsatisfactory Service	Number of Calls
1	45	1,000
2	80	1,000
3	52	1,000
4	75	1,000
5	40	1,000
6	68	1,000
7	58	1,000
8	62	1,000
9	42	1,000
10	60	1,000
	$\Sigma = 582$	$\Sigma = 10,000$

This problem is somewhat different from the previous example. Since we know both the number called and the number with unsatisfactory service, the appropriate distribution is the binomial. In Chapter 8, we discussed finding a confidence interval estimate of a population proportion. Using equation 8-15, slightly modified, we find the following three-standard-deviation confidence interval estimate:

$$\bar{p} \pm 3S_{\hat{p}}$$

Note: $\bar{p}$ is equal to the overall proportion of calls with unsatisfactory service. Thus:

$$\bar{p} = \frac{582}{10,000} = 0.0582$$

$$S_{\hat{p}} = \sqrt{\frac{\bar{p}\bar{q}}{n}}$$

$$= \sqrt{\frac{(0.0582)(.9418)}{1,000}}$$

$$= 0.0074$$

$$\text{UCL} = 0.0582 + 3(0.0074) = 0.0804$$

$$\text{LCL} = 0.0582 - 3(0.0074) = 0.0360$$

Note that the sample size used to calculate the standard deviation is 1,000, since we are concerned with the variation associated with the samples.

FIGURE 11-3

p-Chart for
Customer
Complaints
($n = 1,000$)

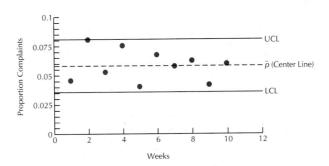

The process control chart constructed using this confidence interval estimate is called a *p*-chart and is shown in Figure 11-3. Looking at this chart, we can conclude that this process is in control since the weekly data appear to be randomly distributed around the mean and no points are outside the control limits.

Example 3

The previous two examples dealt with situations that could be best described by discrete distributions, the Poisson in the first case and the binomial in the second. However, as we mentioned in an earlier chapter, the output of physical processes is often described by a continuous distribution. To describe the possible changes in the output of a physical process requires two process control charts, as the following example will show.

Resistors are being manufactured on a high-speed automated machine. The machine is set up to produce a large run of resistors of 10,000 ohms each. Because of the physical variation in all processes, not all resistors will have the same actual values. To determine the variation of values that the machine is producing throughout the run, fifteen samples were taken with four resistors in each sample. The sample values are listed.

Sample	Resistance in Ohms			
1	9,963	9,862	9,960	10,012
2	10,052	9,891	10,062	10,078
3	9,939	9,997	9,885	9,845
4	9,941	10,018	9,941	10,053
5	9,922	10,375	10,068	9,790
6	10,101	9,910	9,859	9,868
7	9,950	9,963	10,095	9,949
8	9,906	10,038	10,150	10,080
9	10,152	10,206	10,093	9,983
10	10,137	10,198	10,255	10,112
11	9,890	9,924	9,822	10,207
12	9,968	10,066	9,978	9,895
13	10,194	9,968	9,913	10,111
14	9,816	9,913	9,890	10,034
15	10,132	10,022	10,056	9,928

In Chapter 6, when discussing how physical processes change, we identified two sources, sudden failure and gradual change. In the context of this example, sudden change would occur if the average suddenly jumped to 16,000 ohms. Gradual change would occur if the average resistance value started increasing or decreasing. Also, the process may change by becoming more variable, either suddenly or gradually. To identify situations when changes in either the process average or the variability occur, we need to construct two process control charts. One chart will track movements in the mean of the distribution; this is the $\overline{X}$-chart. The second will track movements in the variation of the distribution; this is the **R-chart**.

The $\overline{X}$-chart plots the sample means from the 15 samples of resistors. This chart determines gradual, or sudden, movements in the mean of the distribution of resistor values. Likewise, the range (R), which is the difference between the high and low values in a sample, can be used to analyze the variation within the process. Note that the standard deviation can also be used for this purpose. However, in practice, the range is more common because of its computational advantage. The chart of range values is called an *R*-chart.

To help in the construction of $\overline{X}$- and *R*-charts, a table of coefficients has been developed which makes it easy to construct control limits directly from the values of $\overline{X}$ (mean of the sample means) and $\overline{R}$ (mean of the ranges). This table was named after Walter Shewhart. Selected values from the Shewhart table are shown in Table 11-3. Note that the coefficients in Table 11-3 were derived so that the resulting control limits are 3-sigma limits. This is analogous to developing confidence interval estimates with limits of ± 3(standard deviation) from the center.

TABLE **11-3**

Selected Values from Shewhart Table

Number in Individual Sample, n	Factor for $\overline{X}$-chart, A_2	Factors for *R*-chart	
		Lower Control Limit, D_3	Upper Control Limit, D_4
2	1.880	0	3.276
3	1.023	0	2.575
4	0.729	0	2.282
5	0.577	0	2.115
6	0.483	0	2.004
7	0.419	0.076	1.924
8	0.373	0.136	1.864
9	0.337	0.184	1.816
10	0.308	0.223	1.777
15	0.223	0.348	1.652
20	0.180	0.414	1.586

The values in Table 11-3 are used to calculate the following 3-sigma control limits:

$$\overline{X}\text{-chart:}\quad \text{UCL} = \overline{\overline{X}} + A_2\overline{R}$$
$$\text{LCL} = \overline{\overline{X}} - A_2\overline{R}$$

$$R\text{-chart:}\quad \text{UCL} = D_4\overline{R}$$
$$\text{LCL} = D_3\overline{R}$$

where

$\overline{\overline{X}}$ = Grand mean for all sample data combined

$\overline{R}$ = Average value of R

For the fifteen samples of resistors, we find the following sample values:

Sample	$\overline{X}$	R
1	9,949.25	150
2	10,020.75	187
3	9,916.5	152
4	9,988.25	112
5	10,038.75	585
6	9,934.5	242
7	9,989.25	146
8	10,043.5	244
9	10,108.5	223
10	10,175.5	143
11	9,960.75	385
12	9,976.75	171
13	10,046.5	281
14	9,913.25	218
15	10,034.5	204
	$\overline{\overline{X}} = 10,006.43$	$\overline{R} = 229.53$

Using the sample values to determine the upper and lower control limits for the two charts, we obtain the following:

$$\overline{X}\text{-chart:}\quad \text{UCL} = 10,006.43 + 0.729(229.53)$$
$$= 10,173.76$$

$$\text{LCL} = 10,006.43 - 0.729(229.53)$$
$$= 9,839.10$$

$$R\text{-chart:}\quad \text{UCL} = 2.282(229.53)$$
$$= 523.79$$

$$\text{LCL} = 0(229.53)$$
$$= 0$$

FIGURE **11-4**

$\overline{X}$-Chart for
Sample Resistor
Values

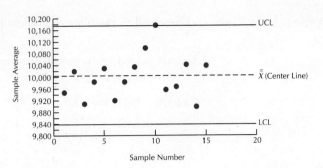

FIGURE **11-5**

R-Chart for
Sample Resistor
Values

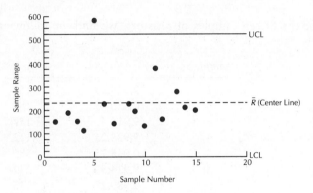

These values are used to construct the $\overline{X}$- and *R*-charts shown in Figures 11-4 and 11-5. Both charts show data points beyond the upper control limit, indicating a source of unstable variation. The cause of this variation should be determined and corrected.

Ideally, new samples of size 4 would be collected after the process is altered to fix the cause of the variation. Then the control limits would be recomputed. However, sometimes practitioners remove the out-of-control points and the control limits are computed from the remaining samples.

The $\overline{X}$-chart is used to monitor the process average. As we said before, if the process suddenly shifts up or down, the $\overline{X}$-chart should detect this shift. The 3-sigma limits, however, should prevent the user from chasing inherent variation in the process. Likewise, if a gradual process shift occurs, the $\overline{X}$-chart should discover this in a reasonably short period of time.

The *R*-chart serves a distinctly different purpose from the $\overline{X}$-chart. It is possible for the process to continue producing average product within the $\overline{X}$ control limits while the variation in individual output has increased (or decreased) from the "normal" levels. The *R*-chart is designed to detect these changes in within-sample variation.

KEY POINTS ABOUT CONTROL CHARTS

The key to understanding process control charts is an understanding of statistical sampling. While some books and companies will rely on lists of rules, the rules will not replace understanding the sampling process itself.

1. We have, for the sake of simplicity, skimped somewhat on the number of data points used to construct the control charts. In general, about thirty data points should be collected before the chart is determined.

2. Since the points plotted on any process control chart should be the result of a random sampling process, they should appear randomly distributed on the chart with about 68% of the points within one standard deviation of the mean and 95% within two standard deviations of the mean. Evidence of nonrandomness includes the following features:

   a. Any point falling outside the control limits. This indicates a source of explainable variation.

   b. Any explainable nonrandom pattern in the data points. This may include a series of points either above or below the center line or a definite upward or downward trend in the data.

   c. Points clustering in the upper or lower part of the chart.

3. From a managerial perspective, control charts are determined by the data—not management directive. In Example 1, no matter what management claims would be an acceptable complaint rate, the process is described by the chart shown in Figure 11-3. If the complaint rate is to be decreased, some change must be made in the system.

4. Control limits are used to establish statistical control, not product specifications. Product specifications should be related to the results of a process capability study as considered in Chapter 2.

5. Control limits are determined by simple statistical formulas. Everyone looking at the same data should find the same control limits.

6. A system in control will randomly generate points falling between the upper and lower control limits.

7. A system may be in control and still generate numerous defective products (customer complaints in Examples 1 and 2, resistors in Example 3).

THE BASIC TOOLS

Many chapters of the text up to this point have contained sections discussing the statistical basis of particular quality control tools. Kaoru Ishikawa, perhaps the most respected Japanese quality control expert, talked about the "basic seven" tools that he claimed, based on 40 years of experience, could solve 95% of all quality problems in a company. While not all the basic tools have statistical foundations, many do, and we have talked about all of them up to this point. The statistical tools needed to improve quality in both goods and services are deceptively simple; the problem arises in correctly implementing these simple tools.

Many statistical techniques yet to be covered in the text can have quality control applications. With the exception of a brief discussion in the next chapter, we will resist the temptation to add additional quality control sections to future chapters. We do this mostly to avoid adding to the often cited U.S. problem of equating the best quality control efforts to the most complicated statistical techniques. Surveys comparing quality control efforts in Japan with those in the United States often identify the complexity of the tools and the timeliness of their feedback as major differences. Japanese companies use simple tools that give immediate feedback to the front-line workers, who are able to make instantaneous changes in the operations to improve the good or service being produced. U.S. companies tend to use complicated tools, used by quality assurance departments. They provide feedback to the front-line workers next week, or even next month, telling them what was done wrong in the past. Based on market results and customers' perceptions of quality, the Japanese may have a better idea.

11-9 CONCLUSIONS

Decision makers often need to estimate population values based on a small sample from the populations. Provided the populations are normally distributed (or at least not highly skewed), the t distribution forms the basis for statistical estimation with a small sample size.

The t distribution has a larger variance than the standard normal distribution, but approaches the normal distribution as the sample size becomes large. The t distribution is symmetrical and has degrees of freedom that depend on the application. We have indicated, for each use, how to calculate the degrees of freedom.

We have also introduced small-sample confidence interval estimation for μ_x, for $(\mu_{x_1} - \mu_{x_2})$ with independent samples, and for $(\mu_{x_1} - \mu_{x_2})$ with dependent samples.

You have probably noticed that statistical estimation and hypothesis testing, for large and small samples, have a lot in common. Some decision makers and statistical authors seem to favor one technique over the other. Both have their place and both should be learned. Estimation procedures are most useful when decision makers have little idea about the population values and are primarily concerned with determining these values. On the other hand, if the decision makers have some idea about the parameter's value, the hypothesis-testing format is most useful.

You should be very familiar with the terminology and equations at the end of this chapter before moving to Chapter 12. The chapter glossary and chapter formulas summarize the concepts and techniques presented in this chapter.

CHAPTER **GLOSSARY**

c-chart Process control chart to monitor number of occurrences per sampling unit.

interval estimator   An interval within which a population parameter may fall. The width of the interval is determined by a combination of sample size, confidence level, and variance.

large sample   In this text, a sample of size $n \geq 30$.

p-chart   Process control chart to monitor percent values over time.

parameter   A measure of the population, such as μ_x, the population mean.

point estimator   A single value calculated from a sample to be used to estimate a population parameter.

pooled variance   A weighted average of two sample variances where the weights are the degrees of freedom associated with each variance.

population   A finite or infinite collection of measurements, items, or individuals of all possible measurements, items, or individuals within the scope of the study.

precision   The width of the confidence interval. The narrower the interval, the greater the precision, and vice versa.

R-chart   Control chart to monitor within-sample variation.

sample   A subset of the population.

small sample   In this text, a sample of size $n < 30$.

stable variation   Normal fluctuations in the output of any physical process.

statistic   A value computed from sample measures, such as $\overline{X}$, the sample mean. The statistic is usually a point estimator of the corresponding population parameter.

Student t distribution   A sampling distribution of

$$t = \frac{\overline{X} - \mu_x}{\dfrac{S_x}{\sqrt{n}}}$$

for samples selected from a normally distributed population with σ_x estimated by S_x, and based on a small sample. The standardized t distribution has a mean of 0 and a variance equal to $(n - 1)/[(n - 1) - 2]$.

unstable variation   Variation that is attributed to some special causes.

$\overline{X}$-chart   Control chart to monitor sample means.

CHAPTER FORMULAS

Sample mean

$$\overline{X} = \frac{\Sigma X}{n}$$

Sample variance

$$S_x^2 = \frac{\Sigma(X - \overline{X})^2}{n - 1}$$

Sample standard deviation—shortcut formula

$$S_x = \sqrt{\dfrac{\Sigma X^2 - \dfrac{(\Sigma X)^2}{n}}{n - 1}}$$

Confidence interval estimate for the population mean—small sample

$$\overline{X} \pm t\dfrac{S_x}{\sqrt{n}}$$

where t has $n - 1$ d.f.

Confidence interval estimate for the difference between two population means—independent small samples

$$(\overline{X}_1 - \overline{X}_2) \pm tS_{\text{pooled}} \sqrt{\dfrac{1}{n_1} + \dfrac{1}{n_2}}$$

where t has $n_1 + n_2 - 2$ d.f.

Pooled standard deviation

$$S_{\text{pooled}} = \sqrt{\dfrac{S_{x_1}^2(n_1 - 1) + S_{x_2}^2(n_2 - 1)}{n_1 + n_2 - 2}}$$

SOLVED PROBLEMS

1. The Artee Corporation makes glass basketball backboards. The company has made ten boards using a new technique. Before it makes any more for commercial sale, Artee needs to estimate the average strength of the new boards. To determine the strength of a board, pressure is applied to each corner until the glass shatters. The pressure at which the glass shatters is recorded.

    Suppose that for the ten glass backboards tested, the mean was 1,526 pounds per square inch and the standard deviation was 15.25 pounds per square inch (psi).

    a. Determine the 90% confidence interval for estimating μ_x, assuming the population is normally distributed.
    b. Determine the 99% confidence interval for estimating μ_x, assuming the population is normally distributed.

Solution

a. The 90% confidence interval for μ_x is determined as follows:

$$\overline{X} \pm t\dfrac{S_x}{\sqrt{n}}$$

where, with 90% confidence and $n - 1 = 9$ degrees of freedom, $t = 1.833$. Then,

$$1,526 \pm 1.833\dfrac{15.25}{\sqrt{10}}$$

$$1,517.16 \text{ psi} \underline{\quad\quad} 1,534.84 \text{ psi}$$

b. The 99% confidence interval is

$$\overline{X} \pm 3.250\frac{S_x}{\sqrt{n}}$$

$$1,526 \pm 3.250\frac{15.25}{\sqrt{10}}$$

$$1,510.33 \text{ psi} \underline{\quad\quad} 1,541.67 \text{ psi}$$

2. Referring to Problem 1, suppose the Artee Corporation wishes to estimate the difference in average strength between the original glass backboards and the new glass backboards. Suppose the company has data for twenty original backboards and the ten new backboards. Calculate the 95% confidence interval estimate of the difference between the two population means, assuming each population is normally distributed and the population variances are equal.

Original	New
$\overline{X}_1 = 1,500$ psi	$\overline{X}_2 = 1,526$ psi
$S_1 = 45.00$ psi	$S_2 = 15.25$ psi
$n_1 = 20$	$n_2 = 10$

Solution

The 95% confidence interval is

$$(\overline{X}_1 - \overline{X}_2) \pm tS_{pooled}\sqrt{\frac{1}{n_1} + \frac{1}{n_2}}$$

where

$$S_{pooled} = \sqrt{\frac{S_1^2(n_1 - 1) + S_2^2(n_2 - 1)}{n_1 + n_2 - 2}}$$

$$= \sqrt{\frac{2,025(19) + 232.56(9)}{28}}$$

$$= 38.06$$

Note that the degrees of freedom for the interval coefficient are $n_1 + n_2 - 2 = 28$ for this problem. Then the interval is

$$(1,500 - 1,526) \pm (2.048)(38.06)\sqrt{\frac{1}{20} + \frac{1}{10}}$$

$$-56.19 \text{ psi} \underline{\quad\quad} 4.19 \text{ psi}$$

The Artee Corporation could be confident that the true difference between the average strengths of the original and new boards is between -56.19 pounds per square inch (new backboard is stronger) and 4.19 pounds per square inch (old backboard is stronger). Since 0 falls within the limits, the company could conclude that the true difference might be 0.

3. A major television manufacturer claims that its average set will be defect-free for more than 2 years of use. A consumer reporting service has decided to test this claim. The service finds a random sample of twenty set owners and

determines the time to the first repair for each. The sample results, in years, are

1.97	3.17	1.34	4.16	2.81	2.75	2.05
2.09	1.01	1.79	3.01	3.10	1.10	1.67
2.24	2.87	3.89	1.62	2.59	0.57	

Based on these sample data, is the manufacturer's claim supported, assuming the burden of proof is on the manufacturer to justify its advertising claim?

Solution

Hypotheses:

H_0: $\mu_x \leq 2$ yr, claim is not true

H_A: $\mu_x > 2$ yr, claim is true

Decision Rule:

Take a sample of size n and determine $\overline{X}$.

If $\overline{X} \leq A$, accept H_0.

If $\overline{X} > A$, reject H_0.

The alpha level is 0.05.

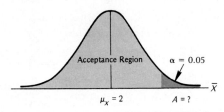

Since σ_x is unknown and the sample size is small, we use the sample standard deviation and the t distribution to determine the A value, if we assume the distribution of time to the first breakdown is normally distributed. Then

$$A = \mu_x + t\frac{S_x}{\sqrt{n}}$$

Next, we calculate $\overline{X}$ and S_x:

$$\overline{X} = \frac{\Sigma X}{n} = 2.29$$

$$S_x = \sqrt{\frac{\Sigma(X - \overline{X})^2}{n - 1}}$$

$$= \sqrt{\frac{17.115}{19}}$$

$$= 0.949$$

The t value for $\alpha = 0.05$ for a one-tailed test with $n - 1 = 19$ degrees of freedom is 1.729. Thus,

$$A = 2 + 1.729\frac{0.949}{\sqrt{20}} = 2.3669$$

Decision Rule:

If $\overline{X} > 2.3669$ yr, reject H_0.

If $\overline{X} \leq 2.3669$ yr, accept H_0.

Since $\overline{X} = 2.29 < 2.3669$, we should accept the null hypothesis and conclude that the manufacturer's claim cannot be supported. Note that the manufacturer would no doubt argue for a larger alpha level or that the burden of proof be shifted to the reporting service.

CONCEPTUAL QUESTIONS AND ASSIGNMENTS

19. A drug manufacturer has asked you to help decide how to test a new drug designed to lower blood pressure. The drug has been tested on animals and found theoretically sound, but has not yet been tested on humans.
    a. Discuss some major considerations in using statistics in this situation. Do you expect to be able to use a large-sample statistical test or a small-sample test?
    b. How important do you expect precision to be in your results and recommendations? Why?
20. Take a good look at the t-distribution table in Appendix D at the back of this text. For a specific level of confidence, what could be said about the value of t as the degrees of freedom increase? Discuss why this occurs.
21. Discuss the basic similarities and differences between the standard normal distribution and the t distribution.
22. Discuss how the t distribution is used in small-sample confidence interval estimation.

ADDITIONAL PROBLEMS

23. The Sweet & Lite Company has recently developed a new angel food cake mix. The company is certain that this mix is "lighter" than the mix of its leading competitor. To test the contention, S&L sends twenty-two numbered, but unidentified, boxes of mix to its testing lab (eleven boxes of its new mix and eleven of the competitor's mix). The cakes are baked and the weights per cubic unit (in grams) are determined. The following values are found.

New	Competition
$\overline{X} = 2.34$ g	$\overline{X} = 2.28$ g
$S_{\overline{x}}^2 = 0.30$ g^2	$S_{\overline{x}}^2 = 0.33$ g^2

Based on these results, would S&L be justified in claiming that its cake is "lighter" than its leading competitor's? Analyze using a 95% confidence level.

24. In Eureka, California, a tax protest group has charged the local real estate appraiser with appraising property higher than the market value, on the average. To refute this claim, the city offered to work with the tax protest group in selecting a random sample of properties sold during the last 6 months. Together they agreed that the sales price would be considered as the market value at the time the house sold. They then would compare the market value with the value assessed by the appraiser to determine whether the appraised values exceeded market values, on the average. The following data were obtained:

Property	Appraised Value	Market Value
1	$88,500	$ 85,400
2	76,200	78,900
3	42,750	23,000
4	96,500	111,000
5	57,400	52,500
6	44,900	45,600
7	88,300	90,100
8	59,000	52,800
9	70,000	76,700
10	83,200	84,700

   a. State the appropriate null and alternative hypotheses to be tested.
   b. Based on these sample data and an alpha level of 0.10, what should be concluded with respect to the average difference in market value and appraised value for homes in the Eureka area? Discuss.

25. Referring to Problem 24, there are two chief appraisers in Eureka who do most of the residential appraising. There has been some concern that the older appraiser tends to underappraise homes, on the average, compared to the younger appraiser. If this is true, then, on the average, residents that have the younger appraiser end up paying an unfair share of the taxes in the city. To test this, each appraiser was asked to appraise a sample of six homes. The following appraisals were recorded in thousands of dollars:

	Home					
	1	2	3	4	5	6
Older Person	40.6	82.6	42.5	90.0	77.5	98.0
Younger Person	56.5	90.0	48.0	87.0	80.6	94.2

   What should be concluded about the difference in average appraisals by the two appraisers, using an alpha level of 0.10? If you conclude that the older person does appraise property on average lower than the younger appraiser, would you recommend that the older appraiser's values be adjusted upward? Discuss.

26. The Go West Exploration Company has recently started drilling exploratory gas wells. The company expects to buy over 100 quick-assembly drill platforms over the next several years, so it is receiving lots of attention from platform manufacturers. Go West has narrowed the possible suppliers to two,

but cannot decide between them. Go West management has placed an initial order for ten platforms from each manufacturer and will choose the type of platform that takes less time to assemble. Management randomly ships the two types of platforms to the next twenty sites and measures the time it takes to assemble them. The results are summarized as follows:

	Type A	Type B
Average time to assemble	5.3 days	4.92 days
Sample standard deviation	0.8 day	0.48 day

Based on this sample information, from which manufacturer should Go West buy the other platforms? Base your response on a 90% confidence interval estimate for the difference in means.

27. Andy Allen, a political-science instructor at State University, is experimenting with a different method of teaching introductory political science. He is teaching two sections this term and decides to use the old method in one section and the new, objective-based method in the other section. At the end of the term he gives a standardized test to each section and wants to estimate the difference in average scores between the two methods. The standardized test gives the following results:

	Old Method	New Method
Class size	18	14
Average score	77.9 points	80.3 points
Sample standard deviation	7.3 points	6.8 points

a. Develop and interpret a 95% confidence interval estimate for the difference in average test scores.

b. Suppose Andy wishes to improve the precision of this estimate. Discuss his alternatives.

28. Health-One, Inc., is a nonprofit company that provides health-care treatment to patients with heart conditions. Health-One, Inc., relies heavily on contributions from around the state to fund its operation. Recently, the company initiated a fund-raising campaign in which it hoped for 20,000 contributions totaling $2.0 million.

In preparation for a board of directors meeting, the treasurer selected a random sample of twenty contributions that had already arrived and found the mean contribution to be $89.00 and the standard deviation to be $26.00.

a. Assuming the organization will receive 20,000 contributions, what is the 95% confidence interval estimate for the total dollars this campaign will generate? Based on this estimate, what should the treasurer report with respect to the $2.0 million goal? Assume the population is normally distributed.

b. How would the treasurer's report differ if the interval estimate were based on a 99% confidence level?

29. The makers of a particular brand of dot-matrix-type printers claim that the average repair costs during the first 2 years of ownership will be less than $40. To test this claim, a random sample of people who have owned this type

of printer for at least 2 years was selected. The people were asked to record their total repair bills during the first 2 years of ownership. These data are as follows for the sample of eight owners:

$58.00 $12.50 $0.00 $0.00
$ 6.75 $32.50 $8.50 $0.00

a. State the appropriate null and alternative hypotheses to be tested.
b. What assumption is required if you are to perform the hypothesis test using the *t* distribution?
c. Perform the hypothesis test at an alpha level of 0.05 and discuss the conclusion that should be reached based on the sample data.

30. According to the magazine *Outdoor Sports,* the average age of people obtaining a fishing license for the first time is on the decrease. The magazine claims that the average age of the first-time fishing licensee is 14 years. If this claim is true, a local Idaho sporting-goods store plans to direct its advertising toward a younger audience.

   In an effort to verify whether the magazine's claim is true, a random sample of the ages of first-time fishing license purchasers was obtained from the Department of Fish and Game. The following results were obtained in years of age:

   17   12   20   21   14   19
   13   18   14   21   12   17
   14   29   15   25   11   22

   Based on this sample, should the sporting-goods store support the magazine's claim? Test at an alpha level of 0.10.

31. The American Tax Institute at Richmond, Virginia, offers courses for individuals in preparing income tax returns. The courses are designed to prepare individuals to complete their own income tax returns rather than taking their tax materials to an accountant or other tax preparer. The course is also designed to help those people who already fill out their own tax returns, but would like to learn to be more efficient in doing the task.

   Recently, the institute recruited a sample of fifteen individuals and had them bring their tax materials to the institute. They were asked to work on their own tax returns and spend as long as they wanted doing so. The actual time spent completing the forms was recorded for each individual. A second sample of individuals was selected and these people were provided with the institute's short course free of charge. Then the time it took each of these people to complete their tax returns was recorded. Two people dropped out of this second sample.

   The following summary statistics were recorded for each of the samples in hours:

No Tax Course	Short Course
$n_N = 17$	$n_S = 15$
$\overline{X}_N = 5.8$ h	$\overline{X}_S = 4.7$ h
$S_N = 2.2$ h	$S_S = 2.8$ h

a. State the appropriate null and alternative hypotheses.

b. Based on the sample data, what should be concluded about the average time it takes to complete an individual's income taxes with and without the short course offered by the American Tax Institute? Test using an alpha level of 0.01.

c. Discuss the assumptions that are necessary in order to use the t distribution to test the null hypothesis.

32. A company personnel director is interested in estimating the difference in absenteeism between the day and night shifts at her company's West Coast distribution center. She takes a random sample of 15 days from the day shift, but only 11 days from the night shift. She finds an average of 8.8 days for the day shift and an average of 10.3 days for the night shift. Based on this evidence, the personnel director concludes that the night supervisor is being lax in hiring practices and recommends a possible change in supervisors.

a. Comment on this conclusion. Should such a conclusion be reached without incorporating the standard deviations into the analysis?

b. The night supervisor, hearing about this possible action, comments strongly about the "evidence." In particular, she states that drawing a conclusion based on this small a sample is wrong. She says, "Anyone who knows anything about statistics knows you have to have a sample size of at least 30 before you can draw any conclusions." Comment on this statement.

33. The Topeka Fire Department has come under pressure from the city council because many citizens have complained about poor response rates. Last year the town had 1,505 fires. The required average response time is 5 minutes or less.

A random sample of thirty fires is selected and the results show a mean of 6 minutes and a variance of 25. Testing at an alpha level of 0.05, determine whether the council should chastise the fire department or if it should conclude that the standard is being satisfied.

34. A local lawn and garden store, The Green Connection, claims that its best-selling brand of lawn mower blades will last at least 6 years. A competitor, D and D Lawn Service, has decided to test The Green Connection's claim. The competition found a random sample of twenty-five people who have used the blades and determined the length of time to the blades' first sharpening. The sample results, in years, are as follows:

5.98	6.30	6.12	4.98	5.75
7.01	6.43	6.88	5.23	5.98
6.10	8.12	5.65	6.78	6.00
6.54	6.37	5.74	7.21	6.90
5.55	6.72	6.39	5.00	6.21

Based on these data, is The Green Connection's claim supported? Use an alpha level of 0.05.

35. The Ludwig Corporation personnel director is interested in determining how effective the company's preventive health care program has been. As part of her analysis, she selected a random sample of employees and recorded the hours of work missed by each employee due to illness in the year immediately

preceding the start of the new program. She also selected another random sample of employees and recorded their hours missed during the new program's first year. The data collected are shown as follows:

Before Plan (h)			After Plan (h)		
16	13	28	30	70	102
72	44	88	5	18	
7	16	90	45	35	

a. What assumptions must be made in order that a 95% confidence interval estimate for the difference in mean hours can be made and interpreted?
b. Develop and interpret the 95% confidence interval estimate for the difference in population mean before versus after.
c. Based on the results of part **b**, what conclusions could the personnel director reach? Discuss.

36. The CSC Corporation is in the design stages for a new microcomputer that will be portable, yet very powerful. CSC plans to market the product primarily to businesses that wish to have very powerful word-processing capabilities in a portable computer. One specific application would be for the secretary to have a way of taking typing work home on evenings and weekends. Thus, it is extremely important that the keyboard layout and touch be acceptable to professional typists.

   CSC is currently considering two companies for the production of the keyboard. The two companies have developed prototypes. CSC plans to test these using a random sample of professional typists from the CSC Corporation. The plan is for each typist to try each keyboard and then provide a rating of the keyboard layout and touch on a 100-point scale, with 100 being the highest rating. The following data were obtained for the twelve typists who participated in the study:

Typist	Keyboard 1	Keyboard 2
1	67	73
2	58	60
3	80	85
4	60	55
5	95	78
6	40	46
7	75	75
8	67	64
9	80	83
10	30	34
11	48	57
12	70	70

a. State the appropriate null and alternative hypotheses.
b. Based on the sample data, what should be concluded about the preferences of typists for the two keyboards? Test using an alpha level of 0.10. Discuss.

c. Discuss why it would be desirable to set up the study of microcomputer keyboards using a paired-sample approach like this. What are the advantages and potential disadvantages?

37. The Nile Company manufactures and distributes cosmetics in the United States and Canada. One of the most difficult problems for the company is forecasting regional demand for its products. The procedure it often uses is to select a random sample of potential customers and ask the people to estimate the number of dollars they will spend on Nile cosmetics in the next forecast period. The marketing vice-president believes that, on the average, there will be no difference between what the customers forecast and what they actually buy.

To test this contention, the marketing department selected a random sample of twenty-five people in Illinois and asked the people to provide forecasts of their Nile cosmetics purchases during the next month. It then did a follow-up survey with these same people and determined the actual expenditure on Nile cosmetics. Since this situation reflects a paired-sample test, the following statistics from the sample data were computed:

$$\bar{d} = \frac{\Sigma(\text{Forecast} - \text{Actual})}{25}$$

$$= \$2.30$$

$$S_d = \$4.20$$

What should the Nile Company conclude about the customers' forecasts, on the average? Test at an alpha level of 0.10. Discuss.

38. The Victory Athletic Shoe Company has a promotional agreement with the Trailmarkers professional basketball team. Victory will supply shoes and monetary consideration to each team member in exchange for rights to feature team members in its advertising. Victory has recently developed a new shoe sole material it thinks provides superior wear compared with the old material. The company gives each of the ten team members one shoe of each material and monitors wear until the shoe, for playing purposes, is worn out. The following times (in hours) are found:

Player	New Material	Old Material
1	47.0	45.5
2	50.0	50.5
3	42.0	48.0
4	47.0	45.5
5	58.0	58.0
6	55.5	49.0
7	39.0	24.5
8	53.0	52.0
9	43.0	48.0
10	61.0	57.5

Based on these data, and assuming a 95% confidence interval, does the evidence indicate that there is a difference between the two shoe materials?

39. The Heaton Furnace Company has just designed a new furnace system that, if it operates as its engineers predict, will allow people to save an average of $40 or more per month on heating. The furnace has been tested at the factory, but Heaton production engineers think that it should be tested under actual conditions. This means that the company will have to install the furnace in a sample of homes and then compare heating bills for the current month with heating bills for the same month the year before. Although not a perfect test because of possible variations in temperature, the company thinks it can test the claim about the savings in this manner. The following data, reflecting the dollar savings, were collected for a random sample of fifteen homes in which the furnace was installed without charge to the homeowner:

$18.50	$21.75	$12.40	$68.00	$35.10
45.00	37.60	52.05	27.60	20.05
36.90	21.76	18.00	41.65	33.84

  a. State the appropriate null and alternative hypotheses.
  b. Using an alpha level of 0.10, develop the appropriate decision rule. What assumption must be made about the population distribution?
  c. Referring to part b, what conclusion should be reached regarding the furnace based on the sample data? Discuss.

40. The Vermont Park and Recreation Department has claimed that the city parks are being used by adults rather than children. In fact, a recent report claims that the average age of park users is at least 32 years. If this claim is true, the city council plans to institute a research study to determine whether a children's park is needed.

    In an effort to verify whether the recreation department's claim is true, a sample of park users has been selected and ages recorded. A random sample of people entering the park was used, giving the following results in years of age:

12	7	17	66	30
59	59	15	16	18

    Based on this sample evidence, should the department's claim be supported? Test at an alpha level of 0.05.

41. A local television station has added a consumer spot to its nightly news. The consumer report has recently bought ten bottles of aspirin from a local drugstore and has counted the aspirins in each bottle. Although the bottles advertised 500 aspirins, the reporter found the following numbers:

493	490	487	498	496
507	501	480	488	495

The consumer report claims this is an obvious case of the public being taken advantage of. Comment. (*Hint:* What is the 95% confidence interval estimate for the average number of aspirins?)

42. The Reach Out Telephone Company manufactures telephones. The company has made twenty phones using a new bonding agent. Before it makes any more for commercial sale, Reach Out needs to estimate the average strength

of the holding mechanism. To determine the strength of the bonding agent, pressure is applied to the sides of the phone until the two parts detach. The pressure at which the parts unfasten is then recorded.

For the twenty phones tested, the mean was 127 pounds per square inch and the standard deviation was 1.30 pounds per square inch (psi).

    a. Determine the 95% confidence interval for estimating μ, assuming the population is normally distributed.

    b. Determine the 99% confidence interval for estimating μ, assuming the population is normally distributed.

43. The Cole Corporation is considering two word-processing systems for its microcomputers. One factor that will influence its decision is the ease of use in preparing a business report. Consequently, Jenn Cole selected a random sample of nine typists from the clerical pool and asked them to type a typical report using both word-processing systems. The typists then rated the systems on a scale of 0 to 100. The results were as follows:

Typist	System 1	System 2
1	82	85
2	78	80
3	90	67
4	53	58
5	44	58
6	82	70
7	95	80
8	45	45
9	70	80

    a. Discuss why it might be appropriate to set up this analysis as a paired-sample estimation problem.

    b. Develop a 95% confidence interval estimate for the difference between population means and interpret it. Do these sample data help Jenn Cole select between the two word-processing systems? Explain.

44. Teton Electronics has decided to place an advertisement on television to be shown three times during a live broadcast of the local university's football game. The sales for each of the 7 days after the ad was placed are to be compared with the sales for the 7 days immediately prior to running the ad. The following data representing the total dollar sales each day were collected:

Sales before the ad	Sales after the ad
$1,865	$2,045
1,543	2,956
2,862	2,090
1,490	1,510
2,300	2,850
1,379	1,755
2,096	2,255

a. State the appropriate null and alternative hypotheses to be tested.

b. What assumptions must be made about the population distributions in order to test the hypothesis using the t distribution?

c. Based on the sample data, what conclusions should be reached with respect to average sales before versus after the advertisement? Test using an alpha level of 0.01.

DATABASE PROBLEMS

The following questions and problems pertain directly to the State Department of Transportation case study and database introduced in Chapter 1. The questions and problems were written assuming that you will have access to a computer and appropriate statistical software. The database contains 100 observations and seventeen variables. *Assume that the data were collected using a simple random sampling process.*

1. Develop and interpret a 95% confidence interval estimate for average age of uninsured motorists in the state. Interpret this estimate.

2. Determine a 90% confidence interval estimate for the average years of formal education for those drivers whose vehicles are not insured.

3. Determine a 95% confidence interval estimate for the difference in average age of drivers of vehicles that are uninsured versus those that are insured.

4. Determine the 90% confidence interval estimate for the difference in average years lived in the state for drivers of vehicles that are insured versus those that are uninsured.

5. Develop a 95% confidence interval estimate for the average number of total convictions for drivers of vehicles that are insured versus those that are uninsured. Be sure to interpret the interval.

6. Determine a 90% confidence interval estimate for the average number of vehicles registered in the state for those who were driving an uninsured vehicle.

CASES

11A   Midcentral Warehousing

Midcentral Warehousing is a contract warehouse operation with locations in several large southern cities. It is open 24 hours a day and services many middle-sized manufacturing and distributing companies that are not large enough to individually afford the extensive inventory control and security provided by Midcentral.

Midcentral has been using a large number of diesel-operated forklifts, but recently has been considering changing to battery-operated lifts. The purchasing chief, Georgeanne Andrews, has been asked to consider the relative merits of battery versus diesel lifts. Georgeanne believes that diesel lifts have definite cost advantages for the moment, but that battery-powered lifts may be more efficient in the future. However, she is worried about how long battery-operated lifts can operate before they need to be recharged. The battery lifts require 1 hour of down time to charge. Naturally, Georgeanne is concerned that there will be too much down time during the three shifts. Her dilemma is whether to start replacing the older-model diesels with battery-operated lifts or with new diesels.

Georgeanne has decided that the critical factor is the time the lifts can operate between charges. The manufacturer's specifications indicate the lifts will operate for at least two shifts, but Georgeanne, having been in the purchasing game for a long time, has learned to distrust specifications.

The lift manufacturer has agreed to supply Midcentral with records from fifty of its customers. The data consist of measurements on the number of hours between charges. Because of the large volume of data, Georgeanne has selected a random sample of eighteen values from all of the data. These values are

8 h	12 h	7 h
10	11	9
13	10	8
3	9	10
12	9	12
11	10	11

Georgeanne reasons that she ought to be able to get an idea about the lasting power of the battery lifts from the sample data without looking at all the data.

11B   U-Need-It Rental Agency

Richard Fundt has operated the U-Need-It rental agency in a northern Wisconsin city for the past 5 years. One of the biggest rental items has always been chain saws; lately, the demand for these saws has increased dramatically. Richard buys chain saws at a special industrial rate and then rents them for $10 per day. The average chain saw is used between 50 and 60 days per year. Although Richard makes money on any chain saw, he obviously makes more on those saws that last the longest.

Richard worked for a time as a repairperson and can make most repairs on the equipment he rents, including the chain saws. However, he would also like to limit the time he spends making repairs. U-Need-It is presently stocking two types of saws—North Woods and Accu-Cut. Richard has an impression that one of the models, Accu-Cut, does not seem to break down as much as the other. Richard presently has eight North Woods saws and eleven Accu-Cut saws. He decides to keep track of the number of hours each saw is used between major repairs. He finds the following values:

her contention. Using the methods introduced in previous chapters, she is interested in testing the following null and alternative hypotheses:

$$H_0: \quad \sigma \le 0.5$$
$$H_A: \quad \sigma > 0.5$$

There is no statistical technique for directly testing hypotheses about a population standard deviation. However, a test is available for testing about a population variance. Thus, the previous hypotheses must be converted to:

$$H_0: \quad \sigma^2 \le 0.25$$
$$H_A: \quad \sigma^2 > 0.25$$

As with all the hypothesis tests introduced in Chapters 9, 10 and 11, the decision to reject or accept the null hypothesis will be based on the statistic computed from a sample. In testing hypotheses about a single population variance, the appropriate statistic is S^2, the sample variance, given in equation 12-1:

$$S^2 = \frac{\Sigma(X - \overline{X})^2}{n - 1}$$

12-1

To test a null hypothesis about a population variance, we compare S^2 with the hypothesized population variance, σ^2. To do this, we need to be able to standardize the distribution of sample variances in much the same way we used the Z distribution and the t distribution when hypothesizing about population means. The standardized distribution for sample variances is a *chi-square distribution*. The standardized chi-square variable is computed by equation 12-2:

$$\chi^2 = \frac{(n - 1)(S^2)}{\sigma^2}$$

12-2

where

χ^2 = Standardized chi-square variable

n = Sample size

S^2 = Sample variance

σ^2 = Hypothesized variance

FIGURE **12-1**

Chi-square
Distributions

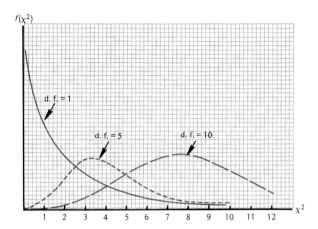

The shape of the standardized chi-square distribution depends on the hypothesized variance and the degrees of freedom, $n - 1$. Figure 12-1 illustrates chi-square distributions for various degrees of freedom. Note that as the degrees of freedom increase, the chi-square distribution approaches a normal distribution.

Returning to the H & L Machines example, suppose Nina Ray took a sample of twenty service calls and found a variance of 0.33 hour squared. Figure 12-2 presents the hypothesis test at an alpha level of 0.10.

FIGURE **12-2**

Chi-square Test
for One
Population
Variance for the
H & L Machines
Example

Hypotheses:
$H_O: \sigma^2 \leq 0.25$
$H_A: \sigma^2 > 0.25$
$\alpha = 0.10$

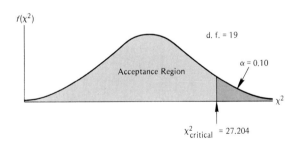

Decision Rule:

If $\chi^2 > \chi^2_{critical} = 27.204$, reject H_0.
Otherwise, do not reject H_0.

The chi-square test is as follows:

$$\chi^2 = \frac{(n-1)(S^2)}{\sigma^2} = \frac{19(0.33)}{0.25}$$

$$= 25.08$$

Since $\chi^2 = 25.08 < \chi^2_{critical} = 27.204$, accept H_0.

Appendix E contains a table of chi-square values for various probabilities and degrees of freedom. The chi-square table is used in a manner similar to the use of the t-distribution table. For example, to find χ^2_{critical} for the H & L Machines example, we first determine the degrees of freedom, $n - 1 = 20 - 1 = 19$, and the desired alpha level, 0.10. Now we go to the chi-square table under the column headed "0.10" (corresponding to the desired alpha) and find the χ^2 value in this column that intersects the row corresponding to the appropriate degrees of freedom. Table 12-1 illustrates how the chi-square table is used to find $\chi^2_{\text{critical}} = 27.204$. If the calculated χ^2 exceeds χ^2_{critical}, the null hypothesis should be rejected.

TABLE 12-1

Finding Critical Values in the Chi-square Table

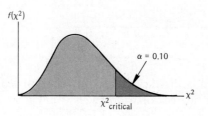

| d.f. | Probabilities (Or Areas under χ^2 Distribution Curve above Given χ^2 Values) | | | | | | | | |
	0.90	0.70	0.50	0.30	0.20	0.10	0.05	0.02	0.01
	Values of χ^2								
1									
2									
.									
.									
.									
.									
.									
.									
17					21.615	24.769			
18					22.760	25.989			
19						27.204	30.144		
20							31.410		
21									
.									
.									
.									
.									
.									
.									
.									

As you can see in Figure 12-2, the sample variance is not significantly larger than the hypothesized variance as to cause the manager to reject the null hypothesis. She will conclude, based on these results, that the service representatives do complete their service calls according to a distribution with a standard deviation of 0.5 hour or less.

In most applications, decision makers are concerned about the variance being too large. However, there are instances in which decision makers are concerned with knowing whether the variance is *higher* or *lower* than a specified level. For instance, the Acme Assembly Company assembles clock radios. The number assembled from day to day varies because of several factors, such as parts availability and employee attitudes. From past records, the production supervisor knows that the assembly variance should be 50. He has selected 25 days at random from this year's production reports and found a sample variance of 20. Figure 12-3 shows the statistical test using an alpha level of 0.20. As the test indicates, this sample information is so different from past information that the production supervisor should infer that the true variance has decreased. Based on this conclusion, the supervisor would, no doubt, try to find out what caused the improved consistency in an effort to ensure that it continues. Of course, he would also want

FIGURE 12-3

Chi-square Test for One Population Variance for the Acme Assembly Company Example

Hypotheses:

$H_0: \sigma^2 = 50$
$H_A: \sigma^2 \neq 50$

$\alpha = 0.20$

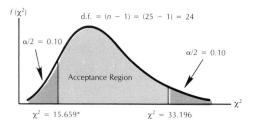

d.f. $= (n - 1) = (25 - 1) = 24$

$\alpha/2 = 0.10$

$\alpha/2 = 0.10$

Acceptance Region

$\chi^2 = 15.659^*$

$\chi^2 = 33.196$

Decision Rule:

If $\chi^2 > \chi^2_{critical} = 33.196$, reject H_0.
If $\chi^2 < \chi^2_{critical} = 15.659$, reject H_0.
If $15.659 \leq \chi^2 \leq 33.196$, accept H_0.

The chi-square test is

$$\chi^2 = \frac{(n - 1)(S^2)}{\sigma^2} = \frac{24(20)}{50}$$

$$= 9.6$$

Since calculated $9.6 < 15.659$, reject H_0.

*Since the hypothesis test is two-tailed, the lower critical value is found from the chi-square table under the column for an area $1 - \alpha/2 = 1 - 0.10 = 0.90$. The upper critical value is found from the chi-square table under the column for an area $\alpha/2 = 0.10$.

to determine whether the assembly process is meeting the standard for average output.

SKILL DEVELOPMENT PROBLEMS FOR **SECTION 12-1**

The following set of problems is meant to test your understanding of the material in this section.

1. Find the value of chi-square when $n = 10$ and the upper tail area (alpha) of the distribution is 0.05.

2. Find the value of chi-square when $n = 20$ and the upper tail area (alpha) of the distribution is 0.10.

3. Given the following null and alternative hypotheses:

$$H_0: \quad \sigma^2 \le 40$$
$$H_A: \quad \sigma^2 > 40$$

   a. Test if $n = 10$, $S = 7$, and $\alpha = 0.05$. Be sure to show the decision rule.
   b. Test if $n = 30$, $S^2 = 54$, and $\alpha = 0.10$. Show the decision rule.

4. Given the following null and alternative hypotheses:

$$H_0: \quad \sigma^2 \le 12$$
$$H_A: \quad \sigma^2 > 12$$

   a. Test if $n = 13$, $S = 4$, and $\alpha = 0.10$. Be sure to show the decision rule.
   b. Test if $n = 30$, $S^2 = 21$ and $\alpha = 0.05$. Show the decision rule.

5. The Haglund Corporation manufactures paint and stain products for interior and exterior home and commercial applications. The new "Apple Wood Stain" product is thought to be a real improvement over some of the company's previous products. One criterion of a quality stain is the consistency of coverage per gallon. Haglund hopes that the standard deviation in coverage will not exceed 20 square feet per gallon. To test this, they have selected a random sample of twelve gallons and found the following coverage in square feet:

245	302	240	280	255	300	290	240	300	270	230	300

   a. State the null and alternative hypotheses.
   b. State the decision rule, assuming an $\alpha = 0.05$.
   c. Perform the test and write a one-paragraph conclusion for the Haglund manager.

6. The National Football League is in the process of renegotiating its television contracts with the networks. At issue is concern over what happens if a game goes too long and runs into the time slot reserved for other programs. As part of the negotiations, the NFL commissioner claimed that the game-time standard deviation does not exceed 8 minutes. To test this claim, a random

sample of fifteen past games was selected, with the following times (in minutes) recorded:

145	136	123	109	145
125	137	134	140	138
120	146	129	135	134

a. State the appropriate null and alternative hypotheses.
b. Determine the decision rule, assuming an alpha level of 0.10.
c. Test the null hypothesis and comment on the result.

12-2 HYPOTHESES ABOUT TWO POPULATION VARIANCES

Just as decision makers are often interested in testing hypotheses regarding two poulation means, they are often faced with decision problems involving *two population variances*. For example, the Midlands Asphalt and Grading Company is considering purchasing a new paving machine. The company has two machines from which to choose. Midlands has decided to select the paver that provides the lesser variation in paving thickness. Variations in asphalt depth can have effects on both material cost and road strength. In addition, penalties are often assessed if testers find the road too thin.

One machine is considerably less expensive than the other, and, although Midlands will buy the more expensive model if necessary, the company does not want to miss out on a good deal if the less expensive machine will spread asphalt with a comparable variation.

The purchasing agent at Midlands has arranged to sample eleven surfaces paved by machine 1 and thirteen surfaces paved by machine 2 to see whether he can detect a difference in thickness variation between the two. The hypotheses are

Hypotheses:

$$H_0: \quad \sigma_1^2 = \sigma_2^2$$
$$H_A: \quad \sigma_1^2 \neq \sigma_2^2$$

Since the population variances are not known, they must be estimated from the sample variances S_1^2 and S_2^2. Intuitively, you might reason that if the two population variances are actually equal, the sample variances should be nearly equal also.

If the samples are selected from two normally distributed populations with σ_1^2 equal to σ_2^2, the ratio of the sample variances, S_1^2/S_2^2, has a probability distribution known as an *F* distribution. The *F* statistic is given in equation 12-3:

$$F = \frac{S_1^2}{S_2^2}$$

12-3

Because S_1^2 and S_2^2 have $n_1 - 1$ and $n_2 - 1$ degrees of freedom, respectively, the F distribution formed by the ratio of sample variances has $D_1 = n_1 - 1$ and $D_2 = n_2 - 1$ degrees of freedom.

The calculated F value gets larger if S_1^2 is greater than S_2^2. Since we have control over which population we label as "1" and which we label as "2" in a two-tailed test, we always select as population 1 the population with the larger sample variance. Therefore, if the calculated F gets too large, we conclude that the two populations have unequal variances.

Suppose the samples for the two paving machines yield variances of $S_1^2 = 0.025$ and $S_2^2 = 0.017$. Figure 12-4(a) presents the test of the hypothesis that the two machines have equal variances. As was the case with the normal, t, and chi-square distributions, the F distribution has been tabulated. The F-distribution values for upper-tail areas of 0.05 and 0.01 are provided in Appendix F.

The relationship between the specified alpha level and the appropriate F table is important. Two situations can occur:

1. If the hypothesis test is two-tailed (that is, $H_0: \sigma_1^2 = \sigma_2^2$), the appropriate F table is the one with an upper-tail area (area above the critical value) equal to one-half alpha. For example, if you have a two-tailed test with an alpha level of 0.10, you should use the F-distribution table containing values of F for the upper 5% of the distribution. If the alpha level is 0.02, you should use the F table containing values of F for the upper 1%.
2. If the hypothesis test is one-tailed (that is, $H_0: \sigma_1^2 \leq \sigma_2^2$), the appropriate F table is the one with the upper-tail area equal to alpha. For example, if the alpha level is 0.05, use the F table containing values of F for the upper 5% of the distribution.

Thus, to determine which F table to use, you must know the alpha level and also whether the test is one- or two-tailed. We can illustrate this concept with two examples. First, take the case of a two-tailed test with a stated alpha level of 0.10 and degrees of freedom D_1 equal to 10 and D_2 equal to 12. We can use Table 12-2 to illustrate how $F_{critical}$ is determined. First, because it is a two-tailed test, go to the F table having an upper-tail area equal to one-half alpha (in this case, $0.10/2 = 0.05$). Next, go to the column corresponding to $D_1 = 10$ and read down to the row corresponding to $D_2 = 12$. The value at the intersection of the row and column is the desired $F_{critical}$ (2.76).

One-tailed tests involving two population variances are performed in a similar manner to the two-tailed tests. To illustrate, suppose the managers at Midlands decided to test two other paving machines. In this instance, prior research indicated that machine 1 should produce greater variation in pavement thickness than machine 2. The managers have sampled seven surfaces paved by machine 1 and eleven surfaces paved by machine 2 with the following results:

$$S_1^2 = 0.035$$
$$S_2^2 = 0.015$$

FIGURE 12-4

F Test for Two
Population
Variances for the
Midlands Asphalt
and Grading
Company
Example

(a) Two-Tailed Test

Hypotheses:

$H_0: \sigma_1^2 = \sigma_2^2$
$H_A: \sigma_1^2 \neq \sigma_2^2$

$\alpha = 0.10$

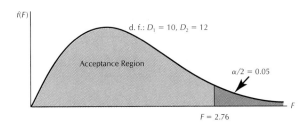

Decision Rule:

If $F \leq F_{\text{critical}} = 2.76$, accept H_0.
If $F > F_{\text{critical}}$, reject H_0.

The *F* test is

$$F = \frac{S_1^2}{S_2^2} = \frac{0.025}{0.017}$$

$$= 1.47$$

Since $F = 1.47 < F_{\text{critical}} = 2.76$ with $D_1 = 10$ and $D_2 = 12$ degrees of freedom, accept H_0.

Note: The right-hand tail of the *F* distribution always contains an area of $\alpha/2$ if the hypothesis test is two-tailed.

(b) One-Tailed Test

Hypotheses:

$H_0: \sigma_1^2 \leq \sigma_2^2$
$H_A: \sigma_1^2 > \sigma_2^2$

$\alpha = 0.01$

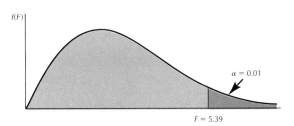

Decision Rule:

If $F \leq F_{\text{critical}} = 5.39$, accept H_0.
If $F > F_{\text{critical}} = 5.39$, reject H_0.

The *F* test is

$$F = \frac{S_1^2}{S_2^2} = \frac{0.035}{0.015} = 2.33$$

Since $F = 2.33 < F_{\text{critical}} = 5.39$ with $D_1 = 6$ and $D_2 = 10$ degrees of freedom, accept H_0.

TABLE 12-2

Finding Critical
Values in the F
Table (Values of
F for Upper 5%)

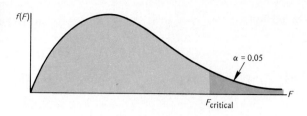

D_2 \ D_1	1	2	3	4	5	6	7	8	10	12
1										
2										
3										
4										
5										
6										
7										
8										
10								3.07	2.97	
12								2.85	2.76	
14									2.60	2.53
16										
20										
24										
.										
.										
.										
.										
.										
.										
.										

Figure 12-4(b) illustrates the one-tailed hypothesis test using an alpha = .01 level. Recall that in a two-tailed test, the F ratio is formed by placing the larger sample variance in the numerator and the smaller variance in the denominator. In a one-tailed test, we look to the alternative hypothesis to determine which sample variance should go in the numerator. If, as in this example, population 1 is thought to have the larger variance, then the sample variance from population 1 forms the numerator regardless of the size of the sample variances. In another example, if population 2 is thought to have the larger variance, the sample variance from population 2 would form the numerator in the F ratio calculation.

It is important that the F ratio be formed correctly for two reasons. First, the correct F ratio is computed. Second, the correct degrees of freedom will be used to determine the critical value to test the null hypothesis. In the Midlands one-tailed example, the numerator represents population 1 and the denominator represents population 2. The F ratio is

$$F = \frac{.035}{.015} = 2.33$$

Thus, the degrees of freedom are $D_1 = 7 - 1 = 6$ and $D_2 = 11 - 1 = 10$. Table 12-3 shows how to locate the appropriate critical value of 5.39 for this one-tailed test with alpha = .01.

As shown in Figure 12-4(b), the calculated F ratio falls in the "acceptance" region so the null hypothesis is not rejected. Based on the sample data, there is no reason to believe that machine 1 produces higher variation than machine 2.

TABLE **12-3**

Finding Critical Values in the F Table (Values of F for Upper 1%)

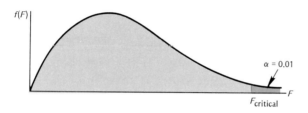

D_2 \ D_1	1	2	3	4	5	6	7	8	10	12
1										
2										
3										
4										
5										
6										
7										
8						6.37				
10					5.64	5.39	5.21			
12					5.06	4.82				
14										
.										
.										
.										
.										
.										
.										
.										
.										

SKILL DEVELOPMENT PROBLEMS FOR SECTION 12-2

The following set of problems is meant to test your understanding of the material in this section.

7. Find the appropriate F value from the F-distribution table for each of the following:
   a. $D_1 = 10$, $D_2 = 14$, $\alpha = 0.05$
   b. $D_1 = 8$, $D_2 = 8$, $\alpha = 0.01$
   c. $D_1 = 14$, $D_2 = 10$, $\alpha = 0.05$

8. Given the following null and alternative hypotheses:

$$H_0: \quad \sigma_1^2 = \sigma_2^2$$
$$H_A: \quad \sigma_1^2 \neq \sigma_2^2$$

and the following sample information:

Sample 1	Sample 2
$n = 11$	$n = 21$
$S = 19$	$S = 23$

   a. If $\alpha = 0.02$, state the decision rule for the hypothesis.
   b. Test the hypothesis and indicate whether the null hypothesis should be rejected.

9. Given the following null and alternative hypotheses:

$$H_0: \quad \sigma_1^2 \leq \sigma_2^2$$
$$H_A: \quad \sigma_1^2 > \sigma_2^2$$

and the following sample information:

Sample 1	Sample 2
$n = 13$	$n = 21$
$S^2 = 1,450$	$S^2 = 1,320$

   a. If $\alpha = 0.05$, state the decision rule for the hypothesis.
   b. Test the hypothesis and indicate whether the null hypothesis should be rejected.

10. Given the following null and alternative hypotheses:

$$H_0: \quad \sigma_1^2 \geq \sigma_2^2$$
$$H_A: \quad \sigma_1^2 < \sigma_2^2$$

and the following sample information:

Sample 1	Sample 2
$n = 21$	$n = 13$
$S^2 = 345.7$	$S^2 = 745.2$

a. If $\alpha = 0.01$, state the decision rule for the hypothesis.
b. Test the hypothesis and indicate whether the null hypothesis should be rejected.

11. The McBurger Company operates fast-food stores throughout the United States and in fourteen other countries. Management is very concerned about making sure that a standard quality of service is achieved. For instance, they are interested in whether there is a difference in variance in service times for customers who use the drive-up window versus those who go inside to the service counter.

The McBurger store in Knoxville, Tennessee, recently was the subject of evaluation. A sample of thirteen drive-through customers was selected and a sample of nine inside-counter customers was selected. The time (in minutes) it took each customer to be serviced was recorded. The following statistics were computed from the sample data:

Drive-Through	Walk-In
$\overline{X} = 4.5$	$\overline{X} = 4.0$
$S = 2.0$	$S = 1.2$

a. State the appropriate null and alternative hypotheses for testing about equality of variances.
b. Based on an alpha level of 0.10, determine the appropriate decision rule and test the null hypothesis.
c. Suppose the managers are also interested in testing whether there is a difference in average time it takes to service the two types of customers. State the appropriate null and alternative hypotheses and test at an $\alpha = 0.05$ level.

12. A national TV telethon committee is interested in determining whether males give donations that have greater variability in amount than do those of females. To test this, random samples of twenty-five males and twenty-five females were selected from people who donated during last year's telethon. The following statistics were computed from the sample data:

Males	Females
$\overline{X} = \$12.40$	$\overline{X} = \$8.92$
$S = \$2.50$	$S = \$1.34$

a. State the null and alternative hypotheses to be tested.
b. Based on an alpha level of 0.05, determine the decision rule and test the null hypothesis.
c. Suppose the committee is also interested in determining whether there is a difference in average donations between men and women. State the appropriate null and alternative hypotheses and test at the $\alpha = 0.05$ level.

12-3

ANALYSIS OF VARIANCE—ONE-WAY DESIGN

The Hudson Company is a diversified manufacturer of electronics products, both for the consumer and manufacturing segments of the economy. The company has always tried to develop numerous small plants as opposed to a few, huge operations. Consequently, it has plants in North America, Asia, and Europe. The company has always maintained a decentralized management style, but does set some corporate goals. A recent goal is to increase the "local content" of goods and services each plant purchases. The purpose of this goal is to add to the stability of the local economy.

The North American division of the Hudson Company is divided into four areas. At the yearly strategic planning meeting, the four regional supervisors decided to determine whether any of the regions were doing better than the others in their efforts to increase the local content. Since "local content" is a difficult value to measure, the supervisors decided to form a working group and sample eight manufacturing sites in each area. Since the working group would expect variation to exist among the sites, it formulated the following null and alternative hypotheses:

$$H_0: \quad \mu_1 = \mu_2 = \mu_3 = \mu_4$$
$$H_A: \quad \text{Not all means are equal.}$$

It also established an alpha level of 0.05 for this test.

WHY TWO-SAMPLE t TESTS WILL NOT WORK

One method to test the null hypothesis involving four population means would be to use the two-sample t test discussed in Chapter 11. The working group could set up a series of null and alternative hypotheses involving *all* possible pairs of sales regions. The two-sample t test could be used to test each null hypothesis. With four populations, there are

$$_4C_2 = \frac{4!}{2!(4-2)!}$$
$$= 6$$

separate pairs of regions. Thus, to test the null hypothesis that all four population means are equal would require six separate t tests of the form

$$H_0: \quad \mu_1 = \mu_2$$
$$H_A: \quad \mu_1 \neq \mu_2$$

with the test statistic as in equation 12-4:

$$t = \frac{(\overline{X}_1 - \overline{X}_2) - 0}{S_{\text{pooled}} \sqrt{\dfrac{1}{n_1} + \dfrac{1}{n_2}}}$$

12-4

If the six separate *t* tests are performed, and the null hypothesis is accepted in each case, we could conclude that all four population means are equal. However, the problem with using a series of two-sample *t* tests is that although each test has an alpha level of 0.05, the true alpha level for all tests combined is greater than 0.05. If we consider the six tests to be independent, the probability of committing at least one Type I error in six tests is given by equation 12-5:

$$
\begin{aligned}
\alpha_{\text{actual}} &\leq [1 - (1 - \alpha_1)(1 - \alpha_2)(1 - \alpha_3) \cdots (1 - \alpha_6)] \\
&\leq [1 - (0.95)(0.95)(0.95)(0.95)(0.95)(0.95)] \\
&\leq 1 - 0.7351 \\
&\leq 0.2649
\end{aligned}
\qquad \textbf{12-5}
$$

Thus, the probability of committing one or more Type I errors using a series of six *t* tests, each with an alpha level of 0.05, is, at most, 0.2649. The logic behind this increase in alpha is that *as more tests are performed, the risk of rejecting at least one true hypothesis is increased.*

Due to this problem, a series of two-sample *t* tests is not generally considered adequate to test hypotheses involving more than two populations. However, a statistical tool known as *analysis of variance* (ANOVA) can be used without "compounding" the probability of committing a Type I error.

THE RATIONALE OF ONE-WAY ANALYSIS OF VARIANCE

In the Hudson Company example, the working group needs to determine whether the average local content is equal among the four North American regions. Analysis of variance is a statistical procedure that, as its name implies, is used to examine population variances to determine whether the population means are equal.

Three assumptions (the same ones as for a two-sample *t* test) must be satisfied before analysis of variance can be applied.

1. The samples must be independent random samples.
2. The samples must be selected from populations with normal distributions.
3. The populations must have equal variances (that is, $\sigma_1^2 = \sigma_2^2 = \cdots = \sigma_k^2 = \sigma^2$).

The rationale behind analysis of variance might best be understood by studying Table 12-4, which presents the data the working group has collected. You should notice several things about the data. First, the plants in the sample do not all have the same percentage of local content in goods and services purchased. Thus, variation exists in the content percentage of the thirty-two plants. This is

TABLE 12-4

Local Content Data for the Hudson Company Example (Values Given as Percentages)

Plant	Region 1	Region 2	Region 3	Region 4
1	4	7	5	12
2	6	9	11	8
3	10	13	6	7
4	12	8	8	9
5	5	9	4	11
6	8	14	9	10
7	4	7	10	6
8	7	5	11	9
Total	56	72	64	72
	$\overline{X}_1 = 7$	$\overline{X}_2 = 9$	$\overline{X}_3 = 8$	$\overline{X}_4 = 9$

Grand total = 264

$$\text{Grand mean} = \overline{\overline{X}} = \frac{264}{32} = 8.25$$

called the **total variation** in the data. Second, within any particular region, not all plants have the same percentage of local content. Thus, variation exists within regions. This variation is called **within-sample variation**. Finally, the sample means for the four regions are not all equal. Thus, variation exists between the regions. As you might have guessed, this is called **between-sample variation**.

The basic principle of one-way analysis of variance is that

Total sample variation = Between-sample variation + Within-sample variation

From our discussion of variance in Chapter 3, we know that the variability in a set of measurements is proportional to the sum of the squared deviations of the measurements from the mean, as given by expression 12-6:

$$\Sigma(X - \overline{X})^2 \qquad \textbf{12-6}$$

Therefore, the total sample variation in the data shown in Table 12-4 is proportional to the sum of the squared deviations of the thirty-two figures around the *grand mean*. This is called the *total sum of squares* (TSS) and is calculated by equation 12-7:

$$\text{TSS} = \sum_{i=1}^{K} \sum_{j=1}^{n_i} (X_{ij} - \overline{\overline{X}})^2$$

12-7

where

$\quad$ TSS = Total sum of squares

$\quad$ K = Number of populations (columns)

$\quad$ n_i = Sample size from population i

$\quad$ X_{ij} = jth measurement from population i (in the present example, the thirty-two different measurements)

$\quad$ $\overline{\overline{X}}$ = Grand mean (here, the mean of all thirty-two measurements)

The total sum of squares for the Hudson Company example is

$$\text{TSS} = (4 - 8.25)^2 + (6 - 8.25)^2 + (10 - 8.25)^2 + \cdots + (9 - 8.25)^2$$
$$= 226$$

As was stated earlier, total variation equals the between-sample variation plus the within-sample variation. Equation 12-8 states this:

$$\underbrace{\sum_{i=1}^{K} \sum_{j=1}^{n_i} (X_{ij} - \overline{\overline{X}})^2}_{\text{TSS}} = \underbrace{\sum_{i=1}^{K} n_i (\overline{X}_i - \overline{\overline{X}})^2}_{\text{SSB}} + \underbrace{\sum_{i=1}^{K} \sum_{j=1}^{n_i} (X_{ij} - \overline{X}_i)^2}_{\text{SSW}}$$

12-8

Equation 12-8 shows that TSS can be *partitioned* into two parts: the *sum of squares between* (SSB) and the *sum of squares within* (SSW).[1] For this example,

$$\text{SSB} = 8(7 - 8.25)^2 + 8(9 - 8.25)^2 + 8(8 - 8.25)^2 + 8(9 - 8.25)^2$$
$$= 22$$
$$\text{SSW} = \text{TSS} - \text{SSB} = 226 - 22$$
$$= 204$$

The working group wants to determine whether the mean local contents in the four regions are equal. However, it must decide this based on a sample from

---

[1] The chapter glossary contains calculation formulas for each of the sum of squares formulas contained in this section.

FIGURE 12-5

Normal
Populations with
Equal Means and
Equal Variances

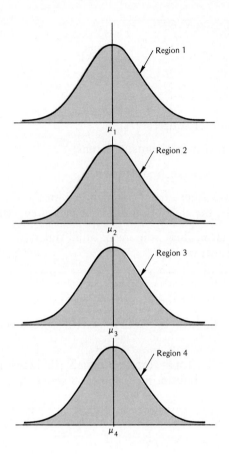

each region. The group wants to know whether the four distributions shown in Figure 12-5 best describe the distributions, or whether Figure 12-6 applies. If Figure 12-5 applies, a null hypothesis that all means are equal should be accepted. If Figure 12-6 applies, the null hypothesis should be rejected. Note that these figures illustrate the assumptions of normal populations and equal population variances.

To determine whether to accept or reject the null hypothesis using analysis of variance, we perform the following:

1. Establish the null hypothesis to be tested:

$$H_0: \quad \mu_1 = \mu_2 = \mu_3 = \cdots$$
$$H_A: \quad \text{Not all means are equal.}$$

2. Make two estimates of the population variance, one based on individual regions and one based on differences in regional averages.

3. If the two estimates are about the same, we conclude that Figure 12-5 applies and that the means are equal. If the variance-estimates are sub-

FIGURE 12-6

Normal
Populations with
Unequal Means
and Equal
Variances

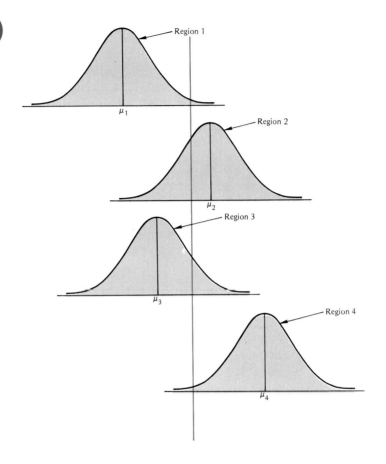

stantially different, we conclude that the population means are not all
equal and reject H_0.

The computational procedures necessary to make the variance estimates are
not complicated if we remember that any variance is a sum of squares divided by
degrees of freedom. The first estimate is given by equation 12-9:

$$\text{MSW} = \frac{\text{SSW}}{N - K} = \text{Unbiased estimate of } \sigma^2 \qquad \textbf{12-9}$$

where

$\quad$ MSW = Mean square within

$\quad$ SSW = Sum of squares within

$\quad\quad$ N = Total number of measurements from all samples

$\quad\quad$ K = Number of groups (here, four regions)

Also, if the region means are truly equal (the null hypothesis is true), the second estimate is given by equation 12-10:

$$MSB = \frac{SSB}{K - 1} = \text{Unbiased estimate of } \sigma^2 \qquad \textbf{12-10}$$

where

MSB = Mean square between

SSB = Sum of squares between

K = Number of groups

Thus, if the null hypothesis is true (that is, all means are equal), MSW and MSB are both estimates of the population variance, σ^2, and we would expect MSW and MSB to be nearly equal.

However, because of the way SSB is calculated, the more the sample means differ, the *larger* SSB becomes. As SSB is increased, MSB begins to differ from MSW. When this difference gets too large, our conclusion will be that the population means are not all equal. Therefore we would reject the null hypothesis. But how do we determine what "too large" is?

Recall the test of two population variances presented in Section 12-2. There we saw that the ratio of two unbiased estimates of the same variance, σ^2, forms an F distribution with D_1 and D_2 degrees of freedom. If the population means are equal, MSW and MSB are both unbiased estimates of σ^2. Their ratio should produce a statistic that is F-distributed when H_0 is true, as shown in equation 12-11:

$$F = \frac{MSB}{MSW} \qquad \textbf{12-11}$$

The calculated F comes from an F distribution with $D_1 = K - 1$ and $D_2 = N - K$ degrees of freedom, if H_0 is true.

A common means of illustrating analysis of variance calculations is in table format. The Hudson working group has formulated Table 12-5. Notice that it has listed the null and alternative hypotheses, and has shown the F distribution and the decision rule for an alpha level of 0.05.

The ratio of MSB to MSW for this example is 1.0065. This value is smaller than the critical F value of approximately 2.92 found in the F-distribution table in

T A B L E 12-5

ANOVA for the
Hudson
Company
Example

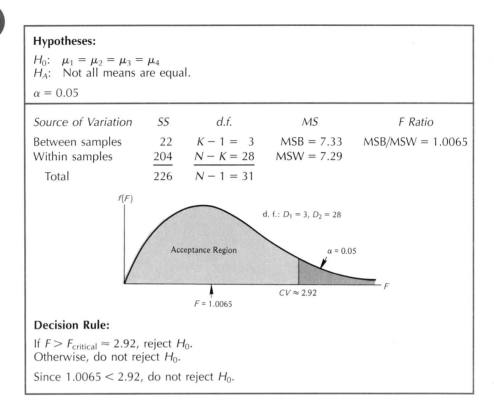

Hypotheses:

H_0: $\mu_1 = \mu_2 = \mu_3 = \mu_4$
H_A: Not all means are equal.

$\alpha = 0.05$

Source of Variation	SS	d.f.	MS	F Ratio
Between samples	22	$K - 1 = 3$	MSB = 7.33	MSB/MSW = 1.0065
Within samples	204	$N - K = 28$	MSW = 7.29	
Total	226	$N - 1 = 31$		

d. f.: $D_1 = 3$, $D_2 = 28$

Acceptance Region

$\alpha = 0.05$

$CV \approx 2.92$

$F = 1.0065$

Decision Rule:

If $F > F_{critical} \approx 2.92$, reject H_0.
Otherwise, do not reject H_0.

Since $1.0065 < 2.92$, do not reject H_0.

Appendix F. Note that we have used degrees of freedom $D_1 = 3$ and $D_2 = 30$ to obtain an approximation for the critical F value. The exact F value could be found from an F table that contains entries for degrees of freedom $D_1 = 3$ and $D_2 = 28$. Since the calculated F value is smaller than the critical F value, the working group should *not* reject the null hypothesis. It would conclude that the average local area contents in the four regions could, in fact, be equal.

The analysis of variance has allowed the Hudson Company to test a null hypothesis involving four population means without compounding alpha above the 0.05 level.

COMPUTER OUTPUT—ANALYSIS OF VARIANCE

Because analysis of variance is such a common statistical technique, all computer packages will perform the calculations necessary to complete the ANOVA output table. Figure 12-7 shows the output for the Hudson Company example given by the GB-STAT package. Notice that the output contains a p-value (PROB) that should be compared with the alpha in the hypothesis. Since the p-value is greater than the 5% level established by the working group in that example, the null hypothesis is not rejected.

FIGURE **12-7**

ANOVA SUMMARY TABLE

GB-STAT Output
for the Hudson
Company Example

SOURCE	SUM SQRES	DF	MEAN SQRES	F-RATIO	PROB
BETWEEN GRPS	22	3	7.33333	1.0065	.4045
WITHIN GRPS	204	28	7.28571		
TOTAL	226	31			

SKILL DEVELOPMENT PROBLEMS FOR **SECTION 12-3**

Several exercises and problems designed to help you understand the material presented in Section 12-3 follow.

13. Given the following sample data:

Item	Group 1	Group 2	Group 3
1	10	8	13
2	9	6	12
3	11	8	12
4	12	9	11
5	13	10	13
6	12	10	15

a. State the appropriate null and alternative hypotheses for determining whether a difference exists in the average value for the three populations.
b. Compute the sum of squares between for the above sample data.
c. Compute the sum of squares within for the above sample data.
d. Based on the computations in parts **b** and **c,** develop the ANOVA table and test the null hypothesis using an $\alpha = 0.05$.

14. Given the following sample data:

Item	Group 1	Group 2	Group 3	Group 4
1	20	28	17	21
2	27	26	15	23
3	26	21	18	19
4	22	29	20	17
5	25	30	14	
6	30	25		
7	23			

a. State the appropriate null and alternative hypotheses for determining whether a difference exists in the average value for the four populations.
b. Compute the sum of squares between for the above sample data.
c. Compute the sum of squares within for the above sample data.
d. Based on the computations in parts **b** and **c,** develop the ANOVA table and test the null hypothesis using an $\alpha = 0.05$.

15. The American Beef Growers Association is trying to promote the consumption of beef products. The organization performs numerous studies, the results of which are often used in advertising campaigns. One such study involved a quality perception test. Three levels of beef gradings—choice, standard, and economy—were involved. A random sample of people was provided a piece of choice-grade beefsteak and asked to rate its quality on a scale of 1 to 100. A second sample of people was given a piece of standard-grade beefsteak and a third sample was given a piece of economy-grade beefsteak, with instructions to rate the beef on the 100-point scale. The following data were obtained.

Choice	Standard	Economy
78	67	65
87	80	62
90	78	70
87	80	66
89	67	70
90	70	73

Based on the sample data, is there sufficient evidence to conclude that there is a difference in perceived quality for the three grades of beefsteak? Test at an $\alpha = 0.05$ level; make sure to state the null and alternative hypotheses and provide the ANOVA table.

12-4 TUKEY'S AND SCHEFFÉ'S METHODS OF MULTIPLE COMPARISONS

Once the analysis of variance leads to rejecting the null hypothesis of equal means, decision makers need a method to determine which means are not equal and that will not compound the alpha error. (Remember that t tests are not acceptable; they compound the probability of Type I errors.) One method, developed by John W. Tukey, can be used when the samples from the populations are the same size. Tukey's method involves establishing a *T range* according to equation 12-12:

$$T \text{ range} = T\sqrt{MSW}$$

12-12

where

$$T = \frac{1}{\sqrt{n}}q$$

q = Value from the Studentized range table (Appendix G), given the alpha level and $D_1 = K$ and $D_2 = N - K$ d.f.

n = Common sample size

If any pair of sample means has an *absolute difference,* $|\overline{X}_1 - \overline{X}_2|$, greater than the T range, we can conclude that the population means are not equal. For example, our Arizona city has three fire districts. The possible *pairwise* comparisons (formally referred to as *contrasts*) are

$$|\overline{X}_1 - \overline{X}_2| = |1.5 - 4.0| = 2.5$$
$$|\overline{X}_1 - \overline{X}_3| = |1.5 - 1.0| = 0.5$$
$$|\overline{X}_2 - \overline{X}_3| = |4.0 - 1.0| = 3.0$$

The calculated T range for this example with an alpha level of 0.05 is

$$T \text{ range} = T\sqrt{\text{MSW}}$$

where

$$T = \frac{1}{\sqrt{n}} q_{(1-\alpha),\, D_1 = K = 3,\, D_2 = N - K = 27}$$

Note that q is from the Studentized range table in Appendix G (value interpolated).

$$= \frac{1}{\sqrt{10}} 3.51$$

$$= 1.110$$

Then

$$T \text{ range} = 1.110\sqrt{1.13}$$
$$= 1.180$$

Thus

$$|\overline{X}_1 - \overline{X}_2| = |1.5 - 4.0| = 2.5 > 1.180$$
$$|\overline{X}_2 - \overline{X}_3| = |4.0 - 1.0| = 3.0 > 1.180$$
$$|\overline{X}_1 - \overline{X}_3| = |1.5 - 1.0| = 0.5 < 1.180$$

Therefore, based on Tukey's method, the city manager can conclude that the mean number of responses for district 1 is *not* equal to the mean for district 2 and that the mean for district 2 is *not* equal to the mean for district 3. However, he does not have enough statistical evidence to conclude that the means of district 1 and district 3 are different.

By examining the sample means, the city manager can infer that district 2 has more responses on the average than district 1 and more than district 3. Thus, district 2 should receive some new firefighters and at least one truck. However, based on this study, the city manager has no statistical basis for assigning a truck or crew to a second district. He cannot conclude that districts 1 and 3 differ with respect to average responses. Some other factor will have to be used to make the final decision.

Tukey's method of multiple comparisons allows decision makers to determine which population means are not equal once analysis of variance leads to rejecting the null hypothesis of equal population means. This method does not compound the alpha level, but applies only when the sample sizes are equal.

The main restriction of Tukey's method is that it requires equal sample sizes. In some controlled applications, managers can guarantee equal sample sizes from each population. However, in many other applications equal sample sizes are not possible. When decision makers have unequal sample sizes, the analysis of variance equations still apply, as does the interpretation of results. But, since Tukey's method does not apply, decision makers need a method of multiple comparisons that allows for unequal sample sizes. H. Scheffé has developed such a procedure.

The Zero Defects Corporation has recently begun bidding on contracts to assemble printed circuit boards. It has received a contract to assemble the main control board for a popular fish finder (a sonar-like unit that locates fish in lakes). The contract is for a fixed cost per board, so the more efficiently the boards can be assembled, the more profitable the contract will be.

While the company has recently purchased an automatic soldering machine, putting the required components on the boards is presently an entirely manual operation. Eduardo Martez, the production manager, is experimenting with five different assembly sequences. To determine which sequence is most effective, he selected a random sample of fifty workers. Ten workers were randomly assigned to each sequence. At the end of a 1-day training period, the workers began assembling circuit boards using their assigned sequence. Table 12-6 shows the average

TABLE 12-6

Printed Circuit Board Assembly Data for the Zero Defects Corporation Example (Number of Boards Assembled)

Sequence 1	Sequence 2	Sequence 3	Sequence 4	Sequence 5
47	86	65	58	49
52	85	63	62	51
46	81	67	63	47
49	90	64	64	55
53	84	59	59	54
39	88	67	55	42
51	77	70	70	53
	79	59	59	57
	82		60	59
			61	58

$n_1 = 7$	$n_2 = 9$	$n_3 = 8$	$n_4 = 10$	$n_5 = 10$	$N = 44$
$\overline{X}_1 = 48.14$	$\overline{X}_2 = 83.56$	$\overline{X}_3 = 64.25$	$\overline{X}_4 = 61.10$	$\overline{X}_5 = 52.50$	$\overline{\overline{X}} = 62.25$

$$\text{TSS} = \sum_{i=1}^{K} \sum_{j=1}^{n_i} (X_{ij} - \overline{\overline{X}})^2 = (47 - 62.25)^2 + (52 - 62.25)^2 + \cdots + (48 - 62.25)^2$$

$$= 7{,}264.25$$

$$\text{SSB} = \sum_{i=1}^{K} n_i (\overline{X}_i - \overline{\overline{X}})^2 = 7(48.14 - 62.25)^2 + \cdots + 10(52.50 - 62.25)^2$$

$$= 6{,}474.27$$

$$\text{SSW} = \text{TSS} - \text{SSB}$$

$$= 789.98$$

number assembled during a 2-week period for each worker for each sequence. As might be expected for a study of this kind, several workers missed work or had other training scheduled and had to be eliminated from the study. Therefore, unequal sample sizes resulted.

Table 12-7 presents the analysis of variance results, the null and alternative hypotheses, and the decision rule. The null hypothesis that the five assembly sequences are equal with respect to the average number of circuit boards assembled is clearly rejected. Eduardo Martez should conclude that not all assembly sequences will produce equal average outputs.

Once the analysis of variance indicates that the null hypothesis should be rejected, *Scheffé's method of multiple comparisons* can determine which means are different. Like Tukey's method, Scheffé's method produces a range to which the absolute differences in pairs of sample means (called contrasts) can be compared. This range is given in equation 12-13:

$$S \text{ range} = S\hat{\sigma}$$

12-13

where

$$S = \sqrt{(K-1)(F_{\alpha, D_1 = K-1, \, D_2 = N-K})}$$

$$\hat{\sigma} = \sqrt{\left(\frac{1}{n_i} + \frac{1}{n_j}\right)(\text{MSW})}$$

One contrast for an alpha level of 0.05 is

$$|\overline{X}_1 - \overline{X}_2| = |48.14 - 83.56| = 35.42$$

If 35.42 is greater than the S range, Martez should conclude that sequences 1 and 2 differ significantly with respect to average output. In this case the S range is

$$S \text{ range} = S\hat{\sigma}$$

where

$$S = \sqrt{(K-1)(F_{\alpha, D_1, D_2})} = \sqrt{4(2.62)}$$
$$= 3.23$$

$$\hat{\sigma} = \sqrt{\left(\frac{1}{n_1} + \frac{1}{n_2}\right)(\text{MSW})} = \sqrt{\left(\frac{1}{7} + \frac{1}{9}\right)(20.26)}$$

$$= 2.27$$

Therefore,

$$S \text{ range} = 3.23(2.27) = 7.332$$

Since the absolute difference of 35.42 is greater than 7.332, Eduardo will conclude that the mean levels for these sequences do differ. Based on the sample

TABLE 12-7

ANOVA for the Zero Defects Corporation Example

Hypotheses:

H_0: $\mu_1 = \mu_2 = \mu_3 = \mu_4 = \mu_5$
H_A: Not all means are equal.

$\alpha = 0.05$

Source of Variation	SS	d.f.	MS	F Ratio
Between methods	6,474.27	4	1,618.57	79.91
Within methods	789.98	39	20.26	
Total	7,264.25	43		

d. f.: $D_1 = 4$, $D_2 = 39$

Acceptance Region

$\alpha = 0.05$

$CV = 2.62$

Decision Rule:

If $F > F_{critical} = 2.62$, reject H_0.
Otherwise, do not reject H_0.

Since $79.91 > 2.62$, reject H_0.

means, he infers that assembly sequence 2 will give significantly higher average output than sequence 1.

The Scheffé method can be applied to any or all possible pairwise contrasts. The S range will differ slightly from contrast to contrast if the sample sizes differ. Table 12-8 shows all possible pairwise contrasts and their associated S ranges for

TABLE 12-8

Scheffé Test for the Zero Defects Corporation Example

Contrast	S Range	Significant?
$\lvert \overline{X}_1 - \overline{X}_2 \rvert = \lvert 48.14 - 83.56 \rvert = 35.42$	7.332	Yes
$\lvert \overline{X}_1 - \overline{X}_3 \rvert = \lvert 48.14 - 64.25 \rvert = 16.11$	7.524	Yes
$\lvert \overline{X}_1 - \overline{X}_4 \rvert = \lvert 48.14 - 61.10 \rvert = 12.96$	7.165	Yes
$\lvert \overline{X}_1 - \overline{X}_5 \rvert = \lvert 48.14 - 52.50 \rvert = 4.36$	7.165	No
$\lvert \overline{X}_2 - \overline{X}_3 \rvert = \lvert 83.56 - 64.25 \rvert = 19.31$	7.064	Yes
$\lvert \overline{X}_2 - \overline{X}_4 \rvert = \lvert 83.56 - 61.10 \rvert = 22.46$	6.680	Yes
$\lvert \overline{X}_2 - \overline{X}_5 \rvert = \lvert 83.56 - 52.50 \rvert = 31.06$	6.680	Yes
$\lvert \overline{X}_3 - \overline{X}_4 \rvert = \lvert 64.25 - 61.10 \rvert = 3.15$	6.896	No
$\lvert \overline{X}_3 - \overline{X}_5 \rvert = \lvert 64.25 - 52.50 \rvert = 11.75$	6.896	Yes
$\lvert \overline{X}_4 - \overline{X}_5 \rvert = \lvert 61.10 - 52.50 \rvert = 8.60$	6.502	Yes

our board assembly example. The only contrasts for which we can conclude that the population means are not different are μ_1 and μ_5, and μ_3 and μ_4. Based on the sample means, the production supervisor infers that sequence 2 will produce a higher average output than the other four sequences.

COMPUTER OUTPUT—TUKEY AND SCHEFFÉ TESTS

While virtually all statistical packages will perform analysis of variance calculations, not all will perform the Tukey and Scheffé tests. Some recent PC packages, including GB-STAT, will perform both tests. These tests are found on the additional statistics menu after analysis of variance is selected. However, while the output for ANOVA tables is fairly consistent between packages, the output formats for the Tukey and Scheffé tests are not as consistent. Figure 12-8 shows the computer output for both the ANOVA table and Tukey (protected t) tests for the Arizona fire district example. Note that the Tukey output is in matrix format. The values in the matrix are equivalent to t values, and the double asterisks (**) found

FIGURE 12-8

GB-STAT Output for the Arizona Fire District Example

SAMPLE DESCRIPTIVE STATISTICS

N 1 = 10
N 2 = 10
N 3 = 10

MEAN GROUP 1 = 1.5
VAR. GROUP 1 = 1.83333
MEAN GROUP 2 = 4
VAR. GROUP 2 = .22222
MEAN GROUP 3 = 1
VAR. GROUP 3 = 1.33333

ANOVA SUMMARY TABLE

SOURCE	SUM SQRES	DF	MEAN SQRES	F-RATIO	PROB
BETWEEN GRPS	51.66669	2	25.83334	22.8689	<.0001
WITHIN GRPS	30.5	27	1.12963		
TOTAL	82.16669	29			

PROTECTED T-TESTS

	1 DIST 1	2 DIST 2	3 DIST 3
DIST 1	0	−5.2597**	1.0519
DIST 2	−5.2597**	0	6.3116**
DIST 3	1.0519	6.3116**	0

**p < .01   *p < .05

next to some values indicate that the means for the corresponding districts have differences significant at the 0.01 level.

Figure 12-9 shows the GB-STAT output for the Zero Defects example. Notice that the Scheffé output is also given in matrix form, with the double asterisks indicating significance at the 0.01 level.

FIGURE 12-9

GB-STAT Output for the Zero Defects Corporation Example

SAMPLE DESCRIPTIVE STATISTICS

N 1 = 7
N 2 = 9
N 3 = 8
N 4 = 10
N 5 = 10

MEAN GROUP 1 = 48.14286
VAR. GROUP 1 = 22.80952
MEAN GROUP 2 = 83.55556
VAR. GROUP 2 = 17.77778
MEAN GROUP 3 = 64.25
VAR. GROUP 3 = 15.07143
MEAN GROUP 4 = 61.1
VAR. GROUP 4 = 16.54445
MEAN GROUP 5 = 52.5
VAR. GROUP 5 = 28.5

ANOVA SUMMARY TABLE

SOURCE	SUM SQRES	DF	MEAN SQRES	F-RATIO	PROB
BETWEEN GRPS	6474.272	4	1618.568	79.9061	<.0001
WITHIN GRPS	789.9794	39	20.25588		
TOTAL	7264.251	43			

SCHEFFE COMPARISONS

	1 SEQ 1	2 SEQ 2	3 SEQ 3	4 SEQ 4	5 SEQ 5
SEQ 1	0	60.9435**	11.9543**	8.5321**	.9648
SEQ 2	60.9435**	0	19.4821**	29.4798**	56.384**
SEQ 3	11.9543**	19.4821**	0	.5443	7.5732**
SEQ 4	8.5321**	29.4798**	.5443	0	4.5641**
SEQ 5	.9648	56.384**	7.5732**	4.5641**	0

$**p < .01$ $*p < .05$

SKILL DEVELOPMENT PROBLEMS FOR **SECTION 12-4**

Several exercises and problems designed to help you understand the material presented in Section 12-4 follow.

16. Under what conditions would Tukey's method of multiple comparison be used and for what purpose is it used?

17. Under what conditions would Scheffé's method of multiple comparison be used and for what purpose is it used?

18. Given the following sample data:

Item	Group 1	Group 2	Group 3
1	12	8	16
2	15	5	12
3	21	7	12
4	15	8	14
5	17	10	15
6	12	10	15

   a. State the appropriate null and alternative hypotheses for determining whether a difference exists in the average value for the three populations.
   b. Compute the sum of squares between for the above sample data.
   c. Compute the sum of squares within for the above sample data.
   d. Based on the computations in parts **b** and **c**, develop the ANOVA table and test the null hypothesis using an $\alpha = 0.05$.
   e. Employ the appropriate method for detecting which means are different, using an $\alpha = 0.05$.

19. Given the following sample data:

Item	Group 1	Group 2	Group 3	Group 4
1	20	28	17	21
2	27	26	15	23
3	26	21	18	19
4	22	29	20	17
5	25	30	14	
6	30	25		
7	23			

   a. State the appropriate null and alternative hypotheses for determining whether a difference exists in the average value for the four populations.
   b. Compute the sum of squares between for the above sample data.
   c. Compute the sum of squares within for the above sample data.
   d. Based on the computations in parts **b** and **c**, develop the ANOVA table and test the null hypothesis using an $\alpha = 0.05$.
   e. Use the appropriate method of multiple comparison to determine which populations have different means. Use an $\alpha = 0.05$.

20. The Green-Checker Cab Company operates twelve taxis in Seattle, Washington. The manager is interested in determining whether there is a difference in average fares collected for the day, swing, and graveyard shifts. To test whether a difference exists, she has collected a random sample of ten observations from each shift. The following summary values have been computed from the sample data:

$$TSS = 156,764 \qquad SSB = 55,600$$

   a. State the appropriate null and alternative hypotheses.
   b. Develop the appropriate ANOVA table and test the hypothesis using an $\alpha = 0.01$.

21. The American Beef Growers Association (see Problem 15) is trying to promote the consumption of beef products. The organization performs numerous studies, the results of which are often used in advertising campaigns. One such study involved a quality perception test. Three levels of beef gradings—choice, standard, and economy—were involved. A random sample of people was provided a piece of choice-grade beefsteak and asked to rate its quality on a scale of 1 to 100. A second sample of people was given a piece of standard-grade beefsteak and a third sample was given a piece of economy-grade beefsteak, with instructions to rate it on the 100-point scale. The following data were observed.

Choice	Standard	Economy
78	67	65
87	80	62
90	78	70
87	80	66
89	67	70
90	70	73

Based on the sample data, is there sufficient evidence to conclude that there is a difference in perceived quality for the three grades of beefsteak? Test at the $\alpha = 0.05$ level; make sure to state the null and alternative hypotheses and provide the ANOVA table. Also, if appropriate, determine which populations have different means, using a method of multiple comparison.

12-5 QUALITY IMPROVEMENT AND ANALYSIS OF VARIANCE

W. Edwards Deming tells the story of an American automobile manufacturer that did not have enough capacity in its plants to make enough automatic transmissions to meet current production schedules. The American company contracted with a Japanese affiliate to produce the transmissions. Later, the company had warranty problems with the transmissions, but discovered the problems were almost entirely with those made in the American plant. Engineers selected samples of both American- and Japanese-made transmissions and broke them down, looking for potential differences. They found that all the American-made transmissions contained parts that varied somewhat, but were all clearly within the design specifications. When the engineers started measuring the Japanese-made parts, they first thought their instruments had failed—all parts measured the same. They soon discovered that they could not measure variation in the parts because virtually no variation existed—the parts *were* all the same!

The Japanese company was following a procedure formulated by Genichi Taguchi, who took to heart Deming's teaching that sources of variation in a process should be identified and reduced using statistically valid methods. The Taguchi method is cited as a key to the quality of Japanese manufacturing and depends heavily on analysis of variance. It starts with gathering enough statistical data to formulate a valid baseline for the existing process and to identify important points of variation in the output. The next step is to formulate experiments to determine the relationship between important variation in the output and alternative actions in the process. The idea is always to select the alternative that minimizes the resulting variation in the output. If sources of variation in the output are continually identified, and alternatives that minimize this variation are selected, eventually all output will appear virtually identical.

Over the last 10 years the Taguchi method has been introduced in numerous American companies, including all three automobile manufacturers, the Bell system, Xerox, and ITT.

12-6 CONCLUSIONS

In many decision-making situations the spread of the distribution is as important as or more important than its center. This chapter has introduced techniques for testing hypotheses involving a single population variance and involving the difference between two population variances. The chi-square and F distributions were used in these two hypothesis-testing applications.

Managers are also often faced with comparing alternatives involving more than two populations. Because hypothesis testing is such a powerful decision-making tool, managers need to be able to extend the hypothesis-testing procedure to more than two populations. Analysis of variance allows this extension.

By using analysis of variance, managers are able to determine whether the sample observations come from the same population or from different populations. Analysis of variance allows managers to separate observations into categories and see whether this separation explains some of the variation in the sample observations. The ability to test for significant relationships between sample observations falling into different categories makes analysis of variance a powerful decision-making tool.

CHAPTER GLOSSARY

between-sample variation (SSB) The variation that exists between the sample means selected from the populations of interest in an analysis of variance test.

one-way ANOVA The analysis of variance design in which only one factor is analyzed and the samples selected from the populations are independent.

total variation (TSS) The variation that exists in the data as a whole.

within-sample variation (SSW) The variation that exists within the sample data from a given population.

CHAPTER FORMULAS

Chi-square test statistic

$$\chi^2 = \frac{(n-1)S^2}{\sigma^2}$$

F-distribution test statistic

$$F = \frac{S_1^2}{S_2^2}$$

Total sum of squares

$$TSS = \sum_{i=1}^{K} \sum_{j=1}^{n_i} (X_{ij} - \overline{\overline{X}})^2$$

Sum of squares between

$$SSB = \sum_{i=1}^{K} n_i(\overline{X}_i - \overline{\overline{X}})^2$$

Sum of squares within

$$SSW = \sum_{i=1}^{K} \sum_{j=1}^{n_i} (X_{ij} - \overline{X}_i)^2$$

Mean square within

$$MSW = \frac{SSW}{N - K}$$

Mean square between

$$MSB = \frac{SSB}{K - 1}$$

F statistic for one-way analysis of variance

$$F = \frac{MSB}{MSW}$$

One-way analysis of variance (calculation formulas)

$$TSS = \sum_{i=1}^{K} \sum_{j=1}^{n_i} X_{ij}^2 - \frac{\left(\sum_{i=1}^{K} \sum_{j=1}^{n_i} X_{ij}\right)^2}{N}$$

$$SBB = \sum_{i=1}^{K} \frac{\left(\sum_{j=1}^{n_i} X_{ij}\right)^2}{n_i} - \frac{\left(\sum_{i=1}^{K} \sum_{j=1}^{n_i} X_{ij}\right)^2}{N}$$

$$SSW = TSS - SSB$$

SOLVED PROBLEMS

1. The plant manager of a small Midwest fishing-equipment manufacturing plant is convinced that he can come up with a method of determining why his workers are sometimes very accurate and at other times very careless. Although he has not had much success up to this point in determining causes, he has recently read a book dealing with biorhythms. This seems to be the final explanation, so he has biorhythm charts prepared for all assembly employees. He divides the employees into four groups according to their positions on their charts: high, low, going up, or going down. He monitors the error rate (number of errors per 100 items produced) for each employee and finds the following results:

High	Low	Going Up	Going Down
2.3	3.2	3.6	1.7
3.1	1.8	2.7	2.5
1.9	2.2	2.9	2.0
2.7	2.5	3.0	1.8
2.1	1.9	3.8	2.1
3.3	2.0	3.4	2.6

a. Formulate the null hypothesis and decision rule necessary to test this situation if you want to control Type I error probability at the 1% level.

b. How many degrees of freedom are associated with the between-group estimate? How do you determine this value?

c. How many degrees of freedom are associated with the within-group estimate?

d. Set up the appropriate analysis of variance table and formulate a conclusion about the possible relationship between error rate and biorhythm level.

e. What is meant by MSW and MSB? What do they estimate?

Solution

a. **Hypotheses:**

$$H_0: \quad \mu_{\text{high}} = \mu_{\text{low}} = \mu_{\text{up}} = \mu_{\text{down}}$$

$H_A:$ Not all means are equal.

Decision Rule:

If $F > F_{\text{critical}}$, reject H_0.

If $F \leq F_{\text{critical}}$, accept H_0.

where $F_{\text{critical}} = 4.94$ (from Appendix F).

b. The degrees of freedom for the between-group estimate equal the number of groups minus 1. In this problem,

$$\text{d.f.} = K - 1 = 4 - 1$$
$$= 3$$

c. For the within-group estimate, the degrees of freedom equal the total sample size minus the number of groups. Here,

$$\text{d.f.} = N - K = 24 - 4$$
$$= 20$$

d.

Source of Variation	SS	d.f.	MS	F Ratio
Between groups	4.411	3	1.470	6.504
Within groups	4.528	20	0.226	
Total	8.939	23		

Since $6.504 > F_{\text{critical}} = 4.94$, the null hypothesis is rejected.

e. MSW is the population variance estimate based on the variation found within the groups after partitioning. MSB is the population variance estimate based on the average values found for each group.

2. An equipment rental firm is trying out three new types of oil in the transmissions of its rental front-end loaders. The maintenance manager is interested in whether any of the oils increase the time before the transmissions have to be repaired. The oils were randomly distributed among a set of new loaders; however, the numbers with each type of oil are not equal. The following data show the hours of use until repair for each front-end loader:

Oil 1	Oil 2	Oil 3
314	401	426
423	307	377
298	267	450
267	217	479
298		503
		532

a. Formulate the appropriate null hypothesis and decision rule to test this situation. Assume an alpha level of 0.01.

b. Construct the analysis of variance table for this situation and either accept or reject your hypothesis.

c. If you conclude one or more oils are associated with a longer average time to repair, determine which oils result in different means.

Solution

a. **Hypotheses**

$$H_0: \quad \mu_1 = \mu_2 = \mu_3$$

$$H_A: \quad \text{Not all means are equal.}$$

Decision Rule

If $F \leq F_{critical}$, accept H_0.

If $F > F_{critical}$, reject H_0.

where $F_{critical} = 6.93$ (from Appendix F).

b.

Source of Variation	SS	d.f.	MS	F Ratio
Between groups	83,098.75	2	41,549.38	10.35
Within groups	48,164.85	12	4,013.736	
Total	131,263.60	14		

Since $F = 10.35 > 6.93$, the null hypothesis should be rejected.

c. Since the number of observations differs between groups, we have to use Scheffé's method, where

$$\text{S range} = S\hat{\sigma}$$

$$S = \sqrt{(K - 1)F_{critical}}$$

$$\hat{\sigma} = \sqrt{\left(\frac{1}{n_1} + \frac{1}{n_2}\right)(\text{MSW})}$$

We have

$$F_{critical} = 6.93$$

so

$$S = \sqrt{(3 - 1)(6.93)} = 3.723$$

For groups 1 and 2:

$$\hat{\sigma} = \sqrt{\left(\frac{1}{5} + \frac{1}{4}\right)(4,013.736)} = 42.50$$

$$\text{S range} = 3.723(42.50) = 158.23$$

For groups 1 *and* 3:

$$\hat{\sigma} = \sqrt{\left(\frac{1}{5} + \frac{1}{6}\right)(4{,}013.736)} = 38.36$$
$$S \text{ range} = 3.723(38.36) = 142.81$$

For groups 2 *and* 3:

$$\hat{\sigma} = \sqrt{\left(\frac{1}{4} + \frac{1}{6}\right)(4{,}013.736)} = 40.89$$
$$S \text{ range} = 3.723(40.89) = 152.23$$

Also, $\overline{X}_1 = 320$, $\overline{X}_2 = 298$, and $\overline{X}_3 = 461.167$.

Contrasts		S Range	Significant?
$\lvert \overline{X}_1 - \overline{X}_2 \rvert = \lvert 320 - 298$ $\rvert = 22$		158.23	No
$\lvert \overline{X}_1 - \overline{X}_3 \rvert = \lvert 320 - 461.167 \rvert = 141.167$		142.81	No
$\lvert \overline{X}_2 - \overline{X}_3 \rvert = \lvert 298 - 461.167 \rvert = 163.167$		152.23	Yes

CONCEPTUAL QUESTIONS AND ASSIGNMENTS

22. Explain in your own terms why, in a two-tailed F test for equal population variances, the alpha level is divided by 2 before the F critical value is looked up in the F-distribution table.

23. Consider some decision-making situations in your major and describe two or more in which tests of one or more population variances are important.

24. Discuss in your own words each of the following:
    a. Within-group variation
    b. Between-group variation
    c. Total sum of squares
    d. Degrees of freedom

25. Discuss in your own words why decision makers should use analysis of variance rather than multiple two-sample t tests when testing hypotheses involving more than two populations.

26. Why is Tukey's procedure for multiple comparisons used instead of performing several t tests?

27. A one-way analysis of variance test has just been performed. The conclusion reached is that the null hypothesis stating that the population means are equal is to be accepted. What would you expect Scheffé's multiple comparison method to show if it were performed for all pairwise comparisons? Discuss.

28. Visit a manufacturing company in your area. Determine what sources of variation exist in its processes. What techniques does the company use to analyze this variation and what efforts does it make to reduce the variation?

ADDITIONAL PROBLEMS

29. The Cranston Company has a contract to provide ball bearings that average 1.25 inches in diameter, with a standard deviation not to exceed 0.04 inch.

To monitor their production, a random sample of ball bearings was selected and Cranston quality control people found the mean bearing to be 1.2552 inches with a standard deviation of 0.061 inch. If the sample size was twenty ball bearings, is Cranston meeting the requirements of the contract? Test the hypotheses using an alpha level of 0.05. Discuss your results.

30. The Phillips Company makes basketball rims used in most college arenas and professional facilities. The basketball standard calls for the rim diameters to have a standard deviation no greater than 0.10 inch. A random sample of twenty-four rims selected from the inventory in the Phillips warehouse showed a variance of 0.032. Given these sample data, what should be concluded about the variation of rim diameters? Be sure to specify the correct null and alternative hypotheses and test at an alpha level of 0.05.

31. The makers of a cattle feed supplement claim that if cattle feeders use the supplement as directed, cattle will gain an average of 1.2 pounds per day over a 30-day period. Further, they say that the range in weight gain will be 12 pounds per cow over this period.

    A test situation has been developed where a random sample of cattle will be checked for weight gain at the end of 30 days. The results of the test involving ten cattle showed a mean gain of 37 pounds, with a standard deviation of 5.2 pounds. What conclusions should be reached with respect to the two claims made by the cattle feed supplement maker? Test at the alpha level of 0.10. (*Hint:* Recall that the standard deviation can be approximated by Range/4.) Discuss your answer.

32. As purchasing agent for the Horner–Williams Company, you have primary responsibility for securing high-quality raw materials at the best possible price. One particular material that the Horner–Williams Company uses a great deal is aluminum. After careful study, you have been able to reduce the prospective vendors to two. It is unclear whether these two vendors produce aluminum that is equally durable.

    To compare durability, the recommended procedure is to put pressure on the aluminum until it cracks. The vendor whose aluminum requires the greatest average pressure will be judged to be the one that provides the most durable product.

    To carry out this test, fourteen pieces from vendor 1 and fourteen pieces from vendor 2 are selected at random. The following results in pounds per square inch were noted.

	Vendor 1	Vendor 2
	$n_1 = 14$	$n_2 = 14$
	$\overline{X}_1 = 2{,}345$ psi	$\overline{X}_2 = 2{,}411$ psi
	$S_1 = 300$	$S_2 = 250$

Before testing the hypothesis about difference in population means, suppose the purchasing agent for the company was concerned whether the assumption of equal population variances was satisfied. Based on the sample data, what would you tell him if you tested at the alpha level of 0.10? Would your conclusion differ if you tested at the alpha level of 0.02? Discuss.

33. Campbell Electronics has decided to place an advertisement on television to be shown three times during a live broadcast of the local university's football game. The sales for each of the 7 days after the ad was placed are to be compared with the sales for the 7 days immediately prior to running the ad. The following data, representing the total dollar sales each day, were collected:

Sales before the Ad	Sales after the Ad
$1,765	$2,045
1,543	2,456
2,867	2,590
1,490	1,510
2,800	2,850
1,379	1,255
2,097	2,255

 a. State the appropriate null and alternative hypotheses to be tested.
 b. What assumptions must be made about the population distributions in order to test the hypothesis using the t distribution?
 c. Based on the sample data, what conclusions should be reached with respect to average sales before versus after the advertisement?
 d. Suppose the Campbell Electronics Company wished to verify whether the assumption of equal population variances was satisfied when it performed the two-sample t test. Based on the sample data, what should it conclude if the alpha level 0.02 is used?

34. The Fister Corporation makes ribbons for computer printers. It is currently considering changing from the current model to a new model expected to last just as long on the average as the current model. However, the new model is thought to be more consistent in terms of how long the individual ribbons will last.

 To test this claim, random samples of twenty-one current-model and seventeen new-model ribbons were selected and tested on the company's quality testing equipment. The following results (measured in tens of thousands of characters) were recorded.

Current	New
$n = 21$	$n = 17$
$S = 3.45$	$S = 2.87$

 a. State the null and alternative hypotheses to be tested.
 b. Test the hypotheses at the $\alpha = 0.05$ level. Be sure to state clearly the decision rule and also discuss the results.

35. Bach Photographs is a large regional photography business with studios in two locations. The owner is interested in monitoring business activity closely at the two locations. Among the factors in which he is interested is the variation in customer orders per day for the two locations. A random sample of 11 days' orders for the two locations showed the following data:

Location A			Location B		
$444	$478	$501	$233	$127	$230
200	400	350	299	250	300
167	250	300	800	340	400
300	600		780	370	

a. State the appropriate null and alternative hypotheses.

b. Based on the sample data, test the hypotheses, using an $\alpha = 0.02$ level. Be sure to state clearly the decision rule.

36. You are responsible for installing emergency lighting in a series of state office buildings. You have bids from four manufacturers of battery-operated emergency lights. The costs are about equal, so you decide to base your decision to buy on which type lasts the longest. You receive a sample of four lights from each manufacturer, turn on the lights, and record the time before each light fails. You find the following values in hours:

Type A	Type B	Type C	Type D
24	27	21	23
21	25	20	23
25	26	25	21
22	22	22	21

Based on this evidence, can you conclude that the mean times to failure of the four types are equal? You will have to specify an alpha level.

37. A nationwide moving company is considering three different types of nylon tie-down straps. The purchasing department randomly selects straps of each type and determines their breaking strengths. The following values are found, in pounds:

Type 1	Type 2	Type 3
1,950	2,210	1,820
1,870	2,300	1,730
1,900	1,990	1,760
1,880	2,190	1,700
2,010	2,250	1,810

a. Construct the analysis of variance table for this set of data.

b. Based on your analysis, with a Type I error rate of 0.05, can you conclude that a difference exists among the types of nylon ropes?

38. A leading manufacturer of beer is considering five different types of advertising displays for a new low-calorie beer. The displays are each tested in five different randomly selected stores. A total of twenty-five stores are in the sample. The average monthly sales (in cases) and variances for the first 3 months for each type of display are as follows:

Display Type	Mean	Variance
A	98	10
B	77	8
C	84	8
D	103	11
E	91	9

Can the manufacturer conclude that it really does not matter which type of display is used? Assume an alpha level of 0.01.

39. Channel 9 television in Bextfort, Washington, recently conducted a study of television news viewers. One item of interest to Channel 9 management was whether the average age of viewers watching Channel 9 was the same as for the other two stations in Bextfort. The sample included twenty-four viewers of each station, with the following results: TSS = 2,900 and SSW = 700.

     Using an alpha level of 0.05, what should Channel 9 conclude about the average ages of news viewers of the three stations? Why?

40. Ajax Mountain Ski Company operates a small snow-skiing operation with two chair lifts. Recently some customers have complained that the lines at chair 1 are too long. The Ajax manager has collected the following data, which represent the number of people in line at the two chair lifts at randomly observed times during a week:

Chair 1	Chair 2
10	14
3	13
14	19
7	7
19	11
33	9
28	12
11	13
26	15

a. Use a two-sample t test to determine whether there is a significant difference in the average numbers of people waiting at the two lifts. Test this at the alpha level of 0.05.

b. Use analysis of variance to test the null hypothesis that the average numbers waiting at the two chair lifts are equal.

c. What observations can you make about the relationship between the two-sample t test and two-sample analysis of variance?

41. The Savouy Corporation recently purchased a bicycle manufacturing plant formerly owned by the American Traveling Company. American had been outfitting its bikes with tires produced by the Leach Corporation. Savouy management is considering whether to stay with Leach tires or to change to another brand. Three other brands are being considered, all of which cost

about the same as the Leach tire. The criterion for tire selection will be average tread life.

Samples of twenty have been selected from the Leach tires and from brands A, B, and C. The following results were found:

$$\overline{X}_{Leach} = 111 \text{ h} \qquad \overline{X}_A = 126 \text{ h} \qquad \overline{X}_B = 100 \text{ h} \qquad \overline{X}_C = 105 \text{ h}$$

$$TSS = 19,620$$

(Note that $\overline{X}$ indicates the average hours of use until the tread was reduced to a specified level.) Using an alpha level of 0.05, test that there is no difference in average tread life for the four brands.

42. A ski resort in Idaho has been charged with discriminating against some nationalities of ski instructors in the wages that they are allowed to earn from private lessons. Instructors of three nationalities teach at this resort: Canadians, Austrians, and Germans. Random samples of six Canadians, eight Austrians, and seven Germans were selected. The following statistics were recorded:

$$\overline{X}_{Canadian} = \$3,111 \qquad \overline{X}_{Austrian} = \$2,005 \qquad \overline{X}_{German} = \$3,511$$

$$TSS = 18,328,128$$

Based on these values, what do you conclude about average salaries for ski instructors at this ski resort? Use an alpha level of 0.05.

43. The Environmental Protection Agency (EPA) performs various tests on automobiles for mileage analysis. Recently, the EPA selected a random sample of people who had purchased a new car within the previous 6-month period. Of the twenty-four people surveyed, eight had purchased big luxury cars, eight medium-sized cars, and eight compact cars. The following data represent the difference between these car owners' mileage compared with the EPA mileage rating as posted on the car window when the car was bought:

Luxury Cars	Medium-Sized Cars	Compact Cars
3.5	3.8	1.5
7.4	4.5	2.3
5.0	3.5	0.5
2.0	3.0	−2.0
3.6	2.7	2.5
5.8	4.0	−3.0
8.0	5.0	3.0
7.0	−1.5	−2.0

Note that positive values indicate that the actual mileage was lower than advertised by the sticker on the car window; negative values indicate the actual mileage exceeded the EPA rating on the sticker.

a. Based on an alpha level of 0.05, what can you conclude about the three types of cars with respect to the average differences between actual mileage and EPA-sticker mileage ratings?

b. If a difference in means is indicated by the test performed in part **a**, which populations of cars have different means? Discuss.

44. The Wicks Advertising Agency recently ran a coupon marketing campaign for one of its retail clients in Denver. Coupons were mailed to several thousand households. In addition, coupons were placed in two daily papers. The coupon offered a 15% discount on any purchases made with the coupon. The Wicks Agency is interested in knowing whether the volume of purchases differs on the average depending on the source from which the customer obtained the coupon. The marketing executive in charge of this client had one of her staff personnel select a random sample of coupons from each source and keep track of the volume of the purchases that accompanied that coupon. The following data represent the dollar amounts rounded to the nearest dollar:

Mailing	Paper 1	Paper 2
38	20	14
27	19	16
33	20	11
12	10	9
33	15	
21	14	
13		
25		

a. Based on the sample data, what can be concluded about the average purchase amounts by customers using coupons from the three sources? Test using an alpha level of 0.05.

b. Which pairs of coupon sources have different population means? Use the appropriate method of multiple comparisons to answer this question.

45. Referring to Problem 44, form the S range using Scheffé's method of multiple comparison and compare this with the T range computed in Problem 44. Which method is appropriate to use and why? Also compare the values of the T range and the S range and comment on what the difference means.

46. The National Basketball Association (NBA) recently performed a survey of fans attending a Celtics game at the Boston Garden Arena. The survey collected data on money spent on concessions at the game. Four types of respondents were identified by the survey: students under 18 years, students over 18 years, professional people, and blue-collar workers. These people, who were selected at random, were observed and the dollar volume spent on concessions at the game recorded. These data are shown as follows:

Under 18	Over 18	Professional	Blue-Collar
$3.10	$2.40	$2.80	$4.20
2.45	2.70	1.25	3.75
3.00	1.75	0.00	5.90
4.50	2.00	2.30	4.20
3.00	0.00	1.50	2.80
	3.00	1.20	6.20
	2.30	0.00	3.00
		2.10	4.00
		0.00	1.25
		4.10	

a. Based on these data, what should the NBA conclude about the average expenditures on concessions by the four groups represented? Test at the alpha level of 0.05.
b. If the test performed in part **a** concluded that there is a difference in the mean amount spent on concessions among the four groups, which groups have different means? Perform the appropriate pairwise test method. Discuss.

DATABASE PROBLEMS

The following questions and problems pertain directly to the State Department of Transportation case study and database introduced in Chapter 1. The questions and problems were written assuming that you will have access to a computer and appropriate statistical software. The database contains 100 observations and seventeen variables. *Assume that the data were collected using a simple random sampling process.*

1. Herb Kriner attended a conference last fall that indicated that female drivers tended to be relatively less variable in the number of convictions (X_5) than male drivers. He would like you to test this claim at the $\alpha = 0.05$ level and prepare a short letter confirming or rejecting the claim based on the sample information from this state. Indicate whether your conclusion can be applied to other states and indicate why or why not.
2. Herb Kriner would like you to test the hypothesis that there is no difference in average years of education for drivers with various employment statuses. Test using an $\alpha = 0.05$ level.
3. Use analysis of variance to test whether there is a difference in average age of male versus female drivers in this state. Then do the same test using a two-sample t test. Compare the results and write a short memo that discusses the relationship between the two approaches.
4. Considering only those drivers who have insured vehicles, is there a difference in average years lived in the state depending on their knowledge of the law? Test at the $\alpha = 0.05$ level and discuss your results.

ADDITIONAL DATABASE PROBLEMS

The questions and problems in this section reference the various databases that accompany this text and which are described in Chapter 1. Your instructor has been provided a diskette with these databases. It is expected that you will be using computer software to access these data and to perform the required calculations and graphs.

DATABASE: **CITIES** (*Refer to the database description in Chapter 1.*)

1. Create a new variable, X_9, which is coded 1 if the labor market stress index is between 100 and 110 inclusive, 2 if the index is between 111 and 120 inclusive, and 3 if it is higher than 120.
    a. Test the hypothesis that there is no difference in average 1989 unemployment rates for cities with the three different labor market stress index levels. Use an $\alpha = 0.05$ level to test the hypothesis. Make sure you state the null and alternative hypotheses and show the appropriate test results.
    b. If it is appropriate, use either Tukey's or Scheffé's (you determine which one) multiple comparison procedure to determine which populations have different means.
2. Suppose it has been claimed that the annual earnings for manufacturing workers is more variable than the earnings for white-collar workers. Assuming that the data represent random samples from the two populations, test the appropriate null and alternative hypotheses at the $\alpha = 0.05$ level. Discuss your conclusions.

DATABASE: **FAST100** (*Refer to the database description in Chapter 1.*)

1. Use the sample data in this database to determine whether there is any difference in the average total sales over the previous four quarters for companies trading on the three stock exchanges. State the appropriate null and alternative hypotheses. If the null hypothesis is rejected, use the appropriate method of multiple comparison to determine which populations have different means. Discuss your results. Test at the $\alpha = 0.05$ level.
2. Based on these sample data, is there a difference in average stock price as of 9/6/91 for companies trading on the three stock exchanges? Assume that these data reflect random samples from the three stock exchanges. Test at the $\alpha = 0.10$ level. If the null hypothesis is rejected, use the appropriate multiple comparison test to determine which populations have different means.
3. Based on these sample data, is there a difference in average price earnings ratio over the past four quarters for companies trading on the three stock exchanges? Assume that these data reflect random samples from the three

stock exchanges. Test at the $\alpha = 0.05$ level. If the null hypothesis is rejected, use the appropriate multiple comparison test to determine which populations have different means.

DATABASE: **PACRIM** (*Refer to the database description in Chapter 1.*)

1. Based on these sample data, can it be concluded that there is a difference in average 1989 annual sales (X_2) for companies located in Japan, South Korea, or Australia? Test the appropriate null and alternative hypotheses at the $\alpha = 0.05$ level. Be sure to discuss your conclusions. If the null hypothesis is rejected, use the appropriate method of multiple comparison to determine which countries have different average sales in 1989.

2. Based on these sample data, can it be concluded that there is a difference in average year-end stockholder's equity for companies located in Japan, South Korea, and Australia? Test the appropriate null and alternative hypotheses at the $\alpha = 0.05$ level. Be sure to discuss your conclusions. If the null hypothesis is rejected, use the appropriate method of multiple comparison to determine which countries have different means.

3. Group the data from Taiwan, Malaysia, and New Zealand together. Can these data be used to show that there is a significant difference in average number of employees for companies in Japan, Australia, South Korea, or the combined countries? Test at the $\alpha = 0.05$ level. Use the appropriate method of multiple comparison to determine which countries have different population means. Discuss your results.

DATABASE: **TRUCKS** (*Refer to the database description in Chapter 1.*)

1. Based on the sample data, is there a difference in average WIM gross weight for trucks weighed in the different months? State the appropriate null and alternative hypotheses and test at the $\alpha = 0.05$ level.

2. Break the data into three groups based on vehicle speed, as follows:

   Group 1: Under 35 mph
   Group 2: 35–45 mph
   Group 3: 46–55 mph
   Group 4: Over 45 mph

   Based on these sample data, can it be concluded that there is no difference in mean POE gross weight for trucks traveling at the four different speeds? Test using an $\alpha = 0.05$ level. If a difference is detected through the ANOVA test, then use the appropriate method of multiple comparison to determine which groups have different means.

3. Suppose it has been stated by representatives of the Idaho transportation department that there is no difference in the variation of gross vehicle weights on the WIM scale or the POE scale. Based on these sample data, can this statement be supported or refuted? State the appropriate null and alternative hypotheses and test at the $\alpha = 0.05$ level. Discuss your results.

CASES

12-A   Consumer Information Association

Yolanda Carson is a newly hired research assistant for the Consumer Information Association. The association is a nonprofit group whose major purpose is to supply information necessary to help consumers make better-informed decisions. Yolanda has been assigned to work with the group studying consumer practices in the banking industry.

Yolanda is aware of studies that indicate that the interest banks charge for loans is related to demographic factors such as the size of the city in which the banks are located and whether the state allows branch banks. She has been asked to determine whether there is a difference in consumer loan charges between major sections of the country.

Yolanda has been assured the cooperation of the American Banking Institute and has been given access to any data the institute has. However, she knows that loan charges may depend on many factors and feels compelled to study banks firsthand. In particular, she has decided to randomly select banks in all parts of the country and apply for an automobile loan at each bank selected. She has decided to make the test during two time periods 6 months apart.

Since consumer interest rates have been changing rapidly lately, Yolanda has recorded all rates in terms of the prime rate plus a certain percentage. (The prime rate is the rate large banks charge their largest corporate customers.) In the first test, Yolanda found the following values charged:

Northeast	Southeast	Midwest	West
Prime + 3.2%	Prime + 2.7%	Prime + 3.4%	Prime + 3.7%
2.9	2.9	3.5	3.6
2.8	3.0	2.9	3.6
3.5	2.9	3.7	3.9
3.4	2.8	3.4	4.0
4.0	2.5	3.5	3.8
3.2	2.7	3.0	3.4
	2.9		3.8

The executive director of the Consumer Information Association is going to be holding a news conference in a few days to discuss the work the organization has been doing. He would like to be able to cite Yolanda's study as an example of its services.

12-B   American Testing Services

When P. T. Miller formed American Testing Services he anticipated that there was a market for consulting services in the market-research area. By the amount of work that his firm has had during the past 3 years, he is sure he was correct.

Recently P. T. was approached by the Convestal Corporation to perform an analysis of the five running shoes Convestal makes. The basic research question to be answered was whether people who own Convestal running shoes share an equal opinion (on the average) of the shoes without regard to the particular type or style of Convestal shoe they own. If not, then the company wants to determine which styles seem to be most liked, and which seem to be most disliked, by the customers.

P. T. suggested that Convestal ask a random sample of shoe customers to rate their shoes on a scale of 1 to 100, with 100 being the highest. The following data represent the results of the sampling:

Style 1	Style 2	Style 3	Style 4	Style 5
84	67	78	60	88
54	56	79	64	79
88	70	89	60	84
90	67	84	72	78
88	59	78	77	68
76	66	84	70	70
	70	90	66	80
	56	85	70	80
	70		59	78
	67		70	84
				75

What should P. T. Miller conclude?

REFERENCES

Berenson, Mark L., and Levine, David M. *Basic Business Statistics Concepts and Applications,* 5th edition. Englewood Cliffs, New Jersey: Prentice-Hall, 1992.

Bowerman, Bruce L., and O'Connell, Richard T. *Linear Statistical Models,* 2nd edition. Boston: PWS-Kent, 1990.

Daniel, Wayne W., and Terrell, James C. *Business Statistics for Management and Economics,* 6th edition. Boston: Houghton Mifflin, 1992.

Iman, Ronald L., and Conover, W. J. *Modern Business Statistics,* 2nd edition. New York: Wiley, 1989.

Levin, Richard I., and Rubin, David S. *Statistics for Management,* 5th edition. Englewood Cliffs, New Jersey: Prentice-Hall, 1991.

Introduction to Regression

and Correlation Analysis

WHY DECISION MAKERS NEED TO KNOW

The statistical techniques discussed thus far have all dealt with a single variable. For example, in Chapter 8, where the fundamentals of statistical estimation were introduced, decision makers were interested in estimating values such as the average weight of a can of corn or the average income of families in a certain geographical area. Chapters 9 through 12 introduced the basic concepts of hypothesis testing. Again the hypothesis involved a single variable from one or more populations.

Although many business applications involve only one variable, in other instances decision makers need to consider the relationship between two or more variables. For example, the sales manager for a tool company may notice his sales are not the same each month. He also knows that the company's advertising expenditures vary from month to month. This manager would likely be interested in learning whether a relationship exists between tool sales and advertising. If he could successfully define the relationship, he might use this information to improve predictions of monthly sales and, therefore, do a better job of planning for his company.

This chapter introduces linear regression and correlation analysis. These techniques are important to decision makers who need to determine the relationship between two variables. Regression and correlation analysis are two of the most often applied statistical tools for decision making.

CHAPTER OBJECTIVES

This chapter will introduce linear regression and correlation techniques. Examples will be used to demonstrate the uses of regression analysis for prediction and description.

This chapter will also show how decision makers can determine whether a significant linear relationship exists between variables. It shows how to determine whether regression analysis is actually useful in a practical decision-making situation. In addition, it shows how to develop confidence intervals for the estimates made using regression analysis.

Finally, this chapter will introduce the assumptions behind regression analysis and discuss some problems that might occur if regression analysis is incorrectly used.

STUDENT OBJECTIVES

After studying the material in this chapter, you should be able to do the following:

1. Calculate the correlation between two variables.
2. Determine whether the correlation is significant.
3. Calculate the linear regression equation for a set of data and know the basic assumptions behind regression analysis.
4. Determine whether a regression model is significant.
5. Develop confidence intervals for the regression coefficients.
6. Interpret the confidence intervals for the regression coefficients.
7. Recognize regression analysis applications for purposes of prediction and description.
8. Apply regression analysis techniques to situations involving two or more independent variables.

13-1 STATISTICAL RELATIONSHIPS BETWEEN TWO VARIABLES

Carl Markowitz has just completed his first year as director of personnel for Software Accessories, a company that specializes in developing and marketing computer packages for small businesses, such as dry cleaners and gas service stations. These smaller companies have mostly been neglected by the larger software development firms. While Software Accessories has been profitable, Carl has been concerned about the rapid turnover in its sales force and has implemented an exit interview procedure for departing sales men and women. In the course of these interviews, he discovered a major concern with the perceived fairness of the wage structure.

Software Accessories has a two-part wage structure, a base salary and a commission based on quarterly sales. On the average, about half of the total wages paid come from the base salary but some people do much better with commissions than others. The idea behind having such a large percentage of total wages associated with commissions is to allow people who want to sell to make the most money. The concern expressed by departing employees is that the training provided on the company's products is so minimal that starting employees cannot make an adequate wage for several years until they learn the product line through experience. Consequently, those with family responsibilities are forced to look for other opportunities.

Carl has decided to look at the relationship between total yearly sales and years with the company. He gathers data from a sample of twelve sales representatives. These data are shown in Table 13-1. By looking at the sample data, Carl is convinced that a relationship exists between total sales and years with the company. He needs to determine what the relationship will tell him.

Figure 13-1 shows **scatter plots** that depict several potential relationships between a dependent variable, Y, and an independent variable, X. A **dependent variable** is the variable whose variation we wish to explain. An **independent variable** is a variable used to explain variation in the dependent variable. For the Software Accessories example, years with the company is the independent variable and total sales the dependent variable. Figures 13-1(a) and (b) are examples of *linear* relationships between X and Y. This means that as the independent variable, X, changes, the dependent variable, Y, tends to change systematically in a straight-line manner. Note that this systematic change can be positive (Y increases as X increases) or negative (Y decreases as X increases). Also notice that the points do not need to fall exactly on a straight line for a linear relationship to be exhibited.

Figures 13-1(c) and (d) are examples of *curvilinear* statistical relationships between variables X and Y. Figures 13-1(e) and (f) are examples showing *no*

TABLE (13-1)

Sales Representative Data for the Software Accessories Example

Years With Company	Total Sales ($ thousands)
3	487
5	445
2	272
8	641
2	187
6	440
7	346
1	238
4	312
2	269
9	655
6	563

FIGURE 13-1

Two-Variable
Relationships

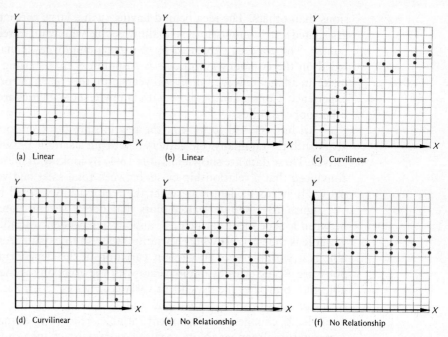

(a) Linear   (b) Linear   (c) Curvilinear

(d) Curvilinear   (e) No Relationship   (f) No Relationship

relationship between X and Y. That is, when X increases, sometimes Y decreases and other times Y increases.

The three situations shown in Figure 13-1 are all possibilities for describing the relationship between sales and advertising for Software Accessories. The first step in determining the appropriate relationship is to plot the data shown in Table 13-1. This plot, shown in Figure 13-2, indicates that total sales and years with the company are related. However, the strength of this relationship is questionable. That is, how close do the points come to falling on a straight line? The scatter plot

FIGURE 13-2

Plot of Sales
Versus Years with
the Company for
the Software
Accessories
Example

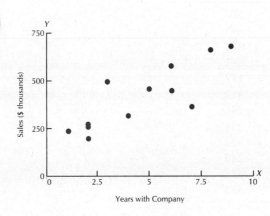

provides a visualization for the answer to this question, but we also need a quantitative measure of the strength of the linear relationship between two variables. The next section introduces a measure called the *correlation coefficient*.

SKILL DEVELOPMENT PROBLEMS FOR **SECTION 13-1**

The following exercises will help you learn the concepts presented in Section 13-1.

1. Develop a scatter plot for the following data:

Y	X
100	88
200	120
150	200
75	100
140	100
160	90
230	125

Based on the scatter plot, describe what, if any, relationship exists between these two variables.

2. Develop scatter plots for the variable Y against variables X_1 and X_2.

Y	X_1	X_2
25	4	7
29	3	9
40	1	13
20	6	6
24	5	8
18	7	5
30	3	11
25	3	5

Describe what, if any, relationship is present in each of the scatter plots.

3. If two variables have a negative linear relationship, what will the value of X tend to do when the corresponding value of Y increases substantially? Show with an example.

4. If the scatter plot of two variables shows a weak positive linear relationship, what will be the general change in Y associated with a downward change in X? Show with an example.

5. If a scatter plot shows that two variables have a curvilinear relationship showing Y increasing at a decreasing rate as X increases, what might the scatter plot look like? Can you think of two variables that might exhibit such a relationship?

13-2

CORRELATION ANALYSIS

The quantitative measure of strength in the linear relationship between two variables is called the **simple correlation coefficient.** The correlation coefficient for two variables (in the case of Software Accessories, sales and years with the company) can be estimated from sample data using equation 13-1:

$$r = \frac{\Sigma(X - \overline{X})(Y - \overline{Y})}{\sqrt{[\Sigma(X - \overline{X})^2][\Sigma(Y - \overline{Y})^2]}}$$

13-1

or by using an algebraic equivalent formula (equation 13-2) more suited to calculators:

$$r = \frac{n\Sigma XY - \Sigma X\Sigma Y}{\sqrt{[n(\Sigma X^2) - (\Sigma X)^2][n(\Sigma Y^2) - (\Sigma Y)^2]}}$$

13-2

where

r = Simple correlation coefficient

n = Sample size

X = Value of the independent variable

Y = Value of the dependent variable

The correlation coefficient can range from a perfect positive correlation, $+1.0$, to a perfect negative correlation, -1.0. If two variables have no linear relationship, the correlation between them is 0. Consequently, the more the correlation differs from 0, the stronger the linear relationship between the two variables. The sign of the correlation coefficient indicates the direction of the relationship, but does not aid in determining the strength.

Figure 13-3 illustrates some possible correlations between two variables. Note that for the correlation coefficient to equal plus or minus 1.0, all the (X, Y) points must be perfectly aligned. The more the points depart from a straight line, the weaker (closer to 0.0) the correlation between the two variables.

The scatter plot of sales and years with company for Software Accessories (Figure 13-2) indicates a *positive* linear relationship, but *not* a *perfect* linear relationship. Table 13-2 lists the calculations necessary to determine the correlation coefficient. The calculated correlation coefficient, r, is 0.8325.

FIGURE 13-3

Correlations
Between Two
Variables

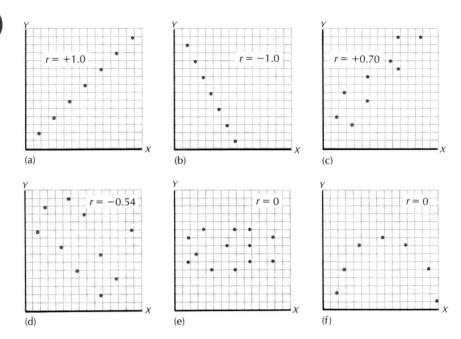

(a) $r = +1.0$

(b) $r = -1.0$

(c) $r = +0.70$

(d) $r = -0.54$

(e) $r = 0$

(f) $r = 0$

TABLE 13-2

Correlation
Coefficient
Calculations for
the Software
Accessories
Example

Sales Y	Years X	YX	Y^2	X^2
487	3	1,461	237,169	9
445	5	2,225	198,025	25
272	2	544	73,984	4
641	8	5,128	410,881	64
187	2	374	34,969	4
440	6	2,640	193,600	36
346	7	2,422	119,716	49
238	1	238	56,644	1
312	4	1,248	97,344	16
269	2	538	72,361	4
655	9	5,895	429,025	81
563	6	3,378	316,969	36
$\Sigma = 4,855$	$\Sigma = 55$	$\Sigma = 26,091$	$\Sigma = 2,240,687$	$\Sigma = 329$

$$r = \frac{n\Sigma XY - \Sigma X\Sigma Y}{\sqrt{[n(\Sigma X^2) - (\Sigma X)^2][n(\Sigma Y^2) - (\Sigma Y)^2]}}$$

$$= \frac{12(26,091) - (55)(4,855)}{\sqrt{[12(329) - (55)^2][12(2,240,687) - (4,855)^2]}}$$

$$= 0.8325$$

Although a correlation coefficient of 0.8325 seems quite high (relative to 0), remember that this value is based on a sample of twelve data points and there is always a chance that the sample may provide misleading information due to extreme sampling error. To determine whether the linear relationship between sales and years with the company is significant, we must test whether the sample data support or refute the hypothesis that the population correlation coefficient, ρ, is 0. The hypothesis that the population correlation coefficient is 0 is tested by computing the t statistic, using equation 13-3:

$$t = \frac{r}{\sqrt{\dfrac{1 - r^2}{n - 2}}}$$

13-3

where

t = Number of standard deviations r is from 0

r = Simple correlation coefficient

n = Sample size

The degrees of freedom for this test are $n - 2$.

Figure 13-4 shows the test for an alpha level of 0.05. Based on these sample data, we should conclude there is a significant linear relationship between years of experience and total sales for Software Accessories sales representatives.

The t test for determining whether the population correlation is significantly different from 0 assumes that the data are interval or ratio level and that two variables (Y and X) are distributed as a *bivariate normal*. Although the formal mathematical representation is beyond the scope of this text, *two variables are bivariate normal if their joint distribution is normally distributed.* Although the t test assumes a bivariate normal distribution, it is robust—that is, correct inferences can be reached even with slight departures from the normal-distribution assumption. (See Neter and Wasserman's *Applied Linear Statistical Models* for further discussion of bivariate normal distributions.)

CAUSE-AND-EFFECT INTERPRETATIONS

Care must be used when interpreting the correlation results. Even though we found a significant linear relationship between years of experience and sales for the Software Accessories sales force, the correlation does not imply cause and

FIGURE 13-4

Correlation
Significance Test
for the Software
Accessories
Example

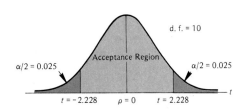

Hypotheses:

$H_0: \rho = 0$
$H_A: \rho \neq 0$

$\alpha = 0.05$

d. f. = 10

$\alpha/2 = 0.025$ Acceptance Region $\alpha/2 = 0.025$

$t = -2.228$ $\rho = 0$ $t = 2.228$ t

Decision Rule:

If $t > t_{\text{critical}} = 2.228$, reject H_0.
If $t < t_{\text{critical}} = -2.228$, reject H_0.
Otherwise, do not reject H_0.

Since $4.752 > 2.228$, reject H_0.
The calculated t value is

$$t = \frac{r}{\sqrt{\dfrac{1 - r^2}{n - 2}}} = \frac{0.8325}{\sqrt{\dfrac{1 - 0.6931}{10}}}$$

$$= 4.752$$

effect. Although a change in experience may, in fact, cause sales to change, simply because the two variables are correlated does not guarantee a cause-and-effect situation. Two seemingly unconnected variables will often be highly correlated. For example, over a period of time, teachers' salaries in North Dakota might be highly correlated with the price of grapes in Spain. Yet we doubt that a change in grape prices will *cause* a corresponding change in salaries for teachers in North Dakota, or vice versa. When a correlation exists between two seemingly unrelated variables, the correlation is **spurious.** You should take great care to avoid basing conclusions on spurious correlations.

Carl Markowitz has a logical reason to believe that years experience with the company and total sales are related. That is, sales theory and customer feedback hold that product knowledge is a major component in successfully marketing a product. However, a statistically significant correlation alone does not prove that this cause-and-effect relationship exists.

SKILL DEVELOPMENT PROBLEMS FOR **SECTION 13-2**

The following exercises will help you learn the concepts presented in Section 13-2.

6. You are given the following data for variables X and Y:

X	Y
20	16
18	12
24	18
20	17
22	21
14	10
18	10

  a. Plot these variables in scatter plot format. Based on this plot, what type of relationship appears to exist between the two variables?

  b. Compute the correlation coefficient for these sample data. Indicate what the correlation coefficient measures.

  c. Test to determine whether the population correlation coefficient is 0. Use the $\alpha = 0.05$ level to conduct the test. Be sure to state the null and alternative hypotheses and show the test and decision rule clearly.

7. You are given the following data for variables X and Y:

X	Y
3.0	1.5
2.0	0.5
2.5	1.0
3.0	1.8
2.5	1.2
4.0	2.2
1.5	0.4
1.0	0.3
2.0	1.3
2.5	1.0

  a. Plot these variables in scatter plot format. Based on this plot, what type of relationship appears to exist between the two variables?

  b. Compute the correlation coefficient for these sample data. Indicate what the correlation coefficient measures.

  c. Test to determine whether the population correlation coefficient is 0. Use the $\alpha = 0.05$ level to conduct the test. Be sure to state the null and alternative hypotheses and show the test and decision rule clearly.

8. A sample of thirty-two people was randomly selected and height and weight measurements were made for each person. The correlation coefficient for the two variables was 0.80.

a. Discuss in your own words what the $r = 0.80$ means with respect to the variables height and weight.

b. Using an $\alpha = 0.10$ level, test to determine whether the population correlation coefficient is significantly different from 0. Be sure to state the null and alternative hypotheses.

9. A random sample of fifty bank accounts was selected from a local branch bank. The account balance and the number of deposits and withdrawals during the past month were the two variables recorded. The correlation coefficient for the two variables was -0.23.

a. Discuss what the $r = -0.23$ measures. Make sure to frame your discussion in terms of the two variables discussed here.

b. Using an $\alpha = 0.05$ level, test to determine whether there is a significant linear relationship between account balance and the number of transactions to the account during the past month. State the null and alternative hypotheses and show the decision rule.

13-3 SIMPLE LINEAR REGRESSION ANALYSIS

Carl Markowitz has determined that the relationship between years of experience with Software Accessories and total sales is linear, and statistically significant, based on the correlation analysis performed in the previous section. Since hiring and training costs have been increasing, he would like to use this relationship to help formulate a more acceptable wage package for the sales force.

The statistical method Carl uses to analyze the relationship between years of experience and total sales is *regression analysis*. Where there are only two variables, a dependent variable such as sales and an independent variable such as years with the company, the technique is **simple regression analysis**. When the relationship between the dependent variable and the independent variable is linear, the technique is *simple linear regression*.

The objective of simple linear regression (which we shall call regression analysis) is to represent the relationship between X and Y with a model of the form shown in equation 13-4:

$$Y_i = \beta_0 + \beta_1 X_i + e_i \qquad \text{13-4}$$

where

Y_i = Value of the dependent variable

X_i = Value of the independent variable

β_0 = Y-intercept

β_1 = Slope of the regression line

e_i = Error term, or residual (i.e., the difference between the actual Y value and the value of Y predicted by the model)

FIGURE **13-5**

Graphical Display
of Linear
Regression
Assumptions

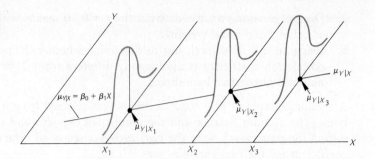

The simple linear regression model described in equation 13-4 has four assumptions:

1. Individual values of the dependent variable, Y, are statistically independent of one another.
2. For a given X value, there can exist many values of Y. Further, the distribution of possible Y values for any X value is normal.
3. The distributions of possible Y values have equal variances for all values of X.
4. The means of the dependent variable, Y, for all specified values of the independent variable, ($\mu_{Y|X}$), can be connected by a straight line called the *population regression model*.

Figure 13-5 illustrates assumptions 2, 3, and 4. The regression model (straight line) connects the averages of Y for each level of the independent variable, X. The regression line (like any other straight line) is determined by two values, β_0 and β_1. These values are the **regression coefficients**. Value β_0 identifies the Y-intercept and β_1 the slope of the regression line. Under the regression assumptions, the coefficients define the true population model. For each observation, the actual value of the dependent variable, Y, for any X, is the sum of two components, as shown by equation 13-5:

$$Y_i = \underbrace{\beta_0 + \beta_1 X_i}_{\text{Linear component}} + \underbrace{e_i}_{\text{Random error component}}$$

13-5

The random error component, e_i, may be positive or negative, depending on whether a single value of Y for a given X falls above or below the regression line.

MEANING OF THE REGRESSION COEFFICIENTS

Coefficient β_1, the slope of the regression line, measures the average change in the dependent variable, Y, for each unit change in X. The slope can be either positive or negative, depending on the relationship between X and Y. For example, a positive slope of 12 ($\beta_1 = 12$) means that for a one-unit increase in X, we can expect an average twelve-unit increase in Y. Correspondingly, if the slope is negative 12 ($\beta_1 = -12$), we can expect an average decrease of twelve units in Y for a one-unit increase in X.

The Y-intercept, β_0, indicates the mean value of Y when X is 0. However, this interpretation holds only if the population could have X values of 0. When this cannot occur, β_0 does not have a meaningful interpretation in the regression model.

Carl Markowitz of Software Accessories has a sample of twelve sales representatives' data available, and he has been able to establish a significant linear relationship between years of experience and total sales using correlation analysis. Now he would like to estimate the *true* linear relationship between years of experience and sales by determining the regression model for the twelve data points.

Figure 13-6 shows the scatter plot for years with the company and sales. Carl needs to use the sample points to estimate β_0 and β_1, the true intercept and slope of the line representing the relationship between the two variables. Statistical theory shows that the best estimates for β_0 and β_1 are the intercept and slope formed from the available sample data. Thus, the *regression line* through the sample data is the estimate of the population regression line. However, there are an infinite number of possible regression lines for a set of points. For example, Figure 13-7 shows three different lines that pass through Software Accessories sales representative experience and sales points. These are but a few of the lines that could have been drawn. Which line should be used to estimate the true regression model?

Since so many possible regression lines exist for a sample of data, we must establish a criterion for selecting the best line. The criterion used is the *least squares criterion*. According to the **least squares criterion,** the best regression line is the one that minimizes the sum of squared distances between the observed (X, Y) points and the regression line. Note that the distance between an (X, Y) point and the regression line is called the *residual* or error.

FIGURE 13-6

Plot of Sales Versus Years with Company for the Software Accessories Example

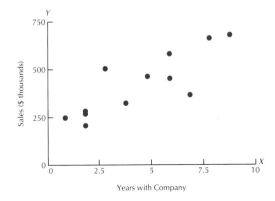

Years with Company

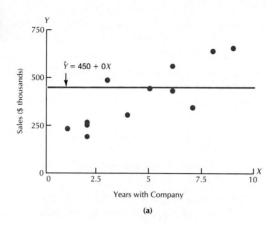

(a)

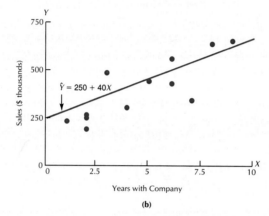

(b)

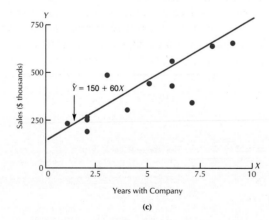

(c)

FIGURE   **13-8**

Computation of
Regression Error
for the Software
Accessories
Example

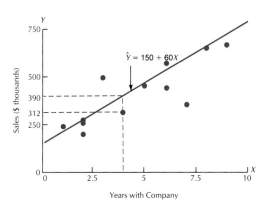

Figure 13-8 shows how the error is calculated when X equals 4 years and the regression line is $\hat{Y} = 150 + 60X$ (where $\hat{Y}$ is the estimated sales value). Notice that when $X = 4$, the difference between the regression line value, $\hat{Y} = 390$, and the observed, $Y = 312$, is 78. Thus, the residual for this line when $X = 4$ is 78.

Table 13-3 shows the calculated errors and sum of squared errors for each of the three regression lines shown in Figure 13-7. Of these three potential regression models, the line with the equation $\hat{Y} = 150 + 60X$ has the smallest sum of squared errors. However, is this line the best of all possible lines? That is, would

$$\sum_{i=1}^{n} (Y_i - \hat{Y}_i)^2 = 97{,}667$$

be smaller than for any other line? One way to determine this is to calculate the sum of squared errors for other regression lines. However, since there are an infinite number of these lines, this approach is not feasible. Fortunately, through the use of calculus, equations can be derived to directly determine the slope and intercept estimates such that $\Sigma(Y_i - \hat{Y})^2$ is minimized.

Let the estimated regression model be of the form shown in equation 13-6:

$$\hat{Y}_i = b_0 + b_1 X_i$$

13-6

where

$\hat{Y}_i$ = Estimated, or predicted, Y value

b_0 = Unbiased estimate of the regression intercept

b_1 = Unbiased estimate of the regression slope

X_i = Value of the independent variable

TABLE 13-3

Sum of Squared
Errors for Three
Linear Equations
for Software
Accessories
Example

From Figure 13-7(a):
$\hat{Y} = 450 + 0X$

X	$\hat{Y}$	Y	$Y - \hat{Y}$	$(Y - \hat{Y})^2$
3	450	487	37	1,369
5	450	445	−5	25
2	450	272	−178	31,684
8	450	641	191	36,481
2	450	187	−263	69,169
6	450	440	−10	100
7	450	346	−104	10,816
1	450	238	−212	44,944
4	450	312	−138	19,044
2	450	269	−181	32,761
9	450	655	205	42,025
6	450	563	113	12,769
				$\Sigma = $ 301,187

From Figure 13-7(b):
$\hat{Y} = 250 + 40X$

X	$\hat{Y}$	Y	$Y - \hat{Y}$	$(Y - \hat{Y})^2$
3	370	487	117	13,689
5	450	445	−5	25
2	330	272	−58	3,364
8	570	641	71	5,041
2	330	187	−143	20,449
6	490	440	−50	2,500
7	530	346	−184	33,856
1	290	238	−52	2,704
4	410	312	−98	9,604
2	330	269	−61	3,721
9	610	655	45	2,025
6	490	563	73	5,329
				$\Sigma = $ 102,307

From Figure 13-7(c):
$\hat{Y} = 150 + 60X$

X	$\hat{Y}$	Y	$Y - \hat{Y}$	$(Y - \hat{Y})^2$
3	330	487	157	24,649
5	450	445	−5	25
2	270	272	2	4
8	630	641	11	121
2	270	187	−83	6,889
6	510	440	−70	4,900
7	570	346	−224	50,176
1	210	238	28	784
4	390	312	−78	6,084
2	270	269	−1	1
9	690	655	−35	1,225
6	510	563	53	2,809
				$\Sigma = $ 97,667

Then the values of b_0 and b_1 are calculated by equations 13-7, 13-8, and 13-9:

$$b_1 = \frac{\Sigma (X - \overline{X})(Y - \overline{Y})}{\Sigma (X - \overline{X})^2} \qquad \text{13-7}$$

$$b_1 = \frac{\Sigma XY - \dfrac{\Sigma X \Sigma Y}{n}}{\Sigma X^2 - \dfrac{(\Sigma X)^2}{n}} \qquad \text{13-8}$$

and

$$b_0 = \overline{Y} - b_1 \overline{X} \qquad \text{13-9}$$

Table 13-4 shows the calculations necessary to estimate the population line for Software Accessories. In this case, the best regression line, given the least squares criterion is

$$\hat{Y}_i = 175.8289 + 49.9101X_i$$

Table 13-5 shows the predicted sales values and the errors and squared errors associated with this best regression line. The errors are called **residuals**. From Table 13-5, the sum of the squared residuals is 84,834.29. This is the smallest sum of squared residuals possible. Any other regression line through these twelve (X, Y) points will produce a larger sum of squared residuals.

Figure 13-9 shows the scatter plot of sales and years of experience and the least squares regression line for Software Accessories.

LEAST SQUARES REGRESSION PROPERTIES

Table 13-5 and Figure 13-9 illustrate several important properties of least squares regression:

1. The sum of the residuals from the least squares regression line is 0 (equation 13-10):

$$\sum_{i=1}^{n} (Y_i - \hat{Y}_i) = 0 \qquad \text{13-10}$$

Calculations for
Least Squares
Regression
Coefficients for
the Software
Accessories
Example

Y	X	YX	X^2
487	3	1,461	9
445	5	2,225	25
272	2	544	4
641	8	5,128	64
187	2	374	4
440	6	2,640	36
346	7	2,422	49
238	1	238	1
312	4	1,248	16
269	2	538	4
655	9	5,895	81
563	6	3,378	36
$\Sigma = 4{,}855$	$\Sigma = 55$	$\Sigma = 26{,}091$	$\Sigma = 329$

$$b_1 = \frac{\Sigma XY - \dfrac{\Sigma X \Sigma Y}{n}}{\Sigma X^2 - \dfrac{(\Sigma X)^2}{n}} = \frac{26{,}091 - \dfrac{(55)(4{,}855)}{12}}{329 - \dfrac{(55)^2}{12}}$$

$$= 49.9101$$

Then,

$$b_0 = \overline{Y} - b_1 \overline{X} = 404.5833 - 49.9101(4.5833)$$
$$= 175.8289$$

The least squares regression line is, therefore,

$$\hat{Y} = 175.8289 + 49.9101X$$

Residuals and
Squared Residuals
for the Software
Accessories
Example

X	$\hat{Y}$	Y	$Y - \hat{Y}$	$(Y - \hat{Y})^2$
3	325.5592	487	161.4408	26,063.13
5	425.3794	445	19.6206	384.9679
2	275.6491	272	−3.6491	13.31593
8	575.1097	641	65.8903	4,341.532
2	275.6491	187	−88.6491	7,858.663
6	475.2895	440	−35.2895	1,245.349
7	525.1996	346	−179.2	32,112.5
1	225.739	238	12.261	150.3321
4	375.4693	312	−63.4693	4,028.352
2	275.6491	269	−6.6491	44.21053
9	625.0198	655	29.9802	898.8124
6	475.2895	563	87.7105	7,693.132
			$\Sigma = 0.0$	$\Sigma = 84{,}834.29$

FIGURE **13-9**

Least Squares
Regression Line
for Software
Accessories
Example

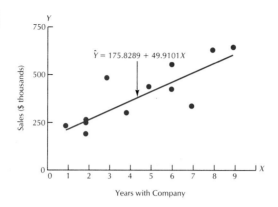

FIGURE **13-9**

Least Squares
Regression Line
for Software
Accessories
Example

2.   The sum of the squared residuals is a minimum (equation 13-11):

$$\sum_{i=1}^{n} (Y_i - \hat{Y}_i)^2 = \text{Minimum} \qquad \textbf{13-11}$$

This property provided the basis for developing the equations for b_0 and b_1.

3.   The simple regression line always passes through the mean of the Y variable, $\overline{Y}$, and the mean of the X variable, $\overline{X}$. This is illustrated in Figure 13-9. Thus, to draw any simple linear regression line, all you need to do is connect the least squares Y-intercept with the $(\overline{X}, \overline{Y})$ point.

4.   The least squares coefficients are unbiased estimates of β_0 and β_1. Thus, the expected values of b_0 and b_1 are β_0 and β_1, respectively.

SKILL DEVELOPMENT PROBLEMS FOR **SECTION 13-3**

The following exercises and problems will help you learn the concepts presented in Section 13-3.

10.   You are given the following sample data for variables Y and X:

Y	140	120	80	100	130	90	110	120	130	130	100
X	5	3	2	4	5	4	4	5	6	5	4

a.   Develop a scatter plot for these data and describe what, if any, relationship exists.

b.   Compute the correlation coefficient. Test to determine whether the correlation is significant at the $\alpha = 0.05$ level.

c. Compute the regression equation based on these sample data and interpret the regression coefficients.

11. The Apex Telephone Company recently performed a study in which ten households were surveyed to determine the number of phone calls made per week (Y) and the number of people living at the residence (X). The sample data were determined as follows:

| Calls (Y) | 37 | 23 | 67 | 21 | 10 | 33 | 46 | 67 | 44 | 38 |
| People (X) | 4 | 2 | 3 | 1 | 2 | 3 | 4 | 5 | 3 | 4 |

a. Develop a scatter plot for these data and describe what, if any, relationship exists.
b. Compute the correlation coefficient. Test to determine whether the correlation is significant at the $\alpha = 0.05$ level.
c. Compute the regression equation based on these sample data and interpret the regression coefficients.

12. At a recent Beach Boys concert, a survey was conducted that asked those sampled their age (X) and how many concerts they have attended since the first of the year (Y). The following data were collected with eleven respondents:

| Age (X) | 24 | 21 | 34 | 45 | 23 | 34 | 47 | 29 | 20 | 37 | 42 |
| Concerts (Y) | 3 | 2 | 1 | 3 | 5 | 2 | 1 | 3 | 5 | 2 | 3 |

a. Develop a scatter plot for these data and describe what, if any, relationship exists.
b. Compute the correlation coefficient. Test to determine whether the correlation is significant at the $\alpha = 0.05$ level.
c. Compute the regression equation based on these sample data and interpret the regression coefficients.
d. Compute the residuals and the sum of squared errors. Also compute the sum of squares for the Y variable and compare the sum of squared errors to this sum. Why do you suppose the sum of squared errors is smaller? Discuss.

13-4 SIGNIFICANCE TESTS IN REGRESSION ANALYSIS

If you recall, Carl Markowitz found that sales varied for the Software Accessories sales force, depending on how many years of experience people had with the company. The statistical measure for total variation in a dependent variable (sales) is TSS (total sum of squares). TSS is computed using equation 13-12:

$$\text{TSS} = \sum_{i=1}^{n} (Y_i - \overline{Y})^2 \qquad \text{13-12}$$

where

TSS = Total sum of squares

n = Sample size

Y_i = ith value of the dependent variable

$\overline{Y}$ = Average value of the dependent variable

The total sum of squares for sales is calculated in Table 13-6. As you can see, the total variation in sales that needs to be explained is 276,434.9.

The least squares regression line minimized the sum of squared residuals. This value (see Table 13-5) is called the *sum of squares error* (SSE) and is calculated by equation 13-13:

$$\text{SSE} = \sum_{i=1}^{n} (Y_i - \hat{Y}_i)^2 \qquad \text{13-13}$$

where

n = Sample size

Y_i = ith value of the dependent variable

$\hat{Y}_i$ = Least squares estimated value for the average of Y for each given X value

TABLE 13-6

Calculation of Total Sum of Squares for the Software Accessories Example

Person	Sales Y	$(Y - \overline{Y})^2$
1	487	6,792.562
2	445	1,633.534
3	272	17,578.25
4	641	55,892.99
5	187	47,342.36
6	440	1,254.364
7	346	3,431.968
8	238	27,749.9
9	312	8,571.612
10	269	18,382.75
11	655	62,708.67
12	563	25,095.95

TSS = $\Sigma(Y - \overline{Y})^2$ = 276,434.9

The SSE represents the amount of variation in the dependent variable that is not explained by the least squares regression line. For Software Accessories, the amount of unexplained variation is 84,834.29. The amount of variation in the dependent variable that is explained by the regression line is called the *sum of squares regression* (SSR) and is calculated by equation 13-14:

$$SSR = TSS - SSE$$

13-14

where

    SSR = Sum of squares regression

    TSS = Total sum of squares

    SSE = Sum of squares error

For the Software Accessories example, the least squares regression line calculated in Table 13-4 produces a sum of squares regression of

$$SSR = 276,434.9 - 84,834.29$$
$$= 191,600.61$$

The percentage of the total variation in the dependent variable that is explained by the independent variable is called the **coefficient of determination** or R^2. We compute R^2 by equation 13-15, 13-16, or 13-17:

$$R^2 = 1 - \frac{\Sigma(Y - \hat{Y})^2}{\Sigma(Y - \overline{Y})^2}$$

13-15

$$R^2 = 1 - \frac{SSE}{TSS}$$

13-16

or, alternatively,

$$R^2 = \frac{SSR}{TSS}$$

13-17

Then, for the Software Accessories example, the percentage of variation in sales that can be explained by the level of advertising is

$$R^2 = 1 - \frac{84,834.29}{276,434.9}$$
$$= 1 - 0.3069$$
$$= 0.6931$$

This means that 69.31% of the variation in the sales data for this sample can be explained by knowing the number of years of experience that accompanied the sales amount.

R^2 can be a value between 0 and 1.0. If there is a perfect linear relationship between two variables, the coefficient of determination, R^2, will be 1.0. This would correspond to a situation in which the least squares regression line would pass through each of the points in the scatter plot.

R^2 is the measure used by many decision makers to indicate how well the linear regression line fits the (X, Y) data points. The better the fit, the closer R^2 will be to 1.0. R^2 will be close to 0 when there is a weak linear relationship or no linear relationship at all.

Finally, when you are employing *simple linear regression* (one independent variable in the model), there is an alternative way of computing R^2, as shown in equation 13-18:

$$R^2 = r^2$$

13-18

where

R^2 = Coefficient of determination

r = Simple correlation coefficient

Thus, by squaring the correlation coefficient we can get R^2 for the simple regression model. Table 13-2 shows the correlation calculation giving $r = 0.8325$. Then using equation 13-18, we get R^2 as follows:

$$R^2 = r^2$$
$$= 0.8325^2$$
$$= 0.6931$$

SIGNIFICANCE OF THE REGRESSION MODEL

Before Carl Markowitz uses the regression model to analyze the relationship between sales and years experience, he should find out if the model itself is statistically significant. To test the model, he uses analysis of variance as shown in Figure 13-10. Based on the analysis of variance F test, he concludes that the proportion of sales variation explained by the least squares regression line is greater than 0. The analysis of variance test has shown that the sample coefficient of determination is significantly greater than 0. This means that the regression model he has developed is statistically significant. That is, predicting sales based on years sales experience using the least squares model would be generally preferable to just using the overall average sales value, $\overline{Y}$.

FIGURE **13-10** Significance Test of the Regression Model for the Software Accessories Example

---

Hypotheses:

H_0: The regression model does not explain any of the total variation in the dependent variable.

H_A: The regression model does explain a proportion of the total variation in the dependent variable greater than 0.0.

$\alpha = 0.05$

Source of Variation	SS	d.f.	MS	F Ratio
Regression	SSR = 191,600.61	$K = 1$	SSR/1 = 191,600.61	MSR/MSE* = 22.59
Unexplained (error)	SSE = 84,834.29	$n - 2 = 10$	SSE/10 = 8,483.43	
Total	TSS = 276,434.9	$n - 1 = 11$		

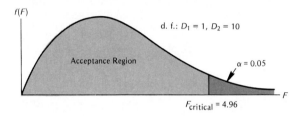

Decision Rule:

If $F > F_{\text{critical}} = 4.96$, reject H_0.

Otherwise, do not reject H_0.

Since $22.59 > 4.96$, we reject H_0 and conclude that the regression model explains a significant amount of variation in the dependent variable.

*MSR = mean square regression; MSE = mean square error.

SIGNIFICANCE OF THE SLOPE COEFFICIENT

To test the significance of the simple linear regression model, we test whether the true regression slope is 0. A slope of 0 would imply that the X variable is of no use in explaining the variation in Y. If the X variable is useful, then we should reject that the regression slope is 0. Because the b_1 value is calculated from a sample, it is subject to sampling error. Thus, even though b_1 is not 0, we must determine whether its difference from 0 is greater than would generally be attributed to sampling error.

If we selected several samples from the same population, and for each sample determined the least squares regression line, we would likely get lines with different slopes and different Y-intercepts. This is analogous to getting different sample means from different samples. Just as the distribution of possible sample means has a standard deviation, the possible regression slopes have a standard deviation, which is given in equation 13-19:

$$\sigma_{b_1} = \frac{\sigma_e}{\sqrt{\Sigma(X - \overline{X})^2}}$$

13-19

where

σ_{b_1} = Standard deviation of the regression slope
(called the **standard error of the slope**)

σ_e = **Standard error of the estimate**

Because we are sampling from the population, we estimate σ_{b_1} as shown in equation 13-20:

$$S_{b_1} = \frac{S_e}{\sqrt{\Sigma(X - \overline{X})^2}} = \frac{S_e}{\sqrt{\Sigma X^2 - \dfrac{(\Sigma X)^2}{n}}}$$

13-20

where

S_{b_1} = Estimate of the standard error of the least squares slope

$S_e = \sqrt{\dfrac{SSE}{n - 2}}$ = Sample **standard error of the estimate** (the measure of deviation of the actual Y values around the regression line)

For Software Accessories, the estimate of the standard error of the slope is

$$S_{b_1} = \frac{\sqrt{\dfrac{84,834.29}{10}}}{\sqrt{329 - \dfrac{(55)^2}{12}}}$$

$$= 10.5021$$

If the standard error of the slope is large, the value of b_1 will be quite variable from sample to sample. On the other hand, if S_{b_1} is small, the slope will be less variable. However, regardless of the standard error, the average value of b_1 will

Standard Error of the Slope

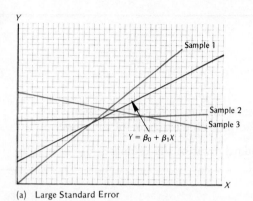

(a) Large Standard Error

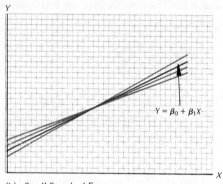

(b) Small Standard Error

Sample Regression Line: $\hat{Y} = b_0 + b_1 X$

True Population Regression Line: $\hat{Y} = \beta_0 + \beta_1 X$

equal β_1, the true regression slope, if the assumptions of the regression analysis are satisfied. Figure 13-11 illustrates what this means. Notice that when the standard error is large, the sample slopes can take on values *much* different from the true population slope. As Figure 13-11(a) shows, a sample slope and the true population slope can even have different signs. However, when S_{b_1} is small, the sample regression lines will cluster closely around the true population line (Figure 13-11(b)).

Because the sample regression slope will most likely not equal the true population slope, we must test to determine whether the true slope could possibly be 0. A slope of 0 in the linear model means that the independent variable will not explain any variation in the dependent variable. To test the significance of a slope coefficient, we use the t test of equation 13-21:

$$t = \frac{b_1 - \beta_1}{S_{b_1}}$$

13-21

where

t = Number of standard errors b_1 is from β_1

b_1 = Sample regression slope coefficient

β_1 = Hypothesized slope

S_{b_1} = Estimate of the standard error of the slope

This test has $n - 2$ degrees of freedom. Figure 13-12 illustrates this test for the Software Accessories example and indicates that we should reject the hypothesis that the true regression slope is 0. Thus, years of experience can be used to help explain the variation in individual representatives' sales.

FIGURE 13-12

Significance Test for the Regression Slope for the Software Accessories Example

Hypotheses:

$H_0: \beta_1 = 0$
$H_A: \beta_1 \neq 0$

$\alpha = 0.05$

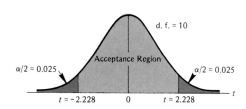

d. f. = 10

Acceptance Region

$\alpha/2 = 0.025$

$\alpha/2 = 0.025$

$t = -2.228$ 0 $t = 2.228$ t

The calculated t is

$$t = \frac{b_1 - \beta_1}{S_{b_1}} = \frac{49.9101 - 0}{10.5021}$$
$$= 4.7524$$

Decision Rule:

If $t > t_{\text{critical}} = 2.228$, reject H_0.
If $t < t_{\text{critical}} = -2.228$, reject H_0.
Otherwise, do not reject H_0.

Since $4.7524 > 2.228$, we should reject the null hypothesis and conclude that the true slope is not zero.

FIGURE **13-13**

Summary of
Simple Regression
Steps

Step 1. Develop a scatter plot of Y and X. You are looking for a linear relationship between the two variables.

Step 2. Calculate the correlation coefficient, r. This measures the strength of the linear relationship between the two variables.

Step 3. Test to see whether r is significantly different from 0. The test statistic is

$$t = \frac{r}{\sqrt{\dfrac{1 - r^2}{n - 2}}}$$

Step 4. Calculate the least squares regression line for the sample data.

Step 5. Calculate the simple coefficient of determination, r^2. This value measures the proportion of variation in the dependent variable explained by the independent variable.

Step 6. Test to see whether the model is significant. The test statistic is

$$F = \frac{\dfrac{SSR}{1}}{\dfrac{SSE}{n - 2}} = \frac{MSR}{MSE}$$

Step 7. Test to determine whether the true regression slope is 0. The test statistic with d.f. $= n - 2$ is

$$t = \frac{b_1 - \beta_1}{S_{b_1}}$$

Note: Steps 3, 6, and 7 are equivalent tests for the simple regression model. Only one of these tests needs to be performed.

Based on the results of his analysis, Carl Markowitz can conclude that a significant relationship exists between sales generated and years of sales experience with Software Accessories. He can also conclude that each year of experience should lead to an increase of about $50,000 in sales. The knowledge generated by this model should help him analyze the present wage scale for sales representatives.

Figure 13-13 outlines the steps involved in developing a simple linear regression model and reviews the various tests of significance. You should recognize that the three tests used thus far to test the significance of the linear relationship between X and Y are actually equivalent. Therefore, the decision maker needs to perform only one of these tests, since they will all lead to the same conclusion. However, you should be familiar with all three since they are each used. When we introduce multiple regression analysis in Chapter 14, the three tests serve different purposes.

COMPUTER APPLICATION

The calculations required to develop a simple linear regression model can be performed with a calculator. However, many computer programs have been developed that will perform the calculations quickly and with great accuracy. These computer programs will also calculate the values necessary to test the significance of the regression model. Table 13-7 shows two sample regression outputs for the Software Accessories example. As in previous chapters, one output is for MINI-TAB (Table 13-7a) and the second is for GB-STAT (Table 13-7b).

As you look at the computer outputs you will see that each labels values a little differently than the text has been doing. For instance, in MINITAB the standard error of the estimate on the printout is s = 92.11, the standard error of the regression slope is Stdev = 10.50, and the intercept is shown on the printout as Constant = 175.83.

Other software packages will use still different labels for the regression values. However, the documentation that accompanies the various packages will indicate what the output labels mean.

SKILL DEVELOPMENT PROBLEMS FOR **SECTION 13-4**

The following exercises are included to help you gain a firm understanding of the concepts presented in this section.

13. You are given the following results from computations pertaining to a simple linear regression application:

$$\hat{Y} = 23.0 + 1.45X$$
$$SSE = 45,000$$
$$n = 25$$
$$\Sigma(X - \overline{X})^2 = 4,000$$

 a. Based on the statistics supplied, can you conclude that there is a significant linear relationship between X and Y? Test at the $\alpha = 0.05$ level.
 b. Interpret the slope coefficient.

14. The following data have been collected by an accountant who is performing an audit of parts inventory for a machinery company. The dependent variable, Y, is the actual number of units counted by the accountant. The independent variable, X, is the number of units on the computer inventory record.

| Y | 233 | 10 | 24 | 56 | 78 | 102 | 90 | 200 | 344 | 120 | 18 |
| X | 245 | 12 | 22 | 56 | 90 | 103 | 85 | 190 | 320 | 120 | 23 |

 a. Develop a scatter plot for these data.
 b. Compute the correlation coefficient and test to determine whether a significant linear relationship exists between the two variables. Test at an $\alpha = 0.05$ level.
 c. Compute the regression model based on the sample data. Compute also the standard error of the estimate. Test to determine whether the regression slope is significantly different from 0. Use an $\alpha = 0.05$ level.

T A B L E 13-7

a. MINITAB Output for the Software Accessories Example

```
MTB > name c1 'years' c2 'sales'
MTB > print c1-c2

ROW     years     sales
 1        3        487
 2        5        445
 3        2        272
 4        8        641
 5        2        187
 6        6        440
 7        7        346
 8        1        238
 9        4        312
10        2        269
11        9        655
12        6        563

MTB > regress c2 on 1 predictor c1
```

The regression equation is
sales = 176 + 49.9 years

Predictor	Coef	Stdev	t-ratio	p
Constant	175.83	54.99	3.20	0.010
years	49.91	10.50	4.75	0.000

s = 92.11   R-sq = 69.3%   R-sq(adj) = 66.2%

Analysis of Variance

SOURCE	DF	SS	MS	F	p
Regression	1	191601	191601	22.59	0.000
Error	10	84834	8483		
Total	11	276435			

b. GB-STAT Output for the Software Accessories Example

$Y = 175.8289 + 49.9101 \cdot X$

UNADJUSTED R^2	= .6931
CORRELATION COEFFICIENT	= .8325
ANOVA FOR PREDICTION F	= 22.5853
CHANCE PROBABILITY P	= .0008
STD ERROR OF ESTIMATE	= 92.1056
VARIANCE OF ESTIMATE	= 8483.445
DEGREES OF FREEDOM	= 1 AND 10

WITH X = YEARS   AND Y = SALES

Note that MINITAB and GB-STAT provide output with slightly different results due to the number of decimal places printed by the software.

15. The National Football League is concerned about the injuries suffered by its players. A sample of players was selected prior to last season. At the end of the year, two variables were measured:

$$Y = \text{Number of days out with an injury}$$
$$X = \text{Weight of the player}$$

The data observed were as follows:

Y	17	9	0	3	26	18	2	8	19	38	20	0	2
X	221	198	234	256	278	197	206	224	234	278	220	199	234

   a. Develop a scatter plot for these data.
   b. Compute the correlation coefficient and test to determine whether a significant linear relationship exists between the two variables. Test at an $\alpha = 0.05$ level.
   c. Compute the regression model based on the sample data. Compute also the standard error of the estimate. Test to determine whether the regression slope is significantly different from 0. Use an $\alpha = 0.05$ level.
   d. Referring to parts **b** and **c**, comment on the relationship between the two hypothesis tests.

13-5 REGRESSION ANALYSIS FOR PREDICTION

One of the main uses of regression analysis is *prediction.* In the Software Accessories sample, Carl Markowitz wanted to know whether years of sales experience was a helpful variable to use to predict sales. As another example, your state government may use regression to forecast annual tax revenues so that elected officials can establish state department budgets.

Using a regression model to predict the dependent variable is quite straightforward once the model has been found. The regression model for Software Accessories individual sales is

$$\hat{Y} = 175.8289 + 49.9101X$$

where

$\hat{Y}$ = Point estimate for the average sales in thousands of dollars, given X

X = Years of experience

To find $\hat{Y}$, the point estimate of expected sales, we substitute the specified years of experience into the regression model. For example, suppose Carl Markowitz is analyzing the performance of someone with 6 years of sales experience. The point estimate for sales becomes

$$\hat{Y} = 175.8289 + 49.9101(6)$$
$$= 475.2895$$

Converting back to dollars, we find the point estimate for sales when $X = 6$ to be $475,289.50.

CONFIDENCE INTERVAL FOR THE AVERAGE Y, GIVEN X

In Chapter 9, we stated that decision makers cannot be confident of the accuracy of any point estimate. In fact, the best they can hope for is that the point estimate is close to the true value being estimated.

In some cases, only a point estimate of the expected value of the dependent variable is required. However, in many other cases the decision maker will want a *confidence interval estimate*. For example, Carl Markowitz might like a 95% confidence interval estimate for average sales, given that a sales representative has 6 years of experience. The prediction interval for the expected value of a dependent variable, given a specific level of the independent variable, is determined by equation 13-22:

$$\hat{Y} \pm t_{\alpha/2} \sqrt{\frac{SSE}{n-2}} \sqrt{\frac{1}{n} + \frac{(X_p - \overline{X})^2}{\Sigma X^2 - \frac{(\Sigma X)^2}{n}}} \qquad \textbf{13-22}$$

where

$\hat{Y}$ = Point estimate of the dependent variable

t = Interval coefficient with $n - 2$ d.f.

n = Sample size

X_p = Value of the independent variable used to arrive at $\hat{Y}$

$\overline{X}$ = Mean of the independent variable observations in the sample

Thus, if X_p equals 6, we get

$$475.2895 \pm 2.228 \sqrt{\frac{84,834.29}{10}} \sqrt{\frac{1}{12} + \frac{(6 - 4.583)^2}{329 - \frac{55^2}{12}}}$$

$$475.2895 \pm 67.8868$$

$$407.4027 \underline{\qquad} 543.1763$$

Therefore, Carl Markowitz can state, at the 95% confidence level, that average sales for a representative with 6 years of experience will be between \$407,402.70 and \$543,176.30. This information would be useful in determining commission levels.

CONFIDENCE INTERVAL FOR A SINGLE *Y*, GIVEN *X*

The prediction interval just calculated is for the expected, or average, sales level, given a sales representative with 6 years of experience with Software Accessories. Carl Markowitz would also be interested in predicting the actual sales for individual sales representatives with 6 years of experience, not the average of the sales for all representatives with 6 years of experience. Developing the interval within which he can be 95% confident that sales will fall requires only a slight modification of equation 13-22. This predictive interval is given by equation 13-23:

$$\hat{Y} \pm t_{\alpha/2} \sqrt{\frac{SSE}{n-2}} \sqrt{1 + \frac{1}{n} + \frac{(X_p - \overline{X})^2}{\Sigma X^2 - \frac{(\Sigma X)^2}{n}}} \qquad \text{13-23}$$

For Software Accessories, the 95% confidence interval estimate for yearly sales for a representative with 6 years of experience is

$$475.2895 \pm 2.228 \sqrt{\frac{84,834.29}{10}} \sqrt{1 + \frac{1}{12} + \frac{(6 - 4.583)^2}{329 - \frac{55^2}{12}}}$$

$$475.2895 \pm 216.1486$$

$$259.1409 \underline{\qquad} 691.4381$$

Thus, the 95% confidence level estimate for yearly sales for a sales representative with 6 years of experience is from \$259,140.90 to \$691,438.10. As you can see, this estimate has extremely poor precision. Although the regression model explains a significant proportion of variation in the dependent variable, it is relatively imprecise for predictive purposes. To improve the precision, Carl might decrease his confidence requirements or increase the sample size and redevelop the model.

Note that the prediction interval for a single value of the dependent variable is wider (less precise) than the interval for predicting the average value of the dependent variable. This will always be the case, as seen in equations 13-22 and 13-23. From an intuitive viewpoint, we should expect to come closer to predicting an average value than a single value. For example, although the average weight of the U.S. population will not be above 250 pounds, many people weigh more than that.

Note that the term $(X_p - \overline{X})^2$ has a particular effect on the confidence interval determined by both equations 13-22 and 13-23. The farther X_p (the value of the independent variable used to predict *Y*) is from $\overline{X}$, the greater $(X_p - \overline{X})^2$. Figure 13-14 shows two regression lines developed from two samples with the same set of *X* values. We have made both lines pass through the same $(\overline{X}, \overline{Y})$

FIGURE 13-14

Regression Lines, Illustrating the Increase in the Potential Variation in Y as X_p Moves Farther from $\overline{X}$

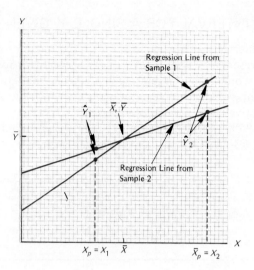

point; however, they have different slopes and intercepts. At $X_p = X_1$, the two regression lines give predictions of Y that are close to each other. However, for $X_p = X_2$, the predictions of Y are quite different. Thus, when X_p is close to $\overline{X}$, the problems caused by variations in regression slopes are not as great as when X_p is far from $\overline{X}$. Figure 13-15 shows the prediction intervals over the range of possible X_p values. The band around the estimated regression line bends away from the regression line as X_p moves in either direction from $\overline{X}$.

SKILL DEVELOPMENT PROBLEMS FOR **SECTION 13-5**

The following exercises will help you better understand the materials presented in this section.

16. You are given the following summary statistics from a regression analysis:

$$\hat{Y} = 200 + 150X$$

$$\text{SSE} = 25.25$$

$$\text{SSX} = \text{Sum of squares } X = \Sigma X^2 - \frac{(\Sigma X)^2}{n} = 99,645$$

$$n = 18$$

$$\overline{X} = 52.0$$

a. Determine the point estimate for Y if $X_p = 48$ is used.
b. Provide a 95% prediction interval estimate for the average Y, given $X_p = 48$. Interpret this interval.
c. Provide a 95% prediction interval estimate for a particular Y, given $X_p = 48$. Interpret.
d. Discuss the difference between the estimates provided in parts **b** and **c**.

FIGURE **13-15**

Confidence
Intervals for $Y|X_p$
and $\overline{Y}|X_p$

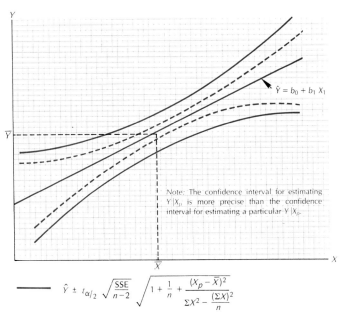

$$\hat{Y} \pm t_{\alpha/2} \sqrt{\frac{SSE}{n-2}} \sqrt{1 + \frac{1}{n} + \frac{(X_p - \overline{X})^2}{\Sigma X^2 - \frac{(\Sigma X)^2}{n}}}$$

Confidence Interval for the Estimate of a Particular Value of $Y|X_p$

$$\hat{Y} \pm t_{\alpha/2} \sqrt{\frac{SSE}{n-2}} \sqrt{\frac{1}{n} + \frac{(X_p - \overline{X})^2}{\Sigma X^2 - \frac{(\Sigma X)^2}{n}}}$$

Confidence Interval for the Estimate of $\overline{Y}|X_p$

17. You are given the following summary statistics from a regression analysis:

$$\hat{Y} = 9,784 - 345.50X$$

$$SSE = 800.25$$

$$SSX = \text{Sum of squares } X = \Sigma X^2 - \frac{(\Sigma X)^2}{n} = 145,789$$

$$\overline{X} = 67.20$$

$$n = 20$$

a. Determine the point estimate for estimating Y if $X_p = 48$ is used.
b. Provide a 90% prediction interval estimate for the average Y, given $X_p = 80$. Interpret this interval.

18. The following data have been collected by an accountant who is performing an audit of account balances for a major retail company. The population from which the data were collected represented those accounts for which the customer had indicated the balance was incorrect. The dependent variable, Y,

is the actual account balance as verified by the accountant. The independent variable, X, is the computer account balance.

| Y | 233 | 10 | 24 | 56 | 78 | 102 | 90 | 200 | 344 | 120 | 18 |
| X | 245 | 12 | 22 | 56 | 90 | 103 | 85 | 190 | 320 | 120 | 23 |

a. Prepare a regression analysis where Y is the dependent variable and X is the independent variable. Show the following results:

$$\text{Regression equation} \qquad SSX = \Sigma X^2 - \frac{(\Sigma X)^2}{n} \qquad S_e$$

b. Determine the point estimate for Y, given $X_p = 100$.
c. Develop a 95% prediction interval estimate for the average value of Y, given $X_p = 100$. Interpret.
d. Develop a 95% prediction interval estimate for the particular value of Y, given $X_p = 100$. Interpret.

13-6 DEVELOPING A MULTIPLE REGRESSION MODEL

Most states have provisions allowing the counties to raise revenue through property taxes. The amount of property taxes a real estate owner will pay depends on the class of property, the appraised value of the property, and the tax rate. Typically, the appraised value for tax purposes is supposed to be the market value for the property. The market value is the value the property would sell for if it were put on the open market. Usually, the county assessor is charged with the responsibility of making property appraisals. Obviously, making a correct property appraisal is important, but trying to determine how much each property would sell for if it were placed on the market is a difficult task, and many assessors are faced with irate taxpayers disputing their property taxes.

American County, located in the Midwest, is just now in the process of changing its appraisal system. The assessor has selected a sample of 531 residential properties that have sold recently in American County. Data for the following variables were obtained for each property:

$$Y = \text{Sales price}$$
$$X_1 = \text{Square feet}$$
$$X_2 = \text{Age of house}$$
$$X_3 = \text{Number of bedrooms}$$
$$X_4 = \text{Number of bathrooms}$$
$$X_5 = \text{Number of fireplaces}$$

The assessor has decided to develop an appraisal model based on multiple regression, an extension of the simple regression techniques discussed in the previous sections.

You will note as we proceed that multiple regression is merely an extension of simple regression analysis. However, as we expand the model from one independent variable to two or more there are some new considerations.

The general format of a **multiple regression model** is given by equation 13-24 (compare with equation 13-4).

$$Y_i = \beta_0 + \beta_1 X_{1i} + \beta_2 X_{2i} + \cdots + \beta_K X_{Ki} + e_i$$

13-24

where

β_0 = Regression constant

β_1 = Regression coefficient for variable X_1

β_K = Regression coefficient for variable X_K

K = Number of independent variables

e_i = Error (residual)

There are three general assumptions of the linear multiple regression model:

1. The errors are normally distributed.
2. The mean of the error terms is 0.
3. The error terms have a constant variance, σ^2, for all combinations of values of the independent variables.

Since the error terms have a mean of 0, the expected value of Y for given values of $X_1, X_2, X_3, \ldots, X_K$ is given by equation 13-25 (compare with equation 13-5).

$$E[Y] = \beta_0 + \beta_1 X_1 + \beta_2 X_2 + \beta_3 X_3 + \cdots + \beta_K X_K$$

13-25

This model is an extension of the simple regression model. The principal difference is that, whereas for the simple model, the regression equation is for a straight line in a two-dimensional space, the multiple regression model forms a *hyperplane* (or *response surface*) through multidimensional space. Each regression coefficient represents a slope. When there are only two independent variables, the **regression plane** can be drawn as shown in Figure 13-16. If there are more than two independent variables, the regression model cannot be visually represented, but the concept remains intact. The next section shows how a multiple regression model is developed.

When a decision maker has sample data available for the dependent variable and for K independent variables, the least squares regression coefficients are esti-

FIGURE 13-16

Illustration of a
Regression Plane

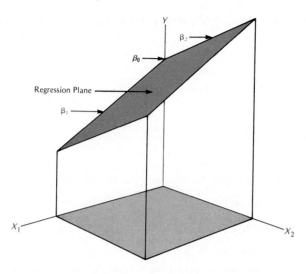

mated, forming the sample regression model of the form shown in equation
13-26:

$$\hat{Y}_i = b_0 + b_1 X_1 + b_2 X_2 + \cdots + b_K X_K$$

13-26

where

$$b_0 = \text{Y-intercept (constant)}$$
$$b_1, b_2, \ldots, b_K = \text{Regression slope coefficients}$$
$$\hat{Y}_i = i\text{th estimated value of the dependent variable}$$
$$X_1, X_2, \ldots, X_K = \text{Independent variables}$$

The estimates of the regression coefficients are determined mathematically so that
$\Sigma(Y_i - \hat{Y}_i)^2$ is minimized. This is referred to as the *least squares criterion*. The
actual procedure for determining the values for the regression coefficients involves matrix algebra. The mathematical derivation is beyond the scope of this
text. (For a more complete treatment of the matrix algebra approach for estimating the multiple regression coefficients, consult *Applied Linear Statistical Models*
by Neter and Wasserman.)

Almost exclusively, multiple regression analysis is performed with the aid of a
computer and appropriate software. The following presentation of examples will
be based on output from either GB-STAT or MINITAB. Note that each software
package presents the results in a slightly different format; however, the same basic
information will appear in all regression output.

Before a multiple regression analysis example is introduced, you should understand this important point: The sample size required to compute a regression model must be at least 1 greater than the number of independent variables. Thus, if we are thinking of developing a regression model with five independent variables, the absolute minimum number of cases required is six. Otherwise, the computer program will indicate an error has been made or will print out meaningless values.

As a practical matter, the sample size should be at least 4 times the number of independent variables. Thus, if we have five independent variables ($K = 5$), we would want at least twenty cases to develop the regression model.

13-7 AMERICAN COUNTY APPRAISAL MODEL

We indicated earlier that the assessor in American County wanted to use multiple regression to develop an appraisal model for residential property in the county.

The assessor gathered data on the following residential property variables for 531 houses:

$$Y = \text{Sales price}$$
$$X_1 = \text{Square feet}$$
$$X_2 = \text{Age of house}$$
$$X_3 = \text{Number of bedrooms}$$
$$X_4 = \text{Number of bathrooms}$$
$$X_5 = \text{Number of fireplaces}$$

Note that sales price is the dependent variable and the other five variables are the independent variables. The assessor hopes to be able to use the variables to predict the market value (price) of residential properties in American County. Table 13-8 illustrates how the data would be arranged. Table 13-9 presents the mean and standard deviation for each variable. The standard deviation for the variable price is high, indicating a large variation in selling prices for houses.

TABLE 13-8

American County Data

Observation	Y	X_1	X_2	X_3	X_4	X_5
1	57,000	1,410	3.0	2.0	1.0	0
2	44,970	1,725	5.0	3.0	2.5	1
.	.	.	.	.	.	.
.	.	.	.	.	.	.
.	.	.	.	.	.	.
$n = 531$	110,790	2,250	1.0	4.0	2.75	2

TABLE 13-9

Means and
Standard
Deviations for
Variables in the
American County
Example

Variable	Mean	Std. Dev.	Cases
Y	79,873.5619	28,034.4579	531
X_1	1,715.5273	588.1123	531
X_2	4.3936	7.7781	531
X_3	3.4038	0.0555	531
X_4	1.9143	0.6094	531
X_5	0.9209	0.5608	531

CORRELATION MATRIX

The first step in developing the appraisal model is to examine the relationship between each independent variable and the dependent variable, *sales price*. As with simple regression analysis, we can measure the strength of the linear relationship between any two variables by calculating the correlation coefficient for each pair of (X, Y) variables using equation 13-27:

$$r = \frac{\Sigma(X_i - \overline{X})(Y_i - \overline{Y})}{\sqrt{\Sigma(X_i - \overline{X})^2 \Sigma(Y_i - \overline{Y})^2}}$$

13-27

The **correlation matrix** found using GB-STAT is shown in Table 13-10. Note that the correlation between Y and each X variable is given, plus the correlation between each pair of independent variables. For example, the correlation between Y and X_2 is -0.068 and between X_3 and X_5 is 0.338. The correlation matrix is very useful for determining which independent variables are likely to help explain variation in the dependent variable. We look for correlations close to ± 1.0, since that indicates changes in one variable are linearly related to changes in the other variable.

TABLE 13-10

Correlation
Matrix Computer
Output for the
American County
Example

	Y	X1	X2	X3	X4	X5
Y	1.000	.841	−.068	.494	.720	.599
X1	.841	1.000	.054	.644	.680	.589
X2	−.068	.054	1.000	.007	−.149	.086
X3	.494	.644	.007	1.000	.551	.338
X4	.720	.680	−.149	.551	1.000	.518
X5	.599	.589	.086	.338	.518	1.000

Also, we can use the correlation matrix to determine the extent to which independent variables are correlated with one another. This can be useful in determining whether certain independent variables are redundant and not needed in the model.

Notice that the correlation matrix has 1.000s running down the main diagonal, indicating the variables are perfectly correlated with themselves. Finally, notice the matrix is symmetric about its diagonal. For example, the correlation between X_2 and X_5 (0.086) is the same as for X_5 and X_2 (0.086).

THE REGRESSION MODEL

The county assessor's goal is to develop a regression model to predict the appropriate selling price for a home, using certain measurable characteristics. The first attempt at developing the model will be to run a multiple regression computer program using all available independent variables except X_2, age. Age (X_2) was excluded in this run since the correlation between age and price was only -0.068 (see Table 13-10). The resulting output, using MINITAB, is shown in Table 13-11. Thus, the multiple regression model (rounding to two significant digits) is

$$Y = 20,494.98 + 29.17X_1 - 5,050.29X_3 + 11,710.94X_4 + 4,450.55X_5$$

These values come from the Coef column of the variables in the equation section of Table 13-11.

TABLE 13-11

MINITAB Output for American County Example

MTB > REGRESS 'Y' on 4 predictors 'X1' 'X2' 'X3' 'X4'

The regression equation is
Y = 20494.980 + 29.173X1 − 5050.290X3 + 11710.938X4 + 4450.552X5

Predictor	Coef	Stddev	t-ratio	p
Constant	20494.980			
X1	29.173	1.496	19.504	0.000
X3	−5050.290	1094.795	−4.613	0.000
X4	11710.938	1250.234	9.367	0.000
X5	4450.552	1210.376	3.677	0.000

s = 13600.502   R-sq = 76.7%   R-sq(adj) = 76.5%

Analysis of Variance

SOURCE	DF	SS	MS	F	p
Regression	4	320033124448.934	80008281112.2334	432.538	0.000
Error	526	97296146146.6557	184973661.875771		
Total	530	417329270595.589			

To obtain a sales price point estimate for any house, we could substitute values for X_1, X_3, X_4, and X_5 into this regression model. For example, suppose a property with the following characteristics is considered:

$$X_1 = \text{Square feet} = 2{,}100$$
$$X_3 = \text{Number of bedrooms} = 4$$
$$X_4 = \text{Number of baths} = 1.75$$
$$X_5 = \text{Number of fireplaces} = 2$$

The point estimate for the sales price is

$$\hat{Y} = 20{,}494.98 + 29.17(2{,}100) - 5{,}050.29(4) + 11{,}710.94(1.75) + 4{,}450.55(2)$$
$$= 90{,}946.31$$

The computer output in Table 13-11 shows a number of other regression statistics. As we proceed, we will discuss these values. Our emphasis will be on interpreting the computer regression results.

INFERENCES ABOUT THE REGRESSION MODEL

Before the American County assessor actually uses this regression model to determine the value of a house, there are several questions that should be answered:

1. Is the overall model significant?
2. Are the individual variables significant?
3. Is the standard error of the estimate too large to provide meaningful results?
4. Is multicollinearity a problem?[1]

We shall answer each of these questions in order.

Is the Overall Model Significant?

Recall that the coefficient of determination measures the percentage of variation in the dependent variable that can be accounted for by the independent variable. With multiple regression, we also use *R-square*, which is calculated by equation 13-28:

$$R\text{-square} = R^2 = \frac{\text{Sum of squares regression}}{\text{Total sum of squares}} = \frac{\text{SSR}}{\text{TSS}}$$

13-28

---

[1] **Multicollinearity** occurs when two independent variables are correlated with each other and therefore contribute redundant information to the model. When highly correlated independent variables are included in the regression model, they can affect the regression results.

The R-square (**multiple coefficient of determination**) for the appraisal model is given in the computer printout in Table 13-11 as 76.7%. Therefore, almost 77% of the variation in sales price can be explained by the four independent variables in the regression model.

We showed earlier that an analysis of variance F test can be used to test whether the regression model explains a significant proportion of variation in the dependent variable. The computer printout in Table 13-11 provides the analysis of variance test for this example. To test the model's significance, we compare the calculated F value, 432.538, with a table F value for a given alpha level and 4 and 526 degrees of freedom. If we specify an alpha level of 0.01, the test is as shown in Figure 13-17.

Clearly, based on the analysis of variance F test, we should conclude that the regression model *does* explain a significant proportion of the variation in sales price.

The computer printout in Table 13-11 also provides a measure called the **adjusted R-square.** This is calculated by equation 13-29:

$$\text{Adjusted } R\text{-square} = R_A^2 = 1 - (1 - R^2)\left(\frac{n - 1}{n - K - 1}\right) \qquad \textbf{13-29}$$

where

n = Sample size

K = Number of independent variables in the model

FIGURE 13-17

Significance Test for American County Example

Hypotheses:

H_0: The regression model does not explain a significant proportion of the total variation in the dependent variable (model is not significant). ($\beta_1 = \beta_3 = \beta_4 = \beta_5 = 0$), $\rho^2 = 0$

H_A: The regression model does explain a significant proportion of the total variation in the dependent variable (model is significant). (At least one $\beta_j \neq 0$; $j = 1, 3, 4, 5$), $\rho^2 > 0$

$\alpha = 0.01$

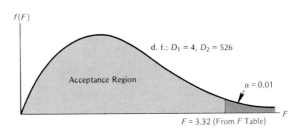

Decision Rule:

If $F > F_{critical} = 3.32$, reject H_0.
Otherwise, do not reject H_0.

The calculated F (see Table 13-11) is 432.54. Since 432.54 > 3.32, the null hypothesis should be rejected.

In the appraisal example,

$$R_A^2 = 1 - (1 - 0.767)\left(\frac{531 - 1}{531 - 4 - 1}\right)$$

$$= 0.765$$

Adding more independent variables to the regression model generally increases R^2. However, the cost in terms of losing degrees of freedom may not justify adding an additional variable. The R_A^2 value takes into account this cost and adjusts the R^2 value accordingly. Therefore, if a variable is added that does not contribute its fair share, the R_A^2 will actually decline.[2] R_A^2 is particularly important when the number of independent variables is large relative to the sample size. It takes into account the relationship between sample size and number of variables. R^2 may appear artificially high if the number of variables is high compared to the sample size.

Are the Individual Variables Significant?

We have concluded that the overall model is significant. This means that *at least* one independent variable explains a significant proportion of the variation in sales price. This does not mean that *all* the variables are significant.

We can test the significance of each independent variable using a *t* test, as discussed earlier. The calculated *t* value for each variable is provided on the computer printout in Table 13-11. Recall that the *t* statistic is determined by dividing the regression coefficient by the standard deviation of the regression coefficient. The test for each variable is performed in Figure 13-18. These *t* tests are *conditional* tests. This means the hypothesis that states that *the value of each slope coefficient is 0* is made recognizing that the other independent variables are already in the model.[3] Based on the *t* tests in Figure 13-18, we conclude that all four independent variables in the model are significant. When a regression model is to be used for prediction, the model should contain no insignificant variables. If insignificant variables are present, they should be dropped and the regression model rerun before it is used for prediction purposes.

Is the Standard Error of the Estimate Too Large?

The purpose of developing the American County regression model is to be able to determine values of the dependent variable when corresponding values of the

---

[2] You might think of R_A^2 as similar to the net income on an income statement and R^2 as the total revenue. Thus R_A^2 is total revenue less expenses.

[3] Note that the *t* tests may be affected if the independent variables in the model are themselves correlated. A procedure known as the *sum of squares drop F test,* discussed by Neter and Wasserman in *Applied Linear Statistical Models,* should be used in this situation. Each *t* test considers only the marginal contribution of the independent variables and may indicate that none of the variables in the model are significant even though the ANOVA procedure indicates otherwise.

FIGURE 13-18

Significance Test for a Single Independent Variable in the American County Example

Hypotheses:

H_0: $\beta_i = 0$, given all other variables are already in the model
H_A: $\beta_i \neq 0$, given all other variables are already in the model

$\alpha = 0.01$

Decision Rule:

If $-2.576 \leq t \leq 2.576$, accept H_0.
Otherwise, reject H_0.

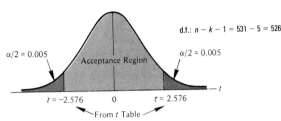

d.f.: $n - k - 1 = 531 - 5 = 526$

$\alpha/2 = 0.005$ Acceptance Region $\alpha/2 = 0.005$

$t = -2.576$ 0 $t = 2.576$

From t Table

The test is:

For β_1: Calculated t (from printout) $= 19.504$.
Since $19.504 > 2.576$, reject H_0.

For β_3: Calculated $t = -4.613$.
Since $-4.613 < -2.576$, reject H_0.

For β_4: Calculated $t = 9.367$.
Since $9.367 > 2.576$, reject H_0.

For β_5: Calculated $t = 3.677$.
Since $3.677 > 2.576$, reject H_0.

Note: the degrees of freedom for the t-distribution is $n - k - 1$, where k is the total number of independent variables in the model.

independent variables are known. An indication of how good the regression model is can be found by looking at the relationship between the measured values of the dependent variable and those values that would be predicted by the regression model. The sample standard deviation of the regression model, often referred to as the **standard error of the estimate** (S_e), measures the dispersion of observed sale values, Y, around values predicted by the regression model. The standard error of the estimate, listed simply as s in Table 13-11, is found by

$$S_e = \sqrt{\frac{SSE}{n - K - 1}}$$

where

$$SSE = \text{Sum of squares error}$$
$$n = \text{Sample size}$$
$$K = \text{Number of independent variables}$$

Notice also in Table 13-11 that the standard error is the square root of the mean square error of the residuals found in the analysis of variance table.

Sometimes, even though the model has a high R^2, the standard error of the estimate will be too large to provide adequate precision for the prediction interval. A rule of thumb that we have found useful is to examine the range $\pm 2S_e$.[4] If this range is acceptable from a practical viewpoint, the standard error of the estimate might be considered acceptable.

In the American County example, as shown in Table 13-11, the standard error is 13,600.50. Thus, the rough prediction range is

$$\pm 2(13,600.50)$$
$$\pm \$27,201$$

From a practical viewpoint, this range is *not* acceptable. The error is over $27,000 in either direction. Not many homeowners would be willing to have their appraisal value set by a model with this possible error. The county assessor needs to take steps to reduce the standard error of the estimate. Subsequent sections of this chapter discuss some ways to reduce this value.

Another measure of whether S_e is too large is the *coefficient of variation*, which is

$$CV = \frac{S_e}{\overline{Y}}(100)$$

where

$$\overline{Y} = \text{Mean of the } Y \text{ variable}$$

In this case,

$$CV = \frac{13,600.50}{79,873.56}(100)$$
$$= 17.03\%$$

As a rule, we like to see a CV of 10% or less. However, each application must be analyzed on an individual basis.

Is Multicollinearity a Problem?

Even if a regression is significant, and if each independent variable is significant, decision makers should still examine the regression model to determine whether it appears reasonable. That is, does any coefficient have an unexpected sign?

---

[4]The actual confidence interval for prediction of a new observation requires the use of matrix algebra as follows:

$$\hat{Y}_p \pm S_e\sqrt{1 + [(X_p')(X'X)^{-1}(X_p)]}$$

where

$\hat{Y}_p$ = Point estimate given values for the independent variables
X_p = Vector of independent variable values used to calculate $\hat{Y}_p$
X = Matrix of independent variable values used to develop the regression model

Refer to *Applied Linear Statistical Models* by Neter and Wasserman (1974) for further discussion.

Before answering this question for our appraisal example, we should review what the regression coefficients mean. First, the constant term, β_0, is the model's Y-intercept. If the data used to develop the regression model contain values of X_1, X_3, X_4, and X_5 that are simultaneously 0 (such as would be the case for vacant land), the constant is the mean value of Y, given that X_1, X_3, X_4, and X_5 all equal 0. Under these conditions β_0 would equal the average value of a vacant lot. However, in the American County example, no vacant land was in the sample, so the constant has no particular meaning.

The coefficient for square feet, β_1, indicates the average change in sales price corresponding to a change in house size of 1 square foot, holding the other independent variables constant. The value shown in Table 13-11 for β_1 is 29.17. The coefficient is positive, indicating that an increase in house size is associated with an increase in sales price. This relationship is expected.

Likewise, the coefficients for X_4, number of bathrooms, and X_5, number of fireplaces, are positive, indicating that an increase in their numbers is also associated with an increase in price. This is also expected. However, the coefficient for variable X_3, number of bedrooms, is $-5{,}050.29$, meaning that, if we hold the other variables constant but increase the number of bedrooms by one, the average price will *drop* by \$5,050.29. This relationship may not be reasonable given the real estate market and buyers' attitudes.

Referring to the correlation matrix in Table 13-10, the correlation between variable X_3 and Y, the sales price, is $+0.494$. This indicates that, without considering the other independent variables, the linear relationship between number of bedrooms and sales price is positive. But why does the regression coefficient turn out negative? The answer lies in what is called *multicollinearity*. **Multicollinearity** occurs when the independent variables are themselves correlated. For example, X_3 and the other independent variables have the following correlations:

$$r_{X_3,X_1} = 0.644$$
$$r_{X_3,X_4} = 0.551$$
$$r_{X_3,X_5} = 0.338$$

In each case, the correlation is significant. Therefore, the other variables in the model are overlapping X_3; hence, to some extent, X_3 becomes unnecessary to the model once X_1, X_4, and X_5 are included. This overlapping is multicollinearity. Multicollinearity can cause problems like those we have seen in this example, where the regression coefficient sign is clearly opposite of what we would expect.

The problems caused by multicollinearity, and how to deal with them, continue to be of prime concern to theoretical statisticians. From a decision maker's viewpoint, you should be aware that multicollinearity can (and usually does) exist and recognize the basic problems it can cause. Some of the most obvious problems and indications of severe multicollinearity are the following:

1. Incorrect signs on the coefficients
2. A change in the values of the previous coefficients when a new variable is added to the model
3. The change to insignificant of a previously significant variable when a new variable is added to the model

4. An increase in the standard error of the estimate when a variable is added to the model

Mathematical approaches exist for dealing with multicollinearity and reducing its impact. Although these procedures are beyond the scope of this text, one suggestion is to eliminate the variables that are the chief cause of the multicollinearity problems. In the American County example, we would drop X_3 from the analysis. This variable is highly correlated with X_1, X_4, and X_5 and has low correlation with Y.

Dealing with multicollinearity problems requires a great deal of experience. This text simply aims to make you aware that such problems may exist and should be considered before the regression model is used.

SKILL DEVELOPMENT PROBLEMS FOR **SECTION 13-7**

The following exercises are included to help you gain a more complete understanding of the material presented in Section 13-7. If possible, use a computer and statistical software to solve the problems and exercises.

19. The Western State Tourist Association gives out pamphlets, maps, and other tourist-related information to people who call a toll-free number and request the information. The association orders the packets of information from a documents printing company and it likes to have enough available to meet the immediate need without having too many sitting around taking up space. The marketing manager decided to develop a multiple regression model to be used in predicting the number of calls that will be received in the coming week. A random sample of 11 weeks is selected, with the following variables:

Y = Number of calls
X_1 = Number of advertisements placed this week
X_2 = Number of calls received last week
X_3 = Number of airline tour bookings into western cities for this week

The following data were collected.

i	Y	X_1	X_2	X_3
1	345	12	297	3,456
2	456	14	502	2,456
3	356	13	340	3,600
4	605	16	450	3,500
5	209	14	350	2,400
6	306	10	340	2,890
7	457	15	401	3,457
8	259	12	340	2,590
9	540	13	400	3,240
10	460	16	440	3,560
11	378	14	348	2,460

Develop a correlation matrix for these variables and write a short report describing the various correlations. Comment on whether you think a multiple regression model will be effectively developed from these data.

20. Referring to the data in Problem 19, compute three simple linear regression models, one for each of the independent variables. Write a report that fully describes each of the models. Indicate in your report which of these models is best.

21. Referring to the data in Problem 19 and to your work in Problem 20, develop a multiple regression model that contains all three independent variables.
    a. Indicate the regression equation.
    b. How much of the total variation in the dependent variable is explained by the three independent variables in the model?
    c. Test to determine whether the overall model is statistically significant. Use $\alpha = 0.05$ to conduct this test.
    d. Which, if any, of the independent variables is statistically significant? Test using $\alpha = 0.05$.
    e. Determine the adjusted R-square and comment on what it means.
    f. As the model stands, comment on whether it will be a useful model for predicting the number of calls to the Western State Tourist Association.

22. Referring to Problems 19–21, prepare a short report that addresses the following points:
    a. Define the term multicollinearity.
    b. Indicate the potential problems that multicollinearity can cause.
    c. Indicate what, if any, evidence there is of multicollinearity problems with this multiple regression model.

23. The athletic director of State University is interested in developing a multiple regression model that might be used to explain the variation in attendance at football games at his school. A sample of sixteen games was selected from home games played during the past ten seasons. Data for the following factors were determined.

$$Y = \text{Game attendance}$$
$$X_1 = \text{Team win/loss percentage to date}$$
$$X_2 = \text{Opponent win/loss percentage to date}$$
$$X_3 = \text{Games played this season}$$
$$X_4 = \text{Temperature at game time}$$

The following data were collected.

i	Y	X_1	X_2	X_3	X_4
1	14,502	33.3	80.0	6	47
2	12,459	25.0	50.0	4	56
3	15,600	80.0	66.6	5	55
4	16,780	75.0	100.0	8	60
5	14,600	60.0	80.0	10	55
6	19,300	100.0	60.0	10	49
7	14,603	66.6	25.0	3	67
8	15,789	50.0	50.0	6	55
9	17,800	80.0	40.0	10	53
10	19,450	75.0	100.0	8	48
11	13,890	20.0	75.0	5	65
12	15,097	70.0	70.0	10	56
13	17,666	83.3	66.6	6	60
14	12,500	20.0	20.0	5	59
15	16,780	80.0	100.0	8	46
16	17,543	80.0	70.0	10	50

Develop a correlation matrix for these variables and write a short report describing the various correlations. Comment on whether you think that a multiple regression model will be effectively developed from these data.

24. Referring to the data in Problem 23, compute four simple linear regression models, one for each of the independent variables. Write a report that fully describes each of the models. Indicate in your report which of these models is best.

25. Referring to the data in Problem 23 and to your work in Problem 24, develop a multiple regression model that contains all four independent variables.
   a. Indicate the regression equation.
   b. How much of the total variation in the dependent variable is explained by the four independent variables in the model?
   c. Test to determine whether the overall model is statistically significant. Use $\alpha = 0.05$ to conduct this test.
   d. Which, if any, of the independent variables is statistically significant? Test using $\alpha = 0.05$.
   e. Determine the adjusted R-square and comment on what it means.
   f. Develop 95% confidence interval estimates for the regression coefficients and interpret these intervals. Write a short report to the athletic director describing the regression model.

13-8 DUMMY VARIABLES IN REGRESSION ANALYSIS

In many cases decision makers may want to use a nominal or ordinal variable (see Chapter 1, Section 1-2) as an independent variable in a regression model. If so, the variable is called a *qualitative variable*. For example, in a model for predicting individual income, a potential variable might be sex—male or female. In another example with GNP (gross national product) as the dependent variable, an interesting independent variable might be the U.S. president's political party—Republican or Democrat. In still another example, where the dependent variable is the number of dollars spent by women on cosmetics, such independent variables as marital status (single, married, widowed, divorced, or separated) and employment status (full time, part time, retired, unemployed, or other) are variables that may help to explain the variation in the dependent variable.

The problem with qualitative variables in a regression analysis is in assigning values to the outcomes. What value should we assign to a male as opposed to a female? What about assigning values for Republican versus Democrat? These classifications do not have unique numerical values, and different decision makers might well assign different values that could affect the regression analysis.

To overcome this problem, qualitative variables are incorporated into a regression analysis by using **dummy variables.** For example, for the qualitative variable sex, which has two categories—male or female, a single dummy variable is created as follows:

$$\text{If sex} = \text{male}, X_2 = 0.$$
$$\text{If sex} = \text{female}, X_2 = 1.$$

For the political party variable, the dummy variable is

$$\text{If party} = \text{Republican}, X_2 = 1.$$
$$\text{If party} = \text{Democrat}, X_2 = 0.$$

Although the qualitative variable is coded (0, 1), it makes no difference which attribute is assigned 0 and which is assigned 1.

When the qualitative variable has more than two possible categories, a series of dummy variables must be used. For example, since marital status could have five categories—single, married, separated, divorced, and widowed, we would develop four $(5 - 1 = 4)$ dummy variables as follows:

$$\text{If single}, X_2 = 1$$
$$\text{Otherwise}, X_2 = 0$$

$$\text{If married}, X_3 = 1$$
$$\text{Otherwise}, X_3 = 0$$

$$\text{If separated}, X_4 = 1$$
$$\text{Otherwise}, X_4 = 0$$

$$\text{If divorced}, X_5 = 1$$
$$\text{Otherwise}, X_5 = 0$$

For a widowed person, X_2, X_3, X_4, and X_5 would all be 0. By default, the person must belong to the remaining category, "widowed."[5]

---

[5] The mathematical reason that the number of dummy variables must be 1 less than the number of possible responses is called the **dummy variable trap.** Perfect multicollinearity is introduced and the least squares regression estimates cannot be obtained if the number of dummy variables equals the number of possible categories.

FIGURE **13-19**

Income Versus
Age

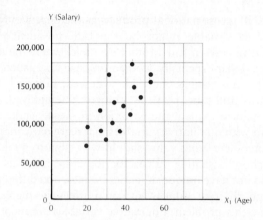

To illustrate the effect of incorporating dummy variables into a regression model, consider the data displayed in the scatter plot in Figure 13-19. The population from which these data were selected consists of executives between the ages of 24 and 60 who are working in U.S. manufacturing business. Data for the dependent variable, annual salary, and the independent variable, age, are available. Even though this model might be statistically significant, we would likely search for other independent variables that could help us to further explain the variation in annual salary.

Suppose we know which of the sixteen people in the sample had an MBA degree. Figure 13-20 shows the scatter plot for these same data with the MBA data circled. We can create a new variable, X_2, which is a dummy variable coded

$$X_2 = 0, \text{ if no MBA}$$
$$X_2 = 1, \text{ if MBA}$$

FIGURE **13-20**

Impact of
Dummy Variables
on Regression
Analysis .

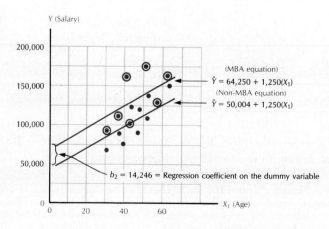

Now we develop a two-variable multiple regression model of the form

$$\hat{Y} = b_0 + b_1 X_1 + b_2 X_2$$

After employing a computer and statistical software, we get the following model:

$$\hat{Y} = 50,004 + 1,250X_1 + 14,246X_2$$

Since the dummy variable, X_2, has been coded 0 or 1 depending on degree status, incorporating it into the regression model is like having two simple linear regression lines with the same slopes, but different intercepts. For instance, when $X_2 = 0$, the regression equation is

$$\hat{Y} = 50,004 + 1,250X_1 + 14,246(0)$$
$$= 50,004 + 1,250X_1$$

This line is shown in Figure 13-20.

However, when $X_2 = 1$ (the executive has an MBA), the regression equation is

$$\hat{Y} = 50,004 + 1,250X_1 + 14,246(1)$$
$$= 64,250 + 1,250X_1$$

This regression line is also shown in Figure 13-20. As you can see, the effect of the dummy variable is on the regression intercept. In this case, the intercept for executives with an MBA degree is $14,246 higher than for those without an MBA.

We interpret the regression coefficient on this degree dummy variable as follows: "Based on these data, on the average and controlling for age (X_1), executives with an MBA degree make $14,246 per year more in salary than their non-MBA counterparts."

Of course, we could develop confidence interval estimates for this regression coefficient and test its significance just as we can with a quantitative variable.

We can also show the effect of including a dummy variable in the American County regression model by starting with the following simple regression equation:

$$\text{Sales price} = 17,590.59 + 36.28X_1$$

Figure 13-21 illustrates this regression line for sales price as a function of square feet, X_1.

Now, suppose a qualitative variable defining whether or not the house has central air conditioning is added. The variable would be

$$\text{If air conditioning, } X_6 = 1$$

$$\text{If no air conditioning, } X_6 = 0$$

Then the regression model would be

$$\hat{Y} = b_0 + b_1 X_1 + b_6 X_6$$

534 Chapter 13

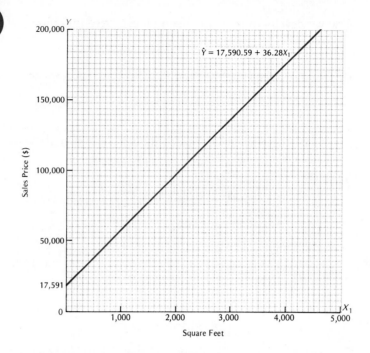

FIGURE 13-21

Simple Regression Line for the American County Example

Table 13-12 shows the computer output for the American County regression model with square feet and air conditioning as the independent variables. The model is

$$\hat{Y} = 15,503.34 + 32.14X_1 + 4,356.99X_6$$

TABLE 13-12

MINITAB Output with Dummy Variable for the American County Example

MTB > REGRESS 'Y' on 2 predictors 'X1' 'X6'

The regression equation is
Y = 15503.336 + 32.138X1 + 4356.988X6

Predictor	Coef	Stddev	t-ratio	p
Constant	15503.336			
X1	32.138	1.247	25.78	0.000
X6	4356.988	1158.773	3.76	0.000

s = 13821.679   R-sq = 75.8%   R-sq(adj) = 75.7%

Analysis of Variance

SOURCE	DF	SS	MS	F	p
Regression	2	316460785892.635	158230392946.318	828.263	0.000
Error	528	100868484702.954	191038796.785898		
Total	530	417329270595.589			

FIGURE **13-22**

Impact of a
Dummy Variable
in the Regression
Model for the
American County
Example

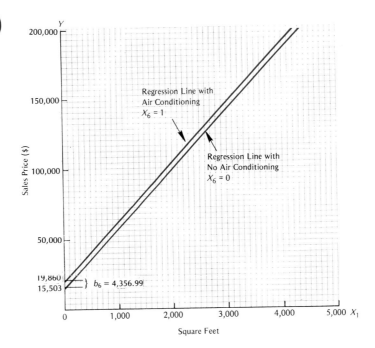

Since variable X_6 can be only 0 or 1, incorporating a dummy variable is equivalent to finding two regression equations with *equal* slopes but *different* intercepts:

$$\hat{Y} = 15,503.34 + 32.14X_1 \quad \text{if } X_6 = 0$$

and

$$\hat{Y} = 19,860.33 + 32.14X_1 \quad \text{if } X_6 = 1$$

The impact of the dummy variable is illustrated in Figure 13-22. The difference in intercepts indicates that, holding square feet constant, the price of a house is on the average $4,356.99 higher if it has central air conditioning.

SKILL DEVELOPMENT PROBLEMS FOR **SECTION 13-8**

The following exercises are included to help you gain a better understanding of the material presented in this section.

26. A manager is considering incorporating a new variable into her regression model. This variable measures education level of the respondent. The variable has been measured on four levels as follows:

 1. No high school degree
 2. High school degree
 3. Some college courses
 4. College degree

a. She is considering this variable and plans to use the codes 1, 2, 3, and 4 to determine which educational level the respondent has achieved. Comment on this.

b. How many dummy variables would you set up to handle this situation? Describe each dummy variable.

27. A study was recently performed by the American Automobile Association in which it attempted to develop a regression model to explain variation in EPA mileage ratings of new cars. At one stage of the analysis, the model took the following form:

$$\hat{Y} = 34.20 - 0.003X_1 + 4.56X_2$$

where

$$X_1 = \text{Vehicle weight}$$
$$X_2 = 1, \text{ if standard transmission}$$
$$= 0, \text{ if automatic transmission}$$

a. Interpret the regression coefficient for variable X_1.
b. Interpret the regression coefficient for variable X_2.
c. Discuss the effect of a dummy variable being incorporated in a regression model like this one. Use a graph if it is helpful.

28. The following data were collected by the Gilmore Accounting Firm in an effort to explain variation in client profitability:

Y	X_1	X_2
2,345	45	1
4,200	56	2
278	26	3
1,211	56	2
1,406	24	2
500	23	3
−700	34	3
3,457	45	1
2,478	47	1
1,975	24	2
206	32	3

where

$$Y = \text{Net profit earned from the client}$$
$$X_1 = \text{Number of hours spent working with the client}$$
$$X_2 = \text{Type of client:}$$
$$\text{1, if manufacturing}$$
$$\text{2, if service}$$
$$\text{3, if governmental}$$

a. Develop a plot of each independent variable against the client income variable. Comment on what, if any, relationship appears to exist.

b. Run a simple linear regression analysis using only variable X_1 as the independent variable. Describe this model fully.

c. Now, incorporate the client type variable into the regression analysis and describe the resulting multiple regression model. Test all appropriate hypotheses, using an $\alpha = 0.05$ level. (*Hint:* You will have to develop dummy variables.)

d. Holding the other factors constant, what is the average difference in profit if the client is governmental? Also state this in terms of a 95% confidence interval estimate.

13-9 CONCLUSIONS

This chapter has introduced the fundamental concepts of simple linear regression and correlation analysis. The techniques of regression and correlation analysis are widely used in business decision making and data analysis. Regression analysis can be applied as a tool for prediction, description, and control within an organization.

Correlation measures the strength of the linear relationship between two variables. The closer the correlation coefficient is to ± 1.0, the stronger the linear relationship between the two variables. When a dependent and an independent variable are highly correlated, the resulting simple linear regression model will tend to explain a substantial proportion of the variation in the dependent variable.

A wide variety of statistical tests have been presented in this chapter. As indicated, many of these tests are equivalent.

Multiple regression is an extension of simple regression analysis. In multiple regression, two or more independent variables are used to explain the variation in the dependent variable. Just as a manager searches for the best combination of employees to perform a job, the decision maker using multiple regression analysis searches for the best combination of independent variables to explain variation in the dependent variable.

CHAPTER **GLOSSARY**

adjusted R-square (R_A^2) A measure of the percentage of explained variation in the dependent variable that takes into account the relationship between the number of cases and the number of independent variables in the regression model. Whereas R^2 will generally increase when an independent variable is added, adjusted R^2 (R_A^2) will decrease if the added variable does not reduce the unexplained variation enough to offset the loss of degrees of freedom.

correlation coefficient   A quantitative measure of the linear relationship between two variables. The correlation ranges from $+1.0$ to -1.0. A correlation of ± 1.0 indicates a perfect linear relationship, whereas a correlation of 0 indicates no linear relationship.

correlation matrix   A table showing the pairwise correlations between all variables (dependent and independent).

dependent variable   The variable to be predicted or explained in a regression model. This variable is assumed to be functionally related to the independent variable.

dummy variables   Variables in a regression model that have two categories, valued 0 and 1. If a qualitative variable has v multiple categories, $v - 1$ dummy variables are formed to represent the qualitative variable in the analysis.

independent variable   A variable related to a dependent variable in a regression equation. The independent variable is used in a regression model to estimate the value of the dependent variable.

least squares criterion   The criterion for determining a regression line that minimizes the sum of squared residuals.

multicollinearity   Correlation among the independent variables. Usually the term is used when the intercorrelation is high.

multiple coefficient of determination (R^2) The percentage of variation in the dependent variable explained by the independent variables in the regression model.

multiple regression model   A regression model having two or more independent variables with a regression equation of the form

$$Y_i = \beta_0 + \beta_1 X_{1i} + \beta_2 X_{2i} + \beta_3 X_{3i} + \cdots + \beta_K X_{Ki} + e_i$$

regression coefficients   In the simple regression model, there are two coefficients: the intercept and the slope.

regression plane   The multiple regression equivalent of the simple regression line. The plane has a different slope for each independent variable.

regression slope coefficient   The average change in the dependent variable for a unit increase in the independent variable. The slope coefficient may be positive or negative, depending on the relationship between the two variables.

residual   The difference between the actual value of the dependent variable and the value predicted by the regression model.

scatter plot   A two-dimensional plot showing the (X, Y) value for each observation. The scatter plot is used as a picture of the relationship between two variables.

simple regression analysis   A regression model that uses one independent variable to explain the variation in the dependent variable. The model takes the form

$$Y_i = \beta_0 + \beta_1 X_i + e_i$$

spurious correlation   Correlation between two variables that have no known cause-and-effect connection.

standard error of the estimate   The square root of the mean square residual in the analysis of variance table for a regression model. The standard error measures the dispersion of the actual values of the dependent variable around the fitted regression plane.

standardized residual   The residual divided by the standard error of the estimate.

CHAPTER FORMULAS

Correlation coefficient

$$r = \frac{n\Sigma XY - \Sigma X\Sigma Y}{\sqrt{[n(\Sigma X^2) - (\Sigma X)^2][n(\Sigma Y^2) - (\Sigma Y)^2]}}$$

Test statistic for significance of the correlation coefficient

$$t = \frac{r}{\sqrt{\dfrac{1 - r^2}{n - 2}}}$$

Coefficient of determination

$$R^2 = \frac{SSR}{TSS} = 1 - \frac{SSE}{TSS}$$

Least squares estimate of the regression slope coefficient

$$b_1 = \frac{\Sigma XY - \dfrac{\Sigma X\Sigma Y}{n}}{\Sigma X^2 - \dfrac{(\Sigma X)^2}{n}} = \frac{\Sigma(X - \overline{X})(Y - \overline{Y})}{\Sigma(X - \overline{X})^2}$$

Least squares estimate of the regression intercept coefficient

$$b_0 = \overline{Y} - b_1\overline{X}$$

Standard error of the slope coefficient

$$S_{b_1} = \frac{S_e}{\sqrt{\Sigma(X - \overline{X})^2}}$$

Standard error of the estimate

$$S_e = \sqrt{\frac{\text{SSE}}{n-2}}$$

Sum of squares error

$$\text{SSE} = \sum_{i=1}^{n} (Y_i - \hat{Y}_i)^2$$

Total sum of squares

$$\text{TSS} = \sum_{i=1}^{n} (Y_i - \overline{Y})^2$$

Test statistic for significance of the slope coefficient

$$t = \frac{b_1 - \beta_1}{S_{b_1}}$$

Test statistic for significance of the simple regression model

$$F = \frac{\dfrac{\text{SSR}}{1}}{\dfrac{\text{SSE}}{n-2}}$$

Prediction interval for average Y, given X_p

$$\hat{Y} \pm t_{\alpha/2} \sqrt{\frac{\text{SSE}}{n-2}} \sqrt{\frac{1}{n} + \frac{(X_p - \overline{X})^2}{\Sigma X^2 - \dfrac{(\Sigma X)^2}{n}}}$$

Prediction interval for a particular Y, given X_p

$$\hat{Y} \pm t_{\alpha/2} \sqrt{\frac{\text{SSE}}{n-2}} \sqrt{1 + \frac{1}{n} + \frac{(X_p - \overline{X})^2}{\Sigma X^2 - \dfrac{(\Sigma X)^2}{n}}}$$

Correlation coefficient

$$r = \frac{\Sigma(X_i - \overline{X})(Y_i - \overline{Y})}{\sqrt{\Sigma(X_i - \overline{X})^2 \Sigma(Y_i - \overline{Y})^2}}$$

Coefficient of multiple determination

$$R^2 = \frac{SSR}{TSS}$$

Adjusted R^2

$$R_A^2 = 1 - (1 - R^2)\left(\frac{n-1}{n-K-1}\right)$$

Standardized residual

$$\frac{e_i}{\sqrt{MSE}}$$

SOLVED PROBLEMS

1. The Cal-Pit Water Company, located in Pittsburg, California, has selected a
    random sample of fifteen customers to see if it can develop a model for
    predicting water usage. Because of the short supply of water in the area,
    predicting water usage is an important part of the company's planning
    activities.

    The company wants to see whether a simple linear regression model, with
    family size as the independent variable and water used as the dependent
    variable, can be a valid predictive tool. The data based on the past month's
    water usage are as follows:

Customer	Water Used (gals) Y	Family Size X
1	1,100	3
2	1,425	5
3	785	2
4	950	3
5	1,200	4
6	1,152	4
7	973	3
8	1,525	5
9	1,600	4
10	700	3
11	1,100	5
12	1,414	4
13	700	2
14	953	2
15	1,063	2

Solution

The first step is to draw the scatter plot.

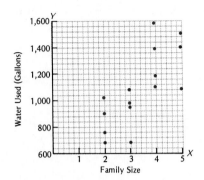

Although not perfect, there does appear to be a positive linear relationship between water used and family size. The next step is to calculate the correlation coefficient, r. Recall that r is a measure of the strength of the linear relationship between two variables and is calculated with the following equation:

$$r = \frac{n\Sigma XY - \Sigma X \Sigma Y}{\sqrt{[n(\Sigma X^2) - (\Sigma X)^2]\,[n(\Sigma Y^2) - (\Sigma Y)^2]}}$$

Instead of calculating this value by hand, a computer was used, and the resulting printout is

```
*********************************************************
VARIABLE SELECTED IS.....X
SUM OF SQUARES REDUCED IN THIS STEP............622130
R-SQUARE.....................................551986
CORRELATION COEFFICIENT......................742958
F FOR ANALYSIS OF VARIANCE (D.F. = 1, 13)........16.1069
STANDARD ERROR OF ESTIMATE...........197.084
VARIABLE    REG. COEFF.    STD. ERR.-COEFF.    COMPUTED T
X             188.011          46.978             4.00212
INTERCEPT 470.094
*********************************************************
```

The correlation coefficient in this computer output is $r = 0.743$. The test of significance is

$$H_0: \quad \rho = 0$$
$$H_A: \quad \rho \neq 0$$
$$\alpha = 0.05$$

$$t = \frac{r}{\sqrt{\dfrac{1 - r^2}{n - 2}}} = \frac{0.743}{\sqrt{\dfrac{1 - (0.743)^2}{13}}}$$

$$= 4.002$$

The critical t for an alpha level of 0.05 and 13 degrees of freedom is 2.160, and, since 4.002 is greater than 2.160, we conclude that there is a significant linear relationship between the two variables.

The next step is to calculate the regression coefficients. This was also done by the computer. The estimates are

$$\hat{Y} = 470.094 + 188.011X$$

The standard error of the estimate is 197.084. The table of residuals printed by the computer program is

OBS. NO.	Y OBSERVED	Y ESTIMATED	RESIDUAL
1	1100	1034.13	65.8713
2	1425	1410.15	14.8486
3	785	846.117	−61.1173
4	950	1034.13	−84.1287
5	1200	1222.14	−22.1401
6	1152	1222.14	−70.1401
7	973	1034.13	−61.1287
8	1525	1410.15	114.849
9	1600	1222.14	377.860
10	700	1034.13	−334.129
11	1100	1410.15	−310.151
12	1414	1222.14	191.860
13	700	846.117	−146.117
14	953	846.117	106.883
15	1063	846.117	216.883

Although our test of significance has indicated that family size has a positive linear relationship to water usage, note that family size explained only 55% of the variation in water usage for the sample data. Also, the standard error of the estimate, 197.084, is quite large, indicating that any prediction interval developed will be imprecise.

2. Referring to Solved Problem 1, suppose a family of five is going to be added to the Cal-Pit Water Company's customer list. Using the regression model developed in Problem 1, determine the 90% confidence interval for the number of gallons of water this family will use.

Solution

The desired prediction interval format is

$$\hat{Y} \pm t_{\alpha/2} \sqrt{\frac{\text{SSE}}{n-2}} \sqrt{1 + \frac{1}{n} + \frac{(X_p - \overline{X})^2}{\Sigma X^2 - \frac{(\Sigma X)^2}{n}}}$$

To obtain the value of $\hat{Y}$, we substitute 5 for X in the regression model.

$$\hat{Y} = 470.094 + 188.011(5)$$
$$= 1{,}410.149$$

Thus, the point estimate of water used by this family of five is roughly 1,410 gallons.

To determine the confidence interval, you should recall that $\sqrt{SSE/(n-2)}$ is the standard error of the estimate. This value is 197.084 and appeared on the computer printout shown earlier. Thus, we have

$$1{,}410 \pm 1.771(197.084) \sqrt{1 + \frac{1}{15} + \frac{(X_p - \overline{X})^2}{\Sigma X^2 - \frac{(\Sigma X)^2}{n}}}$$

Our next step is to complete the calculations under the square root.

Family Size X	X^2	Family Size X	X^2
3	9	4	16
5	25	3	9
2	4	5	25
3	9	4	16
4	16	2	4
4	16	2	4
3	9	2	4
5	25		

$$\Sigma X = 51, \quad \Sigma X^2 = 191$$

Then

$$\overline{X} = \frac{51}{15}$$

$$= 3.4$$

Thus the 90% prediction interval, given $X_p = 5$, is

$$1{,}410 \pm 1.771(197.084) \sqrt{1 + \frac{1}{15} + \frac{(5 - 3.4)^2}{191 - \frac{2{,}601}{15}}}$$

$$1{,}410 \pm 384.28$$

$$1{,}025.72 \text{ gal} \underline{\quad\quad} 1{,}794.28 \text{ gal}$$

The Cal-Pit Water Company can be confident that this family of five will use between 1,026 and 1,794 gallons of water per month. Although this might be helpful information, the precision of the estimate is poor.

ADDITIONAL PROBLEMS

29. The Farmington City Council recently commissioned a study of the park users. Data were collected on the age of the person surveyed and the number of times he or she had been to the park in the past month. The data collected were as follows:

Park Visits	Age
Y	X
7	16
3	15
6	28
5	16
1	29
2	38
4	48
8	18
4	24
5	33
1	56

Draw a scatter plot for these data and discuss what, if any, relationship appears to be present between the two variables.

30. Referring to Problem 29, compute the correlation between age and the number of visits to the park. Write a letter to the Farmington City Council explaining what the correlation measures. Test to determine whether the true correlation might actually equal 0. Use an α level of 0.10. Discuss.

31. A marketing research study performed by the marketing division of the Klondike Company surveyed the income levels and expenditures on recreation for a sample of twenty people. Measurements recorded Y, the expenditures on recreation during the previous year, and X, the total annual family income.

Y	X	Y	X
$1,425	$21,300	900	17,600
1,675	30,200	1,000	16,890
1,356	31,500	2,450	28,000
4,530	45,900	650	14,300
3,200	34,600	300	9,800
1,060	17,800	1,500	24,700
4,090	53,600	890	20,500
1,200	17,400	2,300	31,700
1,800	26,800	3,100	47,800
700	15,700	100	8,400

Draw a scatter plot for these data and discuss what, if any, relationship between the variables appears to exist based on the scatter plot.

32. Refer to Problem 31 and compute the correlation coefficient for the two variables *income* and *dollars spent on recreation*. Test to determine whether the true correlation is different from 0, using an alpha level of 0.05.

33. The Penrose Consulting Company performs studies for universities that want to raise money through their alumni associations. As part of its work, it recently sampled eighteen universities across the United States and determined the number of alumni and the total dollars in gifts received from alumni during the previous academic year. The following data were recorded.

School	Number of Alumni X	Gift Money Y
1	987	$ 234,700
2	1,350	769,000
3	2,345	1,230,000
4	1,300	450,780
5	12,569	6,450,000
6	8,560	2,650,000
7	3,450	1,430,000
8	1,890	230,000
9	23,456	4,560,000
10	12,700	2,678,900
11	4,600	800,000
12	5,700	2,780,000
13	23,600	7,000,000
14	33,450	8,900,000
15	28,900	8,600,000
16	1,800	133,000
17	12,800	5,790,000
18	20,540	2,400,300

a. Draw a scatter plot of these two variables. Based on this plot only, does it appear that a linear relationship exists between the two variables?
b. Compute the correlation coefficient and discuss what it measures.
c. Test to determine whether the population correlation coefficient is actually 0, using an alpha level of 0.05.

34. A company that makes a cattle feed supplement has studied 335 cattle and found the correlation between the amount of supplement fed and the daily weight gain to be 0.104 ($r = 0.104$). Based on these results, what should be concluded about the true correlation between these two variables? Test using an alpha level of 0.05. Comment on the results.

35. The Grinfield Service Company marketing director is interested in analyzing the relationship between her company's sales and the advertising dollars spent. In the course of her analysis, she selected a random sample of 20 weeks and recorded the sales for each week and the amount spent on advertising. These data are shown as follows:

Sales	Advertising	Sales	Advertising
$2,050	$180	3,250	300
3,760	243	4,680	402
1,897	204	4,200	399
2,567	199	2,400	209
4,330	356	1,890	245
5,670	605	3,600	190
2,356	200	5,700	480
3,456	304	5,690	515
1,254	105	2,300	300
4,300	379	1,700	145

a. Identify the independent and dependent variables.
b. Draw a scatter plot with the dependent variable on the vertical axis and the independent variable on the horizontal axis.
c. Compute the correlation coefficient for these two variables and test to determine whether the true population correlation is different from 0 at the alpha level of 0.05.
d. Develop the least squares regression equation for these variables. Plot the regression line on the scatter plot.
e. Perform tests of significance on both the regression model and the slope coefficient.

36. A manager for a major manufacturing company recently delivered a speech to other managers from around the United States. During the course of the speech, he was explaining a study his company had done with respect to sales and price of a particular product. He said that it had developed a simple regression model and found the regression slope coefficient to be $-3,456.98$. He then said that this means that increasing price by 1 dollar will cause sales to drop by 3,456.98 units. Comment on this statement, indicating what, if anything, about the statement you agree with.

37. The Sanders Company production manager is in the process of performing a productivity study of the employees at the Black Hills plant. In the process of performing this study, he has selected a random sample of twenty employees who have worked for the company for 4 years or more. For each employee, he measured the number of hours of special training the employee has taken and the production rate for the employee in pieces per day produced. The following summary data are available:

$$Y = \text{Pieces produced per day}$$
$$X = \text{Hours of special training}$$
$$\overline{X} = 13.50$$
$$S_e = 11.0$$
$$\overline{Y} = 125.0$$
$$\hat{Y} = 88.5 + 1.5X$$
$$\Sigma(X - \overline{X})^2 = 1,245.0$$

a. Develop a 95% prediction interval for the average daily production for people who have taken 15.0 hours of training. Interpret this prediction interval estimate.
b. Develop a 95% prediction interval for a particular individual who has taken 8 hours of special training courses. Interpret these results.
c. Comment on whether you believe the prediction interval computed in part **b** is satisfactory for predicting productivity for individual employees with 8 hours of courses. Discuss.

38. The managerial development director of a major corporation is trying to determine what personal abilities are necessary for a manager to move from middle- to upper-level management. Although she has been relatively successful predicting who will move rapidly from lower- to middle-

the independent variables and the dependent variable and between all possible pairs of independent variables. Write a report that discusses the correlation matrix. Which variables appear to have most promise as predictors of stock price? Discuss.

2. Referring to Problem 1, X_8 is a coded variable indicating on which stock exchange the company's stock is traded. Can this variable be used directly as it is or will you need to make some modification? If so, what is that modification, and why are you making it? Given that a modification is necessary, make the modification and determine the correlation between the new variable(s) and the dependent variable. Discuss.

3. Referring to Problems 1 and 2, develop a multiple regression model with stock price as the dependent variable. Bring in all appropriate independent variables.

    a. Identify the regression model including the intercept and slope coefficients. Comment on whether these coefficients look reasonable given the correlations in Problems 1 and 2. Discuss.

    b. Is the overall model significant? State clearly the null and alternative hypotheses and show your test procedure. Test at the $\alpha = 0.10$ level. Discuss.

    c. What is the coefficient of determination? Does the model explain a significant proportion of the variation in the dependent variable? Test at an $\alpha = 0.10$ level.

    d. Test each of the regression slope coefficients individually to determine which variables are significant in the model. Test at an $\alpha = 0.10$ level. Write a short report describing your results.

DATABASE: **PACRIM** (Refer to the database description in Chapter 1.)

1. It has been suggested that you develop a model that might be used to explain the variation in stockholder's equity, X_7, for companies doing business in the Pacific Rim region. One of the variables that is under consideration is the country in which the company is headquartered. Discuss how you could incorporate this variable into the regression analysis. If new variables are required, go ahead and build the new variables. Discuss what you have done and why.

2. Referring to Problem 1, develop a correlation matrix that includes all independent and dependent variables. Discuss the correlations making note of the size and sign of the correlations.

3. Referring to Problems 1 and 2, develop a multiple regression model with stockholder's equity as the dependent variable. Bring in all appropriate independent variables.

    a. Identify the regression model, including the intercept and slope coefficients. Comment on whether these coefficients look reasonable given the correlations in Problems 1 and 2. Discuss.

Contingency Tables and

Goodness-of-Fit Tests

WHY DECISION MAKERS NEED TO KNOW

The estimation and hypothesis-testing tools introduced in previous chapters are designed to be used
with interval or ratio level data. For instance, a marketing manager may wish to estimate the average
annual income of individuals in a particular region of his state. The
variable of interest, income, is assumed to be measured on a ratio
scale. A production manager might be interested in determining
whether the average set-up time on a machine has decreased after a
training program was initiated. The variable, set-up time, is measured
on a continuous scale and is a ratio level variable. These are but two
examples of the many you might encounter, where the large- and
small-sample estimation and hypothesis-testing procedures introduced
in previous chapters could be applied.

   You will also encounter many business situations in which the
level of data measurement for the variable of interest is either nominal
or ordinal and the estimation and statistical procedures introduced
thus far are not appropriate. For example, a bank may have data on its
customers' automobile loan status that are represented by a code to
indicate whether the customer is a poor risk or a good risk. The bank
may also have data for these customers that indicate, by a code,
whether each person is buying or renting a home. The loan officer may
be interested in determining whether loan classification is independent
of home ownership status. Since both variables are qualitative or categorical variables, their measurement level is nominal and a new statistical tool is needed to assist the manager in reaching an inference
about the customer population. That statistical tool is contingency

analysis. Contingency analysis is a widely used tool for analyzing the relationship between qualitative variables and one that decision makers in all business areas find helpful for data analysis.

Business decision makers also encounter situations in which they need to determine whether output data from a particular process can be described by a known distribution. For example, a food processing company uses an automated machine to fill packages of frozen vegetables. According to the machine's manufacturer, the distribution of individual package weights coming from the machine is normally distributed around a specified mean with a standard deviation of 0.10 pound. Periodically, the production control manager will weigh a sample of packages from the line and from these sample data infer whether the machine is functioning as specified by the manufacturer. To do this, she needs to utilize a statistical technique called goodness of fit. Goodness-of-fit tests are used in many business situations and you will find this tool very useful.

Thus, depending on the situation, as a decision maker you will need an ever-expanding array of statistical tools. The techniques of contingency analysis and goodness-of-fit tests are two additional techniques that will be important additions to tools presented in earlier chapters.

CHAPTER OBJECTIVES

This chapter introduces two important statistical tools: contingency analysis and goodness-of-fit testing. Contingency analysis is a useful tool for determining whether a relationship of statistical independence exists between two or more categorical variables. Goodness-of-fit tests are used to determine whether data coming from a process fit a specified distribution. This chapter will present a variety of real decision-making applications for which these statistical tools are helpful. Included in this discussion will be the introduction of the chi-square test for independence, the phi coefficient, the chi-square goodness-of-fit test, and the Lilliefors goodness-of-fit test.

STUDENT OBJECTIVES

After studying the material in this chapter, you should be able to do the following:

1. Set up a contingency analysis table and perform a chi-square test of independence.
2. Compute and interpret the phi coefficient for a contingency analysis application.
3. Utilize the chi-square goodness-of-fit test to determine whether data from a process fit a specified distribution.
4. Utilize the Lilliefors goodness-of-fit test to determine whether data from a process fit a normal distribution.

14-1

INTRODUCTION TO CONTINGENCY ANALYSIS

During the 1990–1991 academic year, Dalgarno Photo, Inc., undertook the task of surveying yearbook representatives at colleges and universities in its market area. A major part of Dalgarno Photo, Inc.'s business comes from taking photographs for college yearbooks in the eastern United States. A first-year MBA student was hired to develop a survey that would be administered as a mail questionnaire to the yearbook representatives at the colleges and universities.

The primary objective of the survey was to solicit objective views regarding a variety of issues related to the photography and publishing activities associated with yearbook development. For instance, the survey was designed to obtain information about what photographer and publisher services the schools currently use and what factors are most important in making these selections.

The respondents were unaware that Dalgarno Photo, Inc., originated the survey that was mailed to representatives at 850 colleges and universities. A total of 221 usable responses were returned. The survey instrument contained thirty questions, which were coded into 137 separate variables. A portion of the survey instrument is shown in Figure 14-1.

For our purposes here, we will focus on just four of the 137 variables obtained through the survey. They are as follows:

$$X_1 = \text{Source of university funding}$$
$$X_2 = \text{Total undergraduate enrollment}$$
$$X_3 = \text{Sex of the yearbook editor}$$
$$X_4 = \text{Yearbook budget}$$

Among his many interests in this study, Dalgarno's marketing manager has questioned whether funding source and sex of the yearbook editor are related in some manner. To analyze this issue, we examine variables X_1 and X_3 more closely. Variable X_1, source of university funding, is a categorical variable coded as follows:

$$1 = \text{Private funding}$$
$$2 = \text{State-funded}$$

Of the 221 respondents who provided data for this variable, 155 came from privately funded colleges or universities and 66 were from state-funded institutions.

Variable X_3, sex of the yearbook editor, is also a categorical variable with two response categories, coded as follows:

$$1 = \text{Male}$$
$$2 = \text{Female}$$

Of the 221 responses to the survey, 164 were from females and 57 were from males.

FIGURE 14-1

Dalgarno Photo,
Inc., Market
Survey

1. What type of institution is your college/university?
   1. Private   2. State-funded
2. What is the total undergraduate enrollment in your school?
   1. <400
   2. 400–2,000
   3. 2,000–4,000
   4. 4,000–8,000
   5. >8,000
3. What is your major course of study?
   1. Social science/Humanities
   2. Math/Science
   3. Journalism
   4. English
   5. Business/Economics
   6. Engineering/Computer
   7. Other _____
4. What is your grade level?
   1. Sophomore
   2. Junior
   3. Senior
5. What is your gender?
   1. Male
   2. Female
6. What is your title?
   1. Editor-in-chief
   2. Photography editor
   3. Layout editor
   4. Faculty advisor
   5. Other _____
7. What are your related publication experiences?
   1. Yearbook (dates and capacity) _____
   2. Other publication(s) (dates and capacity) _____
   3. No prior related experience
8. Who selected the editor-in-chief?
   1. Former editor-in-chief
   2. Former board of editors
   3. Faculty advisor
   4. Other _____
9. How many people are on the yearbook staff?
   1. <5
   2. 5–10
   3. 10–20
   4. >20

   ⋮

21. How many rolls of film were shot last year? How many were in color?
22. What was your opinion of the quality of last year's yearbook?
    (Low)   1 2 3 4 5 6 7 8 9   (High)
23. When do you normally deliver the yearbook?
    1. Fall   2. Spring   3. Summer
24. Did you meet all your publication deadlines last year? If not, please give the reasons
    for and the extent of the lateness.
    1. Yes. All deadlines were met
    2. No.   Reason(s) for lateness:
             Extent of lateness:

FIGURE **14-1**

Dalgarno Photo,
Inc., Market
Survey
(*Continued*)

25. What publication seminars or conventions are you or your staff planning to attend?
26. How active is your faculty advisor in the management of the yearbook?
    (Inactive)   1   2   3   4   5   6   7   8   9   (Active)
27. Who are your current publisher and photographer? How long have you been associated with them?

	Name	# of years of association
Publisher :		1 2 3 4 5 >6
Photographer:		1 2 3 4 5 >6

28. What are the important factors influencing your selection of the publisher and photographer? Please allocate 100 points among these factors, with the highest number of points for the most important factor.

	Publisher	Photographer
Quality	___	___
Service	___	___
Amount of discount revenue	___	___
Allowance for equipment (computers, cameras)	___	___
Previous experience with your school	___	___
Reputation	___	___
Location (local/national)	___	___
Other _____	___	___
Total	100	100

29. Do you utilize a computer? If so, for what purpose?
    1. No
    2. Yes.   a. Layout
              b. Design
              c. Word processing
              d. Accounting
              e. Other _____
30. Please indicate the annual amount allocated to the yearbook budget.
    _____ Under $20,000   _____ $20,000–$40,000   _____ $40,000–$60,000
    _____ Over $60,000

In cases like this, where the variables of interest are both categorical and the decision maker is interested in determining whether a relationship exists between the two, a statistical technique known as **contingency analysis** is useful. To employ contingency analysis, we set up a two-dimensional table called a **contingency table.** A contingency table is nothing more than a table of the joint frequencies, also called a **cross-tabulation** table (see Chapter 4). The contingency table for variables X_1 and X_3 is shown here:

Sex	Source of Funding		
	Private	State	
Male	14	43	57
Female	141	23	164
	155	66	221

This table shows that 14 of the respondents were males from schools that are privately funded. The numbers at the extreme right and along the bottom are called the **marginal frequencies**. For example, 57 respondents were males and 155 were from privately funded institutions.

The issue of whether there is a relationship between responses to these two variables is formally addressed through a hypothesis test where the null and alternative hypotheses are stated as follows:

H_0: Sex of yearbook editor is independent of source of college's funding.

H_A: Sex of yearbook editor *is not* independent of source of college's funding.

If the null hypothesis is true, the probability that a yearbook editor from a private institution is a male should be equal to the probability that an editor from a state-funded institution is a male. These two probabilities should also equal the probability that an editor is male without considering the school's funding source. To illustrate, we can find the probability (based on the sample data) of an editor being male as follows:

$$P(\text{male}) = \frac{\text{Number of male editors}}{\text{Number of respondents}} = \frac{57}{221}$$
$$= 0.258$$

Then, if the null hypothesis is true, we would expect

$$P(\text{male}|\text{private}) = P(\text{male}) = 0.258$$

and

$$P(\text{male}|\text{state}) = P(\text{male}) = 0.258$$

Thus, in this sample, we would expect 25.8% of the 155 privately funded schools, or 39.99 schools, to have a male yearbook editor. We would also expect 25.8% of the 66 state-funded schools, or 17.028, to have male yearbook editors. (Note, the expected numbers need not be integer values.) We can use this reasoning to determine the expected number of respondents in each cell of the contingency table:

Sex	Source of Funding		
	Private	*State*	
Male	Actual = 14 Expected = 39.99	Actual = 43 Expected = 17.028	57
Female	Actual = 141 Expected = 115.01	Actual = 23 Expected = 48.972	164
	155	66	221

Although sampling error will exist, we would expect, if the null hypothesis is true, the actual frequencies in each cell to closely match the corresponding expected cell frequencies. The greater the difference between the actual and the expected frequencies, the more likely the null hypothesis of independence is false and should be rejected. The statistical test to determine whether the sample data support or refute the null hypothesis is given by equation 14-1:

$$\chi^2 = \sum_{i=1}^{r} \sum_{j=1}^{c} \frac{(f_{A_{ij}} - f_{E_{ij}})^2}{f_{E_{ij}}} \quad \text{with d.f.} = (r - 1)(c - 1) \qquad \textbf{14-1}$$

where

f_A = Actual cell frequency

f_E = Expected cell frequency

r = Number of rows

c = Number of columns

Do not be confused by the double summation in equation 14-1; it merely indicates that all rows and columns must be used in calculating χ^2.

Figure 14-2 presents the hypotheses and test results for this example. Note, the calculated chi-square statistic is compared to the tabled value of chi-square for an $\alpha = 0.05$ and degrees of freedom $= (2 - 1)(2 - 1) = 1$. Since $\chi^2_{\text{calculated}} = 76.15 > 3.841$, the null hypothesis of independence should be rejected and Dalgarno Photo representatives should conclude that the sex of the yearbook editor and the school's source of funding are not independent. The contingency table seems to indicate that males are proportionately underrepresented in privately funded schools and overrepresented in state-supported schools.

THE PHI COEFFICIENT FOR 2 × 2 CONTINGENCY TABLES

In Chapter 13, you were introduced to the correlation coefficient, a statistical measure of the strength of the linear relationship between two variables. Recall that if two variables are perfectly correlated, the correlation coefficient would be $+1$ or -1, depending on the direction of the relationship. However, the correlation coefficient is most applicable when the variables of interest are quantitative and measured by an interval or ratio scale. Thus, the correlation coefficient should not be used to measure the association between the sex variable and school-funding source variable in the Dalgarno Photo, Inc., example we have been discussing. An appropriate measure of association, however, does exist—the

FIGURE 14-2

Chi-Square
Contingency
Analysis Test for
the Dalgarno
Photo, Inc.,
Example

Hypotheses:

H_0: Sex of yearbook editor is independent of college's funding source.
H_A: Sex of yearbook editor *is not* independent of college's funding source.

$\alpha = 0.05$

	Private	State
Male	$f_A = 14$ $f_E = 39.99$	$f_A = 43$ $f_E = 17.028$
Female	$f_A = 141$ $f_E = 115.01$	$f_A = 23$ $f_E = 48.972$

Test Statistic:

$$\chi^2_{calculated} = \sum_{i=1}^{r} \sum_{j=1}^{c} \frac{(f_{A_{ij}} - f_{E_{ij}})^2}{f_{E_{ij}}} = \frac{(14 - 39.99)^2}{39.99} + \frac{(43 - 17.028)^2}{17.028}$$

$$+ \frac{(141 - 115.01)^2}{115.01} + \frac{(23 - 48.972)^2}{48.972}$$

$$= 76.152$$

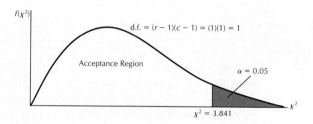

d.f. $= (r - 1)(c - 1) = (1)(1) = 1$

$f(\chi^2)$

Acceptance Region

$\alpha = 0.05$

$\chi^2 = 3.841$

χ^2

Decision Rule:

If $\chi^2_{calculated} > 3.841$, reject H_0.
Otherwise, do not reject H_0.

Since $76.152 > 3.841$, reject H_0.

phi coefficient. In this section, we introduce the phi coefficient for 2 × 2 contingency tables—those with 2 rows and 2 columns.

The **phi coefficient** is used to measure the row and column dependency in 2 × 2 contingency tables. In the contingency table, if all the items in row 1 are in one column, and all the items in row 2 are in the other column, the phi coefficient will equal +1 or −1. A phi coefficient of +1 or −1 then represents the most extreme case of dependency between the row and column variables. Values of phi close to 0 occur when there is independence between the row and column variables. Thus, the phi coefficient is a correlation coefficient computed on the observations in the contingency table.

The Greek symbol phi, ϕ, is used to represent the phi coefficient and is computed using equation 14-2:

$$\phi = \frac{ad - bc}{\sqrt{R_1 R_2 C_1 C_2}}$$

14-2

where

a = Frequency count in row 1, column 1

b = Frequency count in row 1, column 2

c = Frequency count in row 2, column 1

d = Frequency count in row 2, column 2

R_i = Total frequency in row i

C_i = Total frequency in column i

Once again, consider the contingency table for Dalgarno Photo, Inc., with yearbook editor sex and college's funding source as the variables of interest:

	Source of Funding		
Sex	Private	State	
Male	14	43	57
Female	141	23	164
	155	66	221

We compute the phi coefficient using equation 14-2 as follows:

$$\phi = \frac{(14)(23) - (43)(141)}{\sqrt{(57)(164)(155)(66)}}$$

$$= -0.587$$

The phi coefficient shows a reasonably strong negative relationship between editor sex and the college's source of funding. In this case, the implication is that proportionally more editors at state-supported schools are males and proportionally more editors at private schools are females. This means that if an editor is from a state-supported school, it is more likely that the editor is male than female. Likewise, the probability is higher that, if an editor is from a privately funded institution, the editor is female.

Note that the negative sign on the phi coefficient in this example is a result of the order in which the rows and columns were arranged in the contingency table.

For example, if we had reversed the columns to show state schools in column 1 and private schools in column 2, the phi coefficient would be $+0.587$. Check this out for yourself.

USING PHI TO TEST FOR INDEPENDENCE

Previously, we used the chi-square test to determine whether the row and column variables are independent. The chi-square test is strictly a two-tailed test, meaning that, if the null hypothesis of independence is rejected, no direction of dependence is directly supported. However, an alternate test for independence based on the phi coefficient exists that allows the decision maker to use one-tailed tests when a direction of dependence is anticipated.

Consider the Dalgarno Photo example. Suppose the yearbook sales manager thought (before doing the survey) that private schools might favor women editors, while state-supported schools tended to have men editors. Then, given the previous row and column order, the null and alternative hypotheses that the manager wishes to test are as follows:

H_0: Sex of the editor is independent of college's source of funding.

H_A: There is a negative relationship between sex of editor and funding source.

Another way of stating the alternative hypothesis is

H_A: Proportionately more of the editors at private schools will be female and proportionately more editors at state schools will be males.

Testing the null hypothesis involves comparing the computed phi coefficient to a critical value determined as follows:

If H_A predicts a negative dependency, the critical value is $-Z_\alpha/\sqrt{n}$.

If H_A predicts a positive dependency, the critical value is $+Z_\alpha/\sqrt{n}$.

If H_A is nondirectional (two-tailed), the critical values are $\pm Z_{\alpha/2}/\sqrt{n}$.

Here Z_α is the Z value from the standard normal distribution with probability α in the tail of the distribution.

In this example, $\phi = -0.587$ and the alternative hypothesis predicts a negative dependency, so we need to compare $\phi = -0.587$ to $-Z_\alpha/\sqrt{n}$. Figure 14-3 illustrates the result of the test for an alpha level of 0.05. As is seen in Figure 14-3, the null hypothesis is rejected and we conclude that a significant negative relationship exists between the two variables.

The test of significance shown in Figure 14-3 using the phi coefficient is closely related to the chi-square test used in Figure 14-2. In fact, $\chi^2_{calculated} = n\,\phi^2$. Since the two tests are related in this manner, there is no need to compute both tests for a given application. The advantage of the phi coefficient is that it allows one-tailed tests to be performed, whereas the chi-square test is strictly two-tailed.

FIGURE **14-3**

Test of
Independence
Using the Phi
Coefficient for
the Dalgarno
Photo Example

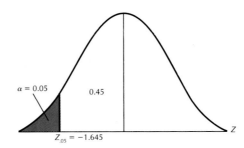

Hypotheses:

H_0: Sex of the editor is independent of college funding source.
H_A: There is a negative relationship between sex of the editor and the college funding source.

$\alpha = 0.05$

Test Statistic:

$\phi = -0.587$
Critical value $= -1.645/\sqrt{221} = -0.111$

Decision Rule:

If $\phi < -Z_\alpha/\sqrt{n}$, reject H_0.
Otherwise, do not reject H_0.

Since $-0.587 < -0.111$, reject H_0 and conclude that there is a negative relationship between the two variables.

This section has introduced the concept of contingency analysis, a very important statistical tool for analyzing categorical data. However, the applications in this chapter have been limited to 2×2 contingency tables. In the next section, we extend the topic of contingency analysis to applications with $r \times c$ tables (tables with r rows and c columns).

SKILL DEVELOPMENT PROBLEMS FOR **SECTION 14-1**

The following problems have been included to provide you with a chance to better understand the material presented in this section.

1. A survey has been conducted at a local company in which various questions about the workplace environment were asked. Two of the questions are listed as follows:

    a. Do you mind if people smoke in the office area? _____ Yes _____ No
    b. Do you smoke? _____ Yes _____ No

Shown are a subset of the responses that came back on these two variables. You are to construct a contingency analysis table from these data.

Respondent	Question 1	Question 2
1	Yes	No
2	Yes	Yes
3	No	Yes
4	No	Yes
5	No	No
6	Yes	No
7	Yes	No
8	Yes	Yes
9	No	No
10	Yes	No

2. Referring to Problem 1, suppose 200 people in the company responded to the survey and the following contingency table has been constructed from the responses.

Do You Care About Smoking in the Office?	*Do You Smoke?*	
	Yes	*No*
Yes	11	139
No	29	21

Based on these data, is attitude about smoking in the office independent of whether an individual smokes or not? Use the chi-square test and test at an $\alpha = 0.10$ level. Discuss the results.

3. Referring to Problems 1 and 2, compute the phi coefficient and interpret.

4. For the ten responses in Problem 1, use the code Yes = 1 and No = 2 for each variable. Then compute the correlation coefficient as discussed in Chapter 13. Also compute the phi coefficient. Compare the two coefficients and discuss.

5. Referring to Problems 1–3, suppose the claim has been made that proportionately more nonsmokers do not want smoking in the office. Thus, the expectation is that a negative relationship will exist between these two variables. Test this claim using the phi coefficient test at an $\alpha = 0.05$ level. Discuss.

6. A contingency analysis table has been constructed from data obtained in a phone survey of customers in a market area in which respondents were asked to indicate whether they owned a domestic or foreign car and whether they were a member of a union or not. The following contingency table is provided.

	Union	
Car	Yes	No
Domestic	155	470
Foreign	40	325

Use the chi-square approach to test whether type of car owned (domestic or foreign) is independent of union membership. Test using an $\alpha = 0.05$ level.

7. Referring to Problem 6, compute the phi coefficient and test the claim that proportionately more union workers will own domestic cars than will be true for nonunion people. Use $\alpha = 0.05$ and discuss.

8. Comment on the relationship between the chi-square statistic and the phi coefficient.

14-2 $r \times c$ CONTINGENCY TABLES

Although you will have occasion to work with 2×2 contingency tables, you will also encounter situations where the row and/or column variable has been divided into more than two categories. This section extends the previous discussion to encompass the general case of analysis involving $r \times c$ contingency tables.

Recall that in the Dalgarno Photo, Inc., example we selected four variables for potential analysis. One of these variables is total undergraduate enrollment, X_2. Variable X_2 could have been treated as a ratio level variable if the survey instrument had simply asked the respondent to record the school's enrollment. However, as can be seen in Figure 14-1, question 2 requires the respondent to indicate which category of enrollment size applies. The categories are as follows:

1: <400

2: 400–2,000

3: 2,000–4,000

4: 4,000–8,000

5: >8,000

(Note that the categories are not mutually exclusive. You should be careful to avoid this error when you construct response categories on survey instruments.)

As part of his analysis of the survey data, the yearbook manager at Dalgarno Photo, Inc., is interested in determining whether university enrollment is independent of source of school funding. The manager can use the sample data to test the following hypotheses:

H_0: Enrollment is independent of school funding source.

H_A: Enrollment *is not* independent of school funding source.

As with 2×2 contingency analysis, the test for independence can be made using the chi-square test, where the expected cell frequencies are compared to the actual cell frequencies using equation 14-1. The logic of the test says that if the actual and expected frequencies closely match, then the null hypothesis of independence is not rejected. However, if the actual and expected cell frequencies are substantially different overall, the null hypothesis of independence is rejected. The calculated chi-square statistic is compared to a tabled critical value for the desired alpha and degrees of freedom equal to $(r - 1)(c - 1)$. Figure 14-4 shows the hypothesis test process.

Note, the expected cell frequencies in Figure 14-4 are determined assuming the row and column variables are independent. This means, for example, that the probability that a school has enrollment under 400 students given that the school is privately funded is assumed to be the same as the overall probability that enrollment is under 400 students for all schools. An easy way to compute f_E, the expected cell frequencies, is given by equation 14-3.

$$f_E = \frac{\text{Row total} \times \text{Column total}}{\text{Total sample size}} \qquad \text{14-3}$$

For row 1 and column 1,

$$f_E = \frac{18 \times 155}{221} = 12.62$$

and for row 3 and column 2,

$$f_E = \frac{41 \times 66}{221} = 12.24$$

Figure 14-4 shows that $\chi^2_{\text{calculated}} = 105.08 > \chi^2_{\text{critical}} = 9.488$ from the chi-square table in Appendix E. Therefore, the null hypothesis of independence is clearly rejected. Dalgarno's yearbook manager should conclude that there is a dependency relationship between source of a school's funding and undergraduate enrollment. A closer look at the contingency table in Figure 14-4 reveals that private schools tend to be overrepresented in the low enrollment categories and state schools tend to be overrepresented in the higher enrollment categories, relative to the expected frequencies.

Another analysis of variables based on the Dalgarno Photo example looks at the relationship between undergraduate enrollment and the yearbook budget, X_4, at the college. The survey questionnaire shown in Figure 14-1 indicates that question 30 requires the respondent to select a category for budget amount. Again, the survey has converted a quantitative variable into a qualitative variable with four

FIGURE 14-4

$r \times c$ Test of
Independence for
the Dalgarno
Photo, Inc.,
Example

Hypotheses:

H_0: Enrollment is independent of school funding source.
H_A: Enrollment *is not* independent of school funding source.

$\alpha = 0.05$

Source of Funding

Enrollment	Private	State	
<400	$f_A = 17$ $f_E = 12.62$	$f_A = 1$ $f_E = 5.38$	18
400–2,000	$f_A = 90$ $f_E = 66.63$	$f_A = 5$ $f_E = 28.37$	95
2,000–4,000	$f_A = 32$ $f_E = 28.76$	$f_A = 9$ $f_E = 12.24$	41
4,000–8,000	$f_A = 12$ $f_E = 25.95$	$f_A = 25$ $f_E = 11.05$	37
>8,000	$f_A = 4$ $f_E = 21.04$	$f_A = 26$ $f_E = 8.96$	30
	155	66	

Test Statistic:

$$\chi^2_{\text{calculated}} = \Sigma \Sigma \frac{(f_A - f_E)^2}{f_E} = \frac{(17 - 12.62)^2}{12.62} + \frac{(1 - 5.38)^2}{5.38} + \cdots + \frac{(4 - 21.04)^2}{21.04}$$

$$+ \frac{(26 - 8.96)^2}{8.96}$$

$$= 105.08$$

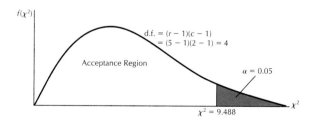

Decision Rule:

If $\chi^2_{\text{calculated}} > 9.488$, reject H_0.
Otherwise, do not reject H_0.

Since $\chi^2_{\text{calculated}} = 105.08 > 9.488$, reject H_0.
Row and column variable are *not* independent.

categories. The yearbook manager at Dalgarno is interested in testing the following null and alternative hypotheses:

H_0: The budget amount is independent of the school enrollment.

H_A: The budget amount *is not* independent of the school enrollment.

Figure 14-5 shows the 5×4 contingency table and the resulting test for independence using the chi-square test. This shows that $\chi^2_{\text{calculated}} = 100.94 > \chi^2_{\text{critical}} = 21.026$. Thus, the null hypothesis of independence is clearly rejected. We see in the contingency table that, generally, bigger schools have larger yearbook budgets.

CHI-SQUARE TEST LIMITATIONS

You should be aware the chi-square distribution is only an approximation for the true distribution of $\chi^2_{\text{calculated}}$ for the previous examples. We use the chi-square approximation because the true distribution is impractical to compute in most instances. However, research has shown that the approximation (and therefore the conclusion reached) is quite good when all expected cell frequencies exceed 1.0. Further, if the number of degrees of freedom $[(r-1)(c-1)]$ is large, the approximation will still be good even though some expected cell frequencies dip below 1.0. However, if any expected cell frequencies drop below 0.5, the general advice is to group categories where appropriate or increase the overall sample size to increase the expected cell frequencies.

If you do decide to group categories together, there should be some logic behind the resulting categories, so you do not lose the meaning of the results through poor groupings. You will need to examine each application individually to determine whether the option of grouping classes to increase expected cell frequencies makes sense.

SKILL DEVELOPMENT PROBLMS FOR **SECTION 14-2**

The following problems have been included to help you better understand the material in this chapter.

9. In a recent study of college graduates, it was hypothesized that income was independent of number of different employers the person has worked for since graduation. The data collected were as follows:

Income Level	1	2	3	4	5 or more
			Number of Employers		
Under $20,000	3	4	3	2	3
20,000–30,000	5	3	7	3	2
30,000–40,000	2	5	3	6	1
40,000–50,000	1	7	9	3	4
Over 50,000	1	3	11	7	4

FIGURE 14-5

r × *c* Test of Independence for the Dalgarno Photo, Inc., Example

Hypotheses:

H_0: Yearbook budget is independent of enrollment.
H_A: Yearbook budget *is not* independent of enrollment.
$\alpha = 0.05$

Budget

Enrollment	*Under $20,000*	*$20,000–$40,000*	*$40,000–$60,000*	*Over $60,000*	
<400	$f_A = 18$ $f_E = 7.82$	$f_A = 0$ $f_E = 6.92$	$f_A = 0$ $f_E = 2.04$	$f_A = 0$ $f_E = 1.22$	18
400–2,000	$f_A = 55$ $f_E = 41.27$	$f_A = 35$ $f_E = 36.54$	$f_A = 5$ $f_E = 10.75$	$f_A = 0$ $f_E = 6.44$	95
2,000–4,000	$f_A = 11$ $f_E = 17.81$	$f_A = 22$ $f_E = 15.77$	$f_A = 7$ $f_E = 4.64$	$f_A = 1$ $f_E = 2.78$	41
4,000–8,000	$f_A = 8$ $f_E = 16.07$	$f_A = 17$ $f_E = 14.23$	$f_A = 9$ $f_E = 4.19$	$f_A = 3$ $f_E = 2.51$	37
>8,000	$f_A = 4$ $f_E = 13.03$	$f_A = 11$ $f_E = 11.54$	$f_A = 4$ $f_E = 3.39$	$f_A = 11$ $f_E = 2.04$	30
	96	85	25	15	221

Test Statistic:

$$\chi^2_{\text{calculated}} = \Sigma\Sigma \frac{(f_A - f_E)^2}{f_E} = \frac{(18 - 7.82)^2}{7.82} + \frac{(0 - 6.92)^2}{6.92} + \cdots + \frac{(4 - 3.39)^2}{3.39}$$

$$+ \frac{(11 - 2.04)^2}{2.04}$$

$$= 100.94$$

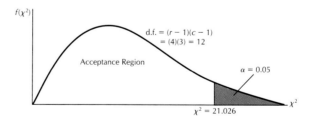

d.f. $= (r - 1)(c - 1)$
$= (4)(3) = 12$

Acceptance Region

$\alpha = 0.05$

$\chi^2 = 21.026$

Decision Rule:

If $\chi^2_{\text{calculated}} > 21.026$, reject H_0.
Otherwise, do not reject H_0.

Since $\chi^2_{\text{calculated}} = 100.94 > 21.026$, we conclude that the row and column variables are not independent.

Assuming that these data reflect observed frequencies, what can be concluded about the hypothesis? Test at an $\alpha = 0.05$ level.

10. Compute Cramer's contingency coefficient for the Problem 9 data and provide an interpretation.

11. A study of automobile drivers was conducted to determine whether the number of traffic citations issued during a 3-year period was independent of the sex of the driver. The following data were collected.

Citations Issued	Sex of Driver Male	Female
0	240	160
1	80	40
2	32	18
3	11	9
Over 3	5	4

Using an $\alpha = 0.05$ level, determine whether the two variables are independent.

12. Based on the information in Problem 11, determine the appropriate measure of association and interpret.

13. A bank in Midvale, Oregon, recently did a study of its customers to determine whether the number of transactions in a checking account was independent of the marital status of the customer. The following data were obtained.

Marital Status	0–10	11–20	21–30	31–40	Over 40
Single	13	23	19	20	11
Married	6	15	33	45	27
Divorced	4	19	22	20	15
Other	2	11	8	5	2

Based on these data, what should the bank conclude? Test at an $\alpha = 0.05$ level.

14. Compute the appropriate measure of association for the data provided in Problem 13 and interpret.

15. In a recent labor negotiation, the union officials collected data from a sample of union members regarding how long they had been with the company and how long they would be willing to stay out on strike if a strike were called. The following data were collected.

Time with Company	Strike Length Toleration		
	Under 1 Week	1–4 Weeks	Over 4 Weeks
Under 1 year	23	6	3
1–2 years	19	15	8
2–5 years	20	23	19
5–10 years	4	21	29
Over 10 years	2	5	18

Based on these data, can the union conclude that the strike length toleration is independent of time with the company? Test at the $\alpha = 0.05$ level.

16. Based on the results in Problem 15, determine the appropriate measure of the association between time with the company and strike length toleration. Comment on what this measure means in this application.

14-3 AN INTRODUCTION TO GOODNESS-OF-FIT TESTS

Gere Memorial Hospital is a privately owned hospital providing a wide range of services to people in a midwestern metropolitan community. Vickie Shelly was recently hired as operations manager from a similar position at a smaller hospital in New Mexico. One of her responsibilities is hospital staffing. A natural concern is that staffing level, consisting of nurses and other support personnel, be balanced appropriately with the patient load in the hospital.

Currently, the staffing level is balanced during the weekdays, Monday through Friday, with a reduced staffing level on Saturday and Sunday. The reasoning behind this, as explained by her predecessor, is that patient demand is fairly level throughout the weekday period and about 25% less on weekends. Although Vickie was willing to operate with this schedule for a while, discussions with other hospital staff soon convinced her to perform a study of patient demand to see whether the pattern may have changed.

To conduct the study, Vickie requested a sample of twenty days for each day of the week, showing the number of patients in the hospital on each of the sample days. A portion of the data that she received follows:

Day	Patient Count
Monday, May 6	325
Monday, October 7	379
Tuesday, July 2	456
Monday, July 15	323
Wednesday, April 3	467
⋮	⋮
etc.	etc.

TABLE 14-1

Patient Count Data for Gere Memorial Hospital Example

Day	Total Patient Count
Sunday	4,502
Monday	6,623
Tuesday	8,308
Wednesday	10,420
Thursday	11,032
Friday	10,754
Saturday	4,361
Total	56,000

FIGURE 14-6

Graph of Actual Frequencies

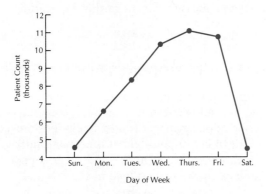

For the 140 days observed, the total count was 56,000 patients. Vickie then computed the total patient count for each day of the week. These results are shown in Table 14-1 and are graphed in Figure 14-6.

Recall that the previous operations manager at Gere Memorial based his staffing on the premise that from Monday to Friday the patient count remained essentially the same and then for Saturdays and Sundays went down 25%. If this is actually the case, how many of the 56,000 patients would have been expected on Monday? How many on Tuesday and so forth? To figure this out, Vickie determined weighting factors by allocating 4 units each to days Monday through Friday and 3 units each (representing the 25% reduction) to Saturday and Sunday. The total number of units is then $(5 \times 4) + (2 \times 3) = 26$ units. The percentage of total patients expected on a weekday is $4/26 = 0.154$ or 15.4% and the percentage expected on a weekend day is $3/26 = 0.115$ or 11.5%. The expected number of patients on a weekday is $0.154 \times 56,000 = 8,624$ and the expected number on each weekend day is $0.115 \times 56,000 = 6,440$.

Figure 14-7 shows a graph with both the actual sample data and the expected values. With the exception of what might be attributed to sampling error, if the distribution claimed by the previous operations manager is correct, the actual frequencies for each day of the week should fit quite closely with the expected

FIGURE **14-7**

Actual and
Expected
Frequencies

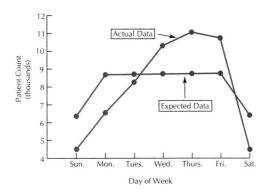

frequencies. As you can see in Figure 14-7, the actual data and the expected data do not match perfectly. Is the difference enough to warrant a change in staffing patterns?

THE CHI-SQUARE GOODNESS-OF-FIT TEST

The situation facing Vickie is one for which a number of statistical tests have been developed. One of the most frequently used is the **chi-square goodness-of-fit test.** The term *goodness of fit* is very appropriate since what Vickie needs to examine is how well the sample data fit the hypothesized distribution. In fact, Vickie wishes to test the following null and alternative hypotheses:

H_0: The patient demand distribution is evenly spread through the weekdays and 25% lower on the weekend.

H_A: The patient demand follows some other distribution.

Equation 14-4 is the equation for the chi-square goodness-of-fit test statistic. You should notice that it is very similar in form to the chi-square contingency analysis test statistic shown earlier as equation 14-1. The difference is the data shown in Table 14-1 actually represent a contingency table with seven rows but only one column.

$$\chi^2_{\text{calculated}} = \Sigma \frac{(f_A - f_E)^2}{f_E}$$

14-4

where

f_A = Actual cell frequency for row i

f_E = Expected cell frequency for row i

As was the case with contingency analysis, if the calculated chi-square statistic gets large this is evidence to suggest the fit of the actual data to the hypothesized distribution is not good, and the null hypothesis should be rejected.

Figure 14-8 shows the hypothesis test process and results for this chi-square goodness-of-fit test. Note the degrees of freedom for the chi-square test are $k - 1$, where k is the number of categories. In this example, we have seven categories

FIGURE 14-8

Chi-Square
Goodness-of-Fit
Test for the Gere
Memorial
Hospital Example

Hypotheses:

H_0: Patient demand is evenly spread through the weekdays and 25% lower on weekends.

H_A: Patient demand follows some other distribution.

$\alpha = 0.05$

	Total Patient Count	
Day	Actual f_A	Expected f_E
Sunday	4,502	6,440
Monday	6,623	8,624
Tuesday	8,308	8,624
Wednesday	10,420	8,624
Thursday	11,032	8,624
Friday	10,754	8,624
Saturday	4,361	6,440
Total	56,000	56,000

Test Statistic:

$$\chi^2_{calculated} = \Sigma \frac{(f_A - f_E)^2}{f_E} = \frac{(4{,}502 - 6{,}440)^2}{6{,}440} + \frac{(6{,}623 - 8{,}624)^2}{8{,}624} + \cdots$$

$$+ \frac{(4{,}361 - 6{,}440)^2}{6{,}440}$$

$$= 3{,}302.7$$

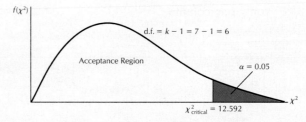

d.f. $= k - 1 = 7 - 1 = 6$

Acceptance Region

$\alpha = 0.05$

$\chi^2_{critical} = 12.592$

Decision Rule:

If $\chi^2_{calculated} > 12.592$, reject H_0.
Otherwise, do not reject H_0.

Since $3{,}302.7 > 12.592$, reject H_0.

corresponding to the days of the week. Thus, the degrees of freedom are $7 - 1 = 6$. The critical value for 6 degrees of freedom and an upper-tail test with $\alpha = 0.05$ is found in Appendix E to be 12.592.

As Figure 14-8 indicates, $\chi^2_{calculated} = 3,302.7 > 12.592$, so the null hypothesis is rejected and Vickie Shelly should conclude the demand pattern does not match the previously defined distribution. She would now most likely wish to make changes in the scheduling to more closely approximate current demand patterns.

THE LILLIEFORS TEST FOR NORMALITY—A QUALITY CONTROL EXAMPLE

Woodtrim Products, Inc., a company based in southern Idaho, makes wood moldings, door frames, and wood frame window products. It purchases lumber from mills throughout Idaho, Washington, Oregon, and Montana. The lumber it purchases is called "dimension lumber" and comes in thicknesses measured as 5 quarter and 6 quarter, in widths ranging from 8 inches to 16 inches. The pieces have knots and other imperfections, such as warp.

The first step in the production process is to cut the dimension lumber into narrower strips ranging from $2\frac{3}{8}$ inches to $3\frac{7}{8}$ inches. A machine called a ripsaw is used for this purpose and is run by a highly skilled operator. The operator starts by aiming a light beam down the length of the board to mark where the saw will cut. The operator's judgment is required to determine what width of pieces to cut from each board to maximize the value to the company. Pieces with no knots or other imperfections can be made into the most profitable products. Each width goes into making a different product. For example, wider pieces with no imperfections are used to make door and window frames. Once the operator makes his decision by lining the light beam along the board, the decision is locked into a computer and when the board reaches the ripsaw a few feet away the saw is automatically adjusted to cut the board at the desired widths. The manufacturer claims that the saw will cut within ± 0.008 inch of the target width.

The company has recently become concerned that the ripsaw may not be cutting the boards at the exact dimension being indicated by the operator. Further downstream in the production process, operators at other machines are finding ripped pieces that are too wide or too narrow. The too wide boards have to be sent through a backripsaw, which trims the pieces to a narrower width. This results in waste and lost profit. The pieces that are too narrow cannot be backripped, so they are sent to a "hogger," which grinds the boards to make woodchips, a low-profit by-product.

A "quality improvement team," QIT, has started to investigate the problem. This means that the QIT will collect data on boards coming off the ripsaw to determine just how capable the saw is of holding the cutting width. To do this, the members selected a random sample of twenty boards just as they came off the ripsaw. To provide a measure of control, the only pieces sampled in the initial study were pieces with stated widths of $2\frac{7}{8}$ inches. The piece was then measured for width at a point halfway between the ends. The difference between $2\frac{7}{8}$ and the

TABLE 14-2

Sample Data of
Board
Thicknesses for
Woodtrim
Products, Inc.,
Example

Sample #	Actual Width	Stated Width	Difference
1	2.870	2.875	−0.005
2	2.863	2.875	−0.012
3	2.885	2.875	0.010
4	2.872	2.875	−0.003
5	2.891	2.875	0.016
6	2.893	2.875	0.018
7	2.868	2.875	−0.007
8	2.861	2.875	−0.014
9	2.889	2.875	0.014
10	2.872	2.875	−0.003
11	2.879	2.875	0.004
12	2.876	2.875	0.001
13	2.869	2.875	−0.006
14	2.890	2.875	0.015
15	2.880	2.875	0.005
16	2.870	2.875	−0.005
17	2.867	2.875	−0.008
18	2.874	2.875	−0.001
19	2.873	2.875	−0.002
20	2.867	2.875	−0.008

measured width was computed. Ideally, the difference would be 0. However, as indicated previously, the manufacturer claims that the saw should cut within ± 0.008 inch and the distribution around 0 is normally distributed. As part of the process capability study, the team wishes to test whether the distribution is normal and then determine what percentage of the product will be within the ± 0.008 inch tolerance.

Table 14-2 shows the data for the sample of twenty boards. Note, the differences have been computed. The chi-square goodness-of-fit test introduced in the previous examples relied on the logic that if the actual sample data closely fit the hypothesized distribution, the null hypothesis would not be rejected. We could employ the chi-square test in this example too, but a better test exists when the hypothesized distribution is normal. This test is the Lilliefors test.

The null and alternative hypotheses for this example are stated as follows:

H_0: The distribution of cut width error is normally distributed.

H_A: The distribution of cut width error is not normally distributed.

In order to use the Lilliefors test, we perform the following steps:

1. Compute the sample mean, $\overline{X}$, and the sample standard deviation, s, on the data in the differences column.
2. Find the Z score for each value in the sample, where $Z = (X - \overline{X})/s$. This is referred to as "standardizing" the data.

3. Arrange the Z scores in order from smallest to largest.
4. Find the probability of a Z value as small as or smaller than each Z score using the standard normal table in Appendix C.
5. Find the percentage of sample points at or below each Z score.
6. Compute the absolute difference between the values found in steps 4 and 5 for each sample value.
7. Compare the maximum absolute difference found in step 6 to the Lilliefors test statistic table in Appendix J for the appropriate sample size and $1 - \alpha$ value.

To demonstrate an application of the Lilliefors test, we first compute the mean and standard deviation for the sample differences in Table 14-2. These values are as follows:

$$\overline{X} = 0.00045$$
$$s = 0.0096$$

We next compute the Z score for each data point. The results are shown in Table 14-3. For example, the Z score for sample 1 difference is calculated as

$$Z = \frac{-0.005 - 0.00045}{0.0096} = -0.57$$

TABLE 14-3

Sample Data of Board Thicknesses for Woodtrim Products, Inc., Example

Sample #	Difference	Z Score
1	−0.005	−0.57
2	−0.012	−1.30
3	0.010	0.99
4	−0.003	−0.36
5	0.016	1.62
6	0.018	1.83
7	−0.007	−0.78
8	−0.014	−1.51
9	0.014	1.41
10	−0.003	−0.36
11	0.004	0.37
12	0.001	0.06
13	−0.006	−0.67
14	0.015	1.52
15	0.005	0.47
16	−0.005	−0.57
17	−0.008	−0.88
18	−0.001	−0.15
19	−0.002	−0.26
20	−0.008	−0.88

TABLE 14-4

Sample Data
of Board
Thicknesses for
Woodtrim
Products, Inc.,
Example

Z Score	Cumulative Probability Z	Cumulative Frequency	Difference
−1.51	0.0655	1/20 = 0.05	0.0155
−1.30	0.0968	2/20 = 0.10	0.0032
−0.88	0.1894	3/20 = 0.15	0.0394
−0.88	0.1894	4/20 = 0.20	0.0106
−0.78	0.2177	5/20 = 0.25	0.0323
−0.67	0.2514	6/20 = 0.30	0.0486
−0.57	0.2843	7/20 = 0.35	0.0657
−0.57	0.2843	8/20 = 0.40	0.1157
−0.36	0.3594	9/20 = 0.45	0.0906
−0.36	0.3594	10/20 = 0.50	0.1406
−0.26	0.3974	11/20 = 0.55	0.1526
−0.15	0.4404	12/20 = 0.60	0.1596
0.06	0.5239	13/20 = 0.65	0.1261
0.37	0.6443	14/20 = 0.70	0.0557
0.47	0.6808	15/20 = 0.75	0.0692
0.99	0.8389	16/20 = 0.80	0.0389
1.41	0.9207	17/20 = 0.85	0.0707
1.52	0.9357	18/20 = 0.90	0.0357
1.62	0.9474	19/20 = 0.95	0.0026
1.83	0.9664	20/20 = 1.00	0.0336

The next step is to arrange the Z scores from lowest to highest and to find the probability of a Z value as small as or smaller than each Z score using the standard normal distribution.

We also establish the cumulative relative frequencies for the sample values and take the absolute difference between the normal distribution probabilities and the cumulative frequencies. These results are shown in Table 14-4.

Note in Table 14-4 that the maximum difference is 0.1596. This figure is compared with the table value, w_p, for the Lilliefors test in Appendix J. The decision rule is as follows:

If $0.1596 > w_p$, reject H_0.

Otherwise, do not reject H_0.

For a sample of size twenty and $1 - \alpha$ level of 0.95, the critical Lilliefors value, w_p, is 0.190. Since the calculated value of $0.1596 \leq 0.190$, the null hypothesis is *not* rejected. Thus, based on the sample data, the Woodtrim quality improvement team will conclude that the cut width error distribution is normal.

The next step for the team is to determine, based on these sample data, the probability of cut widths being within 0.008 inch of the target width. Figure 14-9 shows the computations. Thus, using $\overline{X} = 0.00045$ and $s = 0.0096$, and assuming the cut width error distribution is normal, the percentage of cuts within ± 0.008 inch is computed to be 0.5958, or almost 60% of all boards. This level of capability is probably not as good as the company would like and the quality

FIGURE **14-9**

Process
Capability
Analysis for the
Woodtrim
Products, Inc.,
Example

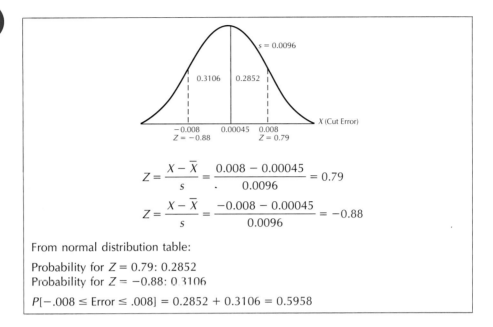

$$Z = \frac{X - \bar{X}}{s} = \frac{0.008 - 0.00045}{0.0096} = 0.79$$

$$Z = \frac{X - \bar{X}}{s} = \frac{-0.008 - 0.00045}{0.0096} = -0.88$$

From normal distribution table:

Probability for $Z = 0.79$: 0.2852
Probability for $Z = -0.88$: 0.3106

$P[-.008 \leq \text{Error} \leq .008] = 0.2852 + 0.3106 = 0.5958$

improvement team will want to begin looking for reasons that the cut width errors are so frequently outside the ± 0.008 range.

CHI-SQUARE VS LILLIEFORS TEST

The chi-square goodness-of-fit test is a very useful tool for testing whether sample data fit certain specified distributions. It is very versatile and can be used to test almost any distribution. However, if the variable of interest is continuous, the chi-square test requires that the data be grouped into classes. For example, Figure 14-10 shows the use of the chi-square test to determine whether the weight distribution of frozen french fry packages is normally distributed with mean equal to 5.0 pounds and standard deviation equal to 0.20 pound. A sample of 1,000 bags has been selected and each package weighed. The data have been grouped into six classes as shown in Figure 14-10. The expected frequencies in each class are determined by finding the probability of an item falling within the specified class limits, if the true distribution is as hypothesized, and multiplying this probability by the sample size of 1,000. As can be seen in Figure 14-10, $\chi^2_{\text{calculated}} = 400.3 > \chi^2_{\text{critical}} = 11.07$, so the null hypothesis is rejected. The distribution must be something other than a normal one with mean 5 and standard deviation 0.20.

Note that the chi-square test requires us to group the raw sample data into classes. The computed value of chi-square will change depending on how the grouping is performed. In fact, it is possible to reach different conclusions with the same data by just changing the way the classes are structured. Because of this, one could easily criticize the goodness-of-fit results on the basis of how the data were grouped.

FIGURE 14-10

Chi-Square Test
of Normal
Distribution for
French Fry
Package Example

Hypotheses:

H_0: Distribution of weights is normal with mean equal to 5 pounds and standard deviation equal to 0.20 pound.

H_A: Distribution of weights is not as hypothesized.

$\alpha = 0.05$

Weight Class	f_A Actual Frequency	f_E Expected Frequency
Under 4.80	18	$(0.1587 \times 1{,}000) = 158.7$
4.80 and under 4.90	102	$(0.1498 \times 1{,}000) = 149.8$
4.90 and under 5.00	305	$(0.1915 \times 1{,}000) = 191.5$
5.00 and under 5.10	360	$(0.1915 \times 1{,}000) = 191.5$
5.10 and under 5.20	140	$(0.1498 \times 1{,}000) = 149.8$
5.20 and over	75	$(0.1587 \times 1{,}000) = 158.7$
	$n = 1{,}000$	$1{,}000$

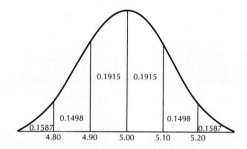

Test Statistic:

$$\chi^2_{calculated} = \Sigma \frac{(f_A - f_E)^2}{f_E} = \frac{(18 - 158.7)^2}{158.7} + \frac{(102 - 149.8)^2}{149.8} + \cdots + \frac{(75 - 158.7)^2}{158.7}$$

$$= 400.3$$

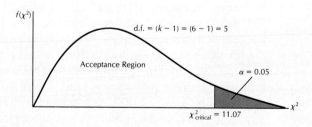

Decision Rule:

If $\chi^2_{calculated} > 11.07$, reject H_0.
Otherwise, do not reject H_0.

Since $\chi^2_{calculated} = 400.3 > 11.07$, reject H_0.

The Lilliefors test, on the other hand, works with the actual raw data and does not require grouping. From that standpoint it is advantageous. It is also preferred to the chi-square for testing hypotheses about normal and exponential distributions because it is more powerful than the chi-square test. This means the Lilliefors test is more likely to reject the null hypothesis when it should be rejected than is the chi-square test using the same data. Thus, we recommend the Lilliefors test be used for normal and exponential distributions and the chi-square test be used for other applications.

SKILL DEVELOPMENT PROBLEMS FOR SECTION 14-3

The following problems have been included to help you better understand the material in this chapter.

17. Daily sales volumes in dollars have been grouped as follows. Can you conclude that the sales are uniformly distributed? Test at $\alpha = 0.05$.

Sales	Frequency
$500 and under $1,000	40
$1,000 and under $1,500	63
$1,500 and under $2,000	55
$2,000 and under $2,500	50
$2,500 and under $3,000	61

18. Use the chi-square goodness-of-fit test to determine whether the number of phone calls coming in to a radio talk show is Poisson distributed with a mean of 5 per hour. The following data, selected over a period of 100 hours, show the frequency distribution for the number of calls in a given hour. Test at the $\alpha = 0.05$ level.

Number of Calls	Frequency
0	0
1	2
2	4
3	10
4	7
5	14
6	11
7	13
8	5
9	10
10	5
11	5
12	7
13	4
14	3
	100

19. The Baltimore Steel and Pipe Company recently selected a random sample of twenty sections of pipe that was designed to measure 2.00 inches in diameter. Company representatives measured the diameter of each of the twenty sections. According to the product specifications, the diameters are supposed to be normally distributed. Based on the following sample data, can the company conclude that the pipe diameters are normally distributed? Use the Lilliefors test at an $\alpha = 0.05$ level.

Pipe Section	Diameter (inches)
1	2.04
2	2.13
3	2.07
4	1.99
5	1.90
6	2.06
7	2.19
8	2.01
9	2.05
10	1.98
11	1.95
12	1.90
13	2.10
14	2.02
15	2.11
16	1.96
17	1.89
18	1.99
19	2.13
20	1.90

14-4 COMPUTER APPLICATIONS

Both contingency analysis and goodness-of-fit tests require substantial computations for even the most elementary applications. As you might imagine, statistical software packages typically contain modules for performing these functions. In this section we demonstrate examples based on the KIVZ-Channel 5 data introduced in Chapter 2 (see Tables 2-10 and 2-11). The examples shown in this section demonstrate contingency analysis using GB-STAT software.

Table 14-5 shows the GB-STAT output for the relationship between national news rating and local news rating. Since GB-STAT is a menu-driven package, the user accesses the statistics menu, selects the nonparametric statistics option, and then selects the chi-square contingency table option. The computer then prompts the user to identify the variables to form the rows and columns in the table. As seen in Table 14-5, the computed chi-square is 44.09, which is significant at any

TABLE (14-5)

GB-STAT
Contingency
Table Output for
KIVZ-Channel 5
Example

CONTINGENCY TABLE—'Nat ns' X 'Loc ns'

COLS:'Nat ns' C1 BASE = 0, WIDTH = 1

ROWS:'Loc ns' R1 BASE = 1, WIDTH = 1

	1	2	3	4	5	Total
1	0	5	4	0	0	9
2	1	3	3	16	2	25
3	0	5	1	5	0	11
4	0	0	1	0	4	5
TOT	1	13	9	21	6	50

SUMMARY STATISTICS

_____

D.F. = 12

CHI-SQUARE = 44.09455

PROB: <.0001

CRAMER'S V = .5422

CONTINGENCY COEF = .6846

reasonable level of alpha. This implies that national news ratings are not independent of local news ratings. Note that Table 14-5 shows the actual joint frequencies for the two variables. GB-STAT will also print out the expected cell frequencies. Also, the Cramer's V shown in the output is the square root of Cramer's contingency coefficient discussed in Section 14-2.

14-5 CONCLUSIONS

This chapter has introduced two very useful statistical tools: contingency analysis and goodness-of-fit testing. Contingency analysis is a frequently used statistical tool that allows the decision maker to test whether responses to two variables are independent. Market researchers, for example, use contingency analysis in analyzing survey research data when at least one of the variables of interest is categorical. For instance, the marketer may be interested in determining whether attitude about the quality of her company's product is independent of whether the customer is male or female. By using contingency analysis and the chi-square contingency test, she can make this determination based on the sample of customers. If either or both of the variables are continuous in nature, they must be recoded before contingency analysis can be performed. Most software can facilitate this recoding process.

Goodness-of-fit testing is used when a decision maker wishes to determine whether sample data come from a population having specific characteristics. Two goodness-of-fit procedures were introduced in this chapter—the chi-square goodness-of-fit test and the Lilliefors test. Both tests rely on the idea that if the distribution of the sample data is substantially different from the hypothesized population distribution, then the population distribution from which these sample data came must not be what was hypothesized. The Lilliefors test is particularly useful for determining whether a population is normally distributed when the raw data from the sample are available. The chi-square goodness-of-fit test is most effective when the sample data have been organized into a grouped frequency distribution.

Both contingency analysis and goodness-of-fit tests are special examples of statistical procedures that, as a group, are known as nonparametric statistics.

CHAPTER **GLOSSARY**

chi-square goodness-of-fit test This is a test utilizing the chi-square distribution to determine whether sample data come from a specific hypothesized population distribution.

contingency table A table used to classify sample observations according to two or more identifiable characteristics. This table is used as an intermediate step in performing contingency analysis.

Lilliefors test A goodness-of-fit test for testing whether sample data (in raw form) come from a population that is normally distributed.

CHAPTER FORMULAS

Chi-square contingency coefficient

$$\chi^2 = \sum_{i=1}^{r} \sum_{j=1}^{c} \frac{(f_{A_{ij}} - f_{E_{ij}})^2}{f_{E_{ij}}}$$

Cramer's contingency coefficient

$$\Phi = \frac{\chi^2_{\text{calculated}}}{n(q - 1)}$$

Expected cell frequency

$$f_E = \frac{\text{Row total} \times \text{Column total}}{\text{Total sample size}}$$

Chi-square goodness-of-fit statistic

$$\chi^2_{\text{calculated}} = \Sigma \frac{(f_A - f_E)^2}{f_E}$$

SOLVED PROBLEMS

1. Burtco Incorporated designs and manufactures gears for heavy-duty construction equipment. One such gear, #9973, has the following specifications:

   1. Mean diameter 3 inches
   2. Standard deviation 0.001 inch
   3. Output normally distributed around the mean

   An assistant to the production control manager has selected a random sample of 500 gears from the inventory. The raw data are no longer available but the frequency distribution is as follows:

Gear Diameter (inches)	Frequency
Under 2.995	3
2.995 and under 2.996	4
2.996 and under 2.997	5
2.997 and under 2.998	19
2.998 and under 2.999	98
2.999 and under 3.000	146
3.000 and under 3.001	124
3.001 and under 3.002	83
3.002 and under 3.003	11
3.003 and over	7
Total	500

   Based on this sample information, does gear #9973 meet specifications? Use a significance level of 0.05.

Solution

This is an example of a one-sample goodness-of-fit problem. We can hypothesize as follows:

H_0: The diameters of gear #9973 are normally distributed with a mean diameter of 3 inches and standard deviation 0.001 inch.

H_A: Gear #9973 is not within specifications.

$\alpha = 0.05$

Since the raw data are not available, an appropriate statistical procedure is the chi-square goodness-of-fit test. This test calculates the expected frequencies for each interval and compares the expected to the observed frequencies. If the calculated χ^2 gets too large, we will conclude that the fit is not good and reject the null hypothesis.

To determine the expected frequencies, we calculate the probability of a gear having a diameter in each of the intervals, assuming the gear meets the required specifications. Then we multiply the probability by 500 to obtain the expected frequency. The procedure is as follows:

$P(\text{less than } 2.995)$ = Area under normal curve to the left of 2.995

$$Z = \frac{X - \mu_x}{\sigma_x} = \frac{2.995 - 3}{0.001}$$
$$= -5.00$$

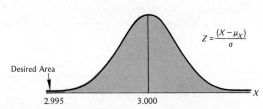

The area to the left of $Z = -5.00$ is essentially 0. Therefore, the expected frequency is $(0)(500) = 0$.

As another example,

$P(2.997 \leq X \leq 2.998)$ = Area under the normal curve between 2.997 and 2.998

$$Z = \frac{2.997 - 3}{0.001} = -3; \text{ area to the right} = 0.4987$$

$$Z = \frac{2.998 - 3}{0.001} = -2; \text{ area to the right} = 0.4772$$

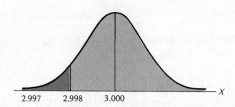

Therefore, the desired probability is $0.4987 - 0.4772 = 0.0215$, and the expected frequency is $(0.0215)(500) = 10.75$.

In a like manner, we find the expected frequencies for each interval:

Gear Diameter (inches)	f_A	f_E
Under 2.997	12	0.650
2.997 and under 2.998	19	10.750
2.998 and under 2.999	98	67.950
2.999 and under 3.000	146	170.650
3.000 and under 3.001	124	170.650
3.001 and under 3.002	83	67.950
3.002 and under 3.003	11	10.750
3.003 and over	7	0.650

Because the chi-square goodness-of-fit test does not work well when more than 20% of the cells have expected cell frequencies below 5.0, as is the case in this example, we must combine the cells.

Gear Diameter (inches)	f_A	f_E	$(f_A - f_E)^2$	$(f_A - f_E)^2/f_E$
Under 2.998	31	11.4	384.16	33.70
2.998 and under 2.999	98	67.95	903.00	13.29
2.999 and under 3.000	146	170.65	607.62	3.56
3.000 and under 3.001	124	170.65	2,176.22	12.75
3.001 and under 3.002	83	67.95	226.50	3.33
3.002 and over	18	11.40	43.56	3.82
				$\chi^2 = 70.45$

$$\chi^2 = \sum_{i=1}^{k} \frac{(f_{A_i} - f_{E_i})^2}{f_{E_i}}$$

$$= 70.45$$

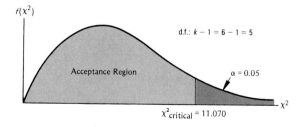

Since $\chi^2 = 70.45 > \chi^2_{\text{critical}} = 11.070$, we reject the null hypothesis and conclude that the gears are *not* within specifications. The production manager would most likely want to halt production and attempt to adjust the process to bring the gears within specifications. However, as often happens, he may discover that the specifications are unreachable with the machinery he has to work with, in which case either new machinery will be required or the specifications will have to be renegotiated.

2. Automobile insurance companies have long used age, sex, and marital status for determining rates. For example, single males under 25 years of age are considered the highest risk and are charged the highest premiums. Single females in the same age group are charged somewhat lower premiums.

Recently, the National Ranch Insurance Company studied 1,000 of its policyholders. The purpose of the study was to determine whether such factors as age, sex, and marital status are independent of whether the policyholder has filed an accident claim. With regard to age for all drivers, both male and female, National Ranch found the following:

	Under 25	25–40	40–55	Over 55	
Reported Claim	93	72	53	63	281
No Claim	115	155	265	184	719
	208	227	318	247	1,000 = N

Age spans the Under 25, 25–40, 40–55, Over 55 columns.

Based on these data, what should National Ranch conclude about age and claim status?

Solution

The basic question facing National Ranch is whether age is independent of claim status. Therefore, we set up our null and alternative hypotheses as follows:

H_0: Whether or not an insurance claim has been filed by a policyholder is independent of the policyholder's age.

H_A: Age and claim status are not independent.

$\alpha = 0.05$

An appropriate test is the chi-square test of independence.

$$\chi^2 = \sum_{i=1}^{r} \sum_{j=1}^{c} \frac{(fA_{ij} - fE_{ij})^2}{fE_{ij}}$$

The expected frequencies are

$$f_{E_{11}} = \frac{281(208)}{1,000} = 58.45$$

$$f_{E_{12}} = \frac{281(227)}{1,000} = 63.79$$

$$f_{E_{13}} = \frac{281(318)}{1,000} = 89.36$$

.

.

.

$$f_{E_{24}} = \frac{719(247)}{1,000} = 177.59$$

The completed contingency table is as follows:

	Age			
	Under 25	*25–40*	*40–55*	*Over 55*
Reported Claim	$f_A = 93.00$ $f_E = 58.45$	$f_A = 72.00$ $f_E = 63.79$	$f_A = 53.00$ $f_E = 89.36$	$f_A = 63.00$ $f_E = 69.41$
No Claim	$f_A = 115.00$ $f_E = 149.55$	$f_A = 155.00$ $f_E = 163.21$	$f_A = 265.00$ $f_E = 228.64$	$f_A = 184.00$ $f_E = 177.59$

Then

$$\chi^2 = \frac{(93.00 - 58.45)^2}{58.45} + \frac{(72.00 - 63.79)^2}{63.79} + \cdots + \frac{(184.00 - 177.59)^2}{177.59}$$

$$= 51.27$$

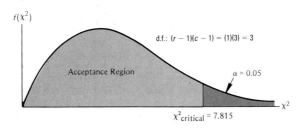

Since $\chi^2 = 51.27 > \chi^2_{\text{critical}} = 7.815$, National Ranch should reject the hypothesis of independence. Based on the data, the insurance company might infer that young drivers have more accident claims than expected, and therefore higher rates might be justified.

CONCEPTUAL QUESTIONS AND ASSIGNMENTS

20. Go to the library and locate a journal article using either contingency analysis or a goodness-of-fit test. Discuss the article, paying particular attention to the reasoning behind using the particular statistical test.

21. In the text we stated that the Lilliefors test is more powerful than the chi-square goodness-of-fit test. Formulate an example to demonstrate this point.

22. Assess the problems you would expect to find if a test that assumes interval or ratio data is used for variables with categorical data. You may want to spend some time in the library for this question.

23. Go to the library and find a marketing research book (or borrow one from a friend). Does it discuss either of the tests considered in this chapter? If yes, outline the discussion. If no, determine where in the text such a discussion would be appropriate.

ADDITIONAL PROBLEMS

24. Linda Stevens, the manager of Arlington Super Discount, always keeps four checkout stands open. However, she frequently notices lines for registers 1 and 2. She is not sure whether the layout of the store channels customers into these registers or whether the check-out clerks in these lines are simply slower than the other two.

    Linda kept a record of which stands 2,000 shoppers chose for checkout. The shoppers checked out of the four stands according to the following pattern:

Stand 1	Stand 2	Stand 3	Stand 4
677	550	402	371

    Based on these data, can Linda conclude that an equal number of shoppers are likely to use each of the stands? (Use an alpha level of 0.05.)

25. A manufacturer of packaged food has decided to market a new cake mix. This venture is rather risky since the new mix will compete with three established brands. The production manager argues that quality will sell the new mix. The marketing manager states that the average consumer cannot tell the difference between brands and that the critical factor in selling the mix will be the advertising campaign.

    To test the marketing manager's contention, the four types of cakes were baked under equal conditions. Shoppers were randomly stopped in several supermarkets and asked to sample each cake and indicate which of the four tasted the best. Which cake was tasted first was randomly determined, and the production manager and the marketing manager believe the process yielded representative results. The following data show how many shoppers rated each brand the tastiest:

	Brand		
A	B	C	New
37	23	27	41

    Which contention do these data support? Use a Type I error rate of 0.01.

DATABASE PROBLEMS

The following questions and problems pertain directly to the State Department of Transportation case study and database introduced in Chapter 1. The questions and problems were written assuming that you will have access to a computer and appropriate statistical software. The database containing 100 observations and seventeen variables was given in Chapter 1. *Assume that the data were collected using a simple random sampling process.*

1. Herb Kriner is interested in determining whether seat belt status is independent of insurance status. Test this at the $\alpha = 0.05$ level. Show the contingency table and the test statistic.
2. Can Herb Kriner conclude that knowledge of the liability insurance law is independent of sex of the respondent? Test at the $\alpha = 0.05$ level.
3. Based on these sample data, can Herb Kriner conclude that the distribution of the time drivers have lived in Idaho is normally distributed? Test using an appropriate goodness-of-fit test at an $\alpha = 0.05$ level.

ADDITIONAL DATABASE PROBLEMS

The questions and problems in this section reference the various databases that accompany this text and which are described in Chapter 1. Your instructor has been provided a diskette with these databases. It is expected that you will be using computer software to access these data and to perform the required calculations and graphs.

DATABASE: **CITIES** (*Refer to the database description in Chapter 1.*)

1. Art Lee is preparing a speech for a trade conference and he intends to use information from the CITIES database that Phillis Rigg compiled. At one point in his speech, he would like to state that the estimate of population growth between 1990 and 1995 in percentage terms is normally distributed. Using an $\alpha = 0.10$ level, would Art be justified in making this statement? If so, what should he conclude that the mean should be? What about the standard deviation?
2. Using contingency analysis, can Art Lee consider the cities' labor market stress index to be statistically independent of 1989 unemployment rate? Break each variable into appropriate categories and conduct the hypothesis test using an $\alpha = 0.05$ level.
3. Referring to Problem 2, break the two variables into different categories and conduct the test again. Did the results change this time? Discuss why it is possible for the contingency analysis results to differ depending on how the categories are formed for a continuous random variable.

DATABASE: **FAST100** (*Refer to the database description in Chapter 1.*)

1. Based on the sample data, would it be appropriate to conclude that price earnings ratios are normally distributed? Test using an $\alpha = 0.05$.
2. Based on these sample data, can we conclude that stock price is independent of where the stock is traded? Break the stock price into three categories and test at an $\alpha = 0.10$ level.
3. Is the annual 3–5-year growth rate for companies in this study described by a uniform distribution? Test using an appropriate goodness-of-fit method at an $\alpha = 0.05$ level.

DATABASE: **PACRIM** (*Refer to the database description in Chapter 1.*)

1. Can it be concluded that profit ranking is independent of asset ranking based on these data for Pacific Rim companies? Break the rankings into four categories and test at an $\alpha = 0.05$ level.
2. Is it appropriate to conclude that the distribution of 1989 annual profits fits a normal distribution? Test using an $\alpha = 0.05$ level.
3. If your software allows you to test data for goodness of fit against several distributions, which of these best fits the data for year-end asset ranking? Discuss the thinking used to reach this conclusion.

DATABASE: **TRUCKS** (*Refer to the database description in Chapter 1.*)

1. Is the WIM gross weight normally distributed? Test this at the $\alpha = 0.05$ level.
2. Compute a variable that is the difference between WIM gross weight and POE gross weight. Then using contingency analysis, determine whether there is reason to support the belief that scale error is independent of the month the data were collected. Test at an $\alpha = 0.05$ level. Break the difference variable into five categories.
3. Referring to Problem 2, would your conclusion change if the difference variable was divided into more or fewer categories? Show two examples to justify your response.
4. Referring to Problem 2, can you conclude that the difference variable is normally distributed? Test this at the $\alpha = 0.05$ level.

CASE

American Oil Company

Chad Williams sat back in his airline seat to enjoy the hour flight between Los Angeles and Oakland, California. The hour would give him time to reflect upon his upcoming trip to Australia and the work he had been doing the past week in Los Angeles.

Chad is one man on a six-man crew for the American Oil Company who literally walks the earth searching for oil. His college degrees in geology and petroleum engineering landed him the job with American, but he never dreamed he would be doing the exciting work he now does. Chad and his crew spend several months in special locations around the world using highly sensitive electronic equipment for oil exploration purposes.

The upcoming trip to Australia is one that Chad has been looking forward to since it was announced that his crew would be going there to search the Outback for oil. In preparation for the Australia trip, the crew has been in Los Angeles at American's engineering research facility working on some new equipment that will be used in Australia in search of oil.

Chad's thoughts centered on the problem he was having with a particular component part on the new equipment. The specifications called for 200 of the components, each having a diameter of between 0.15 and 0.18 inch. The only available supplier of the component in New Jersey manufactures the components to specifications calling for normally distributed output with a mean of 0.16 inch and a standard deviation of 0.02 inch.

Chad faces two problems. First, he is unsure that the supplier actually does produce parts with the mean of 0.16 inch and standard deviation of 0.02 inch according to a normal distribution. Second, if that is the case, he needs to determine how many components to purchase if enough acceptable components are to be received to make two oil exploration devices.

The supplier has sent Chad the following data for 330 randomly selected components. Chad believes that the supplier is honest and that he can rely on the data.

Diameter (inch)	Frequency
Under 0.14	5
0.14 and under 0.15	70
0.15 and under 0.16	90
0.16 and under 0.17	105
0.17 and under 0.18	50
Over 0.18	10
Total	330

Chad needs to have a report ready for Monday indicating whether he believes the supplier delivers at its stated specifications and, if so, how many of the components American should order to have enough acceptable components to outfit two oil exploration devices.

REFERENCES

Berenson, Mark L., and Levine, David M. *Basic Business Statistics Concepts and Applications,* 5th edition. Englewood Cliffs, New Jersey: Prentice-Hall, 1992.

Daniel, Wayne W., and Terrell, James C. *Business Statistics for Management and Economics,* 6th edition. Boston: Houghton Mifflin, 1992.

Iman, Ronald L., and Conover, W. J. *Modern Business Statistics,* 2nd edition. New York: Wiley, 1989.

Levin, Richard I., and Rubin, David S. *Statistics for Management,* 5th edition. Englewood Cliffs, New Jersey: Prentice-Hall, 1991.

Sincich, Terry. *Business Statistics by Example,* 4th edition. New York: Dellen, 1992.

Appendices

APPENDIX A   Binomial Distribution Table

$$P(X_1) = \frac{n!}{X_1!(n - X_1)!} \, p^{X_1}(q)^{n-X_1}$$

(handwritten annotation: $(1-p)$ with arrow pointing to q)

n = 1

X1	P=.01	P=.02	P=.03	P=.04	P=.05	P=.06	P=.07	P=.08	P=.09	P=.10	n−X1
0	.9900	.9800	.9700	.9600	.9500	.9400	.9300	.9200	.9100	.9000	1
1	.0100	.0200	.0300	.0400	.0500	.0600	.0700	.0800	.0900	.1000	0
	q=.99	q=.98	q=.97	q=.96	q=.95	q=.94	q=.93	q=.92	q=.91	q=.90	

X1	P=.11	P=.12	P=.13	P=.14	P=.15	P=.16	P=.17	P=.18	P=.19	P=.20	n−X1
0	.8900	.8800	.8700	.8600	.8500	.8400	.8300	.8200	.8100	.8000	1
1	.1100	.1200	.1300	.1400	.1500	.1600	.1700	.1800	.1900	.2000	0
	q=.89	q=.88	q=.87	q=.86	q=.85	q=.84	q=.83	q=.82	q=.81	q=.80	

X1	P=.21	P=.22	P=.23	P=.24	P=.25	P=.26	P=.27	P=.28	P=.29	P=.30	n−X1
0	.7900	.7800	.7700	.7600	.7500	.7400	.7300	.7200	.7100	.7000	1
1	.2100	.2200	.2300	.2400	.2500	.2600	.2700	.2800	.2900	.3000	0
	q=.79	q=.78	q=.77	q=.76	q=.75	q=.74	q=.73	q=.72	q=.71	q=.70	

X1	P=.31	P=.32	P=.33	P=.34	P=.35	P=.36	P=.37	P=.38	P=.39	P=.40	n−X1
0	.6900	.6800	.6700	.6600	.6500	.6400	.6300	.6200	.6100	.6000	1
1	.3100	.3200	.3300	.3400	.3500	.3600	.3700	.3800	.3900	.4000	0
	q=.69	q=.68	q=.67	q=.66	q=.65	q=.64	q=.63	q=.62	q=.61	q=.60	

X1	P=.41	P=.42	P=.43	P=.44	P=.45	P=.46	P=.47	P=.48	P=.49	P=.50	n−X1
0	.5900	.5800	.5700	.5600	.5500	.5400	.5300	.5200	.5100	.5000	1
1	.4100	.4200	.4300	.4400	.4500	.4600	.4700	.4800	.4900	.5000	0
	q=.59	q=.58	q=.57	q=.56	q=.55	q=.54	q=.53	q=.52	q=.51	q=.50	

n = 2

X1	P=.01	P=.02	P=.03	P=.04	P=.05	P=.06	P=.07	P=.08	P=.09	P=.10	n−X1
0	.9801	.9604	.9409	.9216	.9025	.8836	.8649	.8464	.8281	.8100	2
1	.0198	.0392	.0582	.0768	.0950	.1128	.1302	.1472	.1638	.1800	1
2	.0001	.0004	.0009	.0016	.0025	.0036	.0049	.0064	.0081	.0100	0
	q=.99	q=.98	q=.97	q=.96	q=.95	q=.94	q=.93	q=.92	q=.91	q=.90	

X1	P=.11	P=.12	P=.13	P=.14	P=.15	P=.16	P=.17	P=.18	P=.19	P=.20	n−X1
0	.7921	.7744	.7569	.7396	.7225	.7056	.6889	.6724	.6561	.6400	2
1	.1958	.2112	.2262	.2408	.2550	.2688	.2822	.2952	.3078	.3200	1
2	.0121	.0144	.0169	.0196	.0225	.0256	.0289	.0324	.0361	.0400	0
	q=.89	q=.88	q=.87	q=.86	q=.85	q=.84	q=.83	q=.82	q=.81	q=.80	

X1	P=.21	P=.22	P=.23	P=.24	P=.25	P=.26	P=.27	P=.28	P=.29	P=.30	n−X1
0	.6241	.6084	.5929	.5776	.5625	.5476	.5329	.5184	.5041	.4900	2
1	.3318	.3432	.3542	.3648	.3750	.3848	.3942	.4032	.4118	.4200	1
2	.0441	.0484	.0529	.0576	.0625	.0676	.0729	.0784	.0841	.0900	0
	q=.79	q=.78	q=.77	q=.76	q=.75	q=.74	q=.73	q=.72	q=.71	q=.70	

X1	P=.31	P=.32	P=.33	P=.34	P=.35	P=.36	P=.37	P=.38	P=.39	P=.40	n-X1
0	.4761	.4624	.4489	.4356	.4225	.4096	.3969	.3844	.3721	.3600	2
1	.4278	.4352	.4422	.4488	.4550	.4608	.4662	.4712	.4758	.4800	1
2	.0961	.1024	.1089	.1156	.1225	.1296	.1369	.1444	.1521	.1600	0
	q=.69	q=.68	q=.67	q=.66	q=.65	q=.64	q=.63	q=.62	q=.61	q=.60	

X1	P=.41	P=.42	P=.43	P=.44	P=.45	P=.46	P=.47	P=.48	P=.49	P=.50	n-X1
0	.3481	.3364	.3249	.3136	.3025	.2916	.2809	.2704	.2601	.2500	2
1	.4838	.4872	.4902	.4928	.4950	.4968	.4982	.4992	.4998	.5000	1
2	.1681	.1764	.1849	.1936	.2025	.2116	.2209	.2304	.2401	.2500	0
	q=.59	q=.58	q=.57	q=.56	q=.55	q=.54	q=.53	q=.52	q=.51	q=.50	

n = 3

X1	P=.01	P=.02	P=.03	P=.04	P=.05	P=.06	P=.07	P=.08	P=.09	P=.10	n-X1
0	.9703	.9412	.9127	.8847	.8574	.8306	.8044	.7787	.7536	.7290	3
1	.0294	.0576	.0847	.1106	.1354	.1590	.1816	.2031	.2236	.2430	2
2	.0003	.0012	.0026	.0046	.0071	.0102	.0137	.0177	.0221	.0270	1
3	.0000	.0000	.0000	.0001	.0001	.0002	.0003	.0005	.0007	.0010	0
	q=.99	q=.98	q=.97	q=.96	q=.95	q=.94	q=.93	q=.92	q=.91	q=.90	

X1	P=.11	P=.12	P=.13	P=.14	P=.15	P=.16	P=.17	P=.18	P=.19	P=.20	n-X1
0	.7050	.6815	.6585	.6361	.6141	.5927	.5718	.5514	.5314	.5120	3
1	.2614	.2788	.2952	.3106	.3251	.3387	.3513	.3631	.3740	.3840	2
2	.0323	.0380	.0441	.0506	.0574	.0645	.0720	.0797	.0877	.0960	1
3	.0013	.0017	.0022	.0027	.0034	.0041	.0049	.0058	.0069	.0080	0
	q=.89	q=.88	q=.87	q=.86	q=.85	q=.84	q=.83	q=.82	q=.81	q=.80	

X1	P=.21	P=.22	P=.23	P=.24	P=.25	P=.26	P=.27	P=.28	P=.29	P=.30	n-X1
0	.4930	.4746	.4565	.4390	.4219	.4052	.3890	.3732	.3579	.3430	3
1	.3932	.4015	.4091	.4159	.4219	.4271	.4316	.4355	.4386	.4410	2
2	.1045	.1133	.1222	.1313	.1406	.1501	.1597	.1693	.1791	.1890	1
3	.0093	.0106	.0122	.0138	.0156	.0176	.0197	.0220	.0244	.0270	0
	q=.79	q=.78	q=.77	q=.76	q=.75	q=.74	q=.73	q=.72	q=.71	q=.70	

X1	P=.31	P=.32	P=.33	P=.34	P=.35	P=.36	P=.37	P=.38	P=.39	P=.40	n-X1
0	.3285	.3144	.3008	.2875	.2746	.2621	.2500	.2383	.2270	.2160	3
1	.4428	.4439	.4444	.4443	.4436	.4424	.4408	.4382	.4354	.4320	2
2	.1989	.2089	.2189	.2289	.2389	.2488	.2587	.2686	.2783	.2880	1
3	.0298	.0328	.0359	.0393	.0429	.0467	.0507	.0549	.0593	.0640	0
	q=.69	q=.68	q=.67	q=.66	q=.65	q=.64	q=.63	q=.62	q=.61	q=.60	

X1	P=.41	P=.42	P=.43	P=.44	P=.45	P=.46	P=.47	P=.48	P=.49	P=.50	n-X1
0	.2054	.1951	.1852	.1756	.1664	.1575	.1489	.1406	.1327	.1250	3
1	.4282	.4239	.4191	.4140	.4084	.4024	.3961	.3894	.3823	.3750	2
2	.2975	.3069	.3162	.3252	.3341	.3428	.3512	.3594	.3674	.3750	1
3	.0689	.0741	.0795	.0852	.0911	.0973	.1038	.1106	.1176	.1250	0
	q=.59	q=.58	q=.57	q=.56	q=.55	q=.54	q=.53	q=.52	q=.51	q=.50	

n = 4

X1	P=.01	P=.02	P=.03	P=.04	P=.05	P=.06	P=.07	P=.08	P=.09	P=.10	n-X1
0	.9606	.9224	.8853	.8493	.8145	.7807	.7481	.7164	.6857	.6561	4
1	.0388	.0753	.1095	.1416	.1715	.1993	.2252	.2492	.2713	.2916	3
2	.0006	.0023	.0051	.0088	.0135	.0191	.0254	.0325	.0402	.0486	2
3	.0000	.0000	.0001	.0002	.0005	.0008	.0013	.0019	.0027	.0036	1
4	.0000	.0000	.0000	.0000	.0000	.0000	.0000	.0000	.0001	.0001	0
	q=.99	q=.98	q=.97	q=.96	q=.95	q=.94	q=.93	q=.92	q=.91	q=.90	

X1	P=.11	P=.12	P=.13	P=.14	P=.15	P=.16	P=.17	P=.18	P=.19	P=.20	n-X1
0	.6274	.5997	.5729	.5470	.5220	.4979	.4746	.4521	.4305	.4096	4
1	.3102	.3271	.3424	.3562	.3685	.3793	.3888	.3970	.4039	.4096	3
2	.0575	.0669	.0767	.0870	.0975	.1084	.1195	.1307	.1421	.1536	2
3	.0047	.0061	.0076	.0094	.0115	.0138	.0163	.0191	.0222	.0256	1
4	.0001	.0002	.0003	.0004	.0005	.0007	.0008	.0010	.0013	.0016	0
	q=.89	q=.88	q=.87	q=.86	q=.85	q=.84	q=.83	q=.82	q=.81	q=.80	

X1	P=.21	P=.22	P=.23	P=.24	P=.25	P=.26	P=.27	P=.28	P=.29	P=.30	n-X1
0	.3895	.3702	.3515	.3336	.3164	.2999	.2840	.2687	.2541	.2401	4
1	.4142	.4176	.4200	.4214	.4219	.4214	.4201	.4180	.4152	.4116	3
2	.1651	.1767	.1882	.1996	.2109	.2221	.2331	.2439	.2544	.2646	2
3	.0293	.0332	.0375	.0420	.0469	.0520	.0575	.0632	.0693	.0756	1
4	.0019	.0023	.0028	.0033	.0039	.0046	.0053	.0061	.0071	.0081	0
	q=.79	q=.78	q=.77	q=.76	q=.75	q=.74	q=.73	q=.72	q=.71	q=.70	

X1	P=.31	P=.32	P=.33	P=.34	P=.35	P=.36	P=.37	P=.38	P=.39	P=.40	n-X1
0	.2267	.2138	.2015	.1897	.1785	.1678	.1575	.1478	.1385	.1296	4
1	.4074	.4025	.3970	.3910	.3845	.3775	.3701	.3623	.3541	.3456	3
2	.2745	.2841	.2933	.3021	.3105	.3185	.3260	.3330	.3396	.3456	2
3	.0822	.0891	.0963	.1038	.1115	.1194	.1276	.1361	.1447	.1536	1
4	.0092	.0105	.0119	.0134	.0150	.0168	.0187	.0209	.0231	.0256	0
	q=.69	q=.68	q=.67	q=.66	q=.65	q=.64	q=.63	q=.62	q=.61	q=.60	

X1	P=.41	P=.42	P=.43	P=.44	P=.45	P=.46	P=.47	P=.48	P=.49	P=.50	n-X1
0	.1212	.1132	.1056	.0983	.0915	.0850	.0789	.0731	.0677	.0625	4
1	.3368	.3278	.3185	.3091	.2995	.2897	.2799	.2700	.2600	.2500	3
2	.3511	.3560	.3604	.3643	.3675	.3702	.3723	.3738	.3747	.3750	2
3	.1627	.1719	.1813	.1908	.2005	.2102	.2201	.2300	.2400	.2500	1
4	.0283	.0311	.0342	.0375	.0410	.0448	.0488	.0531	.0576	.0625	0
	q=.59	q=.58	q=.57	q=.56	q=.55	q=.54	q=.53	q=.52	q=.51	q=.50	

n = 5

X1	P=.01	P=.02	P=.03	P=.04	P=.05	P=.06	P=.07	P=.08	P=.09	P=.10	n-X1
0	.9510	.9039	.8587	.8154	.7738	.7339	.6957	.6591	.6240	.5905	5
1	.0480	.0922	.1328	.1699	.2036	.2342	.2618	.2866	.3086	.3280	4
2	.0010	.0038	.0082	.0142	.0214	.0299	.0394	.0498	.0610	.0729	3
3	.0000	.0001	.0003	.0006	.0011	.0019	.0030	.0043	.0060	.0081	2
4	.0000	.0000	.0000	.0000	.0000	.0001	.0001	.0002	.0003	.0004	1
5	.0000	.0000	.0000	.0000	.0000	.0000	.0000	.0000	.0000	.0000	0
	q=.99	q=.98	q=.97	q=.96	q=.95	q=.94	q=.93	q=.92	q=.91	q=.90	

X1	P=.11	P=.12	P=.13	P=.14	P=.15	P=.16	P=.17	P=.18	P=.19	P=.20	n-X1
0	.5584	.5277	.4984	.4704	.4437	.4182	.3939	.3707	.3487	.3277	5
1	.3451	.3598	.3724	.3829	.3915	.3983	.4034	.4069	.4089	.4096	4
2	.0853	.0981	.1113	.1247	.1382	.1517	.1652	.1786	.1919	.2048	3
3	.0105	.0134	.0166	.0203	.0244	.0289	.0338	.0392	.0450	.0512	2
4	.0007	.0009	.0012	.0017	.0022	.0028	.0035	.0043	.0053	.0064	1
5	.0000	.0000	.0000	.0001	.0001	.0001	.0001	.0002	.0002	.0003	0
	q=.89	q=.88	q=.87	q=.86	q=.85	q=.84	q=.83	q=.82	q=.81	q=.80	

X1	P=.21	P=.22	P=.23	P=.24	P=.25	P=.26	P=.27	P=.28	P=.29	P=.30	n-X1
0	.3077	.2887	.2707	.2536	.2373	.2219	.2073	.1935	.1804	.1681	5
1	.4090	.4072	.4043	.4003	.3955	.3898	.3834	.3762	.3685	.3601	4
2	.2174	.2297	.2415	.2529	.2637	.2739	.2836	.2926	.3010	.3087	3
3	.0578	.0648	.0721	.0798	.0879	.0962	.1049	.1138	.1229	.1323	2
4	.0077	.0091	.0108	.0126	.0146	.0169	.0194	.0221	.0251	.0283	1
5	.0004	.0005	.0006	.0008	.0010	.0012	.0014	.0017	.0021	.0024	0
	q=.79	q=.78	q=.77	q=.76	q=.75	q=.74	q=.73	q=.72	q=.71	q=.70	

X1	P=.31	P=.32	P=.33	P=.34	P=.35	P=.36	P=.37	P=.38	P=.39	P=.40	n-X1
0	.1564	.1454	.1350	.1252	.1160	.1074	.0992	.0916	.0845	.0778	5
1	.3513	.3421	.3325	.3226	.3124	.3020	.2914	.2808	.2700	.2592	4
2	.3157	.3220	.3275	.3323	.3364	.3397	.3423	.3441	.3452	.3456	3
3	.1418	.1515	.1613	.1712	.1811	.1911	.2010	.2109	.2207	.2304	2
4	.0319	.0357	.0397	.0441	.0488	.0537	.0590	.0646	.0706	.0768	1
5	.0029	.0034	.0039	.0045	.0053	.0060	.0069	.0079	.0090	.0102	0
	q=.69	q=.68	q=.67	q=.66	q=.65	q=.64	q=.63	q=.62	q=.61	q=.60	

X1	P=.41	P=.42	P=.43	P=.44	P=.45	P=.46	P=.47	P=.48	P=.49	P=.50	n-X1
0	.0715	.0656	.0602	.0551	.0503	.0459	.0418	.0380	.0345	.0312	5
1	.2484	.2376	.2270	.2164	.2059	.1956	.1854	.1755	.1657	.1562	4
2	.3452	.3442	.3424	.3400	.3369	.3332	.3289	.3240	.3185	.3125	3
3	.2399	.2492	.2583	.2671	.2757	.2838	.2916	.2990	.3060	.3125	2
4	.0834	.0902	.0974	.1049	.1128	.1209	.1293	.1380	.1470	.1563	1
5	.0116	.0131	.0147	.0165	.0185	.0206	.0229	.0255	.0282	.0313	0
	q=.59	q=.58	q=.57	q=.56	q=.55	q=.54	q=.53	q=.52	q=.51	q=.50	

n = 10

X1	P=.01	P=.02	P=.03	P=.04	P=.05	P=.06	P=.07	P=.08	P=.09	P=.10	n-X1
0	.9044	.8171	.7374	.6648	.5987	.5386	.4840	.4344	.3894	.3487	10
1	.0914	.1667	.2281	.2770	.3151	.3438	.3643	.3777	.3851	.3874	9
2	.0042	.0153	.0317	.0519	.0746	.0988	.1234	.1478	.1714	.1937	8
3	.0001	.0008	.0026	.0058	.0105	.0168	.0248	.0343	.0452	.0574	7
4	.0000	.0000	.0001	.0004	.0010	.0019	.0033	.0052	.0078	.0112	6
5	.0000	.0000	.0000	.0000	.0001	.0001	.0003	.0005	.0009	.0015	5
6	.0000	.0000	.0000	.0000	.0000	.0000	.0000	.0000	.0001	.0001	4
7	.0000	.0000	.0000	.0000	.0000	.0000	.0000	.0000	.0000	.0000	3
8	.0000	.0000	.0000	.0000	.0000	.0000	.0000	.0000	.0000	.0000	2
9	.0000	.0000	.0000	.0000	.0000	.0000	.0000	.0000	.0000	.0000	1
10	.0000	.0000	.0000	.0000	.0000	.0000	.0000	.0000	.0000	.0000	0
	q=.99	q=.98	q=.97	q=.96	q=.95	q=.94	q=.93	q=.92	q=.91	q=.90	

X1	P=.11	P=.12	P=.13	P=.14	P=.15	P=.16	P=.17	P=.18	P=.19	P=.20	n-X1
0	.3118	.2785	.2484	.2213	.1969	.1749	.1552	.1374	.1216	.1074	10
1	.3854	.3798	.3712	.3603	.3474	.3331	.3178	.3017	.2852	.2684	9
2	.2143	.2330	.2496	.2639	.2759	.2856	.2929	.2980	.3010	.3020	8
3	.0706	.0847	.0995	.1146	.1298	.1450	.1600	.1745	.1883	.2013	7
4	.0153	.0202	.0260	.0326	.0401	.0483	.0573	.0670	.0773	.0881	6
5	.0023	.0033	.0047	.0064	.0085	.0111	.0141	.0177	.0218	.0264	5
6	.0002	.0004	.0006	.0009	.0012	.0018	.0024	.0032	.0043	.0055	4
7	.0000	.0000	.0000	.0001	.0001	.0002	.0003	.0004	.0006	.0008	3
8	.0000	.0000	.0000	.0000	.0000	.0000	.0000	.0000	.0001	.0001	2
9	.0000	.0000	.0000	.0000	.0000	.0000	.0000	.0000	.0000	.0000	1
10	.0000	.0000	.0000	.0000	.0000	.0000	.0000	.0000	.0000	.0000	0
	q=.89	q=.88	q=.87	q=.86	q=.85	q=.84	q=.83	q=.82	q=.81	q=.80	

X1	P=.21	P=.22	P=.23	P=.24	P=.25	P=.26	P=.27	P=.28	P=.29	P=.30	n-X1
0	.0947	.0834	.0733	.0643	.0563	.0492	.0430	.0374	.0326	.0282	10
1	.2517	.2351	.2188	.2030	.1877	.1730	.1590	.1456	.1330	.1211	9
2	.3011	.2984	.2942	.2885	.2816	.2735	.2646	.2548	.2444	.2335	8
3	.2134	.2244	.2343	.2429	.2503	.2563	.2609	.2642	.2662	.2668	7
4	.0993	.1108	.1225	.1343	.1460	.1576	.1689	.1798	.1903	.2001	6
5	.0317	.0375	.0439	.0509	.0584	.0664	.0750	.0839	.0933	.1029	5
6	.0070	.0088	.0109	.0134	.0162	.0195	.0231	.0272	.0317	.0368	4
7	.0011	.0014	.0019	.0024	.0031	.0039	.0049	.0060	.0074	.0090	3
8	.0001	.0002	.0002	.0003	.0004	.0005	.0007	.0009	.0011	.0014	2
9	.0000	.0000	.0000	.0000	.0000	.0000	.0001	.0001	.0001	.0001	1
10	.0000	.0000	.0000	.0000	.0000	.0000	.0000	.0000	.0000	.0000	0
	q=.79	q=.78	q=.77	q=.76	q=.75	q=.74	q=.73	q=.72	q=.71	q=.70	

X1	P=.31	P=.32	P=.33	P=.34	P=.35	P=.36	P=.37	P=.38	P=.39	P=.40	n-X1
0	.0245	.0211	.0182	.0157	.0135	.0115	.0098	.0084	.0071	.0060	10
1	.1099	.0995	.0898	.0808	.0725	.0649	.0578	.0514	.0456	.0403	9
2	.2222	.2107	.1990	.1873	.1757	.1642	.1529	.1419	.1312	.1209	8
3	.2662	.2644	.2614	.2573	.2522	.2462	.2394	.2319	.2237	.2150	7

X1	P=.41	P=.42	P=.43	P=.44	P=.45	P=.46	P=.47	P=.48	P=.49	P=.50	n−X1
4	.2093	.2177	.2253	.2320	.2377	.2424	.2461	.2487	.2503	.2508	6
5	.1128	.1229	.1332	.1434	.1536	.1636	.1734	.1829	.1920	.2007	5
6	.0422	.0482	.0547	.0616	.0689	.0767	.0849	.0934	.1023	.1115	4
7	.0108	.0130	.0154	.0181	.0212	.0247	.0285	.0327	.0374	.0425	3
8	.0018	.0023	.0028	.0035	.0043	.0052	.0063	.0075	.0090	.0106	2
9	.0002	.0002	.0003	.0004	.0005	.0006	.0008	.0010	.0013	.0016	1
10	.0000	.0000	.0000	.0000	.0000	.0000	.0000	.0001	.0001	.0001	0
	q=.69	q=.68	q=.67	q=.66	q=.65	q=.64	q=.63	q=.62	q=.61	q=.60	

X1	P=.41	P=.42	P=.43	P=.44	P=.45	P=.46	P=.47	P=.48	P=.49	P=.50	n−X1
0	.0051	.0043	.0036	.0030	.0025	.0021	.0017	.0014	.0012	.0010	10
1	.0355	.0312	.0273	.0238	.0207	.0180	.0155	.0133	.0114	.0098	9
2	.1111	.1017	.0927	.0843	.0763	.0688	.0619	.0554	.0494	.0439	8
3	.2058	.1963	.1865	.1765	.1665	.1564	.1464	.1364	.1267	.1172	7
4	.2503	.2488	.2462	.2427	.2384	.2331	.2271	.2204	.2130	.2051	6
5	.2087	.2162	.2229	.2289	.2340	.2383	.2417	.2441	.2456	.2461	5
6	.1209	.1304	.1401	.1499	.1596	.1692	.1786	.1878	.1966	.2051	4
7	.0480	.0540	.0604	.0673	.0746	.0824	.0905	.0991	.1080	.1172	3
8	.0125	.0147	.0171	.0198	.0229	.0263	.0301	.0343	.0389	.0439	2
9	.0019	.0024	.0029	.0035	.0042	.0050	.0059	.0070	.0083	.0098	1
10	.0001	.0002	.0002	.0003	.0003	.0004	.0005	.0006	.0008	.0010	0
	q=.59	q=.58	q=.57	q=.56	q=.55	q=.54	q=.53	q=.52	q=.51	q=.50	

n = 15

X1	P=.01	P=.02	P=.03	P=.04	P=.05	P=.06	P=.07	P=.08	P=.09	P=.10	n−X1
0	.8601	.7386	.6333	.5421	.4633	.3953	.3367	.2863	.2430	.2059	15
1	.1303	.2261	.2938	.3388	.3658	.3785	.3801	.3734	.3605	.3432	14
2	.0092	.0323	.0636	.0988	.1348	.1691	.2003	.2273	.2496	.2669	13
3	.0004	.0029	.0085	.0178	.0307	.0468	.0653	.0857	.1070	.1285	12
4	.0000	.0002	.0008	.0022	.0049	.0090	.0148	.0223	.0317	.0428	11
5	.0000	.0000	.0001	.0002	.0006	.0013	.0024	.0043	.0069	.0105	10
6	.0000	.0000	.0000	.0000	.0000	.0001	.0003	.0006	.0011	.0019	9
7	.0000	.0000	.0000	.0000	.0000	.0000	.0001	.0001	.0003		8
	q=.99	q=.98	q=.97	q=.96	q=.95	q=.94	q=.93	q=.92	q=.91	q=.90	

X1	P=.11	P=.12	P=.13	P=.14	P=.15	P=.16	P=.17	P=.18	P=.19	P=.20	n−X1
0	.1741	.1470	.1238	.1041	.0874	.0731	.0611	.0510	.0424	.0352	15
1	.3228	.3006	.2775	.2542	.2312	.2090	.1878	.1678	.1492	.1319	14
2	.2793	.2870	.2903	.2897	.2856	.2787	.2692	.2578	.2449	.2309	13
3	.1496	.1696	.1880	.2044	.2184	.2300	.2389	.2452	.2489	.2501	12
4	.0555	.0694	.0843	.0998	.1156	.1314	.1468	.1615	.1752	.1876	11
5	.0151	.0208	.0277	.0357	.0449	.0551	.0662	.0780	.0904	.1032	10
6	.0031	.0047	.0069	.0097	.0132	.0175	.0226	.0285	.0353	.0430	9
7	.0005	.0008	.0013	.0020	.0030	.0043	.0059	.0081	.0107	.0138	8
8	.0001	.0001	.0002	.0003	.0005	.0008	.0012	.0018	.0025	.0035	7
9	.0000	.0000	.0000	.0000	.0001	.0001	.0002	.0003	.0005	.0007	6
10	.0000	.0000	.0000	.0000	.0000	.0000	.0000	.0000	.0001	.0001	5
	q=.89	q=.88	q=.87	q=.86	q=.85	q=.84	q=.83	q=.82	q=.81	q=.80	

X1	P=.21	P=.22	P=.23	P=.24	P=.25	P=.26	P=.27	P=.28	P=.29	P=.30	n−X1
0	.0291	.0241	.0198	.0163	.0134	.0109	.0089	.0072	.0059	.0047	15
1	.1162	.1018	.0889	.0772	.0668	.0576	.0494	.0423	.0360	.0305	14
2	.2162	.2010	.1858	.1707	.1559	.1416	.1280	.1150	.1029	.0916	13
3	.2490	.2457	.2405	.2336	.2252	.2156	.2051	.1939	.1821	.1700	12
4	.1986	.2079	.2155	.2213	.2252	.2273	.2276	.2262	.2231	.2186	11
5	.1161	.1290	.1416	.1537	.1651	.1757	.1852	.1935	.2005	.2061	10
6	.0514	.0606	.0705	.0809	.0917	.1029	.1142	.1254	.1365	.1472	9
7	.0176	.0220	.0271	.0329	.0393	.0465	.0543	.0627	.0717	.0811	8

n = 20

X1	P=.01	P=.02	P=.03	P=.04	P=.05	P=.06	P=.07	P=.08	P=.09	P=.10	n−X1
0	.8179	.6676	.5438	.4420	.3585	.2901	.2342	.1887	.1516	.1216	20
1	.1652	.2725	.3364	.3683	.3774	.3703	.3526	.3282	.3000	.2702	19
2	.0159	.0528	.0988	.1458	.1887	.2246	.2521	.2711	.2818	.2852	18
3	.0010	.0065	.0183	.0364	.0596	.0860	.1139	.1414	.1672	.1901	17
4	.0000	.0006	.0024	.0065	.0133	.0233	.0364	.0523	.0703	.0898	16
5	.0000	.0000	.0002	.0009	.0022	.0048	.0088	.0145	.0222	.0319	15
6	.0000	.0000	.0000	.0001	.0003	.0008	.0017	.0032	.0055	.0089	14
7	.0000	.0000	.0000	.0000	.0000	.0001	.0002	.0005	.0011	.0020	13
8	.0000	.0000	.0000	.0000	.0000	.0000	.0000	.0001	.0002	.0004	12
9	.0000	.0000	.0000	.0000	.0000	.0000	.0000	.0000	.0000	.0001	11
	q=.99	q=.98	q=.97	q=.96	q=.95	q=.94	q=.93	q=.92	q=.91	q=.90	

X1	P=.11	P=.12	P=.13	P=.14	P=.15	P=.16	P=.17	P=.18	P=.19	P=.20	n-X1
0	.0972	.0776	.0617	.0490	.0388	.0306	.0241	.0189	.0148	.0115	20
1	.2403	.2115	.1844	.1595	.1368	.1165	.0986	.0829	.0693	.0576	19
2	.2822	.2740	.2618	.2466	.2293	.2109	.1919	.1730	.1545	.1369	18
3	.2093	.2242	.2347	.2409	.2428	.2410	.2358	.2278	.2175	.2054	17
4	.1099	.1299	.1491	.1666	.1821	.1951	.2053	.2125	.2168	.2182	16
5	.0435	.0567	.0713	.0868	.1028	.1189	.1345	.1493	.1627	.1746	15
6	.0134	.0193	.0266	.0353	.0454	.0566	.0689	.0819	.0954	.1091	14
7	.0033	.0053	.0080	.0115	.0160	.0216	.0282	.0360	.0448	.0545	13
8	.0007	.0012	.0019	.0030	.0046	.0067	.0094	.0128	.0171	.0222	12
9	.0001	.0002	.0004	.0007	.0011	.0017	.0026	.0038	.0053	.0074	11
10	.0000	.0000	.0001	.0001	.0002	.0004	.0006	.0009	.0014	.0020	10
11	.0000	.0000	.0000	.0000	.0000	.0001	.0001	.0002	.0003	.0005	9
12	.0000	.0000	.0000	.0000	.0000	.0000	.0000	.0000	.0001	.0001	8
	q=.89	q=.88	q=.87	q=.86	q=.85	q=.84	q=.83	q=.82	q=.81	q=.80	

X1	P=.21	P=.22	P=.23	P=.24	P=.25	P=.26	P=.27	P=.28	P=.29	P=.30	n-X1
0	.0090	.0069	.0054	.0041	.0032	.0024	.0018	.0014	.0011	.0008	20
1	.0477	.0392	.0321	.0261	.0211	.0170	.0137	.0109	.0087	.0068	19
2	.1204	.1050	.0910	.0783	.0669	.0569	.0480	.0403	.0336	.0278	18
3	.1920	.1777	.1631	.1484	.1339	.1199	.1065	.0940	.0823	.0716	17
4	.2169	.2131	.2070	.1991	.1897	.1790	.1675	.1553	.1429	.1304	16
5	.1845	.1923	.1979	.2012	.2023	.2013	.1982	.1933	.1868	.1789	15
6	.1226	.1356	.1478	.1589	.1686	.1768	.1833	.1879	.1907	.1916	14
7	.0652	.0765	.0883	.1003	.1124	.1242	.1356	.1462	.1558	.1643	13
8	.0282	.0351	.0429	.0515	.0609	.0709	.0815	.0924	.1034	.1144	12
9	.0100	.0132	.0171	.0217	.0271	.0332	.0402	.0479	.0563	.0654	11
10	.0029	.0041	.0056	.0075	.0099	.0128	.0163	.0205	.0253	.0308	10
11	.0007	.0010	.0015	.0022	.0030	.0041	.0055	.0072	.0094	.0120	9
12	.0001	.0002	.0003	.0005	.0008	.0011	.0015	.0021	.0029	.0039	8
13	.0000	.0000	.0001	.0001	.0002	.0002	.0003	.0005	.0007	.0010	7
14	.0000	.0000	.0000	.0000	.0000	.0000	.0001	.0001	.0001	.0002	6
	q=.79	q=.78	q=.77	q=.76	q=.75	q=.74	q=.73	q=.72	q=.71	q=.70	

X1	P=.31	P=.32	P=.33	P=.34	P=.35	P=.36	P=.37	P=.38	P=.39	P=.40	n-X1
0	.0006	.0004	.0003	.0002	.0002	.0001	.0001	.0001	.0001	.0000	20
1	.0054	.0042	.0033	.0025	.0020	.0015	.0011	.0009	.0007	.0005	19
2	.0229	.0188	.0153	.0124	.0100	.0080	.0064	.0050	.0040	.0031	18
3	.0619	.0531	.0453	.0383	.0323	.0270	.0224	.0185	.0152	.0123	17
4	.1181	.1062	.0947	.0839	.0738	.0645	.0559	.0482	.0412	.0350	16
5	.1698	.1599	.1493	.1384	.1272	.1161	.1051	.0945	.0843	.0746	15
6	.1907	.1881	.1839	.1782	.1712	.1632	.1543	.1447	.1347	.1244	14
7	.1714	.1770	.1811	.1836	.1844	.1836	.1812	.1774	.1722	.1659	13
8	.1251	.1354	.1450	.1537	.1614	.1678	.1730	.1767	.1790	.1797	12
9	.0750	.0849	.0952	.1056	.1158	.1259	.1354	.1444	.1526	.1597	11
10	.0370	.0440	.0516	.0598	.0686	.0779	.0875	.0974	.1073	.1171	10
11	.0151	.0188	.0231	.0280	.0336	.0398	.0467	.0542	.0624	.0710	9
12	.0051	.0066	.0085	.0108	.0136	.0168	.0206	.0249	.0299	.0355	8
13	.0014	.0019	.0026	.0034	.0045	.0058	.0074	.0094	.0118	.0146	7
14	.0003	.0005	.0006	.0009	.0012	.0016	.0022	.0029	.0038	.0049	6
15	.0001	.0001	.0001	.0002	.0003	.0004	.0005	.0007	.0010	.0013	5
16	.0000	.0000	.0000	.0000	.0000	.0001	.0001	.0001	.0002	.0003	4
	q=.69	q=.68	q=.67	q=.66	q=.65	q=.64	q=.63	q=.62	q=.61	q=.60	

X1	P=.41	P=.42	P=.43	P=.44	P=.45	P=.46	P=.47	P=.48	P=.49	P=.50	n-X1
0	.0000	.0000	.0000	.0000	.0000	.0000	.0000	.0000	.0000	.0000	20
1	.0004	.0003	.0002	.0001	.0001	.0001	.0001	.0000	.0000	.0000	19
2	.0024	.0018	.0014	.0011	.0008	.0006	.0005	.0003	.0002	.0002	18
3	.0100	.0080	.0064	.0051	.0040	.0031	.0024	.0019	.0014	.0011	17
4	.0295	.0247	.0206	.0170	.0139	.0113	.0092	.0074	.0059	.0046	16
5	.0656	.0573	.0496	.0427	.0365	.0309	.0260	.0217	.0180	.0148	15
6	.1140	.1037	.0936	.0839	.0746	.0658	.0577	.0501	.0432	.0370	14
7	.1585	.1502	.1413	.1318	.1221	.1122	.1023	.0925	.0830	.0739	13
8	.1790	.1768	.1732	.1683	.1623	.1553	.1474	.1388	.1296	.1201	12
9	.1658	.1707	.1742	.1763	.1771	.1763	.1742	.1708	.1661	.1602	11
10	.1268	.1359	.1446	.1524	.1593	.1652	.1700	.1734	.1755	.1762	10
11	.0801	.0895	.0991	.1089	.1185	.1280	.1370	.1455	.1533	.1602	9
12	.0417	.0486	.0561	.0642	.0727	.0818	.0911	.1007	.1105	.1201	8
13	.0178	.0217	.0260	.0310	.0366	.0429	.0497	.0572	.0653	.0739	7
14	.0062	.0078	.0098	.0122	.0150	.0183	.0221	.0264	.0314	.0370	6
15	.0017	.0023	.0030	.0038	.0049	.0062	.0078	.0098	.0121	.0148	5
16	.0004	.0005	.0007	.0009	.0013	.0017	.0022	.0028	.0036	.0046	4
17	.0001	.0001	.0001	.0002	.0002	.0003	.0005	.0006	.0008	.0011	3
18	.0000	.0000	.0000	.0000	.0000	.0000	.0001	.0001	.0001	.0002	2
	q=.59	q=.58	q=.57	q=.56	q=.55	q=.54	q=.53	q=.52	q=.51	q=.50	

n = 25

X1	P=.01	P=.02	P=.03	P=.04	P=.05	P=.06	P=.07	P=.08	P=.09	P=.10	n-X1
0	.7778	.6035	.4670	.3604	.2774	.2129	.1630	.1244	.0946	.0718	25
1	.1964	.3079	.3611	.3754	.3650	.3398	.3066	.2704	.2340	.1994	24
2	.0238	.0754	.1340	.1877	.2305	.2602	.2770	.2821	.2777	.2659	23
3	.0018	.0118	.0318	.0600	.0930	.1273	.1598	.1881	.2106	.2265	22
4	.0001	.0013	.0054	.0137	.0269	.0447	.0662	.0899	.1145	.1384	21
5	.0000	.0001	.0007	.0024	.0060	.0120	.0209	.0329	.0476	.0646	20
6	.0000	.0000	.0001	.0003	.0010	.0026	.0052	.0095	.0157	.0239	19
7	.0000	.0000	.0000	.0000	.0001	.0004	.0011	.0022	.0042	.0072	18
8	.0000	.0000	.0000	.0000	.0000	.0001	.0002	.0004	.0009	.0018	17
9	.0000	.0000	.0000	.0000	.0000	.0000	.0000	.0001	.0002	.0004	16
10	.0000	.0000	.0000	.0000	.0000	.0000	.0000	.0000	.0000	.0001	15
	q=.99	q=.98	q=.97	q=.96	q=.95	q=.94	q=.93	q=.92	q=.91	q=.90	

X1	P=.11	P=.12	P=.13	P=.14	P=.15	P=.16	P=.17	P=.18	P=.19	P=.20	n-X1
0	.0543	.0409	.0308	.0230	.0172	.0128	.0095	.0070	.0052	.0038	25
1	.1678	.1395	.1149	.0938	.0759	.0609	.0486	.0384	.0302	.0236	24
2	.2488	.2283	.2060	.1832	.1607	.1392	.1193	.1012	.0851	.0708	23
3	.2358	.2387	.2360	.2286	.2174	.2033	.1874	.1704	.1530	.1358	22
4	.1603	.1790	.1940	.2047	.2110	.2130	.2111	.2057	.1974	.1867	21
5	.0832	.1025	.1217	.1399	.1564	.1704	.1816	.1897	.1945	.1960	20
6	.0343	.0466	.0606	.0759	.0920	.1082	.1240	.1388	.1520	.1633	19
7	.0115	.0173	.0246	.0336	.0441	.0559	.0689	.0827	.0968	.1108	18
8	.0032	.0053	.0083	.0123	.0175	.0240	.0318	.0408	.0511	.0623	17
9	.0007	.0014	.0023	.0038	.0058	.0086	.0123	.0169	.0226	.0294	16
10	.0001	.0003	.0006	.0010	.0016	.0026	.0040	.0059	.0085	.0118	15
11	.0000	.0001	.0001	.0002	.0004	.0007	.0011	.0018	.0027	.0040	14
12	.0000	.0000	.0000	.0000	.0001	.0002	.0003	.0005	.0007	.0012	13
13	.0000	.0000	.0000	.0000	.0000	.0000	.0001	.0001	.0002	.0003	12
14	.0000	.0000	.0000	.0000	.0000	.0000	.0000	.0000	.0000	.0001	11
	q=.89	q=.88	q=.87	q=.86	q=.85	q=.84	q=.83	q=.82	q=.81	q=.80	

X1	P=.21	P=.22	P=.23	P=.24	P=.25	P=.26	P=.27	P=.28	P=.29	P=.30	n-X1
0	.0028	.0020	.0015	.0010	.0008	.0005	.0004	.0003	.0002	.0001	25
1	.0183	.0141	.0109	.0083	.0063	.0047	.0035	.0026	.0020	.0014	24
2	.0585	.0479	.0389	.0314	.0251	.0199	.0157	.0123	.0096	.0074	23
3	.1192	.1035	.0891	.0759	.0641	.0537	.0446	.0367	.0300	.0243	22
4	.1742	.1606	.1463	.1318	.1175	.1037	.0906	.0785	.0673	.0572	21
5	.1945	.1903	.1836	.1749	.1645	.1531	.1408	.1282	.1155	.1030	20
6	.1724	.1789	.1828	.1841	.1828	.1793	.1736	.1661	.1572	.1472	19
7	.1244	.1369	.1482	.1578	.1654	.1709	.1743	.1754	.1743	.1712	18
8	.0744	.0869	.0996	.1121	.1241	.1351	.1450	.1535	.1602	.1651	17
9	.0373	.0463	.0562	.0669	.0781	.0897	.1013	.1127	.1236	.1336	16
10	.0159	.0209	.0269	.0338	.0417	.0504	.0600	.0701	.0808	.0916	15
11	.0058	.0080	.0109	.0145	.0189	.0242	.0302	.0372	.0450	.0536	14
12	.0018	.0026	.0038	.0054	.0074	.0099	.0130	.0169	.0214	.0268	13
13	.0005	.0007	.0011	.0017	.0025	.0035	.0048	.0066	.0088	.0115	12
14	.0001	.0002	.0003	.0005	.0007	.0010	.0015	.0022	.0031	.0042	11
15	.0000	.0000	.0001	.0001	.0002	.0003	.0004	.0006	.0009	.0013	10
16	.0000	.0000	.0000	.0000	.0000	.0001	.0001	.0002	.0002	.0004	9
17	.0000	.0000	.0000	.0000	.0000	.0000	.0000	.0000	.0001	.0001	8
	q=.79	q=.78	q=.77	q=.76	q=.75	q=.74	q=.73	q=.72	q=.71	q=.70	

X1	P=.31	P=.32	P=.33	P=.34	P=.35	P=.36	P=.37	P=.38	P=.39	P=.40	n-X1
0	.0001	.0001	.0000	.0000	.0000	.0000	.0000	.0000	.0000	.0000	25
1	.0011	.0008	.0006	.0004	.0003	.0002	.0001	.0001	.0001	.0000	24
2	.0057	.0043	.0033	.0025	.0018	.0014	.0010	.0007	.0005	.0004	23
3	.0195	.0156	.0123	.0097	.0076	.0058	.0045	.0034	.0026	.0019	22
4	.0482	.0403	.0334	.0274	.0224	.0181	.0145	.0115	.0091	.0071	21
5	.0910	.0797	.0691	.0594	.0506	.0427	.0357	.0297	.0244	.0199	20
6	.1363	.1250	.1134	.1020	.0908	.0801	.0700	.0606	.0520	.0442	19
7	.1662	.1596	.1516	.1426	.1327	.1222	.1115	.1008	.0902	.0800	18
8	.1680	.1690	.1681	.1652	.1607	.1547	.1474	.1390	.1298	.1200	17
9	.1426	.1502	.1563	.1608	.1635	.1644	.1635	.1609	.1567	.1511	16
10	.1025	.1131	.1232	.1325	.1409	.1479	.1536	.1578	.1603	.1612	15
11	.0628	.0726	.0828	.0931	.1034	.1135	.1230	.1319	.1398	.1465	14
12	.0329	.0399	.0476	.0560	.0650	.0745	.0843	.0943	.1043	.1140	13
13	.0148	.0188	.0234	.0288	.0350	.0419	.0495	.0578	.0667	.0760	12
14	.0057	.0076	.0099	.0127	.0161	.0202	.0249	.0304	.0365	.0434	11
15	.0019	.0026	.0036	.0048	.0064	.0083	.0107	.0136	.0171	.0212	10

16	.0005	.0008	.0011	.0015	.0021	.0029	.0039	.0052	.0068	.0088	9
17	.0001	.0002	.0003	.0004	.0006	.0009	.0012	.0017	.0023	.0031	8
18	.0000	.0000	.0001	.0001	.0001	.0002	.0003	.0005	.0007	.0009	7
19	.0000	.0000	.0000	.0000	.0000	.0000	.0001	.0001	.0002	.0002	6
	q=.69	q=.68	q=.67	q=.66	q=.65	q=.64	q=.63	q=.62	q=.61	q=.60	

	P=.41	P=.42	P=.43	P=.44	P=.45	P=.46	P=.47	P=.48	P=.49	P=.50	
X1											n-X1
0	.0000	.0000	.0000	.0000	.0000	.0000	.0000	.0000	.0000	.0000	25
1	.0000	.0000	.0000	.0000	.0000	.0000	.0000	.0000	.0000	.0000	24
2	.0003	.0002	.0001	.0001	.0001	.0000	.0000	.0000	.0000	.0000	23
3	.0014	.0011	.0008	.0006	.0004	.0003	.0002	.0001	.0001	.0001	22
4	.0055	.0042	.0032	.0024	.0018	.0014	.0010	.0007	.0005	.0004	21
5	.0161	.0129	.0102	.0081	.0063	.0049	.0037	.0028	.0021	.0016	20
6	.0372	.0311	.0257	.0211	.0172	.0138	.0110	.0087	.0068	.0053	19
7	.0703	.0611	.0527	.0450	.0381	.0319	.0265	.0218	.0178	.0143	18
8	.1099	.0996	.0895	.0796	.0701	.0612	.0529	.0453	.0384	.0322	17
9	.1442	.1363	.1275	.1181	.1084	.0985	.0886	.0790	.0697	.0609	16
10	.1603	.1579	.1539	.1485	.1419	.1342	.1257	.1166	.1071	.0974	15
11	.1519	.1559	.1583	.1591	.1583	.1559	.1521	.1468	.1404	.1328	14
12	.1232	.1317	.1393	.1458	.1511	.1550	.1573	.1581	.1573	.1550	13
13	.0856	.0954	.1051	.1146	.1236	.1320	.1395	.1460	.1512	.1550	12
14	.0510	.0592	.0680	.0772	.0867	.0964	.1060	.1155	.1245	.1328	11
15	.0260	.0314	.0376	.0445	.0520	.0602	.0690	.0782	.0877	.0974	10
16	.0113	.0142	.0177	.0218	.0266	.0321	.0382	.0451	.0527	.0609	9
17	.0042	.0055	.0071	.0091	.0115	.0145	.0179	.0220	.0268	.0322	8
18	.0013	.0018	.0024	.0032	.0042	.0055	.0071	.0090	.0114	.0143	7
19	.0003	.0005	.0007	.0009	.0013	.0017	.0023	.0031	.0040	.0053	6
20	.0001	.0001	.0001	.0002	.0003	.0004	.0006	.0009	.0012	.0016	5
21	.0000	.0000	.0000	.0000	.0001	.0001	.0001	.0002	.0003	.0004	4
22	.0000	.0000	.0000	.0000	.0000	.0000	.0000	.0000	.0000	.0001	3
	q=.59	q=.58	q=.57	q=.56	q=.55	q=.54	q=.53	q=.52	q=.51	q=.50	

n = 50

	P=.01	P=.02	P=.03	P=.04	P=.05	P=.06	P=.07	P=.08	P=.09	P=.10	
X1											n-X1
0	.6050	.3642	.2181	.1299	.0769	.0453	.0266	.0155	.0090	.0052	50
1	.3056	.3716	.3372	.2706	.2025	.1447	.0999	.0672	.0443	.0286	49
2	.0756	.1858	.2555	.2762	.2611	.2262	.1843	.1433	.1073	.0779	48
3	.0122	.0607	.1264	.1842	.2199	.2311	.2219	.1993	.1698	.1386	47
4	.0015	.0145	.0459	.0902	.1360	.1733	.1963	.2037	.1973	.1809	46
5	.0001	.0027	.0131	.0346	.0658	.1018	.1359	.1629	.1795	.1849	45
6	.0000	.0004	.0030	.0108	.0260	.0487	.0767	.1063	.1332	.1541	44
7	.0000	.0001	.0006	.0028	.0086	.0195	.0363	.0581	.0828	.1076	43
8	.0000	.0000	.0001	.0006	.0024	.0067	.0147	.0271	.0440	.0643	42
9	.0000	.0000	.0000	.0001	.0006	.0020	.0052	.0110	.0203	.0333	41
10	.0000	.0000	.0000	.0000	.0001	.0005	.0016	.0039	.0082	.0152	40
11	.0000	.0000	.0000	.0000	.0000	.0001	.0004	.0012	.0030	.0061	39
12	.0000	.0000	.0000	.0000	.0000	.0000	.0001	.0004	.0010	.0022	38
13	.0000	.0000	.0000	.0000	.0000	.0000	.0000	.0001	.0003	.0007	37
14	.0000	.0000	.0000	.0000	.0000	.0000	.0000	.0000	.0001	.0002	36
15	.0000	.0000	.0000	.0000	.0000	.0000	.0000	.0000	.0000	.0001	35
	q=.99	q=.98	q=.97	q=.96	q=.95	q=.94	q=.93	q=.92	q=.91	q=.90	

	P=.11	P=.12	P=.13	P=.14	P=.15	P=.16	P=.17	P=.18	P=.19	P=.20	
X1											n-X1
0	.0029	.0017	.0009	.0005	.0003	.0002	.0001	.0000	.0000	.0000	50
1	.0182	.0114	.0071	.0043	.0026	.0016	.0009	.0005	.0003	.0002	49
2	.0552	.0382	.0259	.0172	.0113	.0073	.0046	.0029	.0018	.0011	48
3	.1091	.0833	.0619	.0449	.0319	.0222	.0151	.0102	.0067	.0044	47
4	.1584	.1334	.1086	.0858	.0661	.0496	.0364	.0262	.0185	.0128	46
5	.1801	.1674	.1493	.1286	.1072	.0869	.0687	.0530	.0400	.0295	45
6	.1670	.1712	.1674	.1570	.1419	.1242	.1055	.0872	.0703	.0554	44
7	.1297	.1467	.1572	.1606	.1575	.1487	.1358	.1203	.1037	.0870	43
8	.0862	.1075	.1262	.1406	.1493	.1523	.1495	.1420	.1307	.1169	42
9	.0497	.0684	.0880	.1068	.1230	.1353	.1429	.1454	.1431	.1364	41
10	.0252	.0383	.0539	.0713	.0890	.1057	.1200	.1309	.1376	.1398	40
11	.0113	.0190	.0293	.0422	.0571	.0732	.0894	.1045	.1174	.1271	39
12	.0045	.0084	.0142	.0223	.0328	.0453	.0595	.0745	.0895	.1033	38
13	.0016	.0034	.0062	.0106	.0169	.0252	.0356	.0478	.0613	.0755	37
14	.0005	.0012	.0025	.0046	.0079	.0127	.0193	.0277	.0380	.0499	36
15	.0002	.0004	.0009	.0018	.0033	.0058	.0095	.0146	.0214	.0299	35

X1	q=.89	q=.88	q=.87	q=.86	q=.85	q=.84	q=.83	q=.82	q=.81	q=.80	n-X1
16	.0000	.0001	.0003	.0006	.0013	.0024	.0042	.0070	.0110	.0164	34
17	.0000	.0000	.0001	.0002	.0005	.0009	.0017	.0031	.0052	.0082	33
18	.0000	.0000	.0000	.0001	.0001	.0003	.0007	.0012	.0022	.0037	32
19	.0000	.0000	.0000	.0000	.0000	.0001	.0002	.0005	.0009	.0016	31
20	.0000	.0000	.0000	.0000	.0000	.0000	.0001	.0002	.0003	.0006	30
21	.0000	.0000	.0000	.0000	.0000	.0000	.0000	.0000	.0001	.0002	29
22	.0000	.0000	.0000	.0000	.0000	.0000	.0000	.0000	.0000	.0001	28

X1	P=.21	P=.22	P=.23	P=.24	P=.25	P=.26	P=.27	P=.28	P=.29	P=.30	n-X1
0	.0000	.0000	.0000	.0000	.0000	.0000	.0000	.0000	.0000	.0000	50
1	.0001	.0001	.0000	.0000	.0000	.0000	.0000	.0000	.0000	.0000	49
2	.0007	.0004	.0002	.0001	.0001	.0000	.0000	.0000	.0000	.0000	48
3	.0028	.0018	.0011	.0007	.0004	.0002	.0001	.0001	.0000	.0000	47
4	.0088	.0059	.0039	.0025	.0016	.0010	.0006	.0004	.0002	.0001	46
5	.0214	.0152	.0106	.0073	.0049	.0033	.0021	.0014	.0009	.0006	45
6	.0427	.0322	.0238	.0173	.0123	.0087	.0060	.0040	.0027	.0018	44
7	.0713	.0571	.0447	.0344	.0259	.0191	.0139	.0099	.0069	.0048	43
8	.1019	.0865	.0718	.0583	.0463	.0361	.0276	.0207	.0152	.0110	42
9	.1263	.1139	.1001	.0859	.0721	.0592	.0476	.0375	.0290	.0220	41
10	.1377	.1317	.1226	.1113	.0985	.0852	.0721	.0598	.0485	.0386	40
11	.1331	.1351	.1332	.1278	.1194	.1089	.0970	.0845	.0721	.0602	39
12	.1150	.1238	.1293	.1311	.1294	.1244	.1166	.1068	.0957	.0838	38
13	.0894	.1021	.1129	.1210	.1261	.1277	.1261	.1215	.1142	.1050	37
14	.0628	.0761	.0891	.1010	.1110	.1186	.1233	.1248	.1233	.1189	36
15	.0400	.0515	.0639	.0766	.0888	.1000	.1094	.1165	.1209	.1223	35
16	.0233	.0318	.0417	.0529	.0648	.0769	.0885	.0991	.1080	.1147	34
17	.0124	.0179	.0249	.0334	.0432	.0540	.0655	.0771	.0882	.0983	33
18	.0060	.0093	.0137	.0193	.0264	.0348	.0444	.0550	.0661	.0772	32
19	.0027	.0044	.0069	.0103	.0148	.0206	.0277	.0360	.0454	.0558	31
20	.0011	.0019	.0032	.0050	.0077	.0112	.0159	.0217	.0288	.0370	30
21	.0004	.0008	.0014	.0023	.0036	.0056	.0084	.0121	.0168	.0227	29
22	.0001	.0003	.0005	.0009	.0016	.0026	.0041	.0062	.0090	.0128	28
23	.0000	.0001	.0002	.0004	.0006	.0011	.0018	.0029	.0045	.0067	27
24	.0000	.0000	.0001	.0001	.0002	.0004	.0008	.0013	.0021	.0032	26
25	.0000	.0000	.0000	.0000	.0001	.0002	.0003	.0005	.0009	.0014	25
26	.0000	.0000	.0000	.0000	.0000	.0001	.0001	.0002	.0003	.0006	24
27	.0000	.0000	.0000	.0000	.0000	.0000	.0000	.0001	.0001	.0002	23
28	.0000	.0000	.0000	.0000	.0000	.0000	.0000	.0000	.0000	.0001	22
	q=.79	q=.78	q=.77	q=.76	q=.75	q=.74	q=.73	q=.72	q=.71	q=.70	

X1	P=.31	P=.32	P=.33	P=.34	P=.35	P=.36	P=.37	P=.38	P=.39	P=.40	n-X1
4	.0001	.0000	.0000	.0000	.0000	.0000	.0000	.0000	.0000	.0000	46
5	.0003	.0002	.0001	.0001	.0000	.0000	.0000	.0000	.0000	.0000	45
6	.0011	.0007	.0005	.0003	.0002	.0001	.0001	.0000	.0000	.0000	44
7	.0032	.0022	.0014	.0009	.0006	.0004	.0002	.0001	.0001	.0000	43
8	.0078	.0055	.0037	.0025	.0017	.0011	.0007	.0004	.0003	.0002	42
9	.0164	.0120	.0086	.0061	.0042	.0029	.0019	.0013	.0008	.0005	41
10	.0301	.0231	.0174	.0128	.0093	.0066	.0046	.0032	.0022	.0014	40
11	.0493	.0395	.0311	.0240	.0182	.0136	.0099	.0071	.0050	.0035	39
12	.0719	.0604	.0498	.0402	.0319	.0248	.0189	.0142	.0105	.0076	38
13	.0944	.0831	.0717	.0606	.0502	.0408	.0325	.0255	.0195	.0147	37
14	.1121	.1034	.0933	.0825	.0714	.0607	.0505	.0412	.0330	.0260	36
15	.1209	.1168	.1103	.1020	.0923	.0819	.0712	.0606	.0507	.0415	35
16	.1188	.1202	.1189	.1149	.1088	.1008	.0914	.0813	.0709	.0606	34
17	.1068	.1132	.1171	.1184	.1171	.1133	.1074	.0997	.0906	.0808	33
18	.0880	.0976	.1057	.1118	.1156	.1169	.1156	.1120	.1062	.0987	32
19	.0666	.0774	.0877	.0970	.1048	.1107	.1144	.1156	.1144	.1109	31
20	.0463	.0564	.0670	.0775	.0875	.0965	.1041	.1098	.1134	.1146	30
21	.0297	.0379	.0471	.0570	.0673	.0776	.0874	.0962	.1035	.1091	29
22	.0176	.0235	.0306	.0387	.0478	.0575	.0676	.0777	.0873	.0959	28
23	.0096	.0135	.0183	.0243	.0313	.0394	.0484	.0580	.0679	.0778	27
24	.0049	.0071	.0102	.0141	.0190	.0249	.0319	.0400	.0489	.0584	26
25	.0023	.0035	.0052	.0075	.0106	.0146	.0195	.0255	.0325	.0405	25
26	.0010	.0016	.0025	.0037	.0055	.0079	.0110	.0150	.0200	.0259	24
27	.0004	.0007	.0011	.0017	.0026	.0039	.0058	.0082	.0113	.0154	23
28	.0001	.0003	.0004	.0007	.0012	.0018	.0028	.0041	.0060	.0084	22
29	.0000	.0001	.0002	.0003	.0005	.0008	.0012	.0019	.0029	.0043	21
30	.0000	.0000	.0001	.0001	.0002	.0003	.0005	.0008	.0013	.0020	20
31	.0000	.0000	.0000	.0000	.0001	.0001	.0002	.0003	.0005	.0009	19
32	.0000	.0000	.0000	.0000	.0000	.0000	.0001	.0001	.0002	.0003	18
33	.0000	.0000	.0000	.0000	.0000	.0000	.0000	.0000	.0001	.0001	17
	q=.69	q=.68	q=.67	q=.66	q=.65	q=.64	q=.63	q=.62	q=.61	q=.60	

X1	P=.41	P=.42	P=.43	P=.44	P=.45	P=.46	P=.47	P=.48	P=.49	P=.50	n−X1
8	.0001	.0001	.0000	.0000	.0000	.0000	.0000	.0000	.0000	.0000	42
9	.0003	.0002	.0001	.0001	.0000	.0000	.0000	.0000	.0000	.0000	41
10	.0009	.0006	.0004	.0002	.0001	.0001	.0001	.0000	.0000	.0000	40
11	.0024	.0016	.0010	.0007	.0004	.0003	.0002	.0001	.0001	.0000	39
12	.0054	.0037	.0026	.0017	.0011	.0007	.0005	.0003	.0002	.0001	38
13	.0109	.0079	.0057	.0040	.0027	.0018	.0012	.0008	.0005	.0003	37
14	.0200	.0152	.0113	.0082	.0059	.0041	.0029	.0019	.0013	.0008	36
15	.0334	.0264	.0204	.0155	.0116	.0085	.0061	.0043	.0030	.0020	35
16	.0508	.0418	.0337	.0267	.0207	.0158	.0118	.0086	.0062	.0044	34
17	.0706	.0605	.0508	.0419	.0339	.0269	.0209	.0159	.0119	.0087	33
18	.0899	.0803	.0703	.0604	.0508	.0420	.0340	.0270	.0210	.0160	32
19	.1053	.0979	.0893	.0799	.0700	.0602	.0507	.0419	.0340	.0270	31
20	.1134	.1099	.1044	.0973	.0888	.0795	.0697	.0600	.0506	.0419	30
21	.1126	.1137	.1126	.1092	.1038	.0967	.0884	.0791	.0695	.0598	29
22	.1031	.1086	.1119	.1131	.1119	.1086	.1033	.0963	.0880	.0788	28
23	.0872	.0957	.1028	.1082	.1115	.1126	.1115	.1082	.1029	.0960	27
24	.0682	.0780	.0872	.0956	.1026	.1079	.1112	.1124	.1112	.1080	26
25	.0493	.0587	.0684	.0781	.0873	.0956	.1026	.1079	.1112	.1123	25
26	.0329	.0409	.0497	.0590	.0687	.0783	.0875	.0957	.1027	.1080	24
27	.0203	.0263	.0333	.0412	.0500	.0593	.0690	.0786	.0877	.0960	23
28	.0116	.0157	.0206	.0266	.0336	.0415	.0502	.0596	.0692	.0788	22
29	.0061	.0086	.0118	.0159	.0208	.0268	.0338	.0417	.0504	.0598	21
30	.0030	.0044	.0062	.0087	.0119	.0160	.0210	.0270	.0339	.0419	20
31	.0013	.0020	.0030	.0044	.0063	.0088	.0120	.0161	.0210	.0270	19
32	.0006	.0009	.0014	.0021	.0031	.0044	.0063	.0088	.0120	.0160	18
33	.0002	.0003	.0006	.0009	.0014	.0021	.0031	.0044	.0063	.0087	17
34	.0001	.0001	.0002	.0003	.0006	.0009	.0014	.0020	.0030	.0044	16
35	.0000	.0000	.0001	.0001	.0002	.0003	.0005	.0009	.0013	.0020	15
36	.0000	.0000	.0000	.0000	.0001	.0001	.0002	.0003	.0005	.0008	14
37	.0000	.0000	.0000	.0000	.0000	.0000	.0001	.0001	.0002	.0003	13
38	.0000	.0000	.0000	.0000	.0000	.0000	.0000	.0000	.0001	.0001	12

| | q=.59 | q=.58 | q=.57 | q=.56 | q=.55 | q=.54 | q=.53 | q=.52 | q=.51 | q=.50 | |

n = 100

X1	P=.01	P=.02	P=.03	P=.04	P=.05	P=.06	P=.07	P=.08	P=.09	P=.10	n−X1
0	.3660	.1326	.0476	.0169	.0059	.0021	.0007	.0002	.0001	.0000	100
1	.3697	.2707	.1471	.0703	.0312	.0131	.0053	.0021	.0008	.0003	99
2	.1849	.2734	.2252	.1450	.0812	.0414	.0198	.0090	.0039	.0016	98
3	.0610	.1823	.2275	.1973	.1396	.0864	.0486	.0254	.0125	.0059	97
4	.0149	.0902	.1706	.1994	.1781	.1338	.0888	.0536	.0301	.0159	96
5	.0029	.0353	.1013	.1595	.1800	.1639	.1283	.0895	.0571	.0339	95
6	.0005	.0114	.0496	.1052	.1500	.1657	.1529	.1233	.0895	.0596	94
7	.0001	.0031	.0206	.0589	.1060	.1420	.1545	.1440	.1188	.0889	93
8	.0000	.0007	.0074	.0285	.0649	.1054	.1352	.1455	.1366	.1148	92
9	.0000	.0002	.0023	.0121	.0349	.0687	.1040	.1293	.1381	.1304	91
10	.0000	.0000	.0007	.0046	.0167	.0399	.0712	.1024	.1243	.1319	90
11	.0000	.0000	.0002	.0016	.0072	.0209	.0439	.0728	.1006	.1199	89
12	.0000	.0000	.0000	.0005	.0028	.0099	.0245	.0470	.0738	.0988	88
13	.0000	.0000	.0000	.0001	.0010	.0043	.0125	.0276	.0494	.0743	87
14	.0000	.0000	.0000	.0000	.0003	.0017	.0058	.0149	.0304	.0513	86
15	.0000	.0000	.0000	.0000	.0001	.0006	.0025	.0074	.0172	.0327	85
16	.0000	.0000	.0000	.0000	.0000	.0002	.0010	.0034	.0090	.0193	84
17	.0000	.0000	.0000	.0000	.0000	.0001	.0004	.0015	.0044	.0106	83
18	.0000	.0000	.0000	.0000	.0000	.0000	.0001	.0006	.0020	.0054	82
19	.0000	.0000	.0000	.0000	.0000	.0000	.0000	.0002	.0009	.0026	81
20	.0000	.0000	.0000	.0000	.0000	.0000	.0000	.0001	.0003	.0012	80
21	.0000	.0000	.0000	.0000	.0000	.0000	.0000	.0000	.0001	.0005	79
22	.0000	.0000	.0000	.0000	.0000	.0000	.0000	.0000	.0000	.0002	78
23	.0000	.0000	.0000	.0000	.0000	.0000	.0000	.0000	.0000	.0001	77
24	.0000	.0000	.0000	.0000	.0000	.0000	.0000	.0000	.0000	.0000	76

| | q=.99 | q=.98 | q=.97 | q=.96 | q=.95 | q=.94 | q=.93 | q=.92 | q=.91 | q=.90 | |

X1	P=.11	P=.12	P=.13	P=.14	P=.15	P=.16	P=.17	P=.18	P=.19	P=.20	n-X1
0	.0000	.0000	.0000	.0000	.0000	.0000	.0000	.0000	.0000	.0000	100
1	.0001	.0000	.0000	.0000	.0000	.0000	.0000	.0000	.0000	.0000	99
2	.0007	.0003	.0001	.0000	.0000	.0000	.0000	.0000	.0000	.0000	98
3	.0027	.0012	.0005	.0002	.0001	.0000	.0000	.0000	.0000	.0000	97
4	.0080	.0038	.0018	.0008	.0003	.0001	.0001	.0000	.0000	.0000	96
5	.0189	.0100	.0050	.0024	.0011	.0005	.0002	.0001	.0000	.0000	95
6	.0369	.0215	.0119	.0063	.0031	.0015	.0007	.0003	.0001	.0001	94
7	.0613	.0394	.0238	.0137	.0075	.0039	.0020	.0009	.0004	.0002	93
8	.0881	.0625	.0414	.0259	.0153	.0086	.0047	.0024	.0012	.0006	92
9	.1112	.0871	.0632	.0430	.0276	.0168	.0098	.0054	.0029	.0015	91
10	.1251	.1080	.0860	.0637	.0444	.0292	.0182	.0108	.0062	.0034	90
11	.1265	.1205	.1051	.0849	.0640	.0454	.0305	.0194	.0118	.0069	89
12	.1160	.1219	.1165	.1025	.0838	.0642	.0463	.0316	.0206	.0128	88
13	.0970	.1125	.1179	.1130	.1001	.0827	.0642	.0470	.0327	.0216	87
14	.0745	.0954	.1094	.1098	.1098	.0979	.0817	.0641	.0476	.0335	86
15	.0528	.0745	.0938	.1067	.1111	.1070	.0960	.0807	.0640	.0481	85
16	.0347	.0540	.0744	.0922	.1041	.1082	.1044	.0941	.0798	.0638	84
17	.0212	.0364	.0549	.0742	.0908	.1019	.1057	.1021	.0924	.0789	83
18	.0121	.0229	.0379	.0557	.0739	.0895	.0998	.1033	.1000	.0909	82
19	.0064	.0135	.0244	.0391	.0563	.0736	.0882	.0979	.1012	.0981	81
20	.0032	.0074	.0148	.0258	.0402	.0567	.0732	.0870	.0962	.0993	80
21	.0015	.0039	.0084	.0160	.0270	.0412	.0571	.0728	.0859	.0946	79
22	.0007	.0019	.0045	.0094	.0171	.0282	.0420	.0574	.0724	.0849	78
23	.0003	.0009	.0023	.0052	.0103	.0182	.0292	.0427	.0576	.0720	77
24	.0001	.0004	.0011	.0027	.0058	.0111	.0192	.0301	.0433	.0577	76
25	.0000	.0002	.0005	.0013	.0031	.0064	.0119	.0201	.0309	.0439	75
26	.0000	.0001	.0002	.0006	.0016	.0035	.0071	.0127	.0209	.0316	74
27	.0000	.0000	.0001	.0003	.0008	.0018	.0040	.0076	.0134	.0217	73
28	.0000	.0000	.0000	.0001	.0004	.0009	.0021	.0044	.0082	.0141	72
29	.0000	.0000	.0000	.0000	.0002	.0004	.0011	.0024	.0048	.0088	71
30	.0000	.0000	.0000	.0000	.0001	.0002	.0005	.0012	.0027	.0052	70
31	.0000	.0000	.0000	.0000	.0000	.0001	.0002	.0006	.0014	.0029	69
32	.0000	.0000	.0000	.0000	.0000	.0000	.0001	.0003	.0007	.0016	68
33	.0000	.0000	.0000	.0000	.0000	.0000	.0000	.0001	.0003	.0008	67
34	.0000	.0000	.0000	.0000	.0000	.0000	.0000	.0001	.0002	.0004	66
35	.0000	.0000	.0000	.0000	.0000	.0000	.0000	.0000	.0001	.0002	65
36	.0000	.0000	.0000	.0000	.0000	.0000	.0000	.0000	.0000	.0001	64
37	.0000	.0000	.0000	.0000	.0000	.0000	.0000	.0000	.0000	.0000	63
	q=.89	q=.88	q=.87	q=.86	q=.85	q=.84	q=.83	q=.82	q=.81	q=.80	

X1	P=.21	P=.22	P=.23	P=.24	P=.25	P=.26	P=.27	P=.28	P=.29	P=.30	n-X1
7	.0001	.0000	.0000	.0000	.0000	.0000	.0000	.0000	.0000	.0000	93
8	.0003	.0001	.0001	.0000	.0000	.0000	.0000	.0000	.0000	.0000	92
9	.0007	.0003	.0002	.0001	.0000	.0000	.0000	.0000	.0000	.0000	91
10	.0018	.0009	.0004	.0002	.0001	.0000	.0000	.0000	.0000	.0000	90
11	.0038	.0021	.0011	.0005	.0003	.0001	.0001	.0000	.0000	.0000	89
12	.0076	.0043	.0024	.0012	.0006	.0003	.0001	.0001	.0000	.0000	88
13	.0136	.0082	.0048	.0027	.0014	.0007	.0004	.0002	.0001	.0000	87
14	.0225	.0144	.0089	.0052	.0030	.0016	.0009	.0004	.0002	.0001	86
15	.0343	.0233	.0152	.0095	.0057	.0033	.0018	.0010	.0005	.0002	85
16	.0484	.0350	.0241	.0159	.0100	.0061	.0035	.0020	.0011	.0006	84
17	.0636	.0487	.0356	.0248	.0165	.0106	.0065	.0038	.0022	.0012	83
18	.0780	.0634	.0490	.0361	.0254	.0171	.0111	.0069	.0041	.0024	82
19	.0895	.0772	.0631	.0492	.0365	.0259	.0177	.0115	.0072	.0044	81
20	.0963	.0881	.0764	.0629	.0493	.0369	.0264	.0182	.0120	.0076	80
21	.0975	.0947	.0869	.0756	.0626	.0494	.0373	.0269	.0186	.0124	79
22	.0931	.0959	.0932	.0858	.0749	.0623	.0495	.0376	.0273	.0190	78
23	.0839	.0917	.0944	.0919	.0847	.0743	.0621	.0495	.0378	.0277	77
24	.0716	.0830	.0905	.0931	.0906	.0837	.0736	.0618	.0496	.0380	76
25	.0578	.0712	.0822	.0893	.0918	.0894	.0828	.0731	.0615	.0496	75
26	.0444	.0579	.0708	.0814	.0883	.0906	.0883	.0819	.0725	.0613	74
27	.0323	.0448	.0580	.0704	.0806	.0873	.0896	.0873	.0812	.0720	73
28	.0224	.0329	.0451	.0580	.0701	.0799	.0864	.0886	.0864	.0804	72
29	.0148	.0231	.0335	.0455	.0580	.0697	.0793	.0855	.0876	.0856	71
30	.0093	.0154	.0237	.0340	.0458	.0580	.0694	.0787	.0847	.0868	70
31	.0056	.0098	.0160	.0242	.0344	.0460	.0580	.0691	.0781	.0840	69
32	.0032	.0060	.0103	.0165	.0248	.0349	.0462	.0579	.0688	.0776	68
33	.0018	.0035	.0063	.0107	.0170	.0252	.0352	.0464	.0579	.0685	67
34	.0009	.0019	.0037	.0067	.0112	.0175	.0257	.0356	.0466	.0579	66
35	.0005	.0010	.0021	.0040	.0070	.0116	.0179	.0261	.0359	.0468	65
36	.0002	.0005	.0011	.0023	.0042	.0073	.0120	.0183	.0265	.0362	64
37	.0001	.0003	.0006	.0012	.0024	.0045	.0077	.0123	.0187	.0268	63
38	.0000	.0001	.0003	.0006	.0013	.0026	.0047	.0079	.0127	.0191	62
39	.0000	.0001	.0001	.0003	.0007	.0015	.0028	.0049	.0082	.0130	61
40	.0000	.0000	.0001	.0002	.0004	.0008	.0016	.0029	.0051	.0085	60

41	.0000	.0000	.0000	.0001	.0002	.0004	.0008	.0017	.0031	.0053	59
42	.0000	.0000	.0000	.0000	.0001	.0002	.0004	.0009	.0018	.0032	58
43	.0000	.0000	.0000	.0000	.0000	.0001	.0002	.0005	.0010	.0019	57
44	.0000	.0000	.0000	.0000	.0000	.0000	.0001	.0002	.0005	.0010	56
45	.0000	.0000	.0000	.0000	.0000	.0000	.0000	.0001	.0003	.0005	55
46	.0000	.0000	.0000	.0000	.0000	.0000	.0000	.0001	.0001	.0003	54
47	.0000	.0000	.0000	.0000	.0000	.0000	.0000	.0000	.0001	.0001	53
48	.0000	.0000	.0000	.0000	.0000	.0000	.0000	.0000	.0000	.0001	52

q=.79 q=.78 q=.77 q=.76 q=.75 q=.74 q=.73 q=.72 q=.71 q=.70

X1	P=.31	P=.32	P=.33	P=.34	P=.35	P=.36	P=.37	P=.38	P=.39	P=.40	n−X1
15	.0001	.0001	.0000	.0000	.0000	.0000	.0000	.0000	.0000	.0000	85
16	.0003	.0001	.0001	.0000	.0000	.0000	.0000	.0000	.0000	.0000	84
17	.0006	.0003	.0002	.0001	.0000	.0000	.0000	.0000	.0000	.0000	83
18	.0013	.0007	.0004	.0002	.0001	.0000	.0000	.0000	.0000	.0000	82
19	.0025	.0014	.0008	.0004	.0002	.0001	.0000	.0000	.0000	.0000	81
20	.0046	.0027	.0015	.0008	.0004	.0002	.0001	.0001	.0000	.0000	80
21	.0079	.0049	.0029	.0016	.0009	.0005	.0002	.0001	.0001	.0000	79
22	.0127	.0082	.0051	.0030	.0017	.0010	.0005	.0003	.0001	.0001	78
23	.0194	.0131	.0085	.0053	.0032	.0018	.0010	.0006	.0003	.0001	77
24	.0280	.0198	.0134	.0088	.0055	.0033	.0019	.0011	.0006	.0003	76
25	.0382	.0283	.0201	.0137	.0090	.0057	.0035	.0020	.0012	.0006	75
26	.0496	.0384	.0286	.0204	.0140	.0092	.0059	.0036	.0021	.0012	74
27	.0610	.0495	.0386	.0288	.0207	.0143	.0095	.0060	.0037	.0022	73
28	.0715	.0608	.0495	.0387	.0290	.0209	.0145	.0097	.0062	.0038	72
29	.0797	.0710	.0605	.0495	.0388	.0292	.0211	.0147	.0098	.0063	71
30	.0848	.0791	.0706	.0603	.0494	.0389	.0294	.0213	.0149	.0100	70
31	.0860	.0840	.0785	.0702	.0601	.0494	.0389	.0295	.0215	.0151	69
32	.0833	.0853	.0834	.0779	.0698	.0599	.0493	.0390	.0296	.0217	68
33	.0771	.0827	.0846	.0827	.0774	.0694	.0597	.0493	.0390	.0297	67
34	.0683	.0767	.0821	.0840	.0821	.0769	.0691	.0595	.0492	.0391	66
35	.0578	.0680	.0763	.0816	.0834	.0816	.0765	.0688	.0593	.0491	65
36	.0469	.0578	.0678	.0759	.0811	.0829	.0761	.0685	.0591	64
37	.0365	.0471	.0578	.0676	.0755	.0806	.0824	.0807	.0757	.0682	63
38	.0272	.0367	.0472	.0577	.0674	.0752	.0802	.0820	.0803	.0754	62
39	.0194	.0275	.0369	.0473	.0577	.0672	.0749	.0799	.0816	.0799	61
40	.0133	.0197	.0277	.0372	.0474	.0577	.0671	.0746	.0795	.0812	60
41	.0087	.0136	.0200	.0280	.0373	.0475	.0577	.0670	.0744	.0792	59
42	.0055	.0090	.0138	.0203	.0282	.0375	.0476	.0576	.0668	.0742	58
43	.0033	.0057	.0092	.0141	.0205	.0285	.0377	.0477	.0576	.0667	57
44	.0019	.0035	.0059	.0094	.0143	.0207	.0287	.0378	.0477	.0576	56
45	.0011	.0020	.0036	.0060	.0096	.0145	.0210	.0289	.0380	.0478	55
46	.0006	.0011	.0021	.0037	.0062	.0098	.0147	.0212	.0290	.0381	54
47	.0003	.0006	.0012	.0022	.0038	.0063	.0099	.0149	.0213	.0292	53
48	.0001	.0003	.0007	.0012	.0023	.0039	.0064	.0101	.0151	.0215	52
49	.0001	.0002	.0003	.0007	.0013	.0023	.0040	.0066	.0102	.0152	51
50	.0000	.0001	.0002	.0004	.0007	.0013	.0024	.0041	.0067	.0103	50
51	.0000	.0000	.0001	.0002	.0004	.0007	.0014	.0025	.0042	.0068	49
52	.0000	.0000	.0000	.0001	.0002	.0004	.0008	.0014	.0025	.0042	48
53	.0000	.0000	.0000	.0000	.0001	.0002	.0004	.0008	.0015	.0026	47
54	.0000	.0000	.0000	.0000	.0000	.0001	.0002	.0004	.0008	.0015	46
55	.0000	.0000	.0000	.0000	.0000	.0000	.0001	.0002	.0004	.0008	45
56	.0000	.0000	.0000	.0000	.0000	.0000	.0000	.0001	.0002	.0004	44
57	.0000	.0000	.0000	.0000	.0000	.0000	.0000	.0001	.0001	.0002	43
58	.0000	.0000	.0000	.0000	.0000	.0000	.0000	.0000	.0001	.0001	42
59	.0000	.0000	.0000	.0000	.0000	.0000	.0000	.0000	.0000	.0001	41

q=.69 q=.68 q=.67 q=.66 q=.65 q=.64 q=.63 q=.62 q=.61 q=.60

X1	P=.41	P=.42	P=.43	P=.44	P=.45	P=.46	P=.47	P=.48	P=.49	P=.50	n−X1
23	.0001	.0000	.0000	.0000	.0000	.0000	.0000	.0000	.0000	.0000	77
24	.0002	.0001	.0000	.0000	.0000	.0000	.0000	.0000	.0000	.0000	76
25	.0003	.0002	.0001	.0000	.0000	.0000	.0000	.0000	.0000	.0000	75
26	.0007	.0003	.0002	.0001	.0000	.0000	.0000	.0000	.0000	.0000	74
27	.0013	.0007	.0004	.0002	.0001	.0000	.0000	.0000	.0000	.0000	73
28	.0023	.0013	.0007	.0004	.0002	.0001	.0000	.0000	.0000	.0000	72
29	.0039	.0024	.0014	.0008	.0004	.0002	.0001	.0000	.0000	.0000	71
30	.0065	.0040	.0024	.0014	.0008	.0004	.0002	.0001	.0001	.0000	70
31	.0102	.0066	.0041	.0025	.0014	.0008	.0004	.0002	.0001	.0001	69
32	.0152	.0103	.0067	.0042	.0025	.0015	.0008	.0004	.0002	.0001	68
33	.0218	.0154	.0104	.0068	.0043	.0026	.0015	.0008	.0004	.0002	67
34	.0298	.0219	.0155	.0105	.0069	.0043	.0026	.0015	.0009	.0005	66
35	.0391	.0299	.0220	.0156	.0106	.0069	.0044	.0026	.0015	.0009	65
36	.0491	.0391	.0300	.0221	.0157	.0107	.0070	.0044	.0027	.0016	64
37	.0590	.0490	.0391	.0300	.0222	.0157	.0107	.0070	.0044	.0027	63
38	.0680	.0588	.0489	.0391	.0301	.0222	.0158	.0108	.0071	.0045	62
39	.0751	.0677	.0587	.0489	.0391	.0301	.0223	.0158	.0108	.0071	61
40	.0796	.0748	.0675	.0586	.0488	.0391	.0301	.0223	.0159	.0108	60

41	.0809	.0793	.0745	.0673	.0584	.0487	.0391	.0301	.0223	.0159	59
42	.0790	.0806	.0790	.0743	.0672	.0583	.0487	.0390	.0301	.0223	58
43	.0740	.0787	.0804	.0788	.0741	.0670	.0582	.0486	.0390	.0301	57
44	.0666	.0739	.0785	.0802	.0786	.0739	.0669	.0581	.0485	.0390	56
45	.0576	.0666	.0737	.0784	.0800	.0784	.0738	.0668	.0580	.0485	55
46	.0479	.0576	.0665	.0736	.0782	.0798	.0783	.0737	.0667	.0580	54
47	.0382	.0480	.0576	.0665	.0736	.0781	.0797	.0781	.0736	.0666	53
48	.0293	.0383	.0480	.0577	.0665	.0735	.0781	.0797	.0781	.0735	52
49	.0216	.0295	.0384	.0481	.0577	.0664	.0735	.0780	.0796	.0780	51
50	.0153	.0218	.0296	.0385	.0482	.0577	.0665	.0735	.0780	.0796	50
51	.0104	.0155	.0219	.0297	.0386	.0482	.0578	.0665	.0735	.0780	49
52	.0068	.0105	.0156	.0220	.0298	.0387	.0483	.0578	.0665	.0735	48
53	.0043	.0069	.0106	.0156	.0221	.0299	.0388	.0483	.0579	.0666	47
54	.0026	.0044	.0070	.0107	.0157	.0221	.0299	.0388	.0484	.0580	46
55	.0015	.0026	.0044	.0070	.0108	.0158	.0222	.0300	.0389	.0485	45
56	.0008	.0015	.0027	.0044	.0071	.0108	.0158	.0222	.0300	.0390	44
57	.0005	.0009	.0016	.0027	.0045	.0071	.0108	.0158	.0223	.0301	43
58	.0002	.0005	.0009	.0016	.0027	.0045	.0071	.0108	.0159	.0223	42
59	.0001	.0002	.0005	.0009	.0016	.0027	.0045	.0071	.0109	.0159	41
60	.0001	.0001	.0002	.0005	.0009	.0016	.0027	.0045	.0071	.0108	40
61	.0000	.0001	.0001	.0002	.0005	.0009	.0016	.0027	.0045	.0071	39
62	.0000	.0000	.0001	.0001	.0002	.0005	.0009	.0016	.0027	.0045	38
63	.0000	.0000	.0000	.0001	.0001	.0002	.0005	.0009	.0016	.0027	37
64	.0000	.0000	.0000	.0000	.0001	.0001	.0002	.0005	.0009	.0016	36
65	.0000	.0000	.0000	.0000	.0000	.0001	.0001	.0002	.0005	.0009	35
66	.0000	.0000	.0000	.0000	.0000	.0000	.0001	.0001	.0002	.0005	34
67	.0000	.0000	.0000	.0000	.0000	.0000	.0000	.0001	.0001	.0002	33
68	.0000	.0000	.0000	.0000	.0000	.0000	.0000	.0000	.0001	.0001	32
69	.0000	.0000	.0000	.0000	.0000	.0000	.0000	.0000	.0000	.0001	31
	$q=.59$	$q=.58$	$q=.57$	$q=.56$	$q=.55$	$q=.54$	$q=.53$	$q=.52$	$q=.51$	$q=.50$	

APPENDIX B   Poisson Probability Distribution—Values of $P(X) = (\lambda t)^X e^{-\lambda t}/X!$

Probability $P(X)$

Example:
$\mu = .60, X = 1$
$P(1) = .3293$

X_1	λt									
	.005	.01	.02	.03	.04	.05	.06	.07	.08	.09
0	.9950	.9900	.9802	.9704	.9608	.9512	.9418	.9324	.9231	.9139
1	.0050	.0099	.0192	.0291	.0384	.0476	.0565	.0653	.0738	.0823
2	.0000	.0000	.0002	.0004	.0008	.0012	.0017	.0023	.0030	.0037
3	.0000	.0000	.0000	.0000	.0000	.0000	.0000	.0001	.0001	.0001

X_1	λt									
	0.10	0.20	0.30	0.40	0.50	0.60	0.70	0.80	0.90	1.00
0	.9048	.8187	.7408	.6703	.6065	.5488	.4966	.4493	.4066	.3679
1	.0905	.1637	.2222	.2681	.3033	.3293	.3476	.3595	.3659	.3679
2	.0045	.0164	.0333	.0536	.0758	.0988	.1217	.1438	.1647	.1839
3	.0002	.0011	.0033	.0072	.0126	.0198	.0284	.0383	.0494	.0613
4	.0000	.0001	.0002	.0007	.0016	.0030	.0050	.0077	.0111	.0153
5	.0000	.0000	.0000	.0001	.0002	.0004	.0007	.0012	.0020	.0031
6	.0000	.0000	.0000	.0000	.0000	.0000	.0001	.0002	.0003	.0005
7	.0000	.0000	.0000	.0000	.0000	.0000	.0000	.0000	.0000	.0001

X_1	λt									
	1.10	1.20	1.30	1.40	1.50	1.60	1.70	1.80	1.90	2.00
0	.3329	.3012	.2725	.2466	.2231	.2019	.1827	.1653	.1496	.1353
1	.3662	.3614	.3543	.3452	.3347	.3230	.3106	.2975	.2842	.2707
2	.2014	.2169	.2303	.2417	.2510	.2584	.2640	.2678	.2700	.2707
3	.0738	.0867	.0998	.1128	.1255	.1378	.1496	.1607	.1710	.1804
4	.0203	.0260	.0324	.0395	.0471	.0551	.0636	.0723	.0812	.0902
5	.0045	.0062	.0084	.0111	.0141	.0176	.0216	.0260	.0309	.0361
6	.0008	.0012	.0018	.0026	.0035	.0047	.0061	.0078	.0098	.0120
7	.0001	.0002	.0003	.0005	.0008	.0011	.0015	.0020	.0027	.0034
8	.0000	.0000	.0001	.0001	.0001	.0002	.0003	.0005	.0006	.0009
9	.0000	.0000	.0000	.0000	.0000	.0000	.0001	.0001	.0001	.0002

X_1	λt									
	2.10	2.20	2.30	2.40	2.50	2.60	2.70	2.80	2.90	3.00
0	.1225	.1108	.1003	.0907	.0821	.0743	.0672	.0608	.0550	.0498
1	.2572	.2438	.2306	.2177	.2052	.1931	.1815	.1703	.1596	.1494
2	.2700	.2681	.2652	.2613	.2565	.2510	.2450	.2384	.2314	.2240
3	.1890	.1966	.2033	.2090	.2138	.2176	.2205	.2225	.2237	.2240
4	.0992	.1082	.1169	.1254	.1336	.1414	.1488	.1557	.1622	.1680
5	.0417	.0476	.0538	.0602	.0668	.0735	.0804	.0872	.0940	.1008
6	.0146	.0174	.0206	.0241	.0278	.0319	.0362	.0407	.0455	.0504
7	.0044	.0055	.0068	.0083	.0099	.0118	.0139	.0163	.0188	.0216
8	.0011	.0015	.0019	.0025	.0031	.0038	.0047	.0057	.0068	.0081
9	.0003	.0004	.0005	.0007	.0009	.0011	.0014	.0018	.0022	.0027
10	.0001	.0001	.0001	.0002	.0002	.0003	.0004	.0005	.0006	.0008
11	.0000	.0000	.0000	.0000	.0000	.0001	.0001	.0001	.0002	.0002
12	.0000	.0000	.0000	.0000	.0000	.0000	.0000	.0000	.0000	.0001

X_1	3.10	3.20	3.30	3.40	3.50	3.60	3.70	3.80	3.90	4.00
					λt					
0	.0450	.0408	.0369	.0334	.0302	.0273	.0247	.0224	.0202	.0183
1	.1397	.1304	.1217	.1135	.1057	.0984	.0915	.0850	.0789	.0733
2	.2165	.2087	.2008	.1929	.1850	.1771	.1692	.1615	.1539	.1465
3	.2237	.2226	.2209	.2186	.2158	.2125	.2087	.2046	.2001	.1954
4	.1734	.1781	.1823	.1858	.1888	.1912	.1931	.1944	.1951	.1954
5	.1075	.1140	.1203	.1264	.1322	.1377	.1429	.1477	.1522	.1563
6	.0555	.0608	.0662	.0716	.0771	.0826	.0881	.0936	.0989	.1042
7	.0246	.0278	.0312	.0348	.0385	.0425	.0466	.0508	.0551	.0595
8	.0095	.0111	.0129	.0148	.0169	.0191	.0215	.0241	.0269	.0298
9	.0033	.0040	.0047	.0056	.0066	.0076	.0089	.0102	.0116	.0132
10	.0010	.0013	.0016	.0019	.0023	.0028	.0033	.0039	.0045	.0053
11	.0003	.0004	.0005	.0006	.0007	.0009	.0011	.0013	.0016	.0019
12	.0001	.0001	.0001	.0002	.0002	.0003	.0003	.0004	.0005	.0006
13	.0000	.0000	.0000	.0000	.0001	.0001	.0001	.0001	.0002	.0002
14	.0000	.0000	.0000	.0000	.0000	.0000	.0000	.0000	.0000	.0001

X_1	4.10	4.20	4.30	4.40	4.50	4.60	4.70	4.80	4.90	5.00
					λt					
0	.0166	.0150	.0136	.0123	.0111	.0101	.0091	.0082	.0074	.0067
1	.0679	.0630	.0583	.0540	.0500	.0462	.0427	.0395	.0365	.0337
2	.1393	.1323	.1254	.1188	.1125	.1063	.1005	.0948	.0894	.0842
3	.1904	.1852	.1798	.1743	.1687	.1631	.1574	.1517	.1460	.1404
4	.1951	.1944	.1933	.1917	.1898	.1875	.1849	.1820	.1789	.1755
5	.1600	.1633	.1662	.1687	.1708	.1725	.1738	.1747	.1753	.1755
6	.1093	.1143	.1191	.1237	.1281	.1323	.1362	.1398	.1432	.1462
7	.0640	.0686	.0732	.0778	.0824	.0869	.0914	.0959	.1002	.1044
8	.0328	.0360	.0393	.0428	.0463	.0500	.0537	.0575	.0614	.0653
9	.0150	.0168	.0188	.0209	.0232	.0255	.0280	.0307	.0334	.0363
10	.0061	.0071	.0081	.0092	.0104	.0118	.0132	.0147	.0164	.0181
11	.0023	.0027	.0032	.0037	.0043	.0049	.0056	.0064	.0073	.0082
12	.0008	.0009	.0011	.0014	.0016	.0019	.0022	.0026	.0030	.0034
13	.0002	.0003	.0004	.0005	.0006	.0007	.0008	.0009	.0011	.0013
14	.0001	.0001	.0001	.0001	.0002	.0002	.0003	.0003	.0004	.0005
15	.0000	.0000	.0000	.0000	.0001	.0001	.0001	.0001	.0001	.0002

X_1	5.10	5.20	5.30	5.40	5.50	5.60	5.70	5.80	5.90	6.00
					λt					
0	.0061	.0055	.0050	.0045	.0041	.0037	.0033	.0030	.0027	.0025
1	.0311	.0287	.0265	.0244	.0225	.0207	.0191	.0176	.0162	.0149
2	.0793	.0746	.0701	.0659	.0618	.0580	.0544	.0509	.0477	.0446
3	.1348	.1293	.1239	.1185	.1133	.1082	.1033	.0985	.0938	.0892
4	.1719	.1681	.1641	.1600	.1558	.1515	.1472	.1428	.1383	.1339
5	.1753	.1748	.1740	.1728	.1714	.1697	.1678	.1656	.1632	.1606
6	.1490	.1515	.1537	.1555	.1571	.1584	.1594	.1601	.1605	.1606
7	.1086	.1125	.1163	.1200	.1234	.1267	.1298	.1326	.1353	.1377
8	.0692	.0731	.0771	.0810	.0849	.0887	.0925	.0962	.0998	.1033
9	.0392	.0423	.0454	.0486	.0519	.0552	.0586	.0620	.0654	.0688
10	.0200	.0220	.0241	.0262	.0285	.0309	.0334	.0359	.0386	.0413
11	.0093	.0104	.0116	.0129	.0143	.0157	.0173	.0190	.0207	.0225
12	.0039	.0045	.0051	.0058	.0065	.0073	.0082	.0092	.0102	.0113
13	.0015	.0018	.0021	.0024	.0028	.0032	.0036	.0041	.0046	.0052
14	.0006	.0007	.0008	.0009	.0011	.0013	.0015	.0017	.0019	.0022
15	.0002	.0002	.0003	.0003	.0004	.0005	.0006	.0007	.0008	.0009
16	.0001	.0001	.0001	.0001	.0001	.0002	.0002	.0002	.0003	.0003
17	.0000	.0000	.0000	.0000	.0000	.0001	.0001	.0001	.0001	.0001

					λt					
X_1	6.10	6.20	6.30	6.40	6.50	6.60	6.70	6.80	6.90	7.00
0	.0022	.0020	.0018	.0017	.0015	.0014	.0012	.0011	.0010	.0009
1	.0137	.0126	.0116	.0106	.0098	.0090	.0082	.0076	.0070	.0064
2	.0417	.0390	.0364	.0340	.0318	.0296	.0276	.0258	.0240	.0223
3	.0848	.0806	.0765	.0726	.0688	.0652	.0617	.0584	.0552	.0521
4	.1294	.1249	.1205	.1162	.1118	.1076	.1034	.0992	.0952	.0912
5	.1579	.1549	.1519	.1487	.1454	.1420	.1385	.1349	.1314	.1277
6	.1605	.1601	.1595	.1586	.1575	.1562	.1546	.1529	.1511	.1490
7	.1399	.1418	.1435	.1450	.1462	.1472	.1480	.1486	.1489	.1490
8	.1066	.1099	.1130	.1160	.1188	.1215	.1240	.1263	.1284	.1304
9	.0723	.0757	.0791	.0825	.0858	.0891	.0923	.0954	.0985	.1014
10	.0441	.0469	.0498	.0528	.0558	.0588	.0618	.0649	.0679	.0710
11	.0245	.0265	.0285	.0307	.0330	.0353	.0377	.0401	.0426	.0452
12	.0124	.0137	.0150	.0164	.0179	.0194	.0210	.0227	.0245	.0264
13	.0058	.0065	.0073	.0081	.0089	.0098	.0108	.0119	.0130	.0142
14	.0025	.0029	.0033	.0037	.0041	.0046	.0052	.0058	.0064	.0071
15	.0010	.0012	.0014	.0016	.0018	.0020	.0023	.0026	.0029	.0033
16	.0004	.0005	.0005	.0006	.0007	.0008	.0010	.0011	.0013	.0014
17	.0001	.0002	.0002	.0002	.0003	.0003	.0004	.0004	.0005	.0006
18	.0000	.0001	.0001	.0001	.0001	.0001	.0001	.0002	.0002	.0002
19	.0000	.0000	.0000	.0000	.0000	.0000	.0000	.0001	.0001	.0001

					λt					
	7.10	7.20	7.30	7.40	7.50	7.60	7.70	7.80	7.90	8.00
0	.0008	.0007	.0007	.0006	.0006	.0005	.0005	.0004	.0004	.0003
1	.0059	.0054	.0049	.0045	.0041	.0038	.0035	.0032	.0029	.0027
2	.0208	.0194	.0180	.0167	.0156	.0145	.0134	.0125	.0116	.0107
3	.0492	.0464	.0438	.0413	.0389	.0366	.0345	.0324	.0305	.0286
4	.0874	.0836	.0799	.0764	.0729	.0696	.0663	.0632	.0602	.0573
5	.1241	.1204	.1167	.1130	.1094	.1057	.1021	.0986	.0951	.0916
6	.1468	.1445	.1420	.1394	.1367	.1339	.1311	.1282	.1252	.1221
7	.1489	.1486	.1481	.1474	.1465	.1454	.1442	.1428	.1413	.1396
8	.1321	.1337	.1351	.1363	.1373	.1382	.1388	.1392	.1395	.1396
9	.1042	.1070	.1096	.1121	.1144	.1167	.1187	.1207	.1224	.1241
10	.0740	.0770	.0800	.0829	.0858	.0887	.0914	.0941	.0967	.0993
11	.0478	.0504	.0531	.0558	.0585	.0613	.0640	.0667	.0695	.0722
12	.0283	.0303	.0323	.0344	.0366	.0388	.0411	.0434	.0457	.0481
13	.0154	.0168	.0181	.0196	.0211	.0227	.0243	.0260	.0278	.0296
14	.0078	.0086	.0095	.0104	.0113	.0123	.0134	.0145	.0157	.0169
15	.0037	.0041	.0046	.0051	.0057	.0062	.0069	.0075	.0083	.0090
16	.0016	.0019	.0021	.0024	.0026	.0030	.0033	.0037	.0041	.0045
17	.0007	.0008	.0009	.0010	.0012	.0013	.0015	.0017	.0019	.0021
18	.0003	.0003	.0004	.0004	.0005	.0006	.0006	.0007	.0008	.0009
19	.0001	.0001	.0001	.0002	.0002	.0002	.0003	.0003	.0003	.0004
20	.0000	.0000	.0001	.0001	.0001	.0001	.0001	.0001	.0001	.0002
21	.0000	.0000	.0000	.0000	.0000	.0000	.0000	.0000	.0001	.0001

					λt					
X_i	8.10	8.20	8.30	8.40	8.50	8.60	8.70	8.80	8.90	9.00
0	.0003	.0003	.0002	.0002	.0002	.0002	.0002	.0002	.0001	.0001
1	.0025	.0023	.0021	.0019	.0017	.0016	.0014	.0013	.0012	.0011
2	.0100	.0092	.0086	.0079	.0074	.0068	.0063	.0058	.0054	.0050
3	.0269	.0252	.0237	.0222	.0208	.0195	.0183	.0171	.0160	.0150
4	.0544	.0517	.0491	.0466	.0443	.0420	.0398	.0377	.0357	.0337
5	.0882	.0849	.0816	.0784	.0752	.0722	.0692	.0663	.0635	.0607
6	.1191	.1160	.1128	.1097	.1066	.1034	.1003	.0972	.0941	.0911
7	.1378	.1358	.1338	.1317	.1294	.1271	.1247	.1222	.1197	.1171
8	.1395	.1392	.1388	.1382	.1375	.1366	.1356	.1344	.1332	.1318
9	.1256	.1269	.1280	.1290	.1299	.1306	.1311	.1315	.1317	.1318
10	.1017	.1040	.1063	.1084	.1104	.1123	.1140	.1157	.1172	.1186
11	.0749	.0776	.0802	.0828	.0853	.0878	.0902	.0925	.0948	.0970
12	.0505	.0530	.0555	.0579	.0604	.0629	.0654	.0679	.0703	.0728
13	.0315	.0334	.0354	.0374	.0395	.0416	.0438	.0459	.0481	.0504
14	.0182	.0196	.0210	.0225	.0240	.0256	.0272	.0289	.0306	.0324
15	.0098	.0107	.0116	.0126	.0136	.0147	.0158	.0169	.0182	.0194
16	.0050	.0055	.0060	.0066	.0072	.0079	.0086	.0093	.0101	.0109
17	.0024	.0026	.0029	.0033	.0036	.0040	.0044	.0048	.0053	.0058
18	.0011	.0012	.0014	.0015	.0017	.0019	.0021	.0024	.0026	.0029
19	.0005	.0005	.0006	.0007	.0008	.0009	.0010	.0011	.0012	.0014
20	.0002	.0002	.0002	.0003	.0003	.0004	.0004	.0005	.0005	.0006
21	.0001	.0001	.0001	.0001	.0001	.0002	.0002	.0002	.0002	.0003
22	.0000	.0000	.0000	.0000	.0001	.0001	.0001	.0001	.0001	.0001

					λt					
	9.10	9.20	9.30	9.40	9.50	9.60	9.70	9.80	9.90	10.00
0	.0001	.0001	.0001	.0001	.0001	.0001	.0001	.0001	.0001	.0000
1	.0010	.0009	.0009	.0008	.0007	.0007	.0006	.0005	.0005	.0005
2	.0046	.0043	.0040	.0037	.0034	.0031	.0029	.0027	.0025	.0023
3	.0140	.0131	.0123	.0115	.0107	.0100	.0093	.0087	.0081	.0076
4	.0319	.0302	.0285	.0269	.0254	.0240	.0226	.0213	.0201	.0189
5	.0581	.0555	.0530	.0506	.0483	.0460	.0439	.0418	.0398	.0378
6	.0881	.0851	.0822	.0793	.0764	.0736	.0709	.0682	.0656	.0631
7	.1145	.1118	.1091	.1064	.1037	.1010	.0982	.0955	.0928	.0901
8	.1302	.1286	.1269	.1251	.1232	.1212	.1191	.1170	.1148	.1126
9	.1317	.1315	.1311	.1306	.1300	.1293	.1284	.1274	.1263	.1251
10	.1198	.1210	.1219	.1228	.1235	.1241	.1245	.1249	.1250	.1251
11	.0991	.1012	.1031	.1049	.1067	.1083	.1098	.1112	.1125	.1137
12	.0752	.0776	.0799	.0822	.0844	.0866	.0888	.0908	.0928	.0948
13	.0526	.0549	.0572	.0594	.0617	.0640	.0662	.0685	.0707	.0729
14	.0342	.0361	.0380	.0399	.0419	.0439	.0459	.0479	.0500	.0521
15	.0208	.0221	.0235	.0250	.0265	.0281	.0297	.0313	.0330	.0347
16	.0118	.0127	.0137	.0147	.0157	.0168	.0180	.0192	.0204	.0217
17	.0063	.0069	.0075	.0081	.0088	.0095	.0103	.0111	.0119	.0128
18	.0032	.0035	.0039	.0042	.0046	.0051	.0055	.0060	.0065	.0071
19	.0015	.0017	.0019	.0021	.0023	.0026	.0028	.0031	.0034	.0037
20	.0007	.0008	.0009	.0010	.0011	.0012	.0014	.0015	.0017	.0019
21	.0003	.0003	.0004	.0004	.0005	.0006	.0006	.0007	.0008	.0009
22	.0001	.0001	.0002	.0002	.0002	.0002	.0003	.0003	.0004	.0004
23	.0000	.0001	.0001	.0001	.0001	.0001	.0001	.0001	.0002	.0002
24	.0000	.0000	.0000	.0000	.0000	.0000	.0000	.0001	.0001	.0001

X_1	λt									
	11.0	12.0	13.0	14.0	15.0	16.0	17.0	18.0	19.0	20.0
0	.0000	.0000	.0000	.0000	.0000	.0000	.0000	.0000	.0000	.0000
1	.0002	.0001	.0000	.0000	.0000	.0000	.0000	.0000	.0000	.0000
2	.0010	.0004	.0002	.0001	.0000	.0000	.0000	.0000	.0000	.0000
3	.0037	.0018	.0008	.0004	.0002	.0001	.0000	.0000	.0000	.0000
4	.0102	.0053	.0027	.0013	.0006	.0003	.0001	.0001	.0000	.0000
5	.0224	.0127	.0070	.0037	.0019	.0010	.0005	.0002	.0001	.0001
6	.0411	.0255	.0152	.0087	.0048	.0026	.0014	.0007	.0004	.0002
7	.0646	.0437	.0281	.0174	.0104	.0060	.0034	.0019	.0010	.0005
8	.0888	.0655	.0457	.0304	.0194	.0120	.0072	.0042	.0024	.0013
9	.1085	.0874	.0661	.0473	.0324	.0213	.0135	.0083	.0050	.0029
10	.1194	.1048	.0859	.0663	.0486	.0341	.0230	.0150	.0095	.0058
11	.1194	.1144	.1015	.0844	.0663	.0496	.0355	.0245	.0164	.0106
12	.1094	.1144	.1099	.0984	.0829	.0661	.0504	.0368	.0259	.0176
13	.0926	.1056	.1099	.1060	.0956	.0814	.0658	.0509	.0378	.0271
14	.0728	.0905	.1021	.1060	.1024	.0930	.0800	.0655	.0514	.0387
15	.0534	.0724	.0885	.0989	.1024	.0992	.0906	.0786	.0650	.0516
16	.0367	.0543	.0719	.0866	.0960	.0992	.0963	.0884	.0772	.0646
17	.0237	.0383	.0550	.0713	.0847	.0934	.0963	.0936	.0863	.0760
18	.0145	.0256	.0397	.0554	.0706	.0830	.0909	.0936	.0911	.0844
19	.0084	.0161	.0272	.0409	.0557	.0699	.0814	.0887	.0911	.0888
20	.0046	.0097	.0177	.0286	.0418	.0559	.0692	.0798	.0866	.0888
21	.0024	.0055	.0109	.0191	.0299	.0426	.0560	.0684	.0783	.0846
22	.0012	.0030	.0065	.0121	.0204	.0310	.0433	.0560	.0676	.0769
23	.0006	.0016	.0037	.0074	.0133	.0216	.0320	.0438	.0559	.0669
24	.0003	.0008	.0020	.0043	.0083	.0144	.0226	.0329	.0442	.0557
25	.0001	.0004	.0010	.0024	.0050	.0092	.0154	.0237	.0336	.0446
26	.0000	.0002	·0005	.0013	.0029	.0057	.0101	.0164	.0246	.0343
27	.0000	.0001	.0002	.0007	.0016	.0034	.0063	.0109	.0173	.0254
28	.0000	.0000	.0001	.0003	.0009	.0019	.0038	.0070	.0117	.0181
29	.0000	.0000	.0001	.0002	.0004	.0011	.0023	.0044	.0077	.0125
30	.0000	.0000	.0000	.0001	.0002	.0006	.0013	.0026	.0049	.0083
31	.0000	.0000	.0000	.0000	.0001	.0003	.0007	.0015	.0030	.0054
32	.0000	.0000	.0000	.0000	.0001	.0001	.0004	.0009	.0018	.0034
33	.0000	.0000	.0000	.0000	.0000	.0001	.0002	.0005	.0010	.0020
34	.0000	.0000	.0000	.0000	.0000	.0000	.0001	.0002	.0006	.0012
35	.0000	.0000	.0000	.0000	.0000	.0000	.0000	.0001	.0003	.0007
36	.0000	.0000	.0000	.0000	.0000	.0000	.0000	.0001	.0002	.0004
37	.0000	.0000	.0000	.0000	.0000	.0000	.0000	.0000	.0001	.0002
38	.0000	.0000	.0000	.0000	.0000	.0000	.0000	.0000	.0000	.0001
39	.0000	.0000	.0000	.0000	.0000	.0000	.0000	.0000	.0000	.0001

Source: Stephen P. Shao. *Statistics for Business and Economics.* 3d ed. (Columbus, Ohio: Merrill Publishing Company, 1976), pp. 782–86. Used with permission.

APPENDIX C Standard Normal Distribution Table

To illustrate: 19.85% of the area under a normal curve lies between the mean, μ_x, and a point 0.52 standard deviation units away.

Example:
Z = 0.52 (or −0.52)
A(Z) = 0.1985 or 19.85%

Z	.00	.01	.02	.03	.04	.05	.06	.07	.08	.09
0.0	.0000	.0040	.0080	.0120	.0160	.0199	.0239	.0279	.0319	.0359
0.1	.0398	.0438	.0478	.0517	.0557	.0596	.0636	.0675	.0714	.0753
0.2	.0793	.0832	.0871	.0910	.0948	.0987	.1026	.1064	.1103	.1141
0.3	.1179	.1217	.1255	.1293	.1331	.1368	.1406	.1443	.1480	.1517
0.4	.1554	.1591	.1628	.1664	.1700	.1736	.1772	.1808	.1844	.1879
0.5	.1915	.1950	.1985	.2019	.2054	.2088	.2123	.2157	.2190	.2224
0.6	.2257	.2291	.2324	.2357	.2389	.2422	.2454	.2486	.2517	.2549
0.7	.2580	.2611	.2642	.2673	.2704	.2734	.2764	.2794	.2823	.2852
0.8	.2881	.2910	.2939	.2967	.2995	.3023	.3051	.3078	.3106	.3133
0.9	.3159	.3186	.3212	.3238	.3264	.3289	.3315	.3340	.3365	.3389
1.0	.3413	.3438	.3461	.3485	.3508	.3531	.3554	.3577	.3599	.3621
1.1	.3643	.3665	.3686	.3708	.3729	.3749	.3770	.3790	.3810	.3830
1.2	.3849	.3869	.3888	.3907	.3925	.3944	.3962	.3980	.3997	.4015
1.3	.4032	.4049	.4066	.4082	.4099	.4115	.4131	.4147	.4162	.4177
1.4	.4192	.4207	.4222	.4236	.4251	.4265	.4279	.4292	.4306	.4319
1.5	.4332	.4345	.4357	.4370	.4382	.4394	.4406	.4418	.4429	.4441
1.6	.4452	.4463	.4474	.4484	.4495	.4505	.4515	.4525	.4535	.4545
1.7	.4554	.4564	.4573	.4582	.4591	.4599	.4608	.4616	.4625	.4633
1.8	.4641	.4649	.4656	.4664	.4671	.4678	.4686	.4693	.4699	.4706
1.9	.4713	.4719	.4726	.4732	.4738	.4744	.4750	.4756	.4761	.4767
2.0	.4772	.4778	.4783	.4788	.4793	.4798	.4803	.4808	.4812	.4817
2.1	.4821	.4826	.4830	.4834	.4838	.4842	.4846	.4850	.4854	.4857
2.2	.4861	.4864	.4868	.4871	.4875	.4878	.4881	.4884	.4887	.4890
2.3	.4893	.4896	.4898	.4901	.4904	.4906	.4909	.4911	.4913	.4916
2.4	.4918	.4920	.4922	.4925	.4927	.4929	.4931	.4932	.4934	.4936
2.5	.4938	.4940	.4941	.4943	.4945	.4946	.4948	.4949	.4951	.4952
2.6	.4953	.4955	.4956	.4957	.4959	.4960	.4961	.4962	.4963	.4964
2.7	.4965	.4966	.4967	.4968	.4969	.4970	.4971	.4972	.4973	.4974
2.8	.4974	.4975	.4976	.4977	.4977	.4978	.4979	.4979	.4980	.4981
2.9	.4981	.4982	.4982	.4983	.4984	.4984	.4985	.4985	.4986	.4986
3.0	.4987	.4987	.4987	.4988	.4988	.4989	.4989	.4989	.4990	.4990

APPENDIX D   Values of *t* for Selected Probabilities

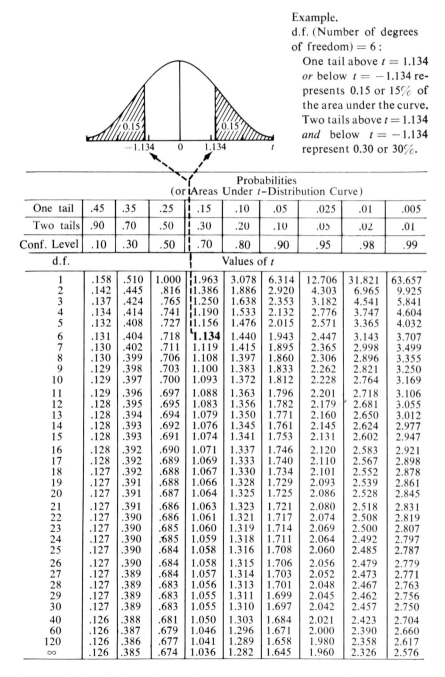

Example.
d.f. (Number of degrees
of freedom) = 6:
One tail above $t = 1.134$
or below $t = -1.134$ represents 0.15 or 15% of
the area under the curve.
Two tails above $t = 1.134$
and below $t = -1.134$
represent 0.30 or 30%.

				Probabilities (or Areas Under *t*–Distribution Curve)					
One tail	.45	.35	.25	.15	.10	.05	.025	.01	.005
Two tails	.90	.70	.50	.30	.20	.10	.05	.02	.01
Conf. Level	.10	.30	.50	.70	.80	.90	.95	.98	.99
d.f.				Values of *t*					
1	.158	.510	1.000	1.963	3.078	6.314	12.706	31.821	63.657
2	.142	.445	.816	1.386	1.886	2.920	4.303	6.965	9.925
3	.137	.424	.765	1.250	1.638	2.353	3.182	4.541	5.841
4	.134	.414	.741	1.190	1.533	2.132	2.776	3.747	4.604
5	.132	.408	.727	1.156	1.476	2.015	2.571	3.365	4.032
6	.131	.404	.718	1.134	1.440	1.943	2.447	3.143	3.707
7	.130	.402	.711	1.119	1.415	1.895	2.365	2.998	3.499
8	.130	.399	.706	1.108	1.397	1.860	2.306	2.896	3.355
9	.129	.398	.703	1.100	1.383	1.833	2.262	2.821	3.250
10	.129	.397	.700	1.093	1.372	1.812	2.228	2.764	3.169
11	.129	.396	.697	1.088	1.363	1.796	2.201	2.718	3.106
12	.128	.395	.695	1.083	1.356	1.782	2.179	2.681	3.055
13	.128	.394	.694	1.079	1.350	1.771	2.160	2.650	3.012
14	.128	.393	.692	1.076	1.345	1.761	2.145	2.624	2.977
15	.128	.393	.691	1.074	1.341	1.753	2.131	2.602	2.947
16	.128	.392	.690	1.071	1.337	1.746	2.120	2.583	2.921
17	.128	.392	.689	1.069	1.333	1.740	2.110	2.567	2.898
18	.127	.392	.688	1.067	1.330	1.734	2.101	2.552	2.878
19	.127	.391	.688	1.066	1.328	1.729	2.093	2.539	2.861
20	.127	.391	.687	1.064	1.325	1.725	2.086	2.528	2.845
21	.127	.391	.686	1.063	1.323	1.721	2.080	2.518	2.831
22	.127	.390	.686	1.061	1.321	1.717	2.074	2.508	2.819
23	.127	.390	.685	1.060	1.319	1.714	2.069	2.500	2.807
24	.127	.390	.685	1.059	1.318	1.711	2.064	2.492	2.797
25	.127	.390	.684	1.058	1.316	1.708	2.060	2.485	2.787
26	.127	.390	.684	1.058	1.315	1.706	2.056	2.479	2.779
27	.127	.389	.684	1.057	1.314	1.703	2.052	2.473	2.771
28	.127	.389	.683	1.056	1.313	1.701	2.048	2.467	2.763
29	.127	.389	.683	1.055	1.311	1.699	2.045	2.462	2.756
30	.127	.389	.683	1.055	1.310	1.697	2.042	2.457	2.750
40	.126	.388	.681	1.050	1.303	1.684	2.021	2.423	2.704
60	.126	.387	.679	1.046	1.296	1.671	2.000	2.390	2.660
120	.126	.386	.677	1.041	1.289	1.658	1.980	2.358	2.617
∞	.126	.385	.674	1.036	1.282	1.645	1.960	2.326	2.576

Source: Stephen P. Shao. *Statistics for Business and Economics.* 3d ed. (Columbus,
Ohio: Merrill Publishing Company, 1976), p. 789. Used with permission.

APPENDIX E   Values of χ^2 for Selected Probabilities

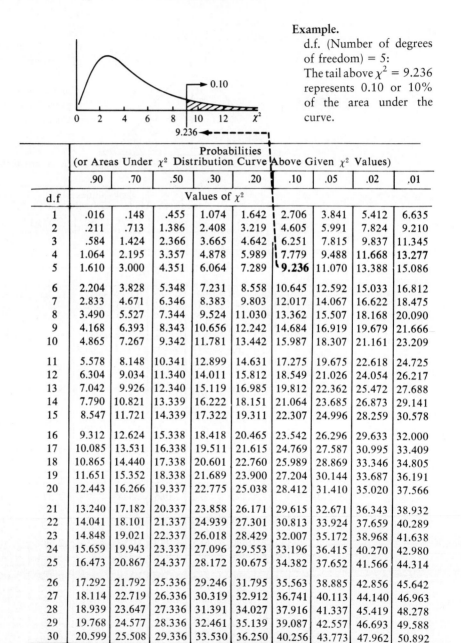

Example.

d.f. (Number of degrees of freedom) = 5:
The tail above χ^2 = 9.236 represents 0.10 or 10% of the area under the curve.

	Probabilities (or Areas Under χ^2 Distribution Curve Above Given χ^2 Values)								
	.90	.70	.50	.30	.20	.10	.05	.02	.01
d.f	Values of χ^2								
1	.016	.148	.455	1.074	1.642	2.706	3.841	5.412	6.635
2	.211	.713	1.386	2.408	3.219	4.605	5.991	7.824	9.210
3	.584	1.424	2.366	3.665	4.642	6.251	7.815	9.837	11.345
4	1.064	2.195	3.357	4.878	5.989	7.779	9.488	11.668	13.277
5	1.610	3.000	4.351	6.064	7.289	**9.236**	11.070	13.388	15.086
6	2.204	3.828	5.348	7.231	8.558	10.645	12.592	15.033	16.812
7	2.833	4.671	6.346	8.383	9.803	12.017	14.067	16.622	18.475
8	3.490	5.527	7.344	9.524	11.030	13.362	15.507	18.168	20.090
9	4.168	6.393	8.343	10.656	12.242	14.684	16.919	19.679	21.666
10	4.865	7.267	9.342	11.781	13.442	15.987	18.307	21.161	23.209
11	5.578	8.148	10.341	12.899	14.631	17.275	19.675	22.618	24.725
12	6.304	9.034	11.340	14.011	15.812	18.549	21.026	24.054	26.217
13	7.042	9.926	12.340	15.119	16.985	19.812	22.362	25.472	27.688
14	7.790	10.821	13.339	16.222	18.151	21.064	23.685	26.873	29.141
15	8.547	11.721	14.339	17.322	19.311	22.307	24.996	28.259	30.578
16	9.312	12.624	15.338	18.418	20.465	23.542	26.296	29.633	32.000
17	10.085	13.531	16.338	19.511	21.615	24.769	27.587	30.995	33.409
18	10.865	14.440	17.338	20.601	22.760	25.989	28.869	33.346	34.805
19	11.651	15.352	18.338	21.689	23.900	27.204	30.144	33.687	36.191
20	12.443	16.266	19.337	22.775	25.038	28.412	31.410	35.020	37.566
21	13.240	17.182	20.337	23.858	26.171	29.615	32.671	36.343	38.932
22	14.041	18.101	21.337	24.939	27.301	30.813	33.924	37.659	40.289
23	14.848	19.021	22.337	26.018	28.429	32.007	35.172	38.968	41.638
24	15.659	19.943	23.337	27.096	29.553	33.196	36.415	40.270	42.980
25	16.473	20.867	24.337	28.172	30.675	34.382	37.652	41.566	44.314
26	17.292	21.792	25.336	29.246	31.795	35.563	38.885	42.856	45.642
27	18.114	22.719	26.336	30.319	32.912	36.741	40.113	44.140	46.963
28	18.939	23.647	27.336	31.391	34.027	37.916	41.337	45.419	48.278
29	19.768	24.577	28.336	32.461	35.139	39.087	42.557	46.693	49.588
30	20.599	25.508	29.336	33.530	36.250	40.256	43.773	47.962	50.892

Source: Stephen P. Shao. *Statistics for Business and Economics.* 3d ed. (Columbus, Ohio: Merrill Publishing Company, 1976), p. 790. Used with permission.

APPENDIX F   Values of *F*

Upper 5% Probability
(or 5% Area under *F*-Distribution Curve)

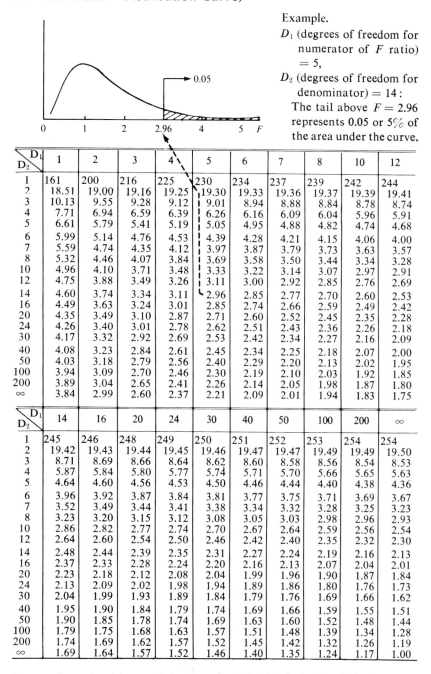

Example.
D_1 (degrees of freedom for numerator of F ratio) $= 5$,
D_2 (degrees of freedom for denominator) $= 14$:
The tail above $F = 2.96$ represents 0.05 or 5% of the area under the curve.

D_2 \ D_1	1	2	3	4	5	6	7	8	10	12
1	161	200	216	225	230	234	237	239	242	244
2	18.51	19.00	19.16	19.25	19.30	19.33	19.36	19.37	19.39	19.41
3	10.13	9.55	9.28	9.12	9.01	8.94	8.88	8.84	8.78	8.74
4	7.71	6.94	6.59	6.39	6.26	6.16	6.09	6.04	5.96	5.91
5	6.61	5.79	5.41	5.19	5.05	4.95	4.88	4.82	4.74	4.68
6	5.99	5.14	4.76	4.53	4.39	4.28	4.21	4.15	4.06	4.00
7	5.59	4.74	4.35	4.12	3.97	3.87	3.79	3.73	3.63	3.57
8	5.32	4.46	4.07	3.84	3.69	3.58	3.50	3.44	3.34	3.28
10	4.96	4.10	3.71	3.48	3.33	3.22	3.14	3.07	2.97	2.91
12	4.75	3.88	3.49	3.26	3.11	3.00	2.92	2.85	2.76	2.69
14	4.60	3.74	3.34	3.11	2.96	2.85	2.77	2.70	2.60	2.53
16	4.49	3.63	3.24	3.01	2.85	2.74	2.66	2.59	2.49	2.42
20	4.35	3.49	3.10	2.87	2.71	2.60	2.52	2.45	2.35	2.28
24	4.26	3.40	3.01	2.78	2.62	2.51	2.43	2.36	2.26	2.18
30	4.17	3.32	2.92	2.69	2.53	2.42	2.34	2.27	2.16	2.09
40	4.08	3.23	2.84	2.61	2.45	2.34	2.25	2.18	2.07	2.00
50	4.03	3.18	2.79	2.56	2.40	2.29	2.20	2.13	2.02	1.95
100	3.94	3.09	2.70	2.46	2.30	2.19	2.10	2.03	1.92	1.85
200	3.89	3.04	2.65	2.41	2.26	2.14	2.05	1.98	1.87	1.80
∞	3.84	2.99	2.60	2.37	2.21	2.09	2.01	1.94	1.83	1.75

D_2 \ D_1	14	16	20	24	30	40	50	100	200	∞
1	245	246	248	249	250	251	252	253	254	254
2	19.42	19.43	19.44	19.45	19.46	19.47	19.47	19.49	19.49	19.50
3	8.71	8.69	8.66	8.64	8.62	8.60	8.58	8.56	8.54	8.53
4	5.87	5.84	5.80	5.77	5.74	5.71	5.70	5.66	5.65	5.63
5	4.64	4.60	4.56	4.53	4.50	4.46	4.44	4.40	4.38	4.36
6	3.96	3.92	3.87	3.84	3.81	3.77	3.75	3.71	3.69	3.67
7	3.52	3.49	3.44	3.41	3.38	3.34	3.32	3.28	3.25	3.23
8	3.23	3.20	3.15	3.12	3.08	3.05	3.03	2.98	2.96	2.93
10	2.86	2.82	2.77	2.74	2.70	2.67	2.64	2.59	2.56	2.54
12	2.64	2.60	2.54	2.50	2.46	2.42	2.40	2.35	2.32	2.30
14	2.48	2.44	2.39	2.35	2.31	2.27	2.24	2.19	2.16	2.13
16	2.37	2.33	2.28	2.24	2.20	2.16	2.13	2.07	2.04	2.01
20	2.23	2.18	2.12	2.08	2.04	1.99	1.96	1.90	1.87	1.84
24	2.13	2.09	2.02	1.98	1.94	1.89	1.86	1.80	1.76	1.73
30	2.04	1.99	1.93	1.89	1.84	1.79	1.76	1.69	1.66	1.62
40	1.95	1.90	1.84	1.79	1.74	1.69	1.66	1.59	1.55	1.51
50	1.90	1.85	1.78	1.74	1.69	1.63	1.60	1.52	1.48	1.44
100	1.79	1.75	1.68	1.63	1.57	1.51	1.48	1.39	1.34	1.28
200	1.74	1.69	1.62	1.57	1.52	1.45	1.42	1.32	1.26	1.19
∞	1.69	1.64	1.57	1.52	1.46	1.40	1.35	1.24	1.17	1.00

Source: Reproduced by permission from *Statistical Methods*, 5th ed., by George W. Snedecor. © 1956 by the Iowa State University Press.

Upper 1% Probability
(or 1% Area under *F*-Distribution Curve)

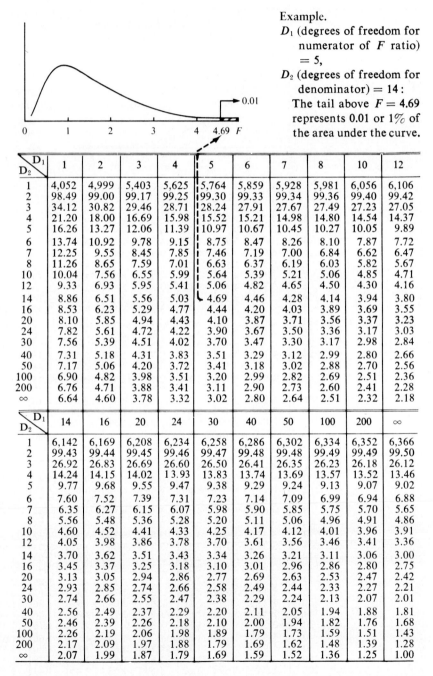

Example.
D_1 (degrees of freedom for numerator of F ratio) = 5,
D_2 (degrees of freedom for denominator) = 14 :
The tail above $F = 4.69$ represents 0.01 or 1% of the area under the curve.

D_2 \ D_1	1	2	3	4	5	6	7	8	10	12
1	4,052	4,999	5,403	5,625	5,764	5,859	5,928	5,981	6,056	6,106
2	98.49	99.00	99.17	99.25	99.30	99.33	99.34	99.36	99.40	99.42
3	34.12	30.82	29.46	28.71	28.24	27.91	27.67	27.49	27.23	27.05
4	21.20	18.00	16.69	15.98	15.52	15.21	14.98	14.80	14.54	14.37
5	16.26	13.27	12.06	11.39	10.97	10.67	10.45	10.27	10.05	9.89
6	13.74	10.92	9.78	9.15	8.75	8.47	8.26	8.10	7.87	7.72
7	12.25	9.55	8.45	7.85	7.46	7.19	7.00	6.84	6.62	6.47
8	11.26	8.65	7.59	7.01	6.63	6.37	6.19	6.03	5.82	5.67
10	10.04	7.56	6.55	5.99	5.64	5.39	5.21	5.06	4.85	4.71
12	9.33	6.93	5.95	5.41	5.06	4.82	4.65	4.50	4.30	4.16
14	8.86	6.51	5.56	5.03	4.69	4.46	4.28	4.14	3.94	3.80
16	8.53	6.23	5.29	4.77	4.44	4.20	4.03	3.89	3.69	3.55
20	8.10	5.85	4.94	4.43	4.10	3.87	3.71	3.56	3.37	3.23
24	7.82	5.61	4.72	4.22	3.90	3.67	3.50	3.36	3.17	3.03
30	7.56	5.39	4.51	4.02	3.70	3.47	3.30	3.17	2.98	2.84
40	7.31	5.18	4.31	3.83	3.51	3.29	3.12	2.99	2.80	2.66
50	7.17	5.06	4.20	3.72	3.41	3.18	3.02	2.88	2.70	2.56
100	6.90	4.82	3.98	3.51	3.20	2.99	2.82	2.69	2.51	2.36
200	6.76	4.71	3.88	3.41	3.11	2.90	2.73	2.60	2.41	2.28
∞	6.64	4.60	3.78	3.32	3.02	2.80	2.64	2.51	2.32	2.18

D_2 \ D_1	14	16	20	24	30	40	50	100	200	∞
1	6,142	6,169	6,208	6,234	6,258	6,286	6,302	6,334	6,352	6,366
2	99.43	99.44	99.45	99.46	99.47	99.48	99.48	99.49	99.49	99.50
3	26.92	26.83	26.69	26.60	26.50	26.41	26.35	26.23	26.18	26.12
4	14.24	14.15	14.02	13.93	13.83	13.74	13.69	13.57	13.52	13.46
5	9.77	9.68	9.55	9.47	9.38	9.29	9.24	9.13	9.07	9.02
6	7.60	7.52	7.39	7.31	7.23	7.14	7.09	6.99	6.94	6.88
7	6.35	6.27	6.15	6.07	5.98	5.90	5.85	5.75	5.70	5.65
8	5.56	5.48	5.36	5.28	5.20	5.11	5.06	4.96	4.91	4.86
10	4.60	4.52	4.41	4.33	4.25	4.17	4.12	4.01	3.96	3.91
12	4.05	3.98	3.86	3.78	3.70	3.61	3.56	3.46	3.41	3.36
14	3.70	3.62	3.51	3.43	3.34	3.26	3.21	3.11	3.06	3.00
16	3.45	3.37	3.25	3.18	3.10	3.01	2.96	2.86	2.80	2.75
20	3.13	3.05	2.94	2.86	2.77	2.69	2.63	2.53	2.47	2.42
24	2.93	2.85	2.74	2.66	2.58	2.49	2.44	2.33	2.27	2.21
30	2.74	2.66	2.55	2.47	2.38	2.29	2.24	2.13	2.07	2.01
40	2.56	2.49	2.37	2.29	2.20	2.11	2.05	1.94	1.88	1.81
50	2.46	2.39	2.26	2.18	2.10	2.00	1.94	1.82	1.76	1.68
100	2.26	2.19	2.06	1.98	1.89	1.79	1.73	1.59	1.51	1.43
200	2.17	2.09	1.97	1.88	1.79	1.69	1.62	1.48	1.39	1.28
∞	2.07	1.99	1.87	1.79	1.69	1.59	1.52	1.36	1.25	1.00

Source: Reproduced by permission from *Statistical Methods*, 5th ed., by George W. Snedecor. © 1956 by the Iowa State University Press.

APPENDIX G   Distribution of the Studentized Range

$p = 0.95$

Percentage points of the Studentized range,
$q = (x_{D_1} - x_1)/s_{D_2}.$

D_2 \ D_1	2	3	4	5	6	7	8	9	10
1	17·97	26·98	32·82	37·08	40·41	43·12	45·40	47·36	49·07
2	6·08	8·33	9·80	10·88	11·74	12·44	13·03	13·54	13·99
3	4·50	5·91	6·82	7·50	8·04	8·48	8·85	9·18	9·46
4	3·93	5·04	5·76	6·29	6·71	7·05	7·35	7·60	7·83
5	3·64	4·60	5·22	5·67	6·03	6·33	6·58	6·80	6·99
6	3·46	4·34	4·90	5·30	5·63	5·90	6·12	6·32	6·49
7	3·34	4·16	4·68	5·06	5·36	5·61	5·82	6·00	6·16
8	3·26	4·04	4·53	4·89	5·17	5·40	5·60	5·77	5·92
9	3·20	3·95	4·41	4·76	5·02	5·24	5·43	5·59	5·74
10	3·15	3·88	4·33	4·65	4·91	5·12	5·30	5·46	5·60
11	3·11	3·82	4·26	4·57	4·82	5·03	5·20	5·35	5·49
12	3·08	3·77	4·20	4·51	4·75	4·95	5·12	5·27	5·39
13	3·06	3·73	4·15	4·45	4·69	4·88	5·05	5·19	5·32
14	3·03	3·70	4·11	4·41	4·64	4·83	4·99	5·13	5·25
15	3·01	3·67	4·08	4·37	4·59	4·78	4·94	5·08	5·20
16	3·00	3·65	4·05	4·33	4·56	4·74	4·90	5·03	5·15
17	2·98	3·63	4·02	4·30	4·52	4·70	4·86	4·99	5·11
18	2·97	3·61	4·00	4·28	4·49	4·67	4·82	4·96	5·07
19	2·96	3·59	3·98	4·25	4·47	4·65	4·79	4·92	5·04
20	2·95	3·58	3·96	4·23	4·45	4·62	4·77	4·90	5·01
24	2·92	3·53	3·90	4·17	4·37	4·54	4·68	4·81	4·92
30	2·89	3·49	3·85	4·10	4·30	4·46	4·60	4·72	4·82
40	2·86	3·44	3·79	4·04	4·23	4·39	4·52	4·63	4·73
60	2·83	3·40	3·74	3·98	4·16	4·31	4·44	4·55	4·65
120	2·80	3·36	3·68	3·92	4·10	4·24	4·36	4·47	4·56
∞	2·77	3·31	3·63	3·86	4·03	4·17	4·29	4·39	4·47

D_2 \ D_1	11	12	13	14	15	16	17	18	19	20
1	50·59	51·96	53·20	54·33	55·36	56·32	57·22	58·04	58·83	59·56
2	14·39	14·75	15·08	15·38	15·65	15·91	16·14	16·37	16·57	16·77
3	9·72	9·95	10·15	10·35	10·52	10·69	10·84	10·98	11·11	11·24
4	8·03	8·21	8·37	8·52	8·66	8·79	8·91	9·03	9·13	9·23
5	7·17	7·32	7·47	7·60	7·72	7·83	7·93	8·03	8·12	8·21
6	6·65	6·79	6·92	7·03	7·14	7·24	7·34	7·43	7·51	7·59
7	6·30	6·43	6·55	6·66	6·76	6·85	6·94	7·02	7·10	7·17
8	6·05	6·18	6·29	6·39	6·48	6·57	6·65	6·73	6·80	6·87
9	5·87	5·98	6·09	6·19	6·28	6·36	6·44	6·51	6·58	6·64
10	5·72	5·83	5·93	6·03	6·11	6·19	6·27	6·34	6·40	6·47
11	5·61	5·71	5·81	5·90	5·98	6·06	6·13	6·20	6·27	6·33
12	5·51	5·61	5·71	5·80	5·88	5·95	6·02	6·09	6·15	6·21
13	5·43	5·53	5·63	5·71	5·79	5·86	5·93	5·99	6·05	6·11
14	5·36	5·46	5·55	5·64	5·71	5·79	5·85	5·91	5·97	6·03
15	5·31	5·40	5·49	5·57	5·65	5·72	5·78	5·85	5·90	5·96
16	5·26	5·35	5·44	5·52	5·59	5·66	5·73	5·79	5·84	5·90
17	5·21	5·31	5·39	5·47	5·54	5·61	5·67	5·73	5·79	5·84
18	5·17	5·27	5·35	5·43	5·50	5·57	5·63	5·69	5·74	5·79
19	5·14	5·23	5·31	5·39	5·46	5·53	5·59	5·65	5·70	5·75
20	5·11	5·20	5·28	5·36	5·43	5·49	5·55	5·61	5·66	5·71
24	5·01	5·10	5·18	5·25	5·32	5·38	5·44	5·49	5·55	5·59
30	4·92	5·00	5·08	5·15	5·21	5·27	5·33	5·38	5·43	5·47
40	4·82	4·90	4·98	5·04	5·11	5·16	5·22	5·27	5·31	5·36
60	4·73	4·81	4·88	4·94	5·00	5·06	5·11	5·15	5·20	5·24
120	4·64	4·71	4·78	4·84	4·90	4·95	5·00	5·04	5·09	5·13
∞	4·55	4·62	4·68	4·74	4·80	4·85	4·89	4·93	4·97	5·01

D_1: Size of sample from which range obtained. D_2: Degrees of freedom of independent s_{D_1}.

$p = 0.99$

D_1 / D_2	2	3	4	5	6	7	8	9	10
1	90·03	135·0	164·3	185·6	202·2	215·8	227·2	237·0	245·6
2	14·04	19·02	22·29	24·72	26·63	28·20	29·53	30·68	31·69
3	8·26	10·62	12·17	13·33	14·24	15·00	15·64	16·20	16·69
4	6·51	8·12	9·17	9·96	10·58	11·10	11·55	11·93	12·27
5	5·70	6·98	7·80	8·42	8·91	9·32	9·67	9·97	10·24
6	5·24	6·33	7·03	7·56	7·97	8·32	8·61	8·87	9·10
7	4·95	5·92	6·54	7·01	7·37	7·68	7·94	8·17	8·37
8	4·75	5·64	6·20	6·62	6·96	7·24	7·47	7·68	7·86
9	4·60	5·43	5·96	6·35	6·66	6·91	7·13	7·33	7·49
10	4·48	5·27	5·77	6·14	6·43	6·67	6·87	7·05	7·21
11	4·39	5·15	5·62	5·97	6·25	6·48	6·67	6·84	6·99
12	4·32	5·05	5·50	5·84	6·10	6·32	6·51	6·67	6·81
13	4·26	4·96	5·40	5·73	5·98	6·19	6·37	6·53	6·67
14	4·21	4·89	5·32	5·63	5·88	6·08	6·26	6·41	6·54
15	4·17	4·84	5·25	5·56	5·80	5·99	6·16	6·31	6·44
16	4·13	4·79	5·19	5·49	5·72	5·92	6·08	6·22	6·35
17	4·10	4·74	5·14	5·43	5·66	5·85	6·01	6·15	6·27
18	4·07	4·70	5·09	5·38	5·60	5·79	5·94	6·08	6·20
19	4·05	4·67	5·05	5·33	5·55	5·73	5·89	6·02	6·14
20	4·02	4·64	5·02	5·29	5·51	5·69	5·84	5·97	6·09
24	3·96	4·55	4·91	5·17	5·37	5·54	5·69	5·81	5·92
30	3·89	4·45	4·80	5·05	5·24	5·40	5·54	5·65	5·76
40	3·82	4·37	4·70	4·93	5·11	5·26	5·39	5·50	5·60
60	3·76	4·28	4·59	4·82	4·99	5·13	5·25	5·36	5·45
120	3·70	4·20	4·50	4·71	4·87	5·01	5·12	5·21	5·30
∞	3·64	4·12	4·40	4·60	4·76	4·88	4·99	5·08	5·16

D_1 / D_2	11	12	13	14	15	16	17	18	19	20
1	253·2	260·0	266·2	271·8	277·0	281·8	286·3	290·4	294·3	298·0
2	32·59	33·40	34·13	34·81	35·43	36·00	36·53	37·03	37·50	37·95
3	17·13	17·53	17·89	18·22	18·52	18·81	19·07	19·32	19·55	19·77
4	12·57	12·84	13·09	13·32	13·53	13·73	13·91	14·08	14·24	14·40
5	10·48	10·70	10·89	11·08	11·24	11·40	11·55	11·68	11·81	11·93
6	9·30	9·48	9·65	9·81	9·95	10·08	10·21	10·32	10·43	10·54
7	8·55	8·71	8·86	9·00	9·12	9·24	9·35	9·46	9·55	9·65
8	8·03	8·18	8·31	8·44	8·55	8·66	8·76	8·85	8·94	9·03
9	7·65	7·78	7·91	8·03	8·13	8·23	8·33	8·41	8·49	8·57
10	7·36	7·49	7·60	7·71	7·81	7·91	7·99	8·08	8·15	8·23
11	7·13	7·25	7·36	7·46	7·56	7·65	7·73	7·81	7·88	7·95
12	6·94	7·06	7·17	7·26	7·36	7·44	7·52	7·59	7·66	7·73
13	6·79	6·90	7·01	7·10	7·19	7·27	7·35	7·42	7·48	7·55
14	6·66	6·77	6·87	6·96	7·05	7·13	7·20	7·27	7·33	7·39
15	6·55	6·66	6·76	6·84	6·93	7·00	7·07	7·14	7·20	7·26
16	6·46	6·56	6·66	6·74	6·82	6·90	6·97	7·03	7·09	7·15
17	6·38	6·48	6·57	6·66	6·73	6·81	6·87	6·94	7·00	7·05
18	6·31	6·41	6·50	6·58	6·65	6·73	6·79	6·85	6·91	6·97
19	6·25	6·34	6·43	6·51	6·58	6·65	6·72	6·78	6·84	6·89
20	6·19	6·28	6·37	6·45	6·52	6·59	6·65	6·71	6·77	6·82
24	6·02	6·11	6·19	6·26	6·33	6·39	6·45	6·51	6·56	6·61
30	5·85	5·93	6·01	6·08	6·14	6·20	6·26	6·31	6·36	6·41
40	5·69	5·76	5·83	5·90	5·96	6·02	6·07	6·12	6·16	6·21
60	5·53	5·60	5·67	5·73	5·78	5·84	5·89	5·93	5·97	6·01
120	5·37	5·44	5·50	5·56	5·61	5·66	5·71	5·75	5·79	5·83
∞	5·23	5·29	5·35	5·40	5·45	5·49	5·54	5·57	5·61	5·65

Source: Reprinted with permission from E. S. Pearson and H. O. Hartley, *Biometrika Tables for Statisticians* (New York: Cambridge University Press, 1954).

APPENDIX H   Random Number Table

1260	5529	9540	3569	8381	9742	2590	2516	4243	8130
8979	2446	7606	6948	4519	2636	6655	1166	2096	1137
5470	0061	1760	5993	4319	0825	6874	3753	8362	1237
9733	0297	0804	4942	7694	9340	2502	3597	7691	5000
7492	6719	6816	7567	0364	2306	2217	5626	6526	6166
3715	2248	2337	6530	1660	7441	1598	0477	6620	1250
9491	4842	6210	9140	0180	5935	7218	4966	0537	4416
5192	7719	0654	4428	9771	4677	3291	4459	7432	2054
1714	3725	9397	9648	2550	0704	1239	5263	1601	5177
1052	8415	3686	4239	3272	7135	5768	8718	7582	8366
6998	3891	9352	6056	3621	5395	4551	4017	2405	0831
4216	4724	2898	1050	2164	8020	5274	6688	8636	2438
7115	2637	3828	0810	4598	2329	7953	4913	0033	2661
6647	4252	1869	9634	1341	7958	9460	1712	6060	0638
3475	2925	5097	8258	8343	7264	3295	8021	6318	0454
0415	1533	7670	0618	5193	9291	2205	2046	0890	6997
7064	4946	2618	7116	3784	2007	2326	4361	4695	8612
9772	4445	0343	5238	0317	7531	5916	8229	3296	2321
5365	4306	4036	9873	9669	8505	8675	3116	1484	9975
6395	4681	9319	6908	8154	5415	5728	1593	9452	8213
1554	0411	3436	1101	0966	5188	0225	5615	8568	5169
6745	7372	6984	0228	1920	6710	3459	0663	1407	9211
2217	3801	5860	1673	0264	6911	7623	7137	0774	5898
9255	9297	4305	5060	8312	9192	6016	7238	5193	4908
1615	9761	5744	2733	5314	6985	6670	0975	5487	6107
6679	4951	5716	5889	4413	1513	5023	7313	0317	0517
5221	3207	0351	2452	1072	3830	5518	5972	6111	9352
7720	5131	4867	6501	6970	4075	4869	4798	7104	5342
2767	6055	2801	7033	5305	9382	2354	4135	5975	7830
9202	6815	8211	5274	2303	1437	8995	2514	6515	0049
9359	2754	8587	2790	9524	5068	1230	4165	7025	4365
1078	7661	0999	4413	3446	2971	7576	3385	3308	0557
5732	4853	2025	1145	9743	8646	4918	3674	8049	1622
1596	0578	1493	4681	3806	8837	4241	4123	6513	3083
0602	8144	8976	9195	9012	7700	1708	5724	0315	8032
3624	8592	7942	4289	0736	4986	4839	4507	4997	7407
9328	3001	1462	1101	0804	9724	4082	2384	9631	8334
1981	1295	1963	3391	5757	4403	5857	4329	3682	3823
6001	4295	1488	6702	9954	6980	4027	8492	8195	7934
3743	0097	4798	6390	6465	6449	7990	3774	3577	3895

3343	6936	1449	2915	6668	8543	3147	1442	6022	0056
9208	3820	5165	3445	2642	2910	8336	1244	6346	0487
4581	3768	1559	7558	6660	0116	7949	5609	2887	4156
3206	5146	7191	8420	2319	4650	3734	0501	0739	2025
5662	8315	4226	8395	2931	1812	3575	9341	5894	3691
4631	6278	9444	4058	0505	4449	5959	7483	8641	1311
1046	6653	8333	5813	6586	9820	0190	9214	1947	9677
5231	2788	7198	5904	8370	8347	6599	7304	6430	3495
5349	6641	3234	8692	4424	9179	2767	9517	1173	4160
8363	9625	3329	5262	5360	8181	9298	6629	2433	9414
5967	1261	2470	8867	1962	1630	8360	6024	6232	8386
6716	3916	8712	6673	1156	0001	6760	6287	4546	5743
0323	3514	8550	3709	6614	5764	0600	7444	2795	4426
1765	0918	8972	9924	5941	0331	6909	4872	5693	8957
4345	6886	2032	4817	2725	9471	2443	9532	4770	1271
9614	8571	2174	0071	7824	0504	9600	6414	5734	1371
1291	8246	5019	6559	5051	5265	1184	9030	6689	2776
3867	3915	8311	2430	1235	7283	6481	2012	8487	0226
1056	1880	3610	7796	7192	6663	5810	3512	1572	2921
1691	2237	6713	4048	8865	5794	3419	4372	6996	8342
7920	8490	2822	2647	1700	5335	0732	9987	7501	1223
1646	4251	7732	2136	4339	0331	9293	1061	2663	4821
7928	2575	2139	2825	3806	2082	9285	7640	6166	5758
3563	9078	1979	1141	7911	6981	0183	7479	1146	8949
6546	3459	3824	2151	3313	0178	9143	7854	3935	7300
8315	8778	1296	3434	9420	3622	3521	0807	5719	7764
8442	4933	8173	6427	4354	3523	3492	2816	9191	6261
7446	1576	2520	6120	8546	3146	6084	1260	3737	1333
2619	1261	2028	7505	0710	4589	9632	2347	1975	6839
0814	8542	1526	1202	8091	9441	0456	0603	8297	1412

Source: Reprinted from Richard J. Hopeman, *Production and Operations Management*, 4th ed. (Columbus, Ohio: Merrill Publishing Company, 1980), 569–70. Used with permission.

Answers to Selected Problems

Chapter 2

7. a. 8 classes, $20 width

b.

Balance	Frequency
$ 0.00–$ 19.99	15
20.00– 39.99	11
40.00– 59.99	8
60.00– 79.99	9
80.00– 99.99	8
100.00– 119.99	4
120.00– 139.99	2
140.00– 159.99	3

9. 0.083, 0.292, 0.250, 0.125, 0.083, 0.083, 0.083

17. a. 9

b. 3,300

c. midpoints: 1,650; 4,950; 8,250; 11,550; 14,850; 18,150; 21,450; 24,750; 28,050

19.

Class	Frequency
0 to under 3	22
3 to under 6	14
6 to under 12	5
12 to under 15	4
15 to under 18	2

21.

Lawn Size	Frequency
0 and under 400	8
400 and under 800	12
800 and under 1,200	20
1,200 and under 1,600	50
1,600 and under 2,000	125
2,000 and under 2,400	103
2,400 and under 2,800	24

Chapter 3

1. Mean = 16.4376; median = 16; mode = 16

3. Range = 15; For population: variance = 19.621; sandard deviation = 4.43
For sample: variance = 20.929; standard deviation = 4.57

5. Mean = 98.196; variance = 494.195; standard deviation = 22.23

7. Variance = 195.068; standard deviation = 13.967

9. 20.91

17. a. 15.3 **b.** 14.5 **c.** 12 **d** 25.69474, 5.069 **e.** Increases the mean **f.** Median

19. a. 530.25 **b.** 425

21. Pine: mean = 1.93; standard deviation = 1.28
Redwood: mean = 1.3; standard deviation = 1.06
Cedar: mean = 2.43; standard deviation = 1.46

23. **a.** 41.26 **b.** 29.5 **c.** 240.69, 15.51

   d.
Class	f	M
15 and under 25	10	20
25 and under 35	10	30
35 and under 45	11	40
45 and under 55	8	50
55 and under 65	5	60
65 and under 75	5	70
75 and under 85	1	80

   f. 41.4 **g.** 39.55 **h.** 281.67, 16.78

25. **a.** Seed Type C
   b. CV_A = 18.18; CV_B = 26.79; CV_C = 25; seed type A

Chapter 4

1. 30,240
3. 630,630
5. 10
7. **a.** 0.056 **b.** 0.167 **c.** 0.111 **d.** 0.028 **e.** 0.019 **f.** 0.019
9. **a.** 0.4 **b.** 0.4 **c.** 0.04 **d.** 0.6 **e.** 0.66 **f.** 0
11. **a.** 0.007 **b.** 0.115 **c.** 0.007 **d.** 0.0063
17. **a.** 1/500 **b.** 3/500
19. **a.** 12 **b.** 1,056
21. 6,435
23. 462
25. **a.** 56 **b.** 336
27. Not independent
29. 0.26272
31. **a.** 0.44 **b.** 0.194 **c.** 0.927
33. **a.** 0.596 **b.** 0.087 **c.** Not independent
35. **a.** Tennis P(tennis/Jones wins) = 0.727
      P(golf/Jones wins) = 0.273
   b. Tennis

Chapter 5

3. **a.** 0.2013 **b.** 0.0008 **c.** 0.2253 **d.** 0.0401
7. Mean = 22.50; variance = 16.875; standard deviation = 4.108
9. **b.** Mean = 4.5; standard deviation = 0.67
11. 0.1356
13. **a.** 0.9161 **b.** 0.744 **c.** 0.682
15. Mean = 10; Standard Deviation = 3.1623
17. More than 100
25. **b.** 0.0288 **c.** 2.0998
27. **a.** 0 **b.** 0.0035 **c.** 0.001; 0.1719
29. **a.** 0.0378 **b.** 0.2503 **d.** 0.2018
33. **a.** 0.0681 **b.** 0.6376 **c.** 0.5438
35. **a.** 0.0009 **b.** 0.0267 **c.** 6 mistakes
37. **b.** 2.6 **c.** variance = 2.6; standard deviation = 1.612

Chapter 6

1. **a.** 0.5 **b.** 0.1587 **c.** 0.6826 **d.** 0.0228
3. **a.** 0.0668 **b.** 0.0336 **c.** 0.0038 **d.** 0.3642
5. **a.** 0.8638 **b.** 0.9147 **c.** 0.2296 **d.** 0.9772
7. **a.** 0.9974
15. **a.** 0.5 **b.** 0.5375 **c.** 0.0918
17. **a.** 0.3594 **b.** 0.9441 **c.** 0.7458
19. **a.** 10 feet 5.4675 inches **b.** 0.892
21. P(more than 74) = 0.1271; P(more than 90) = 0.110
23. 76
25. **a.** 0.1598 **b.** 0
27. **a.** 0.0336 **b.** 0.0237
29. **a.** 0.512 **b.** 1

Chapter 7

1. **a.** Mean = 27.375; standard deviation = 7.78 **b.** 70

3. **a.** 14,322.71 **b.** 35
5. **a.** Mean = 245.5; standard deviation = 93.85 **b.** 120
7. **a.** 58 **b.** 3.33 **c.** 2.236
9. **a.** 0.5 **b.** 0.86
11. Mean = 36.7; standard deviation = 0.94
13. **a.** 0.1469 **b.** 0.3156 **c.** 0.3212 **d.** 0.6995
15. **a.** 0.0038 **b.** 0.9982
35. Mean = 45; standard deviation = 3.13
39. 1.195
41. 0.3446; 0.1867
45. 0.2389
47. 0
49. **a.** 0 **b.** 0 **c.** 0.0119, not in adjustment

Chapter 8

1. **a.** 571.28 —— 588.72 **b.** 569.61 —— 590.39
3. **a.** 171 **b.** 385
5. 13.945 —— 14.515
7. **a.** 0.131 —— 0.219 **b.** 0.122 —— 0.228
9. 601
13. 0.0815 —— 0.1435
15. **a.** −16.56 —— −13.44 **b.** −17.21 —— −12.79
17. **a.** −0.044 —— 0.104 **b.** −0.058 —— 0.118
19. −0.0436 —— 0.0348
29. 14,000.97 —— 14,409.03
31. −0.0449 —— 0.0209
33. **a.** 0.232 —— 0.768
35. Additional sample size = 8,375; Total added cost = \$14,656.25
37. **a.** 2.893 —— 5.107
39. −0.023 —— 0.013
41. 0.588 —— 0.732
43. **a.** 451

45. **a.** 17.817 —— 19.303
47. **a.** 26,570.8 —— 27,139.2
49. **a.** Sample 3 largest **b.** 97.4 percent confidence **c.** Sample 3 **d.** Sample 1 − 36.31; Sample 2 − 36; Sample 3 − 24.2; Sample Size = 240 **e.** Sample 1

Chapter 9

1. **a.** Reject H_0 if $Z > 1.645$ or if $\overline{X} > 205.23$
   b. $Z = 1.41$; accept H_0
3. **a.** Reject H_0 if $\overline{X} < 4,394.07$ or $\overline{X} > 4,505.93$
   b. $\overline{X} = 4,475.60$; accept H_0
5. **a.** $H_0: \mu = 24$; $H_A: \mu \neq 24$
   b. Reject H_0 if $Z < -1.96$ or $Z > 1.96$; $Z = 4.57$, Reject H_0
7. **a.** Beta = 0.6480
   b. Reject H_0 if $\overline{X} < 1,205.20$; $\overline{X} = 1,201.3$; accept H_0
9. **a.** Beta = 0.9492
   b. Beta = 0.9489
   c. 0.0508; 0.0511
11. **b.** Beta = 0.0268
    c. Beta = 0.5871
17. $Z = 1.98$; reject H_0
19. **a.** $H_0: \mu = 70$; $H_A\ \mu \neq 70$
    b. $A_L = 67.74$; $A_U = 72.26$; accept H_0
21. $A = 9.95$; reject H_0
23. **a.** $H_0: \mu \leq 3$; $H_A\ \mu > 3$
    c. 0.298
    d. 0.9066
25. **a.** $H_0: \mu \leq 10$; $H_A\ \mu > 10$
    c. 0.4247
    d. 0.5753
27. **a.** $H_0: \mu \geq 50$; $H_A\ \mu < 50$
    b. Reject H_0 if $\overline{X} < 47.208$; Accept H_0
29. $Z = 1.197$
31. $Z = -1.37$ when standard deviation = 40
    $Z = -2.74$ when standard deviation = 20

33. a. $H_0: \mu \geq 900$; H_A $\mu < 900$
    b. Reject H_0 if $\overline{X} < 866.95$
    c. 0.6217
    d. 0.5636
35. a. $H_0: \mu \geq 3.4$; H_A $\mu < 3.4$
    b. Reject H_0 if $Z < -1.645$; $Z = -8.49$; Reject H_0
    c. $Z = -2.4$; Reject H_0
    d. $Z = -2.28$; Reject H_0
37. b. $H_0: \mu \leq 2.75$; H_A $\mu > 2.75$
    c. $A_L = 2.845$

Chapter 10

1. Reject H_0 if $Z > 1.645$; $Z = 0.675$; Accept H_0
3. Reject H_0 if $\hat{p} < 0.12$ or $\hat{p} > 0.28$; $\hat{p} = 0.225$; Accept H_0
5. $H_0: p \geq 0.4$; $H_A: p < 0.4$; Reject H_0 if $\hat{p} < 0.319$; $\hat{p} = 0.38$; Accept H_0
7. a. Reject H_0 if $Z < -1.96$ or $Z > 1.96$
    b. $Z = 8.43$; Reject H_0
9. a. Reject H_0 if $Z > 1.645$
    b. $Z = 0.99$; Accept H_0
11. a. $H_0: \mu_1 - \mu_2 \geq 0$; $H_A: \mu_1 - \mu_2 < 0$
    b. Reject H_0 if $Z < -1.28$; $Z = -1.89$; Reject H_0
13. Reject H_0 if $Z < -1.645$; $Z = -0.79$; Do not reject H_0
15. Reject H_0 if $Z < -1.96$ or $Z > 1.96$; $Z = -0.74$; Do not reject H_0
17. 0.6591; 0.9457
19. $H_0: p_1 \leq p_2$; $H_A: p_1 > p_2$; Reject H_0 if $Z > 1.645$; $Z = -1.72$; Accept H_0
21. a. $H_0: p \geq 0.75$; $H_A: p < 0.75$
    b. Reject H_0 if $\hat{p} < 0.717$; $\hat{p} = 0.919$; Accept H_0
23. a. $H_0: p \geq 0.5$; $H_A: p < 0.5$
    b. Reject H_0 if $\hat{p} < 0.44$
    c. $\hat{p} = 0.47$; Accept H_0
25. $H_0: p_1 = p_2$; Reject H_0 if $Z < -1.645$ or $Z > 1.645$; $Z = 0.658$; Accept H_0

27. a. $H_0: p_1 \leq p_2$ $H_A: p_1 > p_2$
    c. Reject H_0 if $Z > 2.05$; $Z = 2.03$; Accept H_0
29. $H_0: p \geq 0.5$; $H_A: p < 0.5$; Reject H_0 if $\hat{p} < 0.432$; $\hat{p} = 0.477$; Accept H_0

Chapter 11

1. a. 3.055 b. 1.833 c. 2.080 d. 1.734
3. -1.12
7. a. 2,229.95 —— 2,451.85 b. 2,272.50 —— 2,409.30
9. 2.629 —— 4.271
11. a. -8.9 b. -17.22 —— -0.58
13. a. -0.476 —— 1.176
15. -12.814 —— 4.814
23. -0.439 —— 0.559
25. $H_0: \mu_1 \geq \mu_2$; $H_A: \mu_1 < \mu_2$; Reject H_0 if $t < -1.476$; $t = -1.71$; Accept H_0
29. a. -6.558 —— 3.758
29. a. $H_0: \mu \geq 40$; $H_A < 40$
    c. Reject H_0 if $t < -1.895$; $t = -3.48$; Reject H_0
31. a. $H_0: \mu_1 - \mu_2 \leq 0$; $H_A: \mu_1 - \mu_2 > 0$
    b. Reject H_0 if $t > 2.75$; $t = 1.24$; Accept H_0
33. $H_0: \mu \leq 5$; $H_A: \mu > 5$; Reject H_0 if $t > 2.045$; $t = 1.095$; Accept H_0
35. b. -37.925 —— 33.895
37. $H_0: \mu_1 = \mu_2$; $H_A: \mu_1 \neq \mu_2$; Reject H_0 if $t < -1.711$ or $t > 1.711$; $t = 2.738$; Reject H_0
39. a. $H_0: \mu \geq 40$; $H_A: \mu < 40$
    b. Reject H_0 if $t < -1.345$
    c. $t = -1.89$; Reject H_0
41. 487.988 —— 499.012
43. b. -7.651 —— 11.207

Chapter 12

1. 16.919

3. **a.** Reject H_0 if $\chi^2 > 16.919$; $\chi^2 =$ 11.025; Accept H_0
   b. Reject H_0 if $\chi^2 > 39.087$; $\chi^2 = 39.15$; Reject H_0

5. **a.** $H_0: \sigma^2 \leq 400$; $H_A: \sigma^2 > 400$
   b. Reject H_0 if $\chi^2 > 19.675$
   c. $\chi^2 = 21.155$; Reject H_0

7. **a.** 2.06 **b.** 6.03 **c.** 2.86

9. **a.** Reject H_0 if $F > 2.28$
   b. $F = 1.21$; Accept H_0

11. **a.** $H_0: \sigma_1^2 = \sigma_2^2$
    b. Reject H_0 if $F > 3.28$; $F = 2.78$; Accept H_0
    c. $H_0: \mu_1 = \mu_2$; Reject H_0 if $t < -2.086$ or $t > 2.086$; $t = 0.668$; Accept H_0

13. **a.** $H_0: \mu_1 = \mu_2 = \mu_3$; H_A: Not all means are equal
    b. SSB = 53.54 **c.** SSW = 30.96
    d. Reject H_0 if $F > 3.68$; $F = 13.0$; Reject H_0

15. SSB = 1.152.6; SSW = 386.3; Reject H_0 if $F > 3.68$; $F = 22.33$; Reject H_0

19. **a.** $H_0: \mu_1 = \mu_2 = \mu_3 = \mu_4$; H_A: Not all means are equal
    b. SSB = 317.73
    c. SSW = 163.72
    d. Reject H_0 if $F > 3.16$; $F = 11.64$; Reject H_0
    e. Group 1 & 3 are different; Group 2 & 4 are different

21. Reject H_0 if $F > 3.68$; $F = 22.33$; Reject H_0; T-range = 7.60; Difference 1 & 2 = 13.16; Difference 2 & 3 = 6.00; Difference 1 & 3 = 19.16

29. $H_0: \sigma^2 \leq 0.0016$; $H_A: \sigma^2 > 0.0016$; Reject H_0 if $\chi^2 > 30.144$; $\chi^2 = 44.186$; Reject H_0

31. $H_0: \sigma^2 \leq 9$; $H_A: \sigma^2 > 9$; Reject H_0 if $\chi^2 > 14.684$; $\chi^2 = 27.04$; Reject H_0
    $H_0: \mu = 36$; $H_A: \mu \neq 36$; Reject H_0 if $t < -1.833$ or $t > 1.833$; $t = 0.608$; Accept H_0

33. **a.** $H_0: \mu_1 \geq \mu_2$; $H_A: \mu_1 < \mu_2$

   c. Reject H_0 if $t < -2.681$; $t = -0.45$; Accept H_0
   d. Reject H_0 if $F > 8.47$; $F = 1.15$; Accept H_0

35. $H_0: \sigma_1^2 = \sigma_2^2$; $H_A: \sigma_1^2 \neq \sigma_2^2$; Reject H_0 if $F > 4.85$; $F = 2.61$; Accept H_0

37. **a.** SSB = 459,160.0; SSW = 80.080; $F = 34.40$
    b. Reject H_0 if $F > 3.88$; Reject H_0

39. Reject H_0 if $F > 3.145$; $F = 108.42$; Reject H_0

41. Reject H_0 if $F > 2.74$; $F = 16.09$; Reject H_0

43. **a.** Reject H_0 if $F > 3.49$; $F = 10.36$; Reject H_0
    b. Differences = 2.16; 4.94; 2.78; T range = 2.76

45. 5.57

Chapter 13

7. **b.** 0.9239
   c. Reject H_0 if $t < -2.306$ or $t > 2.306$; $t = 6.8295$; Reject H_0

9. **b.** Reject H_0 if $t < -2.02$ or $t > 2.02$; $t = -1.637$; Accept H_0

11. **b.** 0.7068; Reject H_0 if $t < -2.306$ or $t > 2.306$; $t = 2.8260$; Reject H_0
    c. $\hat{Y} = 4.6202 + 10.9612X$

13. **a.** Reject H_0 if $t < -2.069$ or $t > 2.069$; $t = 207.44$; Reject H_0

15. **b.** 0.5259; Reject H_0 if $t < -2.201$ or $t > 2.201$; $t = 2.0507$; Accept H_0
    c. $-38.4106 + 0.2220X$; Reject H_0 if $t < -2.201$ or $t > 2.201$; $t = 2.0518$; Accept H_0

17. **a.** $-6,800$
    b. $-6,811.8616$ ——— $-6,797.3501$

19. Reject H_0 if $t < -2.262$ or $t > 2.262$; (Y, X_1) $t = 2.12$; (Y, X_2) $t = 2.91$; (Y, X_3) $t = 1.83$; (X_1, X_2) $t = 2.55$; (X_1, X_3) $t = 0.81$; (X_2, X_3) $t = 0.09$

21. a. $-476 + 0.742X_1 + 1.31X_2 + 0.119X_3$
  b. 0.735
  c. Reject H_0 if $F > 4.35$; $F = 6.461$; Reject H_0
  d. X_2, X_3
  e. 0.621

23. Reject H_0 if $t < -2.145$ or $t > 2.145$; $(Y, X_1)\ t = 6.01$; $(Y, X_2)\ t = 1.70$; $(Y, X_3)\ t = 2.80$; $(Y, X_4)\ t = -2.03$; $(X_1, X_2)\ t = 1.12$; $(X_1, X_3)\ t = 2.65$; $(X_1, X_4)\ t = -1.31$; $(X_2, X_3) = 1.65$; $(X_2, X_4)\ t = -1.87$; $(X_3, X_4)\ t = -2.46$

25. a. $14,133 + 63.2X_1 + 10.1X_2 + 31.5X_3 - 55.5X_4$
  b. 0.775
  c. Reject H_0 if $F > 3.36$; $F = 9.45$; Reject H_0
  d. X_1
  e. 0.693
  f. X_1: 30.27 —— 96.03; X_2: -21.40 —— 41.60; X_3: -358.30 —— 421.30; X_4: -192.12 —— 81.20

33. b. 0.891
  c. Reject H_0 if $t < -2.12$ or $t > 2.12$; $t = 7.85$; Reject H_0

35. a. independent: advertising; dependent: sales
  c. 0.914; Reject H_0 if $t < -2.101$ or $t > 2.101$; $t = 9.56$; reject H_0
  d. $460.6 + 9.70X$
  e. Reject H_0 if $F > 4.41$; $F = 91.01$; Reject H_0; Reject H_0 if $t < -2.101$ or $t > 2.101$; $t = 23.95$; Reject H_0

37. a. 105.533 —— 116.47
  b. 76.55 —— 124.45

39. $A_L = -0.5139\ A_H = 0.5139$

43. Reject H_0 if $t < -2.201$ or $t > 2.201$; t for $X_1 = 1.99$; t for $X_2 = 0.86$; t for $X_3 = 1.52$; accept H_0 for all variables

47. Reject H_0 if $t < -2.16$ or $t > 2.16$; t for $(Y, X_1) = 2.877$; t for $(Y, X_2) = 1.371$; t for $(Y, X_3) = 2.85$; t for $(Y, X_4) = 2.00$

49. 0.844; Reject H_0 if $F > 3.48$; $F = 13.607$; Reject H_0

51. Reject H_0 if $t < -2.228$ or $t > 2.228$; t for $X_1 = 4.422$; t for $X_2 = -0.788$; $X_3 = 3.581$; $X_4 = 2.581$

Chapter 14

3. -0.5485

5. Reject H_0 if $\phi_{cal} < \dfrac{-Z_{.05}}{\sqrt{n}}$; $-0.5485 < -0.1163$; Reject H_0

7. 0.1679; Reject H_0 if $\phi_{cal} > \dfrac{-Z_{.05}}{\sqrt{n}}$; $0.1679 > 0.05228$; Reject H_0

9. Reject H_0 if $\chi^2 > 26.296$; $\chi^2 = 17.5467$; Accept H_0

11. Reject H_0 if $\chi^2 > 9.488$; $\chi^2 = 2.35$; Accept H_0

13. Reject H_0 if $\chi^2 > 21.026$; $\chi^2 = 28.44$; Reject H_0

15. Reject H_0 if $\chi^2 > 15.507$; $\chi^2 = 61.5267$; Reject H_0

17. Reject H_0 if $\chi^2 > 9.488$; $\chi^2 = 6.13$; Accept H_0

19. Reject H_0 if $0.075 > w_p$; $w_p = .19$; Accept H_0

25. Reject H_0 if $\chi^2 > 11.34$; $\chi^2 = 6.625$; Accept H_0

27. Reject H_0 if $\chi^2 > 4.605$; $\chi^2 = 404.336$; Reject H_0

29. Reject H_0 if $\chi^2 > 11.07$; $\chi^2 = 41.74$; Reject H_0

31. Reject H_0 if $\chi^2 > 11.07$; $\chi^2 = 80.944$; Reject H_0

33. a. Reject H_0 if $\chi^2 > 3.84$; $\chi^2 = 3.338$; Accept H_0
  b. Reject H_0 if $Z < -1.96$ or $Z > 1.96$; $Z = -1.828$; Accept H_0

Index

STANDARD NORMAL DISTRIBUTION TABLE

To illustrate: 19.85% of the area under a normal curve lies between the mean, μ_x, and a point 0.52 standard deviation units away.

Example:
Z = 0.52 (or −0.52)
A(Z) = 0.1985 or 19.85%

Z	.00	.01	.02	.03	.04	.05	.06	.07	.08	.09
0.0	.0000	.0040	.0080	.0120	.0160	.0199	.0239	.0279	.0319	.0359
0.1	.0398	.0438	.0478	.0517	.0557	.0596	.0636	.0675	.0714	.0753
0.2	.0793	.0832	.0871	.0910	.0948	.0987	.1026	.1064	.1103	.1141
0.3	.1179	.1217	.1255	.1293	.1331	.1368	.1406	.1443	.1480	.1517
0.4	.1554	.1591	.1628	.1664	.1700	.1736	.1772	.1808	.1844	.1879
0.5	.1915	.1950	.1985	.2019	.2054	.2088	.2123	.2157	.2190	.2224
0.6	.2257	.2291	.2324	.2357	.2389	.2422	.2454	.2486	.2517	.2549
0.7	.2580	.2611	.2642	.2673	.2704	.2734	.2764	.2794	.2823	.2852
0.8	.2881	.2910	.2939	.2967	.2995	.3023	.3051	.3078	.3106	.3133
0.9	.3159	.3186	.3212	.3238	.3264	.3289	.3315	.3340	.3365	.3389
1.0	.3413	.3438	.3461	.3485	.3508	.3531	.3554	.3577	.3599	.3621
1.1	.3643	.3665	.3686	.3708	.3729	.3749	.3770	.3790	.3810	.3830
1.2	.3849	.3869	.3888	.3907	.3925	.3944	.3962	.3980	.3997	.4015
1.3	.4032	.4049	.4066	.4082	.4099	.4115	.4131	.4147	.4162	.4177
1.4	.4192	.4207	.4222	.4236	.4251	.4265	.4279	.4292	.4306	.4319
1.5	.4332	.4345	.4357	.4370	.4382	.4394	.4406	.4418	.4429	.4441
1.6	.4452	.4463	.4474	.4484	.4495	.4505	.4515	.4525	.4535	.4545
1.7	.4554	.4564	.4573	.4582	.4591	.4599	.4608	.4616	.4625	.4633
1.8	.4641	.4649	.4656	.4664	.4671	.4678	.4686	.4693	.4699	.4706
1.9	.4713	.4719	.4726	.4732	.4738	.4744	.4750	.4756	.4761	.4767
2.0	.4772	.4778	.4783	.4788	.4793	.4798	.4803	.4808	.4812	.4817
2.1	.4821	.4826	.4830	.4834	.4838	.4842	.4846	.4850	.4854	.4857
2.2	.4861	.4864	.4868	.4871	.4875	.4878	.4881	.4884	.4887	.4890
2.3	.4893	.4896	.4898	.4901	.4904	.4906	.4909	.4911	.4913	.4916
2.4	.4918	.4920	.4922	.4925	.4927	.4929	.4931	.4932	.4934	.4936
2.5	.4938	.4940	.4941	.4943	.4945	.4946	.4948	.4949	.4951	.4952
2.6	.4953	.4955	.4956	.4957	.4959	.4960	.4961	.4962	.4963	.4964
2.7	.4965	.4966	.4967	.4968	.4969	.4970	.4971	.4972	.4973	.4974
2.8	.4974	.4975	.4976	.4977	.4977	.4978	.4979	.4979	.4980	.4981
2.9	.4981	.4982	.4982	.4983	.4984	.4984	.4985	.4985	.4986	.4986
3.0	.4987	.4987	.4987	.4988	.4988	.4989	.4989	.4989	.4990	.4990